HOTELS AND COUNTRY INNS
OF CHARACTER AND CHARM
IN FRANCE

Fodor's RIVAGES

HOTELS AND COUNTRY INNS
of Character and Charm
IN FRANCE

Founding editors
Michelle Gastaut, Jean and Tatiana de Beaumont,
Bénédicte Darblay, Anne Deren

Editorial director
Michelle Gastaut

Fodor's Travel Publications, Inc.
New York • Toronto • London • Sydney • Auckland

While every care has been taken to ensure the accuracy of the information in this guide, time brings change, and consequently the publisher cannot accept responsibility for errors that may occur. Prudent travelers will therefore want to call ahead to verify prices and other "perishable" information.

Published in the United States by Fodor's Travel Publications, Inc.
Published in France by Payot/Rivages

Fodor's is a registered trademark of Fodor's Travel Publications, Inc.

ISBN 0-679-02872-2
First Edition

**Hotels and Country Inns
of Character and Charm in France**
Translators: Marie Elise Palmier Chatelaine, Anne Norris, Edmund Swinglehurst,
Christina Thistlethwayte
Rewriting: Marie Gastaut
Creative director: Fabrizio La Rocca
Front cover photograph: Auberge de Kerhinet (Pays-de-la-Loire),
photo by François Tissier; back cover: Château de Valmer (Provence)

Special Sales

Manufactured in Italy by Litho Service
10 9 8 7 6 5 4 3 2 1

BIENVENUE

Welcome to the world of hotels with character and charm in France. This edition contains 580 hotels, including 66 small hotels in Paris, 40 properties appear in the guide for the first time. All have been selected for charm, quality of welcome, food and hotelkeeping. They range from the comparatively simple to the luxurious.

When choosing among them, remember that you cannot expect as much of a room costing 200F as you can of one costing 600F or more. Please also note that the prices given were quoted to us at the end of 1994 and may change.

When you make your reservation be sure to ask for the exact prices for half board *(demi-pension)* or full board *(pension)* as they can vary depending on the number in your party and the length of your stay. Half board is often obligatory. Note that rooms are generally held only until 6 or 7PM; if you are going to be late, let the hotel know.

STAR RATING

The government's hotel roting organisation assigns stars, from one to four, based on the comfort of a hotel, with special weight given to the number of bathrooms and toilets in relation to the number of rooms. This star rating has nothing at all to do with subjective criteria such as charm or the quality of the hospitality which are among our most important criteria. Some of the hotels in this guide have no stars–and that is because the hoteliers have never asked the gouvernement to rate them.

HOW TO USE THE GUIDE

Hotels are listed by regions, and within each region in alphabetical order by *département* and district. The number of the page on which a hotel is described corresponds to the number on the flag that pinpoints the property's location on the road map and to the numbers in the table of contents and index. The phrase "major credit cards" means that Diner's, Amex, Visa, Eurocard and MasterCard are all accepted.

PLEASE LET US KNOW . . .

If you are impressed by a small hotel or inn not featured here, one that you think ought to be included in the guide, let us know so that we can visit it.

Please also tell us if you are disappointed by one of our choices. Write us at Fodor's Travel Publications, 201 E. 50th Str., New York, NY 10022.

CONTENTS LIST

Hotels listing by region
Map of France
Road maps

Hotels:

CONTENTS

P A R I S

A L S A C E — L O R R A I N E

A Q U I T A I N E

A U V E R G N E - L I M O U S I N

C E N T R E

FRANCHE-COMTÉ

ILE-DE-FRANCE

LANGUEDOC-ROUSSILLON

N O R D - P A S - D E - C A L A I S

N O R M A N D Y

PAYS DE LA LOIRE

ALPES-MARITIMES

BOUCHES-DU-RHÔNE

R H Ô N E - A L P E S

★ Prices shown in brackets are prices for a double room, sometimes with half board. For precise details, go to the page mentioned.

KEY TO THE MAPS

Scale: 1:1,000,000
Maps 30 & 31: scale: 1:1,180,000

MOTORWAYS

① Interchange
② Half-interchange
③ Toll-barrier

Kilometre-distance
① in total
② partial

Motorway
① under construction
② projected

ROAD CLASSIFICATION

Dual-carriageways

High traffic road

Trunk road

Other road

Road **①** under construction
     ② projected

TOWNS CLASSIFICATION

① by the population

— less than 10,000 inhabitants
- from 10.000 to 30.000
— from 30.000 to 50.000
— from 50.000 to 100.000
— more than 100.000
— towns with over
   50.000 inh.

② Administrative
— Chief-town of
   department
— Main subdivision of
   department
— Districts
— Commune, hamlet

TARBES

CARPENTRAS

Combeaufontaine
Andrézieux-Bouthéon

ROAD WIDTH

4 carriageways

3 lane or
2 wide lane
2 lane

Narrow road
Kilometre-distance
① in total
② partial

BOUNDARIES

National boundary
County boundary

TOURISM

Picturesque locality

Very picturesque locality

Interesting site or
natural curiosity

Historic castle
Ruins of outstanding beauty
Abbey
National park

Chenonceaux

Amboise✳

Roches de Ham

DIVERS

Civil Airport
Dam

Canal
Car-ferries

Motorail

Pass

Summit

▲ 2392

1

DIEPPE

ROUEN

HAUTE-
NORMANDIE

LE HAVRE

8

EVREUX

6

ST.LO

7

CAEN

AVRANCHES

BASSE-
NORMANDIE

LANNION

BREST

BRETAGNE

ST.BRIEUC

ST.MALO

RENNES

LAVAL

4

5

QUIMPER

LORIENT

VANNES

PAYS
DE LA LOIRE

CENTRE

BELLE-ILE

ANGERS

TOURS

14

NANTES

15

16

LA ROCHE
S-YON

POITIERS

NIORT

LA ROCHELLE

POITOU-
CHARENTES

LIMOGES

ANGOULEME

22

23

PERIGUEUX

BORDEAUX

CORSE

AQUITAINE

CAHOR

BASTIA

CALVI

36

TOULOUSE

28

BAYONNE

29

30

AJACCIO

PAU

TARBES

BONIFACIO

MIDI-
PYRENEES

C. GRAVIER

côte

Île

Plouguerneau

Ploudalmézeau
D 28
D 27
D 16
D 13
D 26
D 68
St-Renan

Ouessant
PARC
Lampaul
Plouarzel
Gouesnou
D 5
D 67
Guilers
I. Molène
D'ARMORIQUE
le Conquet
BREST
Plouzané
P.te St-Mathieu
D 789

Camaret
P.te de Pen-Hir
Crozon
D 255
Morgat
Gro
Cap de la Chèvre

p.nte ✳
I. de Sein   du Raz
De
D 784
Pont-Croix
Audierne
Ploz
172
Po

N.-D.-de-

P
p.nte de Pen-

6

Cap de la Hague ✳

I. of Alderney

Rochers

Nez de Jobourg

Querqueville **CHER**

Beaumont

Equeurdreville
Octeville

Diélette

les Pieux

Ouett

I. of Guernsey

✈ St-Peter-Port

I. of Sark

Carteret

Barneville
Carteret

Portbail

la Hay
du Pu

I. of Jersey

St-Hélier

St-Mal
de-la-Land

Coutainville

Agon

Montmart

I. Bréhat

Iles Chausey

362 Bré

Granville

eux l'Arcouest

Paimpol

Côte d'É....

Carolles

159

160

184-185

183

178-179

Kermaria **Plouha**

Cap Fréhel ✳

St-MALO ✳

Paramé

Pnte du Grouin

AV

vollon St-Quay-Portrieux

Etables

157

erquy

St-Cast

St-Lunaire

St-Briac

Cancale

✳ le Mont-
St-Michel

NGAMP

Châtelaudren

Pléneuf-
Val-André

le-Val-André

Matignon

Dinard

Sérvan

le Vivier

uagat

35

Plérin

Hénanbihen

le Guildo

Ploubalay

Châteauneuf

E 401

N 176

Ploufragan

St-BRIEUC

Languéux

Plédran

Lamballe

Plancoët

la Motte

Dol-
de-Bretagne

Ple
Fou

5

Quintin

22

Côtes-d'Armor

Plédran

158

Plélan-le Pit

E 401

DINAN

Lanvallay

182

Trans

26

Ploeuc

Moncontour

le Gouray

Jugon **33**

153

Évran

Combourg

Antra

Bazouges-
la-Pérouse

Uzel

Collinée
Plouguenast

Broons

Caulnes

Bécherel

Tinténiac

St-Rémy
-du-Plain

Mûr-
de-Bretagne

St-Caradec

St-Jouan

les Iffs

Hédé

Fin

St-Aubin
d'Aubigné

Gos

44

guère

Loudéac

Merdrignac

Quédillac

Montauban

N 164

Bettor

St-Grégoire
Pacé

Thor

PONTIVY

la Chèze

St-Méen-
le-Grand

Bédée

E 50

RENNE

Chantepie

Rohan

la Trinité-
Porhoët

Gaël

Montfort

le Rheu

St-Jacques

Vern

461

Mohon

Mauron

181

Paimpont

180

Plélan-le-Grand

Maxent

Mordelles

Corps

Bruz

Chartres Châteaugir

losselin

14

Campénéac

Corps

RECTA FOLDEX
MAPS
EXPLORE FRANCE

AND THE WHOLE WORD

RÉALISATIONS ET ÉTUDES CARTOGRAPHIQUES
TOURISTIQUES ET ADMINISTRATIVES
40, 48 rue des Meuniers - 93100 MONTREUIL-SOUS-BOIS (FRANCE)
Tél. (1) 49 88 92 10 - Télex : 234 018 - Télécopie : (1) 49 88 92 09

Hôtel de Notre-Dame★★★

19, rue Maître-Albert
75005 Paris
Tel. (1) 43.26.79.00
Fax (1) 46.33.50.11
M. Fouhety

Rooms 34 with bath or shower and WC, soundproofing, telephone, cable TV, hairdryer, safe and minibar. **Price** Double 690-790F. **Meals** Breakfast 40F with orange juice, no restaurant. **Credit cards** All major. **Pets** No dogs allowed. **Parking** At 1 rue Lagrange. **Open** All year. **How to get there** (Map 38): Metro Saint-Michel, RER Cluny-Saint-Michel, Bus 21, 24, 27, 38, 47, 85 and 96.

You will have no difficulty in spotting the Hôtel de Notre-Dame, in a small street typical of this old quarter of Paris: its wide frontage was once the window of a shop on the ground floor of the building. In the hotel, which has recently been refurbished, partition walls have been put up without spoiling the original beamed ceilings. A few antiques and a fine tapestry lend a strong period atmosphere to the lobby, bar and lounges. The bedrooms are attractively furnished and have rather spacious bathrooms. Its position close to Notre-Dame and the quais of the Seine, with their barges and second-hand booksellers, adds to the hotel's many charms.

Hôtel Esmeralda★★

4, rue Saint-Julien-le-Pauvre
75005 Paris
Tel. (1) 43.54.19.20
Fax (1) 40. 51. 00. 68
Mme Bruel

Rooms 19 with bath or shower or basin and WC, telephone. **Price** Double 320-480F, suite 520-620F. **Meals** Breakfast 45F (in rooms, no breakfast room), no restaurant. **Credit cards** Not accepted. **Pets** Dogs allowed. **Parking** At 1 rue Lagrange, Maubert and Notre-Dame. **Open** All year. **How to get there** (Map 38): Metro Saint-Michel, RER Cluny-Saint-Michel, Bus 21, 24, 27, 38, 47, 85 and 96.

Many a passer-by must wonder, walking through the cloisters of the tiny church of Saint-Julien-le-Pauvre, what the subdued lighting and the air of privacy of this house conceal: a private dwelling or an antique shop? Indeed it could be both, were it not for the fact that Mme Bruel receives guests. Flowery wallpapers, rustic floor tiles and waxed parquet floors, period furniture and curios create a charmingly old-fashioned atmosphere. Ask for one of the bedrooms with a view of Notre-Dame, which are also the most comfortable (some can even accommodate a family of four). But the rooms overlooking the courtyard are just as charming, and even more reasonably priced This is a truly delightful hotel.

Les Rives de Notre-Dame★★★

15, Quai Saint-Michel
75005 Paris
Tel. (1) 43.54.81.16
Fax (1) 43.26.27.09
M. Degravi

Rooms 10 with air-conditioning, telephone, bath or shower, TV and minibar. **Price** Singles and doubles 850F, 1345F; suite 1990F. **Meals** Breakfast 80F **Credit card** All major. **Pets** Small dogs allowed. **Parking** Square in front of Notre-Dame and 1, rue Lagrange. **Open** All year. **How to get there** (Map 38): Metro Cluny, RER Cluny-Saint-Michel, Bus 21, 24, 27, 47, 63, 67, 86, 87 and 96.

Your windows at Les Rives de Notre-Dame look out over a postcard setting between the Place Saint-Michel and Notre Dame: the quays of the Seine with its bookstalls, and the banks (*rives*) down below where lovers stroll and watch the *bateaux mouches* wending their way upstream. Excellent soundproofing means that you can enjoy this view from a quiet room, of which there are ten. Not one is the same but all are handsomely decorated with a tasteful combination of motifs and colors. The rooms are large and include shaped sitting areas with a sofa-bed and pretty bathrooms. On the ground floor, there are three small bedrooms that are equally charming; they are usually for one person, but a couple could stay here if spaciousness is not important. The service is attentive.

Hôtel du Parc Saint-Séverin★★★

22, rue de la Parcheminerie
75005 Paris
Tel. (1) 43.54.32.17
Fax (1) 42.54.70.71
Mme Bonnafoux

Rooms 27 with telephone, bath or shower, soundproofing, cable TV, hairdryer and minibar. **Price** Singles and doubles 476F, 562-1512F. **Meals** Breakfast 45F, snacks available. **Credit cards** Amex, Visa, Eurocard and MasterCard. **Pets** Dogs not allowed. **Parking** Square in front of Notre-Dame and 1, rue Lagrange. **Open** All year. **How to get there** (Map 38): Metro Cluny, RER Cluny-Saint-Michel, Bus 21, 24, 27, 47, 63, 67, 86, 87 and 96.

Although the Hôtel Parc Saint-Séverin is located in the heart of the Latin Quarter, it is quiet because it is on a pedestrian street away from the crowds. The beautiful spaces of the handsome building have been well preserved it is airy and full of light. The muted colors and contemporary or 1930s furniture in the lounge further reenforce the atmosphere of spaciousness. There is the same spirit in the large, bright bedrooms which are pleasantly decorated with antique furniture and paintings. For a beautiful view of the rooftops, the Saint-Séverin Cloister and the gardens of the Cluny Museum, ask for a room on the *cinquième étage* (6th floor) or above; the largest are those on a corner, and on the last floor, you can even have a lovely terrace.

Hôtel des Deux Iles★★★

59, rue Saint-Louis-en-l'Ile
75004 Paris
Tel. (1) 43. 26. 13. 35
Fax (1) 43. 29. 60. 25
Mme Buffat

Rooms 17 with bath or shower and WC, soundproofing, telephone, cable TV, hairdryer. **Price** 695-795F.
Meals Breakfast 42F, snacks available. **Credit cards** Not accepted. **Pets** Dogs not allowed. **Parking** At
2 rue Geoffroy-l'Asnier and square in front of Notre-Dame. **Open** All year. **How to get there** (Map 38):
Metro Pont-Marie, Bus 24, 63, 67, 86 and 87.

Monsieur and Mme Buffat have converted two buildings into charming hotels between a former Archbishop's Palace, the Church of Saint-Louis-en-l'Ile, and Bertillot, famous for ice creams. We have chosen this one for its atmosphere, English with a tinge of exoticism: flowery fabrics and painted cane and bamboo furniture are the main features of the decor. The bedrooms are not very large, but they are delightful. Provençal fabrics replace the chintzes used in the lounge, and the bathrooms are lined with gleaming blue tiles. Everything here is comfortable, including the beautiful vaulted breakfast room. This hotel has a faithful following and often there are no vacancies. If this is the case, you might be able to reserve a room in the Buffat's Hôtel de Lutèce just next door, which is also very charming.

Hôtel du Jeu de Paume★★★★

54, rue Saint-Louis-en-l'Ile
75004 Paris
Tel. (1) 43 26 14 18
Fax (1) 40 46 02 76
Mme Prache

Rooms 32 with bath or shower and WC, telephone, cable TV, hairdryer and minibar. **Price** Double 795-
1250F. **Meals** Breakfast 75F, snacks available. **Credit cards** All major. **Pets** Dogs allowed.
Facilities Sauna. **Parking** At 2 rue Geoffroy-l'Asnier and square in front of Notre-Dame. **Open** All year.
How to get there (Map 38): Metro Pont-Marie, Bus 24, 63, 67, 86 and 87.

This hotel is an authentic old palm-tennis court. The spacious interior has been entirely and artfully restructured by creating a series of galleries and mezzanines to form a dynamic and very decorative architectural arrangement. Several areas have thus been created: On the ground-floor, there is an intimate lounge-bar and a warm, inviting breakfast room; on a mezzanine, you will find a reading room, and off the galleries there are the elegant bedrooms with beautiful baths. The delicious breakfasts include excellent homemade preserves.

Hôtel Relais Christine★★★★

3, rue Christine
75006 Paris
Tel. (1) 43.26.71.80
Fax (1) 43.26.89.38
M. Regnault

Rooms 34 and 17 duplex, with air-conditioning, bath or shower and WC, soundproofing, telephone, cable TV, hairdryer and minibar. **Price** 1580-1780F, suite 2300F, duplex 2150-2700F. **Meals** Breakfast 95F, snacks available. **Credit cards** All major. **Pets** Dogs allowed. **Facilities** Free private parking. **Open** All year. **How to get there** (Map 38): Metro Odéon, Saint-Michel, RER Cluny-Saint-Michel, Bus 24, 27, 58, 63, 70, 86, 87 and 96.

This hotel occupies a former Augustinian convent, entered through a paved courtyard/garden but the interior has nothing monastic about it. On the contrary, it is decorated with a rainbow of warm colors, in both the panelled lounge – which has a handsome collection of portraits – and in the spacious, elegant bedrooms, some of which look onto the garden. Note also the duplexes, which are ideal for long stays. The breakfast room is in one of the most beautiful vaulted rooms of the cloister. The personnel is very attentive, discreet and efficient. Le Relais Christine has become a classic Paris *hôtel de charme*.

Hôtel de Nesle★

7, rue de Nesle
75006 Paris
Tel. (1) 43. 54. 62. 41
Mme Busillet

Rooms 20 with shower or basin and WC. **Price** Single and double 200-360F. **Meals** Breakfast incl., no restaurant. **Credit cards** Not accepted. **Pets** Dogs allowed. **Parking** At 27, rue Mazarine. **Open** All year. **How to get there** (Map 38): Metro Odéon, RER Cluny-Saint-Michel, Bus 24, 27, 58, 63, 70, 86, 87 and 96.

It is hard to find better prices than at this small hotel, which is very popular with foreign guests. A room here in the middle of the Quartier Latin, with its own shower room, will cost you less than three-hundred francs! The hotel is very simple, but each bedroom has been individually decorated by Mme Busillet. For a small extra charge you can treat yourself to the *Arabe, Egyptienne* or *Molière* bedrooms, which are larger and have impeccable bathrooms. On the first floor, there is a charming, small garden for guests. A friendly and informal atmosphere prevails. The only drawback is that you can't reserve your room in advance.

Left Bank
Saint-Germain Hôtel★★★

9, rue de l'Ancienne-Comédie
75006 Paris
Tel. (1) 43.54.01.70
Fax (1) 43.26.17.14
M. Teil

Rooms 30 and 1 suite with air-conditioning, bath or shower and WC, soundproofing, telephone, cable TV, safe, hairdryer and minibar. **Price** 895-990F, suite 1400F. **Meals** Breakfast 25F. **Credit cards** All major. **Pets** Dogs not allowed. **Parking** Opposite 21, rue de l'Ecole-de-Médecine and 27, rue Mazarine. **Open** All year. **How to get there** (Map 38): Metro Odéon, RER Cluny-Saint-Michel, Bus 58, 63, 70, 86, 87 and 96.

The Left Bank is in the heart of Saint-Germain-des-Prés next door to the *Procope* Restaurant, which is steeped in the history of the Revolutionaries, the Encyclopedists and the romantic writers. The small lobby opens onto a pretty lounge which immediately sets the style of the hotel. Oak and walnut panelling and 17th-century-style chairs were made for the hotel and are well coordinated with the antique furniture and Aubusson tapestry. The same style can be seen in the bedrooms, where fabric-upholstered walls enhance the warm and very comfortable atmosphere. (The rooms whose numbers end with 4 and 6 are the largest). All have beautiful, fully equipped bathrooms. The breakfast buffets are delicious and copious.

Hôtel du Lys★★

23, rue Serpente
75006 Paris
Tel. (1) 43.26.97.57
Mme Decharme

Rooms 22 with bath or shower and WC, telephone, hairdryer. **Price** 360-420F. **Meals** Breakfast incl. **Credit cards** Not accepted. **Pets** Dogs allowed. **Parking** Square in front of Notre-Dame. **Open** All year. **How to get there** (Map 38): Metro Saint-Michel, RER Cluny-Saint-Michel, Bus 21, 24, 27, 38, 63, 85, 86, 87 and 96.

This is a very special hotel. In the heart of the Latin Quarter, you can have a room for an undreamed-of price in a small, charming hotel. At reception, you will be greeted by charming Madame Decharne. The hotel is simple but the bedrooms are charming and cheerful and have renovated baths. Likewise, the 17th-century staircase has been restored. (There is no elevator). The mansard bedrooms are the largest and some even have small balconies, but you have to climb the stairs. The prices and the friendly personnel have attracted a faithful clientèle, and you should thus reserve early.

Hôtel Prince de Conti★★★

8, rue Guénégaud
75006 Paris
Tel. (1) 44.07.30.40
Fax (1) 44.07.36.34
Mme Etienne

Rooms 26 with air-conditioning, bath or shower and WC, soundproofing, telephone, cable TV, hairdryer and minibar - Elevator. **Price** Single 700-800F, double 950F, suite 1200F. **Meals** Breakfast 50F. **Credit cards** All major. **Pets** Dogs allowed. **Parking** At 20, rue Soufflot and place du Panthéon. **Open** All year. **How to get there** (Map 38): Metro Odéon,Saint-Michel, RER Cluny-Saint-Michel, Bus 70, 58, 27, 87, 63 and 96.

The Hôtel Prince de Conti is located in an 18th-Century building in the heart of artistic and literary Saint-Germain-des-Prés. The newly renovated hotel's bedrooms, we must note, are not large, but they are very beautiful. The choice of the various coordinated fabrics is superb and there are modern amenities like double windows, air-conditioning, and beautiful, well-equipped bathrooms. The duplex suites are also charming and are larger, with lounges and upstairs bedrooms. Note that there are two single rooms on the ground floor opening onto the courtyard. There is a refined, British atmosphere here, and the people are very friendly.

Hôtel des Grands Hommes★★★

17, place du Panthéon
75005 Paris
Tel. (1) 46.34.19.60
Fax (1) 43.26.67.32
Mlle Brethous

Rooms 32 with air-conditioning, bath and WC, telephone, cable TV, hairdryer and minibar. **Price** Single 600F, double 750F. **Meals** Breakfast 40F with orange juice, no restaurant. **Credit cards** All major. **Pets** Dogs allowed. **Parking** At 20, rue Soufflot and Place du Panthéon. **Open** all year. **How to get there** (Map 38): Metro Cardinal-Lemoine, RER Luxembourg, Bus 21, 27, 38, 82, 84, 85 and 89.

The Hôtel des Grands Hommes is named for such great men of France as Mirabeau, Voltaire and Victor Hugo, who are buried in the Panthéon. The reception area, with its ornate moldings, 1930s armchairs and subtle orange-pink color scheme, sets the style for the entire building. The atmosphere is both classic and refined. Delicate color's have also been used in the bedrooms, which have brass beds and bathrooms tiled in beige. The most charming rooms are those located on the top floor of the building, with sloping ceilings and balconies looking out onto the Place du Panthéon.

Hôtel du Panthéon★★★

19, place du Panthéon
75005 Paris
Tel. (1) 43.54.32.95
Fax (1) 43.26.64.65
Mlle Brethous

Rooms 32 with air-conditioning, bath and WC, telephone, cable TV, hairdryer and minibar. **Price** Single 600F, double 750F. **Meals** Breakfast 40F with orange juice, no restaurant. **Credit cards** All major. **Pets** Dogs allowed. **Parking** At 20, rue Soufflot and Place du Panthéon. **Open** All year. **How to get there** (Map 38): Metro Cardinal-Lemoine, RER Luxembourg, Bus 21, 27, 38, 82, 84, 85 and 89.

The Hotel du Panthéon is next door to the Hôtel des Grands Hommes, which is run by the same family. The entrance and the lounges are very welcoming. The interior is vast and very airy, there is lacquered pale-wood furniture, the travertine floors are immaculate, and color is provided by the carpets and numerous green plants. The elegant bedrooms are more intimate. (The largest are those ending in 1). The staff is attentive and the reception clerks will help you with reservations and such practical problems as baby-sitting.

Hôtel des Trois Collèges★★

16, rue Cujas
75005 Paris
Tel. (1) 43.54.67.30
Fax (1) 46.34.02.99

Rooms 44 with bath or shower and WC, soundproofing, telephone and hairdryer. **Price** Single 360-500F, double 450-600F, suite 750F. **Meals** Breakfast 40F with orange juice, no restaurant. **Credit cards** All major. **Pets** Dogs not allowed. **Parking** At 20, rue Soufflot. **Open** All year. **How to get there** (Map 38): Metro Saint-Michel, Odeon, RER Luxembourg and Cluny-Saint-Michel, Bus 21, 27, 38, 63, 82, 84, 86 and 87.

This small, discreet hotel is located in the shadow of three famous, ancient seats of learning: La Sorbonne; the 15th-century Collège Sainte-Barbe, the oldest private school in France; and the prestigious Collège de France. The decoration of the hotel is deliberately simple in style, and white is the dominant colour. The bedrooms are comfortable and fully equipped, with pretty bathrooms or shower rooms. The largest rooms are on the top floor and overlook the Sorbonne and the Panthéon. The delicious breakfast here, with homemade jam is served in a pleasant small dining-room.

Résidence Les Gobelins★★

9, rue des Gobelins
75013 Paris
Tel. (1) 47.07.26.90
Fax (1) 43.31.44.05
M. and Mme Poirier

Rooms 32 with bath or shower and WC, telephone, TV. **Price** Single 360F, double 400-450F. **Meals** Breakfast 36F with orange juice, no restaurant. **Credit cards** All major. **Pets** Dogs not allowed. **Parking** At place d'Italie and 1, rue Lagrange. **Facilities** Patio. **Open** All year. **How to get there** (Map 38): Metro Gobelins, RER Port-Royal, Bus 27, 47, 83 and 91.

Close to the Manufacture Royale des Gobelins tapestries after which it is named, this hotel is a haven of peace in a busy, colorful neighborhood. The rue Mouffetard and its popular, bustling market are within a short walking distance, as well as the souks, hammam, cafés and restaurants surrounding the Mosquée de Paris (the city's oldest and most important mosque). The decoration of the hotel is bright and pleasant. In the bedrooms bamboo furniture sets the style and imposes the color scheme. Some of the rooms on the upper floors command pretty views of the courtyard and of a garden, and those on the top floor have sloping ceilings. The breakfast room leads out into a flowery patio with teak furniture. You will receive a friendly welcome.

Hôtel du Parc Montsouris★★

4, rue du Parc-Montsouris
75014 Paris
Tel. (1) 45.89.09.72
Fax (1) 45.80.92.72
M. Grand and Mme Piguet

Rooms 35 with bath or shower and WC, telephone, TV. **Price** Single and double 310-370F, suite 420-480F. **Meals** Breakfast 35F with orange juice. **Credit cards** Amex, Visa, Eurocard and MasterCard. **Pets** Dogs allowed. **Parking** In private road. **Open** All year. **How to get there** (Map 37): Metro Porte d'Orléans, RER Cité Universitaire. Bus for Orly from Porte d'Orléans, Bus PC, 27, 38 and 47.

The Hôtel du Parc Montsouris is located in a former villa near the beautiful park of that name. It has been fully renovated, and its columns and Art Deco paintings convey something of the original atmosphere of the house. The decoration is classic in style, and the bedrooms and bathrooms are comfortably arranged. The neighbourhood is quiet, and a stay in this part of the 14th *arrondissement* will show you a new side of Paris, with its quiet *cul-de-sacs* and 1930s villas, among them some interesting works of Sauvage, Le Corbusier and Lurçat. But the 14th arrondissement also boasts two large parks: that of the Cité Internationale Universitaire and, of course, the Parc Montsouris.

Hôtel Raspail–Montparnasse★★★

203, boulevard Raspail
75014 Paris
Tel. (1) 43.20.62.86
Fax (1) 43.20.50.79
M. and Mme Branche

Rooms 36 and 2 suites with air-conditioning, bath or shower and WC, soundproofing, telephone, cable TV and safe. **Price** Single 550F, double 600-850F, suite 1200F. **Meals** Breakfast 50F. **Credit cards** All major. **Pets** Dogs not allowed. **Parking** At 116, boulevard du Montparnasse. **Open** All year. **How to get there** (Map 37): Metro Porte Vavin, Raspail, RER Port-Royal. Bus 68, 82, 83 and 91.

Shortly before he died, the famous decorator Serge Pons became fond of this Art Deco hotel. In 1992, he restored the noble, vast and light-filled lobby with its large rounded bay windows and its ceilings outlined with beautiful geometric moldings. He opened up the monumental stairway, brought back the lounge-bar, and restored the superb canopy of the façade. The bedrooms are tastefully decorated with grey tones enhanced with brighter fabrics on the walls. Each bedroom bears the name of, and is decorated with, a fine reproduction of a painting by an artist who lived in Montparnasse. Pierre Branche and his wife are always here, personally ensuring that guests are well taken care of.

Hôtel Lenox–Montparnasse★★★

15, rue Delambre
75014 Paris
Tel. (1) 43.35.34.50
Fax (1) 43.20.46.64
M. Destouches

Rooms 52 with bath or shower and WC, soundproofing, telephone, TV and safe. **Price** 520-640F, suite 930-960F. **Meals** Breakfast 45F, snacks available. **Credit cards** All major. **Pets** Dogs allowed. **Parking** At 116, boulevard du Montparnasse. **Open** All year. **How to get there** (Map 37): Metro Porte Vavin, Edgar-Quinet, Montparnasse, RER Port-Royal, Denfert-Rochereau. Bus for Orly and Orlyval: Denfer-Rochereau, Bus 28, 58, 68, 82, 91 and 95.

The vast, light reception area is immediately very welcoming. The lounge and bar are furnished with several antiques and deep sofas. The bedrooms are of varying sizes, with the largest on the upper floors. All are pleasantly decorated and personalized with elegant details and nice bathrooms. The bar is very pleasant, as it is at the Lenox-Saint-Germain, and the staff is friendly.

Hôtel Danemark★★★

21, rue Vavin
75006 Paris
Tel. (1) 43.26.93.78
Fax (1) 46.34.66.06
M. and Mme Nurit

Rooms 15 with bath and WC, soundproofing, telephone, cable TV, hairdryer and minibar. **Price** Single and double 550-660F, with Jacuzzi 760F. **Meals** Breakfast 50F. **Credit cards** All major. **Pets** Dogs allowed. **Parking** At 116, boulevard du Montparnasse. **Open** All year. **How to get there** (Map 37): Metro Vavin and Notre-Dame-des-Champs, RER Port-Royal, Bus 58, 68, 75, 82, 83 and 91 - Montparnasse station.

The Hôtel Danemark stands just opposite the remarkable *maison à gradin*s *sportive* (house with a tiered façade), which is covered in white ceramic tiles and was built in 1912 by Sauvage. Perhaps as a tribute to that building, or simply as a reminder of Danish enthusiasm for contemporary design, the decoration of this hotel is resolutely modern in style. Bright and strongly contrasting colors have been chosen for the reception area and lounge. A more subdued color scheme prevails in the bedrooms, to match the 1930s furniture. There are few rooms, all extremely comfortable and well soundproofed. You will find a friendly and attentive welcome.

L'Atelier Montparnasse★★★

49, rue Vavin
75006 Paris
Tel. (1) 46.33.60.00
Fax (1) 40.51.04.21
Mme Tible

Rooms 17 with bath or shower and WC, soundproofing, telephone, TV, hairdryer and minibar. **Price** Single and double 700F, "Fujita room" 950F. **Meals** Breakfast 40F. **Credit cards** All major. **Pets** Small dogs allowed. **Parking** At 116, boulevard du Montparnasse. **Open** All year. **How to get there** (Map 37): Metro Notre-Dame-des-Champs and Montparnasse, RER Port-Royal, Bus 68, 82, 83 and 91 - Montparnasse station.

Very near La Coupole restaurant, the Atelier Montparnasse makes the earlier spirit of the quarter come to life. The hotel has kept the 30s style in the entrance, which harmonizes with the carpet-mosaic of the floor. There is a permanent exhibit of paintings, thus renewing the Montparnasse tradition. The bedrooms are sober, pleasant and comfortable, but the bathrooms—with glass mosaics evoking a great painter from the grand days of Montparnasse—are simply splendid. Madame Tible's dynamism and professionalism are everywhere in evidence in this friendly hotel.

Hôtel Ferrandi★★★

92, rue du Cherche-Midi
75006 Paris
Tel. (1) 42.22.97.40
Fax (1) 45.44.89.97
Mme Lafond

Rooms 41 and 1 suite, with air-conditioning, bath or shower and WC, soundproofing, telephone, TV, hairdryer. **Price** Double 440-920F, suite 950-1250F. **Meals** Breakfast 60F with fresh fruit juices and traditional jams; snacks available. **Credit cards** All major. **Pets** Dogs allowed. **Parking** Garage at hotel (120F per day) and at Bon Marché. **Open** All year. **How to get there** (Map 37): Metro Saint-Placide and Sèvres-Babylone, Bus 39, 48, 84, 89, 94, 95 and 96.

The Hôtel Ferrandi is a classic hotel, with vast reception rooms, Restoration-style mahogany furniture and lavishly draped hangings. The bedrooms are also spacious, and no two are alike. In each one, a different bed creates the style and color scheme. The bathrooms are immaculate. The Hôtel Ferrandi stands just opposite the delightful Hôtel de Montmorency, which now houses the works of the 19th-century French artist Ernest Hébert, whom you might like to discover.

Hôtel Sainte-Beuve★★★

9, rue Sainte-Beuve
75006 Paris
Tel. (1) 45.48.20.07
Fax (1) 45.48.67.52
Mme Compagnon

Rooms 23, with bath and WC, telephone, TV, safe and minibar. **Price** 680-1250F, suite 1500F, apart. 1600F. **Meals** Breakfast 80F, snacks available. **Credit cards** Amex, Visa, Eurocard and MasterCard. **Pets** Dogs not allowed. **Parking** At 116, boulevard du Montparnasse. **Open** All year. **How to get there** (Map 37): Metro Vavin and Notre-Dame-des-Champs, Bus 68, 82, 83 and 91.

The Sainte-Beuve is the model of a charming hotel. For the decoration, David Hicks's Paris ateliers were called in and the spirit of the master is seen in the hotel's comfortable, simple luxury. A great refinement, created by the subtle harmony of colors and materials, distinguishes the neo-Gothic architecture of the lounge. Decoration apart, the amenities are modern and the bedrooms are spacious and bright with delicate colors which are well coordinated with the print wall-fabrics and antique furniture. The breakfasts are delicious and the service impeccable in this beautiful hotel.

Hôtel le Saint Grégoire★★★

43, rue de l'Abbé-Grégoire
75006 Paris
Tel. (1) 45.48.23.23
Fax (1) 45.48.33.95
Mme Agaud and M. Bouvier

Rooms 20 with bath or shower and WC, soundproofing, telephone, TV and hairdryer. **Price** Double 760-890F, suites and rooms with terrasse: 1290F. **Meals** Breakfast 60F, snacks available. **Credit cards** All major. **Pets** Small dogs allowed. **Parking** At rue de l'Abbé-Grégoire. **Open** All year. **How to get there** (Map 37): Metro Saint-Placide, Bus 48, 89, 94, 95 and 96.

The Saint Grégoire is located halfway between Montparnasse and Saint Germain in a small 18th-century building. The intimate decor beautifully blends a range of colors, subtly mixing shades of orange and mauve in the lounge, and pink and brown in the bedrooms. The rooms are well appointed with period furniture and very functional bathrooms. Some have terraces. You can have breakfast in a beautiful room with a vaulted ceiling, and you will enjoy a warm and pleasant welcome.

L'Abbaye Saint-Germain★★★

10, rue Cassette
75006 Paris
Tel. (1) 45.44.38.11
Fax (1) 45.48.07.86
M. Lafortune

Rooms 42 and 4 suites (duplex with balcony and minibar) with bath, WC, telephone and TV. **Price** Standard room 880-960F, large room 1465F, duplex or apartment 1765-1915F. **Meals** Breakfast incl., snacks available. **Credit cards** Amex, Visa, Eurocard and MasterCard. **Pets** Dogs not allowed. **Parking** At place Saint-Sulpice. **Facilities** Patio, bar. **Open** All year. **How to get there** (Map 37): Metro Saint-Sulpice and Sèvres-Babylone, Bus 48, 63, 70, 84, 87, 95 and 96.

Recent renovations have made the Hotel de L'Abbaye even more charming. The ground floor now has a broader view onto the flowering patio, where breakfast is served and bar service is provided in good weather. The plush couches around the fireplace in the lounge are ideal for relaxing in cooler weather. All the rooms are very comfortable, refined, and homey; some are air-conditioned. Among the most recently renovated rooms are the largest ones, which are lovely garden-level duplexes with balconies.

Hôtel de Seine★★★

42, rue de Seine
75006 Paris
Tel. (1) 46.34.22.80
Fax (1) 46.34.04.74
M. Henneveux

Rooms 30 with bath, telephone , soundproofing, cable TV and safe. **Price** 880-900F. **Meals** Breakfast 45F. **Credit cards** Not accepted. **Pets** Dogs not allowed. **Parking** At 27, rue Mazarine. **Open** All year. **How to get there** (Map 37): Metro Mabillon, Saint-Germain-des-Prés, Bus 58, 63, 70, 86, 87, 95 and 96.

After a complete renovation, the Hôtel de Seine has become a very appealing hotel, beginning with the provincial charm of the lounge, where a wood fireplace and panelling are brightened with a prettily colored floral tapestry. The bedrooms are as pleasantly decorated, with Provençal fabrics and patinated painted furniture. Their amenities have also been improved with the recent renovation as have their bathrooms. The staff are energetic and welcoming in this hotel, which is under the same management as the Hôtel des Marronniers.

Relais Saint-Germain★★★

9, carrefour de l'Odéon
75006 Paris
Tel. (1) 43.29.12.05
Fax (1) 46.33.45.30
M. Laipsker

Rooms 21 with air-conditioning, bath, WC, telephone, soundproofing, cable TV, hairdryer, safe and minibar. **Price** Single 1250F, double 1580F, suite 1880F. **Meals** Breakfast incl., snacks available. **Credit cards** All major. **Pets** Dogs allowed. **Parking** At place Saint-Sulpice, opposite 21, rue de l'Ecole-de-Médecine. **Open** All year. **How to get there** (Map 37): Metro Odéon and RER Cluny-Saint-Michel, Bus 58, 63, 70, 86, 87 and 96.

This is a small hotel of great luxury and charm. The very elegant lobby gives onto a small, luxurious lounge with beautiful 18th-century paintings and a Louis XIV chest of drawers. The Relais Saint-Germain has only 17 bedrooms, all beautiful, spacious and furnished with antiques. All are different, with lovely print or striped fabrics that harmonize with the air individual color schemes. The suite on the top floor is especially attractive. Modern amenities and service are, of course, flawless.

Hôtel de l'Odéon★★★

13, rue Saint-Sulpice
75006 Paris
Tel. (1) 43.25.70.11
Fax (1) 43.29.97.34
M. and Mme Pilfert

Rooms 30 with air-conditioning in some rooms, bath or shower and WC, soundproofing, telephone, cable TV, hairdryer and safe. **Price** Single 610F, double 740-920F, suite 1050F. **Meals** Breakfast 48F, snacks available. **Credit cards** All major. **Pets** Dogs allowed. **Parking** At place Saint-Sulpice and opposite 21, rue de l'Ecole-de-Médecine. **Open** All year. **How to get there** (Map 37): Metro Odéon, Saint-Sulpice and Saint-Germain-des-Prés, RER Cluny-Saint-Michel, Bus 58, 63, 70, 86, 87 and 96.

This handsome 16th-century building incorporates a skilful blend of decorative styles. Thus, in the ground-floor lounges, you find Louis-Philippe armchairs and pedestal tables beside a large church pew, and Persian rugs with a flowery English fitted carpet all creating a warm, intimate atmosphere. The bedrooms are individually decorated: Haute Epoque rooms with canopied beds and romantic rooms with large brass beds or Sicilian painted-iron twin beds. All have small writing or sitting areas. As this is the center of Paris, the rooms overlooking the street are well soundproofed, and the more exposed ones have air-conditioning for the summer. Lavish amounts of care and attention have been devoted to creating a stunning decor.

Relais Médicis★★★

23, rue Racine
75006 Paris
Tel. (1) 43.26.00.60
Fax (1) 40.46.83.39

Rooms 16 with air-conditioning, bath and WC, soundproofing, telephone, cable TV, hairdryer, safe and minibar. **Price** Single 920F, double 980-1380-1480F. **Meals** Breakfast incl. **Credit cards** All major. **Pets** Dogs not allowed. **Parking** At place Saint-Sulpice and opposite 21, rue de l'Ecole-de-Médecine. **Open** All year. **How to get there** (Map 37): Metro Odéon, RER Cluny-Saint-Michel, Bus 58, 63, 70, 86, 87 and 96.

The Relais Médicis appropriately defines itself as a hotel with the colors of Provence and the scent of Italy. This is very much the atmosphere inside, with its warm and sunny decoration. Waxed beamed ceilings, garden furniture, antique paintings and photos decorate the reception rooms downstairs. The bedrooms are fresh, cheerful and delightful with bathrooms as pretty as they are comfortable. The largest are on the street side. There is the same charm in the breakfast room with its checked tablecloths and its vacation atmosphere. This is a hotel where you'll love returning in the evening.

Le Clos Médicis★★★

43, rue de l'Abbé-Grégoire
75006 Paris
Tel. (1) 45.48.23.23
Fax (1) 45.48.33.95
Mme Agaud and M. Bouvier

Rooms 38 with air-conditioning, bath, WC, soundproofing, telephone, cable TV, hairdryer, safe and minibar - 1 room for disabled persons; elevator. **Price** Single 700F, double 850-900F, duplex 1200F. **Meals** Breakfast 60F. **Credit cards** All major. **Pets** Dogs allowed (+60F). **Parking** At rue Soufflet. **Open** All year. **How to get there** (Map 37): Metro Odéon, RER Luxembourg, Bus 21, 27, 38, 58, 82, 84, 85 and 89.

The Clos Médicis, like many hotels in this quarter, is named after the Medici Palace which was built in the Luxembourg Gardens for Marie de Medicis. At Number 54 next door, Blaise Pascal wrote a large part of *Les Provinciales* and *Les Pensées*. It has just been entirely renovated, with a beautiful and inviting reception area brightened by a cheerful fireplace in winter. With the first fine days of spring, breakfasts are served in the leafy courtyard which is just off the breakfast room. The bedrooms are generally spacious, and very comfortable, with modern conveniences and well-designed bathrooms; double windows and air-conditioning ensure that they are quiet. The walls are a pretty yellow, and the draperies and bedspreads are coordinated with lovely prints. The staff is very courteous.

Hôtel Le Régent★★★

61, rue Dauphine
75006 Paris
Tel. (1) 46.34.59.80
Fax (1) 40.51.05.07

Rooms 25 with air-conditioning, bath or shower and WC, telephone, TV, hairdryer and safe. **Price** 750-950F. **Meals** Breakfast 55F. **Credit cards** All major. **Pets** Dogs not allowed. **Parking** At 27, rue Mazarine. **Open** All year. **How to get there** (Map 37): Metro Odéon, RER Cluny-Saint-Michel, Bus 58, 63, 70, 86, 87 and 96.

The Hôtel Le Régent has recently opened in a former 18th-century town house between the boulevard Saint-Germain and the Seine. In the lobby, a mirrored wall reflects the painted beams and old stones of the house. The lounge is classic, and the bedrooms, more fanciful, are light and very cheerful with their assorted printed fabrics. The harmonizing bathrooms have beautiful tiles. The owners of the hotel also own the legendary *Café des Deux Magots*, where you can conveniently have your meals.

Hôtel de Fleurie★★★

32, rue Grégoire-de-Tours
75006 Paris
Tel. (1) 43.29.59.81
Fax (1) 43.29.68.44
Famille Marolleau

Rooms 29 with air-conditioning, bath or shower and WC, soundproofing, telephone, cable TV, hairdryer, safe and minibar. **Price** Single 610F, double 810-1200F. **Meals** Breakfast 50F, snacks available. **Credit cards** All major. **Pets** Dogs not allowed. **Parking** Opposite 21, rue de l'Ecole-de-Médecine. **Open** All year. **How to get there** (Map 37): Metro Odéon, RER Cluny-Saint-Michel and Luxembourg, Bus 58, 63, 70, 86, 87 and 96.

We were immediately attracted by the white façade of this hotel, which is highlighted on each level with a white niche and statue. There are the same light tones inside, with white stones or panelling and 18th-century-style caned chairs in the lounge and breakfast room. The bedrooms, which are not very spacious, are tastefully decorated in the same soft shades, and the bathrooms are comfortably equipped. (The rooms ending in 4 are the largest). The staff is efficient and welcoming.

Hôtel les Marronniers★★★

21, rue Jacob
75006 Paris
Tel. (1) 43.25.30.60
Fax (1) 40.46.83.56
M. Henneveux

Rooms 37 with bath or shower and WC (15 with TV). **Price** Single 510F, double 700-850F, suite 1020F. **Meals** Breakfast 45F, no restaurant. **Credit cards** Not accepted. **Pets** Dogs not allowed. **Parking** Opposite 169, boulevard Saint-Germain and at place Saint-Sulpice. **Open** All year. **How to get there** (Map 37): Metro Saint-Germain-des-Prés, Bus 39, 48, 63, 68, 69, 86, 87 and 95.

The Hôtel Les Marronniers is truly a delightful place, especially with its lovely garden. An ornate Napoleon III verandah houses the lounge and breakfast room. It is elegantly decorated with white cast-iron garden furniture, flowery carpets and graceful drapes in soft tones of pink and green. The bedrooms and bathrooms are more conventional. For a view of the garden, ask for a room on the *troisième étage* or higher, with a number ending in 1 or 2. The mansard rooms on the *cinquième* and *sixième étages* overlook the courtyard and have a pretty view of the rooftops. The staff is very pleasant.

Hôtel d'Anglete..

44, rue Jacob
75006 Paris
Tel. (1) 42.60.34.72
Fax (1) 42.60.16.93
Mme Soumier

Rooms 29 with bath, WC, telephone and TV. **Price** Single and double 850-1100F. **Meals** Breakfast 50F with orange juice. **Credit cards** All major. **Pets** Dogs not allowed. **Parking** Opposite 169, boulevard Saint-Germain. **Open** All year. **How to get there** (Map 37): Metro Saint-Germain des Prés, Bus 39, 48, 63, 70, 86, 87, 95 and 96.

This beautiful house is historic, for it was here that the independence of the United States was recognized. It is now a marvelous hotel, with high-ceilinged rooms, ornate panelling, ancient beams and antique furniture. The bedrooms are all individually decorated. In one of the most remarkable rooms, a wall with exposed stonework provides a stunning backdrop for beautiful 17th-century furniture, including a canopy bed. Note that the largest rooms are those overlooking the garden. The service is excellent and the staff will make theatre and restaurant reservations and do everything to make your stay in Paris pleasant.

Hôtel des Saints-Pères★★★

65, rue des Saints-Pères
75006 Paris
Tel. (1) 45.44.50.00
Fax (1) 45.44.90.83

Rooms 39 rooms and suites with bath or shower and WC, soundproofing, telephone, TV, safe and minbar. **Price** Single and double 456-1512F, suite 1512F. **Meals** Breakfast 50F, snacks available. **Credit cards** Amex, Visa, Eurocard and MasterCard. **Pets** Dogs not allowed. **Parking** Opposite 169, boulevard Saint-Germain. **Facilities** Bar, patio. **Open** All year. **How to get there** (Map 37): Metro Saint-Germain-des-Prés, Bus 39, 48, 63, 70, 84, 86, 87 and 95.

An atmosphere of elegance and comfort prevails in this lovely hotel. The spacious bedrooms and bathrooms have been tastefully decorated with simplicity and refinement. Worthy of special note is the *chambre à la fresque*, which has retained its lovely period ceiling. Most of the rooms overlook the hotel patio, and the ground-floor reception rooms lead out into this delightful courtyard full of flowers, where comfortable cane chairs are set in the shade in summer. The service is extremely efficient and professional.

Hôtel Lenox-Saint-Germain★★★

9, rue de l'Université
75007 Paris
Tel. (1) 42.96.10.95
Fax (1) 42.61.52.83
M. Destouches

Rooms 34 (5 duplex) with bath or shower and WC, telephone and TV. **Price** Single and double with shower 590F, with bath 670-830F, duplex 960F. **Meals** Breakfast 45F, snacks available. **Credit cards** All major. **Pets** Dogs not allowed. **Parking** At 9, rue Montalembert and opposite 169, boulevard Saint-Germain. **Facilities** Bar. **Open** All year. **How to get there** (Map 37): Metro rue du Bac and Saint-Germain-des-Prés, RER Gare d'Orsay, Bus 39, 48, 63, 70, 84, 86, 87 and 95.

Admirably located on the corner of the rue du Pré-aux-Clercs and the rue de l'Université, the Lenox has long attracted a young and chic regular clientele. The 1930s rosewood-panelled bar, which is open late, adds greatly to the atmosphere of the hotel. The bedrooms are pretty but some are small; in general, it is best to ask for a room on the upper floors. They are somewhat larger and, above all, less noisy. (The hotel should be soundproofed.) The Lenox Saint-Germain nevertheless is comfortable and the prices are very reasonable.

Hôtel de l'Université★★★

22, rue de l'Université
75007 Paris
Tel. (1) 42.61.09.39
Fax (1) 42.60.40.84
Mme Bergmann

Rooms 27 with air-conditioning, bath or shower and WC, telephone, TV and safe. **Price** Single 600-700F, double 800-1400F. **Meals** Breakfast 45F, with fruit juice and cheese; snacks available. **Credit cards** Visa, Eurocard and MasterCard. **Pets** Dogs not allowed. **Parking** At 9, rue de Montalembert and opposite 169, boulevard Saint-Germain. **Facilities** Bar. **Open** All year. **How to get there** (Map 37): Metro rue-du-Bac and Saint-Germain-des-Prés, RER Gare d'Orsay, Terminal Invalides, Bus 24, 27, 39, 48, 63, 68, 69, 70, 87 and 95.

This is an excellent hotel which owes its long-established reputation to an attentive and discriminating management committed to creating the atmosphere and charm of a family house rather than a hotel. The original vaulted ceilings, their oak supporting pillars, the staircase and fireplaces have been preserved. A subtle ochre color scheme has been chosen for the damask and velvet upholstery on the chairs and sofas in the lounges. The comfortable bedrooms are decorated with antique furniture and curios.

Hôtel de l'Académie★★★

22, rue des Saints-Pères
75007 Paris
Tel. (1) 45.48.36.22
Fax (1) 45.44.75.24
M. Chekroun

Rooms 34 (some with air-conditioning) with bath or shower and WC, telephone, cable TV, hairdryer. **Price** Single 490-720F, double 590-840F, suite 1100F. **Meals** Breakfast 45F, served 7:00-11:00; snacks available. **Credit cards** All major. **Pets** Dogs allowed. **Facilities** Bar, private parking. **Open** All year. **How to get there** (Map 37): Metro Saint-Germain-des-Prés, Bus 34, 48, 63, 70, 84, 86, 87 and 95.

The Hôtel de l'Académie is being handsomely refurbished. The reception area, bar, a small lounge and the breakfast room are now quite separate areas. Beautiful 18th-century and Directoire furniture, enhanced by original beams and old stone walls are stunningly highlighted with superb green and red fabrics. The bedrooms, which all have fully equipped bathrooms, are decorated in pastel shades. Ask for a room overlooking the courtyard, as these are quieter. The only reproach is the carpets in the hallways, which are already showing signs of wear.

Hôtel Montalembert★★★★

3, rue de Montalembert
75007 Paris
Tel. (1) 45.48.68.11
Fax (1) 42.22.58.19
J.-M. Desnos

Rooms 51 and 5 suites with air-conditioning, bath and WC, telephone, TV, video, hairdryer, safe and minibar. **Price** Single 1625F, double 1960-2080F, suite 2750-3600F. **Meals** Breakfast 100F. Restaurant. **Credit cards** All major. **Pets** Dogs allowed on request. **Parking** Montalembert opposite to the Hotel. **Facilities** bar. **Open** All year. **How to get there** (Map 37): Metro rue-du-Bac, Bus 24, 63, 68, 69, 83, 84 and 95.

The new "grand hotels" have changed in style and the Montalembert is one of the most beautiful examples of them. There is no nostalgic reference to the past; instead, modernity is employed to beautiful advantage: Clients of the grand hotels will surely enjoy the Montalembert's discreet luxury. The sobriety of the lobby enhances the interior architecture. The decoration of the lounge, which is both chic and warm, is centered around a fireplace-library at guests' disposal. The bedrooms and their refined baths have every favurious amenity, and the service and welcome are on a par with the hotel's class.

Hôtel Bersoly's★★★

28, rue de Lille
75007 Paris
Tel. (1) 42.60.73.79
Fax (1) 49.27.05.55
Mme Carbonnaux

Rooms 16 with bath or shower and WC, soundproofing, telephone, cable TV, hairdryer and safe. **Price** Single and double 580-680F. **Meals** Breakfast 50F with fruit juice, snacks available. **Credit cards** Visa, Eurocard and MasterCard. **Pets** Dogs allowed on request. **Parking** At 9, rue de Montalembert and opposite 169, boulevard Saint-Germain. **Facilities** Bar. **Open** All year except 3 weeks in Aug. **How to get there** (Map 37): Metro rue-du-Bac and Solférino, RER Gare d'Orsay. Terminal Invalides, Bus 24, 27, 39, 48, 63, 68, 69, 86, 87 and 95.

Bersoly's is a small hotel with an intimate atmosphere. The Louis XIII furniture in the reception area harmonizes handsomely with the rustic décor of the hotel, while the breakfast room in the vaulted cellars is more exotic. The bedrooms are decorated in a charming country style, and all have large fans for summer. The largest rooms are on the ground floor. You will find a warm and friendly welcome.

Hôtel de Nevers★★

83, rue du Bac
75007 Paris
Tel. (1) 45.44.61.30
Fax (1) 42.22.29.47
Mme Ireland

Rooms 11 with bath or shower and WC, telephone, TV, hairdryer and safe. **Price** Single 370F, double 400-430F. **Meals** Breakfast 30F. **Credit cards** Not accepted. **Pets** Dogs allowed. **Parking** At 30, boulevard Raspail. **Facilities** Bar. **Open** All year. **How to get there** (Map 37): Metro rue-du-Bac, Bus 63, 68, 69, 83, 84 and 94.

This is a small, simple, unpretentious hotel whose charming service and very reasonable prices are rare in Paris. A former outbulding of the Récolettes Convent, the building still has some of the original architectural details, which add further charm. The bedrooms are quite simple but have the usual amenities. Those on the top floor even have summery terraces on the roofs. The owner takes very good care of her clients.

Hôtel de Suède★★★

31, rue Vaneau
75007 Paris
Tel. (1) 47.05.00.08
Fax (1) 47.05.69.27
M. Chesnot

Rooms 41 with bath or shower and WC, soundproofing, telephone, cable TV, hairdryer, safe and minibar. **Price** Single 570F, double 635F, suite 845-1105F. **Meals** Breakfast incl. **Credit cards** Amex, Visa, Eurocard and MasterCard. **Pets** Dogs allowed. **Parking** At 30, boulevard Raspail and square Boucicault. **Open** All year. **How to get there** (Map 37): Metro Saint-François-Xavier and Sèvres-Babylone, Bus 82, 87 and 92.

The Hôtel de Suède enjoys the quiet which prevails in this quarter of embassies and the Musée d'Orsay. The reception and lounge are entirely panelled. The bedrooms are decorated in shades of grey, white and blue and furnished with white Directoire period furniture, with checked bedspreads and curtains in the same tones. Ask for those giving onto the courtyard and on the top floors with a view over the trees of the Matignon Garden.

Hôtel de la Tulipe★★

33, rue Malar
75007 Paris
Tel. (1) 45.51.67.21
Fax (1) 47.53.96.37
M. Fortuit

Rooms 20 with bath or shower and WC, soundproofing, telephone, TV, minibar. **Price** Single 438F, double 518-568F. **Meals** Breakfast 40F with cheese. **Credit cards** Amex, Visa, Eurocard and MasterCard. **Pets** Dogs allowed. **Parking** At Esplanade des Invalides. **Facilities** Patio. **Open** All year. **How to get there** (Map 37): Metro Latour-Maubourg and Invalides, RER Pont de l'Alma. Terminal Invalides, Bus 28, 49, 63, 69, 80, 83 and 92.

A delightful cobblestone courtyard engulfed in greenery is all that remains of the former convent which is now this small hotel. It is rustic in style, with beamed ceilings, Louis XIII furniture and bunches of dried flowers in the reception area. The bedrooms, many of which have exposed stone walls, are very quiet. The management is efficient and welcoming, and there is a friendly, informal atmosphere.

Hôtel Saint-Dominique★★

62, rue Saint-Dominique
75007 Paris
Tel. (1) 47.05.51.44
Fax (1) 47.05.81.28
Mme Petit and M. Tible

Rooms 34 with bath or shower and WC, telephone, TV, hairdryer, safe and minibar. **Price** Single and double 470-500F, suite 600-700F. **Meals** Breakfast 40F with orange juice and cheese. **Credit cards** All major. **Pets** Dogs allowed. **Parking** At Esplanade des Invalides. **Open** All year. **How to get there** (Map 37): Metro Latour-Maubourg and Invalides, RER Pont de l'Alma. Terminal Invalides, Bus 28, 42, 49, 69, 80 and 92.

Its convenient location and reasonable prices make the Saint-Dominique a very popular hotel. There is English-style decor in the lobby, where the pale pine furniture blends with the soft colors of the walls and the pink-beige fabrics. A charming country style has been chosen for the bedrooms, which have well equipped bathrooms. Some rooms are larger, with sitting areas, and most overlook patios full of flowers in summer. Those on the street are soundproofed. This is a lovely place to stay.

Hôtel de Tourville★★★★

16, av. de Tourville
75007 Paris
Tel. (1) 47.05.62.62
Fax (1) 47.05.43.90
M. Bouvier - Mme Agaud
Mlle Maas

Rooms 30 with air-conditioning, bath or shower and WC, telephone, cable TV, hairdryer, safe and minibar. **Price** Single and double 760-960F, suite 1390-1990F. **Meals** Breakfast 50F. **Credit cards** All major. **Pets** Dogs allowed (+70F). **Parking** At Esplanade des Invalides. **Open** All year. **How to get there** (Map 37): Metro Ecole-Militaire. Terminal Invalides, Bus 28, 82, 92 and 95.

The Hôtel de Tourville was very recently opened in a beautiful building between the dome of the Invalides and the Rodin Museum. There is an intimate atmosphere in the elegant lounge which was decorated by the David Hicks Atelier. The muted lighting and colors lend softness also to the bedrooms, which are personalized with antique furniture and paintings. The bathrooms are immaculate, with beautiful tiles and veined grey marble, and some open onto pleasant private terraces. This is also a hotel where you will enjoy the charm and quiet of this part of the Left Bank, not to mention the very attractive prices.

Hôtel du Bailli de Suffren★★★

149, av. de Suffren
75015 Paris
Tel. (1) 47.34.58.61
Fax (1) 45.67.75.82
M. and Mme Tardif

Rooms 25 with bath or shower and WC, soundproofing, telephone, TV, hairdryer. **Price** Single 545-596F, double 605-660F, suite 1080-1280F. **Meals** Breakfast 40-65F. **Credit cards** All major. **Pets** Dogs allowed (+50F). **Parking** Garage Bonvin, rue F. Bonvin (90F). **Open** All year. **How to get there** (Map 37): Metro Segur, Sèvres-Lecourbe, Bus 28, 49 and 92.

Located in the UNESCO quarter, the Hôtel du Bailli de Suffren has just been taken over by a dynamic couple who are renovating the hotel reviving the memory of the 18th-century French sailor and member of the Order of Malta called the Bailli de Suffren. They are beginning with very functional, modern bathrooms in most of the bedrooms. Decoration in the bedrooms has not yet been finished but the newly redone Versailles room and the Bailli suite are very lovely, while the older rooms also have their charm. The quietest and the lightest rooms look onto the courtyard. In the small lounge, you will find newspapers and magazines. The service is excellent and the owners are very anxious to help you enjoy your stay.

Hôtel Pergolèse ★★★★

3, rue Pergolèse
75016 Paris
Tel. (1) 40.67.96.77
Fax (1) 45 00 12 11
Mme Vidalenc

Rooms 40 with air-conditioning, bath or shower and WC, telephone, TV, hairdryer and minibar. **Price** Single 950F, double 1050F, suite 1500F. **Meals** Breakfast 75F. **Credit cards** All major. **Pets** Small dogs allowed. **Open** All year. **How to get there** (Map 37): Metro Argentine.

Clients attending conferences at the nearby Palais des Congrès are delighted to stay in this beautiful hotel, very near the Etoile, and to do their morning jogging in the Bois de Boulogne. Artfully restructured by Rena Dumas, the interior design is resolutely contemporary but the materials and colors used lend great gaiety and softness to the decoration. The bedrooms all have the same ash furniture and leather armchairs, which were designed especially for the hotel and which differ in their color schemes. The white marble bathrooms are very modern. In the lounge and dining room, other well-known designers have contributed to the decor, including Philippe Stark for the tables and Hilton McConnico for the wall decoration.

Hôtel de Banville★★★

166, boulevard Berthier
75017 Paris
Tel. (1) 42.67.70.16
Fax (1) 44.40.42.77
Mme Lambert

Rooms 39 with bath or shower and WC, telephone, soundproofing, TV, hairdryer and safe. **Price** Single 600F, double 700F. **Meals** Breakfast 45-75F, snacks available. **Credit cards** Amex, Visa, Eurocard and MasterCard. **Pets** Dogs allowed. **Parking** At 210, rue de Courcelles. **Facilities** Bar. **Open** All year. **How to get there** (Map 37): Metro Péreire and Porte-de-Champerret. Bus for Roissy-Charles-de-Gaulle at Porte Maillot, Bus PC, 83, 84, 92 and 93.

The Hôtel de Banville is a good hotel in a small 1930s building near the Palais des Congrès and the Etoile, on a quiet street lined with plane-trees. The Hôtel de Banville is a hotel of taste: its lounge is elegant, with antique furniture and beautiful Rubelli fabrics. The original elevator leads to the bedrooms, which are bright and spacious and overlook the leafy boulevard. From the *septième étage* up they have panoramic views. Breakfast is served amid the romantic *trompe l'oeil* decor of the dining room.

Le Jardin de Neuilly★★★

5, rue Paul-Déroulède
92200 Neuilly-sur-Seine
Tel. (1) 46.24.51.62
Fax (1) 46.37.14.60
Mme Rouah

Rooms 39 with bath or shower and WC, telephone, soundproofing, cable TV, hairdryer and minibar. **Price** Single and double 650-1050F. **Meals** Breakfast incl., snacks available. **Credit cards** Amex, Visa, Eurocard and MasterCard. **Pets** Dogs allowed. **Parking** At 210, rue de Courcelles. **Facilities** Bar. **Open** All year. **How to get there** (Map 37): Metro Sablons. Bus for Roissy-Charles-de-Gaulle at Porte Maillot.

This is an ideal place for those attending meetings at the Palais des Congrès and those who like returning to a charming, quiet hotel in the evening: A lovely garden separates the hotel from the street. The reception area is spacious, though somewhat impersonal, while the bedrooms are more appealing. Some are elegant while others are more rustic, but all are comfortable and decorated with antique furniture. The marble bathrooms are modern and functional. With the first beautiful days of spring, guests can enjoy their breakfast outside, but a verandah opening onto the garden makes this possible in fine weather all year. Note that this hotel is especially quiet on the weekend, when many residents of Neuilly are away.

Hôtel Galileo★★★

54, rue Galilée
75008 Paris
Tel. (1) 47.20.66.06.
Fax (1) 47.20.67.17
M. Mencaroni

Rooms 27 with air-conditioning, bath and WC, telephone, safe, hairdryer and minibar - Elevator, 2 rooms for disabled persons. **Price** Single and double 800-950F. **Meals** Breakfast 50F. **Credit cards** Amex, Visa, Eurocard and MasterCard. **Pets** Dogs not allowed. **Parking** Georges V (70-80F). **Open** All year. **How to get there** (Map 37): Metro and RER Charles-de-Gaulle-Etoile and Georges V, Bus 22, 30, 31, 52 and 73.

Well located between the Champs Elysées and the Avenue Georges V, the Galiléo is truly a *hôtel de charme*. Refinement and modernity are in evidence throughout, from the elegant lounge with its 18th-century fireplace and Aubusson tapestry to the breakfast room with its lovely soft colors and lighting. The elegant bedrooms also have very modern amenities with air-conditioning, good reading lamps, an office area with fax plug and extremely comfortable bathrooms with radio. The most spacious are the two ground-floor rooms and the two on the *cinquième étage* with a lovely verandah, which are our favorites.

Hôtel du Bois★★

11, rue du Dôme
75116 Paris
Tel. (1) 45.00.31.96
Fax (1) 45.00.90.05
M. Byrne

Rooms 41 with bath or shower and WC, soundproofing, telephone, cable TV, minibar. **Price** Single 405-435F, double 490-585F. **Meals** Breakfast 47F with orange juice. **Credit cards** Amex, Visa, Eurocard and MasterCard. **Pets** Dogs allowed. **Parking** At 8, avenue Foch and 2, rue Lauriston. **Open** All year. **How to get there** (Map 37): Metro Kléber and Etoile, RER and bus for Roissy-Charles-de-Gaulle, Bus 22, 30, 31, 52, 73 and 92.

A small stairway from the avenue Victor-Hugo to the small rue du Dôme leads to the Hôtel du Bois, which is very near the Etoile. Managed by an Englishman, the hotel has a British atmosphere. The bedrooms are decorated with prints in pastel colors and Kashmiri designs. They are comfortable and soundproofed to keep out noise from the large avenues around the Etoile. The staff is very courteous and friendly, and the hotel offers excellent value for the price in this very elegant quarter.

Hôtel Raphaël-Paris★★★★

17, avenue Kléber
75016 Paris
Tel. (1) 44.28.00.28
Fax (1) 45.01.21.50
M. Astier

Rooms 55 and 28 suites (some with air-conditioning) with bath or shower and WC, soundproofing, telephone, TV, minibar. **Price** Double 1950-2500F, suite and apart. 5000-7000F. **Meals** Breakfast 110-150F. Restaurant. **Credit cards** All major. **Pets** Dogs allowed. **Parking** At 8, avenue Foch. **Open** All year. **How to get there** (Map 37): Metro Kléber, RER and bus for Roissy-Charles-de-Gaulle. Bus 22, 30, 31, 52, 73, 92.

The Raphaël has its faithful following and we are among them because it remains a model of what great French hotels were and still can be. In the lounges and bedrooms, there is classic decor of wood panelling, ornate mirrors, Louis XV chairs and Persian carpets. The bedrooms are very spacious and comfortable. You will also enjoy the courtesy and attentiveness of a discreet, distinguished staff. The hotel bar is a very chic meeting spot: have a drink there and you will discover one of the most elegant hotels in Paris.

Hôtel Franklin-Roosevelt★★★

18, rue Clément-Marot
75008 Paris
Tel. (1) 47.23.61.66
Fax (1) 47.20.44.30
Mme Prudhon

Rooms 45 with bath or shower and WC, soundproofing, telephone, TV, hairdryer and minibar. **Price** Single and double 790-890F. **Meals** Breakfast 55F. **Credit cards** Amex, Visa, Eurocard and MasterCard. **Pets** Dogs not allowed. **Parking** At Georges V, opposite 103, avenue des Champs-Elysées and François Ier. **Open** All year. **How to get there** (Map 37): Metro Franklin-Roosevelt and Alma-Marceau, RER Charles-de-Gaulle, Bus 32, 42, 63, 80 and 92.

Hotelkeeping has been a tradition in this family for three generations, and you will find professionalism throughout. The hotel today has been entirely renovated. The bedrooms are romantically exotic, with panoramic scenes above the bedsteads, inspired by the paintings of Zuber. All are different and comfortable, and there are good bathrooms. The lounge and bar are pleasant, as is the breakfast room, which is designed like an interior patio. The staff is charming and attentive and the location is ideal.

Hôtel Queen Mary★★★

9, rue Greffulhe
75008 Paris
Tel. (1) 42.66.40.50
Fax (1) 42.66.94.92
M. Byrne

Rooms 36 with air-conditioning, bath and WC, soundproofing, telephone, cable TV, hairdryer and minibar. **Price** Single 710F, double 810-890F, suite 1175F. **Meals** Breakfast 67F. **Credit cards** Amex, Visa, Eurocard and MasterCard. **Pets** Dogs allowed. **Parking** At place de la Madeleine. **Open** All year. **How to get there** (Map 37): Metro Madeleine and Havre-Caumartin, Opéra, RER Auber, Bus 22, 24, 28, 32, 48, 80, 84 and 94.

Sheltered from the traffic in this busy quarter of large department stores, the Queen Mary has opened following a successful renovation. The lightefilled lounge is handsomely decorated with 18th-century French furniture. The colors chosen for the bedrooms are well coordinated with the mahogany furniture, and beautiful striped fabrics are used for the walls, the chairs and the bedspreads. There are, of course, the usual modern conveniences and very thoughtful details like the trouser press and the carafe of sherry awaiting your arrival. The efficient staff will help you make the most of your vacation or business trip.

Hôtel Lido★★★

4, passage de la Madeleine
75008 Paris
Tel. (1) 42.66.27.37
Fax (1) 42.66.61.23
Mme Teil

Rooms 32 with air-conditioning, bath and WC, telephone, cable TV, hairdryer, safe and minibar. **Price** Single 800F, double 930F. **Meals** Breakfast incl. **Credit cards** Amex, Visa, Eurocard and MasterCard. **Pets** Dogs allowed. **Parking** At place de la Madeleine, rue Chauveau-Lagarde. **Open** All year. **How to get there** (Map 37): Metro Madeleine, RER Auber, Bus 24, 42, 43, 52, 84 and 94.

The first hotel in a small group, including the Beau Manoir next door, the Lido remains a good model of personalized hotelkeeping. This is greatly due to Madame Teil, who personally makes sure that her clients are pleased. Haute-Epoque-period carpets, tapestries and chairs add warmth to the reception area and lounge. The bedrooms, which have their original beamed ceilings, are also very tastefully furnished; there are beautiful warm-colored fabrics on the walls and the well-thought-out details include functional closets and elegant toiletries in the comfortable bathrooms. (The rooms with numbers ending with 3 are the most spacious). The good breakfast includes homemade croissants and old-fashioned preserves.

Hôtel Beau Manoir★★★★

6, rue de l'Arcade
75008 Paris
Tel. (1) 42.66.03.07
Fax (1) 42.66.03.00
Mlle Veyrieras

Rooms 32 with air-conditioning, bath and WC, telephone, soundproofing, cable TV, hairdryer, safe and minibar. **Price** Single and double 995-1155F, suite 1365F. **Meals** Breakfast incl. **Credit cards** All major. **Pets** Dogs allowed. **Parking** At place de la Madeleine, rue Chauveau-Lagarde. **Open** All year. **How to get there** (Map 37): Metro Madeleine, RER Auber, Bus 24, 42, 43, 52, 84 and 94.

The owners have put their knowhow to good use here and created a lovely small *hôtel de prestige*. In the lounge, antique-style panelling is a beautiful complement to an 18th-century Aubusson tapestry. Damask-covered sofas and armchairs also contribute to the atmosphere, which is both luxurious and intimate. The decoration in the bedrooms includes a tasteful combination of coordinated prints. The rooms are spacious and most have corner sitting areas. (We prefer the rooms ending with 1). Note that you can have a meal or a tray brought to your room, prepared by Daniel Metery, who trained with the Troisgros brothers and whose acclaimed restaurant is just across the street.

Hôtel Mansart★★★

5, rue des Capucines
75001 Paris
Tel. (1) 42.61.50.28
Fax (1) 49.27.97.44
M. Dupain

Rooms 57 with with bath and WC, telephone, soundproofing, cable TV, hairdryer, safe and minibar. **Price** Single 526-826F, double 656-960F, suite 1206-1512F. **Meals** Breakfast 45F, snacks available. **Credit cards** Amex, Visa, Eurocard and MasterCard. **Pets** Dogs not allowed. **Parking** At place Vendôme. **Open** All year. **How to get there** (Map 37): Metro Madeleine, RER Auber. Bus Opéra, Madeleine, Concorde, Tuileries, RER Auber-Opéra, Bus 21, 27, 52, 68, 81 and 95.

On the corner of the Place Vendôme and the Rue des Capucines, the Hôtel Mansart has an idyllic location. The refurbishment was conceived in homage to Louis XIV's architect, Jules Mansart. Thus, you will find a tastefully baroque décor in the lobby, with mauve damask-covered 18th-century-style furniture and large paintings inspired by the famous formal gardens of Le Nôtre, Mansart's contemporary. The bold decorative scheme has been carried out tastefully. The spacious bedrooms are marvelously comfortable and decorated in pretty shades of coordinated colors. If you would like to be a neighbor of the Ritz and look out over the Place Vendôme, ask for the Mansart Room, which is superb.

Hôtel de la Place du Louvre★★★

21, rue des Prêtres Saint-Germain-
l'Auxerrois
75001 Paris
Tel. (1) 42.33.78.68
Fax (1) 42.33.09.95
M. Chevalier

Rooms 20 with bath and WC, telephone, cable TV, safe and hairdryer. **Price** Single 495-620F, double 680-830F, suite 820F. **Meals** Breakfast 40F, snacks available. **Credit cards** All major. **Pets** Dogs not allowed. **Parking** At Place du Louvre-Saint-Germain-l'Auxerrois. **Facilities** Bar. **Open** All year. **How to get there** (Map 38): Metro Louvre-Rivoli and Pont-Neuf, RER Châtelet-les-Halles, Bus 21, 24, 27, 67, 69, 74, 76, 81 and 85.

A room with a view awaits you at this hotel. And what a view! You will look out over the famous Louvre itself. A few beautiful vestiges of this ancient building have been preserved and successfully incorporated with modern decorative elements. The lounge and bar are located beneath a glass roof, while breakfast is served in a beautiful vaulted cellar called the *Salle des Mousquetaires,* which once communicated with the Louvre. The bright, sunny bedrooms have up-to-date amenities, and each is named after a painter. The service is efficient.

Le Relais du Louvre ★★★

19, rue des Prêtres-Saint-
Germain-l'Auxerrois
75001 Paris
Tel. (1) 40.41.96.42
Fax (1) 40.41.96.44
Mlle Aulnette

Rooms 18 and 2 suites with bath and WC, telephone, soundproofing, cable TV, safe, hairdryer and minibar. **Price** Single 580-750F, double 780-890F, suite 1040-1400F. **Meals** Breakfast 50F. **Credit cards** All major. **Pets** Small dogs allowed. **Parking** At 2 private locations (65F) and at place du Louvre-Saint-Germain-l'Auxerrois. **Open** All year. **How to get there** (Map 38): Metro Louvre-Rivoli and Pont-Neuf, RER Châtelet-les-Halles, Bus 21, 24, 27, 67, 69, 74, 76, 81 and 85.

From the day it opened, the Relais du Louvre has been obviously a *hôtel de charme.* This is in evident beginning with the reception area, where pretty lighting and warm colors on the walls complement the chairs and antique furniture, all creating a lovely effect. There is the same tasteful décor in the comfortable bedrooms, which can be made into apartments, and in the suites. Here you will live in one of the most prestigious areas of Paris, near the Grand Louvre and in the shadow of Saint-Germain-l'Auxerrois Church, the former parish of the Kings of France.

Hôtel Brighton★★

218, rue de Rivoli
75001 Paris
Tel. (1) 42.60.30.03
Fax (1) 42.60.41.78
M. Hashimoto

Rooms And suites 70 with bath or shower and WC, telephone, soundproofing, TV and minibar. **Price** Single 590-820F, double 620-850F, suite 1260F. **Meals** Breakfast incl. **Credit cards** All major. **Pets** Dogs not allowed. **Parking** At place Vendôme and place du Marché-Saint-Honoré. **Open** All year. **How to get there** (Map 38): Metro Tuileries and Concorde, Bus 68, 69 and 72.

The Brighton has been refurbished but nonetheless has kept all the features that made it, and still make it, a grand hotel with charm. Marble, velvets, carpets and crystal create a quiet, refined atmosphere, and the discreet staff are anxious to make your stay a pleasant one. We recommend the bedrooms giving onto the Tuileries Gardens or, better still, those on the top floors (some can be noisy), which have a lovely view. They are vast, with large windows, period furniture and modern bathrooms. (The bath in Room 115 is exceptional). The bedrooms on the courtyard have been partly renovated, and they have the advantage of being quiet.

Hôtel de la Tamise★★★

4, rue d'Alger
75001 Paris
Tel. (1) 42.60.51.54
Fax (1) 42.86.89.97
Mme Bellec

Rooms 20 with bath or shower and WC, telephone. **Price** Single 480-500F, double 720F, 3 pers. 930F. **Meals** Breakfast 40F. **Credit cards** Visa, Eurocard and MasterCard. **Pets** Dogs allowed. **Parking** At place Vendôme and place du Marché-Saint-Honoré. **Open** All year. **How to get there** (Map 38): Metro Tuileries and Concorde, Bus 68, 69 and 72.

Very near the Tuileries, the Hôtel de la Tamise occupies a house which once belonged to the Noailles and Mac-Mahon families. Its modest size creates an atmosphere of intimacy, which is enhanced by the small, ground-floor lounges; here, lovely English furniture, curios, engravings and paintings lend a personal touch to the interior, as if this were a private home. The bedrooms are classically charming and comfortable. The prices are still reasonable for such a prized quarter, making the Tamise an especially attractive hotel.

Hôtel Louvre Saint-Honoré★★★

141, rue Saint-Honoré
75001 Paris
Tel. (1) 42.96.23.23
Fax (1) 42.96.21.61
M. Maranzana

Rooms 40 with bath and WC, telephone, soundproofing, cable TV, hairdryer, safe and minibar. **Price** Single 490-735F, double 840-945F. **Meals** Breakfast 45F. **Credit cards** Amex, Visa, Eurocard and MasterCard. **Pets** Dogs allowed. **Parking** Louvre des Antiquaires, Croix des Petits-Champs, Forum des Halles. **Open** All year. **How to get there** (Map 38): Metro Palais-Royal, Louvre, RER Châtelet-Les Halles, Bus 21, 67, 69, 74, 75, 76, 81 and 85.

Next to the Louvre and Les Halles, this hotel comprises two buildings connected by a skylight, and the decor and accommodations are modern without being austere. The bedrooms are bright, quiet (thirty-five give onto the courtyard) and the bathrooms are well equipped. The staff are very friendly, and the quarter is extremely picturesque. The open market on the Rue Montorgueil on Sunday morning offers the visitor a chance to revisit the authentic Old Paris. And then, around the Place des Victoires nearby, you will find the fashionable boutiques of the city's leading *créateurs*.

Hôtel de la Bretonnerie★★★

22, rue Sainte-Croix-de-la-Bretonnerie
75004 Paris
Tel. (1) 48.87.77.63
Fax (1) 42.77.26.78
M. and Mme Sagot

Rooms 30 with bath or shower and WC, telephone, soundproofing, TV, safe and minibar. **Price** Single and double 620-730F, suite 900F. **Meals** Breakfast 45F. **Credit cards** Visa, Eurocard and MasterCard. **Pets** Small dogs allowed. **Parking** Hôtel-de-Ville. **Open** All year except in Aug. **How to get there** (Map 38): Metro Hôtel-de-Ville, Bus 29, 38, 47, 58, 67, 69, 70, 72, 74, 75 and 76.

With each season, the Hôtel de la Bretonnerie has pleasant surprises for us. Now, guests can enjoy new bedrooms as well as seven rooms which have been transformed and redecorated. Most are very large and some have a mezzanine. They are decorated in sober tones of beige, brown and burgundy, which harmonize with the exposed beams and antique-style furniture, and with the bathrooms. The suite has been redone in shades of pink. The staff is very welcoming.

Hôtel Saint–Paul–le–Marais★★★

8, rue de Sévigné
75004 Paris
Tel. (1) 48.04.97.27
Fax (1) 48.87.37.04
Mmes Leguide and Marcovici

Rooms 27 with bath and WC, soundproofing, telephone, cable TV, hairdryer and safe. **Price** Single 500F, double 630F. **Meals** Breakfast 45F with fruit juice, cheese and fresh fruit, no restaurant. **Credit cards** All major. **Pets** Dogs not allowed. **Facilities** Patio and bar. **Parking** At 2, rue Geoffroy-l'Asnier and 16, rue Saint-Antoine. **Open** All year. **How to get there** (Map 38): Metro Saint-Paul, Bus 29, 67, 69, 76 and 96.

This hotel is ideal for those who love the Marais quarter with its impressive private mansions, craftsmen's workshops, boutiques and the famous Place des Vosges. Only a few beams and pillars remain of the old building and the rest of the decoration is modern. The reception area, with wide windows onto the street, is light and airy, and it is decorated with black leather armchairs contrasting with pastel-colored walls. The same soft colors are repeated in the bedrooms, which have beamed ceilings and comfortable bathrooms. There is a delicious breakfast and the prices are reasonable.

Hôtel Caron de Beaumarchais★★★

12, rue Vieille-du-Temple
75004 Paris
Tel. (1) 42.72.34.12
Fax (1) 42.72.34.63
M. Bigeard

Rooms 19 with air-conditioning, bath or shower and WC, soundproofing, telephone, cable TV, hairdryer, safe and minibar - Elevator. **Price** Single and double 620-690F. **Meals** Breakfast 48-78F. **Credit cards** All major. **Pets** Dogs not allowed. **Parking** Rue Lobeau. **Open** All year. **How to get there** (Map 38): Metro Hôtel-de-Ville, Saint-Paul-le-Marais, Bus 54, 68, 74, 80, 81 and 95.

The Marais quarter now has a new hotel in keeping with its history. This comfortable 18th-century house has been restored in homage to the famous author of *The Marriage of Figaro*, who lived on this street. The decoration was carried out by Alain Bigeard, who researched and took inspiration from documents of the time. Thus, in the lobby, the walls are covered with embroidered fabric reproduced from the original designs, and there are Burgundian stone floors with period furniture. The same elegance is found in the beautifully comfortable bedrooms and the bathrooms, whose tiles are modeled on those of Rouen and Nevers. In addition, the prices are very attractive.

Pavillon de la Reine★★★★

28, place des Vosges
75003 Paris
Tel. (1) 42.77.96.40
Fax (1) 42.77.63.06
M. Sudre

Rooms 30 with air-conditioning, bath and WC, telephone, cable TV, hairdryer and minibar. **Price** Single 1400F, double 1600F, duplex 1800-2100F, suite 2500-2950F. **Meals** Breakfast 95F. **Credit cards** All major. **Pets** Dogs allowed. **Parking** Private garage. **Open** All year. **How to get there** (Map 38): Metro Bastille, Saint-Paul, Bus 20, 29, 65, 69 and 96.

This is an admirable hotel in an admirably historic place. The hotel consists of two buildings, one part dating from the 17th century, and one harmoniously rebuilt around a small courtyard. The Haute Epoque interior reflects the architectural style, with oak panelling on the walls of the very comfortable lounge, chairs upholstered in *petit point* tapestry and canopied beds. The colors and materials are very elegant and the bedrooms, which look out on the garden or the flower courtyard, are comfortable and quiet. The service is discreet, efficient and attentive.

TimHôtel Montmartre★★

11, rue Ravignan
75018 Paris
Tel. (1) 42.55.74.79
Fax (1) 42.55.71.01
Mme Fournier

Rooms 63 with bath or shower and WC, telephone, cable TV and hairdryer. **Price** Single 440F, double 540F, 3 pers. 680F. **Meals** Breakfast 49F. **Credit cards** All major. **Pets** Dogs allowed. **Parking** Impasse Marie-Blanche. **Open** All year. **How to get there** (Map 38): Metro Abbesses, Bus 30, 54, 67 and 80.

The TimHôtel enjoys one of the most charming locations in Montmartre. The rooms with the most beautiful views over Paris are those on the *quatrième* and *cinquième étages*, on the street side. Those on the top floor, on the *place* side, look out over the rooftops and Sacré-Cœur. The decoration of the bedrooms is ordinary but the hotel is comfortable and very functional; there's a baby's bottle-warmer, a diaper-changing table, a crib and even an iron and ironing board for guest use. The breakfast-buffet is a veritable brunch. You will find also that, despite its touristic reputation, Montmartre is still a village, with little squares, tiny stairway-streets which wind down from the Butte and its neighborhood spirit, all in evidence around the TimHôtel.

Hôtel Arnold ★★★
Route du Vin
67140 Itterswiller (Bas-Rhin)
Tel. 88.85.50.58 – Fax 88.85.55.54 – Mme Arnold

Rooms 28 with telephone, bath or shower, WC, TV and minibar. **Price** Double 380-595F. **Meals** Breakfast 48F, served 8:00-10:00; half board and full board 450-550F (per pers., 3 days min.). **Restaurant** Service 11:30-14:30, 19:30-21:00 (closed Sunday evening and Monday); menus 130-395F, also à la carte. Specialties: Noisette de chevreuil, civet de sanglier, choucroute, baeckeoffe, foie gras. **Credit cards** Visa, Eurocard and MasterCard. **Pets** Dogs not allowed. **Facilities** Parking. **Nearby** Alsace Wine Route from Marlenheim to Thann, church in Andlau, church of Sainte-Marguerite d'Epfig. **Open** All year.

The Hôtel Arnold lies in the heart of the Alsatian vineyards at the foot of the Vosges Mountains. It is composed of three buildings in the most traditional Alsatian style. Windows and balconies overflow with flowers. The interior decoration is warm and the recently renovated bedrooms are all extremely comfortable. Many have balconies with a beautiful view of the valley and the vineyards. Intent on maintaining Alsatian traditions, the Arnold family will invite you to try the regional specialties in the restaurant. Or you can buy them in the hotel's shop, which offers wines, *foie gras* and other products from the family estate.

How to get there *(Map 12): 41km south of Strasbourg via A35; Obernai exit; then N422 to Epfig; turn right on D 335 to Itterswiller.*

Hôtel Gilg ★★

1, route du Vin
67140 Mittelbergheim (Bas-Rhin)
Tel. 88.08.91.37 - Fax 88.08.45.17 - M. Gilg

Rooms 10 with telephone, bath, WC and TV. **Price** Single 215-250F, double 360-400F. **Meals** Breakfast 33F, served 7:30-10:00. **Restaurant** Service 12:00-14:00, 19:00-21:00; menus 125-325F, also à la carte. Specialties: Feuilleté chaud du vigneron, sandre à la moutarde de Meaux, émincé d'agneau au curry, cyrano glacé au croquant. **Credit cards** All major. **Pets** Dogs allowed. **Facilities** Parking. **Nearby** Barr, church in Andlau, church of Sainte-Marguerite in Epfig, Mont Sainte-Odile. **Open** Feb 2 – Jan 8 (closed Tuesday evening and Wednesday).

This imposing *winstub* is located on the corner of two small streets in a lovely village whose principal activity is winegrowing. The rooms here are quiet, warm and cozy, with furniture that is somewhat old-fashioned but charming in its own way. However, the pink bedroom, with its extraordinary bathroom, is outstanding. Meals (the quality is irregular) are served in the Gilg's large dining room with its beautiful traditional decor. The location and quality of this hotel make it a noteworthy place to stay near the Alsatian vineyards and many typical villages, often very old.

How to get there *(Map 12): 37km north of Colmar via N83 to Sélestat and N422 towards Barr.*

Hôtel Anthon ★★
40, rue Principale
67510 Obersteinbach (Bas-Rhin)
Tel. 88.09.55.01 – Mme Flaig

Rooms 9 with telephone, bath (1 with shower) and WC (7 with minibar). **Price** Double 250-280F. **Meals** Breakfast 45F, served 8:00-10:00. **Restaurant** Service 12:00-14:00, 18:30-21:00; menus 250-330F (also 105F weekdays), also à la carte. Specialties: Foie gras frais de canard, game in season. **Credit cards** Visa, Eurocard and MasterCard. **Pets** Dogs allowed. **Facilities** Parking. **Nearby** Lake at Hanau, Châteaux of Lutzelhardt and Falkenstein – 18-hole golf course in Bitche. **Open** Feb. – end Dec. (closed Aug. 21 – 30 and Tuesday and Wednesday).

The hotel-restaurant Anthon is located in a small picturesque village in the heart of the Vosges du Nord Park. It has nine pleasant, well-renovated bedrooms, all overlooking the surrounding countryside as far as the wooded slopes of the Vosges. The dining room is spacious; it is circular in shape and its large bay windows give the impression of dining in a garden full of flowers: perfect surroundings for the very high-quality food that is served there. The hotel also has a lively bar and a quiet lounge. The hotel itself, surrounded by extensive grounds, is very quiet.

How to get there *(Map 13): 66km north of Strasbourg via A4 and D44 to Haguenau, then D27 to Lembach, and D3 to Obersteinbach.*

Auberge d'Imsthal ★★

Route Forestière d'Imsthal
67290 La Petite-Pierre (Bas-Rhin)
Tel. 88.70.45.21 - Fax 88.70.40.26 - M. Michaely

Rooms 23 (2 with lounge), with telephone, bath or shower (20 with WC and TV).
Price Single 200-320F, double 280-600F. **Meals** Breakfast (buffet) 48F, served 8:00-
10:00; half board 300-460F, full board 380-540F (per pers., 3 days min.).
Restaurant Service 12:00-14:00, 19:00-21:00; menus 80-250F, also à la carte.
Specialties: Regional cooking. **Credit cards** All major. **Pets** Dogs allowed (+30F).
Facilities Health center, sauna (50F), parking. **Nearby** Vosges du Nord regional park,
Neuwiller-les-Saverne, Bouxvillier, Lichtenberg, crystal and glass factory in Wingen-
sur-Moder – 18-hole golf course in Bitche. **Open** All year.

The Auberge d'Imsthal is located in the splendid region of the
Northern Vosges Mountains. The interior is authentically
rustic and warm. We particularly recommend the renovated
bedrooms, which are very pleasant with their antiqued wood
furniture and colorful fabrics. Some look out onto a small lake and
the others face the back, which is much less beautiful but still
pleasant. They are comfortable and tasteful. There are many fitness
installations such as whirlpools and saunas. The cuisine is good,
nourishing and is charmingly served, which compensates for the
welcome, which could at times be better.

How to get there *(Map 12): 59km northwest of Strasbourg via A4, Saverne
exit, N4, D122, D133 and D178 to the Lake of Imsthal.*

Hôtel Neuhauser **
Les Quelles
67130 Schirmeck (Bas-Rhin)
Tel. 88.97.06.81 - Fax 88.97.14.29 - M. Neuhauser

Rooms 14 with telephone, bath or shower and WC (6 with TV). **Price** Single and double 200-310F. **Meals** Breakfast 38F, served 8:00-10:00; half board 250-300F, full board 300-370F (per pers., 3 days min.). **Restaurant** With air-conditioning. Service 12:00-14:00, 19:00-21:00 (closed 10–31 January); menus 110-300F, also à la carte. Specialties: Foie gras maison, filet de lapereau farçi, noisette de chevreuil forestière. **Credit cards** Visa, Eurocard and MasterCard. **Facilities** Heated swimming pool and parking. **Nearby** Belvédère de la chatte pendue. **Open** All year.

This hotel, and the few small houses which make up the hamlet, are ringed on all sides by meadows and forests. This isolation guarantees absolute tranquillity. The hotel does not have many rooms, but they are comfortable, well kept up and tastefully decorated in a traditional style (country furniture, beams...). The food is varied and well prepared, and meals are served in a vast panoramic dining room decorated like a winter garden. The wine list is worth close attention, as is the list of liqueurs and *eaux de vie*. Reasonably priced, this hotel is well worth a visit and has a covered swimming pool for use in the summer months.

How to get there *(Map 12): 56km southwest of Strasbourg via A35 and A352, then N420 or D392 to Schirmeck, then Les Quelles.*

Hôtel du Dragon ★★★

2, rue de l'Ecarlate - 12, rue du Dragon
67000 Strasbourg (Bas-Rhin)
Tel. 88.35.79.80 - Telex 871 102 - Fax 88.25.78.95 - M. Iannarelli

Rooms 32 with telephone, bath, WC and TV - Wheelchair accessible. **Price** Single 435-565F, double 475-605F, suite 760-865F. **Meals** Breakfast 54F, served 6:45-10:00. No restaurant. **Credit cards** All major. **Pets** Dogs not allowed. **Nearby** La Wantzenau, Alsace Wine Route – 18-hole golf courses in Illkirch-Graffenstaden and Plobsheim. **Open** All year.

We tend to equate charming with picturesque and old; and yet the 17th-century Hôtel du Dragon, which has been done in a very modern style, certainly has its own charm. The grey tones of the interior decoration and the designer furniture create a somewhat cold atmosphere, but the friendly, welcoming staff and the beautiful contemporary paintings quickly compensate for this. The very comfortable bedrooms face onto one of the quiet streets of the historic quarter. There is no restaurant, but delicious breakfasts are served on pretty china from the Café Coste. (If you admire the paintings, some are for sale). For restaurants, Monsieur Iannarelli will give you good recommendations, but be sure to visit *Chez Yvonne*, one of the most popular wine bars in the city.

How to get there *(Map 13): in the center of Strasbourg via the Quai Saint-Nicolas and the Quai Ch. Frey.*

Parc Hôtel ★★★

39, rue du Géneral-de-Gaulle
67710 Wangenbourg (Bas-Rhin)
Tel. 88.87.31.72 - Fax 88.87.38.00 - M. Gihr

Rooms 34 with telephone, bath or shower and WC. **Price** Single 240-265F, double 333-405F. **Meals** Breakfast 48F, served 7:30-9:30; half board 312-350F, full board 326-370F (per pers., 3 days min.). **Restaurant** Service 12:00-13:30, 19:00-20:30; menus 115-270F, also à la carte. Specialties: Munster chaud sur canapé, magret de canard. **Credit cards** Visa, Eurocard and MasterCard. **Pets** Dogs not allowed. **Facilities** Covered swimming pool, tennis, mountain-bike, sauna (50F), garage. **Nearby** Château de Wangenbourg, Haslach Forest, château and waterfall in Nideck, Château de Saverne, Abbey of Marmoutier. **Open** March 20 – Nov 4, Dec 22 – Jan 2.

The hotel lies in the heart of the village and is made up of a number of houses of different periods. It has a lovely park with its own nature trail, and is most attractively decorated, particularly the delightful lounge and the billiard room. All the bedrooms are large and well equipped, some with balconies looking over the garden. With the enjoyment of their guests in mind, the owners (who represent the sixth generation) have provided facilities for sport and relaxation, including a very charming covered swimming pool giving onto the lawn. Those who want to go on excursions or sightseeing will find all the information they need at the desk. Every Thursday evening in the restaurant food is grilled on an open fire and the atmosphere is very convivial. This is a family hotel to which many guests return every year, creating a vacation–club atmosphere which may not be to everyone's taste.

How to get there *(Map 12): 38km west of Strasbourg via A4, Saverne exit, then N4 towards Wasselonne, D224 and D218.*

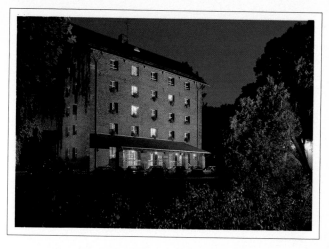

Le Moulin de La Wantzenau ★★

3, impasse du Moulin
67610 La Wantzenau (Bas-Rhin)
Tel. 88.59.22.22 - Fax 88.59.22.00 - Mmes Dametti and Wolff

Rooms 20 with telephone, bath or shower, WC and TV. **Price** Single and double 310-410F, suite 510F. **Meals** Breakfast 45F. **Restaurant** (Independent but at the hotel) Service 12:15-13:45, 19:15-21:15 (closed Wednesday, Sunday evening, national holidays in the evening); menus 150-250F. **Credit cards** All major. **Pets** Dogs allowed (+40F). **Facilities** Garage (+35F). **Nearby** Strasbourg, Alsace Wine Route – 18-hole golf course in La Wantzenau. **Open** Jan 2 – Dec 24.

Though close to Strasbourg, this hotel is in the quiet countryside. It is a beautifully restored old mill with lovely, comfortable bedrooms decorated with pale wood furniture and Laura Ashley fabrics. Most are spacious and have immaculate bathrooms. We also loved the lounge-bar, which is equally warm with its large fireplace and big armchairs which invite you to relax – and to enjoy the library here. (It also has children's books). The various services are much appreciated: the morning newspaper is brought with your breakfast and the hotel will press your clothes. The Moulin de La Wantzenau is a very friendly hotel with good value for the money. The restaurant is separate but just in front of the hotel.

How to get there (Map 13): 12km north of Strasbourg via A4, Reichstett exit, D63, and D301 towards Zone Industrielle La Wantzenau, then D468; 1.5km from La Wantzenau.

Hostellerie Saint-Barnabé ★★★

Buhl
68530 Murbach (Haut-Rhin)
Tel. 89.76.92.15 - Fax 89.76.67.80 - M. and Mme Orban

Rooms 27 with telephone, bath or shower, WC, TV and minibar. **Price** Single and double 310-560F, Suite 695-750F. **Meals** Breakfast 50F, 60F (in room), served 7:30-10:30. **Restaurant** Service 12:00-14:00, 19:00-21:00 (closed Sunday evening Nov – March); menus 125F-315F, also à la carte. Specialties: Chaud-froid de foie gras au vieux gewurztraminer, langoustines aux morilles, aiguillettes de pigeon au vin d'épice. **Credit cards** All major. **Pets** Dogs allowed (+25F). **Nearby** Lauch Valley, Murbach Abbey, Unterlinden Museum in Colmar, Automobile and Rail Museums in Mulhouse, Alsace Wine Route – 9-hole Rouffach golf course. **Open** March 1 – Jan 14.

Now that the Saint-Barnabé has been beautifully refurbished, we are pleased to put it it back into the Guide. Located in a beautiful forest setting, the Hostellerie has several dining rooms, lounges, and smoking rooms with beautiful views. The atmosphere is tranquil and the decoration is classic and pleasant. The bedrooms are attractive and very comfortable, with beautiful bathrooms. (Rooms 11 and 16 can be noisy during meal times). Certain suites are ideal for families, and nature lovers will enjoy the Pavillon Vert rooms on the ground floor. Note also the irresistible Chalet room with a cheerful fireplace. The fabrics throughout have been beautifully chosen. The regional cuisine is excellent – you are served on the terrace in summer – and there is a delightful choice of Alsatian wines. The owners are young and friendly.

How to get there *(Map 20): 3km from Guebwiller. Go straight through the center of town to Bulh; then turn left for Murbach.*

Hostellerie Le Maréchal ★★★★

4-6, place des Six Montagnes Noires
68000 Colmar (Haut-Rhin)
Tel. 89.41.60.32 – Fax 89.24.59.40 – M. and Mme Bomo

Rooms 30 with air-conditioning, telephone, bath or shower, WC and TV. **Price** Single 450-500F, double 550-700F, suite 900-1400F. **Meals** Breakfast 60F, served 7:30-10:00; half board 650F, full board 800F (per pers., 3 days min.). **Restaurant** Service 12:00-14:00, 19:00-22:00; menus 150-380F, also à la carte. Specialties: Soupe de grenouilles à la bière, selle de lapereau à la pistache et aux pignons de pin. **Credit cards** All major. **Pets** Dogs allowed (+35F). **Facilities** Parking (+35F). **Nearby** Issenheim altarpiece at the Unterlinden Museum in Colmar, Alsace Wine Route, Neuf-Brisach, Trois-Epis, Munster – 18-hole golf course in Ammerschwihr. **Open** All year.

Well located in the old quarter of Petite Venise (Little Venice) in Colmar, the Hostellerie Le Maréchal occupies four old houses on the edge of the canals. The interior is delightful. Beams and stone go well with the Louis XIII furniture in the lounge and dining room. Each bedroom has its own style, and you can choose between medieval or 18th-century decor. They are elegant, comfortable and well equipped, and though some are rather small, this fits in perfectly with the cozy atmosphere of the hotel. Ask for a room on the canal side. The candlelit dinners in the long dining room beside the Lauch, the specialties offered there, and the warm, solicitous welcome make the Hostellerie Le Maréchal the best hotel in Colmar.

How to get there (Map 12): in the center of old Colmar.

Hôtel La Clairière ★★★

50, route d'Illhaeusern
68970 Guémar - Illhaeusern (Haut-Rhin)
Tel. 89.71.80.80 - Fax 89.71.86.22 - M. Loux

Rooms 25, and 2 apartments, with telephone, bath, WC, TV and minibar - Elevator.
Price Single 420F, double 540-840F, suite 1200-1600F. **Meals** Breakfast 65F, served
7:30-10:00. No restaurant. **Credit cards** Visa, Eurocard and MasterCard. **Pets** Dogs
allowed. **Facilities** Tennis, swimming pool, parking. **Nearby** Colmar, Alsace Wine
Route from Marlenheim to Thann – 18-hole golf course in Ammerschwihr (25km).
Open March 1 – Dec 31.

Off the main road at the edge of the forest, the Hôtel La Clairière offers 25 country-style bedrooms; most are magnificently decorated, very comfortable and have a lovely view over the plain and the Vosges. The excellent breakfasts are served in your room, enabling you to take further advantage of the view. Comfortable armchairs and a beautiful fireplace make the lounge wecoming and restful. There is no restaurant in the hotel, but the famous, three-star *Auberge de L'Ill* is nearby. The Clairière has its own tennis courts and is also a good starting point for lovely walks. The owners are very hospitable.

How to get there *(Map 12): 17km north of Colmar via N83 towards Sélestat; at Guémar D106 towards Marckolsheim.*

Les Hirondelles ★★

33, rue du 25 janvier
68970 Illhaeusern (Haut-Rhin)
Tel. 89.71.83.76 - Fax 89.71.86.40 - Mme Muller

Rooms 14 with telephone, shower, WC and TV. **Price** Double 220-250F. **Meals** Breakfast 30F, served 8:00-10:00; half board 220-255F (per pers., 3 days min.). **Restaurant** On reservation, service from 19:30 (closed Sunday evening and Nov1 – Easter). Specialties: Traditional country cooking, Alsatian specialties. **Credit cards** Visa, Eurocard and MasterCard. **Pets** Small dogs allowed. **Facilities** Parking. **Nearby** Colmar, Alsace Wine Route from Marlenheim to Thann, Haut-Koenigsbourg – 18-hole golf course in Ammerschwihr. **Open** March – Jan.

L es Hirondelles is an ancient farm of vast dimensions lying near the famous Auberge de l'Ill Restaurant and the lovely Ill River. The bedrooms are located in a large outbuilding which has been entirely refurbished. Decorated for comfort and practicality, they are furnished with new but typically Alsatian wardrobes of polychromed wood. You may choose between rooms giving onto flowery balconies and the courtyard, or a more rural view over small vegetable gardens. There is a welcoming lounge on the ground floor where breakfast is served, along with good dinners based on regional cooking. The welcome is charming and informal at "The Swallows," this pleasant hotel near the vineyards; and the prices are very reasonable.

How to get there (Map 12): 12km north of Colmar via RN83 in the Strasbourg direction.

Hostellerie de L'Abbaye d'Alspach ★★

2-4, rue Foch - Kintzheim
68240 Kaysersberg (Haut-Rhin)
Tel. 89.47.16.00 - Fax 89.78.29.73 - Mme Schwartz

Rooms 29 with telephone, bath or shower and WC (13 with TV). **Price** Single 240-320F, double 320-420F. **Meals** Breakfast (buffet) 44F, served 8:00-10:00. No restaurant. **Credit cards** All major. **Pets** Dogs not allowed. **Facilities** Parking. **Nearby** Issenheim altarpiece at the Unterlinden Museum in Colmar, Alsace Wine Route, Kayersberg, Riquewihr – 18-hole golf course in Ammerschwihr. **Open** All year.

The Alsatian notion of comfort finds full expression in this hotel. The predominance of wood, the comfortable furniture, the hunting trophies on the walls, all contribute to the warm atmosphere which strikes you as soon as you enter. The bedrooms have all been completely renovated and are very pleasant; they are reached via a splendid stone spiral staircase and a wooden footbridge identical to the one once used by the nuns of the order of Saint Clare in the Middle Ages. The restaurant we recommend is *L'Auberge Saint-Martin* in Kintzheim.

How to get there *(Map 12): 10km northwest of Colmar; at Kaysersberg take the Ribeauvillé road for 2km.*

Auberge Les Alisiers **

5, rue Faude
68650 Lapoutroie (Haut-Rhin)
Tel. 89.47.52.82 – Fax 89.47.22.38 – M. and Mme Degouy

Rooms 10 with telephone, bath or shower and WC. **Price** Single 190F, double 350F.
Meals Breakfast (buffet) 42F, served 7:30-10:00; half board 280-340F.
Restaurant Service 12:00-13:00, 19:00-21:00 (closed Monday evening except for
guests on half board, and Tuesday); menus 75-189F, also à la carte. Specialties:
Pigeonneau rôti, truite saumonée à la crème de lard, cervelas rôti sur salade de
choucroute, pommes de terre coiffées de munster fondu. **Credit cards** Visa, Eurocard
and MasterCard. **Pets** Dogs allowed. **Facilities** Parking. **Nearby** Colmar, Alsace
Wine Route from Marlenheim to Thann – 18-hole golf course in Ammerschwihr.
Open Feb 1 – Dec 31.

The Auberge Les Alisiers lies 700 meters up in the mountains;
the view from it over the Hautes Vosges and the Béhine Valley
is stunning, and the hotel itself is very pleasant. The bedrooms,
with their pale wood furniture, are all different, cozy and
comfortable. Some have been recently renovated and these have
the best bathrooms. An attractive dining room offers panoramic
views across the Vosges Mountains. The cooking is varied and
good (with an excellent sauerkraut). The intimate and relaxed
atmosphere of the auberge owes much to the friendliness of its
owners.

*How to get there (Map 12): 19km northwest of Colmar via N415; at
Lapoutroie go left in front of the church and follow the signs for 3km.*

Hôtel Le Clos Saint-Vincent ★★★★
Route de Bergheim
68150 Ribeauvillé (Haut-Rhin)
Tel. 89.73.67.65 – Fax 89.73.32.20 – M. Chapotin

Rooms 11, and 3 apartments, with telephone, bath, WC, TV and minibar. **Price** Single 650F, double 700-935F, apart. 1000-1100F. **Meals** Breakfast incl., served 8:15-10:30. **Restaurant** Service 12:00-14:00, 19:00-20:30 (closed Tuesday and Wednesday); menus 260F, also à la carte. **Credit cards** Visa, Eurocard and MasterCard. **Pets** Dogs allowed (+30F). **Facilities** Covered swimming pool, parking. **Nearby** Hunawihr, swan reproduction center, ruins of the Château of St-Ulrich, Riquewihr, Alsace Wine Route from Marlenheim to Thann, Le Haut-Koenigsbourg; local festivities: Wine Festival in July-Aug, Minstrel Festival in Sept, Baroque Music Festival in autumn – 18-hole golf course in Ammerschwihr. **Open** March 15 – Nov 15.

In the heart of the Riesling wine country, the Clos Saint Vincent looks out on the Alsace plateau, the Black Forest, and to the east, the Alps. The hotel has three floors. On the *premier étage* there is a lobby and a pleasant restaurant with a panoramic view. The rooms are richly decorated in Directoire style with magnificent fabrics. (The "rustic" rooms are less charming). They are light, very comfortable, and very quiet. The pool is beautiful but the service is sometimes lacking.

How to get there *(Map 12): 19km north of Colmar via N83 and D106 towards Ribeauvillé, then D1b towards Bergheim (follow the signs).*

Hostellerie des Seigneurs de Ribeaupierre ★★★

11, rue du château
68150 Ribeauvillé (Haut-Rhin)
Tel. 89.73.70.31 - Fax 89.73.71.21 - Mmes Barth

Rooms 10 with telephone, bath or shower and WC. **Price** Doubles 440-480F, suite 540-670F. **Meals** Breakfast 47F, served 8:00-11:00. No restaurant. **Credit cards** Amex, Visa, Eurocard and MasterCard. **Pets** Dogs not allowed. **Nearby** Hunawihr, swan reproduction center, ruins of the Château of Saint-Ulrich, Riquewihr, Alsace Wine Route from Marlenheim to Thann, Le Haut-Koenigsbourg; local festivities: Wine Festival in July-Aug., Minstrel Festival in Sept., Baroque Music Festival in autumn – 18-hole golf course in Ammerschwihr. **Open** All year (Jan and Feb on reservation by fax).

The Hostellerie des Seigneurs de Ribeaupierre is a remarkable small hotel in one of the most beautiful villages of Alsace: There are several delicious rooms in this 18th-century auberge, which is located in a quiet spot outside the center. All are charming and comfortable, with beautiful old regional furniture, soft beds, light-colored woodwork and half-timbering, and ravishing fabrics. The bathrooms are superb and there is a lovely corner sitting area in many rooms. On the ground floor, there is a small lounge where a fireplace is often blazing and, several steps down, you come to the breakfast room. Breakfasts are delicious and copious and you may even ask for a veritable brunch, with cold cuts, eggs and, as this is Alsace, a slice of *foie gras*. This is a magnificent hotel, where you are greeted warmly by two very dynamic sisters. For restaurants, we suggest the gastronomic *La Winstub Zum Pfifferhüs*; and the simpler *La Flammerie* (delicious *jambonneau*) and *L'Auberge Zahnacker*.

How to get there *(Map 12): 19km north of Colmar via N83 and D106 towards Ribeauvillé.*

Hôtel de la Rochette **
La Rochette
68910 Labaroche (Haut-Rhin)
Tel. 89.49.80.40 - M. Preiss

Rooms 7 with shower and WC. **Price** Double 250F, suite 400F. **Meals** Breakfast (buffet) 45F, served 8:00-9:30; half board 265-300F (child 190F). **Restaurant** Service 12:30-13:30, 19:30-21:00; menus 85-185F, also à la carte. Specialties: Traditional Alsatian cooking, foie gras maison, bouillabaisse (Nov – April). **Credit cards** Amex, Visa, Eurocard and MasterCard. **Pets** Dogs not allowed. **Facilities** Parking. **Nearby** Turckheim, Colmar, Alsace Wine Route from Marlenheim to Thann – 18-hole golf course in Ammerschwihr (5km). **Open** All year (closed Sunday evening and Wednesday).

Standing on a plateau in the heart of the green forests of the Vosges, the Hôtel de la Rochette is to be found a little way from the village. It is difficult not to be charmed by this small house – a hotel for fifty years – with its antique furniture, polished floors, and collections of folk art and local pottery. The bedrooms reflect the spirit of the house: they are all comfortable and number 8 is quite charming, but some could do with new carpets. Note that this is actually a restaurant with rooms, which is why some of the communal areas are not very big, though there is a bar. The welcome here is warm. When the weather is good, drinks and snacks are served on the terrace.

How to get there *(Map 12): 18km northwest of Colmar via D417 to Turckheim, then D11 towards Trois-Epis, Orbay.*

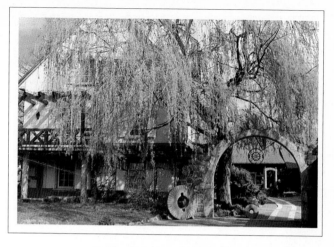

Hôtel Au Moulin ★★

Sainte-Croix-en-Plaine
68127 Herrlisheim (Haut-Rhin)
Tel. 89.49.31.20 - Fax 89.49.23.11 - M. and Mme Wœlffle

Rooms 16 and 1 suite with telephone, bath and WC (4 with TV). **Price** Single and double 210-400F, suite 500F. **Meals** Breakfast 40F, served 7:30-10:00. No restaurant. **Credit cards** Visa, Eurocard and MasterCard. **Pets** Dogs allowed (+30F). **Facilities** Parking. **Nearby** Colmar, Neuf-Brisach, Munster, Trois-Epis, Alsace Wine Route from Marlenheim to Thann – 18-hole golf course in Ammerschwihr. **Open** End March – Nov 15.

This former flour mill was built in the 17th-century by a colony of Mennonites and was converted into a hotel in 1982. It is a large white building with windows brightened by geraniums. The owners, the Wœlffle family, live in adjoining buildings, the ensemble forming a pretty courtyard with banks of flowers surrounding an old stone well. Spread over three floors, the bedrooms face either east, towards the Vosges, or across the fields. Most are spacious and all have very well equipped bathrooms. (There is no television, as peace and quiet are the main concern). Finally, there are three further rooms in another building facing onto the courtyard, where breakfast can be enjoyed to the sound of water flowing down the Thur River, also called the "canal of the twelve mills" (two still work). This is a hotel with a very friendly atmosphere and very attractive prices. For fine dining, we recommend in Eguisheim, *Le Caveau d'Eguisheim* and *Hostellerie du Pape*; in Colmar, *La Maison des Têtes* and *Au Fer Rouge*.

How to get there (Map 12): 6km south of Colmar via N422, then D1 towards Sainte-Croix-en-Plaine.

51

Auberge La Meunière ★★

30, rue Sainte-Anne
68590 Thannenkirch (Haut-Rhin)
Tel. 89.73.10.47 - Fax 89.73.12.31 - M. Dumoulin

Rooms 15 with telephone, shower and WC (6 with TV). **Price** Double 260-310F, suite 650F. **Meals** Breakfast 30F, served 8:30-9:30; half board 230-290F, full board 300-360F. **Restaurant** Service 12:15-14:00, 19:15-21:00; menus 95-190F, also à la carte. Specialties: Foie gras de canard au gewürztraminer, langue de bœuf à la crème de radis noir, Kouglof glacé. **Credit cards** Amex, Visa, Eurocard and MasterCard. **Pets** Dogs allowed (+20F). **Facilities** Health center and sauna (150F for 2 pers.), mountain bikes, parking. **Nearby** Haut-Koenigsbourg, Ribeauvillé, Riquewihr, Kaysersberg – 18-hole golf course in Ammerschwihr. **Open** Easter – Nov 1.

It is impossible not to notice the typically Alsatian facade of this lovely auberge in the little village of Thannenkirch in the foothills of the Vosges. You will find the same charm in the dining room, with its almond-green table linens and low ceilings and the wooden partitions that create several little intimate corners. The bedrooms, some furnished with antiques and some in more modern style, all have the same cozy and comfortable feel. Instead of numbers, the bedroom doors have enameled plaques inscribed with women's names. We particularly liked the *Sophie* and *Josephine* rooms with their glassed-in balconies looking over the countryside towards the fortress of Haut-Koenigsbourg in the distance. The view is superb from the large terrace, where meals are also served.

How to get there (Map 12): 25km north of Colmar via N83 to Guémar, N106 and D42.

Les Violettes ★★★

68500 Jungholtz-Thierenbach (Haut-Rhin)
Tel. 89.76.91.19 - Fax 89.74.29.12
M. Munsch

Rooms 24 with telephone, bath or shower and WC (20 with TV, 12 with minibar).
Price Single 220F, double 540-740F. **Meals** Breakfast 55F, served 8:00-10:00.
Restaurant Service 12:00-14:00, 19:00-21:00 (closed Monday evening and
Tuesday); menus 170-400F, also à la carte. Specialties: Brioche de foie gras,
cassolette de turbot et langouste aux morilles. **Credit cards** All major. **Pets** Dogs
allowed (+40F). **Facilities** Sauna (150F for 2 pers.), parking. **Nearby** Walks,
Automobile and Rail Museums in Mulhouse, Unterlinden Museum in Colmar – 18-
hole golf course in Ammerschwihr. **Open** All year.

Monsieur and Mme Munsch have devoted much care and
attention to their small hotel. It is quiet, on the edge of a
forest and has a lovely view over the valley and the little village of
Thierenbach which lies just below. Inside, antique furniture,
beautiful carpets, paintings and *objets d'art* create a warm and
cheerful ambience. In the dining room with its panoramic windows
and floral fabrics you will enjoy M. Munsch's excellent cooking.
All the bedrooms, whether in the main building or the annex, are
prettily decorated with beautiful fabrics, lace, pictures and white
lacquered or natural wood furniture. Some have a terrace looking
out on the forest. This is a charming place to stay.

*How to get there (Map 20): 5km south of Guebwiller in the direction of
Soultz, at Thierenbach go left of the basilica, then 300m to the edge of the
forest.*

Château d'Adoménil ★★★
Rehainviller
54300 Lunéville (Meurthe-et-Moselle)
Tel. 83.74.04.81 - Fax 83.74.21.78 - M. Million

Rooms 8 with telephone, bath, WC, TV and minibar. **Price** Single and double 480-850F, suite 1200F. **Meals** Breakfast 70F, served 8:00-11:00; half board 710F (per pers., 3 days min.). **Restaurant** Service 12:00-14:00, 19:30-21:30 (closed Sunday evening and Monday and Tuesday lunchtime Nov 1– March 31, and Monday and Tuesday lunchtime April 1 – Oct 31); menus 230-430F, also à la carte. Specialties: Sandre aux lardons, gris de Toul, foie gras poêlé. **Credit cards** All major. **Pets** Dogs allowed. **Facilities** Parking. **Nearby** Château de Lunéville, Crystal Museum in Baccarat, Place Stanislas, School of Nancy Museum and Emile Gallé Museum in Nancy, Saint-Etienne Cathedral in Toul. **Open** All year except Feb (closed Monday).

Some ten years ago, Monsieur Million left his restaurant in Lunéville to move into this beautiful chateau. He has opened a successful restaurant here, and the old stables have been converted into five spacious rooms which open onto the orchard. They all have beautiful tiled floors, modern Italian furniture and decorative objects, and luxurious bathrooms. In the chateau there are three other rooms of a more classical charm. The chateau is on a beautiful seventeen–acre estate, which is disturbed only occasionally by a little railway nearby. The cuisine lives up to its reputation, and you will enjoy delicious breakfasts with croissants and assorted pastries.

How to get there *(Map 12): 30km southeast of Nancy via N4 to Lunéville; 3km south of Lunéville via D914.*

La Bergerie **

15, rue des Vignes
57640 Rugy (Moselle)
Tel. 88.77.82.27 - Fax 87.77.87.07 - Mme Keichinger

Rooms 42 with telephone, bath or shower, WC and TV. **Price** Single and double 300-380F. **Meals** Breakfast 40F, served 6:30-10:30. **Restaurant** Service 12:00-13:45, 19:00-21:30; menus 120-200F, also à la carte. Specialties: Traditional cooking. **Credit cards** Visa, Eurocard and MasterCard. **Pets** Dogs allowed. **Facilities** Parking. **Nearby** Saint-Etienne Cathedral in Metz, Waliby Park (Schtroumpf) – 18-hole golf course in Metz. **Open** All year.

La Bergerie is conveniently placed for the autoroute but nevertheless stands in a green and quiet spot. The hotel consists of several buildings, some of which are very old. The bedrooms are modern, airy and functional and are furnished with lovely country fabrics. Their bathrooms are pleasant and well equipped, but the soundproofing is not always perfect. We particularly recommend those that overlook the park. There are two large and prettily decorated dining rooms to choose between, but, weather permitting, you will probably prefer to sit under the shady trellis with its little white tables. Professional and attentive service and the charm of the place make this a very pleasant place to stay, which could be even moreso if the breakfasts were better.

How to get there *(Map 12): 10km north of Metz via A4, Ennery exit.*

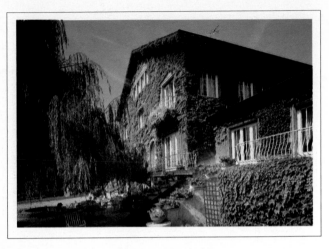

L'Horizon ***
50, route du Crève-Cœur
57100 Thionville (Moselle)
Tel. 82.88.53.65 – Fax 82.34.55.84 – Speck Family

Rooms 10 with telephone, bath, WC and TV. **Price** Single 480F, double 680-780F.
Meals Breakfast 62F, served 7:15-10:30; half board 560-660F (per pers., 3 days
min.), 840-980F (per 2 pers., 3 days min.). **Restaurant** Service 12:00-13:45, 19:00-
21:30 (closed Saturday lunchtime); menus 215-325F, also à la carte. Specialties:
Escargotière de petits gris, sandre en mode lorraine, le mirabellier (dessert).
Credit cards Amex, Visa, Eurocard and MasterCard. **Pets** Dogs allowed (+70F).
Facilities Parking, garage (+70F). **Nearby** St-Etienne Cathedral in Metz, Waliby Park
(Schtroumpf) – 18-hole golf course in Metz. **Open** March 1 – Jan 31.

Although it's only a few minutes from the center of Thionville,
the Horizon is surrounded by greenery, and its hillside location
gives you a panoramic view out over the city. When it was built
some thirty years ago, the hotel was a vast family residence. Even
though it is a luxury hotel today, you are very much aware of the
family feeling, which has been maintained. The bedrooms are very
comfortable, and period furniture lends a personal touch to each.
Those on the *deuxième étage* are smaller but pleasant, and obviously
less expensive. On the ground floor, the living room, dining room
(magnificent) and bar are very warm and inviting. Like many of
the bedrooms, they look out over Thionville and the Moselle Plain.
The Horizon is a half-city, half-country place to stay, offering
famous gastronomy and a warm welcome.

How to get there *(Map 12): 30km south of Luxembourg. 30km north of Metz
via A 31, exit 40. At Thionville, follow the signs "Bel Air," then "Crève-Cœur."*

Auberge du Kiboki ★★

Route du Donon (D993)
57560 Turquestein (Moselle)
Tel. 87.08.60.65 - Fax 87.08.65.26 - M. Schmitt

Rooms 15 with telephone, bath or shower, WC and TV. **Price** Double 350F, suite 550F. **Meals** Breakfast (buffet) 42F, served 8:00-10:00; half board 350F (per pers., 3 days min.). **Restaurant** Service 12:00-14:00, 19:00-21:00; à la carte 130-180F. Specialties: Jambon fumé de gibier, ballotin de saumon au blanc de poireaux, médaillon de biche flambé au whisky, mirabelles flambée sur fleur de vanille. **Credit cards** Visa, Eurocard and MasterCard. **Pets** Dogs not allowed. **Facilities** Covered swimming pool, whirlpool, sauna, tennis, parking. **Nearby** Dabo Rock, crystal factories, potteries in Niderviller. **Open** March 1 – Jan 31 (closed Tuesday).

In the middle of the forest in the Turquestein-Blancrupt Valley lies the traditional Auberge du Kiboki. A very cozy atmosphere is created by the warm decor in this hotel. The dining rooms are very appealing: one is bright with checked tablecloths, matching curtains and lampshades; the other is decorated in soft colors and has a handsome, large china cabinet filled with local pottery. The comfortably furnished bedrooms reflect the same style, with warm beige and brown tones, canopied beds and antique wardrobes. This authentic forest inn is an ideal place for a restful stay. The cuisine is excellent and the owners are very hospitable, all making the Kiboki one of the outstanding hotels in this guide.

How to get there (Map 12): 73km west of Strasbourg via A35 and D392 towards Saint-Dié; at Schirmeck D392 towards Donon and D993 towards Turquestein-Blancrupt.

Hostellerie des Bas–Rupts ★★★

Les Bas–Rupts
88400 Gérardmer (Vosges)
Tel. 29.63.09.25 – Fax 29.63.00.40 – M. Philippe

Rooms 32 with telephone, bath or shower, WC and TV. **Price** Single and double 380-780F, suite 900F. **Meals** Breakfast 80F, served 7:00-10:00; half board 540-720F. **Restaurant** Service 12:00-14:00, 19:00-21:30; menus 160-450F, also à la carte. Specialties: Tripes au riesling, aiguillettes de canard, andouille fumée sur choucroute. **Credit cards** Amex, Visa, Eurocard and MasterCard. **Pets** Dogs allowed (+50F). **Facilities** Swimming pool, tennis, garage, parking. **Nearby** Les Cuves Waterfall, Longemer Lake, Retournemer Lake, Epinal – 18-hole golf course in Epinal. **Open** All year.

The Hostellerie des Bas–Rupts, with its flower-bedecked chalet and famous restaurant, is located just outside Gérardmer, once a favorite Alsace-Lorraine resort where the well-heeled enjoyed spending time (and money, in the casino). The nostalgic town was almost completely destroyed at the end of World War II. The Hostellerie des Bas–Rupts is a veritable celebration of flowers, which are found painted on beams, doors, bedsteads; and in fresh and dried bouquets throughout, adding much charm to the comfortable bedrooms in the annex. Some rooms in the hotel itself are more ordinary. The service is both professional and extremely courteous.

How to get there *(Map 12): 56km west of Colmar via D417 and D486 towards La Bresse.*

Auberge du Spitzemberg **

La Petite-Fosse
88490 Provenchères-sur-Fave (Vosges)
Tel. 29.51.20.46 - Fax 29.51.10.12 – M. and Mme Duhem

Rooms 10 with telephone, bath or shower and WC (5 with TV). **Price** Double 245-325F. **Meals** Breakfast 40F, served 8:00-9:00; half board 440-470F, full board 540-570F (per pers., 2 days min.). **Restaurant** Service 12:00-14:00, 19:00-21:00; menus 80-130F, 120-145F on Sundays and national holidays, also à la carte. Specialties: salade Spitzemberg, tournedos cordon rouge sauce morilles, noix de Saint-Jacques au champagne, noisette d'agneau à la Chartres. **Credit cards** All major. **Pets** Dogs allowed. **Facilities** Parking, garage (35F). **Nearby** Cathedral and Cloisters of Saint-Dié. **Open** Dec 16 – Nov 22.

In the middle of the forests of the Vosges, the Auberge du Spitzemberg is a former farmhouse transformed into a charming small hotel, from which there are exceptional views across the countryside. The bedrooms are plainly decorated but are all comfortably equipped. The dining room is very cheerful, and you'll be served good traditional cooking there. A miniature golf course in a large field in front of the hotel offers a pleasant place to spend an afternoon, when you're not exploring the surrounding area.

How to get there (Map 12): 63km northwest of Colmar via N83 to Sélestat, then N59 to Ste-Marie-aux-Mines, N159 via the tunnel to Provenchères-sur-Faves, and D45 to La Petite-Fosse.

Hôtel de la Fontaine–Stanislas **

Fontaine-Stanislas
88370 Plombières-les-Bains (Vosges)
Tel. 29.66.01.53 - Fax 29.30.04.31 - Mme Lemercier

Rooms 19 with telephone, 14 with bath or shower, 11 with WC and 7 with TV.
Price Single 135-200F, double 145-300F. **Meals** Breakfast 34F, served 7:30-
9:30; half board 230-290F, full board 270-360F (per pers., 3 days min.).
Restaurant Service 12:00-13:30, 19:00-20:30; menus 90-260F, also à la carte.
Specialties: Cassolette d'escargots aux cèpes, coupe plombières. **Credit cards** Amex,
Visa, Eurocard and MasterCard. **Pets** Dogs allowed (+25F). **Facilities** Parking.
Nearby Epinal, Augronne and Semouse Valleys, Guéhand Waterfall, la Feuillée
Nouvelle – 18-hole golf course in Epinal. **Open** April 1 – Sept 30.

This hotel is sublimely situated in the heart of the woods, close
to the fountain that bears the name of the former King of
Poland. Apart from the peace and charm of this lovely spot, we
enjoyed the old-fashioned flavor of the hotel with its 1950s
furniture. The bedrooms have the same character. We particularly
liked the two bedrooms in the annex and numbers 2, 3 and 11,
which have small terraces. The garden is ideally arranged for
enjoying the surroundings: you can have a drink there or just relax
and admire the view over the woods and the valley. The welcome
is a warm one, and the four generations who have successively run
the hotel since 1933 are a guarantee of its professionalism.

How to get there *(Map 20): 30km south of Epinal via D434 to Xertigny,*
then D3, D63 and D20; at Granges-de-Plombières take the forest road on
the right.

Auberge de la Cholotte

Les Rouges-Eaux 88600 Bruyères (Vosges)
Tel. 29.50.56.93 - Fax 29.50.24.12
Mme Cholé

Rooms 5 with bath or shower and WC. **Price** Double 350F. **Meals** Breakfast incl.; half board 300F, full board 400F (per pers., 3 days min.). **Restaurant** Service 12:00-14:00, 19:00-21:00 (closed Sunday evening and Monday); menus 120F, also à la carte. Specialties: Jambon cuit au foin, rapées de pomme de terre, tarte aux myrtilles. **Credit cards** Visa, Eurocard and MasterCard. **Pets** Dogs allowed. **Facilities** Parking. **Nearby** Skiing in winter, Cathedral and Cloisters of Saint-Dié, Epinal, Gérardmer Lake – 18-hole golf course in Epinal. **Open** March 1 – Dec 31 (closed Sunday evening and Monday).

Nestling in a small valley, the Auberge de la Cholotte is an irresistibly charming 18th-century farmhouse. In the bedrooms, which have been carefully restored, fabric and wall colors are tastefully coordinated in shades of yellow, blue and soft green, with an occasional brighter color. There are permanent art exhibits on view and a collection of regional objects, along with 19th-century furniture and handsome old Alsatian pieces in polychromed wood. All combine to create a cheerful, refined atmosphere in the comfortable lounges and the two small dining rooms. Concerts are often given in a third, larger dining room with 18th-century paneling and a Steinway piano. The simple bedrooms are charming, and one has a balneotherapy installation. All have a pretty view of the flower garden and the pines which cover this magnificent countryside. The seasonal cuisine is succulent and healthful, and the welcome is very friendly.

How to get there *(See Map 12): 15km west of Saint-Dié via D420, towards Bruyères.*

Chalets des Ayes ★★★
Chemin des Ayes
88160 Le Thillot (Vosges)
Tel. 29.25.00.09 - Fax 29.25.36.48 - M. Marsot

Rooms 2, and 14 chalets (4-10 pers.), with bath or shower, WC and TV - Wheelchair accessible. **Price** Double 320-420F. **Meals** Breakfast 55F, served 8:00-10:00. **Restaurant** Open during the vacations, service 19:30-21:00; menu 128F. Specialties: Cooking from Alsace and the Vosges. **Credit cards** Visa, Eurocard and MasterCard. **Pets** Dogs allowed only in the chalets. **Facilities** Swimming pool, tennis (38F), parking. **Nearby** Cross-country and Alpine skiing, riding, overland biking, walks. **Open** All year.

The Chalets des Ayes calls itself a hotel, though it isn't really one. It does however provide a practical and pleasant solution to the problem of lodging in the wild and seductively beautiful Vosges region, where it is sometimes hard to find a hotel with rural charm. At the Chalets des Ayes, two rooms are available on a bed-and-breakfast basis. These are bright and cheerful, and there are also five small chalets which are well-equipped and attractively presented. Strictly speaking, the chalets are rented by the week, but like the bedrooms, they can be taken for a few nights subject to availability. There is a garden and a swimming pool and the valley is a cheerful place even in bad weather.

How to get there (Map 20): *51km west of Mulhouse via N66 towards Remiremont and towards Mulhouse to Le Thillot.*

Auberge du Val Joli **
88230 Le Valtin (Vosges)
Tel. 29.60.91.37 – Fax 29.60.81.73
M. Laruelle

Rooms 12 with telephone, 2 with bath, 7 with shower, 8 with WC and TV. **Price** Single and double 150-275F. **Meals** Breakfast 30F, served 8:00-10:00; half board 241-367F, full board 347-480F. **Restaurant** Service 12:30-14:00, 19:30-21:00; menus 60-230F, also à la carte. Specialties: Truite fumée maison, pâté lorrain, tarte aux myrtilles. **Credit cards** Visa, Eurocard and MasterCard. **Pets** Dogs allowed (+20F). **Facilities** Tennis, parking. **Nearby** Saint-Dié Cathedral, Gérardmer Lake – 18-hole golf course in Epinal. **Open** All year (closed Sunday evening and Monday in low season).

The little village of Valtin has only 99 inhabitants, and the mayor is also the owner of this auberge which stands at the bottom of one of the prettiest valleys of the Vosges. You only have to open the door to feel its character: low ceilings, beams, flagstones and fireplace create a completely authentic atmosphere. The dining room is very attractive with its many small windows and particularly its carved wood ceiling is the work of an Alsatian carpenter. The comfort of the bedrooms and their bathroom facilities is rather variable. The best are those that have been renovated. Even though the hotel is on the road, there is not much noise; if in doubt reserve a room overlooking the mountain, such as number 16, 5, or 4. This is a place without pretensions in an unspoiled village.

How to get there *(Map 12): 40km west of Colmar via D417 (by the Schlucht pass) to le Collet, then right on D23 to Le Valtin.*

Château de Lalande ★★★

24430 Annesse et Beaulieu (Dordogne)
Tel. 53.54.52.30 - Fax 53.07.46.67
M. and Mme Sicard

Rooms 22 with telephone, bath or shower and WC (TV on request). **Price** Double 245-400F, apart. 380F. **Meals** Breakfast 37F, served 8:00-9:30; half board 295-380F, full board 375-460F (per pers.). **Restaurant** Service 12:00-13:30, 19:00-21:00 (closed Wednesday lunchtime in low season); menus 95-295F (child 45F), also à la carte. Specialties: Croustade de pigeonneau aux truffes, foie frais maison, magret de canard en croûte. **Credit cards** All major. **Pets** Dogs allowed. **Facilities** Swimming pool, parking. **Nearby** Périgueux, Echourgnac and forest of La Double, Chancelade Abbey, Saltgourde estate, Marsac – 18-hole golf course in Périgueux. **Open** March 15 – Nov 15.

This 19th-century chateau is in countryside not far from Périgueux. Far from stiff, the atmosphere is homey and relaxed. The lounge is in Louis-Philippe style, the dining room has a high ceiling and is decorated in shades of brown. The bedrooms are simple but pleasant, with an old-fashioned charm; they all face towards the grounds. On the *deuxième étage* the attic bedrooms would be improved with some renovation. The lawn, with tables and *chaise longues*, looks over the countryside. In summer you can lunch and dine here in the shade of a large lime tree. A member of the Professional Restaurateur's Association, Monsieur Sicard prepares delicious Périgourdine specialties; equally noteworthy are the pastries and cakes.

How to get there (Map 23): *12km southwest of Périgueux via N89, Montaceix exit, Razac-sur-l'Isle.*

Hostellerie Les Griffons ***

Le Pont
24310 Bourdeilles (Dordogne)
Tel. 53.03.75.61 – Fax 53.04.64.45 – Mme Deborde and M. Laly

Rooms 10 with telephone, bath and WC. **Price** Single and double 390-420F.
Meals Breakfast 48F, served 8:00-10:30; half board 390-420F (per pers.).
Restaurant Service 12:30, 21:00 (closed Tuesday in low season); menus 140-240F,
also à la carte. Specialties: Escalope de foie gras de canard frais, saumon grillé au
beurre de truffe, filet de bœuf aux truffes. **Credit cards** Amex, Visa, Eurocard and
MasterCard. **Pets** Dogs allowed (+30F). **Facilities** Parking. **Nearby** Chancelade,
Merlande, Bourdeilles, Brantôme, Saint-Jean-de-Côle, Jumilhac-le-Grand – 18-hole
golf course in Périgueux. **Open** April – Oct.

The Griffons is a very comfortable inn charmingly located on
the banks of the River Dronne. The luminous local stone of
the building lends special beauty to the decor, as does the period
furniture throughout. From the dining room and the terrace, you
can contemplate the lush Dordogne countryside and the river as
it flows gently at the foot of this historic and lovely village, which
is dominated by an imposing medieval chateau. This is altogether
a beautiful place but the welcome is irregular.

How to get there *(Map 23): 25km northwest of Périgueux.*

Le Chatenet

Le Chatenet
24310 Brantôme (Dordogne)
Tel. 53.05.81.08 - Fax 53.05.85.52 - M. and Mme Laxton

Rooms 10 with telephone, bath or shower and WC (3 with TV) - 1 for disabled persons. **Price** Double 490-580F, suite 810F. **Meals** Breakfast 60F, served 8:30-10:00. No restaurant. **Credit cards** Visa, Eurocard and MasterCard. **Pets** Dogs allowed. **Facilities** Heated swimming pool, tennis (40F), parking. **Nearby** Bell tower of the abbey church in Brantôme, "Peiro-Levado" dolmen, châteaux of Hierce, Puymarteau and Saint-Jean-de-Côle, Chancelade Abbey, Saltgourde estate, Marsac – 18-hole golf course in Périgueux. **Open** All year.

Le Chatenet, which owner Philippe Laxton describes as "a family house open to friends and to friends of friends" in the pretty countryside of Brantôme, is a very pleasant place to stay. It is composed of two buildings built in local style. One accommodates the comfortable and spacious bedrooms as well as a dining-room and a lounge, and the other acts as a club-house, with bar and billiards. This family home has a very congenial atmosphere. There is no restaurant because the Laxtons opened Le Chatenet to provide a service for their restaurant-owning friends. However, an ample breakfast is served on the patio whenever you like. For fine dining try: *Le Moulin de l'Abbaye* and the *Brasserie Saint-Sicaire* in Brantôme.

How to get there *(Map 23): 27km north of Périgueux, 1.5km from Brantôme via D78 towards Bourdeilles.*

Domaine de la Roseraie ★★★

24310 Brantôme (Dordogne)
Tel. 53.05.84.74 - Fax 53.05.77.94
M. Roux

Rooms 7 with telephone, bath or shower, WC and TV - Wheelchair accessible.
Price Double 250-680F, suite 750F. **Meals** Breakfast 50F, served 7:30-10:30. No
restaurant but tea room. **Credit carts** All major. **Pets** Dogs allowed. **Nearby** Bell
tower of the abbey church in Brantôme, "Peiro-Levado" dolmen, châteaux of Hierce,
Puymarteau and St-Jean-de-Côle, Chancelade Abbey, Saltgourde estate, Marsac –
18-hole golf course in Périgueux. **Open** March – Jan.

Nestling in the countryside outside Brantôme, La Roseraie is
composed of two buildings set at an angle and a Perigourdine
tower. With the first sunny days, breakfasts and drinks are served
here. Inside, the Roseraie is very inviting. There are two lounges
(one is for television exclusively) which are furnished with pleasant,
comfortable period furniture and decorated with Impressionist-
style paintings. The bedrooms and baths are equally attractive and
they are kept impeccably clean. Families should note the splendid
duplex suite. All rooms are on the ground floor and have
independent entrances. It is beautifully quiet here, the service is
friendly, and while there is no restaurant at the hotel, there are
several excellent ones in the region. Try *Le Moulin de l'Abbaye* and
the *Brasserie Saint-Sicaire* in Brantôme.

How to get there *(Map 23): 27km north of Périgueux via D939; in the
center of the town, 1km in the direction of Angoulême.*

Hôtel du Manoir de Bellerive ★★★

Route de Siorac
24480 Le Buisson de Cadouin (Dordogne)
Tel. 53.27.16.19 - Fax 53.22.09.05 - Mme Huin

Rooms 16 with air-conditioning, telephone, bath or shower, WC, TV and minibar.
Price Single 400F, double 750F. **Meals** Breakfast 50-65F, served 8:00-11:00.
Restaurant Service 19:30-21:30 (12:00-15:00 only Sunday and national holidays);
menu 160F, also à la carte. Specialties: "Cuisine inventive." **Credit cards** Visa,
Eurocard and MasterCard. **Pets** Dogs allowed. **Facilities** Swimming pool, tennis,
sauna (100F), parking. **Nearby** Le Bugue, cave of Bara-Bahau and Proumeyssac
chasm, Limeuil, National Museum of Prehistory in Les Eyzies – 18-hole golf course
in la-Croix-de-Mortemart. **Open** Easter – Nov 1.

Situated off the road in beautiful English parklike grounds, this 19th-
century manor borders the Dordogne. It has been delightfully
converted by two interior decorators. On the ground floor, the
lounge, bar and dining room open off a vast central colonnaded hall,
from which a double staircase sweeps up to the *premier étage* bedrooms.
The pervading atmosphere of aestheticism and refinement has been
created by a sensitive and masterly combination of colors, fabrics and
trompe l'œil marble. There are also antiques, beautiful carpets,
engravings... Among the very comfortable bedrooms you have the
choice of those with a view over the park or those overlooking the
river. The bathrooms are luxurious. In good weather breakfast is
served on the terrace, which overlooks the Dordogne. You will find
a very hospitable welcome. The restaurant is inaugurating a new menu
called "Dinner Around a Specialty", which is designed to enhance
authentic food tastes with the use of good fresh products.

How to get there *(Map 23): 47km southeast of Périgueux via N89 to
Niversac, D710 to Le Bugue, and D31.*

Le Relais du Touron ★★

Le Touron
24200 Carsac-Aillac (Dordogne)
Tel. 53.28.16.70 – Mme Carlier and M. Amriah

Rooms 12 with telephone, bath or shower and WC. **Price** Double 275-400F, triple 345-500F. **Meals** Breakfast 34F, served 8:00-10:00; half board 288-338F. **Restaurant** Closed at lunchtime and Wednesday diner in low season, Tuesday and Wednesday in high season; menus 90-265F, also à la carte. Specialties: Foie gras d'oie poélé aux pommes caramélisées, feuilleté d'escargots aux cèpes, filet d'agneau au beurre de foie gras, sandre à l'orange. **Credit cards** Visa, Eurocard and MasterCard. **Pets** Dogs allowed. **Facilities** Swimming pool, parking. **Nearby** Walk along the valley of the Enéa from Carsac to Sainte-Nathalène, old town and house of La Boétie in Sarlat, Château de Puymartin – 9-hole golf course in Vitrac. **Open** April 1 – Nov 14.

The Relais du Touron is a peaceful country inn which lies at the end of the village. The rustling leaves of the poplar trees and the murmuring of the Enea as it flows tranquilly along create a romantic pastoral atmosphere. Comfortable bedrooms all alike are in the building facing the swimming pool. In the neighboring Périgourdine house, you will find No. 11 and No. 12, which is the most attractive although; it is, for 3 or 4 people. (It has a beautiful high ceiling and exposed beams.) A beautiful swimming pool, surrounded by shade trees and lawns, a terrace where meals and breakfasts are served facing the garden: all contribute to making the Touron a pleasant place to stay.

How to get there *(Map 23): 75km southeast of Périguex to Sarlat, then D704 towards Gourdon (600m before the village of Carsac).*

Manoir d'Hautegente ★★★

24120 Coly (Dordogne)
Tel. 53.51.68.03 – Fax 53.50.38.52
Mme Hamelin

Rooms 10 with telephone, bath, WC, TV and minibar. **Price** Double 500-850F.
Meals Breakfast 50F, served 8:30-10:00; half board 490-700F (per pers.).
Restaurant Service from 20:00; menus 180-230F, also à la carte. Specialties: Duo
de langoustines au foie gras; pigeon farci au foie gras et sa sauce aux truffes.
Credit cards Visa, Eurocard and MasterCard. **Pets** Dogs allowed. **Facilities** Heated
swimming pool, fishing, parking. **Nearby** Lascaux caves, Abbey of Aubazines,
Argentat, Collonges-la-Rouge. **Open** April 1 – Nov 11.

Formerly a mill and forge of the warrior monks of Saint Amand-
du–Coly and the property of the Hamelin family for almost
three centuries, this Perigord manor has been an elegant hotel for
several years now. It is in a beautiful valley where graceful old
walnut and oak trees line the roads. Ducks roam freely along the
banks of the winding, babbling brook in front of the manor. The
rooms and lounges have all been tastefully decorated with the family
furniture in a perfect blend of style and comfort. The fabrics on
the walls and in the curtains are splendid, especially in the *Liserons*
room. It is very large and has a private balcony overlooking the
river. You will receive a warm and attentive welcome at this very
charming hotel.

How to get there *(Map 23): 30km southwest of Brive-la-Gaillarde via N89*
towards Périgueux to Le Lardin-Saint-Lazare, then D704 and D62 towards
Sarlat-Souillac.

Hôtel Cro-Magnon ★★★
24620 Les Eyzies-de-Tayac (Dordogne)
Tel. 53.06.97.06 - Fax 53.06.95.45
M. and Mme Leyssales

Rooms 18, and 4 apartments, with telephone, bath or shower and WC (10 with TV).
Price Double 350-550F, suite 600-800F. **Meals** Breakfast 50F, served 8:00-10:00;
half board 350-500F (per pers., 3 days min.). **Restaurant** Service 12:00-14:00,
19:30-21:00 (closed Wednesday lunchtime except national holidays); menus 140-
350F, also à la carte. Specialties: Consommé de canard glacé, truffe en croustade.
Credit cards All major. **Pets** Dogs allowed (+30F). **Facilities** Swimming pool,
parking. **Nearby** Le Bugue, Bara-Bahau cave and Proumeyssac chasm, Limeuil,
National Museum of Prehistory in Les Eyzies – 18-hole La-Croix-de-Mortemart golf
course in Le Bugue. **Open** End April – Oct 11.

This old coaching inn has been in the family for many
generations. The two reception rooms, whose colors
harmonize well with the open stonework and old furniture, are
very charming. There is a small museum in one. You can choose
between a pretty dining room in local style or another modern
one, which has been very well integrated and which opens onto
a shady terrace. Excellent regional cuisine is complemented by a
well-chosen wine list. The bedrooms are comfortable and
charmingly decorated; for peace and quiet, we prefer those in the
annex, which all look out onto a very large park with a swimming
pool. The staff is very friendly.

How to get there *(Map 23): 45km southeast of Périgueux via N89 and
D710, then D47.*

Hôtel Les Glycines ★★★

24620 Les Eyzies-de-Tayac (Dordogne)
Tel. 53.06.97.07 - Fax 53.06.92.19
M. and Mme Mercat

Rooms 25 with telephone, bath and WC. **Price** Single 315-390F, double 360-410F. **Meals** Breakfast 50F, served 8:00-10:00; half board 395-450F, full board 493-550F (per pers., 3 days min.). **Restaurant** Service 12:00-14:00, 19:30-21:30 (closed Saturday lunchtime except national holidays); menus 140-290F, also à la carte. Specialties: Pavé de bœuf fourré de son escalope de foie frais et sa sauce truffes, pain perdu à la gelée d'abricot aux amandes. **Credit cards** All major. **Pets** Dogs allowed. **Facilities** Swimming pool, park, parking. **Nearby** Le Bugue, cave de Bara-Bahau and Proumeyssac chasm, Limeuil, National Museum of Prehistory in Les Eyzies – 18-hole La-Croix-de-Mortemart golf course in Le Bugue. **Open** April 15 – End Oct.

Dating back to 1862, this old coaching inn is a large house where stone, wood and prolific vegetation blend happily together. As the name indicates, there is a pergola covered with an abundance of wisteria; trimmed lime trees shade the terrace. The lounge and bar have a restful atmosphere and have been furnished and decorated with great care. The lovely dining room opens onto the garden, but meals may also be taken on a new veranda that gives onto the lawn. All the bedrooms are very comfortable and the furnishings have been well selected; fabrics, papers and colors are in a contemporary style. The cuisine makes good use of fresh produce from the garden.

How to get there *(Map 23): 45km southeast of Périgueux via N89 and D710, then D47.*

Moulin de la Beune ★★

24620 Les Eyzies-de-Tayac (Dordogne)
Tel. 53.06.94.33 – Fax 53.06.98.06
M. and Mme Soulié

Rooms 20 with telephone, bath or shower and WC. **Price** Single 260F, double 280-300F. **Meals** Breakfast 40F, served 8:00-10:30; half board 320F, full board 420F (per pers., 2 days min.). **Restaurant** Service 12:00-14:30, 19:00-21:30 (closed Tuesday lunchtime); menus 85-315F, also à la carte. Specialties: Saint-Jacques aux truffes, raviolis de foie gras, écrevisses. **Credit cards** Amex, Visa, Eurocard and MasterCard. **Pets** Dogs allowed. **Facilities** Parking, **Nearby** Le Bugue, cave of Bara-Bahau and Proumeyssac chasm, Limeuil, National Museum of Prehistory in Les Eyzies – 18-hole la-Croix-de-Mortemart golf course in Le Bugue. **Open** Feb 16 – Jan 2.

When you arrive at this old mill, it is hard to believe that you are in one of the most touristic areas of France. The River Beune runs quietly at your feet; the small garden dotted with tables is a peaceful haven. In the lounge, beside the large fireplace, there are armchairs and little tables arranged comfortably for reading and writing. To one side there is a room where drinks and breakfast are served. The decor of the recently refurbished bedrooms has been tastefully chosen. The restaurant, Le Vieux Moulin, occupies another adjacent mill, and is also charmingly decorated. In the large dining room with its exposed stonework and beams, or in the garden at the foot of ancient cliffs, truffle-based Périgourdine specialties are served.

How to get there *(Map 23): 45km southeast of Périgueux via N89 and D710, then D47; in the middle of the village.*

A Q U I T A I N E

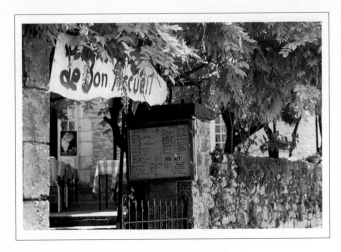

Au Bon Accueil
24510 Limeuil (Dordogne)
Tel. 53.63.30.97
M. and Mme Palazy

Rooms 10 (5 with shower). **Price** Double 125-150F. **Meals** Breakfast 25F, served 8:00-9:30; half board 170-200F, full board 210-250F (per pers., 3 days min.). **Restaurant** Service 12:00-14:30, 19:30-21:30; menus 65-135F, also à la carte. Specialties: Filet de perche au Monbazillac, civet de lièvre ou sanglier, assiette gabare. **Credit cards** Visa, Eurocard and MasterCard. **Pets** Dogs allowed. **Nearby** Le Bugue, cave of Bara-Bahau and Proumeyssac chasm, Limeuil, National Museum of Prehistory in Les Eyzies – 18-hole La-Croix-de-Mortemart golf course in Le Bugue. **Open** March 15 – end Oct.

At the top of the magnificent medieval village of Limeuil M. and Mme Palazy have opened Le Bon Acceuil. The charm of this very simple inn is due to its owners' wish to create a "real" place. The welcome is warm and professional, the food plain and good, the atmosphere relaxed and calm. At these very reasonable prices the bedrooms are a bit basic, but they are very quiet. We recommend this inn especially in good weather, when you may take a meal or a cup of tea in the charming pergola. A pleasant terraced garden has been added at the base of an ancient battlement. Finally, weather permitting, you can set out at dawn with M. Palazy to fish in the river, and later dine on your catch at the hotel.

How to get there *(Map 23): 37km south of Périgueux via D710 towards Villeneuve-sur-Lot to Le Bugue, then D31 towards Trémolat.*

La Grande Marque ★★

24220 Marnac-Saint-Cyprien (Dordogne)
Tel. 53.31.61.63 - Fax 53.28.39.55
M. and Mme Devaux d'Hangest

Rooms 16 (4 duplex) with telephone, bath or shower, WC and TV - 1 for disabled persons. **Price** Single and double 270F, duplex 392F. **Meals** Breakfast 35F, served 8:30-9:30; half board 260-328F, full board 350-406F (per pers., 3 days min.). **Restaurant** Service 12:30-13:30, 19:30-21:00; menus 98-200F, also à la carte. Specialties: Papitons de lotte et saumon, local cooking. **Credit cards** Visa, Eurocard and MasterCard. **Pets** Small dogs allowed. **Facilities** Salt-water swimming pool, parking. **Nearby** Châteaux of Veyrignac, Les Milandes and Montfort, Beynac and Cazenac, Domme – 9-hole Rochebois golf course in Vitrac. **Open** April – Nov 1 and school vacations.

Surrounded by lush vegetation on the side of a hill, La Grande Marque, on a registered historic site, offers an extraordinary panoramic view of the Dordogne. The bedrooms are in an old tobacco barn that has been completely renovated. You enter a modern, soberly furnished reception room lit by immense picture windows. Exhibitions of paintings are held here. Upstairs, the bedrooms are simple though comfortably appointed. The garden, dotted with sculptures by one of the owners' sons, is a mass of flowers and has many pretty nooks and crannies. On a shady terrace tables are laid for summer breakfasts, while in winter dinner is served in a pleasantly rustic dining room. The creative cuisine is excellent and the people are very friendly.

How to get there (Map 23): *57km southeast of Périgueux via N89 to Niversac, D710 to Le Bugue, D31 to Le Buisson, then Siorac and D703. Turn left in 1km.*

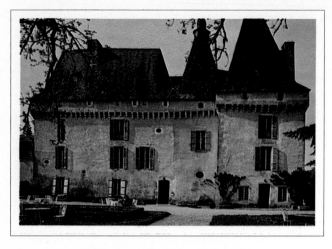

Château de Mavaleix ★★★

Mavaleix
24800 Thiviers (Dordogne)
Tel. 53.52.82.01 - Fax 53.62.03.80 - Mme Ruel

Rooms 18 with telephone, bath or shower and WC (10 with TV). **Price** Double 260-410F. **Meals** Breakfast 45F, served 8:00-10:00; half board 410F, full board 490F (per pers., 3 day min.). **Restaurant** Service 12:00-13:45, 19:30-21:00 (closed Jan and Wednesday); menus 85-220F, also à la carte. Specialties: Civet de canard aux pruneaux d'Agen et à l'hysope, sauté de cèpes en coque de Saint-Jacques, foie frais de canard cuit au torchon, tarte Tatin. **Credit cards** Visa, Eurocard and MasterCard. **Pets** Dogs allowed. **Facilities** Swimming pool, jogging path, fishing, parking. **Nearby** Chancelade, Bourdeilles, Brandôme, Saint-Jean-de-Côle, Jumilhac-le-Grand – 18-hole golf course in Périgueux. **Open** Feb – Dec.

A magnificent vault of trees extending out from a side entrance leads into the courtyard of this chateau, which was built in the 12th-century. This was home to the Knights Templars, and pilgrims stopped here on their way to Compostela. The inside is agreeable: The bedrooms located in the *commanderie* - the knights' apartments - have a somewhat old-fashioned charm, but they are comfortable, well kept, and the new owners are renovating those in the main part of the chateau. All the bedrooms look out onto a beautiful park planted with trees several hundred years old, which stretches into the countryside as far as the eye can see. There is total peace and quiet here, and the atmosphere and welcome are extremely pleasant.

How to get there (Map 23): 35km north of Périgueux via RN21, in the direction of Limoges.

La Métairie ★★★

24150 Mauzac (Dordogne)
Tel. 53.22.50.47 - Fax 53.22.52.93
Mme Vigneron and M. Culis

Rooms 10 with telephone, bath, WC and TV (6 with minibar). **Price** Double 450-600F (low season), 500-650F (high season), suite 950-1110F. **Meals** Breakfast 60F, served 8:00-10:00, half board 450-550F (per pers., 2 days min.). **Restaurant** Service 12:30-13:45, 19:30-21:00 (closed Tuesday April 1 – June 1, and Tuesday lunchtime from July 1); menus 120-300F, also à la carte. Specialties of Périgord. **Credit cards** Visa, Eurocard and MasterCard. **Pets** Dogs allowed (+30F). **Facilities** Swimming pool, parking. **Nearby** Les Eyzies, Limeuil, Le Bugue, Bergerac – 18-hole la-Croix-de-Mortemart golf course in Le Bugue. **Open** April 1 – Oct 15.

A few kilometers from the famous horse shoe-shaped Cingle de Trémolat, in a beautiful valley where great loops of the Dordogne River wind through a mosaic of cultivated fields, lies La Métairie. It is a charming and beautiful house converted with comfort, delicacy and good taste. The garden is also very well done. At the same level as the lawn a pleasant terrace runs along the side of the house, and in summer there is a grill near the swimming pool. The cuisine is very appetizing and aromatic. Finally, it is worth noting that the hotel is close to a superb lake where every type of water sport is available.

How to get there *(Map 23): 68km south of Périgueux via N89 and D70 to Le Bugue, then D703 and branch off for Mauzac.*

Le Mas de Montet ★★★

24600 Petit Bersac près Ribérac (Dordogne)
Tel 53.90.08.71 - Fax 53.90.55.87
Mme Duvert

Rooms 14 with telephone, bath, shower, WC and TV. **Price** 475-650F. **Meals** Breakfast 38F, served 7:00-10:30; half board 450-550F, full board 550-650F (per pers.). **Restaurant** Service 12:30-20:00; menus 120-290F, also à la carte. Specialties of Périgord and foie gras. **Credit cards** Amex, Visa, Eurocard and MasterCard. **Pets** Dogs allowed. **Facilities** Parking. **Nearby** Roman museum in Petit-Bersac, Tourtoirac Abbey, Château de Hautefort, Brantôme, Bourdeilles, Saint-Emilion, foie gras market in Ribérac – 18-hole golf course in Périgueux. **Open** Feb 1 – Dec 31.

Lying in a large park planted with hundred–year–old sequoia trees, this small château does not seem like a hotel but more like a family mansion with beautiful antique furniture, pottery and copperware. The entrance is almost entirely glassed–in and contains a garden room with white lacquered cane furniture and lush green plants. The good smell of polish accompanies the visitor into the lounge and the dining room, which are kept as they have been for years. The bedrooms are very charming, with pretty fabrics, walnut wardrobes, draped dressing tables, and antique armchairs; each one is arranged differently. Some of the the bathrooms are enormous. We preferred number 2 with its extension into the tower, and number 9. A terrace on the *premier étage* means that you can have breakfast in the sunshine and enjoy a panoramic view of the park. This is a superb hotel with an excellent gourmet restaurant whose clientele includes distinguished guests.

How to get there *(Map 23): 50km west of Périgueux via D710 to Ribérac, D20 towards Aubeterre; Petit Bersac road, on the right. 60km from Angoulême towards Aubeterre.*

L'Auberge du Noyer ★★

Le Reclaud-de-Bouny-Bas
24260 Le Bugue (Dordogne)
Tel. 53.07.11.73 - Fax 53.54.57.44 - M. and Mme Dyer

Rooms 10 with telephone, bath and WC. **Price** Single 320F, double 400-520F.
Meals Breakfast 48F, served 8:15-10:00; half board 408-468F (per pers.).
Restaurant Service 19:30-21:00; menu 160F. Specialties: Coussin de truite farcie
aux pleurotes, magret à l'orange, tarte aux noix. **Credit cards** Visa, Eurocard and
MasterCard. **Pets** Dogs not allowed. **Facilities** Swimming pool, parking. **Nearby** Le
Bugue, Proumeyssac chasm, Limeuil, Les Eyzies, Vézère Valley from Limeuil to
Montignac, Lascaux – 18-hole La-Croix-de-Mortemart golf course in Le Bugue.
Open Palm Sunday – Nov 1.

Five kilometers from Le Bugue, this 18th-century Périgourdine
farm has been completely renovated by an English couple, Paul
and Jenny Dyer, who fell in love with the region. The Auberge
du Noyer is a charming, tranquil place to stay, even in August.
The bedrooms are spacious and have impeccable bathrooms: five
have their own private terraces on which to have breakfast; (ask
for number 8). The cooking is simple but refined and meals are
served in a pretty, rustic dining room. Breakfast is a high point,
with home-made jams, freshly squeezed orange juice and toasted
farmhouse bread. The owners are charming, very informal, and
this is an ideal place for a stay of several days, for which the owners
recommend half-board.

How to get there *(Map 23): 37km south of Périgueux via D710 towards*
Villeneuve-sur-Lot, then D703 towards Sainte-Alvère.

La Plume d'Oie

Au Bourg
24250 La Roque-Gageac (Dordogne)
Tel. 53.29.57.05./53.28.94.93 - Fax 53.31.04.81 - M. and Mme Walker

Rooms 4 with telephone, bath or shower, WC, TV and minibar. **Price** Single 275F, double 350-380F. **Meals** Breakfast 55F, served 8:00-9:30. **Restaurant** Service 12:15-13:30, 19:30-21:00; menus 155-260F, also à la carte. Specialties: Foie gras et confit de canard cuits en terrine à la fleur de sel, charlotte de canard aux oignons confits, tarte au lait caillé et coulis de fruits rouges. **Credit cards** Visa, Eurocard and MasterCard. **Pets** Dogs allowed (+25-40F). **Nearby** Old Town and La Boétie's house in Sarlat, châteaux of Puymartin and Commarques, Carsac, Lascaux – 9-hole golf course in Vitrac. **Open** March – Jan (closed Monday)

La Plume d'Oie is a restaurant with an excellent reputation to which four charming bedrooms have just been added. Light and bright, comfortably modern, they are decorated like guest rooms, with pretty chestnut furniture and cream-colored fabrics with occasional splashes of color; the bathrooms are impeccable. Three rooms open onto the river, which is just across the narrow street. Built on the flank of a gigantic cliff right on the Dordogne, La Roque-Gageac is a simply superb site. There's another side to the coin, however: you hear the cars somewhat, which can be a problem in the high season – July and August. If you want complete silence, it's best to reserve the bedroom looking out on the cliff. Breakfasts are served in your room when you wish. The jovial, thoughtful owners will welcome you warmly.

How to get there *(Map 23): 8km south of Sarlat-la-Canéda.*

Hôtel de L'Abbaye ★★★
Rue de l'Abbaye
24220 Saint-Cyprien-en-Périgord (Dorgogne)
Tel. 53.29.20.48 – Fax 53.29.15.85 – M. and Mme Schaller

Rooms 24 with telephone, bath or shower and WC (11 with TV and minibar).
Price Single 340-360F, double 550-680F, suite 650-800F. **Meals** Breakfast 50F,
served 8:00-10:00; half board 390-560F (per pers.). **Restaurant** Service 12:00-
14:00, 19:30-21:00; menus 140-320F, also à la carte. Specialties: Foie gras frais,
poulet sauté aux langoustines, escargots à la crème de persil. **Credit cards** Amex,
Visa, Eurocard and MasterCard. **Pets** Dogs allowed. **Facilities** Swimming pool,
parking. **Nearby** Cave of Proumeyssac, Le Bugue, Château de Campagne, Les Eyzies –
18-hole La-Croix-de-Mortemart golf course in Le Bugue. **Open** April 15 – Oct 15.

The exterior of this large house in the pretty village of Saint-
Cyprien has been left untouched, so that the local stone acts
as decoration. The same feeling is echoed in the lounge, with its
stone walls and fireplace and the original stone floor. The bedrooms
are all comfortably appointed, and some are more luxurious than
others. In one of the annexes, some bedrooms can be combined
to form a family apartment, and the bedrooms in the new building
are really luxurious. A lovely terrace and pleasant gardens with
swimming pool add to the charm of L'Abbaye, where the cuisine
is very good and the owners warm and welcoming.

*How to get there (Map 23): 54km southeast of Périgueux via N89 and
D710 to Le Bugue, then D703 and D35 to St-Cyprien.*

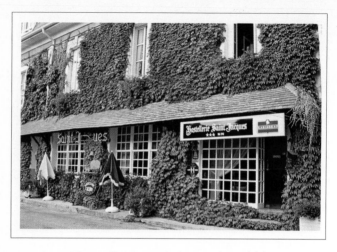

Hostellerie Saint-Jacques ★★★

24470 Saint-Saud-Lacoussière (Dordogne)
Tel. 53.56.97.21 – Fax 53.56.91.33
M. and Mme Babayou

Rooms 22 and 3 apartments, with telephone, bath or shower and WC (10 with TV and minibar). **Price** Single 300F, double 330-450F, suite 750F. **Meals** Breakfast 45F, brunch by the swimming pool; half board 255-385F, full board 335-465F (per pers., 3 days min.). **Restaurant** Service 12:30-13:30, 19:30-21:00 (closed Sunday evening and Monday except for residents, and Oct 15 – Easter except Sunday and national holidays); menus 115-290F, also à la carte. Specialties: Foie gras maison aux figues, pied de porc farci aux ris de veau, parmentier au confit de canard. **Credit cards** Visa, Eurocard and MasterCard. **Pets** Dogs allowed. **Facilities** Heated swimming pool, tennis, parking. **Nearby** Brantôme Abbey, Villars caves, Saint-Jean-de-Côle – 18-hole Saltgourde golf course in Marsac. **Open** April 1 – Oct 15 (closed Sunday evening and Monday in low season).

The Hostellerie Saint-Jacques has the generous proportions of an 18th-century Périgourdine house. The bedrooms all have different fabrics and furniture. Those on the *premier étage* have just been renovated; on the *deuxième étage*, they are all cheerful, bright, and well decorated, and most have wonderful views of the countryside. The attractive dining room (the cuisine is excellent) is a vast room which extends through glass doors into a well-shaded garden generously provided with prettily laid tables. Full of flowers, the garden leads to the swimming pool and tennis court. The owners are very welcoming.

How to get there *(Map 23): 58km north of Périgueux via N21 to La Coquille, then D79.*

Le Chaufourg en Périgord

24400 Sourzac (Dordogne)
Tel. 53.81.01. 56 – Fax 53.82.94.87
M. Dambier

Rooms 10 (2 suites) with telephone, bath, WC and TV (4 with minibar). **Price** Double 700-1050F, suite 1300F. **Meals** Breakfast 65F, served 8:00-11:30. No restaurant. **Credit cards** Amex, Visa, Eurocard and MasterCard. **Pets** Dogs allowed on request. **Facilities** Heated swimming pool, parking. **Nearby** Périgueux, Echourgnac and forest of la Double, Chancelade Abbey, Saltgourde estate, Marsac – 18-hole golf course in Périgueux. **Open** All year.

This very beautiful and elegant 17th-century family mansion is not really a hotel: Le Chaufourg en Périgord is Monsieur Dambier's childhood home, which he has restored "to create the elegant decor I dreamed of for entertaining." You will, not surprisingly, find everything here you could wish for when you travel: very comfortable accommodations, warm hospitality, and those extra details that make all the difference, the tasteful decoration combines antiques with handsome personal objects, magazines and books. There is a billiard table at your disposal. The garden overlooking the Isle River is heavenly. You can relax around the swimming pool, stroll in the shady park or take a boat ride down the river. There is no restaurant, but on request, Monsieur Dambier will prepare a truly memorable meal of the specialties for which the Périgord is renowned. He will also point out the many good local restaurants. Ask him for his native son's tips on making the most of your visit to this enchanting region.

How to get there *(Map 23): 30km southwest of Périgueux via N 89, towards Mussidan.*

Le Vieux Logis ★★★
24510 Trémolat (Dordogne)
Tel. 53.22.80.06 – Fax 53.22.84.89
M. Giraudel

Rooms 24 with telephone, bath, WC, TV, and minibar. **Price** Single and double 720-1240F, suite 1580F. **Meals** Breakfast 72F, served 8:00-11:00. **Restaurant** Service 12:30-14:30, 19:00-21:30, carte. **Credit cards** All major. **Pets** Dogs allowed. **Facilities** Swimming pool, parking. **Nearby** Tobacco Museum in Bergerac, Lanquais, bastide town of Sainte-Foy-la-Grande – 18-hole La Croix-de-Montemart golf course in Le Bugue. **Open** All year.

For four centuries, the same family has lived on this superb estate, which was made into a hotel by Monsieur Giraudel's mother. The different buildings are all charming: In addition to the main building, there is the tobacco barn, the lodge, the gardener's house... No two bedrooms are alike but they have one point in common: They are extremely comfortable, quiet and elegantly decorated down to the last detail; the antique furniture and the *souleiado* Provençal fabrics go together beautifully. The two dining rooms are magnificent. One is small, with pale wood paneling; the other is immense, overlooked by a balustraded lounge (the former hayloft). Gourmets will love it, and so will those who appreciate interior design.

How to get there *(Map 23): 54km south of Périgueux via N 89 to Niversac. D 710 to Le Bugue and D 81.*

Château de Vieux-Mareuil ★★★

Vieux-Mareuil
24340 Mareuil (Dordogne)
Tel. 53.60.77.15 - Fax 53.56.49.33 - Mme Lefranc

Rooms 14 with telephone, bath, WC, TV and minibar. **Price** Double 400-1000F.
Meals Breakfast 60F, served 8:00-10:30; half board 450-750F, full board 550-850F
(per pers., 3 days min.). **Restaurant** Service 12:00-14:30, 19:00-21:45; menus 120-
320F, also à la carte. **Credit cards** All major. **Pets** Dogs not allowed.
Facilities Swimming pool, parking. **Nearby** Brantôme Abbey, château de Bourdeilles,
St-Jean-de-Côle, Jumilhac-le-Grand – 18-hole Saltgourde golf course in Marsac.
Open March 1 – Jan 15 (closed Sunday evening and Monday Nov 1 – Easter).

Perched on a little hill in 50 acres of woods and fields, this old château has been tastefully converted into a very comfortable hotel. In the main part of the building there are two attractive dining rooms, a small living room with a lovely fireplace, and in the tower of the chateau three beautiful bedrooms furnished in antique style. The other bedrooms, more modern but also very pleasing, are in a wing overlooking the park. For sunny days there is a swimming pool. The delicious cooking varies according to the season, and the very good *demi-pension* menu changes every day. The pleasant atmosphere created by the owners, and the excellent service, make this an ideal place to stay in one of the loveliest regions of France.

How to get there *(Map 23): 42km northwest of Périgueux via D939 to Vieux-Mareuil.*

Hauterive Hôtel Saint-James ★★★★

3, place Camille-Hostein
33270 Bouliac (Gironde)
Tel. 57.97.06.00 - Telex 573 001 - Fax 56.20.92.58 - M. Amat

Rooms 17 with telephone, bath, WC, TV and minibar. **Price** Single 600-800F, double 650-850F, suite 1150-1350F. **Meals** Breakfast 70F, served from 7:00. **Restaurant** Service 12:00-14:00, 20:00-22:00; menus 250F, also à la carte. Specialties: Fondant d'aubergine au cumin, pigeon aux épices et sa pastilla, salade d'huîtres au caviar et sa crépinette. **Credit cards** All major. **Pets** Dogs allowed (+100F). **Facilities** Swimming pool, tennis, sauna, health center, parking. **Nearby** Museum of Contemporary Art, Museum of Fine Art, Port-de-la-Lune Theatre, Cité Mondiale du Vin (25, quai des Chartons) in Bordeaux; Le Bordelais (renowned world-wide for its wines) – 18-hole Cameyrac golf course, 18-hole Bordelais golf course. **Open** All year.

To make an exception and include this ultra-modern place means that it must be out of the ordinary. And so it is, owing to the immense talents of two people: the owner and chef, Jean-Marie Amat, and the architect Jean Nouvel. The result of their combined efforts is amazing. Occupying three buildings, all the bedrooms have picture windows with extensive views over vineyards and the plain of Bordeaux. The decor is in tones of white and cream, broken by brightly-colored carpets or the flash of steel grey. This high-tech approach combines with bunches of flowers, sculpture and books to create the intimacy of a private house: what could have been cold, is warm instead. There is no need to describe the famous cuisine of Jean-Marie Amat. His celebrated restaurant and an excellent bistro adjoin the hotel.

How to get there *(Map 22): 5km east of Bordeaux. On "Rocade-road," Bouliac exit (no. 23).*

Château du Foulon

33480 Castelnau-de-Médoc (Gironde)
Tel. 56.58.20.18 - Fax 56.58.23.43
M. and Mme de Baritault du Carpia

Rooms 5 with bath and WC. **Price** Double 400F, suite 500-600F. **Meals** Breakfast incl. No restaurant. **Credit cards** Not accepted. **Pets** Dogs not allowed. **Facilities** Parking. **Nearby** Médoc peninsula on the left bank of the Garonne, then the Gironde (day trip, 150km), Mouton-Rothschild Museum in Pauillac – 18-hole Bordelais golf course, 18-hole Bordeaux-le-Lac golf course. **Open** All year.

The very elegant Château du Foulon stands at the end of a long avenue of trees which leads into a wood and then an immense park where you will discover magnificent peacocks and snow-white swans. Monsieur and Madame de Baritault, who will greet you with great hospitality, have tastefully decorated each bedroom with beautiful antique furniture and great comfort. There are also two charming apartments, which are ideal for a long stay. Breakfasts are served at a large table in the magnificent dining room, a model of elegance and refinement. For dinner or for discovering the region, your hosts will give you a wealth of good advice.

How to get there (Map 22): 28km northwest of Bordeaux via D1 to Le Verdoux, then go south to Foulon.

Hostellerie du Vieux Raquine

Lugon
33240 Saint-André-de-Cubzac (Gironde)
Tel. 57.84.42.77 - Fax 57.84.83.77 - Mme de Raquine

Rooms 10 with telephone, bath or shower and WC (3 with TV). **Price** Single 450F, double 450-600F, suite 650F. **Meals** Breakfast 50F, served 8:00-10:00. No restaurant. **Credit cards** Visa, Eurocard and MasterCard. **Pets** Dogs not allowed. **Facilities** Parking. **Nearby** Church of Saint-André-de-Cubzac, château de Bouilh, Bourg, Saint-Emilion – 18-hole Bordelais golf course. **Open** All year.

The ground floor of this hotel covers the whole top of a hill. Completely renovated, it is furnished in an old-fashioned style. The bedrooms are impeccably kept and, except one, all are at ground level. There are two reception rooms including the one used as the dining room; it has windows all along one side opening onto a large terrace with an outstanding view of the vineyards of Fronsac, bordered by the Dordogne in the distance. Mme Raquine makes the hotel feel like a family house. Tranquillity and fresh air are guaranteed. For fine dining, try a restaurant near the hotel or *Au Sarment* in Saint-Gervais.

How to get there *(Map 22): 23km northeast of Bordeaux; A10 St-André-de-Cubzac exit, D670.*

Château Lardier ★★

33350 Ruch - Castillon-la-bataille (Gironde)
Tel. 57.40.54.11 - Fax 57.40.70.38
M. and Mme Bauzin

Rooms 9 with telephone, bath or shower and WC (2 with TV). **Price** Double 230-340F. **Meals** Half board 270-330F, full board 340-440F (per pers., 3 days min.). **Restaurant** Service 12:00-13:30, 19:30-21:30; menus 80-270F, also à la carte. Specialties: Croquant de Saint-Jacques, terrine de foie gras, confit de canard, saladine d'aiguillettes de canard avec maïs à l'aigre-doux. **Credit cards** Visa, Eurocard and MasterCard. **Pets** Dogs allowed. **Facilities** Parking. **Nearby** Libourne and the Libournais (Pomerol, Château Pétrus, St Emilion), Blasimon, Duras. **Open** March – end Nov (closed Sunday evening and Monday except July, Aug and Sept).

This charming country hotel on a little hill overlooking vineyards is very peaceful and you will receive a warm welcome from the young owners, who have furnished it very comfortably and in discreet good taste. The bedrooms vary in size; they are light and airy and have pleasant turn-of-the-century furniture. Ask for the *Green* room as your first choice. The cooking is good traditional fare, with some well meals are prepared specialties, and served in a dining room where a log fire burns in winter. In summer the tables are placed outside on the terrace in the shade of a cedar, facing the view. The hotel is well kept and for guests' amusement there is a billiard table upstairs. This is a good family place from which to visit the vineyards or explore the nearby Romanesque abbeys.

How to get there (Map 22): 9km south of Castillon-la-Bataille via D15 and D17 towards Sauveterre, then D232 (2km from the town).

La Closerie des Vignes ★★

Village des Arnauds
33710 Saint-Ciers-de-Canesse (Gironde)
Tel. 57.64.81.90 - Fax 57.64.94.44 - Mme Robert-Broy

Rooms 9 with telephone, bath, WC and TV. **Price** Double 350F. **Meals** Breakfast 35F, served 8:00-10:00; half board 315F (per pers., 3 days min.). **Restaurant** Service 12:00-13:30, 19:30-21:00 (closed Sunday evening and Tuesday in low season); menus 120-160F, also à la carte. Specialties: Gambas flambées au whisky, lamproie bordelaise, magret confit, foie gras. **Credit cards** Visa, Eurocard and MasterCard. **Pets** Dogs allowed. **Facilities** Swimming pool, parking. **Nearby** Citadel in Blaye, Bourg, cave of Pair-non-Pair near Prignac, Château de Bouilh, Church of St-André-de-Cubzac. **Open** March 1 – Jan 31

The Closerie des Vignes is not an old building but this small auberge is truly delightful and the ambience so welcoming and friendly that it cries out to be included in this guide. Lying amid vineyards, it is very comfortable, admirably well cared for, and its decor includes: modern furniture, soft pastel colors, pretty floral fabrics and comfortable sofas and chairs. The dining room opens onto the vineyards and there is a pleasant swimming pool for summer visitors.

How to get there *(Map 22): 8km southeast of Blaye via D669 to Villeneuve, then D250.*

Le Couvent aux Herbes ★★★★
40320 Eugénie-les-Bains (Landes)
Tel. 58.05.06.07 - Fax 58.51.13.59
M. Hardy - M. Leclercq

Rooms 8 with telephone, bath, WC, TV and minibar. **Price** Double 1000-1650F, suite 1450-2000F. **Meals** Breakfast 100F, served 7:30-10:15. **Restaurant** "Les Prés d'Eugénie". Service 13:00-14:30, 19:00-22:30 (closed Wednesday and Thursday lunchtime); menus 390-650F, also à la carte. **Credit cards** All major. **Pets** Dogs allowed (+150F). **Facilities** Swimming pool, tennis, sauna (110F), health center, parking. **Nearby** Aire-sur-Adour, Mont-de-Marsan, Samadet, Saint-Sever. **Open** Feb 15 – Dec 31.

This village in the heart of Gascony which was made famous in the 19th-century by Empress Eugénie, who came here "to take the waters". Le Couvent aux Herbes is a former 18th-century convent and girls' boarding school lying on the edge of a lovely park lush with magnolias, palms and banana trees. It has today been exquisitely restored by Christine Guérard of *Les Prés d'Eugénie* in the village, which is famous for the cuisine of her husband, Michel, as well as for her own gracious hospitality and decorative talents. Madame Guérard has decorated the Couvent aux Herbes with soft, refined, harmonious touches throughout the eight exquisite bedrooms/salons. They are so beautiful we wanted to try them all: *Le Temps des Cerises* for its delicious scent of old roses; or *Belle Nonette* for its magnificent oak beams; or, finally, *Jardin Secret*, which opens onto the luscious herb garden for which Le Couvent aux Herbes is named. If a week's slimming and exercising is part of your vacation plan, this is the place to come.

How to get there *(Map 29): 35km south of Mont-de-Marsan.*

La Maison Rose **
40320 Eugénie-les-bains (Landes)
Tel. 58.05.05.05 - Fax 58.51.13.59
M. and Mme Guérard - M. Hardy and M. Leclercq

Rooms 32, and 5 suites, with telephone, bath, WC and TV. **Price** Single 400-480F, double 480-550F, suite with kitchen 550-800F. **Meals** Breakfast 70F, served 8:00-9:15; full board 600-800F (per pers., 3 days min.). **Restaurant** "Cuisine minceur" Service 13:00 and 20:00; menus 170-190F. **Credit cards** All major. **Pets** Dogs allowed (+50F). **Facilities** Swimming pool, tennis, sauna, health center, parking. **Nearby** Aire-sur-Adour cathedral and organs, Mont-de-Marsan museums and keep, Samadet pottery museum, Saint-Sever Dominican monastery. **Open** Feb 14 – Dec 4.

Michel and Christine Guérard have always been successful at combining their respective arts. There is Michel's gastronomic art, of course, which has made his Prés d'Eugénie into one of the greatest restaurants in France. And Christine's art of gracious hospitality has made the couple's three houses in Eugénie into models of charm. While Les Prés has a colonial touch and Le Couvent des Herbes has become one of their prettiest hotels, La Maison Rose is decorated in a more country manner. We especially like this one for its *"Feather Weight, Feather Price"* menu, with five daily thermal treatments and the possibility of following a slimming regime, for a reasonable full room-and-board price. Throughout your stay, you can enjoy the master's famous *Cuisine Minceur*, or a rustic festive meal at *La Ferme aux Grives*, the couple's third auberge. Be prepared for a week-long dream in a decor of charm.

How to get there *(Map 29): 35km south of Mont-de-Marsan via D124 towards Pau.*

La Ferme aux Grives ***

40320 Eugénie-les-Bains (Landes)
Tél. 58.51.19.08 - Fax 58.51.13.59
M. Hardy - M. Leclercq

Rooms 4 with telephone, bath, WC, TV and minibar. **Price** Double 550-600F, suite 750F. **Meals** Breakfast in lounge 70F, served 8:30-10:00. **Restaurant** Service 12:00-13:30, 20:00-22:30 (closed Mon. evening, Tues. lunchtime except July 12 – Sep 12); menus 170-190F. **Credit cards** Visa, Eurocard and MasterCard. **Pets** Dogs allowed (+50F). **Facilities** Swimming pool, tennis, sauna, health center, parking. **Nearby** Aire-sur-Adour, Mont-de-Marsan, Samadet, Saint-Sever. **Open** Fev 15 – Dec 31.

La Ferme aux Grives is yet another of our newly selected hotels in the small village of Eugénie-les-Bains, a belonging to the Guérards. We have included it rustic auberge because it offers real quality and country charm at affordable prices. This old farmhouse has been entirely restored in the finest regional tradition: its walls of large rocks from the Adour River, its big stone fireplaces and terra cotta floors have all been charmingly renewed. There are two dining rooms: the Café du Village, where you can sample the excellent wines of the region and enjoy the chef's special; and the large auberge dining room where a beautiful menu highlights authentic family recipes of this gastronomic region. Here, plump, farm-raised Landes chickens turn roasting on the spit and hams are hung from the ceilings to cure, while fresh seasonal vegetables and magnificent country breads are displayed on a large butcher block in the center. There are several bedrooms in a small building, which have all the delightful rusticity and charm of the country.

How to get there *(Map 29): 35km south of Mont-de-Marsan towards Pau.*

Pain, Adour et Fantaisie ★★★

7, place des tilleuls
40270 Grenade-sur-Adour (Landes)
Tel. 58.45.18.80 - Fax 58.45.16.57 - M. Garret

Rooms 11 with air-conditioning, telephone, bath (9 with whirlpool), WC, TV, safe and minibar - wheelchair accessible. **Price** Double 380-700F, apart. 1200F. **Meals** Breakfast 75F; "Week-end de charme" 2500-3000F (per 2 pers.); "soirée fantaisie" 1300F (per 2 pers.). **Restaurant** Service 12:00-14:15, 19:45-22:30 (closed Sunday evening and Monday; Monday lunchtime in July and Aug); menus, also à la carte. **Credit cards** All major. **Pets** Dogs allowed (+50F). **Facilities** Parking, garage (+50F). **Nearby** Landes de Gascogne Regional Park, Bastides tour– 9- and 18-hole golf courses in Mont-de-Marsan. **Open** All year.

On the village side, this superb, half-timbered 17th-century auberge looks out onto the arcades of the large public square. On the river side, a cool, shady terrace (a summer dining room), the large traditional balconies and certain bedrooms look out directly onto the river Adour. Here is a place of peace and pleasure. The bedrooms, with evocative names from nature, are vast and bright. Decorated with great talent, they all have charm and character; and the bathrooms are very well equipped. The original old wood paneling graces the dining room. Henceforth, guests will enjoy the cuisine prepared by Philippe Garret, who has taken over the hotel and who was long Didier Oudill's second in the kitchen; (the well-known Monsieur Oudill is today at the Café de Paris in Biarritz). This is yet another very good auberge, and is reason enough to make the trip to the Landes staying here.

How to get there *(Map 29): 15km south of Mont-de-Marsan via N 124.*

La Vieille Auberge ★★★

Port-de-Lanne
40300 Peyrehorade (Landes)
Tel. 58.89.16.29 – Fax 58.89.12.89 – M. and Mme Lataillade

Rooms 10 with telephone, bath or shower and WC (2 with TV). **Price** Single and double 230-450F, suite 500-600F. **Meals** Breakfast 40-50F, served 8:30-10:30; half board 320-450F (per pers.). **Restaurant** Service 12:00-13:30, 19:30-21:00; menus 120-235F, also à la carte. Specialties: Magret, mousseline de saumon, saumon frais, confits de canard et de porc à l'ail. **Credit cards** Not accepted. **Pets** Dogs allowed. **Facilities** Swimming pool, parking. **Nearby** Biarritz, Peyrehorade, abbey of Arthous, Sorde-l'abbaye, Romanesque church in Cagnotte, Bonnat and Basque museums in Bayonne – 18-hole Hossegor golf course. **Open** May 31 – Oct 1 (closed Monday).

Both Monsieur Lataillade and his father were born in this old coaching inn whose rustic beams, walls and floors bear the imprint of time. The inviting reception rooms are disturbed only by the slow rhythm of an antique pendulum clock or occasional music from an old piano. The bedrooms, located in the former stables and barns, are charming and comfortable, and there is a lovely garden with a swimming pool. M. Lataillade has built up an interesting museum, which is located in the old hay barn. It contains objects retracing the history of the port of Lanne and its seafarers, who were known as *Gabariers*. La Vieille Auberge is a friendly Gascon inn, where you will enjoy Madame Lataillade's homemade preserves at breakfast, and her excellent cuisine.

How to get there *(Map 29): 30km northwest of Bayonne via N117; on the church square.*

Auberge des Pins **

Route de la Piscine
40630 Sabres (Landes)
Tel. 58.07.50.47 – Fax 58.07.56.74 – M. and Mme Lesclauze

Rooms 26 with telephone, bath or shower and WC (21 with TV). **Price** Single and double 230-450F, suite 500-600F. **Meals** Breakfast 40-50F, served 7:30-10:00; half board 320-450F (per pers., 3 days min.). **Restaurant** Service 12:00-14:00, 19:30-21:00; menus 100-235F, also à la carte. Specialties: Foie gras poêlé pointe d'asperges, filets de rouget, langoustines aux cèpes, pigeon en croûte. **Credit cards** Visa, Eurocard and MasterCard. **Pets** Dogs not allowed. **Facilities** Parking. **Nearby** Church in Sabres, local history museum in Marquèze, Les Landes de Gascogne Regional park. **Open** All year (closed Sunday evening and Monday in low season).

You will be enchanted by this hotel amid the pines on the way out of the village of Sabres. Generations of good hotel keeping ensure high-quality service and a faultless welcome. The bedrooms in the main building have every comfort and an old-fashioned charm, but the bedrooms in the newer building, which blends very well with the old, are our favorites. They are large, light, airy and elegantly modern, with lovely fabrics, superb bathrooms and a small terrace. The dining room, with its antique furniture, copperware, ceramics and fireplace laden with a collection of rare old Armagnacs, is a place to linger in over the beautiful cooking of Michel Lesclauze, who uses the best local produce to make truly memorable meals, and we strongly recommend the Auberge des Pins.

How to get there *(Map 29): 40km east of Mimizan via D44.*

La Bergerie ★★★

Avenue du Lac
40140 Soustons (Landes)
Tel. 58.41.11.43 – Mme Clavier

Rooms 12 with telephone, bath, WC and TV. **Price** Single 300F, double 350-400F, suite 550F. **Meals** Breakfast 40F, served 8:00-10:00; half board 380-440F (per pers., 3 days min.). **Restaurant** For residents on half board only. Specialties: Foie gras, confit des Landes, vins de sable. **Credit cards** Visa, Eurocard and MasterCard. **Pets** Dogs not allowed. **Facilities** Parking. **Nearby** The Lit-et-Mixe Marensin in Dax (100km), Bonnat and Basque museums in Bayonne – 9- and 18-hole Côte d'Argent golf course. **Open** Mar 15 – Nov 15.

Drive past the village church, take the road lined with gigantic plane trees, and you will arrive at La Bergerie. A typically Landaise private house built at the beginning of the century, it is surrounded by large gardens. The oak floor in the entrance hall shines nearly as brightly as the polished copperware and there are two small and prettily furnished lounges. The bedrooms are simple; their furnishings remind you that Spain isn't very far away. This homey charm is also found in the living room and dining room, where every morning the menu of the day is posted. On summer mornings a very pretty verandah opening onto the patio is set for breakfast. The hospitality makes you soon feel part of the household. If the hotel is full, ask for a room at the Château Bergeron, the Clavier family's other establishment; and in any case, you can enjoy its swimming pool.

How to get there *(Map 28): 38km north of Bayonne via A63 to Saint-Vincent-de-Tyrosse, then D112 to Tosse, D632 to Soustons.*

A la Belle Gasconne

47170 Poudenas (Lot-et-Garonne)
Tel. 53.65.71.58 – Fax 53.65.87.39
M. and Mme Gracia

Rooms 7 with telephone, bath or shower and WC (3 with TV). **Price** Single 430F, double 500-555F, suite 655F. **Meals** Breakfast 50F; half board 540-715F (per pers.) **Restaurant** Service 12:00-14:15, 19:30-21:30; menus 80-285F, also à la carte. Specialties: Foie gras frais, civet de canard au vin vieux de Buzet. **Credit cards** All major. **Pets** Dogs allowed. **Facilities** Swimming pool. **Nearby** Beauville, Auvillar (pottery museum), Nérac – 18-hole golf courses in Albret and Barbaste. **Open** Feb 1 – Dec 31 (closed Sunday evening and Monday in low season).

Who hasn't dreamed of spending a few romantic days in an old mill lulled by the sound of water trickling beneath the window? Lying at the foot of a stunningly beautiful medieval village, the Belle Gasconne has a vast living room, all wood and stone, and it still has some of the old mill machinery; you can actually see the water running under the floor through a glass paving stone. From this room there is access to a small island where you can relax in the shade of the trees. The bedrooms, which have specially built elm furniture, are comfortable and beautifully decorated. Colors have been delicately coordinated, and in the bathrooms, which are done with Salernes tiles, even the dressing gowns are changed daily. Madame Gracia's restaurant is famous and the owners' hospitality is discreet and attentive.

How to get there *(Map 30): 47km southwest of Agen via D656 towards Nérac.*

Hôtel Ohantzea ★★

Rue Principale
64250 Aïnhoa (Pyrénées-Atlantiques)
Tel. 59.29.90.50 - M. and Mme Ithurria

Rooms 9 with telephone, 8 with bath and 1 with shower. **Price** Single 230F, double 300F. **Meals** Breakfast 30F, served 8:00-9:30; half board 300F, full board 360F (per pers., 3 days min.). **Restaurant** Service 12:00-14:00, 20:00-20:45; menus 120-215F, also à la carte. Specialties: Magret de canard aux poires, turbot braisé au Jurançon. **Credit cards** Visa, Eurocard and MasterCard. **Nearby** Espelette, Sare, Ascain, Villa Arnaga in Cambo-les-Bains, Bonnat and Basque museums in Bayonne – 18-hole Chantaco golf course in Saint-Jean-de-Luz. **Open** Feb 15 – Nov 15 (closed Sunday evening and Monday).

In the middle of the village opposite the church, an attractive whitewashed façade hides this old 17th-century farm, renovated at the beginning of this century, and a lovely garden, invisible from the road. The paintings hanging in the small living room were offered as payment by passing artists. At one side is the *salle*, one of the most beautiful rooms and authentic in the Pays Basque now used for dining. Be sure to notice the old wooden stairs, the handsome furniture, decorative objects, copper and prints. The bedrooms and bathrooms are delightfully old-fashioned and all are comfortable. Many retain their original wallpaper and those on the garden side have balconies covered with wisteria. The hospitality is expecially warm.

How to get there *(Map 28): 26km south of Bayonne via D932 and D918 towards Espelette, then D20.*

Chez Chilo ★★

64130 Barcus (Pyrénées–Atlantiques)
Tel. 59.28.90.79 – Fax 59.28.93.10
M. and Mme Chilo

Rooms 14, 11 with telephone, 6 with bath, 5 with shower, 10 with WC and 9 with TV. **Price** Single 120-420F, double 140-440F. **Meals** Breakfast 35F; half board 170-320F, full board 250-410F (per pers., 3 days min.). **Restaurant** Service 12:00-14:30, 19:00-22:00 (closed Sunday evening and Monday in low season); menus 75-200F, also à la carte. Specialties: Croustillant "Piquiuos" au merlu à l'ail, carré d'agneau de lait des Pyrénées, puits croquant aux fruit frais. **Credit cards** All major. **Pets** Dogs allowed. **Facilities** Parking. **Nearby** Châteaux of Moumour and Aven, Saint-Blaise-Hospital, Pau – Golf course in Artiguelouve. **Open** All year except Jan 2 – 14 (closed Sunday evening and Monday in low season).

You have to have an adventurous spirit to turn off onto this tiny winding road in the heart of the green Béarn mountains. Yet it's only a few kilometers from the villages of Aramits and Lanne, immortalized in Alexandre Dumas's *The Three Musketeers*. You won't regret your detour. Awaiting you in this beautiful countryside is a restaurant offering sumptuous cuisine and a hotel worthy of the most discriminating. This family auberge has recently been enlarged and redecorated with taste and originality by young Madame Chilo, whose husband is the chef. The most recent bedrooms are the most luxurious; those in the old part are simpler but still comfortable and have been newly carpeted. So there is a room for everyone's taste. And the welcome is extremely courteous.

How to get there *(Map 29): 16km west of Oloron-Sainte-Marie via D24; towards Mauléon-Licharre.*

Hôtel Laminak ★★★

Route de Saint-Pée
64210 Artonne (Pyrénées-Atlantiques)
Tel. 59.41.95.40 - Fax 59.41.87.65 - M. and Mme Cauderlier

Rooms 10 with telephone, 6 with bath, 4 with shower, WC, TV and minibar - Wheelchair access. **Price** Double 350-550F. **Meals** Breakfast 45F, served 8:00-11:00. No restaurant. **Credit cards** Amex, Visa, Eurocard and MasterCard. **Pets** Dogs allowed (fee). **Facilities** Parking. **Nearby** Biarritz, Anglet and the forest of Chiberta, Arcangues, Bidart, Saint-Jean-de-Luz – 18-hole golf courses in Arcangues and Bussussary. **Open** All year.

Perched on a hilltop on the edge of Biarritz between the Atlantic and the Pyrenees, this old 18th-century Basque farmhouse has just been entirely converted into a charming small hotel. Surrounded by hilly countryside, the Laminak is calm and peaceful. The bedrooms have been carefully decorated, combining the latest amenities with original touches which lend an individual character to each. Some are larger and have corner sitting areas, but all are in exquisite taste. You can enjoy a copious, elegant breakfast in the colonial-style winter garden, which also serves light snacks if you don't want to go out. There are many good restaurants nearby, including *L'Epicerie d'Ahetze* and *Les Frères Ibarboure* in Bidart, and *La Tantine de Burgos* in Biarritz.

How to get there (*Map 28*): *4km south of Biarritz. On A 63 exit Biarritz-La Négresse, then D 255 towards of Arbonne.*

Le Château du Clair de Lune ★★★

48, avenue Alan-Seeger
64200 Biarritz (Pyrénées-Atlantiques)
Tel. 59.23.45.96 - Fax 59.23.39.13 - Mme Beyrière

Rooms 16 with telephone, bath, WC and TV (8 with minibar). **Price** Double 420-700F. **Meals** Breakfast 50F, served 8:00-11:00. No restaurant. **Credit cards** All major. **Pets** Dogs allowed (+35F). **Facilities** Parking. **Nearby** Rock of the Virgin, Museum of the Sea in Biarritz, Anglet and the Forest of Chiberta, Arcangues, Bidard – 18-hole Biarritz golf course, 18-hole Chiberta golf course in Anglet. **Open** All year.

This turn-of-the-century house above Biarritz is very peaceful and stands in a serene garden of roses, flower beds, trees and lawns. It is the sort of house which conjures up nostalgic memories of childhood. The bathrooms and bathtubs have the huge proportions of another era, and the floor tiles and basins are antique. The large lounge on the ground floor opens onto and merges with the garden: cheerful, airy and bright, it is furnished with yellow sofas and a grand piano. The dining room, where guests breakfast together around a large table, makes you wish that you could dine here as well. This lovely family house on the Basque coast, though a hotel, begins to feel as if it were your own. The restaurants we recommend are: *La Tantina de Burgos* and *Le Calejon* (Spanish specialties), *La Bodega* and *les Trois Salsas* (surfers' favorite), and *Chez Albert* (fish and sea food).

How to get there *(Map 28): 4km south of the town center via the Pont de la Négresse and D255 (Arbonne route).*

Le Saint-Charles ★★
47, avenue Reine-Victoria
64200 Biarritz (Pyrénées-Atlantiques)
Tel. 59.24.10.54 - Fax 59.24.56.74 - A. Faget-Marc

Rooms 13, 9 with telephone, 3 with bath, 10 with shower, WC and cable TV. **Price** 260-380F. **Meals** Breakfast 35F, served 7:30-11:00; half board 490-560F, full board 610-690F (per 2 pers., 3 days min.). **Restaurant** For residents only. Service 12:30-13:00, 19:30-20:00; menu 90F. Specialties: Regional cooking. **Credit cards** Visa, Eurocard and MasterCard. **Pets** Dogs allowed. **Nearby** Biarritz, Anglet and the Forest of Chiberta, Arcangues, Bidard, Saint-Jean-de Luz – 18-hole Biarritz golf course, Le Phare; 18-hole Chiberta golf course in Anglet. **Open** Feb 16 – Nov 30.

Don't be misled: Behind the old-fashioned façade of this charming family *pension* is hidden a small hotel which is quite comfortable. The simply decorated bedrooms are all well equipped with newly redone baths or showers. The small lounge and the dining room have an atmosphere of the past. In the garden, where your breakfast is served in summer, there are lush geraniums, hydrangeas, plumbagos and pink oleander. The only drawback is the traffic in the street, which can be quite noisy in the summer. It's the price you pay when you're just a few steps from the center of town, the beach, and the Louison Bobet Thassalotherapy Center!

How to get there *(Map 28): Signs in the center of Biarritz.*

Hôtel du Pont d'Enfer ★★

64780 Bidarray (Pyrénées–Atlantiques)
Tel. 59.37.70.88 – Fax 59.37.76.60
Mme Gagnant

Rooms 17 with telephone, bath or shower (13 with WC, 10 with TV). **Price** Double 150-330F. **Meals** Breakfast 30F, served 8:00-9:30; half board 195-260F, full board 265-325F (per pers., 3 days min.). **Restaurant** Service 12:00-14:00 and 19:00-20:30; menus 88-168F, also à la carte. Specialties: Foie gras, confit de canard,truite du Pont-d'Enfer, zarzuela, merlu Koskera. **Credit cards** All major. **Pets** Dogs allowed. **Facilities** Parking. **Nearby** Saint-Jean-Pied-de-Port, caves of Isturits and Oxocelhaya, Bonnat and Basque museums in Bayonne — 18-hole Arcangues golf course in Argelous. **Open** Feb 15 – Dec 15 (closed Sunday evening and Wednesday except for the residents).

To reach this hotel you cross the River Nive on the Pont d'Enfer Bridge, after which the hotel is named. Situated at the foot of a hill at the entrance to the village, the hotel is old but comfortable. We liked the huge dining room, furnished faithfully in Basque country style, as well as the atmosphere of the bedrooms. Some of the bedrooms are in a separate building and of these, numbers 14, 16 and 18 look out directly onto the river. In summer you can have your meals on the terrace beside the Nive. Mme Gagnant is very kind and welcoming.

How to get there *(Map 28): 35km southeast of Bayonne via D932 and D918.*

Hôtel Errobia ★★★

Avenue Chantecler
64250 Cambo-les-Bains (Pyrénées-Atlantiques)
Tel. 59.29.71.26 - Fax 59.29.96.36 - Mme Garra

Rooms 15 with telephone, bath or shower and TV (9 with WC). **Price** Single 300F,
double 400F, suite 500F. **Meals** Breakfast 30F, served 7:30-11:00. No restaurant.
Credit cards Visa, Eurocard and MasterCard. **Pets** Dogs allowed. **Facilities**
Swimming pool, parking. **Nearby** Villa Arnaga in Cambo, Artzamendi, Church of
Itxassou, Bonnat and Basque museums in Bayonne – 18-hole Arcangues golf course
in Argelous. **Open** Easter and May 1 – Oct 30.

In the residential area of Cambo-des-Bains, on the edge of a
plateau overhanging the river Nive facing the Pyrenees, this large
Basque villa stands in magnificent gardens. The interior is
completely furnished in Basque style, from the antique furniture
to the kitchens and the wall tiles. Our only reservation: some of
the beds are uncomfortable. All around, the green and flowering
gardens bear witness to the gentle climate here. To enjoy their
peace and beauty stroll among the trees and the abundant
hydrangeas, mimosas, and camellias. *Tante Ursule* and *Le Relais de
la Poste* are two good restaurants near the hotel.

How to get there *(Map 28): 20km south of Bayonne via D932; near the
church.*

Lehen Tokia

64500 Ciboure (Pyrénées-Atlantiques)
Tel. 59.47.18.16 – Fax 59.47.38.04
M. Taboulet

Rooms 6 with telephone, bath or shower, WC and TV. **Price** Single and double 550-800F, suite 1200F. **Meals** Breakfast 50F, served 8:30-10:00. **Restaurant** Only for residents and by reservation. Menu. Specialties: Turbot, foie gras, paëlla. **Credit cards** Visa, Eurocard and MasterCard. **Pets** Dogs not allowed. **Facilities** Swimming pool, parking. **Nearby** Saint-Jean-Baptiste church in Saint-Jean-de-Luz, coast road, Ciboure, Bayonne, Biarritz – 18-hole Nivelle and Chantaco golf courses. **Open** All year.

Built in 1925, this splendid Basque villa has recently been classed as a Historic Monument, notably because of its remarkable stained glass. The original owner used to come here on vacation with his family. Today, two of his grandchildren have opened Lehen Tokia to guests. The interior has been refurbished, but the original splendid decoration is intact. There is a subtle combination of magnificent objects and Art Déco furniture with antique regional furniture and family paintings, and the rooms are of superb size. You enter the vestibule, then go up several steps to the salon, which in turn is surrounded by an elegant curving stairway leading to the bedrooms. Ravishingly beautiful and very comfortable, they have a marvelous view out over the Atlantic. In the foreground, you also see the garden which slopes down to the swimming pool and the charming small pavilion. In summer, several pretty dining tables are set out here for residents. You will enjoy good home cooking with Basque specialties at this very beautiful hotel.

How to get there *(Map 28): 2km from Saint-Jean-de-Luz. On A 63, exit Saint-Jean-de-Luz south.*

Artzaïn Etchea★★

Route d'Iraty
64220 Esterençuby (Pyrénées–Atlantiques)
Tel. 59.37.11.55 – Fax 59.37.20.16 – M. Arriaga

Rooms 22 with telephone, bath or shower and WC (8 with TV) - Wheelchair access to 2 rooms. **Price** Single 180F, double 220F, suite 290F. **Meals** Breakfast 36F; half board 200-240F, full board 226-272F (per pers., 2 days min.). **Restaurant** Service 12:30-14:00, 19:30-21:00; menus 94-190F (child 60F), also à la carte. Specialties: Foie de canard chaud aux raisins, saumon frais au champagne, salmis de palombe. **Credit cards** Not accepted. **Pets** Dogs allowed (+20F). **Facilities** Parking. **Nearby** Saint-Jean-Pied-de-Port (Pilgrim's Route), Saint-Etienne-de-Baïgorry, Saint-Jean-le-Vieux. **Open** Dec 20 – Nov 11 (closed Wednesday in low season).

A small road lined with low walls, trees and streams brings you to the crossroads where Artzaïn Etchea stands. As its Basque name indicates, this was once a shepherd's dwelling which has been converted into a simple but good country hotel. The bedrooms are comfortable but you will do well to choose one of the more recent ones, some of which have wonderful views of the valley. The pleasant dining room also has beautiful prospects. In summer tables are placed outside, and you can hear the sound of the stream which runs below. The people are very welcoming

How to get there *(Map 28): 52km southeast of Bayonne via D918 to Saint-Jean-Pied-de Port, then D301.*

Hôtel Arcé ★★★

64430 Saint-Etienne-de-Baïgorry (Pyrénées-Atlantiques)
Tel. 59.37.40.14 - Fax 59.37.40.27
M. Arcé

Rooms 22 with telephone, bath or shower, WC and TV. **Price** Single and, double 420-680F, suite 1030F. **Meals** Breakfast 47F, served 7:45-10:30; half board 400-540F, 730F in suites (per pers., 3 days min.). **Restaurant** Service 12:30-13:45, 19:30-20:30 (closed Monday lunchtime in low season); menus 110-230F, also à la carte. Specialties: Truite au bleu du vivier, tête de veau vinaigrette, carré d'agneau farçi à la fleur de thym. **Credit cards** Visa, Eurocard and MasterCard. **Pets** Dogs allowed. **Facilities** Heated swimming pool, tennis, parking. **Nearby** Saint-Jean-le-Vieux, Saint-Jean-Pied-de-Port, village of Béhérobie – 18-hole Arcangues golf course in Argelous. **Open** March 15 – Nov 15.

This old inn, typical of the region and luxuriously restored, has been managed by the same family for the last five generations. The large picture windows are in keeping with the beautiful proportions of the dining room, and outside, long terraces are laid out at the water's edge. The bedrooms are extremely comfortable, newly decorated and overlook the river and the Pyrenees; a variety of reading matter is supplied. Bouquets of flowers are placed all over the hotel. The little annex is a pleasing addition, with its balconies overhanging the river: you can fish without even leaving your bedroom! You will enjoy good classic regional cooking and a very friendly welcome.

How to get there *(Map 28): 50km southeast of Bayonne via D932 and D918 to Saint-Martin d'Arossa, then D948 to St-Etienne-de-Baïgorry.*

La Devinière ★★★

5, rue Loquin
64500 Saint-Jean-de-Luz (Pyrénées-Atlantiques)
Tel. 59.26.05.51 - Fax 59.51.26.38 - M. Carrère

Rooms 8 with telephone, bath and WC. **Price** 500-600F. **Meals** Breakfast 50F, served all morning. No restaurant. **Credit cards** Visa, Eurocard and MasterCard. **Pets** Dogs allowed on request (+50F). **Nearby** Saint-Jean-Baptiste Church in Saint-Jean-de-Luz, Basque coast road, Ciboure, Bayonne, Biarritz – 18-hole Nivelle and Chantaco golf courses. **Open** All year.

There is no obvious reason why M. and Mme Carrère should have taken on and renovated this residential family hotel – he is a lawyer and she an antiques dealer – other than the pleasure of opening a charming place in the heart of Saint-Jean-de-Luz. Good taste and discernment are apparent everywhere. The eight bedrooms are ravishingly pretty and are furnished with beautiful antiques, as are the music room and library, which are open for the use of the guests. The pedestrian street and the garden ensure quiet nights even in the heart of the town. The welcome is warm. For fine dining, try: *Chez Pablo* (piperades and chipirons), *Kaïku* (sole aux cèpes) or *Jourasse* in town, or *La Ferme Penzia* in Ascain (open only in the summer) and *Chez Mattin* in Ciboure (specialty: "ttorro").

How to get there (Map 28): 15km southwest of Biarritz via A63.

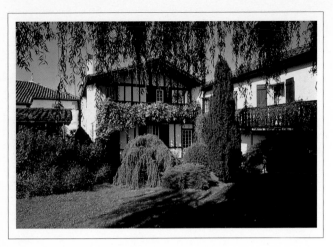

Hôtel Arraya ★★★
Place du village
64310 Sare (Pyrénées–Atlantiques)
Tel. 59.54.20.46 – Fax 59.54.27.04 – M. Fagoaga

Rooms 20 with telephone, bath or shower, WC and TV. **Price** Single 395-400F, double 480-540F, suite 755-855F. **Meals** Breakfast 50F, served 8:00-10:00. **Restaurant** Service 12:00-14:00, 19:30-22:00; menus 120-198F, also à la carte. Specialties: Ravioles de xanguro (crab), gâteau de morue, gratin de fraises et de framboises au sabayon d'orange. **Credit cards** Amex, Visa, Eurocard and MasterCard. **Pets** Dogs not allowed. **Facilities** Parking. **Nearby** Villa Arnaga in Cambo, Espelette, Ascain, Saint-Jean-de-Luz, Bonnat and Basque museums in Bayonne – 18-hole La Nivelle and Chantaco golf courses. **Open** May 1 – Nov 6.

Do not be put off by the Arraya's somber facade, which is typical of the region. This superb Basque hotel, set on the corner of two streets in the center of the village, is made up of three old houses;, the garden, invisible from the street, effectively screens out the noise. On the ground floor, the lovely lounges and the comfortable dining room are charming with patinated rustic furniture and bright bowls of flowers. The bedrooms are all different but equally attractively furnished: the prettiest is on the garden side. There is a boutique selling regional delicacies which you can eat on the spot or take away. The restaurant menu is long and varied, but regional dishes remain the specialties of the house.

How to get there *(Map 28): 36km south of Bayonne via A63, Saint-Jean-de-Luz exit, D918 to Ascain and D4 to Sare.*

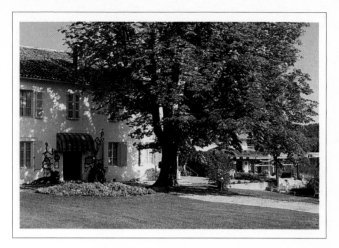

Hôtel La Patoula ★★★

64480 Ustaritz (Pyrénées–Atlantiques)
Tel 59.93.00.56 – Fax 59.93.16.54
M. Guilhem

Rooms 9 with telephone, bath or shower and WC. **Price** Double 300-430F.
Meals Breakfast 55F, served 8:00-10:00; half board 325-390F, full board 445-510F
(per pers., 3 days min.). **Restaurant** Service 12:00-14:00, 20:00-22:00; menus 130-
290F (child 90F), also à la carte. Specialties: Alose grillée, saumon sauvage,
palombes rôties, agneau de lait. **Credit cards** Visa, Eurocard and MasterCard.
Pets Dogs allowed (+35F). **Facilities** Parking. **Nearby** Villa Arnaga in Cambo,
Biarritz, Bonnat and Basque museums in Bayonne – 18-hole Biarritz golf course,
18-hole Chantaco golf course in Saint-Jean-de-Luz. **Open** Feb 15 – Jan 5 (closed
Sunday evening and Monday in low season).

This hotel is set back from the road in a park bordered by the tranquil waters of the River Nive. This romantic view can be enjoyed either from the dining room, from the pergola where breakfast tables are laid in summer, or from the *chaise longues* in the garden. In the winter, when there are fewer tourists, the dining room with its open fire provides an intimate setting, and people come for the cooking from all over the region. The bedrooms are spacious, comfortable and very prettily decorated. We preferred the two which overlook the river and the four which overlook the garden. The modest number of rooms and Madame Guilhem's friendliness give La Patoula a very pleasant atmosphere.

How to get there *(Map 28): 11km south of Bayonne via A10, Bayonne-sud exit number 5, towards Cambo-les-Bains, then D982; in the center of Ustaritz, opposite the church.*

Le Chalet ★★★

03000 Coulandon (Allier)
Tel. 70.44.50.08 – Fax 70.44.07.09
M. Hulot

Rooms 28 with telephone, bath or shower, WC and TV. **Price** Single 280-320F, double 340-430F. **Meals** Breakfast 42F, served 7:00-11:00; half board 280-320F, full board 340-430F (per pers., 3 days min.). **Restaurant** Service 12:30-13:30, 19:30-21:00; menus 105-220F, also à la carte. Specialties: Filet d'agneau en croûte, poêlée de langoustines aux pâtes fraîches, délice glacé au chocolat, crème de miel. **Credit cards** All major. **Pets** Dogs allowed. **Facilities** Lake, fishing, swimming pool, parking. **Nearby** Souvigny priory, châteaux of the Besbre Valley and of Lapalisse in Dompierre (half day's journey), triptych of the Maître de Moulins at Notre Dame cathedral in Moulins – 9-hole Avenelles golf course in Moulins. **Open** Feb 1 – Dec 15.

This turn-of-the-century hotel is set in the hilly Bourbonnais countryside. The bedrooms are located in the main house and the outbuildings: numbers 8, 3 and 4, which still have the charm of the past, are beautifully spacious and they have a pretty balcony. Numbers 16, 17 and 19, which have been renovated, are comfortable and well-decorated. Avoid number 1, which is too close to the parking lot. The other rooms have varying amenities but they are all pleasant, with prettily coordinated wallpapers and fabrics. The restaurant is in a building somewhat too new for our taste. In summer, tables are set out on the terrace, and you can dine with a beautiful view past the swimming pool below to a landscape of fields and trees all around. The staff is very courteous, but an additional person would perhaps improve the service. This is a lovely country setting just several minutes from Moulins.

How to get there *(Map 18): 6km west of Moulins via D945.*

Château de Boussac

Target
03140 Chantelle (Allier)
Tel. 70.40.63.20 – Fax 70.40.60.03 – M. and Mme de Longueil

Rooms 5 with bath and WC. **Price** Single and double 600-800F, suite 950-1100F.
Meals Breakfast 50F, served 8:00-10:00; half board 1100F (per pers., 5 days min.).
Restaurant Set meal in the evening only and on reservation; menu 260-320F incl.
wine and alcohol. **Credit cards** Amex, Visa, Eurocard and MasterCard. **Pets** Dogs
allowed (fee). **Facilities** Parking. **Nearby** Church of Sainte-Croix and museum of the
Vine in Saint-Pourçain-sur-Sioule, priory in Souvigny, triptych of the Maître de
Moulins at Notre Dame cathedral in Moulins – 18-hole golf course in Montluçon.
Open April 1 – Nov 15.

The many faces of this beautiful chateau blend medieval austerity
with the grace of the 18th-century. The owners receive you
like friends and spontaneously include you in their aristocratic
country life. Each very comfortable bedroom is superbly furnished
with antiques (often Louis XV or Louis XVI), family mementos,
and beautiful fabrics. The lounges have been charmingly restored.
Finally, the large dining room table sets the scene for festive dinner
parties which are very popular with sportsmen in the hunting
season. The elegant silverware, the conversation, and the cuisine
all contribute towards making each evening a lovely and
memorable event.

*How to get there (Map 25): 40km south of Moulins via A71, number 11
Montmarault exit, then D42 to Boussac (between Chantelle and
Montmarault).*

Le Tronçais ★★

Avenue Nicolas-Rambourg
Tronçais – 03360 Saint-Bonnet-Tronçais (Allier)
Tel. 70.06.11.95 – Fax 70.06.16.15 – M. and Mme Bajard

Rooms 12 with telephone, bath or shower, WC and TV. **Price** Single 198F, double 252-334F. **Meals** Breakfast 31F, served 8:00-10:30; half board 237-278F, full board 288-3307F (per pers., 3 days min.). **Restaurant** Service 12:00-13:30, 19:30-21:00; menus 98-180F, also à la carte. Specialties: Terrine d'anguille aux mûres, sandre au gratin, côte de veau aux cèpes, game. **Credit cards** Visa, Eurocard and Mastercard. **Pets** Dogs allowed only in bedrooms. **Facilities** Tennis, parking. **Nearby** Oak forest of Tronçais, château d'Ainay-le-Vieil, Château Meillant – 18-hole Nassigny golf course. **Open** March 15 – Dec 15 (closed Sunday evening and Monday in low season).

Once the private house of a forge owner, the Tronçais is located at the edge of the forest in a garden bordered by a lake. From the entrance steps to the bedrooms, the hotel is calm, comfortable and civilized. A small annex close by is as attractive and comfortable as the house itself. The graveled garden in front of the two buildings serves as the terrace and bar in the summer. The hotel grounds stretch all the way to the banks of the lake, in which you can fish.

How to get there *(Map 17): 45km north of Montluçon. On A71 Forêt-de-Tronçais exit, then N144 and D978A to Tronçais.*

Auberge de Concasty ★★★

15600 Boisset (Cantal)
Tel. 71.62.21.16 – Fax 71.62.22.22
Mme Causse

Rooms 16 with telephone, bath, WC and TV. **Price** Single 260-290F, double 300-470F. **Meals** Breakfast 50F, brunch 80F, served 9:00-11:30; half board 340-430F (per pers., 2 days min.). **Restaurant** On reservation; closed Wednesday except for residents. Service 12:30-13:30, 20:00-21:30; menus 135-200F. Specialties: Fresh local produce. **Credit cards** All major. **Pets** Dogs allowed (+35F). **Facilities** Swimming pool, whirlpool, Turktish bath, parking. **Nearby** Château de Conros, valleys of the Lot and the Truyère, Champollion museum in Figeac. **Open** All year (on reservation).

The Auberge de Concasty is an old family mansion surrounded by its farm and fields. It has been completely restored and equipped with a swimming pool and whirlpool. The inn nonetheleess looks like a traditional family vacation house. It is very comfortable, the rooms have again been improved, and the reception rooms are pleasantly decorated. At Concasty, Madame Causse will delight you with fine seasonal cuisine featuring local specialties, (*cèpe* mushrooms, *foie gras*). You can also enjoy a good Auvergnat breakfast in this lovely vacation spot.

How to get there (*Map 24*): *25km southwest of Aurillac. In Aurillac via Cahors/Montauban by N122 for 20km; then in Manhes, turn left on D64 and follow signs.*

Château de Lavendès ★★★
15350 Champagnac (Cantal)
Tel. 71.69.62.79 - Fax 71.69.65.33
M. and Mme Gimmig

Rooms 8 with telephone, bath or shower, WC and TV. **Price** Double 420-550F.
Meals Breakfast 50F, served until 10:00; half board 400-500F (per pers, 3 days min.).
Restaurant Service 12:30-13:45, 19:30-21:00; menus 160-260F, also à la carte.
Specialties: Omble chevalier, volailles fermières, fromages au lait cru, glace à la
chicorée, tarte aux pruneaux, crème brulée. **Credit cards** Visa, Eurocard and
MasterCard. **Pets** Dogs not allowed. **Facilities** Swimming pool, sauna (100F), parking.
Nearby Bort-les-Orgues, Bort dam and château de Val, gorges of the Dordogne from
Bort to the Aigle dam (3 hours) – 9-hole Mont-Dore golf course. **Open** March 1 – Nov 15
(closed Monday in low season).

This 17th-century manor house is set in the middle of a 2-1/2-
acre park. In the lobby, which has an imposing fireplace,
afternoon tea is also served. In the two dining rooms, one furnished
in Louis XV style and the other in Louis XIII, you will dine on
the *specialités de la maison* and modernized regional cuisine prepared
by Madame Gimmig, a professional chef. A splendid staircase (on
which you will find many curiosities including old wooden
mechanisms and children's toys) leads to the comfortably furnished
bedrooms. The only sound you will hear is the tinkling of cow
bells in the surrounding meadows. (Salers beef is a prized regional
specialty).

How to get there *(Map 24): 78km north of Aurillac via D922 to Vendes
via Mauriac, then left on D12 or D112 to Champagnac; (the château is on
D15).*

Auberge du Vieux Chêne **
34, route des Lacs
15270 Champs-sur-Tarentaine (Cantal)
Tel. 71.78.71.64 - Fax 71.78.70.88 - Mme Moins

Rooms 15 with telephone, bath or shower, WC and TV. **Price** Double 320-420F.
Meals Breakfast 45F, served 8:00-10:00; half board 280-300F, full board 320-380F
(per pers., 3 days min.). **Restaurant** Service 12:00-13:30, 19:00-20:30; menus 130-
230F, also à la carte. Specialties: Foie gras d'oie maison, ris de veau aux morilles,
escalope de saumon à l'oseille. **Credit cards** Visa, Eurocard and MasterCard.
Pets Dogs allowed. **Facilities** Parking. **Nearby** Bort-les-Orgues, Bort dam and
château de Val, gorges of the Dordogne from Bort to the Aigle dam (3 hours)– 9-hole
Mont-Dore golf course. **Open** March 15 – Nov 15 (closed Sunday evening and Monday
except July and Aug).

This old stone and timber farmhouse, which is set well away
from the road, has been charmingly restored and enlarged.
The bedrooms have been beautifully renovated with cheerful,
refined colors, coordinated fabrics and wallpapers and many
charming decorative details. At one end of the ground floor, there
is a pleasant bar, while the rest of the area is occupied by a salon
and a vast dining room whose end wall is one immense fireplace.
Outside, a garden–terrace is set for breakfast. The hospitality is
warm and the cuisine is excellent.

*How to get there (Map 24): 93km north of Aurillac via D922 to Bort-les-
Orgues, then D979.*

Auberge du Pont de Lanau **

Lanau
15260 Chaudes–Aigues (Cantal)
Tel. 71.23.57.76 - Fax 71.23.53.84 - M. Cornut

Rooms 8 with telephone, bath, WC and TV. **Price** Single and double 270-350F.
Meals Breakfast 35F; half board 260-300F, full board 350-400F (per pers., 3 days
min.). **Restaurant** Service 12:30-14:00, 19:30-21:30; menus 90-300F, also à la
carte. **Credit cards** Visa, Eurocard and MasterCard. **Pets** Dogs allowed (+35F).
Facilities Parking. **Nearby** Saint-Flour, gorges of the Truyère. **Open** All year except
in Jan (closed Tuesday evening and Wednesday in low season).

Courtesy is the tradition in this old farmhouse–auberge built in
1855. In the past, clients were served meals on the left (today
the restaurant) and horses were stabled on the right (today the
lounge, breakfast room and bar). The beautifully decorated rustic
restaurant has stone walls and is dominated by a immense fireplace.
Guests once slept in bed recesses close to the fireplace to keep
warm, and you can still see traces of the original wooden partitions.
Today the inn is primarily a restaurant serving very good, refined
regional cooking. Monsieur Cornut often prepares specialties
which are little known today and which are sometimes delicious
new versions of traditional regional dishes. The eight bedrooms
are pleasant, some decorated in floral motifs while others, more
elegant, are salmon pink. They have fabric–covered walls and are
well insulated with double windows. The auberge is located beside
a country road and is a lovely place to stay.

How to get there *(Map 25): 20km south of Saint-Flour via D921.*

Hostellerie de la Maronne ★★★
Le Theil
15140 Saint-Martin-Valmeroux (Cantal)
Tel. 71.69.20.33 - Fax 71.69.28.22 - Mme Decock

Rooms 21 with telephone, bath, WC and minibar (6 with TV). **Price** Single 350-500F, double 350-550F, suite 700F. **Meals** Breakfast 40-50F, served 8:30-10:00; half board 355-480F. **Restaurant** Service 19:30-21:00; menus 140-300F, also à la carte. Specialties: Escalope de sandre aux mousserons, foie gras chaud au caramel de porto, gâteau tiède aux marrons et chocolat amer. **Credit cards** Visa, Eurocard and MasterCard. **Pets** Dogs allowed. **Facilities** Swimming pool, tennis, parking. **Nearby** Medieval city of Salers, basilica of Notre-Dame-des-Miracles in Mauriac, Puy Mary. **Open** April 3 – Nov 5.

Monsieur and Madame Decock have marvelously transformed this 19th-century Auvergnat house into a hotel. Everything has been provided for guests' rest and recreation. The living room, reading room and bar have been elegantly decorated with comfortable armchairs and some antique furniture. The modern, very comfortable bedrooms are done in pale colors and they have splendid views – the best are found in the rooms with large terraces and balconies. (There is also an apartment which is ideal for families). The cuisine is increasingly renowned and the dining room is beautiful, with a lovely view over the countryside. Walking in the area is a pleasure here, and there are a swimming pool and tennis courts. Last but not least, the hospitality and service are charming.

How to get there *(Map 24): 33km north of Aurillac via D922 to Saint-Martin Valmeroux, then D37 towards Fontanges.*

Auberge de la Tomette ★★

15220 Vitrac (Cantal)
Tel. 71.64.70.94 - Fax 71.64.77.11
M. and Mme Chausi

Rooms 21 with telephone, bath or shower, WC and TV. **Price** Single 240-260F, double 280-300F, suite 390-460F. **Meals** Breakfast 30F; half board 220-270F, full board 280-330F (per pers., 3 days min.). **Restaurant** Service 12:00-14:00, 19:00-20:30; menus 65-175F, also à la carte. Specialties: Truite paysanne aux noix, caille forestière, ris de veau crémaillère, tartes maison. **Credit cards** Amex, Visa, Eurocard and MasterCard. **Pets** Dogs allowed in bedrooms only. **Facilities** Swimming pool, sauna (45F). **Nearby** Conques, Salers, monts du Cantal, château d'Anjony, Vic-sur-Cère. **Open** March 15 – Dec 31.

Vitrac, surrounded by chestnut plantations, is a beauty spot in the south of the Cantal, and the Auberge de la Tomette is right in the heart of the village. Several bedrooms open onto a delightful little garden in the back, but the greater part of the hotel is a few steps away in a vast flowery park with a very beautiful view of the countryside. The bedrooms are comfortable, impeccably kept and decorated in sober, modern style which is brightened with pretty fabrics. Note the duplex, which is ideal for families. The atmosphere in the rustic dining room, with its exposed beams and wood paneling, is very friendly, and the cuisine is excellent. Madame Chausi will greet you charmingly and advise you on what to do and where to go in the region. This is a picturesque place to stay, where you become part of the village life.

How to get there *(Map 24): 25km south of Aurillac via N122 towards Figeac; at Saint-Mamet-La Salvetat take D66.*

Hôtel de l'Echo et de l'Abbaye **

Place de L'Echo
43160 La Chaise-Dieu (Haute-Loire)
Tel. 71.00.00.45 - Fax 71.00.00.22 - Mme Chirouzé

Rooms 11 with telephone, bath or shower and 9 with TV. **Price** Single 250-300F, double 300-350F **Meals** Breakfast 38F, served 7:30-9:30; half board 300-330F (per pers., 3 days min.). **Restaurant** Service 12:00-14:00, 19:30-21:00; menus 90-250F, also à la carte. Specialties: Flan aux cèpes sauce forestière, mignon de porc à la crème de myrtilles, tournedos de saumon aux lentilles vertes du Puy, entrecôte à la fourme d'Ambert, tarte aux fruits des bois. **Credit cards** All major. **Pets** Dogs not allowed. **Nearby** Basilica of Notre-Dame du Puy, church of Saint-Laurent and Aiguille au Puy, Mont Mezenc, Mont Gerbier-de-Jonc, village of Arlempdes. **Open** Easter – Nov 1.

This auberge is part of the enclave formed by the splendid La Chaise Dieu Abbey, and is the ideal place for visiting the historic village. Its name refers to the "Room of Echoes" nearby, which is known for its strange acoustical phenomenon. The hotel is a very old house, beautifully maintained by Madame Chirouzé, who is always warm and welcoming. The small bedrooms are charming and comfortable, and some have a view of the cloister. There is always a contemporary painting exhibit on view in the restaurant dining room, which is decorated in Haute Epoque style. Often complimented in the guest book, the regional Auvergnate cuisine is excellent. Cocktails and refreshments can be served outside on the terrace, which is reserved exclusively for the hotel.

How to get there *(Map 25): 35km north of Le Puy-en-Velay.*

Le Pré Bossu ★★★

43150 Moudeyres (Haute-Loire)
Tel. 71.05.10.70 – Fax 71.05.10.21
M. Grootaert

Rooms 10 with telephone, bath or shower and WC. **Price** Double in half board 430-590F (per pers.). **Meals** Breakfast incl., served 8:00-10:00. **Restaurant** In low season closed lunchtime except Sunday. Service 12:00-13:30, 19:30-21:00; menus 165-360F (child 65F), also à la carte. Specialties: Ecrevisses aux petits légumes, andouillette d'escargot au coulis de céleri. **Credit cards** All major. **Pets** Dogs allowed in bedrooms (+35F). **Facilities** Parking. **Nearby** Basilica of Notre-Dame-du-Puy in Puy-en-Velay, Gerbier-des-Joncs, Mézenc forest – 9-hole Chambon-sur-Lignon golf course in Romières. **Open** Palm Sunday – Nov 11.

Located in the lovely village of Moudeyres, this old thatched cottage built in local stone is named for the meadow which surrounds it. The atmosphere is cozy and welcoming. To one side there is a reception room with a large fireplace, TV and library. In the beautiful stone dining room with its smartly set tables, you will be served out-standing gourmet specialties of the region, which are made with fresh produce from the kitchen garden. The bedrooms are very comfortable and attractively furnished. The garden and terrace overlook the countryside and drinks can be served there. If you wish to go out for the day, picnic baskets can be prepared, and the welcome is very friendly.

How to get there *(Map 25): 25km east of Le Puy via D15 to Les Pandreaux, then D36 to Moudeyres via Laussonne.*

Relais de Saint-Jacques-de-Compostelle ★★

19500 Collonges-la-Rouge (Corrèze)
Tel. 55.25.41.02 - Fax 55.84.08.51
M. Guillaume

Rooms 24 (14 in the annex) with telephone, 10 with bath or shower and WC and 2 with TV. **Price** Double 150-300F. **Meals** Breakfast 36F. **Restaurant** Service 12:30-13:30, 19:30-21:30; menus 100-250F, also à la carte. Specialties: Feuilleté de Saint-Jacques, filet de bœuf fourré au foie gras, terrine de cèpes au coulis de jambon de pays, marquisette aux deux chocolats. **Credit cards** All major. **Pets** Dogs allowed. **Facilities** Parking. **Nearby** Collonges, Turenne, church in Beaulieu-sur-Dordogne, Argentat – 18-hole Coiroux golf course in Aubazines. **Open** Mid-March – mid-Jan (closed Tuesday evening and Wednesday in low season).

Its fascinating medieval houses in red sandstone make Collonges-la-Rouge a very beautiful and much visited place. Located in the heart of the village, the hotel has just been very tastefully restored; the general effect is light and flowery. On the ground floor are two dining rooms, a small reception room furnished with amusing "toad" armchairs, and an intimate bar. The small bedrooms are all very attractive. Excellent cooking is served with a smile. In summer, tables are laid on three lovely shaded terraces. M. and Mme Guillaume's welcome even in this highty touristy town, is reason enough for a visit.

How to get there *(Map 24): 45km south of Tulle via D940 as far as Le Colombier, then right on D38 to Collonges-la-Rouge.*

Au Rendez-Vous des Pêcheurs ★★

Pont du Chambon
19320 Saint-Merd-de-Lapleau (Corrèze)
Tel. 55.27.88.39 - Fax 55.27.83.19 - Mme Fabry

Rooms 8 with telephone, bath or shower, WC and TV. **Price** Single and double 235F.
Meals Breakfast 30F, served 8:00-9:30; half board 245F, full board 285F (per pers.,
3 days min.). **Restaurant** Service 12:15-13:30, 19:45-21:00; menus 75-195F, also
à la carte. Specialties: Sandre au beurre blanc, ris de veau aux cèpes, mousse de
noix glacée. **Credit cards** Visa, Eurocard and MasterCard. **Pets** Dogs allowed.
Facilities Parking. **Nearby** Merle, château of Sédières, viaduc des Rochers Noirs –
18-hole Coiroux golf course in Aubazines. **Open** Dec 20 – Nov 11 (closed Friday
evening and Saturday evening Oct 1 – March 30).

Built on the banks of the Dordogne, this large house backs onto
wooded hills and owes much of its appeal to its exceptional
location. On the ground floor, a light, large and well decorated
dining room with flowered curtains and pretty tables has beautiful
views across the river. At one side, a small lounge and bar give
access to a lovely terrace overlooking the river. The bedrooms have
been well refurbished but, again, it is the view that makes them
special; though they are comfortable, they would be improved
with soundproofing. There is good fishing here, and you can try
the local perch, pike and trout cooked by Elise. Pedalboats are for
rent at the hotel, and you can also cruise on the Dordogne in a
traditional *gabare*. This is a good hotel, and very moderately priced.

How to get there *(Map 24): 45km east of Tulle via D978 to Saint-Merd-
de-Lapleau via Marcillac-la-Croisille, then D13 to Pont-du-Chambon.*

La Maison Anglaise

Saint-Robert
19310 Ayen (Corrèze)
Tel. 55.25.19.58 – Fax 55.25.23.00 – M. and Mme Baldwin

Rooms 6 with shower and WC. **Price** Double 200-350F. **Meals** Breakfast 45-65F, served 8:00-10:00; half board 270F, full board 345F (per pers., 3 days min.). **Restaurant** Service 12:00-14:00, 19:30-21:30; menus 70-230F, also à la carte. Specialties: Croquettes de camembert chaud, parapluies de champignons chauds, magret de canard aux cerises, feuilleté d'estouffade de bœuf et rognons. **Credit cards** Amex, Visa, Eurocard and MasterCard. **Pets** Dogs allowed. **Facilities** Swimming pool, parking. **Nearby** Château de Hautefort, abbey of Tourtoirac, Brive-la-Gaillarde, Périgueux. **Open** Dec 13 – Nov 11.

The Maison Anglaise was opened four years ago in this lovely little village perched on a green hill. The hotel, whose charm and quality have added much to the village, occupies a small and ancient house. It has a real country-style bar with wooden furniture, a handsome dining room and, adjoining it, a comfortable lounge, beautifully furnised, with paintings and *objets d'art*. The fireplaces are huge and fires are always lit in winter. There are six bedrooms on the *premier étage*, some of them large. We liked their white walls, their curtains and thick quilts, all enhanced by the lovely pale wooden furniture, wide floorboards and pink table skirts. The bathrooms are simple and well kept. Some are partitioned off in the rooms but this has been done discreetly. In summer there is a grill by the swimming pool and tables are set on the terrace, where the view is superb.

How to get there *(Map 23): 30km northwest of Brive-la-Gaillarde towards Objat, then Ayen, to Saint-Robert.*

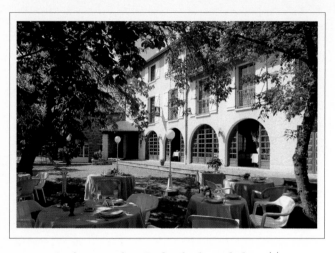

Auberge des Prés de la Vézère **
19240 Saint-Viance (Corrèze)
Tel. 55.85.00.50 – Fax 55.84.25.36
M. Parveaux

Rooms 11 with telephone, bath, WC and TV. **Price** Single and double 240-330F.
Meals Breakfast 35F, served 7:30-10:00; half board 300-345F. **Restaurant** Service
12:00-14:00, 19:30-21:00; menus 105-220F, also à la carte. Specialties: Saumon
fumé maison, dorade à l'ail et au thym, civet de canard tradition. **Credit cards** Visa,
Eurocard and MasterCard. **Pets** Dogs allowed. **Facilities** Parking. **Nearby** Abbey of
Aubazines, Uzerches, Argentat, Collonges-la-Rouge, Pompadour stud farm,
Beaulieu-sur-Dordogne – 18-hole Coiroux golf course in Aubazines. **Open** May – mid-
Nov.

Saint-Viance is a very well preserved small town, with its old
houses and the lovely bridge that spans the Vézère, which is
very popular with fishermen. The hotel is at the entrance to the
village beside a quiet road. There is a large dining room which
extends onto a beautiful shaded terrace. On the *premier étage*,
although the corridor is somewhat dark, you will be agreeably
surprised by the bedrooms, which have lovely pale wallpapers and
pretty curtains matching the bedcovers. The rooms are cheerful
and well kept and all have well equipped bathrooms. This is a good
place for a family holiday.

How to get there *(Map 23): 11km northwest of Brive-la-Gaillarde, towards
Objat then Allassac.*

Domaine des Mouillères ★★

Les Mouillères
Saint-Georges-la-Pouge – 23250 Pontarion (Creuse)
Tel. 55.66.60.64 – Fax 55.66.68.80 – M. and Mme Thill

Rooms 7 with telephone (3 with bath, 4 with WC). **Price** Single 110F, double 190-370F. **Meals** Breakfast incl., served 8:00-9:30. **Restaurant** For residents only. Service 20:00-20:30; menus 90-150F, also à la carte. Specialties: Truite montagnarde, feuilleté aux cèpes, rognons de veau au chinon. **Credit cards** Visa, Eurocard and MasterCard. **Pets** Dogs not allowed. **Facilities** Parking. **Nearby** Hôtel de Moneyroux and Guéret Museum, abbey church of Moutier-d'Ahun – 18-hole la Jonchère golf course in Montgrenier-Gouzon. **Open** March 20 – Oct 1.

Standing in a 15-acre park, the Domaine is an ancient farm which has been restored and converted into a charming hotel. The lovely small lounge has a mixture of furniture and old-fashioned objects. We prefer the bedrooms with bathrooms, but the others have been totally refurbished and are equipped with basins. They are all pretty and pleasant. In the warm and countrified dining room, the simple cooking is made with fresh produce from the estate, but the quality is irregular. If you want to explore the magnificent countryside, the owner will lend bicycles. Drinks and meals can be served on the lovely garden terrace. The staff is very courteous.

How to get there *(Map 24): 34km south of Guéret via D942 towards Limoges to Pontarion; then towards La Chapelle-Saint-Martial, D3.*

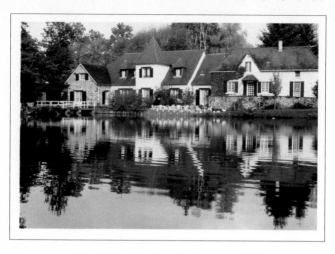

Au Moulin de la Gorce ★★★

87800 La Roche l'Abeille (Haute-Vienne)
Tel. 55.00.70.66 – Fax 55.00.76.57
M. Bertranet

Rooms 9 and 1 apartment, with telephone, bath, WC and TV. **Price** Single 350F, double 700-900F, suite 1300F. **Meals** Breakfast 70F, served from 8:00; half board 1500F, full board 1800-1950F (2 pers., 3 days min.). **Restaurant** Service 12:00-13:30, 19:30-21:00; menus 180-480F, also à la carte. Specialties: Œufs brouillés aux truffes dans leur coque, foie poêlé aux pommes, lièvre à la royale. **Credit cards** All major. **Pets** Dogs allowed. **Facilities** Parking. **Nearby** Saint Etienne cathedral and Adrien-Dubouché ceramics museum in Limoges, abbey of Solignac, church of Saint-Léonard-de-Noblat – 18-hole Porcelaine golf course in Limoges. **Open** March 1 – Dec 31 (closed Sunday evening and Monday Sept 20 – April 30).

Converted into a sumptuous hotel-restaurant by a family of pastry cooks/caterers from Limoges, this flour mill dates back to 1569. Today entirely renovated, it consist of several buildings set around a beautiful lake with a stream that tumbles down into the garden. The interior decoration is very tasteful, intimate and comfortable. The bedrooms are pleasant and elegantly furnished. Drinks are served on the terrace overlooking the lake and garden, and there is fine, gourmet cuisine with an interesting "Saint Jacques de Compostelle" menu. This is a luxurious, professionally run hotel which has nevertheless retained its family-style hospitality.

How to get there (Map 23): 30km south of Limoges via D704 then D17.

Castel-Hôtel 1904 ★★

Rue du Castel
63390 Saint-Gervais-d'Auvergne (Puy-de-Dôme)
Tel. 73.85.70.42 – Fax 73.85.84.39 – M. Mouty

Rooms 17 with telephone, bath or shower, WC and TV (3 with minibar). **Price** Single and double 250-270F. **Meals** Breakfast 38F, served 7:30-10:00; half board 225-235F, full board 290-300F (per pers., 3 days min.). **Restaurant** Service from 12:30 and 19:30; menus 69-300F, also à la carte. Specialties: Tournedos roulé aux pieds de porc, sandre, crêpe Célina. **Credit cards** Visa, Eurocard and MasterCard. **Pets** Dogs not allowed. **Facilities** Parking. **Nearby** Gorges of the Sioule, church in Ménat, Fades viaduct, Mandet museum and museum of the Auvergne in Riom – 9- and 18-hole Volcans golf course in Orcines. **Open** Easter – Nov 11.

This ancient château, built in 1616, was converted into a hotel in 1904 and has been run by the same family ever since. All the charm of an old French hotel is to be found in its warm and welcoming rooms, the bar and above all the large dining room, whose parquet floors gleam. The fireplaces, the antique furniture and the ochre tones of the walls and curtains all contribute to the old-fashioned but very charming character of the hotel The comfortable bedrooms are all different and in keeping with the spirit of the hotel. You have the choice of two restaurants: the *Castel,* which has an inventive menu, and the *Comptoir à Moustache,* an authentic country bistro. The Castel is welcoming and friendly – the kind of place you become attached to.

How to get there *(Map 24): 55km northwest of Clermont-Ferrand via N9 to Châtelguyon, then D227 to Saint-Gervais-d'Auvergne via Manzat.*

Hôtel Clarion ★★★

21420 Aloxe-Corton (Côte-d'Or)
Tel. 80.26.46.70 - Fax 80.26.47.16
M. and Mme Voarick

Rooms 10 with telephone, bath, WC, TV and minibar. **Price** Single 485F, double 585-790F. **Meals** Breakfast 75F, served 8:00-13:00. No restaurant. **Credit cards** Visa, Eurocard and MasterCard. **Pets** Dogs allowed. **Facilities** Parking. **Nearby** Hôtel-Dieu, basilica of Notre Dame in Beaune, Hôtel de la Rochepot and Bourgogne Wine museum in Beaune, Côte de Beaune between Serrigny and Chagny, château du Clos-Vougeot, Nolay, Rochepot – 18-hole Beaune-Levernois golf course. **Open** All year.

At the Clarion, behind the village of Aloxe-Corton, only 2 miles from Beaune, the Voaricks have successfully blended natural beauty and modern comfort. The former mansion is surrounded by a large lawn which extends down to a vineyard. But behind this traditional appearance, there is a tastefully decorated contemporary interior, which combines old exposed beams and fireplaces with the clean lines of a simple modern design. The result is a warm, intimate atmosphere. The rooms have soft lights, antiqued furniture, comfortable armchairs and magnificent bathrooms. The breakfasts are marvelous, and you can have brunch anytime next to the fireplace or under the linden trees in the garden. The service is attentive and discreet in this truly lovely hotel. For local restaurants, we recommend *Le Benaton* in Beaune and *Les Coquines* in Ladoix-Serrigny.

How to get there *(Map 19): 5km north of Beaune via N74.*

Chez Camille ★★★

1, place Edouard-Herriot
21230 Arnay-le-Duc (Côte-d'Or)
Tel. 80.90.01.38 - Fax 80.90.04.64 - M. and Mme Poinsot

Rooms 14 with telephone, bath and TV. **Price** Double 395F, suite 500F (free for children under 11 years). **Meals** Breakfast 50F, served 7:00-12:00; half board 400F (per pers.). **Restaurant** Service 12:00-14:30, 19:30-22:00; menus 100-450F, also à la carte. Specialties: Rissoles d'escargots aux pâtes fraîches et champagne, le charolais. **Credit cards** All major. **Pets** Dogs allowed. **Facilities** Garage. **Nearby** Basilica of Saint-Andoche in Saulieu, château de Commarin, Châteauneuf – 18-hole Château de Chailly golf course. **Open** All year.

This charming hotel is peaceful and quiet despite its town location in small Arnay-le-Duc. There is a large, comfortable lobby with a piano, and a lovely 17th-century stairway leads to the bedrooms. They are restful, comfortable and beautifully decorated, some with antique furniture. We especially liked Number 17. (Reserve ahead of time). Not only an excellent hotel, Chez Camille is also a famous restaurant. The ravishing dining room is set in a winter garden with a glass roof: a perfect setting for trying the fine specialties of Burgundy, which are made with products from the Poinsots' farm. The regional cuisine is light and inventive, making Chez Camille a Burgundian must.

How to get there (Map 19): 28km northeast of Autun via N81.

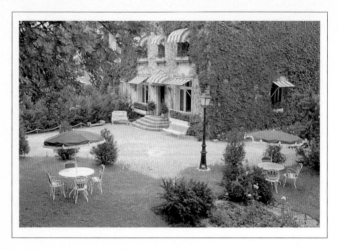

Hôtel Le Home **

138, route de Dijon
21200 Beaune (Côte-d'Or)
Tel. 80.22.16.43 – Fax 80.24.90.74 – Mme Jacquet

Rooms 23 with telephone, bath or shower and WC (8 with TV). **Price** Single and double 315-450F. **Meals** Breakfast 32F. No restaurant. **Credit cards** Visa, Eurocard and MasterCard. **Pets** Dogs allowed. **Facilities** Garage. **Nearby** Hôtel Dieu, basilica of Notre-Dame in Beaune, Côte de Beaune between Serrigny and Chagny, château du Clos-Vougeot, Nolay, Rochepot – 18-hole Beaune-Levernois golf course. **Open** All year.

The inspiration for this small hotel, at the entrance to Beaune, is definitely English. The Virginia-creeper – covered house is surrounded by a flowery garden where breakfast is served. Well-chosen antiques, lamps and carpets give a personal touch to every room. The bedrooms are pretty, comfortable and quiet; the living room inviting. The proximity of the road is noticeable only from outside and the interior is well-insulated from noise. The hospitable Mme Jacquet loves her house, which explains the care that is evident; you will be received here as a friend. For restaurants see page 133.

How to get there *(Map 19): In Beaune, on the Dijon road; beyond the church of Saint-Nicolas.*

Hôtel Le Parc ⋆⋆
Levernois
21200 Beaune (Côte-d'Or)
Tel. 80.22.22.51/80.24.63.00 - Fax 80.24.21.19 - Mme Oudot

Rooms 25 with telephone and TV (19 with shower, 6 with bath and 22 with WC).
Price Double 200-460F. **Meals** Breakfast 33F, served 7:30-9:30. No restaurant.
Credit cards Visa, Eurocard and MasterCard. **Pets** Dogs allowed (fee).
Facilities Parking. **Nearby** Hôtel Dieu, basilica of Notre-Dame in Beaune, Côte de
Beaune between Serrigny and Chagny, château du Clos-Vougeot, Nolay, Rochepot –
18-hole Beaune-Levernois golf course. **Open** All year except a few days in Dec.

The Hôtel Le Parc is an old, ivy-covered Burgundian house on
the doorstep of the charming international wine capital of
Beaune. It has a flowery courtyard where breakfast is served, and
a garden with huge, ancient trees. Hôtel Le Parc has the feel of a
much smaller hotel despite the number of bedrooms. The
atmosphere of every bedroom is different, created in one by the
wallpaper, in another by a chest of drawers and in yet another by
a quilt. Monsieur and Madame Oudot refurbish the rooms
regularly. Those which have just been redecorated have pretty
floral-bordered English wallpapers coordinated with the curtains
and bedspreads. Some of them are very large and luxurious, but
always in good taste. Although not far from the town, you will
feel as if you are in the country, and, most important, you will be
charmingly welcomed. For restaurants, try the famous *Hostellerie
de Levernois*, or in Beaune the elegant *Jardin des Remparts*, the
charming *Le Bénaton*, or *Le Gourmandin*.

How to get there *(Map 19): 4km southeast of Beaune via D970, towards
Verdun.*

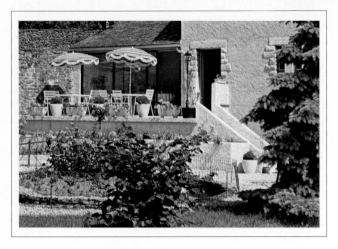

Hostellerie du Château ★★

21320 Châteauneuf-en-Auxois (Côte-d'Or)
Tel. 80.49.22.00 - Fax 80.49.21.27
M. and Mme Poirier

Rooms 17 with telephone, bath or shower and WC. **Price** Single 210F, double 380-450F, suite 450F. **Meals** Breakfast 40F; half board 300-400F. **Restaurant** Service 12:00-13:30, 19:00-21:00; menus 130-240F, also à la carte. Specialties: Fondue d'Epoisse au Calvados, cassolette de canard et foie gras, langoustines poêlée aux deux poireaux, marquise au chocolat. **Credit cards** All major. **Pets** Dogs allowed. **Nearby** Château of Châteauneuf and of Commarin, basilica of Saint-Andoche in Saulieu, Hôtel-Dieu and basilica of Notre-Dame in Beaune – 18-hole château de Chailly golf club in Chailly-sur-Armançon. **Open** Feb 15 – Nov 15 (closed Monday evening and Tuesday except July 1 – Sep 5).

This old parsonage is at the top of an old market town which stands sentinel above the Bourgogne Canal and overlooks the château. The ancient canal is visible from the terraced gardens, set out with tables and swings. Inside, an old fireplace and exposed stone walls reming you of the age of the Hostellerie, but the rest has been much renovated. The restaurant has large windowed bays overlooking the garden. The bedrooms are simply furnished and comfortable, but the ones in the annex, though large, lack charm. The cuisine varies according to the season and offers tempting Burgundian specialties. Don't leave without wandering through the village, whose old houses border a maze of narrow, quiet streets with an occasional dizzying view over the plain below.

How to get there *(Map 19): 30km northwest of Beaune via A6, Pouilly-en-Auxois exit, then D977bis towards Vandenesse, then Crugey; after the cemetry turn left; it's on the other side of the canal.*

Le Manassès

21220 Curtil-Vergy (Côte-d'Or)
Tel. 80.61.43.81 – Fax 80.61.42.79
M. Chaley

Rooms 7 with telephone, bath, WC, TV and minibar. **Price** Single and double 380F.
Meals Breakfast 50F, served 7:45-10:00. No restaurant. **Credit cards** Visa, Eurocard
and MasterCard. **Pets** Small dogs allowed. **Facilities** Parking. **Nearby** Abbey of Saint-
Vivant in Curtil-Vergy, abbey of Cîteaux, château de Cussigny, château du Clos-
Vougeot, Côte de Nuits – 18-hole Dijon-Bourgogne golf course. **Open** March – Dec 31.

To reach this small, quiet hotel you go under a little porch and
then across an inner courtyard. M. Chaley is a wine grower
and as a jovial host, he well upholds the profession's reputation!
His house has been totally renovated and transformed into a hotel.
References to wine abound: in the barn which houses an interesting
wine museum, in the big room where breakfast is served and in
the corridors and bedrooms – each picture is a reminder. From the
cellars close by comes the faint aroma of casks in which the wine
is aging. The communal rooms are furnished with beautiful old
furniture, while the comfortable bedrooms are more modern, with
pretty color combinations and marble-lined bathrooms. The view
over the wild green valley is superb. Good restaurants include
L'Orée du Bois in Quémigny-Poisot and *La Gentilhommière* in Nuits-
Saint-Georges.

How to get there *(Map 19): 24km northwest of Beaune. A31, Nuits-Saint-
Georges exit, D25 and D35.*

Les Grands Crus ★★★

Route des Grands-Crus
21220 Gevrey-Chambertin (Côte-d'Or)
Tel. 80.34.34.15 - Fax 80.51.89.07 - Mme Farnier

Rooms 24 with telephone, bath and WC. **Price** Single and double 350-430F.
Meals Breakfast 45F, served 7:00-10:30. No restaurant. **Credit cards** Visa, Eurocard
and MasterCard. **Pets** Dogs allowed (+10F). **Facilities** Parking. **Nearby** Château of
Gevrey, church of Notre-Dame and art museum in Dijon, Côte de Nuits, châteaux of
Clos-Vougeot and Cussigny, abbey of Cîteaux – 18-hole Dijon-Bourgogne golf course.
Open March – Dec 31.

Encircled by the famous vineyards of Gevrey-Chambertin, Les
Grands Crus, "the great wines," is aptly named. The bedrooms
overlook the splendid rows of vines, and some have a view of the
ancient château. Opening off a wide corridor, the bedrooms are
light and comfortable and are furnished with beautiful copies of
Louis XV furniture. The almost traffic-free road and excellent
sound-proofing ensure a quiet stay. On the ground floor a large
living room with fireplace acts as both breakfast room and lounge.
Mme Farnier will receive you charmingly. To enjoy the fine
cuisine, and above all the great vintages of Gevrey-Chambertin,
the two best restaurants are *Les Millésimes* and *Rôtisserie du
Chambertin*. For simpler and less expensive fare, try *La Sommellerie*.

How to get there *(Map 19): 12km south of Dijon via N74 towards Beaune.*

Hostellerie du Val–Suzon ★★★

R.N. 71 - 21121 Val-Suzon (Côte-d'Or)
Tel. 80.35.60.15 - Fax 80.35.61.36
M. and Mme Perreau

Rooms 17 with telephone, of which 16 with bath and WC, 1 with shower, 10 with TV and minibar. **Price** Single 300-350F, double 400-500F, suite 600-800F. **Meals** Breakfast 52F, served 7:30-9:30; half board 442-517F, full board 632-707F (per pers., 3 days min.). **Restaurant** Closed Thursday noon in low season. Service 12:00-14:00, 19:30-21:45; menus 128-400F, also à la carte. Specialties: Œufs coque homard et foie gras, millefeuille d'escargots au beurre de persil. **Credit cards** All major. **Pets** Dogs allowed (+50F). **Facilities** Parking. **Nearby** Château de Vantoux-lès-Dijon, Dijon, Carthusian monastery in Champmol, Côte de Nuits – 18-hole Dijon-Bourgogne golf course. **Open** Dec 16 – Nov 17 (closed Wednesday).

The Hostellerie is composed of two houses separated by a ravishing, vast garden laid out on a slight rise. The restaurant is located in the main house; a fireplace, a few prettily set tables and thick draperies make a pleasant decor, which adds to the pleasure of tasting delicious, creative cuisine of Yves Perreau. The other house resembles a chalet and overlooks the garden. The bedrooms are located here. All are comfortable (some beds have been replaced), bright and decorated in a somewhat strict modern style, with a traditional note added by 19th-century-style armchairs or antique tables. The staff in the hotel could be somewhat more attentive.

How to get there (Map 19): 15km northwest of Dijon via N71 towards Troyes.

Le Grand Monarque ★★

10, rue de l'Etape
58220 Donzy (Nièvre)
Tel. 86.39.35.44 – Fax 86.39.37.09 – M. Lesort

Rooms 11 with telephone, bath or shower, WC and TV. **Price** Double 230-270F.
Meals Breakfast 35F, served 7:30-9:30. **Restaurant** Closed Sunday evening and
Monday. Service 12:00-13:30, 19:30-21:30; menus 70-155F, also à la carte.
Specialties: Saupiquet donziais, magret de canard, coq au vin. **Credit cards** Visa,
Eurocard and MasterCard. **Pets** Dogs allowed (+25F). **Facilities** Parking, garage.
Nearby Museum of La Meunière in Donzy, châteaux of Menou, La Motte-Josserand
and Saint Fargeau (son et lumière in July and Aug) – 9-hole Saint Satur golf course.
Open All year (Jan and Feb on reservation).

In the very lovely Burgundian village of Donzy, three beautiful
old stone buildings form the hotel Grand Monarque. The bar-
lounge is furnished with bistro tables and is next to the kitchen
with its gleaming copper pans. Beside it is the dining room, where
good regional cooking is served. A 15th-century spiral staircase
leads to the small and charmingly simple bedrooms. Situated in the
heart of the village, the hotel gives the impression of being a world
away from frenzied tourists. Good value and good quality make
this an excellent place to stay.

*How to get there (Map 18): 65km southwest of Auxerre via N151 to
Courson-les-Carrières, then D104 to Entrain-sur-Nohain and D1 to Donzy;
(the hotel is near the church).*

Manoir de Sornat ***

Allée de Sornat
71140 Bourbon-Lancy (Saône-et-Loire)
Tel. 85.89.17.39 - Fax 85.89.29.47 - M. Raymond

Rooms 13 with telephone, bath or shower, WC, TV and minibar. **Price** Single and double 350-650F, suite 700F. **Meals** Breakfast 55F, served 7:30-11:00; half board 450-700F, full board 550-850F (per pers., 3 days min.). **Restaurant** Closed Monday lunchtime. Service 12:00-14:00, 19:30-21:30; menus 160-400F, also à la carte. Specialties: Galette d'escargots de Bourgogne, filet de bœuf. **Credit cards** All major. **Pets** Dogs allowed (+30F). **Facilities** Parking. **Nearby** Château de Saint-Aubin-sur-Loire, church in Ternant, abbey at Paray-le-Monial. **Open** All year (closed Sunday evening in low season).

This house was built in the 19th-century at the whim of an affluent Lyonnais who was fond of horse racing at Deauville. He chose a pure Anglo-Norman style of architecture which, though common in Deauville, is unusual here. Adjoining the Manoir are the remains of a racecourse where up to World War II the Bourbon Lancy stakes race was run. The bedrooms are spacious, light, airy and tastefully decorated. If you reserve a room with a terrace looking out over the park, you can enjoy your hearty breakfast while watching the squirrels playing in the century-old trees. In the evenings you can walk down the beautiful carved staircase to enjoy Gérard Raymond's cuisine, which combines traditional dishes with modern presentation. The dining room has large bay windows that look out over the beautiful park. The owners are efficient and kind, and you may find it hard to leave.

How to get there *(Map 18): 25km northeast of Moulins via N79 towards Chevagnes.*

Hostellerie du Château de Bellecroix ★★★

RN 6
71150 Chagny (Saône-et-Loire)
Tel. 85.87.13.86 – Fax 85.91.28.62 – Gautier-Crinquant Family

Rooms 21 with telephone, bath or shower, WC, TV and minibar. **Price** Single and double 580-1000F. **Meals** Breakfast 60F, served 7:30-10:30; half board 590F, full board 690-950F (per pers., 3 days min.). **Restaurant** Closed Wednesday. Service 12:00-14:00, 19:30-21:00; menus 240-340F, also à la carte. Specialties: Poularde de Bresse pochée et morilles, escargots en cocotte lutée. **Credit cards** All major. **Pets** Dogs allowed (+50F). **Facilities** Swimming pool, parking. **Nearby** Hôtel-Dieu in Beaune, Côte de Beaune between Serrigny and Chagny, château du Clos-Vougeot, Nolay, Rochepot – 18-hole Beaune-Levernois golf course. **Open** Feb 15 – Dec 18 (closed Wednesday except July and Aug).

Built in the 12th-century and modified in the 18th, the Hostellerie, which is just out of the town, was once the *commanderie* of the Knights of Malta. At the entrance, a large, beautifully decorated panelled room serves as reception hall and dining room. It is decorated with lovely flowered draperies, comfortable Louis XV-style chairs around, elegantly laid tables, and reproductions of Old Master paintings on the walls. Next to it in a turret, there is a small intimate lounge. The comfortable bedrooms, located in two buildings, all look out onto the lovely 5-acre park with swimming pool, shady terraces and lawns. The rooms in the first building are small but well designed; many are done in handsome 18th-century style. Those in the other building, which is magnificent, with old walls and mullioned windows, are vast, superbly Haute Epoque in decor, but of course more expensive. Some open directly onto the garden. The staff is very courteous.

How to get there (Map 19): 15km south of Beaune via N74, then N6.

Hôtel de Bourgogne ★★★
Place de l'Abbaye
71250 Cluny (Saône-et-Loire)
Tel. 85.59.00.58 – Fax 85.59.03.73 – Mme Gosse

Rooms 15 with telephone, bath or shower and WC (11 with TV). **Price** Single and double 390-490F, suite 890-920F. **Meals** Breakfast 55F, served 7:30-9:30; "Soirée étape gourmande" 900-1000F (2pers.). **Restaurant** Service 12:00-14:00, 19:30-21:00; menus 130F (lunchtime)-420F, also à la carte. Specialties: Foie gras frais de canard, volaille de Bresse à la vapeur de truffes. **Credit cards** All major. **Pets** Dogs allowed (+50F). **Facilities** Garage (+40F). **Nearby** Abbey and Ochier museum in Cluny, caves in Azé, arboretum in Pézanin, château de Chaumont – 18-hole Château de la Salle golf course in Lugny. **Open** March 5 – Nov 18 (closed Tuesday evening).

This hotel was built on part of the site of the ancient abbey of Cluny, the pride of the little town which attracts many visitors every summer. But, the reasonable number of bedrooms and the arrangement of the rooms around a small inner garden ensure peace and quiet. There is a pleasantly proportioned living room, where several styles are nicely combined; a large dining room, and gourmet cooking, that lives up to its excellent reputation. The bedrooms are comfortable and well decorated, and there is a bar where breakfast is served when the weather makes it impossible to use the garden. Everything, including the welcome, contributes to the pleasure of your stay. Lamartine enjoyed the charm of the house, and after him, a number of famous people have signed the visitors' book over the past thirty years.

How to get there *(Map 19): 24km northwest of Mâcon via N79 and D980.*

141

Auberge Aux Trois Saisons

Dracy-le-Fort
71640 Givry (Saône-et-Loire)
Tel. 85.44.41.58 – Fax 85.44.46.53 – MM. Völckers and Sobel

Rooms 5 with telephone, bath and WC (TV on request). **Price** Single 410F, double
465F. **Meals** Breakfast 45F. **Restaurant** Service 20:00; menu 135F. Specialties:
Burgundian and American. **Credit cards** Visa, Eurocard and MasterCard. **Pets** Dogs
allowed with reservation (+25F). **Facilities** Parking. **Nearby** Château de Germolles,
château de Rochepot, Buxy, valley of les Vaux – 18-hole Chalon-sur-Saône golf
course, Saint-Nicolas leisure park. **Open** Easter – mid Oct.

Dr Sobel left Harvard University to come and live in this old
mansion. Five spacious bedrooms have been furnished and
decorated with perfect taste. They have beams and white walls,
while the zebra bedside rugs, patchwork quilts, fresh flowers, and
chocolates on the bedside tables give a touch of sophistication. The
bathrooms, with soft dressing gowns and perfumed soaps, are very
luxurious. Around the house, apple, cherry and peach trees invite
the visitor to stroll to the river that borders the grounds. At 7.30PM
drinks are served, and then the host slips away to the kitchen to
finish the preparation of dinner, served at 8PM. The candlelit tables,
the quality of the food and the discreet background music make
dinner a very pleasant experience. Sad to note, however the auberge
does not welcome children.

How to get there *(Map 19): 28km south of Beaune via N74 and N6 to
Chagny, then D981 until 2km before Givry, turn left towards Dracy-le-Fort.*

Moulin de Bourgchâteau **

Route de Chalon
71500 Louhans (Saône-et-Loire)
Tel. 85.75.37.12 - Fax 85.75.45.11 - M. Gonzales

Rooms 21 with telephone, bath or shower, WC and TV. **Price** Single 220-260F, double 240-300F, suite 400-650F. **Meals** Breakfast 40F, served 7:00-10:00. **Restaurant** Service 12:00-13:30, 19:30-21:00; menus 100-230F, also à la carte. Specialties: Poulet de Bresse. **Credit cards** All major. **Pets** Dogs allowed. **Facilities** Parking. **Nearby** Côte Chalonnaise around Mercurey, Rully, château de Germolles, church in Givry, Buxy, Hôtel-Dieu in Louhans – 18-hole Lons-le Saunier golf course. **Open** Jan 15 – Dec 18.

Louhans is a large town in the part of the Bresse region that lies between Burgundy and the Jura. Once a month on big market days, when the streets and arcades are full of live poultry and farm produce, it is not unusual to hear the local patois spoken. The hotel occupies an old grain mill which was still working less than fifteen years ago; you can see the impressive cog wheels in the bar. The huge building gives the impression of a rock standing on the water. The bedrooms are all similar in comfort and appearance. Their windows look out over the water and sometimes the mist gives you the feeling of being on a ship. You will have the same view from the restaurant, where you can enjoy the wines and food of Bresse and Burgundy. This is a good place to stay in a relatively unknown region of France.

How to get there *(Map 19): 33km southeast of Chalon-sur-Saône via A6, Chalon Sud exit (then D978), or Tournus exit (then D971).*

Moulin d'Hauterive ***
Saint-Gervais-en-Vallière
71350 Chaublanc (Saône-et-Loire)
Tel. 85.91.55.56 - Fax 85.91.89.65 - M. and Mme Moille

Rooms 21 with telephone, bath or shower, WC, TV and minibar. **Price** Double 550-700F, suite 750-850F. **Meals** Breakfast 70F, served 8:00-11:00. **Restaurant** Service 12:00-14:00, 19:00-21:00; menus 160-400F, also à la carte. Specialties: Cassolette d'escargots à la purée de persil, foie gras poêlé à la purée de pomme de terre. **Credit cards** Amex, Visa, Eurocard and MasterCard. **Pets** Dogs allowed. **Facilities** Swimming pool, tennis, sauna, parking. **Nearby** Château de Germolles, château de Rochepot, Buxy, valley of Les Vaux – 18-hole Chalon-sur-Saône golf course, Saint-Nicolas leisure park. **Open** March 1 – Dec 1 (closed Sunday evening and Monday in low season).

Located in the heart of the countryside, this old mill lies in 7 1/2 acres of grounds through which the Dheune River runs. It's an attractive house with two lovely dining rooms, in one of which armchairs are arranged around the fireplace in an inviting little group. The bedrooms are exquisite and have all been decorated and furnished with care and good taste. Outside there are plenty of places to relax: beside the swimming pool, around the house, and on a more private terrace reached by crossing a little wooden bridge over the river. In summer, drinks and food are served outdoors. Christiane Moille has a passion for cooking which adds to the enormous pleasure of staying in this very hospitable place.

How to get there *(Map 19): 15km southeast of Beaune via D970, then D94.*

La Montagne de Brancion ***

Brancion
71700 Tournus (Saône-et-Loire)
Tel. 85.51.12.40 - Fax 85.51.18.64 - M. and Mme Million

Rooms 20 with telephone, bath or shower (hairdryer), WC and minibar. **Price** Single 450-610F, double 450-750F. **Meals** Breakfast 60F, served 8:00-9:30. **Restaurant** Service 19:15-21:00; menus 190-360F, also à la carte. Specialties: regional. **Credit cards** All major. **Pets** Dogs allowed (+50F). **Facilities** Swimming pool, parking. **Nearby** Church of Saint-Philibert in Tournus, church in Chapaize, Blanot, Cluny, Taizé, château de Cormatin – 9- and 18-hole Château-la-Salle golf course. **Open** March 15 – Nov 1.

A ll the bedrooms in this hotel, which is perched on a hill, have views over the Maconnais vineyards and face the rising sun. The landscape is magnificent and the silence impressive. The building and its decor are modern. The cane furniture harmonizes with the fabrics of the cushions, bedcovers and curtains. Breakfasts are served in your room, in the lounge or in the garden by the swimming pool and are very good, with several kinds of pastry, hot toast and fresh fruit juice. Jacques and Nathalie Million are enthusiastic, paying great attention to their guests' needs and providing information to ensure that you enjoy a visit to their part of the country.

How to get there *(Map 19): 35km south of Chalon via A6, Tournus exit; 13 km of Tournus via D14 (it's 1km from Brancion).*

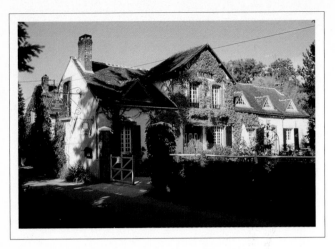

La Fontaine aux Muses ★★
89116 La Celle-Saint-Cyr (Yonne)
Tel. 86.73.40.22 – Fax 86.73.48.66
Pointeau-Langevin Family

Rooms 17 with telephone, bath or shower and WC (4 with TV). **Price** Single 340F, double 390F, suite 550-650F. **Meals** Breakfast 36F, served 8:00-10:00; half board 370-520F (per pers., 3 days min.). **Restaurant** Service 12:30-13:45, 20:00-21:15; menu 185F, also à la carte. **Credit cards** Visa, Eurocard and MasterCard. **Pets** Dogs not allowed. **Facilities** Swimming pool, golf (50F), tennis (35F), parking. **Nearby** Joigny, Othe forest, St-Cydroine, church of St-Florentin, cathedral of St-Etienne in Auxerre. **Open** All year.

The charm of certain hotels is largely due to their owners and that is certainly the case with the Fontaine aux Muses, which was created by a family of artists. Today son Vincent is the dynamic spirit of the place. Obviously in love with this tiny hamlet, he decided to indulge his passion for the country and to share it with his clients. He loves wine and has his own vineyard; he loves to hunt, with the exception of Toto the wild boar who is a great favorite of city children. Vincent also loves music and often invites his musician friends to enliven weekend dinners with ballads and bossa-novas during the meal, finishing with a veritable professional jazz session. Comfortable armchairs await you beside the fire in the bar-lounge, and whether your beautiful bedroom is on the *premier étage* or at ground level opening onto the garden. More bedrooms have just been opened in a small house at the entrance to the golf course. We are delighted that this traditional auberge spirit is being maintained, even though the training given in hotel schools is sometimes neglected.

How to get there *(Map 18): 36km northwest of Auxerre via N6 to Joigny, D943 for 7km, then D194. By A6, Courtenay/Sens exit.*

Château de Prunoy

Prunoy
89120 Charny (Yonne)
Tel. 86.63.66.91 - Fax 86.63.77.79 - Mme Roumilhac

Rooms 11 and 5 suites with telephone, bath and WC. **Price** Double 450-650F, suite 650-900F. **Meals** Breakfast 50F, served 8:00-11:00. **Restaurant** Service 12:00 and 20:00 (closed Monday); menu 160F, also à la carte. Family cooking. **Credit cards** Not accepted. **Pets** Dogs allowed. **Facilities** Tennis, parking. **Nearby** Saint-Fargeau, Boutissaint animal park, château de Ratilly, cathedral of Saint-Etienne d'Auxerre – 18-hole de Roncemay golf course in Chassy. **Open** March 16 – Jan 1.

Surrounded by a 250-acre park on which there are two lakes, the Château de Prunoy is built in the purest 17th-century architectural style. The owner, a former antiques dealer in Paris, will greet you like a member of the family and will point out the lovely walks you can take around her estate. The cuisine is both simple and refined, and meals are served in a charming dining room whose family objects remind you that you are in a private home. Breakfast is served either in the dining room or in your bedroom. There are 16 rooms all together, and all are very special because of their splendid decoration, as well as their spaciousness and comfort. Note also the small living room-library, which is ideal for having a cup of tea and reading in winter. This is fabulous place to stay, midway between a hotel and a bed and breakfast.

How to get there *(Map 18): 45km northwest of Auxerre via A6, exit direction Montargis, then D943 for 4km and D16 to Prunoy (towards Charny then Vézelay).*

Le Castel ★★

Place de l'église
89660 Mailly-le-Château (Yonne)
Tel. 86.81.43.06 - Fax 86.81.49.26 - M. and Mme Breerette

Rooms 12 with telephone, of which 8 with bath, 3 with shower and 8 with WC.
Price Single 160F, double 230-340F. **Meals** Breakfast 36F, served 8:00-9:30; 1 meal
a day obligatory in high season. **Restaurant** Service 12:15-13:30, 19:15-20:30;
menus 75-170F, also à la carte. Specialties: Escargots aux noisettes, pavé de
charolais, pétoncles à la bretonne, gratin de framboises. **Credit cards** Visa, Eurocard
and MasterCard. **Pets** Dogs allowed (+25F). **Nearby** Basilica of Sainte-Madeleine
in Vézelay, Saussois rocks, cathedral of Saint-Etienne in Auxerre, Arcy caves – 18-
hole Roncemay golf course in Chassy. **Open** March 16 – Nov 14 (closed Wednesday).

A pretty garden with a lime-shaded terrace awaits you in front
of this late 19th-Century house. The arrangement of the
ground floor means that the lounge lies between the two dining
rooms, the whole forming a single area. Around the fireplace are
Empire tables and armchairs, and although the furniture in the
dining rooms is in a different style, the ensemble works well. Each
year, two or three bedrooms are renovated. Ask for them when
you reserve because their decor is particularly fresh and elegant.
Located in a historically preserved site in front of the church of
this tiny, typical village, Le Castel is a quiet hotel with a very good
restaurant, and a bar on the terrace. The owners and friendly and
informal.

How to get there (Map 18): 30km northwest of Avallon via N6 to Voutenay-
sur-Cure, then D950 direction Courson-les-Carrières; at the top of the village.

Le Moulin des Templiers ★★

Vallée du Cousin
Pontaubert – 89200 Avallon (Yonne)
Tel. 86.34.10.80 – Mme Hilmoine

Rooms 14 with telephone, bath or shower (11 with WC). **Price** Single 250F, double 350F. **Meals** Breakfast 33F, served 8:00-10:00. No restaurant. **Credit cards** Not accepted. **Pets** Dogs allowed (+40F). **Facilities** Parking. **Nearby** Avallon, Cousin valley, basilica of Sainte-Madeleine in Vézelay. **Open** March 15 – Oct 30.

You take a quiet little tree-lined road winding along the valley beside the River Cousin, and then you arrive at this mill, where a kind welcome and all the comfort you could ask for are yours. Breakfast is delicious and copious and is served in the garden on the river bank when weather permits. There is toast, hot croissants, good jams, and as much tea or coffee as you want. The bedrooms are small but comfortable, and are decorated in good taste. The car park is surrounded by a meadow in which a donkey, a pony, chickens and pigs go about their routines, adding further flavor to this charming place. There is no restaurant, but Pontaubert is only half a kilometer away. Try *Les Capucins, Au Relais des Gourmets* and *Le Moulin des Ruats.*

How to get there *(Map 18): 46km southeast of Auxerre, 4km southwest of Avallon via D957 towards Vézelay.*

BURGUNDY

Auberge des Moulins Banaux ★★
18, route des Moulins-Banaux
89190 Villeneuve-l'Archevêque (Yonne)
Tel. 86.86.72.55 - Fax 86.86.78.94

Rooms 16 with telephone, bath, WC and TV. **Price** Single and double 210-280F.
Meals Breakfast 30F, served 7:00-10:00; half board 240-280F (per pers., 3 days
min.). **Restaurant** Closed Sunday evening and Monday Nov 1 – March 31. Service
12:00-13:30, 19:30-21-30; menus 68-148F, also à la carte. Specialties: Confit de
canard, foie gras et saumon fumé maison, poisson, galette fondante au chocolat.
Credit cards Visa, Eurocard and MasterCard. **Pets** Dogs allowed (+15F).
Facilities Parking. **Nearby** Church of Villeneuve in Archevêque, Notre-Dame church
in Villeneuve-sur-Yonne, cathedral and Synod Palace in Sens, Joigny: Cistercian
abbey in Vauluisant, modern art museum in Troyes. **Open** All year.

After you have crossed the small bridge that spans the River
Vanne, you will glimpse the two superb wheels of this 16th-
century mill, today a hotel built on a 15-acre estate. All the original
old machinery of the mill, which is located in the vast dining room,
is still in perfect working condition. The auberge is warm and
inviting, rustic in style and it has a large fireplace. The bedrooms
are upstairs; most have been comfortably and beautifully renovated,
while the more old-fashioned rooms have their own charm. All
have a lovely view over the river or the garden. The cuisine reflects
the dedication of the chef, and his customers are delighted,
particularly as this is an auberge near Paris where it is possible to
spend a pleasant weekend without paying a fortune!

How to get there *(Map 10): 24km northeast of Sens; via N6 to Sens and
then N60.*

La Lucarne aux Chouettes

14, Quai Bretoche
89500 Villeneuve-sur-Yonne (Yonne)
Tel. 86.87.18.26 - Fax 86.87.22.63 - M. Marc Daniel

Rooms 4 with telephone, bath and WC. **Price** Double 450F; loft, suite and Duplex 650F. **Meals** Breakfast 45F, served 8:30-10:30. **Restaurant** Closed Sunday evening and Monday in winter. Service 12:00-14:30, 19:30-22:30; menu 98F (weekday lunch)-155F, also à la carte. Specialties: Blinis de tourteau, sandre, lieu jaune, caille fermière "désossée," mousseline de poires caramélisée. **Credit cards** Visa, Eurocard and MasterCard. **Pets** Dogs allowed. **Facilities** Parking. **Nearby** Cathedral and Synod Palace, the municipal greenhouses in Sens, Joigny: church of Saint-Florentin, cathedral Saint-Etienne d'Auxerre, Avarollais museum. **Open** All year except Feb 15 – 28.

Originally four village houses, the Lucarne aux Chouettes has recently been converted into a very charming auberge by Leslie Caron herself. On the ground floor, there is a bar-veranda and a superb dining room whose beams and half-timbering create the essential part of the decoration. The cuisine is delicious, inventive, light and refined. (Marc Daniel used to be the chef at Paris' famous Lasserre). The service is attentive and in summer, meals are served on the lovely terrace overlooking the quay. The bedrooms are upstairs and all have a beautiful view over the river. Priority has been given to spaciousness, modern amenities and charm in the bedrooms, where there are antique-style beds, pretty fabrics, family furniture and paintings. The welcome is very hospitable and friendly, making the Lucarne aux Chouettes a delightful place to stay.

How to get there *(Map 10): 15km south of Sens. Via A6 exit Courtenay/ Sens, then D15 towards Piffonds and Villeneuve-sur-Yonne.*

Château Hôtel de Brélidy ★★★

Brélidy
22140 Bégard (Côtes-d'Armor)
Tel. 96.95.69.38 - Fax 96.95.18.03 - Mme Pémezec and M. Yoncourt

Rooms 14 with telephone, bath and WC (4 with TV). **Price** Single 360-410F, double 380-685F, suite 920-1030F. **Meals** Breakfast 50F, served 8:00-10:00; half board 375-510F. **Restaurant** Service 19:30-21:00; menus 135-175F. Specialties: Panaché de poissons, aiguillettes de canard aux pommes caramélisées. **Credit cards** All major. **Pets** Dogs allowed. **Facilities** Fishing, Mountain bikes, parking. **Nearby** Saint-Tugdual cathedral in Tréguier, basilica of Notre-Dame-de-Bon-Secours in Guingamp, château de Tonquedec, Kergrist, Rosambo – 18-hole Ajoncs d'or golf course in Saint-Quai-Portrieux. **Open** Easter – Nov 1.

From this old Breton château buried in the countryside you can see woods, wild hedgerows and deep lanes criss-crossing the hills. The granite walls rise out of banks of hydrangeas. The bedrooms are as comfortable as those of a good hotel. A set menu is served in one of two beautiful dining rooms, featuring cuisine which, like the welcome and the service, is friendly and family-style. After dinner you can retire to the lounge or take advantage of the billiard room. Both are vast and, though a little bare, welcoming nonetheless. The bedrooms are named after flowers and the suite has a canopied bed and beautiful views; but for less money you might prefer the *Jasmine* or *Iris* rooms. This is a place to treasure in the most unspoiled Breton countryside.

How to get there (Map 5): 6km west of Bégard via D15, towards Pontrieux.

Hôtel d'Avaugour ★★★

1, place du Champ-Clos
22100 Dinan (Côtes-d'Armor)
Tel. 96.39.07.49 - Fax 96.85.43.04 - Mme Quinton

Rooms 27 with telephone, bath, WC and TV. **Price** Single 340-450F, double 480-560F. **Meals** Breakfast (Buffet) 48F, served 7:00-10:00. No restaurant. **Credit cards** All major. **Pets** Dogs allowed. **Nearby** Léhon, Pleslin, Pleslin, Pléven, château de la Hunaudaie – 18-hole Dinard golf course in Saint-Briac-sur-Mer. **Open** All year.

The beautiful grey stone façade of the Avaugour overlooks the ramparts in the middle of the town. Inside, you will find the comfortable, intimate atmosphere of a family home. All the rooms are charming, some facing the garden and the ramparts. Mme Quinton will look after you well. In town, *La Caravelle, Les Grands Fossés* and *Chez La Mère Pourcel* are very good addresses for a fine dinner.

How to get there *(Map 6): 29km south of Saint-Malo (in the center of the town).*

Manoir du Cleuziou ★★

22540 Louargat (Côtes-d'Armor)
Tel. 96.43.14.90 – Fax 96.43.52.59
M. and Mme Costan

Rooms 28 with telephone, bath (1 with shower) and WC. **Price** Single 320-380F, double 420F. **Meals** Breakfast 40F, served 7:30-9:30; half board 325F (per pers.). **Restaurant** Service 12:00-13:30, 19:00-21:30; menus 95-210F, also à la carte. **Credit cards** Amex, Visa, Eurocard and MasterCard. **Pets** Dogs allowed. **Facilities** Swimming pool, Tennis (30F), parking. **Nearby** Basilica of Notre-Dame-de-Bon-Secours in Guingamp, Menez-Bré – 18-hole Saint-Samson golf course in Pleumeur-Bodou. **Open** March 1 – Jan 31.

The oldest part of the manor dates back to the 15th–century. It is a beautiful building, the interior a match for its elegant façade. There are magnificent carved stone fireplaces, lovely doors and tapestries. All the small bedrooms are different and, like the bathrooms, are very comfortable. If you have children the prices are excellent because, for a small supplement, some bedrooms can be arranged with two extra bunk beds. The dining room is splendid, but the quality of the cooking is irregular. The bar in the old cellars is open until 1AM. We should point out the presence of a small de luxe camping site a little way away which belongs to the manor and has the use of its leisure facilities.

How to get there *(Map 5): 14km west of Guingamp via N12; in the village follow signs.*

Le Repaire de Kerroc'h ★★★

29, quai Morand
22500 Paimpol (Côtes-d'Armor)
Tel. 96.20.50.13 - Fax 96.22.07.46 - M. Broc

Rooms 13 with telephone, bath, WC, TV and minibar. **Price** Single 250F, double 450F, suite 580-990F. **Meals** Breakfast 45F, served 8:00-10:30; half board 395F, full board 495F (per pers., 3 days min.). **Restaurant** Service 12:15-14:00, 19:15-21:30; menus 95-350F, also à la carte. Specialties: Dorure de saumon breton au vinaigre balsamique, caneton rôti au miel et aux épices, homard en 3 services. **Credit cards** Diners, Visa, Eurocard and MasterCard. **Pets** Dogs allowed. **Facilities** Ocean fishing (150F per pers.). **Nearby** Abbey of Beauport, Guilben Point, l'Arcouest Point, Lanieff, Kermaria-an-Iskuit chapel, Lanloup, Plouézec, Bilfot Point. **Open** All year.

Bréhat and Plougescant are only a few kilometers from the small town of Paimpol. On the quayside stands this very charming hotel, built in 1793 in typical St Malo style. The pretty bedrooms are named after islands off the Brittany coast and are well furnished in old-fashioned style. The hotel has been enlarged by the acquisition of an other part of this former pirate's house. There the bedrooms are larger and decorated with wallpapers and chintzes in bright, cheerful colors. The windows are double , which together with the thick walls of the old house ensures a peaceful night's sleep. Kerroc'h'Kitchen is famous for its excellent fish, unequalled in Paimpol. This is a very pleasant town hotel, full of the spirit of the sea and of Brittany.

***How to get there** (Map 5): 33km east of Lannion via D786 to Paimpol.*

Hôtel Le Sphinx ★★★

67, chemin de la Messe
22700 Perros-Guirec (Côtes-d'Armor)
Tel. 96.23.25.42 - Fax 96.91.26.13 - M. and Mme Le Verge

Rooms 20 with telephone, bath, WC and TV - Wheelchair access, elevator. **Price** Double 470-550F. **Meals** Breakfast 44F, served 7:30-10:00; half board 480-550F (per pers.). **Restaurant** Closed Monday lunchtime except holidays. Service 12:30-14:00, 19:30-21:30; menus 125-265F, also à la carte. **Credit cards** Amex, Visa, Eurocard and MasterCard. **Pets** Dogs not allowed. **Facilities** Direct access to the sea, parking. **Nearby** Footpath to Ploumanac'h, pink granite coast (chapel of Notre-Dame-de-la-Clarté), Sainte-Anne-de-Trégastel, boat excursions to the Sept Iles (Ile aux Moines) — 18-hole Saint-Samson golf course in Pleumeur-Bodou. **Open** Feb 15 – Jan 3.

Located on a small road along the pink granite coast, overlooking the Bay of Trestrignel, this hotel has an exceptional site with a garden going all the way down to the sea, a warmly decorated bar-lounge and adjoining dining room jutting out over the ocean; the owners are very hospitable. The rooms are always comfortable and well kept, although a bit impersonal. They all have a splendid view of the bay. Some have been recently built and are very pleasant with their English-style furniture and bay windows right over the sea. They are modern but elegant and cheerful. Mr. Le Verge's savory cuisine is excellent.

How to get there (Map 5): 11km of Lannion, along the coast.

Domaine du Val ★★★

22400 Planguenoual (Côtes-d'Armor)
Tel. 96.32.75.40 – Fax 96.32.71.50
M. Hervé

Rooms 36 with telephone, bath, WC and TV. **Price** Single and double 450-840F, suite 660-1050F. **Meals** Breakfast 45-55F; half board 450-600F. **Restaurant** Service 12:30-14:00, 19:30-21:30; menus 135-320F, also à la carte. Specialties: Saumon fumé maison, homard à l'armoricaine, pigeonneau à la Valoise, foie gras poêlé. **Credit cards** Visa, Eurocard and MasterCard. **Pets** Dogs allowed. **Facilities** Covered and heated swimming pool, sauna, squash, covered tennis, gym, parking. **Nearby** Château de Bienassis, stud farm and church of Saint-Martin in Lamballe – 18-hole Val d'Armor golf course. **Open** All year.

Set in large grounds stretching down to the sea, the Château du Val is well camouflaged. The covered tennis courts, squash courts, gymnasium and covered swimming pool are virtually hidden from sight. Amidst the greenery only a pretty Renaissance style building is visible. There is also a row of little granite houses, surrounded by shrubs. In these, every bedroom is at ground level and has its own terrace: they are peaceful and comfortable. The bedrooms in the château are a bit more expensive and classic, and their bathrooms, with Plancoët tiles deserve a special mention. On the ground floor the dining room is comfortable and decorated in Neo-Gothic style. Beside it is an attractive verandah where in summer you can dine under bunches of grapes hanging from the vine. In all, the pleasant welcome and the many leisure activities available make the Domaine du Val a good place to stay.

How to get there *(Map 6): 27km northeast of Saint-Brieuc, exit autoroute at Le Val-André; 1km from Planguenoual.*

Manoir du Vaumadeuc ★★★★

22130 Pleven (Côtes-d'Armor)
Tel. 96.84.46.17 - Fax 96.84.40.16
M. O'Neill

Rooms 14 with telephone, bath or shower and WC. **Price** Single 490F, double 490-950F, suite 950F. **Meals** Breakfast 45F, served 8:00-10:00; half board 450-680F (per pers., 3 days min.). **Restaurant** Closed Oct – June. Service 19:00-21:00; menus 190-295F, also à la carte. Specialties: Filet de barbue au miel et aux oranges, live lobster from the fish tank. **Credit cards** All major. **Pets** Dogs allowed (+50F). **Facilities** Fishing in the lake, parking. **Nearby** Château de la Hunaudaie, Dinan, Saint-Malo, Léhon, Preslin – 9-hole Pen Guen golf course, 18-hole Briac-sur-Mer golf course. **Open** Easter – Jan 5.

Dating from the end of the 15th-century, this manor has survived unscathed. In the main building are the dining room, a huge lounge and delightful bedrooms, immaculately decorated and furnished. To one side there are two small houses in the same style, also comfortably arranged. In front of the manor in the 16th-century dovecote is the bar. Set in woods, but only 18km from the sea, this is an excellent place to stay. The regional cooking is excellent.

How to get there *(Map 6): 37km east of Saint-Brieuc via N12 to Lamballe; in the village, D28 to Pléven via La Poterie and the Hunaudaie Forest.*

Le Fanal **

Route du Cap Fréhel
Plévenon - 22240 Fréhel (Côtes-d'Armor)
Tel. 96.41.43.19 - M. and Mme Legros

Rooms 9 with telephone, shower and WC. **Price** Single 230F, double 320F.
Meals Breakfast 33F. **Restaurant** Crêperie, service 18:00-21:00 weekends and
school holidays. **Credit cards** Visa, Eurocard and MasterCard. **Pets** Dogs not allowed.
Facilities Parking. **Nearby** Cap Fréhel, Fort La Latte, rock of la Grande Fauconnière,
market in Matignon (Wednesdays) – 18-hole Sables-d'Or-les-Pins golf course in Cap
Fréhel. **Open** April 1 – Sept 30.

In the middle of the Fréhel region between Plévenon and the
cape, the wooden architecture of Le Fanal blends perfectly with
its surroundings. To experience its secret charm you must go inside
and you will find antique furniture, classical music, books about
Brittany: everything contributes to peace and relaxation. The
tastefully decorated bedrooms are modern and comfortable, and
all have views over the moor and the sea. Nature lovers will enjoy
the bird reserve and the walks, or they can relax in the garden. The
welcome is informal and friendly.

How to get there *(Map 6): 40km west of St-Malo via D786, then D16.*

Relais de Fréhel *
Route du cap Fréhel
22240 Le Fréhel (Côtes-d'Armor)
Tel. 96.41.43.02 - Mme Lemercier

Rooms 13, 2 with bath, 7 with shower and 7 with WC. **Price** 235-285F.
Meals Breakfast 32F, served 8:00-11:00, half board 285F, full board 365F (per pers.,
3 days min.). **Restaurant** Service 12:30-14:00, 19:30-21:00; menus 90-265F, also
à la carte. Specialties: Seafood, lobster, grillades au feu de bois. **Credit cards** Visa,
Eurocard and MasterCard. **Pets** Dog not allowed. **Facilities** Tennis, parking.
Nearby Cape Fréhel, La Latte Fort, Grande Fauconnière rock, Matignon market on
Wednesday – 18-hole Sables-d'Or-les-Pins golf course. **Open** April – Nov 2

The Relais de Fréhel is an old farm which has been restored;
its long low façade of pink stone is surmounted by large slate-
covered mansard roofs and faces a lovely garden of hydrangeas and
a very lush and verdant park. Inside, the warm wood of the window
and ceiling joists softens the stark but beautiful exposed stones
which frame doors and windows, and the white stucco of the walls.
The bedrooms are small, rustic and very simple, but the prices are
in keeping. The dining room is charming; the cuisine,
unfortunately, is nothing to write home about, but the meals grilled
in the fireplace are good. The atmosphere is very family-style, calm
and restful. The Côte Sauvage (Wild Coast) and the bird sanctuary
at Cape Fréhel are several kilometers away, attracting lovers of the
sea as well as bird watchers.

How to get there *(Map 6): 40km west of Saint-Malo via D786, then D16;*
follow the signs in the direction of Cap Fréhel.

Hôtellerie de l'Abbaye

Bon-Repos
22570 Saint-Gelven (Côtes-d'Armor)
Tel. 96.24.98.38 - M. Gadin

Rooms 5 with bath and WC. **Price** Single and double 240-270F. **Meals** Breakfast 32F, served 8:30-9:30; half board 240-340F (per pers., 5 days min.). **Restaurant** Service 12:15-13:30, 19:30-20:30; menus 60-200F, also à la carte. Specialties: Filet de canard au cidre, brochet au beurre blanc. **Credit cards** Visa, Eurocard and MasterCard. **Pets** Dogs allowed (+20F). **Facilities** Parking. **Nearby** Guerlédan lake, abbey of Bon-Repos, gorges of the Daoulas. **Open** All year (closed Tuesday evening and Wednesday).

This hotel occupies the old outbuildings of the Cistercian abbey of Bon Repos, founded in 1184. The site is very peaceful and the main road, though convenient, is far enough away not to be heard. The landscape is very green. The sight of the Nantes-Brest Canal flowing tranquilly below, and the Forest of Quénécan in front the Hôtellerie, makes a wonderful picture. It is an ideal spot for sportsmen in search of woodcock, and for fishermen. (The nearby River Blanet is rated first-class). All five bedrooms comfortable, but you should note that three have only small oval windows. Meals are served in a lovely dining room with big beams and solid stone walls. M. Gadin does the excellent cooking himself. The prices are reasonable and the people are friendly.

How to get there (Map 5): 46km south of Guingamp. On N164 bis (Rennes-Brest), in the village of Bon-Repos, between Caurel and Gouarec.

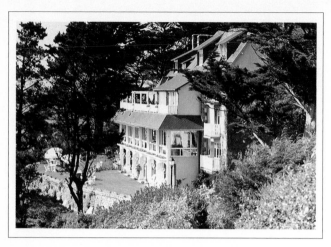

Ti Al-Lannec ★★★

Allée de Mezo-Guen
22560 Trébeurden (Côtes-d'Armor)
Tel. 96.23.57.26 - Fax 96.23.62.14 - M. and Mme Jouanny

Rooms 29 with telephone, bath, WC and cable TV. **Price** Single 385-430F, double 600-1000F. **Meals** Breakfast 65-90F, served 7:15-10:30; half board 535-750F, full board 695-915F. **Restaurant** Service 12:30-14:00, 19:30-21:30; menus 100-380F, also à la carte. Specialties: Noix de coquilles Saint-Jacques dorées sauce curry, caneton rôti aux baies de cassis, la tentation de l'écureuil. **Credit cards** All major. **Pets** Dogs allowed (+45F). **Facilities** Fitness-beauty center, parking. **Nearby** Le Castel, Bihit point, the Breton corniche from Trébeurden to Perros-Guirec – Saint-Samson golf course in Pleumeur-Bodou. **Open** March 18 – Nov 10.

Ti Al-Lannec is exceptionally well decorated and the hotel has a wonderful view of the sea (which is easily accessible by a small path) and terraced gardens. The very comfortable bedrooms are beautifully furnished and decorated, some with English fabrics and wallpaper; most have a sitting area, a charming verandah or terrace. The same care in decoration is evident in the lounges and in the dining room, which extends onto a large verandah overlooking the bay. The service here is perfect and the cuisine excellent. Also worthy of note is the fitness center.

How to get there *(Map 5): 9km northwest of Lannion via D65.*

162

Manoir de Crec'h-Goulifen

Beg Leguer-Servel
22300 Lannion (Côtes-d'Armor)
Tel. 96.47.26.17 - Mme Droniou

Rooms 7 with telephone, bath or shower and WC. **Price** Single 250-280F, double
330-400F. **Meals** Breakfast incl., served 8:00-10:30. No restaurant. **Credit cards**
Not accepted. **Pets** Dogs allowed (+40F). **Facilities** Tennis, parking. **Nearby** Chapel
of Kerfons, châteaux de Tonquédec, de Kergrist and de Rosambo, chapel of the Sept-
Nains – Saint-Samson golf course in Pleumeur-Bodou. **Open** All year.

The manor of Crec'h-Goulifen, originally an 18th-century farm
and, been lovingly renovated. The main room on the ground
floor is arranged with regional country furniture, and breakfast is
served here or on the terrace. The bedrooms are also in country
style, small but comfortable although somewhat dark. We
recommend the two which have a bathroom, (The third room,
called The Studio, is less pleasant). The Manoir is a pleasing and
peaceful place, in a good location. For fine dining, try *Le Serpolet,*
which is located in a pretty house in a small street behind the post
office.

How to get there *(Map 5): 6km northwest of Lannion via D21, then towards*
Servel.

Kastell Dinec'h ★★★

22200 Tréguier (Côtes-d'Armor)
Tel. 96.92.49.39 - Fax 96.92.34.03
M. and Mme Pauwels

Rooms 15 with telephone, bath and WC (6 with TV). **Price** Double 400-480F. **Meals** Breakfast 50F, served 8:00-10:00; half board 420-460F. **Restaurant** Service 19:30-21:30; menus 130-300F, also à la carte. Specialties: Bar en croûte de sel, cassolette de moules aux mousserons, crêpes de seigle au homard. **Credit cards** Visa, Eurocard and MasterCard. **Pets** Dogs allowed (+25F). **Facilities** Heated swimming pool May 15 – Sept 15, parking. **Nearby** Cathedral of Saint-Tugdual and the house of Ernest Renan in Tréguier, Pleubian, chapel of Saint-Gonéry in Plougescrant, château de la Roche-Jagu – 9-hole Saint-Samson golf course in Pleumeur-Bodou. **Open** March 15 – Oct 11 and Oct 27 – Dec 31 (closed Tuesday evening and Wednesday in low season).

In the countryside 2km from Tréguier stands this 17th-century manor-farm. The main building – housing a beautiful dining room, a small comfortable lounge and some of the bedrooms – has two annexes containing the other bedrooms. Together they look onto a lovely garden where drinks and breakfast are served in summer. The bedrooms are small but tastefully decorated, some with antique furniture. The overall effect is simple and elegant. Mme de Pauwels' is very hospitable, and her husband's cooking is delicious.

How to get there (Map 5): 16km east of Lannion via D786, 2km before Tréguier; follow the signs.

Le Minaret ★★

Corniche de l'Estuaire
29950 Bénodet (Finistère)
Tel. 98.57.03.13 - Mme Kervran

Rooms 20 with telephone, bath or shower, WC and TV - Elevator. **Price** Double 260-420F **Meals** Breakfast 40F, served 8:00-10:00; half board (obligatory in high season) 275-390F. **Restaurant** Closed Tuesday in April and May. Service 12:30-14:00, 19:30-21:00; menus 90-210F, also à la carte. Specialties: Gigot de lotte au poivre vert, pavé de poisson grillé à la façon des îles, homard grillé. **Credit cards** Visa, Eurocard and MasterCard **Pets** Dogs allowed except in the restaurant. **Facilities** Parking. **Nearby** Quimper, boat trip on the Odet from Quimper to Bénodet, Breton museum and villages, Notre-Dame de Quilinen chapel. **Open** Easter – Oct 1.

An oasis in the midst of traditional Brittany: That is what Le Minaret looks like! It is a large white house designed in the 1920s by the architect Laprade; from the top of its real minaret, there's a breathtaking view out over the estuary of the River Odet, where sailboats pass regularly on their way in or out of the port. But even more than the exterior architecture, the interior decoration of the house reminds you discreetly of its Oriental character. The bright rooms, three of which have a small terrace, have a view of the sea or the charming small inlet bordering the town of Sainte-Marine. The great curiosity of the house is the *Pacha* bedroom, decorated in pure Moroccan style with wide windows opening onto the estuary. The mixture of the styles is attractive and lends unusual charm to the hotel. A pretty garden surrounds the house, and the terrace on the seafront also affords a superb view.

How to get there *(Map 5): 16km south of Quimper.*

Domaine de Kéréven **

29950 Bénodet (Finistère)
Tel. 98.57.02.46 - Fax 98.66.22.61
Mme Berrou

Rooms 16 with telephone, bath or shower and WC. **Price** Double 280-375F.
Meals Breakfast 38F, served 8:30-10:30; half board 295-340F. **Restaurant** Closed
Sept 25 – May 20. Service 19:30-20:30; menu 120F. Specialties: Seafood.
Credit cards Not accepted. **Pets** Dogs not allowed. **Facilities** Parking. **Nearby** Boat
trip on the Odet from Quimper to Bénodet, chapels of Gouesnac'h and le Drennec,
châteaux of Bodinio and Cheffontaines, Quimper, îles de Glénan – 18-hole l'Odet
golf course in Bénodet. **Open** Easter – Oct 14 (by reservation Easter – May 20 and
Sept 22 – Oct 15).

Surrounded by fields and farmland, the vast Domaine de Kéréven
and its contiguous old farm buildings are eloquent examples of
the unspoiled traditional charm you will still find in this part of the
Breton countryside. (And yet it is still near the sea and beaches). The
family atmosphere of the domaine and the hospitality are very
pleasant. The bedrooms have comfortable, modern amenities, and
they are well kept and very quiet, but greater effort should be made
with decoration to make them more personal and more cheerful.
But the demi-pension is certainly good value for the money. You
have dinner in a large rustic dining room which opens onto a terrace
where it is pleasant to have drinks before dinner. One of the buildings,
has apartments with kitchens, which is very convenient if you are a
family or a group. The Domaine de Kéréven is truly a haven of
comfort and tranquillity.

How to get there *(Map 5): 16km south of Quimper via D34.*

Castel Régis **

Plage du Garo
29890 Brignogan-Plage (Finistère)
Tel.98.83.40.22 – Telex 940 941 – Fax 98.83.44.71 – M. and Mme Plos

Rooms 21 with telephone, bath and WC. **Price** Double 240-650F. **Meals** Breakfast 34F, served 8:00-10:00; half board 390-510F, full board +100F (per pers., 3 days min.). **Restaurant** Service 12:30-14:00, 19:30-21:00; menus 98-198F, also à la carte. Specialties: Blanquette Saint-Jacques, fricassée coquelet, cassolette de pommes chouchen. **Credit cards** Visa, Eurocard and MasterCard. **Pets** Dogs allowed (+35F). **Facilities** Heated swimming pool (June 1 – Sept 30), tennis, mini-golf course, sauna, bicycles, kayak, parking. **Nearby** Pontusual point, church in Goulven, côte des Abers – Abers golf course. **Open** April 14 – Sept 31.

Castel Régis has a marvellous position on a tiny peninsula, with the restaurant at its very end by the water's edge. The bedrooms are scattered about in various buildings with a flowering garden and a mini-golf course in between. All the bedrooms are different, but try to get one directly overlooking the sea. There are bedrooms on the ground floor opening onto the garden, and others suitable for families. Some are decorated with antiques, and some are more ordinary. When you make your reservation the management will be happy to give you descriptions of the bedrooms available. Certain external details like stairs and gangways are unattractive but you feel so good here and the welcome and cooking are so pleasant that you will easily forgive the defects, which will no doubt be dealt with in the future.

How to get there *(Map 5): 37km north of Brest via D788 to Lesneven then D770.*

Hôtel Ty Mad ★★

Plage Saint-Jean
29100 Douarnenez (Finistère)
Tel. 98.74.00.53 – Fax 98.74.15.16 – Mme Martin

Rooms 23 with telephone, bath or shower and WC (TV on request). **Price** Single and double 220-310F. **Meals** Breakfast 35F, served 8:00-11:00. **Restaurant** Service 12:30-14:00, 19:30-21:30; menus, also à la carte. Specialties: fish, seafood. **Credit cards** All major. **Pets** Dogs allowed (+25F). **Facilities** Parking. **Nearby** Douarnenez (port-musée), coast paths of Plomarc'h and Roches Blanches, Beuzec point, Cap Sizun, Quimper, Locronan, church of Confort, Pont-Croix and Sainte-Anne-la-Palud – 18-hole l'Odet golf course in Bénodet. **Open** Easter – Nov 1.

What famous guests for such a small hotel! Many renowned people in search of peace and quiet have sought refuge in this house, including Christopher Wood and Max Jacob, who lived here for more than two years. Located twenty minutes from the house of Françoise Gilot, Picasso's companion, Ty Mad has bedrooms which, from its three upsper floors, look out over a countryside beautiful enough to be painted. Meals are served in a large, bright room with white tablecloths and a glossy parquet floor, which gives onto a terrace. Nearby, there is a small 17th-century chapel and a beach for the clients of the hotel. The Ty Mad is right out of a Jacques Tati film, – an excellent small hotel.

How to get there *(Map 5): 18km northwest of Quimper via D765; at the Tréboul Yacht Harbor, the hotel is signposted.*

Manoir du Stang ★★★★

29940 La Forêt-Fouesnant (Finistère)
Tel. 98.56.97.37
M. and Mme Hubert

Rooms 26 with telephone, bath or shower and WC. **Price** Single 525F, double 590-860F. **Meals** Breakfast 40F, served 8:00-10:00; half board price on request. **Restaurant** Residents only, on reservation. Service 19:30-20:30; menu 160F, also à la carte. **Credit cards** Not accepted. **Pets** Dogs not allowed. **Facilities** Tennis. **Nearby** Concarneau, Cabellou point, Saint-Corentin cathedral and art museum in Quimper, boat trips up the Odet and on the sea (Iles des Glénans) — 18-hole Cornouaille golf course adjoining the Manoir du Stang. **Open** May – Sept.

Le Stang is a family agricultural estate of 100 acres, with large formal gardens, a rose garden, lakes, woods, farm and fields, all very close to the sea. The manor is a civilized and comfortable 16th-century gentleman's residence. The 17th-century dining room opens onto a terrace overlooking the lakes. All the bedrooms are delightful, well furnished and with lovely views, and the cooking is enhanced by the quality of the home-grown produce. This is an excellent hotel from which to enjoy the beaches and water sports (sailing and diving) on the sea, the Port-la-Forêt yacht harbor nearby, and the golf course next to the hotel.

How to get there *(Map 5): 12km southeast of Quimper via D783 to the private drive of the Manoir, follow signs.*

Hôtel Ker–Ansquer ★★★

Lababan
29710 Pouldreuzic (Finistère)
Tel. 98.54.41.83 - Mme Ansquer

Rooms 11 and 2 apartments with telephone, bath, WC and TV. **Price** Double 330F.
Meals Breakfast 40F, served 8:00-10:00; half board 330F (per pers.).
Restaurant Service 12:30-19:30; menus 90-295F. Specialties: Plateau de fruits de
mer, coquilles Saint-Jacques en poêlon, langouste sauce armoricaine, canard à
l'orange. **Credit cards** All major. **Pets** Dogs allowed (+30F). **Facilities** Parking.
Nearby Breton villages between Pont-l'Abbé and Pouldreuzic (D2), Saint-Corentin
cathedral and art museum in Quimper – 18-hole l'Odet golf course in Bénodet.
Open Easter – end Sept and school holidays.

A good example of a modern building in traditional style, this
hotel was built a few years ago and has just been enlarged by
the addition of a new wing. The somewhat plain and austere
architecture of slate roofs and grey stone walls has been enlivened
by the new round tower. The furniture was made by a local cabinet
maker and the crockery came from Quimper. The 2 1/2-acre
garden makes the hotel quiet, and the view stretches out over fields
and the countryside to the sea.

How to get there *(Map 5): 25km west of Quimper via D784 to Landudec,
then D143 towards Pouldreuzic and D40.*

Manoir de Moëllien ★★

29550 Plonévez–Porzay (Finistère)
Tel. 98.92.50.40 – Fax 98.92.55.21
M. and Mme Garet

Rooms 10 with telephone, bath, WC and TV. **Price** Double 330-350F. **Meals** Breakfast 40F, served 8:00-9:30; half board 345-355F, full board 425F (per pers.). **Restaurant** Closed Wednesday in low season. Service 12:30-14:00, 19:30-21:00; menus 120-230F, also à la carte. Specialties: Fish and shellfish. **Credit cards** All major. **Pets** Dogs allowed (+30F). **Facilities** Parking. **Nearby** Saint-Corentin cathedral and art museum in Quimper, Locronan, Sainte-Anne-la-Palud, church in Ploéven – 18-hole l'Odet golf course in Bénodet. **Open** March 20 – Jan 2.

Invisible from the little road leading to it, this château is hidden by a pine forest. The dining room is on the ground floor of the main building, built of stone in the 17th-century. Its rustic Breton furnishings are brightened with bunches of fresh flowers and house plants. Next door is a small, intimate bar. In the relaxing first-floor lounge a stone fireplace takes pride of place. Opposite the noble façade of the manor is a building housing bedrooms at ground-floor level. They are comfortable, pretty, quiet and well kept. The views of the surrounding countryside and the excellent welcome will soon win your heart.

How to get there (Map 5): 20km northwest of Quimper via D63 to Locronan (the Manoir is 3km northwest of Locronan via C10).

Hôtel de L'Iroise

29770 Pointe-du-Raz (Finistère)
Tel. 98.70.64.65
Mme Le Coz

Rooms 10 with shower (3 with WC). **Price** Double 150-200F. **Meals** Breakfast 22F, served 8:30-10:30. No restaurant. **Credit cards** Not accepted. **Pets** Dogs allowed. **Facilities** Parking. **Nearby** Route de la Pointe du Raz, Saint-Tugen chapel, cape Sizun ornithological reserve. **Open** All year

Whipped by the wind, thrust out in the wild moor of the Pointe du Raz, this small white house struggles all alone against the terrible storms which blow in from the Atlantic Ocean. The ten small, simply decorated rooms all have a view of the Baie des Trépassés, an extraordinary, apocalyptic landscape where there is not a single tree growing and where the earth and stones prevent any kind of plants from thriving. The only vegetation that survives in this austere climate is a few clumps of broom. At the Iroise, you can peruse the photos which several great photographers have given Madame Le Coz in gratitude for the combat she has waged for so long for the survival of this magic place. In fact, it is planned to demolish the house in 1996. So you have only a short time left in which to discover this strange and mysterious site, where fairy tales and goblins are still alive. If you love strong emotions, don't miss it. You can have dinner 1km away in Lescaf, at *La Brochette*, or in Audierne at *La Goélette*.

How to get there *(Map 4): 14km northwest of Audierne via D784.*

Moulin de Rosmadec ★★

Venelle de Rosmadec
29930 Pont-Aven (Finistère)
Tel. 98.06.00.22 - Fax 98.06.18.00 - Sébilleau Family

Rooms 4 with telephone, bath, WC and TV. **Price** Double 470F. **Meals** Breakfast 40F.
Restaurant Service 12:30-14:00, 19:30-21:00; menu 160F, 295F, 400F with lobster,
also à la carte. Specialties: Fish, homard grillé Rosmadec. **Credit cards** All major.
Pets Dogs allowed (+25F). **Facilities** Parking. **Nearby** Gauguin Museum in Pont-
Aven, Saint-Corentin cathedral and museum fine arts in Quimper, Tremal chapel,
Nizon, Kérangosquer, the enclosed city of Concarneau, boat ride down Odet River –
18-hole Odet golf course in Bénodet **Open** March 1 – Oct 15 (closed Wednesday and
Sunday exept June 15 – Sep 15).

You will find the Moulin de Rosmadec at the end of a small
lane in the charming village of Pont Aven, immortalized by
Paul Gauguin. Nestling between two branches of a pretty river,
this 15th-century mill is an ideal place to stay in order to explore
this marvelous Breton village with fifteen mills. The Moulin's four
small rooms are all comfortable, and from them you will hear the
peaceful sound of water tumbling through the wheel, which is still
in operation. The hotel's Michelin-starred restaurant, which is run
by the owners' son, has been here for more than sixty years,
specializing in grilled lobster and other succulent Breton fish dishes.
You can have breakfast on the patio, in the center of which stands
a charming old moss-covered well. In short, you will love this
special place to stay!

How to get there *(Map 5): 32km southeast of Quimper via D783, towards
Concarneau.*

173

Château de Kernuz ★★
29120 Pont-L'Abbé (Finistère)
Tel. 98.87.01.59 – Fax 98.66.02.36
M. and Mme du Chatellier

Rooms 19 with telephone, bath and WC. **Price** Single 350F, double 350-450F and 600F. **Meals** Breakfast 35F, served 8:00-10:00; half board 360-410F, full board 510-560F (per pers.). **Restaurant** Service 12:00-13:30, 19:30-21:30; menus 150F, (child 60F), also à la carte in July, Aug. **Credit cards** All major. **Pets** Dogs allowed. **Facilities** Swimming pool, tennis and parking. **Nearby** Cathedral Saint-Corentin and fine arts museum in Quimper, Breton villages, Pont-Aven, Concarneau, boat ride down Odet River – 18-hole Odet golf course in Bénodet. **Open** April – Sept.

This is a family home and a beautiful chateau which became a hotel out of necessity but which has maintained itself proudly and nobly in its park, surrounded, as is its due, by a dovecote, a chapel and a watchtower. There is a very charming lounge whose beautiful dark woodwork is brightened by beige-grey sofas, and farther on a very handsome bar with two Renaissance pillars of painted sculpted wood. The bedrooms are also striking; although not so alluring as the rooms on the main floor, many are very charming, each with different colors and decor. Everything here is in good taste, and the welcome is friendly.

How to get there *(Map 5): 20km south of Quimper; 1km south of Pont-L'Abbé, take D785, towards Plomeur, then the road for Penmarc'h.*

Le Brittany ★★★
Boulevard Sainte-Barbe
29681 Roscoff (Finistère)
Tel. 98.69.70.78 - Fax 98. 61. 13. 29. - Mme Chapalain

Rooms 25 and 1 studio with telephone,bath or shower,WC and TV - Elevator.
Price Single 390-420F, double 440-590F, studio 640-840F. **Meals** Breakfast 58F,
served 7:15-10:30; half board 390-540F. **Restaurant** "Le Yacht man" Service 12:15-
14:00, 19:15-21:30 (closed Monday noon); menus 120-320F, also à la carte.
Specialties: Fish and shellfish. **Credit cards** Amex, Visa, Eurocard and MasterCard.
Pets Dogs allowed except in restaurant. **Facilities** Swimming pool, sauna, parking.
Nearby Balz island (15 min. by boat), Saint-Pol-de-Léon, tour of châteaux of Léon
(château of Kérouzéré, manoir of Tronjoly, château of Kerjéan). **Open** April – Oct 15.

In the delightful small town of Roscoff, the Brittany Hotel is the
last rampart against the winds that beat in from the Atlantic. The
bedrooms are decorated with beautiful old furniture and white fabric
wall coverings; they are calm and pleasant, with well equipped
bathrooms. You might want to have breakfast in your room because
the breakfast room near the swimming pool can be noisy. The dining
room, which is located in a 17th-century manor house, is the most
charming and pleasant part of the hotel: Facing due west, it looks
out over the sea and its large bay windows bathe the room with
light. The hospitality is very British, and the cuisine is typical of the
region, with lots of fresh fish; and there is a very good wine list. The
bar has the discreet atmosphere of a great hotel. The last stop on the
way to Ireland and England, this auberge combines the pleasures of
a comfortable stopover with the tranquillity of an old Breton house.

How to get there (Map 5): 25km north of Morlaix.

Les Grandes Roches ★★★

Route des Grandes-Roches
29910 Trégunc (Finistère)
Tel. 98.97.62.97 - Fax 98.50.29.19 - M. and Mme Henrich

Rooms 22 with telephone, bath or shower and WC. **Price** Single 240F, double 300-390F, suite 530F. **Meals** Breakfast 40F, served 8:00-9:30; half board 280-420F (per pers., 3 days min.). **Restaurant** Closed mid. Nov – mid. March. Service 12:30-14:30 (only Saturday, Sunday and National Holidays), 19:15-21:15 (every night); menus 98-250F, also à la carte. Specialties: Seafood, saumon à la peau, poissons fumés à l'auberge, filets de canard, nougat glacé maison. **Credit cards** Visa, Eurocard and MasterCard. **Pets** Dogs not allowed. **Facilities** Parking. **Nearby** Pont-Aven, Nizon, Kérangosquer, Concarneau, Nevez – 18-hole l'Odet golf course in Bénodet and Queven. **Open** Jan 15 – Dec 15.

This old farmhouse, which has been renovated and is very comfortable, stands in a large and well-shaded garden. There is a bar with a terrace, two dining rooms and a lounge with television. The thatched cottages, an unusual and interesting feature, have been very well restored and turned into apartments furnished in traditional style. A *menhir* can be found in the grounds – evidence of prehistoric occupation – and in the countryside around there are more dolmens, menhirs and monoliths. A number of beaches are close by. The owner's husband is German, which makes this a popular spot for visitors from beyond the Rhine.

How to get there *(Map 5): 28km southeast of Quimper via D783 to Trégunc via Concarneau; (the auberge is just outside the village).*

Hôtel Ménez ★★

Saint–Antoine
29252 Plouézoc'h (Finistère)
Tel. 98.67.28.85 - Mme Ménez

Rooms 8 with telephone, bath or shower and WC. **Price** Single 150F, double 230-260F. **Meals** Breakfast 25F, served 8:00-10:00. No restaurant. **Credit cards** Not accepted. **Pets** Dogs not allowed. **Facilities** Parking. **Nearby** Morlaix River, Plougonyen, parish enclosures of Saint-Thegonnec, Guimiliau and Lampaul-Guimiliau – 18-hole Saint-Samson golf course in Pleumeur-Bodou. **Open** June 1 – Sept 1 only on reservation.

This is another recently built hotel, but this one adheres scrupulously to the Breton style. Standing in a park with countryside around, it has ten very well furnished bedrooms with every modern facility. On the ground floor the light and cozy living room is peaceful and relaxing. The proprietors are kind and welcoming. In Morlaix, try the small restaurant *L'Auberge Saint-Antoine* and *La Marée Bleue*.

How to get there (Map 5): 9km north of Morlaix via D46.

Hôtel Richeux

35260 Cancale (Ille-et-Vilaine)
Tel. 99.89.25.25 - Fax 99.89.88.47
M. and Mme Roellinger

Rooms 11 and 2 suites with telephone, bath, WC, TV and minibar - 1 for disabled persons; elevator. **Price** Double 750-1350F. **Meals** Breakfast 85F, served 8:00-10:00. **Restaurant** Closed Monday and Tuesday noon in low season. Service 12:30-14:00, 19:30-21:30; menu shellfish: from 100F, also à la carte. **Credit cards** All major. **Pets** Dogs allowed (+50F). **Facilities** Parking. **Nearby** Saint-Malo, Côte d'Emeraude, Mont Saint-Michel – 18-hole Dinard golf course in Saint-Briac. **Open** All year.

In this beautiful, spacious house, Olivier and Jeanne Roellinger have just opened a luxurious auberge on the seafront whose discreet charm, comfort and refinement will delight you. In each bedroom, with a view over the Bay of Mont Saint-Michel or the Breton countryside, you will find a different atmosphere, with beautiful old furniture and a bouquet of fresh flowers. All the bathrooms are bright and very pleasant. In the dining room, which opens onto the garden, you will savor the chef's fish specialties, along with fresh vegetables from the garden and fruit from the orchard. This is a very high-quality hotel which will surely satisfy the most demanding guests.

How to get there *(Map 6): 12km east of Saint-Malo; in Cancale, turn towards of Mont Saint-Michel.*

Hôtel Les Rimains

1, rue Duguesclin
35260 Cancale (Ille-et-Vilaine)
Tel. 99.89.64.76 - Fax 99.89.88.47 - M. and Mme Roellinger

Rooms 6 with telephone, bath, WC, TV and minibar. **Price** Double 650-750F.
Meals Breakfast 85F, served 8:00-10:00. **Restaurant** (600 m from hotel) Closed
Tuesday and Wednesday in low season. Service 12:30-14:00, 19:30-21:00; menu,
also à la carte. **Credit cards** All major. **Pets** Dogs allowed (+50F). **Facilities** Parking.
Nearby Saint-Malo, Côte d'Emeraude, Mont Saint-Michel — 18-hole Dinard golf
course in Saint-Briac. **Open** March 1 – Dec 31.

On the edge of a wild and unspoiled cliff overlooking the Bay
of Mont Saint Michel, Les Rimains has six small, bright
bedrooms which are tastefully decorated and have up-to-date
amenities. From the ground floor and the upstairs rooms, the
grandiose panoramic view dominates the hotel. There is no lounge
here but the garden of this authentic Breton house is a lovely place
in which to relax and enjoy the view of the beautiful countryside.
You can also have breakfast (delicious) in the garden. There is no
restaurant but the owners will welcome you to their Relais
Gourmand Olivier Roellinger and ply you with the delicious local
specialties and the fresh products of the region. The welcome is
charming and discreet.

How to get there *(Map 6): 12km east of Saint-Malo; hotel signposted
beginning at the church.*

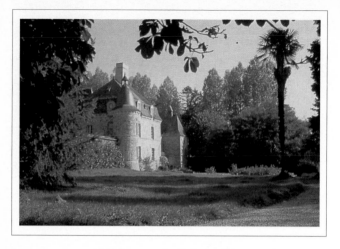

Château de Léauville

35360 Landujan (Ille-et-Vilaine)
Tel. 99.07.21.14 - Fax 99.07.21.80
Mme Desaize

Rooms 8 with telephone, bath and WC. **Price** Single and double 470-720F.
Meals Breakfast 56F, served 8:00-10:00; half board from 476F (per pers.).
Restaurant Service 19:30-20:30; menus from 185F. Specialties: Traditional seasonal
cooking, fish, seafood on request. **Credit cards** All major. **Pets** Dogs allowed (+60F).
Facilities Heated swimming pool, parking. **Nearby** Saint-Malo, Dinan, Mont Saint-
Michel, Brocéliande, Rennes – 18-hole la Freslonnière golf course in Le Rheu, 9-hole
Rennes golf course. **Open** March 16 – Nov 14.

Château de Léauville dates from the 16th and 17th centuries
and incorporates a turret of the 11th-century manor of
Pontelain, on whose ruins it was built. The 16th-century chapel
now serves as an exhibition hall and there are traces of the old
building everywhere. There is a friendly ambience in the dining
room and the cozy, tastefully furnished bedrooms. In the garden
is a large swimming pool, and there are terraces for relaxing and
gazing at the countryside. The owners are very hospitable.

How to get there *(Map 6): 30km northwest of Rennes via N12 to Bédée,
then D72 to Irodouër and D21.*

Manoir du Tertre ★★★

Paimpont
35380 Plélan-le-Grand (Ille-et-Vilaine)
Tel. 99.07.81.02 - Fax 99.07.85.45 - M. Gouguenheim

Rooms 8 with telephone, bath and WC. **Price** Double 350-500F. **Meals** Breakfast 35F, served 8:00-11:00; half board 300-400F, full board 380-500F (per pers., 3 days min.). **Restaurant** Closed Monday. Service 12:30-14:00, 19:30-21:00; menus 130-185F, also à la carte. Specialties: Regional cooking, game and fish. **Credit cards** Amex, Visa, Eurocard and MasterCard. **Pets** Dogs allowed. **Facilities** Parking. **Nearby** Paimpont Forest, les Forges-de-Paimpont, church in Paimpont, lake of le Pas-du-Houx, château de Comper, church in Tréhonrenteuc, Campénéac and château de Trécesson – 18-hole la Freslonnière golf course in Rheu, 9-hole Rennes golf course. **Open** March 1 – Jan 31.

This manor house in the heart of ancient Brocéliande should have belonged to a druidess–perhaps the lady whose portrait you can see in the living room. The interior of the house has much charm, as do the bedrooms, which have just been completely refurbished. Most have a big window overlooking the countryside and the 5-acre grounds. This is an ideal place for a weekend, with walks along the tracks and paths of the forest of Paimpont in the footsteps of Merlin and the fairy Viviane.

How to get there *(Map 6): 40km southwest of Rennes to Plélan-le-Grand, then D38 via N24.*

Château de la Motte Beaumanoir ★★★

35720 Pleugueneuc (Ille-et-Vilaine)
Tel. 99.69.46.01 - Fax 99.69.42.49
M. Bernard

Rooms 6 and 2 suites with telephone, bath and WC (TV on request). **Price** Double 700F, suite 800-900F. **Meals** Breakfast 60F, served 8:00-10:00; half board 560F (per pers.). **Restaurant** Closed Tuesday and Nov 15 – March 15. Service 12:00-13:00, 20:00-22:00; menus 140-250F, also à la carte. Specialties: Traditional cooking. **Credit cards** Amex, Visa, Eurocard and MasterCard. **Pets** Dogs allowed (+60F). **Facilities** Heated swimming pool, boating, fishing, parking. **Nearby** Dinan, Léhon, Pleslin, château de la Hunaudaie – 18-hole Dinard golf course in Saint-Briac-sur-Mer. **Open** Jan 3 – Dec 22.

A landscape of forests, lakes and fields surrounds this tranquil 15th-century château. Behind the graceful austerity of its granite walls lies a cheerful and elegant interior. The bedrooms are huge, with high ceilings, beautiful furniture, and fabrics chosen to give a different personality to each room. Some have a view of the lake, and the bathrooms are modern and comfortable. The young master of the house will welcome you more as a guest than a client. Do not hesitate to ask his advice about local tourist attractions. The cuisine is excellent.

How to get there *(Map 6): 12km southeast of Dinan via N137; then north of Pleugeuneuc turn right at first crossroads from Dinan, toward Plesder.*

Manoir de la Rance ★★★

Château de Jouvente
35730 Pleurtuit (Ille-et-Vilaine)
Tel. 99.88.53.76 - Fax 99.88.63.03 - Mme Jasselin

Rooms 10 with telephone, bath, WC and TV. **Price** Single 400-450F, double 450-800F, suite 800-1100F (-20% Oct – April). **Meals** Breakfast 50F, served 7:00-11:00. No restaurant. **Credit cards** Visa, Eurocard and MasterCard. **Pets** Dogs allowed (+40F). **Facilities** Parking. **Nearby** Banks of the river Rance, castle and walled town of Saint-Malo, Cézembre island, Chausey island, côte d'Emeraude from Dinard to Le Val André – 27-hole Saint-Malo golf course. **Open** March – Dec.

Facing the Rance and surrounded by trees and flowers, this 19th-century manor stands in large and lovely grounds. The big lounge is pleasantly furnished in a mixture of styles, and in the bar and the small living room, where tea is served, the atmosphere is very homey. Refreshments are served outside in the charming gardens and terraces, which have reclining chairs. Located on three floors, all the bedrooms are very comfortable and quiet, and all have a stunning view of the sea, the cliffs and the countryside. Madame Jasselin, the owner, is very friendly. For dining, you will find *Le Petit Robinson* in La Richardais (3km), and many restaurants in Saint-Malo.

How to get there *(Map 6): 15km southeast of Saint-Malo via D168, then left after the Rance Dam on D114 to La Jouvente (via La Richardais). The manor is to the left on the way out of the village.*

La Korrigane ★★★

39, rue Le Pomellec - Saint-Servan
35400 Saint-Malo (Ille-et-Vilaine)
Tel. 99.81.65.85 - Fax 99.82.23.89 - M. Marchon

Rooms 10 with telephone, bath or shower, WC and TV. **Price** Single 300-400F, double 400-800F. **Meals** Breakfast 55F, served 8:00-10:00; brunch 120F. No restaurant. **Credit cards** All major. **Pets** Dogs allowed (+50F). **Facilities** Parking. **Nearby** Ramparts, castle and walled town of Saint-Malo, Chaussey islands, Cézembre island, Jersey, England, Saint-Samson cathedral in Dol-de-Bretagne. **Open** Feb 1 – Dec 31.

This is without doubt one of the most charming little hotels in France. It lies within a turn-of-the-century house which from the outside looks like an old holiday house turned into a family *pension*. The atmosphere is so comfortable that you feel quite at home, and the welcome is warm, discreet and courteous. Everything is restful, exquisitely tasteful and unpretentiously aesthetic. Each bedroom has its own color scheme, with perfectly harmonized colors and fabrics, and lovely furniture and paintings. Behind the house is a small garden where you can have breakfast or enjoy the sunshine. The large, book-lined living room is an invitation to relax as are the tea-room and bar. La Korrigane is better than a hotel: it is your own special *pied-à-terre* in Saint-Malo. *Le Saint Placide* is one of the best restaurants in this part of Saint Malo; note also the *Métairie de Beauregard*, *La Corderie* and *La Duchesse Anne* in the town.

How to get there *(Map 6): In the center of town, on N137 take the Saint-Servan road.*

184

L'Ascott Hôtel ★★★

35, rue du Chapitre - Saint-Servan
35400 Saint-Malo (Ille-et-Vilaine)
Tel. 99.81.89.93 - Fax 99.81.77.40 - M. and Mme Hardouin

Rooms 10 with telephone, bath, WC and TV. **Price** Single 350-400F, double 400-600F. **Meals** Breakfast 50F, served all morning. No restaurant. **Credit cards** Visa, Eurocard and MasterCard. **Pets** Dogs allowed. **Facilities** Parking. **Nearby** Ramparts, castles and walled town of Saint-Malo, Chaussey and Cézembre islands, Jersey, England, Saint-Samson cathedral in Dol-de-Bretagne. **Open** All year.

In an elegantly renovated 19th-century mansion surrounded by a tiny garden, this small hotel is a charming new address in Saint Malo. The hospitality and the atmosphere are very refined. No detail has been overlooked and everything has been carefully thought out. The bedrooms, which are named after racetracks (the hotel is located in front of the Saint Malo racetrack), are snug and quiet. The walls are covered with prettily colored fabrics, which are coordinated with the bedspreads and curtains. Some rooms have a small balcony where you can have breakfast. On the ground floor, there is the lounge, as appealing as the rest of the house, and which opens onto the small, lush garden where drinks are served. Near the hotel, you will find *Le Saint Placide*, one of the best restaurants in this part of Saint Malo; note also the *Métairie de Beauregard*, *La Corderie* and *La Duchesse Anne* in the town.

How to get there *(Map 6): Via N137, take the direction Saint-Servan, then Boulevard Douville and the second street to the left (signposted).*

Hôtel Village La Désirade ★★★

56360 Belle-Ile-en-Mer (Morbihan)
Tel. 97.31.70.70 - Fax 97.31.89.63
Mme Mulon

Rooms 26 with telephone, bath, WC and TV. **Price** Double 390-490F. **Meals** Breakfast 50-70F, served 8:00-11:00. No restaurant but evening meal. **Credit cards** All major. **Pets** Dogs allowed (+20F). **Facilities** Heated swimming pool, parking. **Nearby** Vauban fortifications, cave of l'Apothicairerie, port Donnan, les Aiguilles de Port-Coton – 18-hole Sauzon golf course in Belle-Ile-en-Mer. **Open** March 1 – Jan 6.

Facing the Côte Sauvage 1500 meters from the sea in a hamlet typical of Belle-Ile-en-Mer where Monet painted "Les Aiguilles de Port-Coton," La Désirade is composed of five small houses built around a heated swimming pool. Each of these has four bedrooms, giving a family or group of friends a place entirely to themselves. The decor is simple but in good taste, with brightly colored chintzes creating a cheerful effect all year round. In the morning a breakfast buffet is set out by the swimming pool, allowing everybody to keep his own pace. This is a relaxed place where privacy is respected. There is a restaurant adjoining the hotel.

How to get there *(Map 5): By car, take the Quiberon-Le Palais ferry; by air from Lorient by Finist-Air (20 min. flight); 7km southwest of Le Palais via D190 through Bangor; (the hotel is 2km from Bangor).*

Petit Hôtel Les Pougnots

Rue du Chemin-Neuf - Le Sauzon
56340 Belle-Ile-en-Mer (Morbihan)
Tel. 97.31.61.03 - Mme Guillouët

Rooms 5 with telephone, shower and WC. **Price** Single 450F, double 530F.
Meals Breakfast incl., served 8:30-12:00. No restaurant. **Credit cards** Not accepted.
Pets Dogs not allowed. **Nearby** Vauban fortifications, cave of l'Apothicairerie, Port
Donnan, les Aiguilles de Port-Coton – 18-hole Sauzon golf course in Belle-Ile-en-
Mer. **Open** All year.

The Hôtel des Pougnots is in Sauzon is in a little port surrounded
by whitewashed cottages with colored shutters. Set high up
in the village, this friendly small hotel looks rather like a chalet and
has only five bedrooms to offer. Inside, the decoration is simple,
even somewhat monastic in style, but tasteful and comfortable.
Breakfast can be served on a small balcony overlooking the harbor.
This delightful hotel, until recently known by word of mouth only,
it is superbly located on wild, romantic Belle-Ile with its ocean-
swept cliffs, gorse and heaths. In Le Sauzon, the *Roz-Avel* is a
friendly restaurant which serves delicious cuisine made with very
fresh ingredients.

*How to get there (Map 5): By car, take the Quiberon-Le Palais ferry; by
air from Lorient by Finist-Air (20 min. flight); 5km from Le Palais, at the
port of Le Sauzon.*

Domaine de Rochevilaine ★★★★

Pointe de Pen Lan
56190 Billiers-Muzillac (Morbihan)
Tel. 97.41.61.61 - Fax 97.41.44.85 - M. Cotillard

Rooms 26 and 1 suite with telephone, bath, WC and TV - Handicap access.
Price Double 750-1150F, suite 1400-1600F. **Meals** Breakfast 60F, served 7:00-
10:30; half board 780F, full board 1030F (per pers., 3 days min.). **Restaurant** Service
12:15-14:00 and 19:30-21:15; menu 250-375F (with lobster), also à la carte.
Specialties: Lobster and seafood. **Credit cards** All major. **Pets** Dogs allowed (+50F).
Facilities Heated swimming pool, parking. **Nearby** Rochefort-en-Terre, Morbihan
gulf– 18-hole Kerver golf course. **Open** March 16 – end Jan.

Built on the majestic site of the Pointe de Pen Lan, a former
lookout post, the Domaine de Rochevilaine looks like a small
village. Its several buildings follow the geographic contours of the
Point and face the sea, taking maximum advantage of the
breathtaking view over the Atlantic. This is a luxurious hotel whose
bedrooms are well located and spacious, elegantly classic and
comfortable. The most attractive are the ones with antique
decoration; the more modern rooms are unremarkable. Note also
the suite with a beautiful private terrace. The panoramic restaurant
offers one of the finest cuisines of Brittany, but it is a shame that
the tables are so close together. (Try the lobster menu). The
Rochevilaine is a superb hotel for a very special weekend.

How to get there *(Map 14): 20km southeast of Vannes via the express route
(towards Nantes) to Muzillac; then to Billiers and Pointe de Pen Lan.*

Logis Parc er Gréo ★★★

Mané-Guen-Le Gréo
56610 Arradon (Morbihan)
Tel. 97.44.73.03 - Fax 97.44.80.48 - M. Bermond

Rooms 12 with telephone, bath or shower, WC and TV - Wheelchair accessible. **Price** Single 203-250F, double 224-380F. **Meals** Breakfast 24-35F, served 8:00-12:30; half board 211-320F (per pers., 3 days min.). **Restaurant** Residents only, by reservation in the morning; service from 20:00; menus 75-95F. Specialties: Fish, seasonal cuisine. **Credit cards** All major. **Pets** Dogs allowed (+35F). **Facilities** Swimming pool. **Nearby** Morbihan Gulf, Ile de Gravinis, Ile aux Moines, Carnac – 18-hole Baden golf course. **Open** Feb 1 – Dec 31.

Even though the Logis Parc Er Gréo has been built recently, this small hotel is indeed one of "character and charm," beginning with the welcome you receive. The decoration combines shapes and colors beautifully, with antique furniture here and there, a boat model, or a painting done by an artist friend. Finally, there is the beautiful island setting itself. From the terrace as well as the bedrooms, you have a lovely view of the swimming pool, the fields and trees and, just behind them, one of the small inlets that so charmingly dot the Morbihan Gulf. The bedrooms, which look due south, are a model of taste and comfort. On the ground floor, the living room is also a dining room where excellent breakfasts and dinners are served. When it's sunny, meals are also served on the pretty flowery terrace. There is a small winter garden with luxuriant bougainvillia where you can enjoy a view of the countryside whether it rains or shines.

How to get there *(Map 14): 3km southwest of Vannes via D101 to Le Moustoir, on left, then 6ʰ turn on right.*

Hôtel de la Marine **

7, rue du Général-de-Gaulle
56590 Ile-de-Groix (Morbihan)
Tel. 97.86.80.05 - Fax 97.86.56.37 - Mme Hubert

Rooms 22 with telephone, bath or shower and WC. **Price** Single 186-205F, double 207-420F. **Meals** Breakfast 32F, served 8:00-10:00; half board 210-325F, full board 283-400F (per pers., 2 days min.). **Restaurant** Service 12:00-13:30, 19:30-21:30; menus 68-140F, also à la carte. Specialties: Feuilleté de Saint-Jacques, barbecue de poisson, marquise au chocolat. **Credit cards** Visa, Eurocard and MasterCard. **Pets** Dogs allowed (+18F). **Facilities** Parking. **Nearby** Museum in Groix, L'Enfer point, Saint-Nicolas seaport, Pen-Mer. **Open** Feb 1 – Dec 31.

This is a real find, because many of the hotels on the islands are neglected and seem to count on their isolation (and the necessity of catching the last boat) to keep their clientele. There is none of that attitude here. Mme Hubert, the owner, has lovingly designed and arranged this hotel, and we are certain that you will appreciate her taste. The reception room has pretty, old-fashioned furniture; the dining room, where you can eat very well at reasonable prices, has attractive colored table linens; on the fireplace and the shelves is a collection of pottery; in a corner, a shell-encrusted clock is the only reminder of the passage of time. The bedrooms are simple, painted white and brightened with colored curtains and bedspreads. Ask for those facing the sea (especially No. 1), but all are very pleasant and comfortable. Outside in a paved garden, drinks are served in the shade of the oldest tree on the island. An unreservedly kind welcome awaits you here.

How to get there *(Map 5): boat from Lorient (45 min., tel. 97.21.03.97).*

Le San Francisco ★★

56780 Ile aux Moines (Morbihan)
Tel. 97.26.31.52 – Fax 97.26.35.59
M. Vérien

Rooms 8 with telephone, bath or shower, WC and TV. **Price** Double 270-510F.
Meals Breakfast 40-55F, served 8:00-9:30; half board 255-375F (per pers.).
Restaurant Closed Thursday in winter. Service 12:00-14:00, 19:00-20:30; menu 125-225F, also à la carte. Specialties: Fish and shellfish, sauté de langoustines sauce crustacés, mousse de saumon sur coulis de courgettes. **Credit cards** Amex, Visa, Eurocard and MasterCard. **Pets** Dogs allowed (+30F). **Nearby** Morbihan Gulf – 18-hole La Bretesche golf course. **Open** All year.

The San Francisco enjoys the most beautiful location on the island: facing the port, with the dramatic, jagged coast of the Gulf of Morbihan in the distance. Today a spot that tourists love, the small hotel nevertheless is beautifully quiet. The ambience is refined but not stiff, and the overall decoration is very pleasant. All the rooms are quiet, comfortable and brightened with elegant color schemes. Reserve in advance and ask for a room with a view (superb) over the sea. One room has a small terrace facing the port. There is a pleasant reception area, a charming dining room and, above all, as soon as it's fine weather, you can relax on a delicious terrace where you can have meals and admire the magnificent view. You will always be warmly welcomed to this charming hotel on "Monks' Island".

How to get there *(Map 14): 14km south of Vannes; on Autoroute E60, exit Vannes-Ouest; then follow signs for Ile aux Moines to boat landing. 5 min. crossing; in winter, 7 AM to 8 PM; in summer, 7 AM to 10 PM.*

Au Vieux Chêne **

Kerault
56690 Landévant (Morbihan)
Tel. 97.56.90.01 – M. and Mme Bouteloup

Rooms 7 with telephone (3 with bath, 2 with shower and 3 with WC). **Price** Single and Double 140-220F. **Meals** Breakfast 25F, served until 10:20; half board 265-345F, full board 365-445F. **Restaurant** Closed Tuesday evening and Wednesday in low season. Service 12:15-14:00, 19:15-21:30; menus 70-165F, also à la carte. Specialties: Salade de crevettes tiède au vinaigre de framboise, saumon fumé maison, escargots en croûte, caramel de crème, fondant au chocolat. **Credit cards** All major. **Pets** Dogs allowed (+20F). **Facilities** Parking. **Nearby** Ile de Groix, Hennebont, Citadel of Port-Louis – 18-hole Ploemem golf course. **Open** All year (closed Tuesday evening and Wednesday in low season).

In a small park planted with trees which are more than 300 years old, set between the countryside and the spectacular coastline of the Morbihan, the Vieux Chêne offers seven comfortable rooms where you can enjoy the peace, quiet and lush green beauty of the spot. While the decoration of the bedrooms is simple, and not all have bathrooms, the cuisine is outstanding in both originality and finesse. In the atmosphere of a country inn, the owners will greet you like a member of their family; they do their job with love and professionalism, and you will reap the benefits of their devotion. This is very good quality for the price, and every effort is made so that children are neither a burden for their parents nor a nuisance for other guests. We're sure you will love "The Old Oak" for its simplicity and courtesy.

How to get there *(Map 5): 20km southeast of Lorient via N165, exit Landevant interchange; then follow signs.*

Moulin de Lesnehué **

Lesnevé
56890 Saint-Avé (Morbihan)
Tel. 97.60.77.77 - Mme Cheval

Rooms 12 with telephone, bath or shower and WC. **Price** Single 170F, double 230-250F. **Meals** Breakfast 30F, served 8:00-10:00. No restaurant but "crêperie". **Credit cards** All major. **Pets** Dogs allowed. **Facilities** Parking. **Nearby** Chapel of Notre-Dame-du-Loc in Saint-Avé, ramparts and Saint-Pierre cathedral in Vannes, Conleau peninsula, fortress of Largoët, château du Plessis-Jossot – 18-hole Kerver golf course in Saint-Gildas de Rhuys.**Open** Jan 15 – Dec 15.

This 15th–century stone mill has a lovely location in the middle of the countryside on the banks of a stream. The bedrooms are arranged in the two buildings which form the hotel. All of them are simple and modern, with contemporary furnishings, but charming and comfortable. The hotel has no restaurant, but there is a *crêperie* in one of the buildings. Ferns, flowers, the sound of water and birdsong provide nature's backdrop to this lovely welcoming place.

How to get there *(Map 14): 5km north of Vannes via D126; turn right on the way out of the village of Lesnehué.*

Hôtel de Kerlon ⋆⋆

56680 Plouhinec (Morbihan)
Tel. 97.36.77.03 - Fax 97.85.81.14
M. and Mme Coëffic

Rooms 16 with telephone and WC, (15 with bath or shower and 15 with TV).
Price Single 240-265F, double 270-300F. **Meals** Breakfast 35F, served 8:00-10:00;
half board 260-280F (per pers.). **Restaurant** Service 19:30-21:00; menus 75-150F,
also à la carte. Specialties: Fish, seafood. **Credit cards** Visa, Eurocard and
MasterCard. **Pets** Small dogs allowed (+15F). **Facilities** Parking. **Nearby** Quiberon,
Morbihan Gulf, île de Groix, Port-Louis – 18-hole Queven golf course, 18-hole
Ploemeur-Océan golf course in Saint-Jude. **Open** March 16 – Oct 31.

This hotel is set in the middle of the countryside, 5km from the
sea and midway between Lorient and Carnac. It is a farmhouse
which has been completely renovated. The beams, exposed
stonework and two fireplaces give a rustic air to the dining room,
which has a small terrace where drinks are served or where you
can relax beside the garden. The bedrooms are plainly decorated
and quiet. Being close to the beaches and resorts does not spoil this
hotel's tranquil, rural atmosphere, and you can enjoy biking
everywhere.

How to get there *(Map 5): 30km southeast of Lorient. Leave N165 at
Hennebont, Carnac-Quiberon-Port-Louis exit, then follow signs Carnac-
Quiberon.*

Hostellerie Les Ajoncs d'Or ★★

Kerbachique
56340 Plouharnel (Morbihan)
Tel. 97.52.32.02 - Fax 97.52.40.36 - Mme Le Maguer

Rooms 20 with telephone, bath or shower and WC. **Price** Double 280-340F, suite 600F. **Meals** Breakfast 35F, served 8:00-9:30; half board 280-340F (per pers.). **Restaurant** Service 19:00-21:30; menus 96-145F, also à la carte. Specialties: Regional cooking, seafood. **Credit cards** Visa, Eurocard and MasterCard. **Pets** Small dogs allowed (fee) **Facilities** Parking. **Nearby** Menhirs of Carnac and Erdeven, church in Plouhinec, Belle-Ile – 18-hole Saint-Laurent-Ploëmel golf course. **Open** March – Nov 2.

Les Ajoncs d'Or is a pink granite Breton farmhouse made up of three adjoining buildings and situated outside the village. On the ground floor, a large restaurant with a lovely fireplace happily combines beams, exposed stonework, flowered curtains and pictures. Next door is another very pleasant room for breakfasts. The bedrooms are simple and comfortable. We recommend those above the restaurant, which are well renovated, light and cheerful. Thanks to the hostess, the hotel has a family atmosphere. And the warmth of the welcome makes Les Ajoncs d'Or a very special place to stay.

How to get there *(Map 5): 52km of Lorient via N165 to Auray, then D768 and D781 (between Carnac and Plouharnel).*

Domaine de Bodeuc ★★★

Nivillac
56130 La Roche-Bernard (Morbihan)
Tel. 99.90.89.63 - Fax 99.90.90.32 – M. and Mme Grandpierre

Rooms 8 with telephone, bath or shower, WC and TV - Wheelchair access; elevator. **Price** Double 500F, 200F (1 small room for 1 pers.). **Meals** Breakfast 45F, served 8:00-12:30. **Restaurant** Residents only, by reservation. Service 19:00-21:00; menu 150F. **Credit cards** Amex, Visa, Eurocard and MasterCard. **Pets** Dogs allowed. **Facilities** Swimming pool, Parking. **Nearby** La Baule, tour of La Brière and the Guérande marshes, Morbihan Gulf– 18-hole La Bretesche golf course. **Open** All Year.

Charming Monsieur and Madame Grandpierre will welcome you to this pretty hotel, which is hidden in the Breton countryside but is only 20 minutes from the beach. The lovely little manor house stands in a large 37-acre park, its façade so covered with ivy that you can see only the white shutters and slate roof. The eight bedrooms are spacious, each with its own style, and all are decorated with antique furniture and pretty fabrics. The bathrooms, which have been tiled by a specialized craftsman, are comfortable and bright. As a final touch, a basket of fruit is placed in your bedroom. On the ground floor, there is a large lounge where drinks and coffee are served, and downstairs, there is a billiard table for guests. If you wish, Monsieur Grandpierre will make you dinner of simple but delicious family dishes. He also makes his own jams, which are served with hot croissants for breakfast.

How to get there (Map 14): 40km south of Vannes via E60. At La Roche-Bernard, turn towards Redon for 5km, then follow the signs.

Auberge du Moulin de Chaméron ★★★

18210 Bannegon (Cher)
Tel. 48.61.83.80 - Fax 48.61.84.92
M. Candore

Rooms 13 with telephone, bath or shower, WC and TV. **Price** Single 330F, double 480F, suite 670F. **Meals** Breakfast 50F, served 7:30-10:00. **Restaurant** Service 12:15-14:00, 19:30-21:00; menus 145-195F, also à la carte. Specialties: Seasonal cooking. **Credit cards** Amex, Visa, Eurocard and MasterCard. **Pets** Dogs allowed (+30F). **Facilities** Swimming pool, parking. **Nearby** Basilica and château of Châteauneuf-sur-Cher, church of Saint-Amand-Montrond, abbey of Noirlac, châteaux of Meillant and Ainay-le-Vieil, Bourges – 18-hole Val-de-Cher golf course in Montluçon. **Open** March 1 – Nov 15. (closed Tuesday in low season).

Renovated about 20 years ago, this 18th-century mill lies deep in the countryside. The old mill machinery has been kept intact in the middle of the building and a museum displays a collection of tools and objects used by millers in the past. The bedrooms are very pleasant and comfortable, with antique or reproduction furniture. We particularly liked those on the ground floor with a private terrace where you can have breakfast. In the summer, lunch and dinner are served in the garden by the mill-pond, but if the weather is discouraging meals are served in a delightful, intimate dining room with a fireplace. The cuisine is excellent and the people are charming.

How to get there (Map 17): 42km southeast of Bourges via N76 towards Moulins, then D953 and D41.

La Solognote **

18410 Brinon–sur–Sauldre (Cher)
Tel. 48.58.50.29 – Fax 48.58.56.00
M. and Mme Girard

Rooms 13 with telephone, bath or shower, WC and TV. **Price** Double 290-400F, suite 450F. **Meals** Breakfast 55F; half board 800-900F (per 2 pers., 3 days min.). **Restaurant** Service 12:30-14:00, 19:30-20:30; menus 160-330F, also a la carte. Specialties: Gratin de langoustines et grenouilles aux bettes, tarte fine aux pommes et au foie gras, game in season. **Credit cards** Visa, Eurocard and MasterCard. **Pets** Dogs not allowed. **Facilities** Parking. **Nearby** Orléans Cathedral, La Source flower gardens in Olivet, châteaux on the Jacques-Coeur road, Aubigny-sur-Nère, the Berry from La Chapelle d'Angillon to Saint-Martin-d'Auxigny, Sancerre – 18-hole Sully golf course in Viglains, 18-hole Marcilly golf course. **Open** March 16 – Feb 14 (closed May 9 – 18, Sept 12 – 21; Tuesday and Wednesday noon in July, Aug).

This pink brick inn, located in a small village in Sologne just fifteen minutes from the National Route 20, is famous for its excellent cuisine and beautiful rooms. The restaurant is warm, elegant, and very charming. The rooms are lovely, each one decorated in a different style, with one or two antique pieces, beautiful fabrics, and polished wooden floors. They are comfortable and very quiet, their bathrooms are well equipped, and many look out on a small flower garden. There are apartments available for families. M. and Mme. Girard's gracious welcome and commitment to quality have made this one of our favorite hotels in France.

How to get there *(Map 17): 60km southeast of Orléans via N20 to Lamotte-Beuvron, then D923 towards Aubigny-sur-Nère.*

Auberge des Meaulnes ★★★

Route de Vierzon
18330 Nançay (Cher)
Tel. 48.51.81.15 – Fax 48.51.84.58 – M. and Mme Bisson

Rooms 10 with telephone, bath or shower, WC, TV and minibar. **Price** Singles 450F, double 500F. **Meals** Breakfast 50F. **Restaurant** Service 12:00-14:00, 19:30-21:30; menus 130-180F, also à la carte. Specialties: Foie gras frais de canard, brouillade d'écrevisses, ris de veau aux morilles, pigeon au miel d'acacias, tarte Tatin. **Credit cards** All major. **Pets** Dogs allowed. **Facilities** Parking. **Nearby** Imaginary Museum of Le Grand Meaulnes (souvenirs of Alain Fournier) and the Villâtre barn in Nançay; Bourges, Aubigny-sur-Nère, Sancerre – 9-hole Meaulnes golf course. **Open** All year (closed Tuesday).

Recently taken over by a new owner and redecorated, the delightful Auberge des Meaulnes has several very comfortable rooms. Located in the main building as well as in a charming small house, they are attractively decorated with antique furniture and pretty objects. On the main floor the inviting gourmet restaurant, specializing in succulent regional dishes, is decorated with beautiful furniture, colorful *faïences* and a large fireplace, all combining to create an elegant, traditional ambiance: The auberge is the perfect reflection of this superb region of the Loire hunt country, known for its excellent quality of life. You will find a charming terrace in the small garden outside where it's delightful to read or have drinks in the shade of a large willow. The hospitality at the auberge is very warm.

How to get there *(Map 17): 36km north of Bourges. On A71, exit Salbris, then D944.*

Château de la Beuvrière ★★

18100 Saint-Hilaire-de-Court (Cher)
Tel. 48.75.14.63 - Fax 48.75.47.62
M. and Mme de Brach

Rooms 15 with telephone, bath or shower and WC (4 with minibar). **Price** Single 270F, double 340-460F, duplex 450F, suite 580F. **Meals** Breakfast 38F, served 7:30-10:00. **Restaurant** Closed Sunday evening and Monday. Service 12:00-14:00, 19:30-21:00; menus 140-196F, gastronomic menu 250F, also à la carte. Specialties: Saumon fumé maison, foie gras frais maison, sandre braisé au beurre de truffes, ris de veau braisé à l'orange. **Credit cards** All major. **Pets** Dogs allowed. **Facilities** Swimming pool, tennis, parking. **Nearby** Saint-Etienne cathedral, hôtel Jacques-Coeur in Bourges, Aubigny-sur-Nère – 18-hole La Picardière golf course, 18-hole Vierzon golf course. **Open** March 16 – Dec 14 (closed Sunday evening).

The château has kept its 2562-acre estate intact since the Middle Ages. Inherited by the present owners, it is a very charming hotel today. The family furniture is authentic and dates from the 15th to the 19th-century – the overall effect is one of excellent quality arranged with perfect taste. Lovely and very well kept, the bedrooms overlook the grounds. Those on the *premier étage* are almost sumptuous, and if their bathrooms are a bit on the small side this allows room for the wood-panelled bed alcoves. The *deuxième étage* bedrooms have original beams and some have a mezzanine. You will dine sitting on Empire armchairs at a beautifully laid table. The food is as excellent as the decor, and the welcome is informal and cordial.

How to get there *(Map 17): 39km northwest of Bourges via A71, Vierzon-Nord exit, then N20 towards Châteauroux.*

Hostellerie Saint-Jacques ★★★

Place du Marché-aux-Œufs
28220 Cloyes-sur-le-Loir (Eure-et-Loir)
Tel. 37.98.40.08 – Fax 37.98.32.63 – M. Thureau

Rooms 22 with telephone, bath or shower, WC and TV. **Price** Single and double 320-480F, suite 680F. **Meals** Breakfast 50F, served 8:00-10:30; half board 420F, full board 570F (per pers.). **Restaurant** Service 12:00-13:30, 19:30-21:00; menus 169F. Specialties: Fricassée de poulet fermier à l'ail doux, poêlée de rascasse au romarin. **Credit cards** Visa, Eurocard and MasterCard. **Pets** Dogs allowed. **Facilities** Boats, table tennis, parking. **Nearby** Chapel of Yrou at Châteaudun, Vendôme, valley of the Loir (Montoire-sur-le-Loir, Lavardin, Troo, manoir de la Possonnière) – 9-hole la Bosse golf course in Oucques. **Open** March 1 – Nov 20.

Located on the village square, l'Hostellerie Saint-Jacques is an old 16th-century coaching inn. Here you may go boating on the Loir, which crosses the shady 1 1/2-acre gardens. The 20 bedrooms have been completely modernized (perhaps too much so) and redecorated. The tasteful and intimate dining room overlooks the garden. The house has a reputation for good food, and in summer you can enjoy the double pleasure of eating an excellent lunch outside under the trees in beautiful surroundings. Note also the *Petit Bistrot,* which serves excellent, reasonably priced meals.

How to get there *(Map 16): 53km north of Blois via D957 to Vendôme, then N10 (going north) to Cloyes-sur-le-Loir.*

Château du Vivier

Le Vivier
36200 Argenton-sur-Creuse (Indre)
Tel. 54.24.22.99 - Fax 54.01.12.87 - M. and Mme Longin

Rooms 9 with telephone, bath, WC and TV. **Price** Single and double 300-580F.
Meals Breakfast 65F, served until 12:00; half board 500-650F; full board 650-900F
(per pers., 3 days min.). **Restaurant** Service 12:00-14:00, 19:00-23:00; menus 135-
380F, also à la carte. Specialties: Fish, foie gras, rare mushrooms. **Credit cards** All
major. **Pets** Dogs allowed (+60F). **Facilities** Parking. **Nearby** Pont-Vieux and Saint-
Benoît chapel in Argenton, château de Nohant-Vic, Georges Sand museum in La
Châtre, abbey church of Fontgombault – 18-hole Dryades and Pouligny-Notre-Dame
golf courses. **Open** All year.

There is a romantic air about this small château, built in the
17th-century and renovated in the early 19th. Anxious to keep
the family character of the place and to welcome their guests as
friends, M. and Mme Longin have decorated it delightfully. In the
dining room there is antique furniture, paintings, old photographs,
curios and dried-flower arrangements. The *premier étage* bedrooms
are large, with lovely materials used as wall or bed-hangings, as
well as antique furniture. On the *deuxième étage* the bedrooms are
smaller but very charming, with long windows reaching to the
floor. In good weather tables are set outside under the big trees.
There you can have tea, read Proust or lose yourself in the maze
of greenery in the garden.

How to get there *(Map 16): 30km southwest of Châteauroux, on the way
out of Argenton-sur-Creuse, at "Le Vivier."*

Domaine de l'Etape ★★★

Route de Bélâbre
36300 Le Blanc (Indre)
Tel. 54.37.18.02 – Mme Seiller

Rooms 35 with telephone, bath or shower and WC (20 with TV). **Price** Single 210-380F, double 220-430F. **Meals** Breakfast 45F, served 7:00-11:00. **Restaurant** Residents only. Service 19:30-21:30; menus 125-135F, also à la carte. Specialties: Coq en barbouille, pâté berrichon. **Credit cards** Visa, Eurocard and MasterCard. **Pets** Dogs allowed. **Facilities** Riding, fishing, hunting, boating, parking. **Nearby** Museum of local history in Le Blanc, châteaux of Azay-le-Ferron, le Guillaume and le Bouchet, Benedictine abbey of Fontgombault. **Open** All year.

You will be delighted by the kind welcome in this 19th-century house standing in a 320-acre estate. Everything is charming and a bit old-fashioned. The lounge, with Louis Philippe furniture, is ideal for reading or watching television. The pale wood-panelled dining room is often brightened by an open fire. There is a small garden terrace with a bar. The bedrooms are simple, comfortable, and all different. Country-lovers will enjoy the bedrooms in the farmhouse, which are rustic but also comfortable. The farm provides fresh produce for the kitchen. Fishermen can try their luck in the lake and horse lovers can go riding and inspect the foals in the fields.

How to get there *(Map 16): 59km west of Châteauroux via N20 and N151 to Le Blanc, then D10 towards Bélâbre.*

Château de Bouesse

36200 Bouesse (Indre)
Tel. 54.25.12.20 - Fax 54. 25.12.30
M. and Mme Courtot-Atterton

Rooms 11 with telephone, bath or shower and WC. **Price** Single 300-350F, double 380-480F, suite 720F. **Meals** Breakfast 55F, served 8:00-10:00; half board 395-455F (per pers., 3 days min.). **Restaurant** Service 12:00-14:00, 19:30-21:30; menu 145F, also à la carte. Specialties: Fish, foie gras, rognons de veau à l'ancienne, scallops. **Credit cards** Amex, Visa, Eurocard and MasterCard. **Pets** Dogs not allowed. **Facilities** Parking. **Nearby** Pont-Vieux and Saint-Benoît chapel in Argenton, château de Nohant-Vic, Georges Sand museum in La Châtre, abbey church of Fontgombault – 18-hole Dryades and Pouligny-Notre-Dame golf courses. **Open** Feb 1 – Dec 31 (closed Monday in low season).

M onsieur and Mme Courtot-Atterton love history and have focused their enthusiasm on the restoration of this superb 13th- and 15th-century château. The bedrooms' names refer to the château's history: *Jeanne d'Arc, Raoul VI de Gaucourt*, etc. The bedrooms are all very large, and often have stone fireplaces bearing coats of arms. Some rooms have been redecorated recently in the style of the Middle Ages, using furniture specially made for the château. Others are in the romantic style of the English 19th century. The hotel is totally comfortable and peaceful. The view cannot have changed for centuries. We particularly admired the dining room, which has pale blue and grey panelling and a 17th-century painting on the ceiling. In summer an excellent breakfast is served outside on the terrace.

How to get there *(Map 17): 33km south of Châteauroux, on D927 between Argenton-sur-Creuse and La Châtre.*

Château de la Vallée Bleue ★★★

Saint-Chartier
36400 La Châtre (Indre)
Tel. 54.31.01.91 - Fax 54.31.04.48 - M. Gasquet

Rooms 13 with telephone, bath or shower, WC, TV and minibar. **Price** Single 195-375F, double 315-550F. **Meals** Breakfast 47F; half board 400-450F, full board 500-550F (per pers., 3 days min.). **Restaurant** Service 12:00-13:30, 19:30-21:00; menus 125-325F, also à la carte. Specialties: Home-smoked produce, tartare de langoustines et de crabe, agneau aux pignons de pin et jus anisé, croustillants aux poires épicées. **Credit cards** Visa, Eurocard and MasterCard. **Pets** Dogs allowed (+50F). **Facilities** Swimming pool, health center, parking. **Nearby** Georges Sand museum in La Châtre, château des Maître-Sonneurs in Saint-Chartier, château de Nohant-Vic – 18-hole Dryades golf course. **Open** March – Jan (closed Sunday evening and Monday Oct – March).

The ghosts of George Sand and Chopin float over this small château, which was built by that couple's doctor in a 10-acre park. The entrance hall is lovely, and M. and Mme Gasquet are very welcoming. Everywhere there are pictures and memorabilia to do with the writer and the musician. The bedrooms are identified by small glass plaques with reproduction signatures of George Sand's artist friends. The bedrooms are comfortable, stylishly furnished and pleasantly decorated with Laura Ashley papers and fabrics, and they have lovely views over the park and the countryside. The English-style lounge is warm and a glass of old cognac or liqueur beside the fire is a pleasure. The list of *eaux-de-vie* is amazing. Off the lounge there are two very attractive dining rooms opening onto the park with its two-hundred-year-old oak tree. The cuisine is delicious.

How to get there (Map 17): 27km southeast of Châteauroux via D943 to Saint-Chartier. The hotel is outside the village on the Verneuil road.

Hôtel du Bon Laboureur et du Château ★★★

6, rue du Docteur Bretonneau
37150 Chenonceaux (Indre-et-Loire)
Tel. 47.23.90.02 - Fax 47.23.82.01 - M. Jeudi

Rooms 36 with telephone, bath or shower and WC (18 with TV). **Price** Single 280-500F, double 320-600F, suite 1000F. **Meals** Breakfast 45F, served 7:30-10:30; half board 400-650F. **Restaurant** Service 12:00-14:00, 19:30-21:30; menus 175-300F, also à la carte. Specialties: Tartare de saumon, sole farcie au vouvray, magret de canard au bourgueil, croustillant d'agneau, millefeuilles sablé aux fraises. **Credit cards** All major. **Pets** Dogs allowed. **Facilities** Swimming pool, parking. **Nearby** Château de Chenonceaux, Loire Valley (châteaux de la Loire), Montlouis-sur-Loire via the Cher Valley– 18-hole Touraine golf course in Ballan-Miré. **Open** Dec 16 – Nov 14 and Feb 16 – Jan 1.

The hotel is located in the middle of the village near the château. Made up of various buildings on both sides of the road, and with gardens and a swimming pool, this property has been a hotel for many generations. The pleasant bedrooms are in traditional style; the ones in the small building overlooking the inner courtyard are very charming and merit their higher prices. There are three very comfortable living rooms: the first is English-style, the other two are more contemporary with deep armchairs and soft color schemes. The dining room is light and pleasant, and the cuisine has been repeatedly praised in the visitors' book. The welcome is warm.

How to get there *(Map 16): 35km southeast of Tours; on A10 Tours exit, then via D410, or N76 to Bléré, then D40 to Chenonceaux; (the hotel is in the center of the town).*

Hostellerie du Château de l'Isle ★★

Civray-en-Touraine
37150 Chenonceaux (Indre-et-Loire)
Tel. 47 23 80 09 - Fax 47 23 82 91 - M. Gandon

Rooms 10 with telephone, bath or shower, WC and minibar (4 with TV). **Price** Single and double 270-400F, suite 500F. **Meals** Breakfast 45F, served 8:15-11:00; half board 350F, full board 448F (per pers.). **Restaurant** Service 12:00-14:00, 19:30-21:00; menus 98F (lunch), 140-190F, also à la carte. Specialties: Regional cuisine. **Credit cards** Amex, Visa, Eurocard and MasterCard. **Pets** Dogs allowed. **Facilities** Parking. **Nearby** Loire Valley (châteaux de la Loire), Château de Chenonceaux, Montlouis-sur-Loire via the Cher Valley – 18-hole Touraine golf course in Ballan-Miré. **Open** Dec 12 – Nov 14.

Monsieur Gandon describes his small Hostellerie du Château de l'Isle as "the friends' house"; given his hospitality and the relaxed atmosphere here, the description is fully justified. The bedrooms are all different, simple, comfortable and quite pretty, offering you a pleasant view out over the garden and the gentle countryside of the Loire Valley in the distance. There are two inviting rooms on the garden, whose amenities are more basic but which have a private terrace. A ravishing double-spiral wooden staircase leads to the other rooms. On the main floor, you will find a series of very charming small dining rooms, where there is often a cracking fire in the fireplace. Traditional old furniture and paintings provide the décor for the excellent meals here: good, traditional Loire Valley cuisine made with fresh ingredients from the region. This is truly a hotel of character and charm on the doorstep of exquisite Chenonceaux.

How to get there *(Map 16): 35km southeast of Tours. On A10, Tours exit, then D 140 and D 40 to Civray-en-Touraine.*

Hôtel Diderot ★★

4, rue Buffon
37500 Chinon (Indre-et-Loire)
Tel. 47.93.18.87 - Fax 47.93.37.10 - M. Kazamias

Rooms 28 (4 in annex) with telephone, bath or shower and WC (TV on request).
Price Single 225-300F, double 280-400F. **Meals** Breakfast 40F, served 7:30-10:00.
No restaurant. **Credit cards** All major. **Pets** Dogs not allowed. **Facilities** Parking.
Nearby Château de Chinon, château d'Ussé, château d'Azay-le-Rideau, Saché,
Richelieu, Rabelais country (La Devinière), château du Coudray-Montpensier, Lerné,
château de la Roche-Clermanet – 18-hole Touraine golf course in Ballan-Miré.
Open Jan 15 – Dec 15.

Its position close to the Place Jeanne D'Arc in the center of
Chinon does not spoil the appeal or the tranquillity of this hotel.
On the contrary, the modest size of this 18th-century building
gives visitors the impression of being in a particularly pleasing
private house. There is no restaurant, but a delicious breakfast with
a selection of home made jams is served in front of a 15th-century
fireplace. For fine dining, try l'*Hostellerie Gargantua* and *Au Plaisir
Gourmand.*

How to get there *(Map 16): 48km southwest of Tours via D751. Go along
the Vienne to the Place Jeanne-d'Arc; on the corner of the Rue Diderot.*

Hôtel George Sand ★★★

39, rue Quintefol
37600 Loches (Indre-et-Loire)
Tel. 47.59.39.74 - Fax 47.91.55.75 - M. Loiseau

Rooms 20 with telephone, bath or shower, WC and TV. **Price** Single 200-320F, double 250-450F. **Meals** Breakfast 35F, served 7:00-9:30; half board 260-320F, full board 360-415F (per pers., 3 days min.). **Restaurant** Service 12:00-14:00, 19:30-21:30; menus 85-245F, also à la carte. Specialties: Effeuillé de noix de Saint-Jacques au parfum de cidre, suprême de turbot au pain d'épice. **Credit cards** Visa, Eurocard and MasterCard. **Pets** Dogs allowed (+25F). **Nearby** Château and keep of Loches, Carthusian monastery of Le Liget in the Loches forest, abbey church of Beaulieu-les-Loches, Montrésor, Indre valley, Cormery, Montbazon, Monts, Saché –18-hole Touraine golf course in Ballan-Miré. **Open** All year.

Standing at the foot of the impressive Château de Loches, this ancient 15th-century house once marked the boundary of the medieval town. M. Loiseau will welcome you with great kindness. Entering from the street you will be pleasantly surprised to find that the dining room and its large terrace are on the edge of the river Indre, which at this point forms a large waterfall. The hotel is decorated in a simple countrified style, and is especially recommended for families, as each of the large *premier étage* bedrooms contains several comfortable beds. Quite a few have stone fireplaces and beamed ceilings. Those on the *deuxième étage* are smaller; the best overlook the river and the public gardens on the opposite bank. Some stone arches and a beautiful spiral staircase are reminders of the hotel's age.

How to get there *(Map 16): 42km southeast of Tours via N143.*

Domaine de la Tortinière ★★★

Route de Ballan-Miré - Les Gués de Veigné
37250 Montbazon-en-Touraine (Indre-et-Loire)
Tel. 47.26.00.19 - Fax 47.65.95.70
Mme Olivereau-Capron and M. Olivereau

Rooms 21 (1 with air-conditioning) with telephone, bath, WC and TV. **Price** Double 435-880F, suite 990-1460F. **Meals** Breakfast 65F, served 8:00-11:00; half board 525-860F (per pers., 3 days min.). **Restaurant** Service 12:15-13:45, 19:30-21:00; menus 195-350F, also à la carte. Specialties: Chausson d'asperges et de foie gras truffé, civet de homard et dorade au bourgueil, chibouste aux framboises et citron vert. **Credit cards** Visa, Eurocard and MasterCard. **Pets** Dogs not allowed. **Facilities** Swimming pool, tennis, boat, mountain bikes on request, parking. **Nearby** Keep of Fouques Nerra in Montbazon, Indre valley, Cormery, Monts, Saché, Tours cathedral, château d'Azay-le-Rideau – 18-hole Touraine golf course in Ballan-Miré. **Open** March 1 – Dec 19.

A Renaissance-style chateau built in 1861, the Tortinière is set in a 37-acre park dominating the Indre valley, although it is only 10km from Tours. The two restaurants, the salon and most of the bedrooms are in the chateau. The bedrooms are all different, superbly decorated, and very comfortable; the ones in old pavilions outside are as beautiful and recommendable as those in the chateau. Decorated in a floral, "winter garden" style, the restaurant is beautiful and the cuisine is very good. In autumn, the park is carpeted with cyclamen, and in good weather you can still enjoy the heated swimming pool.

How to get there *(Map 16): 10km south of Tours via A10, Nr. 14 exit, then N10 towards Montbazon; via route of Ballan-Miré it's at Les Gués de Veigné.*

Château de la Bourdaisière

25, rue de la Bourdaisière
37270 Montlouis-sur-Loire (Indre-et-Loire)
Tel. 47.45.16.31 - Fax 47.45.09.11 - M. de Broglie

Rooms 13 (2 suites) with bath or shower and WC (TV on request) - Elevator.
Price Double 500-1100F, suite 750-1050F. **Meals** Breakfast 50F. No restaurant.
Credit cards Visa, Eurocard and MasterCard. **Pets** Dogs allowed. **Facilities** Heated
swimming pool, tennis, riding, parking. **Nearby** Tours, grange de Meslay, Vouvray
wine cellars, Loire valley (châteaux de la Loire) — 18-hole Touraine golf course in
Ballan-Miré. **Open** Feb 15 – Jan 15.

Built on the foundations of a 14th-century citadel by order of
François I, the Château de la Bourdaisière was a gift from the
king to his mistress, Marie Gaudin. Less than a century later, it was
the birthplace of the beautiful Gabrielle d'Estrée, with whom Henri
IV fell in love. It is no wonder, therefore, that the hotel's bedrooms
and two suites are named after women who had an influence on
French history. The bedrooms are superb: large and all different,
their decoration is bright and colorful while respecting the age of
the building. Throughout the house there is a wealth of period
furniture, with some truly sumptuous pieces in the lounge. This
room is dedicated to the Princesse de Broglie, whose young
descendants will welcome you like old friends. The hotel has
splendid and extensive grounds, with formal gardens, a kitchen
garden, an arboretum, a rose garden and an animal park. For
restaurants, we recommend: *Jean Bardet* (one of France's top chefs),
Le Canotier, Les Tuffeaux in Tours; and *L'Oubliette* in Rochecorbon.

How to get there *(Map 16): 11km east of Tours via D152.*

Hostellerie Les Perce-Neige ★★

37210 Vernou-sur-Brenne (Indre-et-Loire)
Tel. 47 52 10 04 – Fax 47 52 19 08
Mme Chemin

Rooms 15 with telephone, bath or shower (14 with WC) and TV. **Price** Double 200-280F. **Meals** Breakfast 30F, served 7:30-10:00; half board 410F, full board 630F (2 pers., 3 days min.). **Restaurant** Service 12:00-14:00, 19:30-22:00; menus 97-139F, also à la carte. Specialties: Traditional cuisine. **Credit cards** Amex, Visa, Eurocard and MasterCard. **Pets** Dogs allowed. **Facilities** Parking. **Nearby** Tours, grange de Meslay, Vouvray wine cellars, Loire valley (châteaux de la Loire) – 18-hole Touraine golf course in Ballan-Miré. **Open** All year.

Now that the management has changed, we are happy to be able to put the Perce-Neige ("Snow Drops") back in this guide because the little hotel is truly one of character and charm. Located in a lovely small winegrowing village in the Loire Valley, it is comfortable and tastefully decorated. On the ground floor, there is a small lounge decorated in warm tones, an inviting bar and two charming dining rooms (the small non-smoking dining room is the prettiest). Apart from two bedrooms which are located in an adjacent building and which give directly onto the park, the others are upstairs in the hotel. Comfortable and charming, many have retro furniture which is painted in the dominant color of the room. In summer, you can have dinner in the park, which is shaded with beautiful trees: a veritable invitation to a romantic stroll before or after dinner. Last but not least, the hospitality is delightful.

How to get there *(Map 16): 11km east of Tours, direction Amboise-Blois; in Vouvray, take direction Vernou.*

La Croix Blanche ★★★

41600 Chaumont-sur-Tharonne (Loir-et-Cher)
Tel. 54 88 55 12- Fax 54 88 60 40
M. and Mme Goacolou

Rooms 12 with telephone, bath, WC, TV and minibar - Wheelchair accessible.
Price Single 250-400F, double 300-500F, suite 500-600F. **Meals** Breakfast 45F,
served 7:30-11:00; half board 420-500F, full board 600-800F (per pers., 2 days
min.). **Restaurant** Service 12:00-13:45, 19:30-21:30; menus 118-250F, also à la
carte. Specialties: Sologne and Périgord cooking. **Credit cards** All major. **Pets** Dogs
allowed. **Facilities** Bicycle, parking. **Nearby** Saint-Viâtre, Marcilly, route des Etangs
to La Ferté-Saint-Aubin (château), châteaux de la Loire (Chambord, Cheverny),
Sologne aquarium – 27-hole Aisses golf course. **Open** All year.

The very old Croix Blanche auberge is located in a ravishing
village in the Sologne forest. Since the 18th century, thirteen
generations of women chefs have presided over the kitchen,
gradually winning a solid gastronomic reputation. The dining room
is tastefully decorated with hunting trophies, antique country
furniture, and the smartly laid tables of a good old-fashioned
restaurant. In the summer, you can have dinner in the pretty flower
garden. Service throughout is both friendly and efficient. The
bedrooms are very comfortable and some have small sitting areas
with rustic, warm decoration (though it is somewhat heavy on
fabric and carpet motifs). The breakfasts are especially pleasant. The
Croix Blanche is a friendly, professionally run old inn, and a long-
time favorite in the Loire Valley.

How to get there *(Map 17): 34km south of Orléans via N20 to La Ferté-
Saint-Aubin, then D922 to Chaumont. Via A71, exit Lamotte-Beuvron.*

Château de Chissay ★★★★

Route de Pierrefitte-sur-Sauldre
Montrichard 41400 Chissay-en-Touraine (Loir-et-Cher)
Tel. 54.32.32.01 - Fax 54.32.43.80 - M. Savry

Rooms 31 with telephone, bath and WC. **Price** Single 390F, double 550-910F, suite or apartment 950-1600F. **Meals** Breakfast 50F, served 7:30-10:30; half board 490-680F, full board 670-860F (per pers.). **Restaurant** Service 12:00-14:00, 19:30-21:30; menus 160-295F, also à la carte. Specialties: Marbré de sandre et langoustines, feuilleté de noix de Saint-Jacques, pigeonneau rôti au jus de truffes, aumônière de fraises au rosé de Touraine. **Credit cards** All major. **Pets** Dogs allowed (+45F). **Facilities** Swimming pool, parking. **Nearby** Tours, grange de Meslay, Vouvray wine cellars, Loire valley (châteaux de la Loire) – 18-hole Touraine golf course in Ballan-Miré. **Open** beg. March – mid. Nov.

This ancient fortified château is full of historic memories: Charles VII, Louis XI and the Duke of Choiseul all stayed here. More recently, General de Gaulle spent several days here in June 1940 before going to England. Entirely renovated in 1986, it has 31 luxurious bedrooms; those in the turrets are especially charming (Nos. 12, 22, 10, 30). The restaurant is elegant, and there are pleasant walks in the surrounding garden and woods, and in the Touraine countryside.

How to get there *(Map 16): 35km east of Tours via D40 to Chenonceaux, then D76; 4km before Montrichard.*

Hôtel Les Charmilles ★★

Route de Pierrefitte-sur-Sauldre
41600 Nouan-le-Fuzelier (Loir-et-Cher)
Tel. 54.88.73.55 - Mme Sené

Rooms 14 with telephone, bath or shower, WC and TV. **Price** Single 310F, double 330-390F, suite 480F. **Meals** Breakfast incl., served 7:30-9:00. No restaurant. **Credit cards** Visa, Eurocard and MasterCard. **Pets** Dogs allowed in the ground-floor bedrooms. **Facilities** Parking. **Nearby** Church of Saint-Viâtre, château du Moulin, lake road from Saint-Viâtre to Romorantin via Selle Saint-Denis, La Source flower garden in Olivet – 12-hole Rivaulde golf and country club in Sallris. **Open** March 16 – Dec 14.

This big, comfortable family house, built at the beginning of the century, has been converted into a hotel. The decor is sober but warm, with recently laid thick carpets. The bedrooms are large and cheerful, with pleasant bathrooms. Breakfast is served in the bedrooms – just hang your breakfast order on the doorknob the evening before. The grounds are delightful. The large garden has a lake, cool shady areas under very old trees, comfortable garden furniture, and a beautiful lawn. The owners are very hospitable. There is no restaurant, but you can picnic on the grounds. For dinner, *Le Dahu* and *Raboliot* in Nohan are good choices.

How to get there *(Map 17): 44km south of Orléans via N20 towards Vierzon; on the way out of the village D122.*

Hôtel Château des Tertres ★★★

Route de Monteaux
41150 Onzain (Loir–et–Cher)
Tel. 54.20.83.88 – Fax 54.20.89.21 – M. Valois

Rooms 14 with telephone, bath or shower and WC. **Price** Double 370-480F.
Meals Breakfast 39F, served 8:00-10:00. No restaurant. **Credit cards** Amex, Visa,
Eurocard and MasterCard. **Pets** Dogs not allowed. **Facilities** Bicycles, parking.
Nearby Châteaux of Chaumont, Blois, Amboise, Chambord, Beauregard and
Chenonceaux – 9-hole la Carte golf course in Onzain, 18-hole château de Cheverny
golf course. **Open** April 1 – Nov 14.

This 19th–century château is a beautiful building and charmingly
decorated. On the ground floor overlooking the garden and
the countryside, the reception area adjoins a lounge with 19th-
century furniture. To one side is a very attractive room where a
delicious breakfast is served. The overall effect is that of a family
house. The bedrooms are very comfortable and pretty. They are
regularly redecorated with beautiful fabrics and the latest
conveniences. Although in a popular tourist area, the château is
quiet and reasonably priced. The welcome is very warm. The hotel
does not serve meals but there are some good restaurants in the
village, notably *Le Pont d'Ouchet* and *Le Domaine des Hauts de Loire*,
which is more elegant and more expensive.

How to get there *(Map 16): 44km northeast of Tours via N152 to the bridge
of Chaumont-sur-Loire, then D1 to Onzain.*

Relais des Landes ★★★

Ouchamps
41120 Les Montils (Loir-et-Cher)
Tel. 54.44.03.33 - Fax 54.44.03.89 - M. Badenier

Rooms 28 with telephone, bath, WC, TV and minibar. **Price** Single and double 495-725F. **Meals** Breakfast 50F, served 7:30-10:00; half board 550-650F. **Restaurant** Service 12:30-13:30, 19:00-21:30; menus 170-295F, also à la carte. Specialties: Foie gras de canard maison, cuisse de canard confit, lotte aux poivrons et pommes croustillantes. **Credit cards** All major. **Pets** Dogs allowed (+35F). **Facilities** Bicycle rent, parking. **Nearby** Châteaux of Chaumont, Blois, Amboise, Chambord, Beauregard and Chenonceaux – 9-hole la Carte golf course in Onzain, 18-hole château de Cheverny golf course. **Open** All year except Dec.

Lying in the middle of the countryside in a 24-acre park, the Relais de Landes is a 17th-century house which has been well restored and is well kept. The lounge/reception also houses the bar and offers corners for conversation or reading. The furniture is comfortable in these rooms and in the dining room, where a fire is lit in winter. Next to it there is a winter garden giving onto the lawn where dining tables are also set. In summer, you can have meals in the flower garden beside its small streams. The bedrooms are very comfortable, prettily decorated and they have beautiful bathrooms. The staff is friendly and helpful.

How to get there *(Map 16): 15km east of Blois towards Montrichard; follow the signs from Les Montils.*

Auberge de la Chichone ★★★

Place de l'Eglise
41210 Saint-Viâtre (Loir-et-Cher)
Tel. 54.88.91.33 - Fax 54.96.18.06 - M. and Mme Clément

Rooms 7 with telephone, bath or shower, WC and TV. **Price** Single and double 290-320F. **Meals** Breakfast 35F, served 8:00-11:00; half board 350F (per pers., 3 days min.). **Restaurant** Service 12:30-14:30, 19:30-22:00; menus 145-195F, also à la carte. Specialties: Game in season, girolles and cèpes mushrooms in season, fish from the lakes. **Credit cards** Amex, Visa, Eurocard and MasterCard. **Pets** Dogs allowed. **Nearby** Church of Saint-Viâtre, château du Moulin, lakes route to la Ferté-Saint-Aubin, La Source flower garden in Olivet – 9-hole Rivaulde golf and country club in Sallris. **Open** April 1 – Feb 28 (closed Tuesday and Wednesday in low season).

This hunting inn, very evocative of the Sologne, is located in a small church square. The bar and dining room are done in a countrified style, with shelves of wine, hunting trophies, gleaming copperware, and small lamps on the tables. No detail has been overlooked in the creation of the overall effect. The bedrooms are warm and decorated in brown tones with cane furniture. The walls are covered with a velvety fabric. A small television room opens onto a charming garden courtyard where breakfast can be served. The cuisine is refined, and there is a good selection of Loire wines.

How to get there *(Map 17): 51km south of Orléans via A71, Lamotte-Beuvron exit, then D923, then D49.*

Château de la Voûte

Troo
41800 Montoire-sur-le-Loir (Loir-et-Cher)
Tel. 54.72.52.52 - MM. Clays and Venon

Rooms 5 with bath or shower and WC. **Price** Double 370-470F, suite 550F.
Meals Breakfast incl., served 8:00-10:00. No restaurant. **Credit cards** Not accepted.
Pets Dogs not allowed. **Facilities** Parking. **Nearby** Benedictine abbey of la Trinité
and church of Rhodon in Vendôme, valley of the Loir, chapel of Saint-Gilles in
Montoire, Gué-du-Loir, Lavardin, Saint-Jacques-des-Guérets, manoir de la
Possonnière – 9-hole La Bosse golf course in Oucques. **Open** All year.

Here is a place for the discerning. The rooms in this old manor are full of beautiful things, reflecting the owners' passion for antiques. The bedrooms are furnished and decorated with some of their finds. Every room is different and has its own style and charm; even the smallest is lovely. Some are suites (named *Pompadour, Louis XIII* and *Empire*) and even apartments *(Les Tours)*. The view is worthy of a 17th-century painting. This is an ideal place for exploring the Tours region and the valleys of the Loir and the Loire. This is a well managed hotel of great quality. For restaurants, we recommend *Le Cheval Blanc* in Troo, *Le Cheval Rouge* in Montoire and *Le Relais d'Antan* in Lavardin.

How to get there *(Map 16): 48km north of Tours via D29 to La Chartre-sur-le-Loir, then right on D305 and D917 to Troo.*

Manoir de la Forêt **

Fort-Girard
41160 La Ville-aux-Clercs (Loir-et-Cher)
Tel. 54.80.62.83 - Fax 54.80.66.03 - Mme Autebon

Rooms 19 with telephone, bath or shower, WC and TV. **Price** Single and double 280-340F, suite 390-480F. **Meals** Breakfast 40F, served 7:30-9:00; half board 500F, full board 550F. **Restaurant** Service 12:15-14:00, 19:30-21:00; menus 145-270F, also à la carte. Specialties: Foie gras frais au Muscat, grenadin de lotte et langoustines au sabayon de champagne, poêlée de ris de veau, fish. **Credit cards** Amex, Visa, Eurocard and MasterCard. **Pets** Dogs allowed. **Facilities** Fishing, parking. **Nearby** Benedictine abbey of la Trinité and church of Rhodon in Vendôme, Loire Valley (châteaux de la Loire), valley of Loir, chapel of Saint-Gilles in Montoire, Gué-du-Loir, Lavardin, Saint-Jacques-des-Guérets, manoir de la Possonnière – 9-hole la Bosse golf course in Oucques. **Open** All year (closed Sunday evening and Monday Oct – March).

The former hunting lodge of the Château de la Gaudinière, which dates from the 18th-century, the Manoir de la Forêt stands in five acres of wooded grounds with a lake. The lounge/reception sets the scene with its restful atmosphere, fresh flowers and pleasant furniture. Two living rooms with deep armchairs and sofas are the ideal place for a drink, morning coffee or afternoon tea. The dining room, whose eleven windows open onto the garden, offers an excellent menu. Throughout, the choice of colors and fabrics is good. The bedrooms overlook the grounds or the forest and number 6 has a pretty terrace. In good weather drinks and meals are served outside.

How to get there (Map 16): *72km northeast of Tours via N10 to 6km beyond Vendôme, then left on D141 to La Ville-aux-Clercs.*

Hôtel de l'Abbaye ★★★

2, quai de l'Abbaye
45190 Beaugency (Loiret)
Tel. 38.44.67.35 - Fax 38.44.87.92 - M. Aupetit

Rooms 18 with telephone, bath, WC and TV. **Price** Single 420-480F, double 510-560F, suite 560-700F. **Meals** Breakfast 42F, served 7:00-10:00. **Restaurant** Service 12:00-14:00, 19:00-21:30; menu 185F, also à la carte. Specialties: Traditional cooking. **Credit cards** All major. **Pet** Dogs allowed (+50F). **Facilities** Parking. **Nearby** Medieval and Renaissance quarters of Beaugency, château de Meung-sur-Loire, basilica and chapel of Saint-Jacques in Cléry-Saint-André – 18-hole Saint-Laurent-Nouan golf course. **Open** All year.

A discreet nameplate announces that this 17th-century former Augustine convent built on the banks of the Loire opposite the old bridge in Beaugency is... a hotel. You will be charmingly welcomed in an immense but comfortable hall. Beside this is the bar and then the dining room, both very well furnished. In summer there are tables on the terrace overlooking the river. An extraordinary stone staircase leads to the bedrooms. The *premier étage* bedrooms make use of their ceiling height to include a mezzanine, well designed to seem like part of the original building, and they contain some pieces of Louis XIII furniture. They are very comfortable and have pleasant bathrooms. The *deuxième étage* bedrooms seem more classic, and some have unusual bathrooms. The Abbaye is quite special.

How to get there *(Map 17): 25km southwest of Orléans via A10, Meung-sur-Loire exit, then N152.*

221

Hôtel de la Sologne **
Place Saint-Firmin
45190 Beaugency (Loiret)
Tel. 38.44.50.27 - Fax 38.44.90.19 - Mme Rogue

Rooms 16 with telephone, bath or shower, WC and TV. **Price** Single and double 250-410F. **Meals** Breakfast 38F, served 7:00-9:30. No restaurant. **Credit cards** Visa, Eurocard and MasterCard. **Pet** Dogs not allowed. **Nearby** Medieval and Renaissance quarters of Beaugency, château de Meung-sur-Loire, basilica and chapel of Saint-Jacques in Cléry-Saint-André – 18-hole les Bordes golf course in Saint-Laurent-Nouan. **Open** All year except Christmas and New Year.

This charming hotel in the heart of old Beaugency is very courteously managed by Mme Rogue. The bedrooms are plain but comfortable, and she has equipped them with television sets with headphones (so as not to disturb the neighbors), wall lamps with pretty shades, hairdryers, and, in as many as possible, electric trouser presses. The living room is rustic and welcoming, with a fireplace, old beams and a huge selection of magazines. There is a pleasant verandah, which is also a lounge and winter garden. There is a good restaurant in the Hôtel de L'Abbaye.

How to get there (Map 17): 29km southwest of Orléans via A10, Meung-sur-Loire exit, then N152.

L'Auberge de Combreux **
45530 Combreux (Loiret)
Tel. 38.59.47.63 – Fax 38.59.36.19
Mme Gangloff

Rooms 20 with telephone, bath or shower, WC and TV (2 with whirlpool). **Price** 315-495F. **Meals** Breakfast 33F, served 8:00-10:00; half board 335-495F (per pers., 2 days min.). **Restaurant** Service 12:00-14:00, 19:15-21:15; menus 90-200F, also à la carte. Specialties: Mousseline de chèvre chaud au cresson, filet de brochet aux échalotes confites, navarin d'agneau, tarte au citron. **Credit cards** Visa, Eurocard and MasterCard. **Pets** Dogs allowed (+30F). **Facilities** Heated swimming pool, tennis (30F), bicycles (50F half-hour), parking. **Nearby** Orléans, arboretum and museum in Châteauneuf-sur-Loire, La Source flower gardens in Olivet – 18-hole Orléans golf course. **Open** Jan 20 – Dec 20.

This is a lovely, simple inn with white walls, white beds, bunches of reeds, and wood everywhere: beams, rustic furniture, mantelpieces. Throughout there is a gentle harmony between the colors of the curtains, the lampshades and, to add brighter tones, bouquets of flowers. The bedrooms too are very attractive, though some of them are in the annex on the other side of the street. In summer the arbor is perfect for a lazy breakfast or uplifting aperitifs. The cuisine is rustic and delicious: real French family cooking. The warmth of the welcome is worth mentioning and so is the pleasure of excursions on the bicycles you can rent at the hotel.

How to get there (Map 17): 35km east of Orléans via N60, Châteauneuf-sur-Loire and Vitry-aux-Loges exit.

Domaine de Chicamour **
45530 Sury-aux-Bois (Loiret)
Tel. 38.55.85.42 - Fax 38.55.80.43
M. Merckx

Rooms 12 with telephone, bath or shower, and WC. **Price** Single 325F, double 360F.
Meals Breakfast 45F, served 8:00-10:00; half board 370F, full board 460F.
Restaurant Service 12:00-14:00, 19:30-21:00; menus 95-350F, also à la carte.
Specialties: Foie gras, boudin de truite au vin de Montlouis, noisettes d'agneau.
Credit cards Visa, Eurocard and MasterCard. **Pets** Dogs allowed (+25F).
Facilities Tennis, riding, bicycles, boules and parking. **Nearby** Orléans, arboretum
and museum in Châteauneuf-sur-Loire, La Source flower gardens in Olivet – 18-
hole Orléans golf course. **Open** March 1 – Nov 30.

Set in a 20-acre park in the heart of the Orléans National Forest,
the small château of Chicamour has been turned into a hotel
with the accent on simplicity and elegance. The result is
remarkable. The lovely lounge has deep sofas surrounding the
fireplace and beautifully chosen curtains and fabrics. The superb
collection of paintings and decorative objects helps to make this a
special place you will not want to leave. The bedrooms also are
beautiful, with pale wood furniture and Laura Ashley fabrics
matching the wallpapers and lampshades. They are all comfortable,
overlook the park and have beautiful bathrooms. In the elegant
dining room, you will enjoy refined cuisine based on regional
produce. The cellar includes a great variety of Loire wines, which
you can buy.

How to get there *(Map 17): 39km west of Montargis on N60, between
Bellegarde and Châteauneuf-sur-Loire.*

Hôtel de l'Abbaye ★★★

8, rue des Tourelles
02600 Longpont (Aisne)
Tel. 23.96.02.44 – M. Verdun

Rooms 12 with telephone, (5 with bath or shower and 6 with WC). **Price** Double 175-320F. **Meals** Breakfast "campagnard" 40F, served any time; half board 290-390F, full board 360-460F (per pers., 3 days min.). **Restaurant** Service 12:00-14:00, 19:30-21:00; menus 95-220F, also à la carte. Specialties: Wood grills, canard aux cerises, game and mushrooms in season. **Credit cards** All major. **Pets** Dogs allowed. **Facilities** Bicycle rent. **Nearby** Abbey and château of Longpont, château, Hôtel de Ville and Alexandre Dumas museum in Villers-Cotterêts, château de Vierzy, forest of Retz – 9-hole Valois golf course in Barbery. **Open** All year.

This fine old house is located in a village in the heart of the Forest of Retz. Its large, heavy dining tables and its fireplace are the scene of warm and friendly gatherings for walkers and sports enthusiasts. The delicious home cooking owes a great deal to the proprietor, who does everything to make you feel at home. The few bedrooms vary in quality; five have full bathroom facilities, and all have a peaceful atmosphere and look out on the forest or the abbey. Other amenities of the hotel are a reading room, a TV room, a delightful garden and a wealth of tourist information about the region.

How to get there (Map 10): 20km south of Soissons via N2 towards Villers-Cotterêts, then D2.

Hostellerie Le Château ★★★

Neuville-Saint-Amand
02100 Saint-Quentin (Aisne)
Tel. 23.68.41.82 - Fax 23.68.46.02 - M. Meiresonne

Rooms 15 with telephone, bath, WC and TV (6 with minibar). **Price** Single and double 330-390F. **Meals** Breakfast 45F, served from 7:30. **Restaurant** Service 12:00-13:30, 19:00-21:00; menus 120-330F, also à la carte. Specialties: Cassolette d'escargots crème d'ail et poivrons, mélange de ris et rognon au genièvre de Houlles, assiette gourmande. **Credit cards** All major. **Pets** Dogs not allowed. **Facilities** Parking. **Nearby** Antoine Lécuyer Museum (pastels by Quentin de la Tour), college and Hôtel de Ville of Saint-Quentin – 9-hole le Mesnil golf course. **Open** All year (closed Saturday noon and Sunday evening, 3 weeks in Aug).

This château lies in the heart of a beautiful wooded park. The ground floor rooms are occupied by its famous restaurant, while other pleasantly furnished rooms extend into a modern wing with bay windows and a view of the park. Viewed from the outside, however, the architectural effect is disappointing. The comfortable, pleasantly furnished bedrooms are very attractive, with pastel wall fabrics. The bathrooms are lovely. At the Hostellerie, you will enjoy a restful stay and welcoming hospitality.

How to get there *(Map 2): 120km south of Lille via A26, exit Saint-Quentin-Gauchy or Saint-Quentin-Center; Rue du General-Leclerc and D12; in the centre 200m from the church.*

Château de Barive ★★★★

Sainte-Preuve
02350 Liesse (Aisne)
Tel. 23.22.15.15 - Fax 23.22.08.39 - M. Bergman

Rooms 15 with telephone, bath or shower, WC and TV. **Price** Single 380F, double 580-680F. **Meals** Breakfast 55F, served from 7:30; half board from 400F (per pers.). **Restaurant** Service 12:00-14:00, 19:00-21:00; menus 150-310F, also à la carte. Specialties: Ravioles de crustacés servis dans leur nage, filet de Saint-Pierre aux truffes et poireaux. **Credit cards** All major. **Pets** Dogs allowed. **Facilities** Swimming pool, sauna, tennis. **Nearby** Laon cathedral, abbey of Prémontrés, forest of Saint-Gobain, ruins of abbeys of Le Tortoir and Saint-Nicolas-aux-Bois. **Open** All year.

Surrounded by countryside, this 17th–Century château was first a hunting lodge, then a boarding house, and has now been fully restored and opened as an impeccable hotel. The bedrooms are large and extremely comfortable, with thick eiderdowns and luxuriously fitted bathrooms. There is no period furniture, but some fine copies recreate something of the historic atmosphere of the chateau. The big breakfast room opens onto the surrounding greenery and is arranged rather like a winter garden. The lounge and dining room are still a little formal, but both rooms are comfortable, and the gourmet cuisine served in the latter certainly contributes much to the atmosphere. Hotel facilities include a large heated indoor swimming-pool, a sauna and a tennis court, so a stay here provides the perfect opportunity to get back into shape. The hospitality is friendly and attentive.

How to get there *(Map 3 and 10): 18km east of Laon via D977.*

Auberge de la Scierie ★★★
La Vove
10160 Aix-en-Othe (Aube)
Tel. 25.46.71.26 - Fax 25.46.65.69 - M. and Mme Duguet

Rooms 15 with telephone, bath or shower, WC and TV. **Price** Single and double 350-480F. **Meals** Breakfast 40F, served 8:00-11:00; half board 450F (per pers.). **Restaurant** Closed Feb, Monday evening and Tuesday Oct 15 – April 15. Service 12:00-14:00, 19:30-21:15; menus 130-230F, also à la carte. Specialties: fish. **Credit cards** All major. **Pets** Dogs allowed. **Facilities** Heated swimming pool, parking. **Nearby** Saint-Urbain Basilica, Cathedral of Saint Pierre and Saint Paul, Modern Art Museum in Troyes – 18-hole la Cordelière golf course in Chaource. **Open** All year except Feb.

This inn, lying in unspoiled countryside, is in an old sawmill. The main structure has been so well restored and refurbished that it seems as if the Auberge has always been a hotel. The beautiful surroundings provide lovely places for al fresco meals and walks in the beautiful 5-acre park which also was pretty stream. The bedrooms, which surround the swimming pool, are quiet and comfortable; some are traditionally furnished. The lounge is pleasant and has a beautiful fireplace and a library. The food is excellent and guests are sure of a warm welcome.

How to get there *(Map 10): 33km west of Troyes via N60 towards Sens, then D374 or via A5 Vulaines exit or Touvilliers exit; on the way out of the village in the Villemoiron-en-Othe direction.*

Château d'Etoges

4, rue Richebourg – 51270 Etoges by Montmort (Marne)
Tel. 26.59.30.08 – Fax 26.59.35.57
Mme Filliette-Neuville

Rooms 20 with telephone, bath or shower and WC (TV on request). **Price** Single 400F, double 500-700F, suite 1000F. **Meals** Breakfast 55F, served 8:00-11:00; half board 450-520F, full board 600-670F (per pers., 2 days min.). **Restaurant** On reservation. Service 12:00-14:00, 19:30-21:30; menu 180F. Specialties: Poisson au champagne, pintade vigneronne, Charlotte au marc de champagne. **Credit cards** All major. **Pets** Dogs allowed (+40F). **Facilities** Parking. **Nearby** Champagne Museum in Epernay, abbey of Hautvillers (where Dom Perignon invented champagne) – 18-hole La Vitarderie golf course in Dormans, 18-hole Val-Secret golf course in Château-Thierry. **Open** Feb 25 – Dec 31.

The splendid Château d'Etoges dates from the 17th-Century. It is set against a low hill beneath which there are springs which emerge as elegant fountains. The interior of the château is equally enchanting; it has been refurbished with good taste to retain the building's character and provide modern amenities. (The bathrooms are beautiful). There is a grand staircase, spacious lounges with decorative panels, delightful percale tablecloths in the dining room, and superb bedrooms. Some are big and sumptuous, others more intimate, but in each there is a delightful blend of antique furniture and pretty materials and romantic views over the moat. A warm, personal welcome at the Château d'Etoges, evokes a way of life in a more graceful age. It is an ideal base for exploring the Champagne vineyards.

How to get there (Map 10): 40km west of Châlons-sur-Marne via D33.

Le Prieuré ★★★

Chevet de l'Eglise
60440 Ermenonville (Oise)
Tel. 44.54.00.44 - Fax 44.54.02.21 - M. and Mme Treillou

Rooms 11 with telephone, bath or shower, WC, TV and minibar. **Price** Double 450-500F. **Meals** Breakfast 50F. No restaurant. **Credit cards** All major. **Pets** Small dogs allowed. **Nearby** Châalis abbey, Ermenonville forest, Astérix park, Eurodisneyland. **Open** All year except in Feb.

You will feel right at home at Le Prieuré, a true gem hidden in an English garden just next to the church. Mr. and Mrs. Treillou love polished antique furniture, paintings, knick-knacks, and rugs. The fabrics they have selected for the curtains and bedspreads reflect the atmosphere of each room. The bedrooms are very large and comfortable, and certain attic rooms have beautiful exposed beams. They are all quiet (the road to Ermenonville is not too far but it is not busy on weekends). On the ground floor, the reception rooms open directly onto the garden. Each one has a fireplace, but when it's nice outside, the sun warms the polished tile floors all over the house and you can have breakfast in a charming country dining room. You can dine very pleasantly at *L'Ermitage*, about 100 yards from the hotel. Le Prieuré is enchanting.

How to get there *(Map 9): 45km northeast of Paris via A1, exit Survilliers, then D104 direction Villepinte, then Ermenonville.*

A la Bonne Idée ★★★

3, rue des Meuniers
60350 Saint-Jean-aux-Bois (Oise)
Tel. 44.42.84.09 - Fax 44.42.80.45 - M. Drieux

Rooms 23 with telephone, bath, WC and TV - 1 wheelchair accessible room.
Price Single and double 385-430F, suite 430F. **Meals** Breakfast 55F, served 7:30-
10:30; half board 560F, full board 725F (2 pers.). **Restaurant** Service 12:15-14:00,
19:15-21:00; menu 120F, also à la carte. Specialties: Escalopine de foie gras aux
pommes et vinaigre de cidre, homard au vieux porto et au pistou. **Credit cards** Amex,
Visa, Eurocard and MasterCard. **Pets** Dogs allowed (+25F). **Facilities** Parking.
Nearby Château and forest of Compiègne, archery museum in Crépy-en-Valois –
18-hole golf course in Compiègne. **Open** All year.

This hotel, a former 18th-century hunding lodge, is located in
a charming little village in the heart of the Forest of
Compiègne. In the entrance hall and the bar the old and the new
blend harmoniously. The lovely dining room provides a handsome
setting for the the chef's excellent cuisine. There is a choice of
bedrooms; those in the main building are charmingly traditional
in style, and the ones in the annex are elegantly furnished and look
out onto flower gardens and the shaded terrace. Visitors will
appreciate its hospitable welcome and its calm ambience, ensured
by the fact that the hotel's proximity to the forest paths.

How to get there (Map 9): 75km northeast of Paris via A1, number 9 exit
in Chevrières direction Verberie, then D200 to La-Croix-Saint-Ouen and
D85 through the Forest of Compiègne to Saint-Jean-aux-Bois.

A l'Orée du Bois **

Futeau
55120 Clermont-en-Argonne (Meuse)
Tel. 29.88.28.41 - Fax 29.88.24.52 - M. and Mme Aguesse

Rooms 7 with telephone, bath, WC and TV. **Price** Single 285F, double 330-350F.
Meals Breakfast 46F, served 7:30-11:00; half board 395F, full board 505F (per pers.,
3 days min.). **Restaurant** Closed Tuesday and Sunday evening in low season. Service
12:00-13:30, 19:00-20:30; menus 110F (in week), 185-350F, also à la carte.
Specialties: Pigeonneau des Hauts de Chée, fricassée d'écrevisses, rognons de lapin
aux champignons, bourgeon de sapin glaçé. **Credit cards** Visa, Eurocard and
MasterCard. **Pets** Dogs allowed (+40F). **Facilities** Parking. **Nearby** Argonne Forest,
Butte de Vauquois, Varennes-en-Argonne, Lachalade Abbey, Verdun, Rarécourt
Museum, Les Islettes pottery factory (open July 1 – August 30). **Open** All year (closed
Jan.,Nov. 1, school holidays, Sunday evening and Tuesday in low season).

With a beautiful forest at the back, the small Orée du Bois
looks out over a beautiful, peaceful countryside. The
interior decoration is pleasant and is lent character by traditional
old furniture. Located in a recently built wing, the bedrooms are
on the ground floor facing the lawn and all have a very beautiful
view. They are large and decorated in a classically rustic style, but
the pretty fabrics give the rooms warmth. The dining room with
large bay windows has the most beautiful view. Monsieur Aguesse
turns out such regional specialties as fricassée of crayfish, while his
wife, who oversees the dining room, will advise you very
competently on wines. Both Monsieur and Madame will see to it
that your stay at "The Edge of the Woods" is memorable.

How to get there *(Map 11): 40km west of Verdun via A4, exit Sainte-Menehould.*
Then take N3 towards Verdun to Islettes, then D2 on the right, towards Futeau.

Hôtel Dolce Vita ***

Route des Sanguinaires
20000 Ajaccio (Corse-du-Sud)
Tel. 95.52.00.93 – Fax 95.52.07.15 – M. Federici

Rooms 32 with telephone, bath, WC, TV and minibar. **Price** Single and double 440-935F. **Meals** Breakfast 55F, served 7:00-10:00; half board and full board (obligatory in July and August) 665-945F. **Restaurant** Service 12:30-13:45, 19:30-21:30; menu 200F, also à la carte. Specialties: Raviolis au broccio, fricassée de langouste. **Credit cards** All major. **Pets** Dogs allowed (+50F). **Facilities** Swimming pool, water skiing, beach. **Nearby** Gulf of Ajaccio via the Route des Iles Sanguinaires, Les Milelli, Château de la Punta, Bastelica. **Open** Easter – Nov. 1.

The Dolce Vita is a modern hotel whose superb location compensates for the functional style of its architecture and its rather flashy interior decor. All the rooms face the sea. They are located on two levels; the lower ones have direct access to a small beach, where the concrete is rather an eyesore. The hotel is very comfortable and the bathrooms have all the usual facilities. There are flowers everywhere and it is a pleasure to stroll among the bougainvillea, oleanders and palm trees. The dining area is composed of a large interior room where the pink tablecloths seem to be waiting for a special occasion, and a spacious shaded terrace which overlooks the sea. At night, with the swimming pool floodlit, the twinkling lights in the trees and the glimmer of lights across the bay, the scene is reminiscent of Hollywood.

How to get there (Map 36): 8km west of Ajaccio via the Route des Sanguinaires. Ajaccio-Campo dell'Oro Airport 15km away, tel. 95.21.03.64.

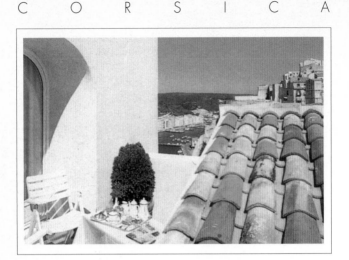

Hôtel Genovese ★★★

Quartier de la Citadelle
20169 Bonifacio (Corse-du-Sud)
Tel. 95.73.12.34 - Fax 95.73.09.03

Rooms 14 with air-conditioning, telephone, bath, WC, TV and minibar. **Price** Double 700-1500F, suite 950-1700F. **Meals** Breakfast 70-80F, served 7:30-11:00. No restaurant. **Credit cards** All major. **Pets** Dogs allowed. **Facilities** Parking. **Nearby** Boat trip to marine grottoes, cave of Sdragonato and tour of the cliffs, gulf of Santa-Manza – 18-hole golf course in Sperone. **Open** All year.

Set out along the walls of the Bonifacio ramparts, this hotel is in an old naval building and has a beautiful view of the sea, the town and the harbor. It is luxuriously and elegantly furnished. The rooms are set around a delightful courtyard and are decorated in pastel shades with flowered curtains. The bathrooms are faultless and there is a whirlpool in every suite. Room 2 also has a balcony which overlooks the port. There is no restaurant but the ground floor has a breakfast area and a lounge where a handsome white settee blends delightfully with the stone walls. An additional asset is that the hotel is fully air conditioned. *La Caravelle* is the popular fish restaurant; *Le Voilier* and *Le Stella d'Oro* (upstairs), are favorites with the region's famous people; and *La Cantina Doria* serves the best authentic Corsican specialties.

How to get there *(Map 36): In Bonifacio, turn right immediately on leaving the road to the Citadelle. Figari Airport 21km away, tel. 95.71.00.22.*

Résidence du Centre Nautique ★★★
Quai Nord
20169 Bonifacio (Corse-du-Sud)
Tel. 95.73.02.11 - Fax 95.73.17.47 - M. Lantieri

Rooms 10 with telephone, shower, WC, TV and minibar. **Price** Double 450-950F.
Meals Breakfast 50-60F. No restaurant. **Credit cards** All major. **Pets** Dogs allowed.
Facilities Parking. **Nearby** Boat trip to the marine grottoes, Sdragonato Cave and
tour of the cliffs, Santa-Manza Gulf – 18-hole golf course in Sperone. **Open** All year.

This hotel on Bonifacio harbor lies below the upper town and
looks out over the moored boats. Despite its name it is a place
that gives a cordial welcome to tourists as well as to sailing
enthusiasts. The ceiling height has made it possible to convert the
rooms into small duplexes. On the lower level there is a small living
room and on the mezzanine the bedroom and bathroom. It is more
like a studio than a conventional hotel bedroom and perfect for
inviting your neighbors in for cocktails. Some units have a view
over the garden and others over the port, which is quiet and
peaceful at night. You can have breakfast on the terrace overlooking
the sailboats and yachts.

How to get there *(Map 36): On the port. Figari Airport 21km away, tel.
95.71.00.22*

Grand Hôtel Cala Rossa ★★★★

Cala Rossa - 20137 Porto-Vecchio (Corse-du-Sud)
Tel. 95.71.61.51 - Fax 95.71.60.11
M. Canarelli and Mme Biancarelli

Rooms 50 with air-conditioning, telephone, bath, WC and TV. **Price** Single 450-2000F, double 640-2700F, suite 1180-2700F. **Meals** Breakfast incl., served 7:30-11:30; half-board obligatory in high season. **Restaurant** Service 12:30-14:30, 19:45-22:00; menus, also à la carte. Specialties: Mesclun de seiches à l'origan, craquant de loup aux aubergines, filet d'agneau à la choucroute de fenouil. **Credit cards** All major. **Pets** Dogs not allowed. **Facilities** Private beach, water skiing, windsurfing, boat trips, parking. **Nearby** Palombaggia beach and Piccovaggia Peninsula, Ospedale Forest – 18-hole golf course in Sperone. **Open** April 15 – Dec 31.

The success of the Grand Hôtel Cala Rossa is due mainly to the enthusiasm of proprietor Toussaint Canarelli and his loyal and hard-working team. The hotel is very well located on the edge of the sea, and the restaurant, which is one of the best in Corsica, has become the summer haunt of famous politicians and actors from the Cala Rossa residential area. The bedrooms are all comfortable, but the suites decorated in Mediterranean style are especially luxurious as are the reception and the salon. The surroundings are magnificent: the garden with its shady pines, oleanders and plumbagos extends as far as the private beach. It is essential to reserve very early for the summer season, but in spring and autumn you can enjoy the pleasures of the maquis and the Ospedale Forest as well as the sea. Note the very attractive low-season rates.

How to get there *(Map 36): 10km northeast of Porto Vecchio via N198, D568 and D468. Figari Airport 33km away, tel. 95.71.00.22.*

L'Aïtone **
20126 Evisa (Corse-du-Sud)
Tel. 95.26.20.04 - Fax 95.26.24.18
M. Ceccaldi

Rooms 32 with telephone, bath or shower, WC and cable TV. **Price** Single 150-400F, double 200-550F. **Meals** Breakfast 35-38F, served 8:00-9:30; half board 250-450F, full board 380-550F (per pers, 3 days min.). **Restaurant** Service 12:00-14:00, 19:30-22:00; menus 85-160F, also à la carte. Specialties: Terrine de sanglier aux châtaignes, omelette broccio et menthe, charcuterie corse, truite. **Credit cards** Amex, Visa, Eurocard and MasterCard. **Pets** Dogs allowed. **Facilities** Swimming pool, parking. **Nearby** Waterfall and pool in the forest of Aïtone, gorges of the Spelunca, forest of Aïtone, calanques of Piana, villages of Ota and Vico, Girolata. **Open** Jan – Nov.

The Aïtone auberge is 850m above sea level on the edge of the spectacular forest of pines and larches of Aïtone and the Valdo-Niello. Toussaint Ceccaldi, the proprietor, has taken over from his parents and is constantly refurbishing and enlarging the hotel. The building is not particularly attractive but it has a superb location, with its large swimming pool overlooking the beautiful Spelunca Valley. The bedrooms - some, with balconies are more luxurious than others - have a magnificent view of the Gulf of Porto. You will enjoy very good cuisine.

How to get there *(Map 36): 23km east of Porto via D84. Ajaccio Airport 70km away, tel. 95.21.03.64.*

Les Roches Rouges **
20115 Piana (Corse-du-Sud)
Tel. 95.27.81.81 - Fax 95.27.81.76
Mme Dalakupeyan

Rooms 30 with telephone, shower and WC. **Price** Double 265-280F. **Meals** Breakfast 40F, served 7:30-11:00; half board 320F (per pers.). **Restaurant** Service 12:00-14:00; menus 100-360F, also à la carte. Specialties: Fish, lobster. **Credit cards** All major. **Pets** Dogs allowed. **Facilities** Parking. **Nearby** Calanques of Piana, boat to Girolata (dep. Porto), villages of Ota, Evisa and Vico, Lava peak, route de Ficajola. **Open** April 1 – Oct 30.

This turn-of-the-century Corsican house, on the edge of the village of Piana and three kilometers from the famous creeks, has been refurbished. There is a spacious, well-lit, handsome restaurant which extends onto a terrace, and from here as well as from the bedrooms there are superb views. The rooms themselves are rather simple and could do with improvement, but this is made up for by the cordial welcome given by Mady and the very reasonable prices.

How to get there *(Map 36): 71km north of Ajaccio via D81. Ajaccio Airport, tel. 95.21.03.64.*

Le Maquis ★★★★

20166 Porticcio (Corse–du–Sud)
Tel. 95.25.05.55 - Fax 95.25.11.70
Mme Salini

Rooms 19 with air-conditioning, telephone, bath, WC, TV and minibar. **Price** 840F in low season, Half board only, double 1780-2480F. **Meals** Breakfast incl., served 8:00-10:30. **Restaurant** Service 12:30-14:00, 19:30-22:00; à la carte 300-450F. **Credit cards** All major. **Pets** Dogs allowed (+60F). **Facilities** Heated swimming pool, tennis, gym, private beach, parking. **Nearby** Gulf of Ajaccio via the Route des Iles Sanguinaires, Les Milelli, Château de la Punta, Bastelica. **Open** All year.

The Maquis is one of the outstanding hotels in this guide. It is splendidly located on a small inlet off the Gulf of Ajaccio, two kilometers from Porticcio. Its pretty private beach, the elegant decor and the comfort of its communal rooms and bedrooms (ask for a room with a terrace facing the sea) make it ideal for a relaxing, comfortable vacation. The terrace, the covered swimming pool and a tennis court complete the picture. At noon, there is a delicious buffet lunch on the terrace and in the evenings an excellent menu, changed every day, is served. What more could we want? Madame Salini has made Le Maquis a veritable oasis on a coast unfortunately has been rather spoiled. But if you do want to leave the hotel, you can explore the beautiful interior of Corsica.

How to get there *(Map 36): 18km southeast of Ajaccio via N196, D55 along the coast. Ajaccio-Campo dell'Oro Airport, tel. 95.21.03.64.*

Hôtel L'Aiglon **
20147 Serriera (Corse-du-Sud)
Tel. 95.26.10.65 - Fax 95.26.14.77
M. Colonna-Ceccaldi

Rooms 18 with telephone, bath or shower (8 with WC). **Price** 200-350F.
Meals Breakfast 30F, served 8:00-9:30; half board 200-300F, full board 250-360F
(per pers., 3 days min.). **Restaurant** Service 12:30-14:00, 20:00-21:30; menus 85-
130F, also à la carte. Specialties: Omelette au broccio, daube de sanglier, cannellonis
à la corse. **Credit cards** All major. **Pets** Dogs allowed. **Facilities** Parking.
Nearby Waterfall and pool in the Forest of Aïtone, Gorges of the Spelunca, Forest of
Aïtone, calanques of Piana, boat to Girolata, villages of Ota and Vico. **Open** May 1
– end Sept.

The Hôtel L'Aiglon, built about thirty years ago out of Porto
stone, is a place for lovers of peace and tranquillity. It is set in
the heart of the maquis. To reach the hotel, you take a winding
road across hilly countryside; but it is not as isolated as this might
suggest for the sea is only five kilometers away. Because it is
patronized by a regular clientele, the bedrooms have not been
updated. They are quite simple and the furniture is very 1950s.
The bathrooms are behind rather thin partitions. To one side of
the building there are six rooms in bungalows, each one with its
own terrace. The moderate rates are interesting if you wish to
explore the interior of Corsica or want inexpensive proximity to
the sea.

How to get there *(Map 36): 5km north of Porto via D81; follow signs. Calvi
Airport 80km, tel. 95.65.08.09.*

Hôtel Balanéa ★★★

6, rue Clémenceau
20260 Calvi (Haute-Corse)
Tel. 95.65.00.45 - Fax 95.65.29.71 - M. Ceccaldi

Rooms 37 with air-conditioning, telephone, bath, WC and TV (32 with minibar).
Price Double 300-1200F, suite 700-1200F. **Meals** Breakfast 60F, served 7:30-10:30.
No restaurant. **Credit cards** All major. **Pets** Dogs allowed (+100F). **Nearby** Citadel
of Calvi, tour of the villages of Balagne (Calenzana, Zilia, Montemaggiore,
Sant'Antonino, church of the Trinity in Aregno, convent of Corbara), Scandola national
park – 9-hole Lumio golf course. **Open** All year.

Located on the harbor in Calvi, the Balanéa is the most pleasant
hotel in the center of town. The bedrooms, which are very
comfortable, are spacious and well decorated; they have large
bathrooms with all the amenities, including hair-dryers. Most have
balconies and some have real terraces from which there are
marvelous views of the fort and citadel. All the rooms are air-
conditioned, making for pleasant sleeping in the hot summer. The
Balanéa is the only hotel open in Calvi during the winter. For an
unforgettable evening, we recommend dinner on the marvelous
terrace of *La Signoria* and the piano-bar of *Chez Tao*.

How to get there *(Map 36): on the port in Calvi. Calvi Airport 7km, tel.
95.65.08.09*

Auberge de la Signoria ★★★
Route de forêt de Bonifato
20260 Calvi (Haute-Corse)
Tel. 95.65.23.73 - Fax 95.65.38.77 - MM. Ceccaldi

Rooms 10 with telephone, bath, WC, TV and minibar. **Price** Single and double 450-1100F, suite 1000-1500F, apart. 1200-2000F. **Meals** Breakfast 70F, served 8:00-11:00; half board 1150-1800F (per 2 pers., 2 days min.). **Restaurant** Service 12:00-13:30, 19:30-22:30; menu 320F (child 130F), also à la carte. Specialties: Carpaccio de saumon aigre doux, salade de pigeonneau, noisettes d'agneau à la croute d'herbes du maquis. **Credit cards** Amex, Visa, Eurocard and MasterCard. **Pets** Dogs allowed. **Facilities** Swimming pool, tennis, Steam bath, parking. **Nearby** Citadel of Calvi, tour of the villages of Balagne (Calenzana, Zilia, Montemaggiore, Sant'Antonino, church of the Trinity in Aregno, convent of Corbara), Scandola national park – 9-hole Lumio golf course. **Open** End March – Oct 15.

L a Signoria is the kind of hotel that dreams are made of. It is in a beautiful old house on a large estate with eucalyptus and palm trees and a beautiful swimming pool in the garden. The owners have converted the house into a hotel, without spoiling any of its charm. The rooms in the main building are the most pleasant and comfortable ones, but you will not feel deprived if you have one in the annex. Dinner by candlelight under the canopy of palm trees on the terrace is one of the many lovely moments you will spend here. This beautiful hotel is perfectly quiet even in the middle of August.

How to get there *(Map 36): 5km from Calvi on the airport road. Calvi Airport 7km, tel. 95.65.08.09.*

Marina d'Argentella

L'Argentella
20260 Calvi (Haute-Corse)
Tel. 95.65.25.08 - M. Grisoli

Rooms 25 with bath and WC. **Price** Double room with half board 350-450F (per pers.), reduced rate for children. **Meals** Breakfast incl. **Restaurant** Service 12:30-14:30, 20:00-22:00; menu 120F, also à la carte. Specialties: Fish and Corsican dishes. **Credit cards** Visa, Eurocard and MasterCard. **Pets** Dogs allowed. **Facilities** Parking. **Nearby** Citadel of Calvi, tour of the villages of Ballagne (Calenzana, Zilia, Montemaggiore, Sant 'Antonino, church of the Trinity in Aregno, convent of Corbara), Scandola regional park – 9-hole Lumio golf course. **Open** May 1 – Oct 1.

The Argentella is a very special place, not only because it is so beautifully located on the beach of Crovani Bay, but also because of Pierre and Dorine's friendly hospitality. The bedrooms, which are in small bungalows in a eucalyptus grove, are simple but charming, and all have comfortable bathrooms. Chef Dhair prepares new recipes regularly. At noon, meals are light and fresh, and in the evening the fare is more ambitious. Swimming, windsurfing, picnics and boat excursions are offered by the hotel. At seven in the evening, you can join in the traditional volleyball game and then enjoy a drink as you admire the wonderful sunset. The Argentella is ideal for a family vacation. And note the special slimming week in June.

How to get there (Map 36): 22km south of Calvi towards Porto by coast road. Calvi Airport 25km away, tel. 95.65.08.09.

Hôtel Mare e Monti **

20225 Feliceto (Haute-Corse)
Tel. 95.61.73.06 - Fax 95.61.78.67
M. Renucci

Rooms 18 with telephone, (14 with shower and 2 with bath and WC). **Price** Single 252-265F, double 283-297F. **Meals** Breakfast 30F, served 8:00-10:00; half board 276F, full board 385F (per pers., 3 days min.). **Restaurant** Service 12:00-14:00, 19:30-22:00; menus 80-180F, also à la carte. Specialties: Truite à la Calamenti, agneau de lait à la mode corse. **Credit cards** All major. **Pets** Dogs allowed. **Facilities** Parking. **Nearby** Citadel of Calvi, tour of the villages of Ballagne (Calenzana, Zilia, Montemaggiore, Sant 'Antonino, church of the Trinity in Aregno, convent of Corbara). **Open** May 1 – Sept 30.

This lovely house, which lies between the sea and the mountains, was built in 1870 and is still lived in by the same family. Behind the hotel there are steep rocky cliffs, and in the distance one can see the sea behind Ile Rousse. On one side of the hotel is a lovely terrace where meals are served. Nearby are two magnificent cedar trees, and an orchard of apple trees provides fruit for breakfast. The *deuxième étage* bedrooms, with high ceilings, simple decor and old paintings, are preferable to those on the *troisième étage*, where the linoleum-covered floor is not attractive. M. Renucci gives a cordial welcome to all his guests and the traditional, delicious cuisine provided by his chef is an attraction for people who want to know a more authentic Corsica than that found in its seaside resorts.

How to get there *(Map 36): 26km northeast of Calvi via N197 to beyond Alcajola, then right on D13 to Feliceto via Santa Reparata. Calvi Airport, Tel. 95.65.08.09.*

La Bergerie ★
Route de Monticello
20220 L'Ile-Rousse (Haute-Corse)
Tel. 95.60.01.28 - Fax 95.60.06.36 - M. Caumer

Rooms 19 with telephone, bath or shower, WC and TV. **Price** Single and double 250-450F. **Meals** Breakfast 30F, served 8:00-10:00; half board 400-460F (per pers., 5 days min.). **Restaurant** Service 12:00 and 19:30; also à la carte. Specialties: Brochettes de liche, araignées farcies, omelette aux oursins, sardines farcies, mérou à la juive. **Credit cards** Visa, Eurocard and MasterCard. **Pets** Dogs allowed. **Facilities** Swimming pool, parking. **Nearby** Citadel of Calvi, tour of the villages of Ballagne (Calenzana, Zilia, Montemaggiore, Sant 'Antonino, church of the Trinity in Aregno, convent of Corbara). **Open** March 15 – Dec 1 (closed Monday in low season).

L a Bergerie is an old sheep farm converted into a small hotel 800 meters from Ile Rousse and the beach. It is famous as a restaurant throughout Ile Rousse and Calvi, and bedrooms have been added in the quiet garden. The owner is an enthusiastic fisherman and delights his guests with dishes he has made using his catch of the day. These might include such refined dishes as sea-urchin omelette and sea-anemone fritters. The atmosphere is relaxed and friendly.

How to get there *(Map 36): 24km northeast of Calvi via N197 to L'Ile Rousse. Calvi Airport, tel. 95.65.08.09.*

U Sant' Agnellu

20247 Rogliano (Haute-Corse)
Tel. 95.35.40.59
M. and Mme Albertini

Rooms 9 with bath and WC. **Price** Double 220-300F. **Meals** Breakfast 25F; half board 250-300F. **Restaurant** Service 12:00-15:00, 19:30-23:00; menu 90F, also à la carte. Specialties: Brandade, boulettes au broccio, cannelonis, tourte Sant 'Agnellu. **Credit cards** Visa, Eurocard and MasterCard. **Pets** Dogs allowed. **Facilities** Parking. **Nearby** Romanesque Cathedral of la Canonica and San Parteo Church, villages of Cap Corse from Bastia to Saint-Florent. **Open** Easter – Oct.

Young Monsieur and Madame Albertini set up a restaurant in this old town hall in 1984 and three years later converted it into a hotel. He deserves encouragement for his delicious cuisine at unbeatable prices, as well as for the charming bedrooms. With white stucco walls and solid wooden furniture, they are simple but very comfortable and the tiled bathrooms are impeccable. Five bedrooms look out onto the sea and the others onto the mountains. In good weather, meals are served on the panoramic terrace: the spacious indoor dining room with its semicircle of large windows also has beautiful views. Visitors who enjoy old buildings will find much to interest them in this picturesque 12th-century village, which has two churches, a convent and the ruins of a château as well as various Genoese towers.

How to get there *(Map 36): 42km north of Bastia via D80 towards Macinaggio (free bus from port of Macinaggio to the hotel). Bastia Airport, tel. 95.54.54.54.*

Hôtel Castel Brando ★★★
20222 Erbalunga (Haute-Corse)
Tel. 95.30.10.30 - Fax 95.33.98.18
M. and Mme Pieri

Rooms 10 and 6 apartments with air-conditioning, telephone, bath, WC and TV, kitchenette. **Price** Double 400-800F. **Meals** Breakfast incl., served 8:30-10:00. No restaurant. **Credit cards** All major. **Pets** Dogs allowed. **Facilities** Swimming pool, parking. **Nearby** Bastia, romanesque cathedral of La Canonica and San Parteo church, villages of Cap Corse from Bastia to Saint-Florent. **Open** April 1 – Oct 30.

Joëlle and Jean-Paul Piéri, who were born in this picturesque fishing village, have restored a beautiful and charming house here, lending it comfort and personality. You can live here at your own pace and the apartments with kitchenette are especially recommendable for long stays. The shady park has a swimming pool, but if you prefer the sea, the pebble beaches in Erbalunga or Piétracorba are nearby. Fairly new to the hotel business, Monsieur and Madame Piéri have quickly become real professionals. They are very enthusiastic and will give you a warm welcome - as well as tips for discovering and enjoying the real Corsica. Erbalunga itself is classed as a preserved site and has inspired numerous painters. For dinner, the owners will give you their special addresses. We recommend *La Citadelle* and *Le Romantique* in Bastia; and in Erbalunga, overlooking the sea, *Le Pirate*.

How to get there *(Map 36): 9km north of Bastia. Bastia-Poretta Airport tel.: 95 54 54 54.*

Hôtel de la Corniche **
San-Martino-di-Lota
20200 Bastia (Haute-Corse)
Tel. 95.31.40.98 - Fax 95.32.37.69 - Mme Anziani

Rooms 19 with telephone, bath or shower and WC (10 with TV). **Price** Single 250-300F, double 300-450F. **Meals** Breakfast 30-35F, served 7:30-10:00; half board 280-360F (per pers., 3 days min.). **Restaurant** Service 12:00-14:00, 19:30-21:30 (closed Sunday evening and Monday, Oct – end March); menus, also à la carte. Specialties: Raviolis au broccio et aux herbes, Pageot du golf en étuvée de fenouil confit olives vertes, grenadins de veau sautés au gingembre et citron vert et ses canellonis de courgette au basilic, pastizzu du Cap Corse et son coulis d'orange caramélisé. **Credit cards** All major. **Pets** Dogs not allowed. **Facilities** Swimming pool. **Nearby** Romanesque cathedral of La Canonica and San Parteo church, villages of Cap Corse from Bastia to Saint-Florent. **Open** Feb 1 – Dec 20.

This hotel at San Martino-di-Lota lies along a winding road ten minutes' drive from Bastia. It has been owned by the same family since 1935 and has incomparable views of the sea. The first thing you will notice is the beautiful terrace and its splendid plane trees. Meals are served here in beautiful weather and on clear days you can see as far as the Italian coast. Home cuisine and Corsican specialties are the keynotes of the menu. The bedrooms are excellent for their price range; they are tastefully and comfortably decorated with classic wooden furniture and attractive bathrooms, and all look out to the sea. You will find a cordial welcome here.

How to get there (Map 36): 6km north of Bastia via D80, then D131 at Pietranera. Bastia Airport, tel. 95.54.54.54.

Auberge Le Moulin du Plain ★★
25470 Goumois (Doubs)
Tel. 81.44.41.99 – Fax 41.44.45.70
M. Choulet

Rooms 22 with telephone, bath or shower and WC. **Price** Single and double 204-275F. **Meals** Breakfast 34F, served 8:00-9:30; half board 220-234F, full board 290-305F (per pers., 3 days min.). **Restaurant** Service 12:00-13:30, 19:00-21:30; menus 94-194F, also à la carte. Specialties: Truite à l'échalote, feuilleté aux morilles, jambon du pays, coq au savagnin. **Credit cards** Visa, Eurocard and MasterCard. **Pets** Dogs allowed. **Facilities** Parking. **Nearby** Circuit from Maîche (D437) to Gière and Indevillers, Corniche of Goumois via the gorges of the Doubs to the Echelles de la Mort, art and clock making museums in Besançon – 18-hole Prunevelle golf course. **Open** Feb. 25 – Nov 2.

This hotel is a great favorite with fishermen. It stands on the banks of the Doubs River with its sand and pebble beach, at the foot of the mountains facing Switzerland. The emphasis here is on calm and simplicity: the steep roof of the building is a typical feature of farmhouses in the Haut-Jura, and the bedrooms are attractively unpretentious. The Auberge du Moulin du Plain is ideal for those seeking a peaceful retreat. It has a small lounge, several fireplaces and a bar area. Its exceptional location has a lot to offer not only to fishermen but also to those in search of simple pleasures: bathing in crystal-clear waters, stunning walks and excursions (Switzerland is within easy reach). The cuisine is of the same calibre as the hotel.

How to get there *(Map 20): 53km south of Montbéliard via D437 towards Maîche, at Maison Rouge D437b to Goumois; 4km before Goumois beside the River Doubs.*

Hôtel Taillard ★★★

25470 Goumois (Doubs)
Tel. 81.44.20.75 – Fax 81.44.26.15
M. Taillard

Rooms 17 with telephone, bath or shower, WC and TV (6 with minibar).
Price Double 275-340F, suite 420-430F. **Meals** Breakfast 50F, served 8:00-9:30;
half board 350-400F (per pers., 3 days min.). **Restaurant** Service 12:00-14:00,
19:15-20:45; menus 135-370F, also à la carte. Specialties: Escalope de foie gras
aux griottes de Fougerolles. **Credit cards** All major. **Pets** Dogs allowed (+30F).
Facilities Swimming pool, parking. **Nearby** The Maîche road (D437) to Gière and
Indevillers, Goumois (coastal road) via the Doubs gorges to Les Echelles de la
Mort, art and clock making museums in Besançon – 18-hole Prunevelle golf
course. **Open** March – Nov (closed Wednesdays in March and Oct).

You will appreciate the hotelkeeping and gastronomic
knowhow of four generations of Taillards in this hotel. It is
in the middle of the Jura countryside on a hillside overlooking a
small valley. You can see the blue foothills of the Swiss Alps on
the horizon. The rooms are comfortable and most of them have a
balcony facing the mountains. The pastures of the Haut-Doubs are
soft green, and you can still hear the tinkling of cow bells there,
the Doubs river is great for trout fishing and kayaking. Everything
is simple and quiet here. We especially liked Monsieur Taillard's
cuisine, which features regional specialties with a local flavor. The
menu is imaginative and the "light" dishes will satisfy many a
gourmet. The service is also outstanding.

How to get there *(Map 20): 53km south of Montbéliard via D437 towards
Maîche, at Maison Rouge D437b to Goumois; near the church.*

Hôtel de la Vouivre ★★★

39 bis, rue Gédéon-David
39300 Champagnole (Jura)
Tel. 84.52.10.44 - Mme Pernot

Rooms 20 with telephone, bath or shower, WC and TV. **Price** Single 297-362F, double 312-404F. **Meals** Breakfast 39F, served 7:00-9:30; half board 270-350F, full board 370-430F (per pers.). **Restaurant** Closed Wednesday noon. Service 12:00-14:00, 19:30-21:30; menus 110-170F, also à la carte. Specialties: Truite au vin jaune, filet de bœuf aux morilles. **Credit cards** Visa, Eurocard and MasterCard. **Pets** Dogs allowed. **Facilities** Swimming pool, tennis, parking. **Nearby** Lake of Chalain, cirque of Beaume-les-Messieurs, château of Syam, Billaude waterfall, Langouette and Malvaux gorges – 18-hole Val-de-Sorne golf course in Lons-le-Saunier. **Open** May 1 – Oct 30.

The Vouivre is a beautiful hotel somewhat on the outskirts of Champagnole. Comfortable bedrooms, a swimming pool, tennis courts and a quiet location make it a restful place to stay in this beautiful region of the Jura. It is very near the La Joux Forest with its famous President fir tree (132 feet high, 12 feet in diameter), which is unfortunately difficult to get to. The lake, which is surrounded by a ten-acre park, provides good fishing. Champagnole itself is a dynamic small town there toys and furniture are made.

How to get there *(Map 20): 43km southwest of Pontarlier via D471.*

Le Moulin de la Mère Michelle ★★

Les Planches
39600 Arbois (Jura)
Tel. 84.66.08.17 - Fax 84.37.49.69 - M. Delavenne

Rooms 22 with telephone, bath or shower, WC, TV and minibar - Elevator. **Price** Double 380-680F. **Meals** Breakfast 55F, served 8:00-10:30; half board 450-600F (per pers., 3 days min.). **Restaurant** Closed Thursdays in low season. Service 12:00-13:30, 19:30-21:00; menus 75-380F, also à la carte. Specialties: Poularde aux morilles et vin jaune, pochouse de truite. **Credit cards** Amex, Visa, Eurocard and MasterCard. **Pets** Dogs allowed (+60F). **Facilities** Swimming pool, tennis, parking. **Nearby** Wine and vineyard Museum, Pasteur's house, Planches cave, Hôtel-Dieu pharmacy in Poligny — 18-hole Val-de-Sorne golf course in Lons-le-Saunier. **Open** All year.

The Moulin de la Mère Michelle stands well off the beaten track on the way to Switzerland and not far from Arbois, a town that delights visitors with the opulent provincial charm of prosperous businesses and vineyards. Formerly a mill where walnuts were ground for oil, the building has been carefully restored by its current owner, who has extensively transformed it into a small fortress with an elevator in tower. The bedrooms also have been modernized and are very comfortable with their warn colors, stone walls, beamed ceiling and a four-poster bed in rooms 10 and 11. This is a good hotel in a peaceful and superb setting near a spectacular waterfall. Note that half-board is compulsory in summer, particularly for guests staying for one night only.

How to get there *(Map 19): 42km northeast of Lons-le-Saunier via N83 to Arbois via Poligny, D107 to Mesnay then D247.*

Hôtel de France ★★

39220 Les Rousses (Jura)
Tel. 84.60.01.45 – Fax 84.60.04.63
Mme Petit

Rooms 33 with telephone, bath or shower, (31 with WC) and TV. **Price** Double 260-460F. **Meals** Breakfast 38F; half board 310-415F, full board 390-495F (per pers., 2 days mim.). **Restaurant** Service 12:15-14:00, 19:15-22:00, menus 120-360F. Specialties: Terrine poularde, raviolis de crustacés, cœur de pigeon au vin rouge, poires caramélisées au fondant de chocolat, crème soufflée au Grand-Marnier. **Credit cards** All major. **Pets** Dogs not allowed. **Nearby** Ski: 200m from the ski lift – 18-hole Rochat golf course. **Open** Dec 13 – Nov 18 (closed June 11 – 27).

The Petit family has been running this hotel for more than thirty years. It is a large chalet whose balconies overflow with flowers in summer. Once you're inside the front door, you will love the Hôtel de France; the large lounge with its wood paneling and beautiful beams beckon you to take a seat by the large stone fireplace. On the left, the dining room is bright and welcoming. The chef, Jean-Pierre Durcrot, who was Roger Petit's apprentice and trained with the famous Paris chefs, puts all his considerable talent in the service of the hotel's clientele. Meals are served on the large shady terrace in summer. All the bedrooms are simply and comfortably decorated and look out on the forest. You can enjoy total relaxation here after a vigorous day of cross-country or downhill skiing. Madame Petit is very friendly and hospitable.

How to get there *(Map 20): 85km southwest of Pontarlier via D72 to Chaffrois; D471 to Champagnole and N5 via Morez.*

Auberge de Courpain ★★★

Courpain
91690 Fontaine-la-Rivière (Essonne)
Tel. (1) 64.95.67.04 – Fax (1) 60.80.99.02 – Mme Tewe

Rooms 18 with telephone, bath or shower and WC (7 with TV). **Price** Single and double 350F, suite 450-700F. **Meals** Breakfast 40F. **Restaurant** Service 12:30-14:00, 19:30-21:00; menus 130 (in week)-180F, also à la carte. Specialties: Filet Waldorff, blanquette de lotte aux morilles, nougat glacé, Pithiviers chaud. **Credit cards** Amex, Visa, Eurocard and MasterCard. **Pets** Dogs allowed. **Facilities** Helicopter pad, parking. **Nearby** Château promenade des parfums in Chamerolles, Juine Valley in Méréville, aérodrome Jean Salis in La Ferté-Alais, Jeurre Park in Morigny-Etampes. **Open** All year except in Feb.

This former coaching's inn consists of a number of buildings lying within a large garden in the middle of the countryside. Unfortunately the road beside the hotel has been considerably widened and the garden can therefore be a bit noisy. A path leads from the inn to a delightful valley where you can stroll along the banks of its trout streams. You will enjoy reading or relaxing in the lounge or by the fireplace of the hotel, where a warm and cozy atmosphere prevails. There are three dining rooms, all spacious and pleasantly furnished. (Our favorite is the summer dining-room, for its vast windows looking out onto the garden). The bedrooms are all different and have been tastefully decorated, and the same amount of care and attention to detail has been devoted to the bathrooms. The cuisine is good.

How to get there *(Map 9): 58km south of Paris via N20 to Etampes, then N191 Malsherbes-Pithiviers to the roundabout, on your right D721 towards Pithiviers.*

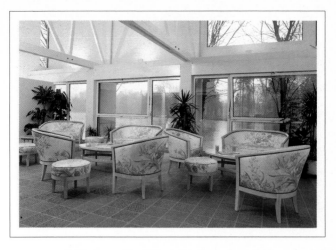

Auberge de l'Ile du Saussay ★★★

Route de Ballancourt
91760 Itteville (Essonne)
Tel. (1) 64.93.20.12 – Fax (1) 64.93.39.88 – M. Lebrun

Rooms 7, 2 apartments (4 pers.), 13 suites with telephone, bath or shower, WC, TV, minibar and safe. **Price** Double 350F, apartment 900F, suite 450F. **Meals** Breakfast 45F, served 7:00-10:30. **Restaurant** Closed Monday. Service 12:00-14:30, 19:00-22:00; menus 145-195F, also à la carte. **Credit cards** All major. **Pets** Dogs allowed. **Facilities** Parking. **Nearby** Dourdan, Arpajon and Renarde Valley, château of Farcheville. **Open** All year except in Aug (closed Monday).

Monsieur and Madame Lebrun fell in love with the beautiful watery setting of the Auberge de l'Ile du Saussay at first sight. Although it is very contemporary in design, the lakes and trees surrounding the Auberge make it perfectly charming. Three different categories of accommodations are proposed, but all share beautiful decor and modern conveniences. Large bay windows open onto a terrace with a view of the lake or, in the back, the trees and a small inlet. You have a choice of bedrooms; suites with a small living room and bedroom on the mezzanine; or apartments with two bedrooms and a living room. The overall effect is very lovely. The restaurant also enjoys a splendid view of these small lakes which were created centuries ago when the River Essonne filled up the old quarries which monks had dug out to extract peat to heat Parisian houses. At the Auberge, you will enjoy very friendly service and hospitality on the part of a couple who want to share their enthusiasm for this very special setting.

How to get there *(Map 9): 40km south of Paris via N 20 to Etampes; then, after Arpajon, take direction La Fertais-Alais.*

Hostellerie de la Clé d'Or ★★★

73, Grande-Rue
77630 Barbizon (Seine-et-Marne)
Tel. (1) 60.66.40.96 - Fax (1) 60.66.42.71 - M. Gayer

Rooms 16 with telephone, bath or shower, WC, cable TV and minibar. **Price** Single 280F, double 420F, suite 850F. **Meals** Breakfast 45F, served 7:45-11:00. **Restaurant** Service 12:00-14:00, 19:30-21:00; menus 190-230F, also à la carte. **Credit cards** All major. **Pets** Dogs allowed. **Facilities** Parking. **Nearby** House of Théodore Rousseau, forest and palace of Fontainebleau – 18-hole Fontainebleau golf course in Barbizon. **Open** All year (closed Sunday evenings in low season).

Located on the edge of the forest in Barbizon, the Hostellerie de la Clé d'Or is a traditional hotel, evocative of opulence and comfort. Formerly a coaching inn, it is the oldest establishment in a village whose peace and beauty have inspired many artists. The cuisine certainly constitutes the highlight of a visit. Skilfully prepared gourmet cuisine is served here, admirably complemented by an interesting wine list. The hotel has much to offer: a beautiful dining-room with a fireplace, a terrace looking out across the garden where meals can be served in summer, and fully-equipped bedrooms with access to the lawn. The elegant atmosphere is enhanced by beautiful antique furniture, copperware, pottery and tastefully hung paintings.

How to get there *(Map 9): 57km southeast of Paris via A6, Fontainebleau exit; then N37 and D64 to Barbizon.*

Château des Bondons ★★★

47/49, rue des Bondons
77260 La Ferté-sous-Jouarre (Seine-et-Marne)
Tel. (1) 60.22.00.98 - Fax (1) 60.22.97.01 - M. Busconi

Rooms 14 with telephone, bath, WC, TV and minibar. **Price** Double 300-500F, suite 550-900F, apart. 500-800F. **Meals** Breakfast 40F. No restaurant. **Credit cards** All major. **Pets** Dogs allowed (+30F). **Facilities** Parking. **Nearby** Jouarre, Eurodisneyland. **Open** All year.

Set in a vast park, this small 19th-century château was sinking into oblivion before the Busconis thoroughly renovated and resuscitated it. The reception rooms on the ground-floor look out onto the surrounding gardens. The entrance hall has an elaborate marble mosaic floor and the same geometrical patterns can be seen in the ivory inlay of the paneling. In the dining-room there is delightful paneling inlaid with small landscape pictures. You will find a wealth of 18th-century style furniture – modern copies, but elegant. The lounge is vast and light, but the tiled floor could do with a few rugs. A beautiful wooden staircase leads up to the bedrooms which are extremely warm and cozy, with thick carpets and lovely flowered fabrics. The bedrooms are individually decorated and have luxuriously equipped bathrooms. Rooms 4 and 8 are particularly noteworthy (albeit more expensive). You will enjoy an extremely friendly welcome and excellent, hearty breakfasts. *L'Auberge de Condé* is the best restaurant in the city; another good choice is *L'Auberge du Petit Morin* in Mourette.

How to get there *(Map 10): 65km east of Paris via A4, Ferté-sous-Jouarre exit, then N3; in the village Chalons-sur-Marne and Montménard direction.*

257

Au Moulin ★★★

2, rue du Moulin
77940 Flagy (Seine-et-Marne)
Tel. (1) 60.96.67.89 - Fax (1) 60.96.69.51 - M. and Mme Scheidecker

Rooms 10 with telephone, bath and WC. **Price** Single 350-438F, double 533-620F.
Meals Breakfast 45F, served 7:45-11:00; half board 350-438F, full board 477-552F
(per 2 pers.). **Restaurant** Service 12:15-14:15, 19:15-21:15; menus 170-220F, also
à la carte. **Credit cards** All major. **Pets** Dogs allowed. **Facilities** Parking.
Nearby Palace and forest of Fontainebleau, Moret-sur-Loing – 18-hole La Forteresse
golf course. **Open** Jan 22 – Sept 17 and Sept 29 – Dec 17 (closed Sunday evenings
and Mondays except Easter, May 1 and 23: Monday evening and Tuesday).

This 13th-century flour mill has been well restored. Beneath
the stucco façade the ancient masonry was discovered in a
remarkable state of preservation. The original half-timbering, the
cob walls, the ground-floor stonework and the beautiful vaulted
gable have all been stripped bare and greatly contribute to the strong
period atmosphere of the building. The hotel accommodates guests
in ten fully equipped and carefully decorated bedrooms. The
dining-room looks out onto the river, and there are also a terrace
and a garden. Dinner is served by candlelight in the evening and
log fires are lit in winter. You are assured of a comfortable stay in
this hotel where a quiet rural setting and beautiful architecture
combine to create an ambience of warmth and well-being only an
hour away from Paris.

How to get there *(Map 9): 88km southeast of Paris via A6, Fontainebleau
exit, then N6 for 18km; at the traffic lights turn right onto D403 and
immediatly on your left D120.*

Hostellerie Aux Vieux Remparts ★★★

3, rue Couverte - Ville Haute
77160 Provins (Seine-et-Marne)
Tel. (1) 64.08.94.00 - Fax (1) 60.67.77.22 - M. Roy

Rooms 25 with telephone, bath or shower, WC, TV and minibar. **Price** Single 340-470F, double 395-650F. **Meals** Breakfast 50F, served 7:00-11:00; half board 490-560F, full board 650-720F (per pers.). **Restaurant** Service 12:00-14:30, 19:30-21:30; menus 180-350F, also à la carte. Specialties: Petite salade de langouste tiède en crudité, gaspacho de tomates, lasagnes de homard breton et ragoût de coquillages, pomme de ris de veau piquée, foie gras braisée au beurre mousseux, confiture de vieux garçon. **Credit cards** All major. **Pets** Dogs allowed (+60F). **Facilities** Parking. **Nearby** Ramparts, tower of César, church of Saint-Quiriace in Provins, spectacle de fauconnerie, tournoi de chevalerie, church of Saint-Loup-de-Naud – 18-hole Fontenaille golf course. **Open** All year.

Located in the most beautiful part of medieval Provins, the Hostellerie Aux Vieux Remparts has twenty-five bedrooms in an adjoining modern building. It successfully blends in with the town's splendid medieval architecture. In the comfortable, quiet bedrooms, the modern decor includes quilted bedcovers, carpets, and many cerused pieces of furniture. In the restaurant, you will have the choice between a highly reputed gastronomic menu or the bistrot fare, which is served in a beautiful half-timbered 16th-century house, or on the terrace in summer. The decoration is in strict keeping with the traditional character of the village and tables are also set up in a very charming small courtyard in good weather. The Hostellerie is very lovely and you will be warmly welcome.

How to get there *(Map 10): 86km southeast of Paris via A4, then D231 to Provins.*

La Louveterie ★★★★

77515 Saint-Augustin (Seine-et-Marne)
10, route de Faremoutiers
Tel. (1) 64.03.37.59 - Fax (1) 64.03.89.00 - Mme Lucia Di-Meo

Rooms 8 with telephone, bath, WC and TV. **Price** Double 500F, apartment 700F. **Meals** Breakfast 50-80F, served 7:30-10:30; half board 500-750F, full board 850-950F (per pers., 3 days min.). **Restaurant** Closed Feb 1 – 20.and Nov 1 – April 30). Service 12:00-14:30, 19:30-21:00; menus 145-370F, also à la carte. Specialties: Parmentier de queue de bœuf, gigot de lapin cuit au foin, raviolis de l'océan au consommé de volaille, agrumes grillés aux écorces d'oranges confites. **Credit cards** All major. **Pets** Dogs allowed. **facilities** Swimming pool, sauna, parking. **Nearby** Meaux, Provins, Jouarre, Grand Morin Valley, Eurodisneyland – Crécy-la-Chapelle golf course. **Open** All year except Feb 1 – 20.

La Louveterie was a private residence before the present owner, a decorator, converted it into a hotel. So it is not surprising that it is so beautifully decorated, and as pleasant to live in as to look at. It is modern, warm, spacious and flooded with light from its bay windows. Several steps lead to the lounge and the dining room, which are furnished with contemporary paintings, comfortable furniture - antique as well as designer pieces - and shimmering rugs. The bedrooms and baths reflect the same intimate, tranquil beauty. There is also an indoor swimming pool whose sliding bay windows open onto a vast terrace; in the summer, several dining tables are set out here. The final touch is the excellent cuisine; the service and hospitality are very friendly.

How to get there *(Map 10): 70km east of Paris via A 4, exit Provins, direction Coulommiers; 8km south of Coulommiers, on the edge of the Malvoisine Forest.*

Hostellerie Le Vieux Logis

5, rue Sadi-Carnot
77810 Thomery (Seine-et-Marne)
Tel. (1) 60.96.44.77 - Fax (1) 60.96.42.71 - M. Plouvier

Rooms 14 with telephone, bath, WC and TV. **Price** Single and double 400F.
Meals Breakfast 50F, served 7:15-10:00. **Restaurant** Service 12:15-14:45, 19:45-21:30; menus 145-240F, also à la carte. **Credit cards** Amex, Visa, Eurocard and MasterCard. **Pets** Dogs allowed (+35F). **Facilities** Heated swimming pool, parking. **Nearby** Palace and forest of Fontainebleau, Barbizon, Milly-la-Forêt (chapel of Saint-Blaise, decorated by Cocteau, and covered market), Moret-sur-Loing — 18-hole Fontainebleau golf course. **Open** All year.

Having restored and opened the beautiful Moulin de Flagy, M. and Mme Plouvier decided to apply all their energy and flair to this handsome late 18th-century house, set in a village once famous for its vineyards and close to Fontainebleau Forest. The fourteen fully equipped bedrooms are decorated in a muted contemporary style combining painted wood and pastel fabrics. The chef's inspired efforts in the kitchen result in exquisite dishes, which are served in a magnificent dining-room. In the conservatory, white tables, a white piano and potted plants create an elegant modern atmosphere which is carried through to the pleasant bar area. The hotel has just added a magnificent heated swimming pool and a beautiful garden where meals are served in good weather. Madame Plouvier is meticulous in every detail, and she will ensure you have an enjoyable stay.

How to get there *(Map 9): 71km southeast of Paris via A6, 9km west of Fontainebleau via N6 towards Sens, then D137 towards Champagne.*

Auberge du Gros Marronnier ★★

3, place de l'Eglise
78720 Senlisse (Yvelines)
Tel. (1) 30.52.51.69 – Fax (1) 30.52.55.91 – Mme Trochon

Rooms 19 with telephone, bath or shower and WC. **Price** Single 290F, double 325-385F. **Meals** Breakfast 40F, served 7:00-11:30; half board and full board 340-690F. **Restaurant** Service 12:00-14:30, 19:30-22:00; menus 135F (165F on Sunday), also à la carte. Specialties: Foie gras et confit de canard maison, fish, game, desserts maison. **Credit cards** All major. **Pets** Dogs allowed (+50F). **Facilities** Parking. **Nearby** Châteaux of Dampierre and Breteuil, abbeys of Vaux-le-Cernay and Port-Royal-des-Champs – Forges-les-Bains golf course. **Open** All year.

This charming inn is on a street in the pretty village of Senlisse, in the Chevreuse Valley regional park. On the far side of the courtyard, there is a lovely walled garden with fruit trees, a well and benches where you can sit and admire the beautiful church next door. You will find the same peaceful country atmosphere inside the house. The rooms and bathrooms are comfortable and have all been renovated. In winter, you can see the beautifully lit stained glass windows of the church and the valley beyond from the enclosed porch of the restaurant. As soon as spring comes, the tables are moved outside. The hotel is only 35 minutes from the center of Paris by subway (RER B line) although the RER station is three and a half miles from Senlisse. This is a good place for those who want to get away from it all, without having to deal with weekend traffic.

How to get there *(Map 9): 35km southwest of Paris; Pont de Sèvres, A10 toward Chartres, Saclay exit, then D906 to Chevreuse and D91 on 6km toward Senlisse.*

Dame Carcas ★★★

15, rue Saint-Louis - La Cité
11000 Carcassonne (Aude)
Tel. 68.71.37.37 - Fax 68.71.50.15 - M. Faidherbe and M. Luraschi

Rooms 30 with air-conditioning, telephone, bath or shower, WC and TV - Wheelchair accessible. **Price** Single 340-470F, double 400-600F. **Meals** Breakfast 60F, served 7:00-11:00. **Restaurant** Closed Wednesday. "Les Coulisses du Théatre". Service 12:00-14:00, 19:00-22:00; menus 80-200F, also à la carte. Specialties: Regional cooking. **Credit cards** All major. **Pets** Dogs allowed. **Facilities** Parking. **Nearby** La Cité, churches of Saint-Vincent and Saint-Nazaire in Carcassonne, château de Pennautier – 9-hole Auriac golf course in Carcassonne. **Open** All year.

Formerly an annex of the Hôtel de la Cité, the Dame Carcas is now a hotel in its own right, and a very pleasant one, too. It has been entirely refurbished with as much flair and attention to detail as its neighbor, but is more sober in style. The bedrooms are all comfortable, with cherry wood beds and beautiful furniture, and their decor is charming and fresh. Rooms 215 to 219 are resolutely rustic in character with floor tiles and a flowery decor, whereas rooms 201 to 210, lavishly equipped with marble bathrooms, are elegance epitomized. The hotel doesn't have a restaurant of its own, but a footbridge allows easy access to the restaurant in the Hôtel de la Cité which isunder the same management.

How to get there *(Map 31): Inside the ramparts.*

Hostellerie du Grand Duc ★★

2, route de Boucheville
11140 Gincla (Aude)
Tel. 68.20.55.02 - Fax 68.20.61.22 - M. and Mme Bruchet

Rooms 10 with telephone, bath or shower and WC. **Price** Single 215-240F, double 250-320F. **Meals** Breakfast 37F, served 8:00-11:00; half board 250-290F, full board 330-390F (per pers., 3 days min.). **Restaurant** Closed Wednesdays in low season. Service 12:15-14:00, 19:30-21:00; à la carte. Specialties: Baignades de sépiole au Fitou, cailles au muscat, faux-filet au foie gras et aux griottes. **Credit cards** Visa, Eurocard and MasterCard. **Pets** Dogs allowed. **Facilities** Parking. **Nearby** Forest of Fanges, Saint-Paul-de-Fenouillet, Belvianes, Saint-Paul-de-Fenouillet, gorges of Galamus. **Open** March 25 – Nov 15.

This hotel of great charm – a carefully restored family mansion – is set in a small village. Their guests' well-being is the young and friendly owners' chief concern and they pride themselves on their warm hospitality. The bedrooms are all individually designed and decorated in a wide range of styles. Whitewashed walls, exposed stonework and beamed ceilings highlight the rustic character of the pleasant dining room. The lounge and the bar area are particularly cozy. In summer, breakfast and dinner can be served in the garden, with candles on the tables in the evening.

How to get there *(Map 31): 63km northwest of Perpignan via D117 to Lapradelle, then D22 to Gincla.*

Relais du Val d'Orbieu ★★★

11200 Ornaisons (Aude)
Tel. 68.27.10.27 – Fax 68.27.52.44
M. and Mme Gonzalvez

Rooms 20 with telephone, bath, WC, TV and minibar. **Price** Single 480F, double 580-690F, suite 790-1450F. **Meals** Breakfast 65F, served 7:30-10:30; half board 615-670F (per pers.). **Restaurant** Service 12:15-13:45, 19:30-21:00; menus 165-295F, also à la carte. Specialties: Langoustines rôties, magret au rancio, gratin de fruits. **Credit cards** All major. **Pets** Dogs allowed (+80F). **Facilities** Swimming pool, tennis, golf practice, parking. **Nearby** Cathedral of Saint-Just in Narbonne, mountain of la Clape, African reserve of Sigean, abbey of Fontfroide, Lagrasse – 9-hole Auriac golf course in Carcassonne. **Open** All year (closed Sunday evenings Nov – March).

Facing the stunningly picturesque Montagne Noire, the Relais couldn't have a better location. The building itself, formerly a mill, has been carefully restored: the rooms are elegantly decorated and an atmosphere of calm and coziness prevails. The bedrooms at garden level are all very comfortable and in the morning delicious and ample breakfasts are served there, with fresh fruit juices, cheese, *pâtisseries* and home-made jams, as well as a large choice of teas and coffees. The Relais' much praised cuisine has earned it a reputation as one of Languedoc's leading restaurants, and it is admirably set off by J.P. Gonzalvez's remarkable selection of regional wines. Guests will find the hospitality attentive.

How to get there *(Map 31): 47km east of Carcassonne via A61, Lézignan exit then D611 to Lézignan and D24 (eastward) to Ornaisons; signposted.*

Castel de Villemagne **
Villemagne
11310 Saissac (Aude)
Tel. 68.94.22.95 - Mme de Vézian Maksud

Rooms 7 with telephone, bath or shower and WC. **Price** Single 255-370F, double
310-430F, suite 600F. **Meals** Breakfast 40F, served 8:00-10:00; half board 292-
355F (per pers., 3 days min.). **Restaurant** Service 19:30-20:30; menus 100-
190F, children 60F, also à la carte. Specialties: Cassoulet, civet de marcassin.
Credit cards Visa, Eurocard and MasterCard. **Pets** Dogs allowed in bedrooms.
Facilities Parking. **Nearby** La Montagne Noire, abbey of Villelongue, belvedere of the
châteaux of Lastours, gorges of la Clamoux – 9-hole Auriac golf course in
Carcassonne. **Open** March 15 – Dec 31.

In a pretty village in the Montagne Noire area, between Mazamet
and Carcassonne, Mme de Vezian-Maksud accommodates guests
in a manor built in the 14th and 18th centuries. The Castel de
Villemagne has throughout the centuries been a private house,
opening as a hotel only ten years ago, and it retains the distinctive
character of a long-established and much-loved family home. In
the bedrooms, tall wardrobes and Napoleon III wing-chairs create
the old-fashioned charm associated with country living. In summer,
the garden is the best place to have breakfast, for the lovely view
of the Pyrenees and the pleasant park. Mme de Vézian-Maksud is
very much attached to her native region and will be delighted to
tell you all about the Languedoc area and the fascinating
Cathars.

How to get there (*Map 31*): *31km northwest of Carcassonne via N113,*
then D629 to Saissac and D103.

Hôtel Les Arcades

23, bd Gambetta
30220 Aigues-Mortes (Gard)
Tel. 66.53.81.13 - Fax 66.53.75.46

Rooms 6 with telephone, bath and WC. **Price** Double 460-550F. **Meals** Breakfast incl.
Restaurant Closed Monday and Tuesday in low season. Menus 120-200F, also à la
carte. Specialties: Gardiane de taureau à l'ancienne, huîtres chaudes, filet de taureau
grillé, crèpes pralinées à l'orange. **Credit cards** All major. **Pets** Small dogs allowed.
Nearby The Camargue, Arles, Saintes-Maries-de-la-Mer (gypsies' pilgrimage May
24 – 25), Tarascon, Nîmes, Montpellier. **Open** All year (closed Feb 3 – 28).

We loved this 16th-century house set in a quiet street in the
old town. Inside, everything is neat and charming. A lovely
aged and patinated paint effect, in colors ranging from lime green
to brown, enhances the corridors and the bedrooms, where
curtains, bedspreads and antique furniture are in perfect harmony.
The bedrooms are vast, with high, elaborate ceilings and tall
mullioned windows, and fully equipped bathrooms provide all the
modern comforts. Breakfast and dinner – which are excellent – are
served in a pleasant dining-room with an ancient terra cotta tiled
floor. It opens on one side into a little garden, and on the other
into an arcade where a few tables are set up. A warm, family
atmosphere prevails.

How to get there *(Map 32): 48km west of Arles towards Saintes-Maries-
de-la-Mer, then D58.*

Hôtel Les Templiers ★★★

23, rue de la République
30220 Aigues-Mortes (Gard)
Tel. 66.53.66.56 - Fax 66.53.69.61 - M. Berdin

Rooms 11 with air-conditioning, telephone, bath or shower, WC and cable TV -
Wheelchair accessible. **Price** Double 400-700F, suite 650-750F. **Meals** Breakfast
50F, served from 7:30. No restaurant. **Credit cards** Amex, Visa, Eurocard and
MasterCard. **Pets** Dogs allowed. **Facilities** Garage. **Nearby** La Camargue, Arles, Les
Sainte-Marie-de-la-Mer (gypsies' pilgrimage May 24 – 25), Tarascon, Nîmes,
Montpellier. **Open** March 2 – Jan 16.

The present owners have, over the last four years, made an
elegant hotel in the center of Aigues-Mortes out of what was
once a 17th-century merchants' house which they retrieved four
years ago from a state of advanced dilapidation. The Polvaras are
in love with the region, the city, the hotel and their work - which
is a very recent discovery for them - and they are anxious to share
their enthusiasm in every way with their guests. After their tasteful
restoration of the house, the couple searched the region for
Provençal furniture, which lend each bedroom a personal touch;
there are few family portraits on the walls. Some rooms look out
onto the street but are nevertheless very quiet except on holidays:
Aigues-Mortes is a pedestrian town. We liked other rooms for their
view onto the interior courtyard and a cool fountain. There is no
restaurant but the hotel serves pleasant snacks and will provided
list of good restaurants. We like *Le Minos*, *La Goulue* and *Les Arcades*.

How to get there *(Map 32): 48km west of Arles, direction Saintes-Maries-
de-la-Mer, then D 58.*

Mas Quayrol ★★

Aulas
30120 Le Vigan (Gard)
Tel. 67.81.12.38 - Fax 67.81.23.84 - M. Grenouillet

Rooms 16 with telephone, bath, WC and TV. **Price** Single and double 360F.
Meals Breakfast 36F. **Restaurant** Service 12:00-14:00, 19:00-21:00; menus 125-260F, also à la carte. Specialties: Champignons de la forêt, truites, foie gras de canard, cuissot de canard confit au vin jaune et aux morilles, duo de poissons à l'oseille, pélardon de chèvres, assiette de gourmandises. **Credit cards** Visa, Eurocard and MasterCard. **Pets** Dogs allowed. **Facilities** Swimming pool, tennis, parking. **Nearby** Château de Roquebois in Meyrueis, cave of the Demoiselles, cirque of Navacelles, La Couvertoirade, Cévenol museum in Le Vigan, Cévennes national park – 9-hole Bombequiols golf course in Ganges. **Open** March 25 – Dec 31.

Set on a hillside above the village of Aulas, this hotel commands stunning views of the valley below. The layout of the building follows the slope, and the different levels have been skillfully put to use to accommodate terraces, small lounges and a panoramic restaurant. Beamed ceilings and wood panelling create a pleasant atmosphere. The brown color scheme chosen to decorate the bedrooms was fashionable in the 70s but makes the rooms seem a bit dark when the sun is not shining. Everywhere else in the hotel, large picture windows afford unimpeded enjoyment of the natural surroundings. (The most remarkable of these many windows is the one in the entrance hall, which opens out onto the swimming pool.)

How to get there *(Map 32): 60km north of Montpellier via D986, then D999 to Le Vigan, then Aulas.*

Hôtel Le Mas du Termes ★★★

Route de Bagnols-sur-Cèze
30430 Barjac (Gard)
Tel. 66.24.56.31 - Fax 66.24.58.54 - M. and Mme Marron

Rooms 19 and 8 apartments with telephone, bath or shower, WC, TV and minibar.
Price Double 330-450F, suite 660-720F. **Meals** Breakfast 45F, served 7:30-
10:00; half board 370-400F, full board 510-535F (per pers., 3 days min.).
Restaurant Service 12:00-14:00, 19:00-22:00; menus 120-220F, also à la carte.
Specialties: Panaché d'agneau de lait au miel de Barjac, suprême de saumon à la
crème d'oseille, nougat glacé au coulis de framboise. **Credit cards** Visa, Eurocard
and MasterCard. **Pets** Dogs allowed. **Facilities** Swimming pool, parking.
Nearby Art Modern Museum in Bagnols-sur-Cèze, Prafrance bamboo garden in
Anduze, gorges of the Ardèche. **Open** March 1 – Dec 31.

This hotel lies only minutes away from the gorges of the Ardèche
and the Cèze Valley, both very popular with visitors in search
of beautiful scenery. Yet its location amidst its own extensive
vineyards ensures you will find peace and quiet. The restaurant is
one of the best in the area and serves wine from the hotel's vineyard.
The building was once used for silkworm breeding, and its
character is still evident in the vaulted lounge, the bar in the interior
courtyard, and the stone walls. In addition to comfortable, pleasant
bedrooms there are eight apartments. The young owners are
considerate and friendly hosts.

How to get there *(Map 32): 64km northwest of Avignon via A7, Bollène
exit, then D994 to Pont-Saint-Esprit, then N86, turn left after 3km onto
D901 to Barjac via Aiguèze.*

Hostellerie Le Castellas ★★★

Grand' Rue
30210 Collias (Gard)
Tel. 66.22.88.88 - Fax 66.22.84.28 - M. and Mme Aparis

Rooms 15 and 1 suite with air-conditioning, telephone, bath or shower, WC, TV and minibar. **Price** Single 400-440F, double 500-590F, suite 800-1000F. **Meals** Breakfast 60F, served 7:30-11:00; half board 495-750F. **Restaurant** Service 12:00-14:00, 19:00-21:15; menus 160-300F, also à la carte. Specialties: Foie gras poêlé et plateau de pommes de terre à la truffe, suprême de pigeon rôti à la provençale, champignons et jus de ses abats. **Credit cards** All major. **Pets** Dogs allowed (+50F). **Facilities** Swimming pool, parking. **Nearby** Pont du Gard, Uzès, Nîmes – 9-hole golf course in Uzès. **Open** March 10 – Jan 6.

In a little street in the center of Collias, two venerable 17th-century dwellings house the Hostellerie Le Castellas. The layout of the buildings forms an enclosed courtyard which makes the perfect location for a beautiful swimming-pool, the terrace of the restaurant, and a delightful little garden *à la Monet*. A favorite haunt of artists and sculptors, the second house has remarkable interior decoration and extraordinary bathrooms. The bedrooms in the main building are also very pleasant, but more classical in style. A friendly welcome and a restaurant serving refined and imaginative cuisine add to the many attractions of the hotel.

How to get there *(Map 33): 26km northeast of Nîmes via A9, Remoulins exit; at Remoulins D981 then D112 to Collias.*

La Bégude Saint-Pierre
D 981
30210 Les Coudoulières (Gard)
Tel. 66.22.10.10 - Fax 66.22.73.73 - M. Griffoul

Rooms 28 with telephone, bath, WC, TV and minibar - Wheelchair accessible.
Price Double 440-700F, suite 800-1300F. **Meals** Breakfast 65F, served 7:00-10:30;
half board 450F, full board 630F (per pers., 3 days min.). **Restaurant** Service 12:00-
14:00, 19:30-22:00; menus 195-360F, also à la carte. Specialties: Foie gras poêlé,
saumon fumé par la maison. **Credit cards** All major. **Pets** Dogs allowed (+40F).
Facilities Swimming pool, parking. **Nearby** Pont du Gard, Uzès, Nîmes, Avignon.
Open All year except in Nov.

A *bégude* used to be a postal relay station with a twin farmhouse
next door. The owner of an auberge in a village near Uzès,
Monsieur Griffoul has extensively restored this pretty Provençal
bégude, creating a comfortable, luxurious hotel with a swimming
pool, bedrooms with large terraces, a bar, a restaurant and a grill
for the summer. We especially liked room 31 for its unusual
spaciousness, and number 15 for its charming mezzanine. All are
decorated with the simplicity which is appropriate to Provençal
houses, including Souleïado fabrics and regional furniture. The
lounges and dining rooms are decorated with similar traditional
charm, conferring homogeneity to the style of this recently
inaugurated hotel. Obviously, special attention is given to the
cuisine because Monsieur Griffoul is first and foremost a chef! He
even smokes his own salmon on the premises.

How to get there *(Map 33): 25km northeast of Nîmes via A9, exit
Remoulins, then D981 direction Uzès.*

La Vieille Fontaine ★★★
30630 Cornillon (Gard)
Tel. 66.82.20.56 – Fax 66.82.33.64
M. Audibert

Rooms 8 (4 with air-conditioning) with bath, WC, TV and minibar. **Price** Double 550-850F. **Meals** Breakfast 55F, from 8:00; half board 450-650F (per pers., 4 night min.). **Restaurant** Service 12:00-13:30, 19:30-21:30; menus from 195F, also à la carte. Specialties: Soupe au pistou, gratiné de langoustine, civet de porcelet, gigot à la ficelle. **Credit cards** Amex, Visa, Eurocard and MasterCard. **Pets** Dogs allowed (+50F). **Facilities** Swimming pool. **Nearby** Avignon, Orange, Modern Art Museum in Bagnols-sur-Cèze, village of Roque-sur-Cèze, Goudargues Abbey Church, gorges of the Cèze. **Open** March 1 – Dec 31.

Restaurant owners for more than twenty years, Monsieur and Madame Audibert have discovered a new calling as hotel keepers. Within the walls of the former medieval castle of Cornillon, they have integrated a very modern structure with eight bedrooms decorated by Madame Audibert. There are two bedrooms per floor. Upstairs, the original small medieval apertures have been kept, providing lovely cool air in the summer. Your climb up to the last floor is rewarded with the view from pleasant balconies, which look out over the chateau walls and the valley. To reach the swimming pool, you must climb up a terraced garden (which is not advisable for people who have difficulty walking). Those who do stroll through the beautiful, carefully arranged garden, however, do not regret it!

How to get there *(Map 33): 45km northwest of Avignon via A9, exit Tavel to Bagnols-sur-Cèze; then D980 direction Barjac. On A7, take Bollène exit.*

A l'Auberge Cévenole ★★★

30110 La Favède (Gard)
Tel. 66.34.12.13 - Fax 66.34.50.50
Mme Burlon

Rooms 20 with telephone, bath or shower and WC (6 with TV and minibar). **Price** Single 300-350F, double 300-600F, suite 550-650F. **Meals** Breakfast 45F, served 7:30-10:30; half board 335-500F (per pers., 3 days min.). **Restaurant** Service 12:00-14:00, 19:30-21:00; menus 165-265F, also à la carte. Specialties: Fricassée de moules aux cèpes des Cévennes, gourmande de ris de veau aux morilles, escalope de canard chaude mille fleurs. **Credit cards** Visa, Eurocard and MasterCard. **Pets** Dogs allowed. **Facilities** Swimming pool, mini-tennis, parking. **Nearby** Mas-Soubeyran and Desert museum, Prafrance bamboo garden in Anduze, caves of Trabuc – 18-hole Haut de Nîmes golf course. **Open** Apr 1 – Oct 1.

There is nothing here to remind you of the austere *Cévennes noires*: this an island of greenery in which the garden gradually merges with the surrounding hills. In the bedrooms and the lounge, carpets, wall-fabrics and pretty tables create a warm and cozy atmosphere. The decoration shows a meticulous attention to detail and your hosts' desire to ensure you have a comfortable and enjoyable stay. The garden is full of flowers, and the large swimming-pool and the secluded location make the hotel a peaceful and pleasant summer retreat. The restaurant serves excellent food.

How to get there *(Map 32): 14km northwest of Alès via N106 to La Grande-Combe and D283.*

L'Hacienda ★★★

30320 Marguerittes – Mas de Brignon (Gard)
Tel. 66.75.02.25 – Fax 66.75.45.58
M. and Mme Chauvin

Rooms 12 with telephone, bath or shower, WC, TV and minibar. **Price** Single 350-450F, double 400-550F. **Meals** Breakfast 60-70F, served 8:00-10:00; half board 450-550F (per pers.). **Restaurant** Service 12:00-13:30, 19:30-21:30; menus 140-320F, also à la carte. Specialties: Salade tiède de St-Jacques au vinaigre de framboise, pigeonneau désossé rôti à l'ail confit. **Credit cards** Visa, Eurocard and MasterCard. **Pets** Dogs allowed (+50F). **Facilities** Swimming pool, tennis (70F), archery, pétanque, bicycles, sauna (70F), parking. **Nearby** Nîmes, Maison Carrée, Art Museum in Nîmes, Pont du Gard, château de Villevieille in Sommières, chapel of Saint-Julien-de-Salinelles – 18-hole Hauts-de-Nîmes and Nîmes Campagne golf course. **Open** All year.

The Hacienda is set in a quiet park enclosed by walls. In the center of the house, we were pleasantly surprised to find a beautiful patio with a few tables where drinks and dinner are served around a magnificent swimming pool. Next to the patio is the dining room very charming and spacious with prettily set tables and an old spiral staircase which leads up to a mezzanine overlooking the room. You will dine by candlelight and enjoy delicious cuisine, which Monsieur Chauvin and his young assistant prepare with the freshest farm products. The bedrooms are comfortable and furnished in rustic English style. Some are lighted by large, half-moon windows and others, on the ground floor, have a terrace on the garden. Not far away, you will find a *pétanque* court set among pink oleanders and roses, and a small Scandinavian chalet which houses a sauna. This is a friendly, lovely place to stay.

How to get there (Map 33): 6km east of Nîmes via A9, Nîmes-Est exit; then N86 and D135; go through Marguerittes and follow signs.

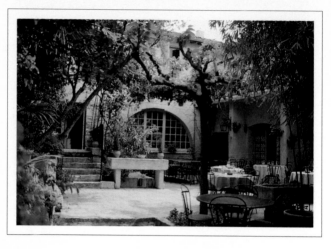

Auberge de la Paillère

Avenue du Puits-Vieux
30121 Mus (Gard)
Tel. 66.73.78.79 - Fax 66.73.79.28 - M. Gastinel

Rooms 7 with telephone, bath or shower, WC, TV, VCR and minibar. **Price** Double 350F (spacial price during Féria). **Meals** Breakfast incl., from 8:30. **Restaurant** Closed Monday and Tuesday noon. Service 12:00-13:30, 20:00-21:30; menus 110-230F, also à la carte. Specialties: Provençale cooking. **Credit cards** Amex, Visa, Eurocard and MasterCard. **Pets** Dogs allowed. **Nearby** Nîmes, Saint-Gilles, Sommières, château de Villevieille – 18-hole Hauts-de-Nîmes golf course. **Open** All year (except Jan).

When you've gone through one of the first gates of the village, you will be beneath the trellis of La Paillère's restaurant, where meals are served as soon as the weather is good. In winter, two intimate dining rooms inside, complete with traditional straw hats on the walls, serve up the aromatic specialties of Provence. Fires blaze in the fireplaces in both dining rooms as well as in the small, carefully decorated lounge. A stairway leads from the lounge to the most beautiful bedrooms: number 6, with a large sandstone bathroom; and number 7, with a balcony overlooking the graceful Virginia creeper vine. Several more functional and somewhat less charming bedrooms are located in a building of much more recent construction, which is nevertheless quite pleasant. For reasonable prices, the Auberge is lovely for festivals, vacations or even for a rainy weekend: the owner gives you a choice of 15 video cassettes to enjoy on the VCR in your bedroom.

How to get there *(Map 32): 15km southwest of Nîmes via A9, exit Gallargues, direction Les Plages, then N113 direction Codognan.*

Royal Hôtel ★★★
3, Boulevard Alphonse-Daudet
30000 Nîmes (Gard)
Tel. 66.67.28.36 - Fax 66.21.68.97 - Mmes Riera and Morel

Rooms 27 with telephone, bath or shower, WC and TV. **Price** Single and double 250-480F. **Meals** Breakfast 40F, served 7:00-12:00; half board 245F, full board 320F (per pers.). **Restaurant** Buffet-brunch. Service 12:00-15:00; menu 100F. Specialties: Mediterranean cooking. **Credit cards** Amex, Visa, Eurocard and MasterCard. **Pets** Dogs allowed (+40F). **Nearby** Maison Carrée, art museum in Nîmes, Pont du Gard, château de Villevieille in Sommiéres, chapel of Saint-Julien-de-Salinelles – 18-hole Haut-de-Nîmes golf course. **Open** All year.

This small hotel is located close to the Quai de la Fontaine and the Maison Carrée, and looks out onto the Place d'Assas renovated by Martial Raysse. The hotel has a clientele of artists and designers and the atmosphere is relaxed and informal. The hotel has been entirely renovated, with white walls and quite sparse decoration including several 1950s and '60s pieces of furniture; it is quite unusual but attractive. An attractive restaurant serves salads and brunches; in summer tables are set up outside in the square. It is better to take a room at the back of the hotel to avoid hearing the clattering of forks deep into the night. During the *férias* the atmosphere is animated and festive, and the bar and restaurant stay open late. There are jazz sessions some evenings.

How to get there *(Map 32): In the town center.*

Le Mas d'Oléandre

Saint-Médiers
30700 Uzès (Gard)
Tel. 66.22.63.43 - Eva and Carl-Heinz Törschen

Rooms 3, 2 apartments and 1 studio, with bath or shower and WC. **Price** Single 160F, double 240F, suite 320-400F. **Meals** Breakfast 40F, served 9:00-10:00. No restaurant. **Credit cards** Not accepted. **Pets** Dogs not allowed. **Facilities** Swimming pool, parking. **Nearby** le Duché, churches of Saint-Etienne and Saint-Théodorit in Uzès, Pont du Gard, Nîmes, Avignon – 9-hole golf course in Uzès. **Open** March 16 – Oct 31.

A secluded location and a stunning view are the main features of this hotel tucked away at the end of a peaceful little village. All around it cypresses, vineyards and hills combine to create a beautifully harmonious landscape and that may be what kept the owners from returning to their native Germany once they had set eyes on it. This doesn't feel like a hotel at all. The farmhouse has been carefully restored to make your stay as pleasant as possible. There are comfortable, cozy bedrooms, fully equipped studios and practical apartments which easily accommodate families with children. The hotel is an ideal base for exploring the beautiful Uzès area, and the swimming-pool proves an irresistible invitation to laze in the sun. In the evening your hosts will gladly indicate the best local restaurants, including *L'Auberge de Cruvier*, or *Le Fou du Roi* in Pougnadoresse, and dinner *L'Auberge Saint-Maximin* in Saint-Maximin. The studios and apartments have small kitchens.

How to get there *(Map 33): 40km west of Avignon via N100 and D981 to Montaren, then D337 to Saint-Médiers; (the Mas is on the edge of the hamlet).*

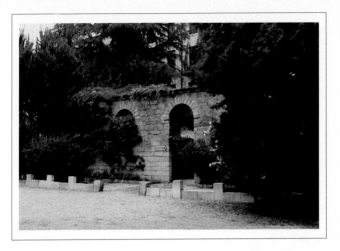

Auberge du Pont Romain ★★★

2, rue Emile-Jamais
30250 Sommières (Gard)
Tel. 66.80.00.58 - Fax 66.80.31.52 - Mme Michel

Rooms 18 with telephone, bath or shower (16 with WC). **Price** Single 260-400F, double 260-440F. **Meals** Breakfast 45F, served 7:45-10:00; half board 395F. **Restaurant** Service 12:15-13:15, 20:15-21:30; menus 155-225F, also à la carte. Specialties: Petit gris des garrigues au roquefort, foie gras maison. **Credit cards** All major. **Pets** Dogs allowed. **Facilities** Swimming pool, parking. **Nearby** Château de Villevieille, chapel of Saint-Julien-de-Salinelles, church of Notre-Dame-des-Pommiers in Beaucaire, Pont du Gard, Nîmes – 18-hole Nîmes-campagne golf course. **Open** March 15 – Jan 15 (closed Wednesdays in low season).

The façade that looks out onto the street is austere and barracks-like, betraying something of the history of the building. It was a carpet factory in the 19th-century, then a laundry, then, until 1968, a distillery. But as soon as you walk through the porch you enter a different world. A garden full of trees and flowers (all the more marvelous for its unlikely location) provides a pleasant setting for a terrace and a swimming-pool, and leads down to the Vidourle River. The vastness of the bedrooms can prompt memories of dormitories, but the best rooms are the ones with views of the garden; our favorite is room number 8 with a terrace among the branches of the plane trees overlooking the river. The cuisine is traditional and generous, but the service can be a bit casual.

How to get there (Map 32): 28km southwest of Nîmes via D40.

Demeures du Ranquet ★★★★

Tornac
30140 Anduze (Gard)
Tel. 66.77.51.63 - Fax 66.77.55.62 - M. and Mme Majourel

Rooms 10 with telephone, bath, WC, TV and minibar - Wheelchair accessible.
Price Single 480-640F, double 580-800F. **Meals** Breakfast 65F, served from 8:00;
half board 500-560F (per pers., 3 days min.). **Restaurant** Service 12:00-13:30,
19:30-21:30; menus 150-350F, also à la carte. Specialties: Daurade aux citrons
confits pommes boulangères, blanquette d'agneau Joseph Delteil et son riz sauvage,
crème brulée à la farine de châtaigne. **Credit cards** Visa, Eurocard and MasterCard.
Pets Dogs allowed (except in the restaurant). **Facilities** Swimming pool, golf practice
green, cooking lessons, parking, helicopter pad. **Nearby** Prafance, Bamboo Grove,
Générargues, Luziers, Mas-Soubeyran (Desert Museum), Trabuc Cave, Saint-Jean-
du-Gard. **Open** March 11 – Nov 10.

The distinguished people who have long been coming here are
still faithfully returning. If you're not immediately charmed
by the bungalows scattered in the woods, you will soon fall under
the spell of the original ambiance of the Ranquet. The beautiful
cuisine adds a great deal to the appeal of the place. The breakfasts
are fabulous, the lunch and dinner menus are varied, and new
recipes (Mediterranean red fish with preserved lemons) are often
created. Everything is made on the premises and wine lovers will
also be enchanted. Then too, you will sense the Majourels' love
of a difficult job, which they handle with skill. If you enjoy painting
and gardening, you will want to discuss both with them.

How to get there *(Map 32): 47km northwest of Nîmes, direction Alès; 6km*
south of Anduze on D982, on the road to Sainte-Hippolyte-du-Fort.

Hôtel Marie d'Agoult ★★★

Château d'Arpaillargues
30700 Uzès (Gard)
Tel. 66.22.14.48 – Fax 66.22.56.10 – M. Savry

Rooms 28 with telephone, bath, WC, TV and minibar. **Price** Single and double 400-1100F, suite 900-1100F. **Meals** Breakfast 55F, served 7:30-10:30; half board 440-790F, full board 635-985F. **Restaurant** Service 12:30-13:30, 19:30-21:00; menus 125-210F, also à la carte. Specialties: Carré d'agneau rôti en croûte de foin. **Credit cards** All major. **Pets** Dogs allowed (+60F). **Facilities** Swimming pool, tennis, parking. **Nearby** Le Duché, churches of Saint-Etienne and Saint-Théodorit in Uzès, Pont du Gard, Nîmes, Avignon – 9-hole golf course in Uzès, 18-hole golf course at 20km. **Open** April 1 – Nov 2.

This hotel is in the beautiful 18th-century Château d'Arpaillargues, once the home of Marie de Flavigny, Franz Liszt's companion. The bedrooms are comfortably furnished and tastefully decorated. If you want one with its own terrace, try room number 1 on the roof of the main building, or rooms 15 or 16 with access to the garden. In the annex, room 28 is a small duplex complete with a covered terrace. The extremely high standards of everything here make up for the somewhat formal atmosphere that prevails. A pleasant bar area, lunch by the swimming-pool, and breakfast and dinner in the garden in summer make a stay here a delightful prospect. The cuisine is light and refined.

How to get there *(Map 33): 40km west of Avignon via N100 to Remoulins (on A9, Remoulins exit), then D981 to Uzès and D982 (westward) to Arpaillargues.*

Hôtel d'Entraigues ★★★

8, rue de la Calade
30700 Uzès (Gard)
Tel. 66.22.32.68 - Fax 66.22.57.01 - Mme Georges

Rooms 36 (9 with air-conditioning) with telephone, bath, WC, TV and minibar - Elevator. **Price** Single 185-195F, double 285-650F. **Meals** Breakfast 45F, served 7:15-11:00; half board +220F (per pers.). **Restaurant** With air-conditioning. Service 12:15-13:30, 19:30-21:30; menus 100-185F, also à la carte. **Credit cards** All major. **Pets** allowed (+35F). **Facilities** Swimming pool,sauna, health center, garage (+50F). **Nearby** Le Duché, churches of Saint-Etienne and Saint-Théodorit in Uzès, Pont du Gard, Nîmes, Avignon – 9-hole golf course in Uzès and 18-hole golf course at 20km. **Open** All year.

The Hôtel d'Entraigues is a beautiful 15th-century mansion in the center of Uzès, just opposite the ancient seat of the barons of Castille and the Bishop's Palace. Some of the bedrooms have views of those impressive buildings (such as room number 9) or of the surrounding countryside, but those without a view make up for it in other ways. The rooms are all attractive and pleasant although different in style and size: some nestle under the eaves; others are much bigger (rooms 14, 15, 16, 18). A small lounge close to the reception area and a vaulted breakfast room provide all the comfort guests can wish for. The gastronomic restaurant *Les Jardins de Castille* is just across the street. and upstairs there is a large flowery terrace with a superb view. The new *Bains Bouches* offers simpler, quick inexpensive meals. This is a hotel and a town full of charm and character.

How to get there *(Map 33): 40km west of Avignon via N100 to Remoulins (on A9, Remoulins exit), then D981 to Uzès.*

Hôtel de l'Atelier ★★

5, rue de la Foire
30400 Villeneuve-lès-Avignon (Gard)
Tel. 90.25.01.84 - Fax 90.25.80.06 - M. and Mme Gounaud

Rooms 19 with telephone, bath or shower and WC (11 with TV). **Price** Double 240-420F. **Meals** Breakfast 34-42F, served 7:00-10:00. No restaurant. **Credit cards** All major. **Pets** Dogs allowed. **Nearby** "The Crowning of the Virgin" by Enguerand Quarton in the Musée Municipal in Villeneuve, Carthusain monastery of the Val-de-Bénédiction, fort Saint-André in Villeneuve, chapel of Notre-Dame-de-Belvezet, Avignon – 18-hole Châteaublanc-les-Plans golf course in Avignon. **Open** Mid-Dec – mid-Nov.

The Hôtel de l'Atelier is in Villeneuve-lès-Avignon, a small town at the foot of the Fort Saint-André which faces Avignon across the Rhône. Avignon was once the City of the Popes, Villeneuve was home to the cardinals. Outwardly a quiet village house, the building has many hidden charms: a sequence of flower-filled patios where fig-trees provide welcome shade, a roof terrace – the perfect setting for a cup of tea or an evening drink – and delightful bedrooms. The latter have all been carefully and individually designed, and their shape and size vary, as do the pieces of period furniture they contain. Our favorite is room 42 on the top floor: it has all the character of attic rooms (with air-conditioning!), and if you stand on the little platform you can see Avignon through the high window. The hotel doesn't have a restaurant of its own but Avignon is just on the doorstep and in Villeneuve itself there are some very good restaurants. Try *La Magnagneraie* or *Le Saint-André* (less expensive).

How to get there *(Map 33): 3km west of Avignon via N100; if on A6, Avignon-Nord exit.*

Château de Madières ★★★★

Madières
34190 Ganges (Hérault)
Tel. 67.73.84.03 - Fax 67.73.55.71 - M. and Mme Brucy

Rooms 10 with telephone, bath or shower, WC, TV and minibar. **Price** Double 560-960F, suite 850-1090F. **Meals** Breakfast 75F, served 8:30-10:30; half board 595-785F (per pers., 3 days min.). **Restaurant** Service 12:30-14:00, 19:30-21:00; menus 190-350F, also à la carte. Specialties: Truite au picpoul, magret de canard flambé. **Credit cards** All major. **Pets** Dogs allowed (+supp.). **Facilities** Heated swimming pool, fitness room, parking. **Nearby** Gorges of the river Vis, cirque de Navacelles, La Couvertoirade, cave of the Demoiselles, church of Saint-Guilhem-le-Désert. **Open** April 1 – Nov 1.

Set on the southern slopes of the Cévennes among the gorges of the River Vis, this 14th-century fortified house juts out like a balcony on the side of the mountain, only 40 minutes away from the Cirque de Navacelles. The Château has been carefully restored to become a hotel of great character. The bedrooms are luxuriously equipped and look out onto a patio. They are extremely comfortable and pleasant, and their individual decoration shows great attention to detail. The elegant lounge still has a Renaissance fireplace and leads out onto a terrace overlooking the river and the village. There are two dining-rooms (one with panoramic views) in which to enjoy Mme Brucy's excellent cooking. In summer, meals can be served by the swimming-pool which has just been completed on a terrace below the hotel.

How to get there *(Map 32): 60km northwest of Montpellier via D986 towards Le Vigan to Ganges, then D25 towards the Cirque de Navacelles, Lodève (18km from Ganges).*

Relais Chantovent
34210 Minerve (Hérault)
Tel. 68.91.14.18
Mme Evenou

Rooms 7 with shower (1 with bath) and WC. **Price** Single 180F, double 220F.
Meals Breakfast 28F, served 8:00-10:00; half board 320F (per pers., 3 days min.).
Restaurant Service 12:30-14:00, 19:30-21:00; menus 95-230F. Specialties:
Croustillant aux deux saumons sur coulis de poivrons doux. **Credit cards** Visa,
Eurocard and MasterCard. **Pets** Dogs not allowed. **Nearby** Lagrasse, château de
Gaussan, abbey of Fontfroide, African reserve of Sigean, gorges of the Tarn.
Open March 15 – Jan 1 (closed Mondays in July and Aug).

Minerve is a village high up between the gorges of the Rivers
Cesse and Briand, and the hotel buildings are scattered in its
narrow alleys. The annex is a tastefully restored old village house
next to the "post-office library" and the rooms are as charming as
the ones in the main building. Two of them share a terrace, and
the one in the attic has kept its original layout, with the bathroom
more or less in the room; all have charm and character. Those
facing the restaurant have just been fully refurbished: fabrics and
contemporary lithographs create a cheerful atmosphere, and the
bathrooms have been redone. The restaurant serves good, simple,
local specialties. The village and its surroundings are splendid and
the welcome is very friendly.

How to get there *(Map 31): 45km northwest of Carcassonne via N113 and
D160 to Homps, then D910 to Olonzac and D10 to Minerve (northward).*

Domaine de Rieumégé ★★★
Route de Saint-Pons
34390 Olargues (Hérault)
Tel. 67.97.73.99 - Fax 67.97.78.52 - M. Sylva

Rooms 14 with telephone, bath or shower and WC. **Price** Single 318-478F, double 350-518F, suite (4 pers.) 619-774F. **Meals** Breakfast (buffet) 55F, served 8:30-10:00; half board 398-509F, full board 493-604F (per pers., 2 days min.). **Restaurant** Service 12:00-14:00, 19:00-21:30; menus 100F (lunchtime)-135-220F, also à la carte. **Credit cards** Amex, Visa, Eurocard and MasterCard. **Pets** Dogs allowed (+40F). **Facilities** Swimming pool (2), tennis, parking. **Nearby** Abbey of Fontcaude, mountains of l'Espinouse, cave of la Devèze. **Open** April – Dec .

The mountains of the Haut-Languedoc provide an impressive backdrop for the Domaine de Rieumégé, a pleasant place to stay in an area where good hotels are few and far between. This is an old 17th-century house which has been restored by the owners with great taste and a feeling for comfort. The terraces, lounges and kitchen have been improved this year. The interior decoration skillfully combines country-style antiques with more modern pieces of furniture, exposed stonework, and well-chosen colors on the walls. Despite the nearby road the hotel is quiet. A luxury accommodation is also possible, offering a bedroom and a suite giving onto a private swimming pool with a tropical garden, which is reserved exclusively for the occupants. The price is 100F extra per person.

How to get there *(Map 31): 50km northwest of Béziers via D14, then D908 towards Olargues; 3km from Olargues in the Saint-Pons-de-Thomières direction.*

Le Sanglier ★★★

Domaine de Cantourras
Saint-Jean-de-la-Blaquière - 34700 Lodève (Hérault)
Tel. 67.44.70.51 - Fax 67.44.72.33 - Mme Plazanet and M. Lormier

Rooms 10 with telephone, bath and WC (2 with TV). **Price** Double 370-400F.
Meals 45F, served 8:00-10:00; half board 385F, full board 495F (per pers., 3 days
min.). **Restaurant** Closed Tuesdays and Wednesday noon in July and Aug. Service
12:00-13:30, 19:30-20:30; menus 90F (lunchtime)-138-210F, also à la carte.
Specialties: Coquilles Saint-Jacques sur chiffonade au Noilly Prat, côtes d'agneau
grillées au feu de bois et crème d'ail, cassolette d'escargots aux noisettes, salade
mêlée au soufflé de chèvre chaud. **Credit cards** Visa, Eurocard and MasterCard.
Pets Small dogs allowed. **Facilities** Swimming pool, tennis, parking. **Nearby** Church
of Saint-Guilhem-le-Désert, cirque de Navacelles, la Couvertoirade, chapel of
Gignac, Villeneuvette. **Open** March 15 – Oct 25.

In the very heart of the Valley of the Hérault, the Sanglier lies
well off the beaten track and close to an extraordinary mini-
canyon, all sand and red rocks, which looks like Arizona. Formerly
a shepherd's house, the building has been completely renovated.
The bedrooms are all on the *premier étage* – try to get one with a
terrace facing the valley (Numbers 1 to 5). Despite their outdated
70s decor, they are all pleasant and comfortable. The large dining-
room is in rustic style and the tables face a big fireplace where meat
is grilled on vine branches. Meals can also be served outside. The
house is surrounded by a pretty terraced garden which leads down
to a swimming-pool. You will be warmly welcomed by attentive
hosts.

How to get there (Map 32): *45km west of Montpellier via N109 towards
Lodève to Rabieux, then D144 on the right.*

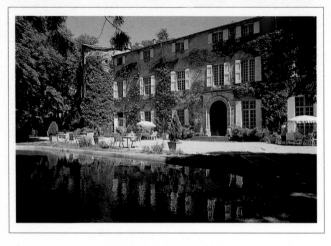

Château d'Ayres ***
48150 Meyrueis (Lozère)
Tel. 66.45.60.10 – Fax 66.45.62.26
M. de Montjou

Rooms 26 with telephone, bath or shower, WC and TV (18 with minibar). **Price** Double 360-800F, suite 830-930F. **Meals** Breakfast 55F; half board 380-560F, full board 490-670F (per pers.). **Restaurant** Service 12:30-13:45, 19:30-22:00; menus 148-300F, also à la carte. Specialties: Feuilleté aux deux saumons, croustillant de magret au foie gras. **Credit cards** All major. **Pets** Dogs allowed (+45F). **Facilities** Swimming pool, tennis, parking. **Nearby** Gorges of the Tarn, Aven d'Armand, gorge of Dargilan, Cévennes national park. **Open** Apr 1 – Nov 15.

The Château d'Ayres has not been spared the many vicissitudes of history. Rebuilt in the 18th-century by the Nogaret family, it was later sold and turned into a hotel. But the woman who inherited it, a Miss Roussel, married one of the Nogarets' cousins, thus bringing the castle back into the family. We can easily understand why the family is so attached to it. Set amidst 12-acres of beautiful parkland planted with age-old oaks and gigantic sequoias, it is lovely. The lounges, bedrooms and library are decorated with beautiful period furniture and attractive paintings. Exquisite taste is in evidence throughout the house, including the lovely dining room, which is more rustic in style. This is a special place.

How to get there *(Map 32): 55km south of Mende via N88, and D986 to Meyrueis via Sainte-Enimie.*

Hôtel Chantoiseau ★★★

48220 Vialas (Lozère)
Tel. 66.41.00.02 - Fax 66.41.04.34
M. Patrick Pagès

Rooms 15 with bath or shower, WC, TV and minibar. **Price** Single and double 400-480F. **Meals** Breakfast 50F, served 8:00-9:30; half board 450F, full board 490F (per pers., 3 days min.). **Restaurant** Service 12:00-13:30, 19:00-20:30; menus 130-750F, also à la carte. Specialties: Ravioles au pélardon, carré d'agneau, suprême au chocolat. **Credit cards** All major. **Pets** Dogs not allowed. **Facilities** Swimming pool, parking. **Nearby** Ridgeway to Alès via Portes; La Garde, Guérin, Florac. **Open** April 8 – Nov 15 (closed Tuesday evenings and Wednesdays).

The Chantoiseau is one of the best hotels in the region. This former 17th-century coaching inn, set 600 meters up on the steep Mediterranean slopes of the Cévennes, provides a sunny stopping place on the doorstep of the Cévennes National Park. The bedrooms are comfortable and look out onto peaceful valleys and mountains. The dining room retains the austere character of houses in the area: walls built in large slabs of granite, deep embrasures, the warm presence of wood. It commands beautiful views over the valley. The menu features specialties of the Cévennes only, prepared by the owner whose talent has earned wide recognition, and who has chosen the finest wines to accompany them. The wine list is outstanding, ranging from modest but charming *vins de pays* to great vintages.

How to get there *(Map 32): Northwest of Alès via D906, direction Genolhac; in Belle-Poèle, D998 to Vialas.*

La Terrasse au Soleil ★★★★
Route de Fontfrède
66400 Céret (Pyrénées-Orientales)
Tel. 68.87.01.94 - Fax 68.87.39.24 - B. and P. Leveillé-Nizerolle

Rooms 27 with air-conditioning, telephone, bath, WC, TV, minibar and safe. **Price** Single and double 595-795F. **Meals** Breakfast 70F, served 8:00-12:00; half board 578-678F, full board +100F (per pers.). **Restaurant** Service 12:00-14:30, 19:30-21:30; menus 160-340F, also à la carte. Specialties: Rosée des Pyrénées poêlés, étuvée de girolles à la catalane, pigeon fermier rôti aux tagliatelles fraîches. **Credit cards** Visa, Eurocard and MasterCard. **Pets** Dogs allowed. **Facilities** Heated swimming pool, tennis, par-3 golf course, parking. **Nearby** Museum of modern art and church of Saint-Pierre in Céret, Cabestany, Prats-de-Mollo, château de Quéribus, Quilhac and the château de Peyrepertuse, Perpignan – 27-hole Saint-Cyprien golf course, 7-hole Amélie-les-Bains golf course, 18-hole Falgos golf course. **Open** Feb 4 – Jan 3.

La Terrasse au Soleil is an old farmhouse which has been completely restored. It occupies an enviable position crowning the village among cherry trees. The bedrooms have all the modern comforts. The largest and best are the upstairs ones with a terrace and views of the mountains. The La Cerisaie Restaurant will delight you with its excellent cuisine; for lunch, it also proposes a simpler *brasserie* menu, in addition to the dessert menu: don't miss the superb *mille-feuille* pastry. In good weather meals can be served in the garden. A heated swimming-pool, tennis court and par-3 golf course add to the many assets of this hotel, where a friendly and informal atmosphere encourages guests to relax.

How to get there *(Map 31): 31km southwest of Perpignan via A9, Le Boulou exit, then D115 towards Céret; it's 2km from the center of the village via D13f in the Fontfrède direction.*

Le Mas Trilles ★★★

66400 Céret-Reynès (Pyrénées-Orientales)
Tel. 68.87.38.37 - Fax 68.87.42.62
M. and Mme Bukk

Rooms 10 with telephone, bath, WC and TV - 1 room for disabled persons. **Price** Double and suite 420-950F. **Meals** Breakfast 60F, served 8:30-10:30; half board 410-675F. **Restaurant** Service 20:00; menus 150-185F. Specialties: Seasonal cooking. **Credit cards** Visa, Eurocard and MasterCard. **Pets** Dogs allowed (+supp.). **Facilities** Swimming pool, parking. **Nearby** Museum of modern art and church of Saint-Pierre in Céret, Cabestany, Prats-de-Mollo, château de Quéribus, Quilhac and the château de Peyrepertuse, Perpignan – 27-hole Saint-Cyprien golf course, 7-hole Amélie-les-Bains golf course, 18-hole Falgos golf course. **Open** April 1 – Oct 31.

The Mas Trilles is an old house surrounded by a garden with fruit trees. From the swimming-pool, when there is a lot of traffic and the wind is blowing in the wrong direction, the rumble of cars on the road above the hotel can sometimes be heard. The bedrooms, however, are quiet at all times. Inside, the house has been fully refurbished and decorated with exquisite taste: there are terra cotta floors, the walls in some rooms have been sponge painted and in others whitewashed, and each fabric has been carefully chosen by Madame Bukk to blend in with, and round off, the decor. The bedrooms have lovely bathrooms and many of them also have a private terrace where breakfast (which always includes fresh fruit) can be served. Dinner (for residents only) is in a charming dining-room or on the terrace. Friendly hospitality adds to the pleasant homey atmosphere that prevails. This is a beautiful, comfortable hotel.

How to get there *(Map 31): 31km southwest of Perpignan via A9, Le Boulou exit, then D115 towards Céret; 3km from the center, in Amélie-les-Bains direction.*

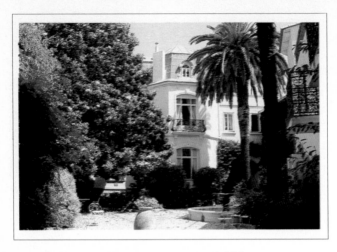

Hôtel Casa Païral ***

Impasse des Palmiers
66190 Collioure (Pyrénées-Orientales)
Tel. 68.82.05.81 – Fax 68.82.52.10 – Mmes De Bon and Lormand

Rooms 28 some with air-conditioning, telephone, bath or shower, WC, cable TV and minibar. **Price** Single 300-600F, double 350-690F, suite 670-900F. **Meals** Breakfast 45-50F. No restaurant. **Credit cards** Amex, Visa, Eurocard and MasterCard. **Pets** Dogs allowed (+30F). **Facilities** Swimming pool, parking (+40F). **Nearby** The Vermeille coast between Argelès-sur-Mer and Cerbère, Balcon de Madeloc, mountain road between Collioure and Banyuls, Château de Salses, museum of modern art in Céret – 27-hole Saint-Cyprien golf course. **Open** April – Oct.

A real gem, Casa Païral is hidden in a small *cul-de-sac*, right in the center of Coullioure, just a few minutes from the beach, restaurants, and cafés. It is perfectly quiet. This luxurious 19th-century town house was built in a Moorish-style with wrought ironwork, marble, and ceramic tilework. On the patio, lush vegetation grows in the shade of a stately palm tree and a hundred-year-old magnolia tree. All the rooms are comfortable, but ask for the ones in the main house, which are nicer. The very pleasant breakfast room and lounges open onto the walled garden and swimming pool. This hotel is very much in demand, so you will need a reservation. For dinner, try the fish at *Pa i Trago* or at *Le Puits* in the old town, or at *La Marinade*, for its pretty terrace on the town square.

How to get there *(Map 31) 26km southeast of Perpignan via N114.*

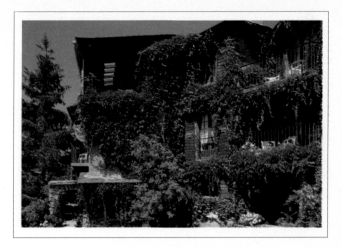

Auberge L'Atalaya ★★★

Llo - 66800 Saillagouse (Pyrénées-Orientales)
Tel. 68.04.70.04 - Fax 68.04.01.29
M. and Mme Toussaint

Rooms 13 with telephone, bath or shower, WC, TV and minibar. **Price** Single 480F, double 620F, suite 715F. **Meals** Breakfast 55F, served 7:30-10:30; half board 460-560F, full board 620-740F (per pers., 3 days min.). **Restaurant** Closed Mondays and Tuesday noon in low season. Service 12:30-14:30, 19:30-21:30; menus 150-380F, also à la carte. **Credit cards** Visa, Eurocard and MasterCard. **Pets** Dogs allowed in the bedrooms. **Facilities** Swimming pool, solarium, parking. **Nearby** Ski in Eyne, Odeillo solar furnace, lake of Les Buoillouses north of Mont-Louis, gorges of the river Aude, château de Quérigut – 18-hole Real Club de Cerdana golf course, 9-hole golf course in Font-Romeu. **Open** April 1– Jan 10.

L lo is the most typical pastoral village of the Cerdagne region on the border between Andorra and Spain, which can be seen from some of the bedrooms. Clustered around its watchtower – called an *atalaya* in old Castilian – and the ruins of its 11th-century castle, the village stands above the gorges of the River Sègre. Needless to say, its location is one of the memorable features of the Auberge. But the building itself is well worth the stay. The magnificent house has been tastefully decorated throughout and the bedrooms are comfortable and attractive. In summer, meals are served outside on a terrace among geraniums and hollyhocks, and there is now also a swimming-pool. In winter, the closest ski stations are Eyne and Err-Puigmal, and there are at least eight others within easy reach. The food is delicious.

How to get there *(Map 31): 90km west of Perpignan via N116 to Saillagouse, then D33.*

293

Lou Rouballou

66210 Mont-Louis (Pyrénées-Orientales)
Tel. 68.04.23.26 - Fax 68.04.14.09
M. and Mme Duval

Rooms 14 with bath or shower and 8 with WC. **Price** Double 150-300F.
Meals Breakfast 30F; half board 210-250F, full board 250-280F (per pers., 3 days
min.). **Restaurant** Service 12:30-13:30, 19:30-20:30; menus 100-190F, also à la
carte. Specialties: Catalan cooking. **Credit cards** Visa, Eurocard and MasterCard.
Pets Small dogs allowed. **Nearby** Romanesque church of Planès, lake of Les
Bouillouses, gorges of the river Aude, château de Quérigut, pass of Saint-Georges.
Open All year except in Oct., Nov. and May (closed Wednesdays in low season).

You will find this auberge among the village houses. Its façade
doesn't stand out, but as soon as you walk through the door
you will feel at ease. Inside, the decor is rustic, cozy and genuine.
Some of the bedrooms are more comfortable than others: we
recommend rooms 3, 18, 19, 20, 21, which Christiane Duval has
lovingly arranged with antique furniture, extremely comfortable
beds and pleasant bathrooms. But Lou Raballou is also renowned
for the gourmet cuisine turned out by Pierre Duval. The menu
features excellent traditional dishes, prepared with only the freshest
products. In the autumn, Pierre will take you hunting for
mushrooms, and then prepare the mushrooms in a delicious dish
for dinner. This is a charming, friendly and unpretentious inn.

How to get there *(Map 31): 10km east of Font-Romeu via N116 (in the
old part of the town).*

Château de Camon

09500 Camon (Ariège)
Tel. 61.68.28.28 - Fax 61.68.81.56
M. du Pont

Rooms 7 with bath or shower and WC. **Price** Single and double 500-1000F, suite 1500F. **Meals** Breakfast incl. **Restaurant** Evening meals on reservation; menu 300F. **Credit cards** All major. **Pets** Dogs allowed. **Facilities** Swimming pool, parking. **Nearby** Mirepoix, châteaux of Lagarde and of Caudeval, Montségur and Foix. **Open** March – Nov.

At the château Camon, in the beautiful region of Ariège on the wooded road into Spain, you will be treated more like a guest than a customer. The château has been in the family of M. du Pont for two centuries: "Only two hundred years," he says as if to apologize for so recent an acquisition. The château is closed to the public unless, of course, you are a guest, but there is an abbey next to it which can be visited; they both overlook the village below. A colorful terraced garden descends to a lawn with a swimming pool. The bedrooms have been admirably decorated by the owner, (who is an interior decorator) with antique. You will be delighted with every aspect of this château, which feels like a private home.

How to get there *(Map 31): 59km southwest of Carcassonne via D119 to Mirepoix, then D7 towards Chalabre. If on A61, Castelnaudary exit.*

Hôtel Eychenne ★★★

8, avenue Paul Laffont
09200 Saint-Girons (Ariège)
Tel. 61.66.20.55 – Fax 61.96.07.20 – M. and Mme Bordeau

Rooms 42 with telephone, bath or shower, WC, 30 with TV and 35 with minibar. **Price** Single and double 280-530F. **Meals** Breakfast 46F, served 7:00-10:30; half board 355-412F, full board 470-527F (per pers., 3 days min.). **Restaurant** Closed Sunday evening and Monday Nov – March. Service 12:15-13:30, 19:45-21:30; menus 128-315F, also à la carte. Specialties: Foie de canard frais aux raisins , pigeonneau au fitou, gigot de lotte safrané, soufflé au grand marnier. **Credit cards** All major. **Pets** Dogs allowed. **Facilities** Swimming pool, parking. **Nearby** Saint-Lizier, Montjoie, Romanesques churches at the valley of Couserans in Oust and Cominac, Ercé Chapel in Garbet Valley, Castillon, Audressein, Sentein, Ayet, Ourtjou-les Bordes. **Open** Feb 2 – Dec 21 (closed Sunday evening and Monday Nov – March).

Managed by the Bordeau family for generations, the Eychenne has preserved its atmosphere of the past while offering the latest in modern amenities. In the two lounges, small bar, and dining room, the furniture, family objects and pictures create a friendly atmosphere. Most of the comfortable bedrooms, which are not very large, are furnished with antiques. Some have a beautiful view out over the Pyrenees. The cuisine – savory specialties of the Southwest – warrants a visit here. In summer, meals are served in the dining room which looks onto a garden, or lighter fare is available by the swimming pool. Breakfasts are generous. The staff is friendly and attentive.

How to get there (Map 30): *In Saint-Girons, head towards Foix and follow the signs.*

Château de Seignan ★★★

Montjoie
09200 Saint-Girons (Ariège)
Tel. 61.96.08.80 - Fax 61. 96.08.20 - M. de Bardies

Rooms 9 with telephone, bath or shower, WC, TV and minibar. **Price** Double 320-850F. **Meals** Breakfast 42F, served 7:00-11:00; half board 395-580F (per pers., 3 days min.). **Restaurant** Closed Monday and Tuesday noon Sep 15 – June 15. Service 12:00-14:30, 19:30-22:00; menus 125F (lunch) and 340F, also à la carte. Specialties: Brochette de poisson à l'indienne, panaché de foies gras, pigeon désossé sauce forestière, gratin de fruits de jardin. **Credit cards** All major. **Pets** Dogs allowed. **Meals** Swimming pool, tennis, parking. **Nearby** Saint-Lizier, Montjoie, Romanesque churches in the Couserans Valleys in Oust and Cominac, Ercé Chapel in the Garbet Valley, Castillon, Audressein, Sentein, Ayet, Ourtjou-les Bordes. **Open** Dec 16 – Oct 31 (closed Tuesday, Wednesday noon).

At the foot of the Pyrenees, on the edge of the mysterious valleys of the Couserans and scarcely 1km from Saint-Girons, this family chateau was opened to guests several years ago by Monsieur de Bardies. There are nine large, comfortable bedrooms furnished with antiques, while the bathrooms are very modern. The dining room is welcoming, as is the small lounge, where a pianist plays during cocktail hour. In summer, meals are served in the garden, which is shaded by century-old chestnut trees along the edge of the River Baup. A tennis court and swimming pool lend further appeal to the site. The staff is kind and courteous.

How to get there *(Map 30): 1km east of Saint-Girons. In Saint-Girons, take D117 in the direction of Foix, on the right.*

Château de Castelpers **

Castelpers
12170 Ledergues (Aveyron)
Tel. 65.69.22.61 - Fax 65.69.25.31 - Mme Tapié de Celeyran

Rooms 9 with telephone, bath or shower, 8 with WC and 6 with TV. **Price** Single 240F, double 375-465F, suite 500F. **Meals** Breakfast 45F, served 8:00-9:30; half board 230-342F, full board 300-412F (per pers., 3 days min.). **Restaurant** Closed Saturday evening and Sunday except for guests. Service 12:30-14:00, 19:30-21:00; menus 130-260F, also à la carte. Specialties: Confit aux cèpes, beignets au roquefort, faux-filet aux morilles, foie gras poêlée au jus de truffes. **Credit cards** Amex, Visa, Eurocard and MasterCard. **Pets** Dogs allowed (+20F). **Facilities** Parking. **Nearby** Châteaux of Le Bosc and Taurines, Sauveterre, Viaduct and Valley of Le Viau, Pareloup Lakes – 18-hole golf course in Albi. **Open** April 1 – Oct 1.

The Château de Castelpers is tucked away in a verdant corner of Rouergue, in the peaceful Viaur Valley, a region where inns are scarce. The rustic dry-stone building adjoins another with Gothic arches where the main lounge has a ceiling resembling a ship's hull. The terrace overlooks a large park with centuries-old trees bordered by a trout stream. Handsome old furniture gives character to the dining room, the lounge and the comfortable bedrooms. Room 5 has leaded windows and a canopied bed; the other rooms are more modern, as are number 9 and its neighbor on the ground floor, which open onto the garden.

How to get there *(Map 31): 40km from Rodez and Albi via N88, then take D80 at Les Peyronnies, 3km from Nancelle-Gare.*

Hôtel Longcol ★★★
La Fouillade
12270 Najac (Aveyron)
Tel. 65.29.63.36 – Fax 65.29.64.28 – Luyckx Family

Rooms 17 with telephone, bath or shower, WC, TV and minibar. **Price** Double 550-750F. **Meals** Breakfast 60F, served 7:30-10:30; half board 515-615F (per pers., 2 days min.). **Restaurant** Service lunchtime (guests only), 19:45-21:30; menus 120-210F, also à la carte. Specialties: Seasonal cuisine, home-made foie gras,salade Longcol. **Credit cards** Amex, Visa, Eurocard and MasterCard. **Pets** Dogs allowed. **Facilities** Swimming pool, tennis, fishing, helicopter landing pad, parking. **Nearby** Château of Najac, Gorges of the Aveyron, Carthusian Monastery, Pénitents Noirs chapel and Place of Cornières in Villefranche-de-Rouergue. **Open** Easter – Nov 15.

This old Rouergue country house is like a miniature village sitting on a wild mountain pass with the Aveyron flowing below. Recently restored and decorated beautifully, each room is furnished with Oriental objects, antique rugs and furniture and old studded doors – all elegantly arranged and comfortable. The lounge and billiards rooms are particularly gracious, a corner fireplace and large leather armchairs creating a convivial atmosphere. The bedrooms are all individually decorated, bright and cheerful. All have views of either the swimming pool or the valley. In summer you can fish in the river that runs through the property and can enjoy lunch by the pool, looking out over the beautiful countryside. The staff is courteous in keeping with the beauty of this hotel.

How to get there *(Map 31): 19km south of Villefranche-de-Rouergue via D922, at La Fouillade (between La Fouillade and Najac, on D638).*

L'Oustal del Barry ★★

Place du Bourg
12270 Najac (Aveyron)
Tel. 65.29.74.32 – Fax 65.29.75.32 – Mme Miquel

Rooms 21 with telephone, bath or shower, WC and TV. **Price** Single 210-290F, double 300-450F. **Meals** Breakfast 48F, served 8:00-10:30; half board 295-330F, full board 380-420F (per pers., 2 days min.). **Restaurant** Service 12:30-14:00, 19:30-21:00; menus 100-320F, also à la carte. **Credit cards** Amex, Visa, Eurocard and MasterCard. **Pets** Dogs allowed. **Facilities** Parking. **Nearby** Château of Najac, Gorges of the Aveyron, Carthusian Monastery, Pénitents Noirs chapel and Place of Cornières in Villefranche-de-Rouergue. **Open** April – Oct (closed Monday, except public holidays, from April – June and Oct).

Five generations of the same family have presided over the Oustal del Barry, which has all the charms of a traditional French hotel. On the whole the bedrooms are rustic but with a curious mixture of other styles, principally Art Deco. The dining room has a panoramic view of the flowers and greenery of the 15-acre grounds. A vegetable garden cultivated by Madame Miguel grows several types of herbs used in the excellent cuisine, which also incorporates other local produce. The kindness of your hosts will make you regret leaving this simple and charming hotel. Hotel rates include free admission to the swimming pool at Najae, one hour of tennis a day and the use of bicycles.

How to get there *(Map 31): 24km south of Villefranche-de-Rouergue via D922, then D239.*

Hostellerie Les Magnolias

12550 Plaisance (Aveyron)
Tel. 65.99.77.34 - Fax 65.99.70.57
M. and Mme Roussel

Rooms 6 with telephone, bath, WC and TV. **Price** Single and double 225-300F.
Meals Breakfast (campagnard) 38-58F; half board 200-260F (per pers.).
Restaurant Service 12:15-14:00, 20:00-21:30; menus 68-300F, also à la carte.
Specialties: Cuisine based on traditional local products. **Credit cards** Amex, Visa,
Eurocard and MasterCard. **Pets** Dogs allowed (+25F). **Nearby** Churches in Plaisance,
Abbey of Sylvanes, Château du Bosc, Toulouse-Lautrec Museum in Albi – 18-hole
golf course in Albi. **Open** April – Dec.

This is one of the outstanding hotels in this guide. A beautiful
14th-century dwelling once owned by Paul Valéry's brother,
it will enchant you at first glance. Carefully chosen, delicate decor
has transformed this village house into a hotel of charming intimacy
and character. The cuisine is truly a labor of love. M. Roussel
speaks with real passion about the sauces and stocks that go into
the succulent dishes he serves; all the produce is local, fresh and
home made. It is with the same enthusiasm that he has collected
the materials and furnishings to decorate and restore his hotel. The
already beautiful bedrooms at the top of a lovely staircase are to be
renovated to further enhance the charm and comfort of this superb
hotel. The Hostellerie is a place where the staff goes to great pains
to ensure that you are content.

How to get there (Map 31): 42km east of Albi via D999 to Alban, then
after 4km take D127.

Hôtel du Midi–Papillon ★★

12230 Saint-Jean-du-Bruel (Aveyron)
Tel. 65.62.26.04 – Fax 65.62.12.97
M. and Mme Papillon

Rooms 19 with telephone, (11 with bath, 3 with shower and 17 with WC). **Price** Single 77-97F, double 95-191F. **Meals** Breakfast 23F, served 8:00-10:00; half board 155-212F, full board 185-243F (per pers., 3 days min.). **Restaurant** Service 12:30-14:00, 19:30-21:30; menus 70-192F, also à la carte. Specialties: Feuilleté de brochet à l'anguille fumée deux beurres, tronçons de lotte avec compote de tomates caviar d'aubergine, pigeon cocotte aux gousses d'aïl fricassée de cèpes, croquant à la gianduja et crème de vanille. **Credit cards** Visa, Eurocard and MasterCard. **Pets** Dogs allowed. **Facilities** Heated swimming pool, whirlpool. **Nearby** Millau Belfry, Montpellier-le-Vieux, Gorges of the Tarn. **Open** Palm Sunday – Nov 11.

On the road to Mont Aigoual, the highest point in the Cévennes, Saint-Jean-du-Bruel is a good stopping place in the Gorges of the Dourbie. The hotel is an old coaching inn run by the same family for four generations. Well located on an outcrop above the river, it offers an outstanding picture–postcard view of the old village houses and a stone bridge. You'll find a friendly atmosphere and good cuisine prepared with homemade ingredients (poultry, *confits, foie gras, charcuteries*). Our favorite rooms are those which have just been renovated and which have terraces overlooking the river. The breakfasts are excellent. The prices are surprisingly reasonable.

How to get there (Map 32): 99km northwest of Montpellier via N109 and N9 in the direction of Le Caylar to La Cavalerie, then D999as you enter the village).

Château Saint Saturnin

12560 Saint-Saturnin-de-Lenne (Aveyron)
Tel. 65.70.36.00 - Fax 65 70 36 19
M. and Mme Lenton

Rooms 12, with telephone, bath, WC and TV (11 for non-smokers, 1 for smokers).
Price 450-980F **Meals** Breakfast 35F, served 8:00-10:00; half board 355-600F, full
board 510-680F (per pers., 3 days min.). **Restaurant** Service 12:00-14:00, 20:00-
21:30; menus 80-110F (lunch), 145-190F (dinner). Specialties: Lapin au cidre,
magret de canard, salade californienne. **Credit cards** Amex, Visa, Eurocard and
MasterCard. **Pets** Dogs allowed. **Facilities** Swimming pool, parking. **Nearby**
Cathedral of Rodez, abbey of Conques, Séverac-le-château, Gorges du Tarn, Valley
of Lot; markets at Saint-Geniez and Séverac-le-château. **Open** April 1 – Jan 14.

A chateau in name only, the Saint-Saturnin is more like a vast
mansion with beautifully large rooms offering panoramic
views over an ancient sheep-farming village. The owners have
successfully combined British hospitality with the American taste
for modern amenities – all done in a very French style. They make
every effort to make their guests feel at home and happy in this
authentic French country house. Upon request, Monsieur and
Madame Lenton are pleased to serve meals - either around a large
communal dining table or even in the immense kitchen. After
dinner, coffee is served in the library, which is the only room (along
with one bedroom) where guests are allowed to smoke. Some of
the rooms are very large and all are as comfortable as those you
would find in the best hotels. The tastefully decorated bathrooms
are supplied with dressing gowns and toiletries.

How to get there (Map 31): A75, exit Campagnac. 46km east of Rodez, take
N88 to Laissac. D28 to Pont-de-Palmas and D45 to Saint-Saturnin-de-Lenne.

Le Sénéchal ★★★
12800 Sauveterre-de-Rouergue (Aveyron)
Tel. 65.71.29.00 - Fax 65.71.29.09
M. Truchon

Rooms 11 with air-conditioning, telephone, bath, WC, TV and minibar - 1 wheelchair accessible room, elevator. **Price** 450-550F, duplex 650-750F, suite 850-950F. **Meals** Breakfast 65F; half board 420F, full board 520F (per pers., 3 days min.). **Restaurant** Closed Sunday evening and Monday except public holidays, July and Aug. Service 12:00-14:00, 19:30-21:30; menus 120-400F, also à la carte. Specialties: Terrine de queues de bœuf en gelée à l'orange, tournedos de pied de porc en écailles de truffes, mousse de verveine fraîche et son sorbet. **Credit cards** All major. **Pets** Dogs allowed. **Facilities** Heated swimming pool. **Nearby** Rodez, Plateau Le Ségala, lakes of Levézou and villages of Saint-Beauzély, Combéroumal, Castelnau-Prégayrols, Montjaux, Chestnut Festival on Nov 1, Saint-Christophe's Feast Day in July, Light Festival in Aug. **Open** All year except Feb.

In a former royal fortified village in the heart of the lovely Avéyron countryside, the big, brand-new Sénéchal is a haven of refinement and hospitality. The bedrooms, decorated in pale lemon colors, are very spacious, and look out over gentle hillsides. Spacious, too, are the bathrooms, the lounge and the dining room. Decor is modern and comfortable, with some antique furniture. The cuisine here is renouned; breakfast is outstanding. Across the street are 15 inexpensive rooms in the Sénéchal's old auberge, but they do not have the charm of the new rooms. You will want to visit the village, which has beautifully preserved medieval arcades, fortifications, and a church-dungeon with a small museum.

How to get there (Map 31): 32km southwest of Rodez.

304

Hôtel des Trois Lys ★★★

38, rue Gambetta
32100 Condom (Gers)
Tel. 62.28.33.33 - Fax 62.28.41.85 - Mme Manet

Rooms 10 with telephone, bath or shower, WC and TV. **Price** Single 280F, double 380-550F. **Meals** Breakfast 38F, served 7:30-10:30. No restaurant. **Credit cards** Visa, Eurocard and MasterCard. **Pets** Dogs allowed. **Facilities** Swimming pool, parking. **Nearby** Armagnac Museum in Condom, châteaux, churches and bastides of Armagnac; Flaran, Larresingle, Fourcès, Tillac, Bassoues, Lavarders, Collegiate Church of La Romieu, Jazz festival in Marciac (August) – 9-hole Guinlet golf course in Eauze. **Open** All year.

When they converted this 18th-century manor house into a hotel, the Manets decorated it with their own fine taste. The ten rooms are done in coordinated colors and furnished with antiques or excellent reproductions finished in splendid fabrics. The rooms are big – some very big – and some of them retain their wood panelling and Louis XV alcoves; double doors, thick carpeting and double windows ensure absolute silence. The bathrooms are also beautiful, with gleaming taps, colored tiles and soft lighting. A monumental stone staircase leads from the bedrooms to the ground floor. Pleasingly decorated in pastel tones, the dining room and the lounge wind to the back of the house where a swimming pool tempts you to plunge into its refreshing depths, especially in the height of summer. Need we add that the hospitality is charming? For restaurants, try *La Table des Cordelies* in Condom, or *Le Moulin du Petit Gascon*.

How to get there *(Map 30): 40km south of Agen.*

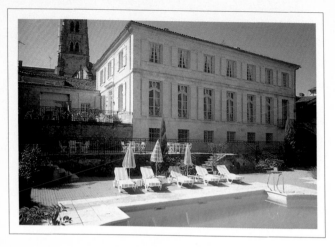

Hôtel de Bastard ★★

Rue Lagrange
32700 Lectoure (Gers)
Tel. 62.68.82.44 - Fax 62.68.76.81 - M. Arnaud

Rooms 28 and 1 suite with telephone, bath or shower, WC and TV. **Price** Single 190-280F, double 220-320F. **Meals** Breakfast 35-40F; half board 270-320F, 460F for the suite (per pers., 3 days min.). **Restaurant** Closed Friday, Saturday noon and Sunday evening Oct 1 – April 30. Service 12:15-13:30, 19:30-21:30; menus 80-240F, also à la carte. Specialties: Foie frais, carpaccio de magret. **Credit cards** All major. **Pets** Dogs allowed (+15F). **Facilities** Swimming pool, parking. **Nearby** Château de Gramont; châteaux, churches and bastides of Armagnac; Flaran, Larresingle, Fourcès, Tillac, Bassoues, Lavarders; Collegiate Church of La Romieu; jazz festival in Marciac (August) – 9-hole Fleurance golf course. **Open** March 1 – Jan 7.

Lectoure is a magnificent small fortified town overlooking the undulating countryside of the Gers. Setting out to explore the narrow streets lined with old houses, you will come across a large carved stone gateway which is the entrance to this 18th-century house. A large paved terrace with a swimming pool overlooks the village rooftops and open countryside. This view can be seen from the reception rooms, which are beautifully decorated, with pretty fabrics, high ceilings and handsome 18th-century style furniture. The bedrooms are small but comfortable; choose a room on the *premier étage* and make sure that the hotel is not giving a wedding party if it is a weekend! The Hôtel de Bastard is a charming place to stay.

How to get there *(Map 30): 35km north of Auch via N21.*

Château de Projan

Projan 32400 Riscles (Gers)
Tel. 62.09.46.21 - Fax 62.09.44.08
J. and C. Vichet

Rooms 11 (5 with shower). **Price** 180-350F. **Meals** Breakfast 30-50F, served 8:00-11:00; half board 210-280F, full board 265-335F (per pers., 5 days min.). **Restaurant** Closed Monday and Jan. Service from 13:00, 20:00; menus 75-185F. Specialties: Assiette gasconne, saumon frais aux champignons, agneau au fenouil, foie chaud aux pommes, magret et pigeonneau forestier. **Credit cards** All major. **Pets** Small dogs allowed on request. **Nearby** Landes and Gascony Regional Parks; bastides; Château of Mascaraas, Museum of Vic-Bilh, the ocean 1 1/2 hr., jazz festival in Marciac (August). **Open** All year (Jan on reservation).

The beautiful, ancient Château de Projan is located in a 7-1/2-acre park on a rocky spur overlooking the two Valleys of the Lees. The present owners, who are veritable patrons of the arts, have gathered an impressive collection of contemporary art, which is exhibited throughout the chateau; combined with several imposing 17th- and 18th-century pieces of furniture, the overall effect is warm and inviting. The bedrooms, impeccably renovated and tastefully decorated, vary from vast to tiny. Some ultra-modern designer baths were cleverly integrated into the chateau, where space was available. Don't be horrified if you have to use the communal showers: the owners have transformed the ancient thermal baths into modern and beautiful facilities. This hôtel, with its reasonable prices, is a true find: It deserves a detour!

How to get there *(Map 29): A 64, exit Pau. 40km north of Pau via N134 to Sarron, and D646 in the direction of Riscles.*

Auberge d'Enrose

32120 Solomiac (Gers)
Tel. 62.65.01.42 – Fax 62.65.02.93
R. Ryan and P. Cuff

Rooms 6 and 1 apartment with shower, WC and TV. **Price** From 300F, apart. 400-450F (per 2 pers.). **Meals** Breakfast incl., served until 10:00. **Restaurant** On reservation. Service 12:00-14-30, 20:00-21:30; menus (lunch) 80F weekdays and 145F Sunday, dinner 125F. Specialties: Regional cooking and English cooking. **Credit cards** Visa, Eurocard and MasterCard. **Pets** Small dogs allowed. **Facilities** Heated swimming pool. **Nearby** Auch, bastides tour: Mauvezin, Beaumont-de-Lomagne, Gimont, Mirande, Fleurance; Lectoure, Vic-Fezensac (bullfights on Whit Sunday). **Open** Feb – Dec.

Perched on a lush, green hilltop, the Auberge d'Enrose is a vast, quiet and comfortable country house in the heart of traditional Gascony. Several bedrooms and a small, well- equipped apartment for two to four people have been elegantly decorated. All are on the ground floor and open onto the lovely countryside. Thoughtful small details include an electric tea kettle in each room and a laundry room at guests' disposal. With the first beautiful days of spring, you can swim in the heated pool and have drinks in the garden while waiting for your hosts' delicious meal and your choice of wines and spirits. (Don't miss the Armagnac of the region, or the more rustic Pousse Rapière.) Your hosts are very welcoming and friendly.

How to get there *(Map 30): 30km northeast of Auch via N 124 in the direction of Gimont. In Aubet, go in the direction of Mauvezin and Solomiac. As you leave Solomiac, take the direction of Montfort (road on the right indicated).*

Le Demeure d'en Jourdou ★★

31480 Cadours (Haute-Garonne)
Tel. 61.85.77.77
M. Lachambre

Rooms 7 with telephone, bath or shower, WC, TV on request and minibar. **Price** Single 250-390F, double 280-420F. **Meals** Breakfast 37-47F, served 8:00-10:00; half board 380-500F, full board 480-600F (per pers., 3 days min.). **Restaurant** By reservation(dinner). **Credit cards** Amex. **Pets** Dogs allowed. **Facilities** Swimming pool, parking. **Nearby** Châteaux of Laréole, Larra and Launac; abbey of Sainte-Marie-du-Désert; bastide of Grenade – Saint-Gabriel, La Ramée, Toulouse-Seih Golf Course near Toulouse. **Open** All year.

This elegant pink brick house, somewhat set back from the road, is surrounded by beautiful countryside and fields as far as the eye can see. Skillful restoration has preserved its traditional charm. The large, comfortable bedrooms on the *premier étage* retain their original flooring and beautiful Louis XIV doors. They are comfortable, the furnishings tasteful and the bathrooms well appointed. The other bedrooms, smaller but well designed, are in the attic; soft blue carpeting and cane furniture lend these rooms an intimate charm. In the dining room, with its pastel fabrics and dark blue walls, an elegant table setting awaits you. The cuisine is in keeping with the rest of the hotel: refined and creative, with classical touches. The hosts are informal and pleasant.

How to get there *(Map 30): 39km west of Toulouse via D1.*

Auberge du Poids Public ★★★

31540 Saint-Félix-Lauragais (Haute-Garonne)
Tel. 61.83.00.20 - Fax 61.83.86.21
M. Taffarello

Rooms 13 with telephone, bath or shower, WC, TV and minibar. **Price** Double 250-300F. **Meals** Breakfast 40F, served 8:00-10:00; half board 540-590F (per 2 pers.). **Restaurant** Closed Sunday evening Oct – April. Service 12:00-13:15, 19:30-21:15; menus 135-300F, also à la carte. Specialties: Terrine de foie gras aux poireaux, gigotin d'agneau de lait des Pyrénées, croustillant aux fruits rouges. **Credit cards** Amex, Visa, Eurocard and MasterCard. **Pets** Dogs allowed. **Facilities** Parking. **Nearby** Cathedral of Saint-Papoul, Toulouse-Lautrec museum in Albi, Toulouse, Pastel road, Midi Canal road – 9 and 18-hole golf courses in Toulouse. **Open** Feb – Dec.

L ocated on the outskirts of the village, this old inn makes a pleasant stopping place. The bedrooms are fairly large and simply furnished with some antique pieces; six of them enjoy a beautiful view. Most are quiet; the few that look onto the street are only used if the others are full. There is a private bar-lounge. Depending on the time of year lunches and dinners are served either in the large, bright and prettily decorated dining room or in the shade of wide umbrellas on the lovely terrace. In either case the marvelous view is enhanced by outstanding cuisine, some of the best in the region.

How to get there (Map 31): 40km southeast of Toulouse via D2 towards Revel.

Hostellerie des 7 Molles ★★★

31510 Sauveterre-de-Comminges (Haute-Garonne)
Tel. 61.88.30.87 – Fax 61.88.36.42
M. Ferran

Rooms 19 with telephone, bath, WC, TV and minibar. **Price** Single 570F, double 600-760F, suite 900-1100F. **Meals** Breakfast 70F, served 8:00-11:00; half board 560-675F, full board 750-900F (per pers., 3 days min.). **Restaurant** Service 12:00-13:30, 19:30-21:30; menus 185-300F, also à la carte. Specialties: Pastis gersois de foie gras à la pomme reinette, agneau de lait des Pyrénées et sa moulinade de haricots. **Credit cards** All major. **Pets** Dogs allowed. **Facilities** Swimming pool, tennis, parking. **Nearby** Saint-Bertrand-de-Comminges, Montréjeau, Gallo-Roman villa of Montmaurin – 18-hole Lannemezan golf course, 9-hole golf course in Luchon. **Open** mid-March – end Oct.

The seven watermills have disappeared but the millstones remain and lend their name to the hotel. The immediate surroundings are superb: meadows, vines and groves of trees surround the house. The spacious, luminous bedrooms are furnished in traditional style. There is a warm ambience in the dining room and reception rooms. The cuisine, both traditional and modern, is made largely from homemade products, including sausages from the hotel's own pig farm, trout from the fish tank, *foie gras* and pastries. The staff is welcoming and friendly.

How to get there *(Map 30): 74km southeast of Tarbes via N117 to Saint-Gaudens, then D8 to Valentine and D9 (follow signs).*

Hôtel du Château **
46500 Alvignac (Lot)
Tel. 65.33.60.14 – Fax 65.33.69.28
M. Darnis

Rooms 36 with telephone, bath or shower and WC. **Price** Single 165F, double 200-260F. **Meals** Breakfast 25F, served 7:30-9:30; half board 250-260F, full board 275-290F. **Restaurant** Service 12:00-13:30, 19:00-20:30; menus 60-180F, also à la carte. Specialties: Cuisine de canard, magret, confit, pâté, cèpes. **Credit cards** All major. **Pets** Dogs allowed. **Facilities** Parking. **Nearby** Padirac chasm, Rocamadour. **Open** April 1 – mid Oct.

Located in the park of the Quercy famous for its waters since the 18th-century, this hotel is built on the foundations of an ancient château. A terrace silled with flowers extends from the large dining room, and there is a small bar hung with paintings by M. Darnis' brother. A courtyard shaded by large trees makes the hotel quiet and cool. Nostalgics may yearn for the charms of the original hotel, but the bedrooms are now more comfortable and quieter, and have been redecorated in pale colors. The annex is similarly styled but we would only recommend it as a last resort as it lacks the appeal of the main house. Guests also have the use of extensive grounds on the other side of the road. The hosts are very friendly.

How to get there *(Map 24): 58km south of Brive-la-Gaillarde via N20 to Cressensac, then N140 and D673.*

Chez Marcel

Rue du 11 mai 1944
46100 Cardaillac (Lot)
Tel. 65.40.11.16 - Fax 63. 96.07.20 - M. Marcel

Rooms 6. **Price** Double 135F. **Meals** Breakfast 30F, served all morning; half board 185F, full board 230F (per pers., 3 days min.). **Restaurant** Closed Monday except in July and August. Service 12:00-13:30, 19:00-20:30; menus 75-170F, also à la carte. Specialties: Foie gras, omelette aux cèpes ou aux truffes, tripoux, agneau du causse, fromage de Rocamadour, gâteau aux noix, clafoutis, profiterolles à la menthe et à la crème. **Credit cards** All major. **Pets** Dogs allowed in restaurant. **Facilities** Parking. **Nearby** "Musée Eclaté" in Cardaillac, Valleys of the Lot and the Célé (Figeac-Cahors-Figeac). **Open** All year (closed Monday in low season).

In tiny Cardaillac, the grocery store is also the tobacco shop and the picturesque village restaurant Chez Marcel has several rooms for visitors. You will enjoy delicious regional dishes as well as a friendly staff here. The bedrooms are furnished in traditional style and while not very large, they are charming – but there is only one shower for the six rooms. Still, the price is right. Chez Marcel is located in a beautiful village which still has many vestiges of the Middle Ages and the time when it was a Protestant refuge. Today, the community takes pride in what is voted "one of the most beautiful villages of France".

How to get there *(Map 24): 9km northwest of Figeac via N140, then D15 on the right.*

313

Hôtel Les Falaises ★★

Gluges
46600 Martel (Lot)
Tel. 65.37.33.59 - Fax 65.37.34.19 - M. Dassiou

Rooms 17 with telephone, bath or shower and WC. **Price** Single 165F, double 210-320F. **Meals** Breakfast 38F, served 8:00-10:00; half board 220-270F, full board 290-350F (per pers., 3 days min.). **Restaurant** Service 12:30-14:00, 19:30-21:00; menus 100-250F, also à la carte. Specialties: Magret de canard au vert jus et raisins confits. **Credit cards** Visa, Eurocard and MasterCard. **Pets** Dogs not allowed. **Facilities** Parking. **Nearby** Quercy region of the Dordogne from Souillac to Saint-Céré, Rocamadour, Padirac, Lacave, Car museum in Souillac – 9-hole Mas del Teil golf course in Souillac. **Open** March 1 – Nov 30.

At the foot of the cliffs bordering the Dordogne, this old residence has been converted into a hotel. A large terrace with an ornamental pool separates it from the main building, and in summer meals are served here in the shade of the trees. The dining room has just been renovated; predominantly blue, its large windows open out onto the terrace. The bedrooms are comfortable and sensibly furnished, and we particularly recommend numbers 10 or 12, all of which have terraces. The hotel has just purchased a 2 1/2-acre park so that guests may enjoy a peaceful stroll before dinner. The beautiful location, warm welcome, excellent cooking and particularly good breakfasts are the trump cards of this family hotel.

How to get there *(Map 24): 70km south of Brive-la-Gaillarde via N140 towards Martel (on the banks of the Dordogne).*

Le Pont de L'Ouysse ***

46200 Lacave (Lot)
Tel. 65.37.87.04 – Fax 65.32.77.41
M. and Mme Chambon

Rooms 13 with telephone, bath, WC, TV and minibar. **Price** Single 350F, double 500F, suite 750F. **Meals** Breakfast 60F, served 8:00-10:00; half board 600-650F (per pers.). **Restaurant** Service 12:30-14:00, 19:30-21:00; à la carte. Specialties: Ecrevisses, foie gras, pigeon aux cèpes, poulette rôtie aux truffes. **Credit cards** All major. **Pets** Dogs allowed. **Facilities** Swimming pool, parking. **Nearby** Quercy region of the Dordogne from Souillac to Saint-Céré, Rocamadour, Padirac – 9-hole Rochebois golf course in Vitrac. **Open** March 1 – Dec (closed Monday in low season).

The same family has always run this hotel, which is attached to the side of a rock surrounded by lush vegetation. The large, light bedrooms are very comfortable, with an attractive decor based on English wallpapers and coordinated fabrics. The bathrooms are equally pleasant. The road which goes over the river and up to the hotel is a dead end, ensuring peace and quiet. The charm of this place is enhanced by its lovely terrace, which is shaded by a horse chestnut and a linden tree, and provides outdoor dining in summer. The menu is not extensive but changes often, and the excellent cooking is a result of the imagination and skill of Monsieur Chambon. Madame Chambon will give you a very friendly welcome.

How to get there *(Map 23): 37km south of Brive-le-Gaillarde via N20 to Souillac, then D43.*

Hostellerie Le Vert **

Le Vert
46700 Mauroux (Lot)
Tel. 65.36.51.36 – M. and Mme Philippe

Rooms 7 with telephone, bath or shower, WC and TV. **Price** Single 230F, double 270-340F. **Meals** Breakfast 35F, served 7:30-10:30; half board 295-330F, full board 375-410F (per pers., 3 days min.). **Restaurant** Closed Thursdays and Friday lunchtime. Service 12:00-13:15, 19:30-20:30; menus 100-150F, also à la carte. Specialties: Foie gras frais aux fruits frais, agneau du Quercy, poêlée de cèpes aux petits gris. **Credit cards** Amex, Visa, Eurocard and MasterCard. **Pets** Dogs allowed (+25F). **Facilities** Swimming pool, parking. **Nearby** Cathedral of Saint-Etienne in Cahors, Cahors wine route (château de Bonaguil), valley of the Lot. **Open** Feb 12 – Nov 26.

The Hostellerie Le Vert is an old converted farmhouse. Its windows shed a soft and gentle light on the spacious, comfortable and refined interior. A lovely terrace looks out over the surrounding countryside – a pleasant spot for a summer breakfast. The cuisine is very good. In summer, ask for the bedroom that has been made in the old vaulted cellar (number 6), which is cool and unusual. Above it a large, bright new bedroom has just been added, with a beamed ceiling, stone floor, a beautiful fireplace and a piano. The bedrooms in the main hotel are not so original but are no less inviting and comfortable.

How to get there *(Map 30): 37km west of Cahors via D911 to Puy-l'Evêque, then D5 in the direction of Mauroux.*

Relais Sainte-Anne ★★★

Rue du Pourtanel
46600 Martel (Lot)
Tel. 65.37.40.56 - Fax 65.37.42.82 - Mme Lachèze

Rooms 10 with telephone, bath or shower, WC, TV and 8 with minibar. **Price** Single and double 280-850F. **Meals** Breakfast 50F, served 8:00-12:00. No restaurant. **Credit cards** All major. **Pets** Dogs allowed (+50F). **Facilities** Swimming pool, parking. **Nearby** Rocamadour, Padirac, grottes de la Cave, Dordogne Valley, Collonges-la-Rouge, abbey of Aubazines - Music festival in summer. **Open** Nov 6 – Easter.

Don't be surprised to find a chapel here: The Relais Sainte Anne was once a boarding house for nuns. There are ten lovely bedrooms located in several recently renovated buildings. All have very modern conveniences but each room is individually decorated in sober, elegant fabrics and colors. The largest room has a fireplace and a terrace; smaller rooms are less expensive. There is a walled-in, old garden with a lovely terrace, small paths and a beautiful swimming pool surrounded by a lawn. Breakfast can be served in your room, in the breakfast room which has a fireplace or, in good weather, on the terrace. In summer, classical music concerts are performed in the chapel. The Relais Sainte Anne radiates with turn-of-the-century charm.

How to get there *(Map 23 and 24): 30km south of Brive.*

Relais de la Dolse ★★★

Montcabrier
46700 Puy-l'Evêque (Lot)
Tel. 65.36.53.42 - Fax 65.24.61.25

Rooms 11 with telephone, bath or shower and WC. **Price** Single and double 390-450F. **Meals** Breakfast 35F, served 8:30-10:00. No restaurant but snacks available. **Credit cards** All major. **Pets** Dogs allowed. **Facilities** Swimming pool, parking. **Nearby** Cahors Wine Route from Mercues to Montcabrier. **Open** May 14 – Oct 2.

This hotel stands in a countryside surrounded by trees and small valleys. It is composed of two buildings about 100 meters apart. The older building, which houses the reception area and the restaurant, has been renovated to emphasize beamed ceilings and exposed stonework. In the dining room, period furniture and finely-worked Indian fabrics create a warm atmosphere, while an impressive, multi-colored wooden horse prances above the big fireplace. There is only one bedroom (our favorite) in the old building; the other rooms occupy the more recent building, and they are large and comfortable, decorated in shades of pink and white. Each has a small private garden. Breakfast is served in an adjoining room. You will be warmly welcomed, and prices are reasonable. There is no longer a restaurant at the Relais, but there are many good small restaurants in the region.

How to get there (Map 30): 8km north of Puy-l'Evêque via D68 (3km from the village).

Hôtel Les Vieilles Tours **

Lafage
46500 Rocamadour (Lot)
Tel. 65.33.68.01 - Fax 65.33.68.59 - M. and Mme Zozzoli

Rooms 18 with telephone, bath or shower and WC. **Price** Double 210-450F.
Meals Breakfast 38-58F, served 8:00-11:00; half board 290-420F. **Restaurant**
Service 19:30-21:00 (at lunchtime by reservation); menus 100-180F, children 57F,
also à la carte. Specialties: Carré d'agneau du Causse, trute au vin de Cahors, foie
gras poëlé aux pommes, charlotte aux fruits. **Credit cards** Visa, Eurocard and
MasterCard. **Pets** Dogs allowed except in the restaurant (+30F). **Facilities** Swimming
pool, parking. **Nearby** Old town, Francis Poulenc museum in Rocamadour, Padirac
chasm, Lascaux caves – 9-hole Saint-Céré golf course. **Open** April 1 – Nov 4.

This hotel is only 2 kilometers from Rocamadour. It has been
well restored using beautiful local stone and enjoys exceptional
views and tranquillity. The reception and dining room have their
original stone walls and the tables are tastefully laid. There are
bedrooms in both the old building and its modern annex, which
was built in the local style. Pleasantly furnished, with some 19th-
century pieces, the bedrooms are all different and have comfortable
amenities, as do the bathrooms. Monsieur Zozzoli is a painter,
engraver and lithographer and you will find frequent examples of
his work, which is inspired by the region. The menu offers delicious
regional dishes, which change according to the season and Madame
Zozzoli's inspiration.

How to get there (Map 24): *53km south of Brive-la-Gaillarde via N20 to
Cressensac, then N140 and D673; 3km from Rocamadour, in the direction of
Payrac/Gourdon.*

Domaine de la Rhue ★★★

La Rhue
46500 Rocamadour (Lot)
Tel. 65.33.71.50 - Fax 65.33.72.48 - M. and Mme Jooris

Rooms 12 with telephone, bath or shower, WC and 4 with TV. **Price** Single 370F, double 370-570F, apart. (4 pers.) 680F. **Meals** Breakfast 42-65F, served 8:00-10:00. No restaurant. **Credit cards** Visa, Eurocard and MasterCard. **Pets** Dogs allowed (+30F). **Facilities** Swimming pool, parking. **Nearby** Old town, Francis Poulenc museum in Rocamadour, truffle market in Gramat, Lascaux caves, Padirac chasm – 9-hole Montal golf course in Saint-Céré. **Open** April 14 – Oct 15.

This hotel is located in the splendid stables of a château which is surrounded by beautiful rolling countryside. The Domaine is tastefully and comfortably furnished throughout. The vast entrance hall retains its original paving and traces of the stalls. Pleasantly furnished in a rustic style, the bedrooms are named after horse breeds, and are all spacious, quiet and attractive, with some antique furniture, elegant fabrics and many original beams. Some of the rooms on the ground floor are like small houses with a private terrace. The Domaine has all the modern amenities, mixed with the charm of the past. For excellent cuisine try the *Sainte-Marie* Restaurant.

How to get there *(Map 24): 55km south of Brive-la-Gaillarde via N20 towards Cressensac, then N140; 1km before junction with D673, take the road on the right.*

320

Hôtel Ric ★★★

Route de Leyme
46400 Saint-Céré (Lot)
Tel. 65.38.04.08 - Fax 65.38.00.14 - M. Ric

Rooms 6 with telephone, bath, WC and TV. **Price** Double 300-350F. **Meals** Breakfast 45F, served until 9:00 (in room); half board 350-380F (per pers.). **Restaurant** Closed Monday in low season except National holidays. Service 12:00-14:00, 19:30-21:30; menus 100-240F, also à la carte. Specialties: Parmentier de foie gras aux oignons frits, fleurs de courgettes farcies aux écrevisses, taboulé de langoustines, fondant au chocolat aux framboises et fraises des bois. **Credit cards** Visa, Eurocard and MasterCard. **Pets** Dogs allowed. **Facilities** Swimming pool, parking. **Nearby** Quercy region of the Dordogne from Souillac to Saint-Céré – 9-hole Saint-Céré golf course. **Open** March –Jan (closed Monday in low season except National holidays).

Surrounded by beautiful foliage, this small hotel has a magnificent view over the hills of Saint-Céré. The accommodations are modern, as is the decor. All the bedrooms are comfortable, but we prefer those on the front. In the pale–green dining room or on the terrace in summer, you will enjoy the inventive cuisine of the owner, Monsieur Ric, who serves such specialties as fresh squash blossoms stuffed with crayfish. The staff is young and friendly.

How to get there (Map 24): 55km south of Brive-la-Gaillarde via D 702, in the direction of Saint-Céré. At 2.5km from Saint-Céré, Leymé road by D48.

Hôtel de la Pelissaria ★★★

46330 Saint-Cirq-Lapopie (Lot)
Tel. 65.31.25.14 - Fax 65.30.25.52
Mme Matuchet

Rooms 10 with telephone, bath, WC and TV - 1 wheelchair accessible room.
Price Double 400-600F, suite 640F. **Meals** Breakfast 48F, served 8:00-10:00.
Restaurant Closed Thursday and Friday. Service 20:00-21:00; à la carte. Specialties:
home-made pasta and sorbets, confit de canard. **Credit cards** Visa, Eurocard and
MasterCard. **Pets** Dogs allowed (+15F). **Facilities** Small swimming pool. **Nearby** Lot
and the Célé valleys. **Open** April 1 – Nov 15.

There is something magical about the village of Saint-Cirq-
Lapopie. It is one of the most beautiful medieval villages in
France, and has been classified as a historic monument. Hôtel de
la Pelissaria, one of the most beautiful hotels listed on this book,
was built in the 13th-century in local stone, and has been carefully
and tastefully restored by its cordial owners. Our favorite bedroom
is number 4, with its little window opening onto the village and
the Lot Valley. Two small cottages nestled in a garden house two
charming rooms. In the dining room, which has a piano and a
lovely fireplace, you will enjoy very good cuisine (and excellent
value for money). The number of seats in the restaurant is limited,
so reservations are a must.

How to get there *(Map 31): 33km east of Cahors via D653 towards Saint-
Géry, then D662.*

322

Auberge du Sombral **
46330 Saint-Cirq-Lapopie (Lot)
Tel. 65.31.26.08 – Fax 65.30.26.37
M. and Mme Hardeveld

Rooms 8 with telephone, 5 with bath, 5 with shower. **Price** Single 300F, double 400F. **Meals** Breakfast 48F, served until 9:30. **Restaurant** Service 12:00-14:00, 19:30-21:00; menus 100-280F, also à la carte. Specialties: Truite au vieux Cahors, feuilleté d'asperges aux morilles, escalope de foie chaud aux pommes, terrine de foie de canard confit. **Credit cards** Visa, Eurocard and MasterCard. **Pets** Dogs allowed. **Nearby** Valleys of the Lot and the Célé. **Open** Apr 1 – Nov 11 (closed Tuesday evening and Wednesday).

This auberge is in an old house which has been perfectly restored. It faces the town square in the heart of this village, now classed as a historic monument. The village is on an escarpment overlooking the Valley of the Lot. The atmosphere is calm, the surroundings exceptional. The bedrooms are pleasant and comfortable. You can explore the village with its alleys and picturesque houses, as well as the auberge itself, which has its own museum with a permanent display of paintings by local artists. The restaurant offers excellent cuisine and emphasizes regional specialties.

How to get there *(Map 31): 33km east of Cahors via D653 towards Saint-Géry, then D662.*

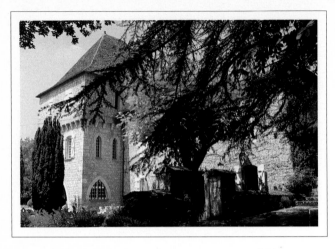

Hostellerie La Source Bleue ★★★

Touzac
46700 Puy-l'Evêque (Lot)
Tel. 65.36.52.01 - Fax 65.24.65.69 - M. and Mme Bouyou

Rooms 16 with telephone, bath, WC and 5 with TV. **Price** Single 250F, double 250-450F. **Meals** Breakfast 35F, served 7:30-9:30; half board from 285F, full board from 385F (per per., 3 days min.). **Restaurant** Service 12:00-13:30, 19:30-21:15 (closed Tuesday lunchtime); menus 100, 140, 200F, also à la carte. Specialties: Saumon cuit sur sa peau, rôti de lotte et sa concassée de tomates fraîches, agneau de pays au parfum de gingembre, feuilleté de fruits frais. **Credit cards** Amex, Visa, Eurocard and MasterCard. **Pets** Dogs allowed (+30F). **Facilities** Swimming pool, sauna (100F), health center (100F), boat, parking. **Nearby** Marguerite-Moréno museum, Cahors wine route (château de Bonaguil) – 18-hole La Chapelle golf course in Auzac, 18-hole Castelnaud-de-Gratecambe golf course. **Open** April – Dec.

La Source Bleue, in a converted 14th-century paper mill on the left bank of the Lot, has been tastefully restored by its owners. The bedrooms, some with modern furniture, are comfortable, and the bathrooms are impeccable. Four new bedrooms have been added in the tower and decorated with antique furniture. The cooking is refined and served in a beautiful dining room. The service is attentive but discreet, and there is soft background music. The gardens and park of "The Blue Spring" are beautiful with their many species of trees, including an impressive bamboo forest.

How to get there (Map 30): 48km west of Cahors via D911 towards Fumel; at Touzac, cross the Lot.

Le Square ★★★
5, place de la Craste
47220 Astaffort (Lot-and-Garonne)
Tel. 53.47.20.40 - Fax 53.47.10.38 - M. Cabrel

Rooms 8 with air-conditioning, telephone, bath, WC, TV and minibar - 1 wheelchair accessible room. **Price** 280F. **Meals** Breakfast 32F, served 8:00-10:00. **Restaurant** Closed Sunday evening and Monday. Service 12:00-14:00, 19:30-22:00; menu 92F, also à la carte. Specialties: Regional cooking. **Credit cards** All major. **Pets** Dogs allowed. **Nearby** Agen, bastides of Villeneuve-sur-Lot and of Beauville, Prades, Auvillar, Nérac, market "fermier" Monday in Astaffort. **Open** All year (except 2-3 weeks in Jan; Sunday evening and Monday).

The pretty pink and blue façade of Le Square seems to beckon you to this brand-new village hotel which is surprisingly refined and comfortable. The ravishing bedrooms are decorated with tasteful combinations of colors and prints, while the bathrooms, in the same color schemes, are superb. There are two dining rooms where you are served delicious cuisine of the Southwest, which is both traditional and inventive. One dining room opens onto a small terrace where you can have meals in summer; in the other, which is cool and informal, you are served on warmly colored enameled-lava tables. Guests enjoy the friendly atmosphere of Le Square, a charming hotel very near Agen.

How to get there *(Map 30): 16km south of Agen via RN 21. Via A62, number 7 Agen exit.*

Hostellerie Saint-Antoine ★★★★
17, rue Saint-Antoine
81000 Albi (Tarn)
Tel. 63.54.04.04 - Fax 63.47.10.47 - MM. Rieux and fils

Rooms 48 with air-conditioning, telephone, bath, WC and TV. **Price** Single 360-450F, double 450-750F, suite 850-950F. **Meals** Breakfast 60F; half board 420-720F (per pers.). **Restaurant** Closed Saturday and Sunday lunchtime. Service 12:00-14:00, 19:00-21:30; menus 150-280F, also à la carte. Specialties: Foie gras, salade de homard, daube de bœuf à l'albigeoise, tournedos Périgueux, tarte à l'ancienne, glace aux noix. **Credit cards** All major. **Pets** Dogs allowed (+55F). **Facilities** Parking. **Nearby** Cathedral of Sainte-Cécile, Toulouse-Lautrec museum in Albi, Viaur viaduct, Ambialet, Gaillac, Cordes – 18-hole golf course in Albi. **Open** All year.

Founded in the 18th-century and run by the same family for five generations, this inn was restored in 1960. Elegantly modernized, each room is enhanced by antique furniture – including Directoire and Louis-Phillippe pieces, and bright fabrics. The bedrooms are extremely comfortable, quiet, well-designed and many have a view of the flower garden. Some of the larger ones have a lounge area. On the ground floor the dining room opens onto the garden. You will enjoy good traditional cooking, attentive service and warm hospitality.

How to get there (Map 31): In the town center.

Cuq-en-Terrasse

Cuq-le-Château
81470 Cuq-Toulza (Tarn)
Tel 63.82.54.00 - Fax 63.82.54.11 - M. and Mme Whitmore

Rooms 7 and 1 apartment (duplex), bath or shower, WC and TV. **Price** 350-450F, suite 650F, apartment 900F. **Meals** Breakfast 40F. **Restaurant** On reservation. Service 12:00-14:30, 19:30-21:30; menus 120F (lunch), 140F (dinner). Specialties: Vichyssoise, gazpacho, mousse de saumon fumé, filet mignon de veau à l'estragon et aux baies roses, noisettes d'agneau aux deux poivrons. **Credit cards** Visa, Eurocard and MasterCard. **Pets** Dogs allowed. **Facilities** Swimming pool. **Nearby** Albi, Carcassonne, Castres market in Revel – 18-hole Fiac Golf Course. **Open** All major.

This ancient house spreads out over an enchanting terraced hillside. From the terraces and the garden swimming pool, you will have a superb view over the patchwork of rich valleys the locals call *Le Pays de Cocagne*, the land of abundance. Le Cuq en Terrasse has been magnificently restored and decorated by an English architect and his wife. Tasteful decoration in the bright bedrooms and baths make this a very beautiful hotel, in which traditional decor has been skillfully combined with the most modern amenities. You will enjoy the sheer serenity of the place, from the terrace to the shady nooks around the swimming pool. Breakfasts are generous and elegant and Zara Whitmore serves delicious regional cuisine. There is an excellent choice of wines, and the owners are friendly and considerate.

How to get there *(Map 31): 35km east of Toulouse, direction Castres. In Cuq, take diretion Revel for 2km. On A61, exit number 17.*

Demeure de Flore ★★★

106, route Nationale
81240 Lacabarède (Tarn)
Tel. 63.98.32.32. – Fax 63.98.47.56 – Mme Tronc

Rooms 8 and 1 suite with telephone, bath, WC and TV - Wheelchair access.
Price Single 340F, double 400F, suite 670F. **Meals** Breakfast 52F. **Restaurant** Service
19:30-21:30; menus 130-200F, also à la carte. **Credit cards** Visa, Eurocard and
MasterCard. **Pets** Dogs not allowed. **Facilities** Swimming pool, parking. **Nearby** Goya
museum in Castres, le Sidobre and the Monts Lacaune de Castres in Mazamet – 18-
hole La Barouge golf course in Pont-de-l'Arn. **Open** All year except in Feb.

This small hotel is hidden from the road by lush vegetation.
Indoors, the decor is elegant; antique furniture, paintings and
curios combine to create a warm and cozy atmosphere. The
comfortable bedrooms are all individually decorated with colorful
designer fabrics and antiques bought locally. The bathrooms are
modern and luxuriously equipped. Our favorite rooms are those
with a small terrace and access to the garden and swimming pool.
Evening meals, based on fresh local produce, are served in the
lovely dining room. This is a marvelous place to stay.

How to get there *(Map 31): 15km east of Mazamet via N112.*

Château de Montlédier ★★★

Route d'Anglès
81660 Pont-de-L'Arn (Tarn)
Tel. 63.61.20.54 – Fax 63.98.22.51 – Mme Thiercelin

Rooms 9 with telephone, bath, WC, TV and minibar. **Price** Single 330-360F, double 430-590F. **Meals** Breakfast 50F; half board 350-410F, full board 430-490F (per pers., 3 days min.). **Restaurant** Closed Sunday evening and Monday except July – Aug. Service 12:00-13:30, 19:30-21:30; menus 100-225F, also à la carte. Specialties: Foie gras maison, carré d'agneau, magret de canard, soufflé léger à la poire. **Credit cards** All major. **Pets** Dogs allowed. **Facilities** Swimming pool, parking. **Nearby** Goya museum in Castres, le Sidobre and the Monts Lacaune de Castres in Mazamet – 18-hole La Barouge golf course in Pont-de-l'Arn. **Open** Feb.1 – Dec 31.

You enter the chateau through the grand courtyard. Inside there are a number of small lounges, equipped so that there is something to please everyone. The bedrooms are spacious and beautifully decorated, each extremely comfortable. The smallest and least expensive rooms (*Victoria* and *Alexandra*) are as charming as the others, and the *Raymond IV* bedroom has a particularly charming bathroom – it is huge and from it you can see through the trees into the ravine. Meals are served in the small dining room or on a shady terrace which forms an extension to the lounge.

How to get there *(Map 31): 19km southeast of Castres via N112 towards Mazamet, then D65 at Bout-du-Pont-de-l'Arn.*

Le Métairie Neuve ★★★
81660 Pont-de-L'Arn (Tarn)
Tel. 63.61.23.31
Mme Tournier

Rooms 11 with telephone, bath, WC, TV and 9 with minibar. **Price** Single 310-500F, double 290-550F. **Meals** Half board 300-550F, full board 450-680F (per pers., 3 days min.). **Restaurant** Closed Saturday in low season, Saturday lunchtime in high season. Service 12:00-13:30, 19:30-21:00; menus 100-250F, also à la carte. Specialties: Terrine de foie gras frais, ris de veau à l'ancienne, salade de homard, fish, game. **Credit cards** Diners, Visa, Eurocard and MasterCard. **Pets** Dogs allowed. **Facilities** pool, parking. **Nearby** Goya museum in Castres, le Sidobre and the Monts Lacaune de Castres in Mazamet – 18-hole La Barouge golf course in Pont-de-l'Arn. **Open** Jan 20 – Dec 13.

This lovely old farmhouse is on the outskirts of a village which is expanding with commercial developments, but the hotel remains in a leafy, quiet area. The bedrooms are all well equipped and elegantly furnished; the colors are harmonious and the old furniture blends perfectly with the more modern pieces. The hotel has a beautiful courtyard, a large garden with a terrace, and a swimming pool. One of the restaurant's two rooms is reserved for non-smokers. But the cuisine itself needs improvement.

How to get there *(Map 31): 19km southeast of Castres via N112 towards Mazamet.*

Château de l'Hoste **

Saint-Beauzeuil
82150 Montaigu-de-Quercy (Tarn-et-Garonne)
Tel. 63.95.25.61 - Fax 63.95.25.50 - M. Poumeyrau

Rooms 32 with telephone, bath and WC. **Price** Single and double 210-260F.
Meals Breakfast 40F, served 8:00-10:00; half board 280F, full board 380F (per pers.,
3 days min.). **Restaurant** Closed Sunday evening and Monday in low season. Service
12:00, 19:45; menus 110-265F, also à la carte. Specialties: Lamproie bordelaise,
trilogie de bœuf, cassoulet d'antan. **Credit cards** Visa, Eurocard and MasterCard.
Pets Dogs allowed (+20F). **Facilities** Swimming pool, parking. **Nearby** Agen
museum, Port-Sainte-Marie, Villeneuve-sur-Lot, Beauville – 18-hole château de
Terrides golf course. **Open** All year.

Monsieur Poumeyrau has just acquired this 18th-century
mansion. You will be charmed by its pale stone walls, lovely
interior courtyard, and the proximity of the swimming pool. The
decoration has been less successful in the bedrooms where the
antique-style furniture is disappointing. They are nevertheless
large, well kept rooms with comfortable beds and impeccable
bathrooms. We recommend rooms 204 and 210, which are smaller
but charming. In summer avoid the rooms that overlook the terrace
where dinner is served; the enthusiasm of the diners enjoying the
chef's excellent cooking (especially the *lamproie à la bordelaise*) may
disturb you if you want to retire early.

How to get there *(Map 30): 40km northeast of Agen via D656; between
Agen and Cahors – 8km east of Montaigu.*

Château de Ligny ★★★

4, rue Pierre-Curie
59191 Ligny-Haucourt (Nord)
Tel. 27.85.25.84 - Fax 27.85.25.84 - M. and Mme Boulard

Rooms 6 and 3 suites with telephone, bath WC, TV and suites with minibar.
Price Single and double 460-600F, suite 700-1100F. **Meals** Breakfast 50F, served
7:45-9:30. **Restaurant** Closed Monday lunchtime and Saturday lunchtime. Service
12:30-13:45, 19:30-21:30; menus 190-380F, also à la carte. Specialties: Foie gras
de canard en terrine, noisette d'agneau à la menthe poivrée. **Credit cards** All major.
Pets dogs allowed in bedrooms (+50F). **Nearby** Church of Saint-Géry in Cambrai
('Entombment' by Rubens), abbey of Vaucelles, Matisse museum in le Cateau-
Cambrésis, art museum in Valenciennes – 9-hole golf course in Valenciennes.
Open All year (closed Monday in low season).

Beside the village church the gates of the château open into a
charming courtyard with a beautiful magnolia tree
overhanging a stone fountain. The size of the building makes this
an inviting place to stay, for it is less grandiose than some other
château hotels. The bedrooms are all individually decorated. The
Rustique bedroom is entirely green, including the carpet; the *Royale*
suite is more modern in inspiration with its pale colors. The owner
is an antiques enthusiast and the *Regent* bedroom in particular has
benefitted from his finds, notably a superb carved wood ram. A
small park surrounding the château makes it beautifully quiet.

How to get there (Map 2): 15km southeast of Cambrai via A2, Cambrai
exit.

Le Jardin Fleuri **

23, rue du Moulin
59990 Sebourg (Nord)
Tel. 27.26.53.31 - Fax 27.26.50.08 - Mme Delmotte

Rooms 13 with telephone, bath or shower, 9 with WC and 8 with TV. **Price** Double 200-300F. **Meals** Breakfast 25F, served 7:00-10:00; half board 260-320F, full board 360-420F (per pers., 4 days min.). **Restaurant** Closed Wednesday. Service 12:00-13:00, 19:00-22:00; menus 110-180F, also à la carte. Specialties: Langue Lucullus, saumon à l'unilatérale, tarte aux pommes. **Credit cards** Visa, Eurocard and MasterCard. **Pets** Dogs allowed. **Facilities** Parking. **Nearby** Art museum in Valenciennes, Bavay, Le Quesnoy, glass museum in Sars-Poterie – 9-hole golf course in Valenciennes. **Open** All year (closed Sept 15 – 30).

In the small rue du Moulin, you first come to the restaurant and then, behind it, the hotel's colorful and charming garden; the little stream with its wooden bridge and the beautiful fir trees are lovely. Beyond it is the hotel, a small brick house. It contains 13 bedrooms on two floors; cozy and comfortable, they look out over the garden and two have a balcony. The Jardin Fleuri is notable for its good cooking and very reasonable prices.

How to get there *(Map 3): 9km east of Valenciennes via A2, Curgies exit, then D8.*

Auberge du Bon Fermier ★★★★

64-66, rue de Famars
59300 Valenciennes (Nord)
Tel. 27.46.68.25 - Fax 27.33.75.01 - M. and Mme Paul

Rooms 16 with telephone, bath or shower WC, TV and minibar. **Price** Single 380-
430F, double 530-700F. **Meals** Breakfast 45F, served 7:00-11:00. **Restaurant** Service
12:00-14:30, 19:00-22:30; menus 160-200F, also à la carte. Specialties: Langue
Lucullus, cochon de lait à la broche, tarte au maroilles (goyère). **Credit cards** All
major. **Pets** Dogs allowed. **Facilities** Parking (+50F). **Nearby** Remains of the ancient
abbey in Saint-Amand-les-Eaux, fortifications of Le Quesnoy, the Helpe valley – 9-
hole golf course in Valenciennes. **Open** All year.

Stop off at the Auberge du Bon Fermier for a comfortable evening
in what used to be a royal carriage house in the 17th-century,
on the road from the Tuileries to Brussels. It has been an inn since
1840, and is now registered a historic monument, scrupulously
restored by its present owners. The red bricks of the outer walls
and many inner ones, the exposed beams, and the oak floors all
help recreate the atmosphere of that era. The rooms are all spacious
and enchanting, and each has a sitting area. The quietest ones are
on the park. Modern conveniences have been carefully blended
into the decor. The restaurant serves regional specialties but also
features fresh lobster and a wide range of spit-roasted meats. The
atmosphere is somewhat theatrical, but this is nonetheless a place
not to be missed.

How to get there *(Map 3): In the town center, between the Place du Canada
and the town hall.*

Grand Hôtel Clément ★★★

91, esplanade du Maréchal-Leclerc
62610 Ardres (Pas-de-Calais)
Tel. 21.82.25.25 - Fax 21.82.98.92 - M. Coolen

Rooms 17 with telephone bath or shower, WC, TV and minibar. **Price** Single and double 240-340F. **Meals** Breakfast 35F, served 7:30-9:30; half board 240-290F, full board 340-390F. **Restaurant** Service 12:00-14:00, 19:00-21:00; menus 95-320F, also à la carte. Specialties: Volaille de Licques, ragoût et produits de la mer, foie gras. **Credit cards** All major. **Pets** Dogs allowed. **Facilities** Parking. **Nearby** The 'Bourgeois de Calais', art and lace museum in Calais, basilica of Notre-Dame and Sandelin museum in Saint-Omer, church of Saint-Eloi and museum in Hazebrouck – 18-hole golf course in Wimereux. **Open** Feb 15 – Jan 15 (closed Monday).

This hotel has been run by the same family since 1917, François Coolen, a member of the Young Restaurateurs of France Association, has furthered the hotel's reputation with his culinary skill. The bedrooms are simple, but a piece of old furniture, a lovely mirror or a beamed ceiling make each room unique. Our favorites are numbers 19, 20 and 21, which look out over the grounds at the rear of the hotel. There is a nostalgic atmosphere in the bar, the lounge and the beautiful dining room. The family is very hospitable.

How to get there *(Map 2): 97km northwest of Arras via A26, Nordausque exit; then N43. 17km southeast of Calais.*

Chartreuse du Val Saint-Esprit ★★★

1, rue de Fouquières
62199 Gosnay (Pas-de-Calais)
Tel. 21.62.80.00 - Fax 21.62.42.50 - M. and Mme Constant

Rooms 56 with telephone, bath, WC, TV and minibar. **Price** Single 330-600F, double 400-900F. **Meals** Breakfast 50F, served 6:30-10:00. **Restaurant** Service 12:00-14:30, 19:00-22:00; menus 195-375F, also à la carte. Specialties: Turbot à la fondue de poireaux, feuilleté de foie gras et ris de veau, médaillon de lotte aux endives, pied de porc truffé, suprême de bar aux fenouils. **Credit cards** Amex, Visa, Eurocard and MasterCard. **Pets** Dogs allowed (+45F). **Facilities** Parking. **Nearby** Golf course at Aa. **Open** All year.

At first sight this splendid brick and stone edifice, with its great courtyard and large park, may seem rather austere. This first impression is, however, immediately dispelled by a warm and friendly welcome and the refinement of the interior decoration. Most of the rooms are vast, and the *premier étage* bedrooms with impressive high-ceilings, are extremely comfortable, with beautiful bathrooms. Lavish amounts of attention have been devoted to features such as bedspreads, curtains and wallpapers, which all blend to perfection. The *deuxième étage* rooms tend to be less bright, but this makes them more cozy and intimate. The breakfast room is delightful, with a row of arched windows overlooking the gardens. The hotel has added new bedrooms which match the charm of the older ones. A recent *brasserie* service has been added for simple meals.

How to get there *(Map 2): 5km south of Béthune via A26, number 6 exit, in the direction of Chartreuses.*

Château de Cocove ★★★

62890 Recques-sur-Hem (Pas-de-Calais)
Tel. 21.82.68.29 - Fax 21.82.72.59
Mme Borel-Pidou

Rooms 24 with telephone, bath or shower, WC and TV. **Price** Single and double 435-690F. **Meals** Breakfast 45F, served 7:30-10:30; "weekend gastronomic" 2250F (per pers.). **Restaurant** Service 12:00-14:00, 19:30-21:30; menus 115-335F, also à la carte. Specialties: Fricassée de soles et langoustines, foie gras maison. **Credit cards** All major. **Pets** Dogs allowed (+45F). **Facilities** Sauna (25F), parking. **Nearby** Basilica of Notre-Dame and Sandelin museum in Valenciennes, blockhouse in Eperlecques, church of Saint-Eloi and museum in Hazebrouck, the 'Bourgeois de Calais', art and lace museum in Calais – 27-hole Saint-Omer golf course in Lumbres. **Open** All year (closed 25 Dec).

Only a few minutes from Calais, this 18th-century château is deep in the countryside surrounded by extensive grounds. The interior has been beautifully restored in keeping with the age of the building. In the same spirit the dining room has been converted from the old stables, its wide doors replaced by bay windows; pale subdued decor adds to the elegance of the room. The bedrooms are light and pleasantly furnished and some are very spacious. Amateur wine enthusiasts can visit the cellars where a large selection of wines can be purchased at a reasonable cost. Last but not least, there is a gastronomic weekend rate for two which includes the room, breakfast and two meals.

How to get there (Map 2): 17km southeast of Calais: from Calais by A26, number 2 Ardres-Licques exit. Or via N43 towards Saint-Omer.

Hôtel Cléry ★★★

62360 Hesdin-l'Abbé (Pas-de-Calais)
Tel. 21.83.19.83 - Fax 21.87.52.59
Mme Osseland

Rooms 20 with telephone, bath or shower, WC and TV. **Price** Single 340F, double 420-640F, pavillon 985F (5 pers.). **Meals** Breakfast 50F, served 7:00-10:00. No restaurant. **Credit cards** All major. **Pets** No dogs allowed. **Facilities** Parking. **Nearby** Castle-museum and national marine center in Boulogne-sur-Mer, pottery museum in Desvres, Opal coast, Cap Gris-Nez, Cap Blanc-Nez – 18-hole golf course in Hardelot. **Open** Jan 15 – Dec 18.

Legend has it that Napoleon stayed at this small château. There are three rooms on the ground floor: a large, light room where breakfast is served, a bar and a beautiful room where you can sit in deep leather armchairs by an open fire. An elegant staircase with a Louis XV style wrought iron banister leads to the *premier étage*. The bedrooms are comfortable and the decor simple. The rooms on the *deuxième étage* have gently sloping mansard roofs, but whether they look out on the chestnut trees in the park or on the drive, all the bedrooms are quiet. Behind a courtyard with old stone paving and geraniums, there are seven other bedrooms in the former stable block. Room eight is on the ground floor and among the others, on the *premier étage*, are two pretty small bedrooms. Finally, located in a pretty corner of the park, there is a pavilion offering two bedrooms with bathrooms and a small lounge with fireplace. Not far from the national highway, the hotel is located on the road to England. The outstanding restaurants in Boulogne are *La Matelote* and *La Liégeoise*. In the Centre National de la Mer, you can also enjoy delicious shellfish lunches at *Le Grand Pavois*.

How to get there (Map 1): *9km southeast of Boulogne via N1.*

Hostellerie du Moulin du Pré **

14860 Bavent (Calvados)
Tel. 31.78.83.68 - Fax 31.78.21.05
Hamchin-Holtz Family

Rooms 10 with telephone, bath or shower and 5 with WC. **Price** Double 210-330F.
Meals Breakfast 40F, served 8:00-10:00. **Restaurant** Service 12:30-13:30, 19:30-
21:00; menus 250-280F, also à la carte. Specialties: Marbré de volailles au foie gras,
turban de sole soufflé au homard, huîtres chaudes maraîchères aux œufs de saumon,
papillottes de poisson, game in season. **Credit cards** All major. **Pets** Dogs not
allowed. **Facilities** Parking. **Nearby** Deauville, Caen, Normandy landing beaches,
Houlgate – 18-hole Le Home Varaville golf course in Cabourg. **Open** All year except
March 1-15 and Oct (closed Sunday evening and Monday except July, August and
national holidays).

On the borders of the Auge region, this renovated country
farmhouse stands on a large property with a small lake. The
sea is only 4 km away. The interior of the hotel is comfortable.
The small bedrooms are delightful, some in a rustic style, and all
of them look out on the peaceful countryside. The bathroom
facilities and soundproofing vary from room to room. The large
dining room and lounge on the ground floor are very welcoming
and mealtimes provide an opportunity to discover excellent French
home cooking.

How to get there *(Map 7): 14km northeast of Caen via D513 towards
Cabourg, then D95 towards Gonneville-en-Auge.*

Hôtel d'Argouges ★★

21, rue Saint-Patrice
14400 Bayeux (Calvados)
Tel. 31.92.88.86 - Fax 31.92.69.16 - M. and Mme Auregan

Rooms 25 with telephone, bath or shower, WC, minibar and 18 with TV. **Price** Single 190-350F, double 190-420F. **Meals** Breakfast 38F, served 7:30-10:30. No restaurant. **Credit cards** All major. **Pets** Dogs allowed (+35F). **Facilities** Parking. **Nearby** Bayeux cathedral, Port-en-Bessin – 27-hole Omaha Beach golf course in Bayeux (10km). **Open** All year.

You will feel at home in this old private hotel run by the Argouges family. It is on the quiet outskirts of the old town and within walking distance of all points of interest. The hotel's rooms, all very quiet and plainly but comfortably furnished, are in two buildings and have high ceilings and exposed beams. Most are quite large. Rooms 23 and 25, built in old barns, are actually small, well designed apartments, each one with a large main bedroom and a small bedroom for children. At the rear of the hotel, behind an 18th-century facade, there is an extensive garden where you can have breakfast, unless you prefer the delightful dining room. This is a beautiful hotel; and a good value. *Le Lion d'Or* is a charming restaurant, while *L'Amaryllis* is simpler.

How to get there (Map 7): 27km west of Caen via N13.

Auberge de la Boule d'Or

14430 Beuvron-en-Auge (Calvados)
Tel. 31.79.78.78
M. and Mme Duval

Rooms 3 with bath or shower and WC. **Price** Double 220F. **Meals** Breakfast 30F, served 7:00-10:00; half board 230F, full board 300F (per pers., 7 days min.). **Restaurant** Closed in Jan. Service 12:00-13:30, 19:00-21:30; menus 98-155F, also à la carte. Specialties: Norman cooking. **Credit cards** All major. **Pets** Small dogs allowed. **Nearby** Lisieux, pays d'Auge from Lisieux to Deauville and Lisieux to Cabourg. **Open** All year (closed Sunday evening and Monday except July – Aug).

In summer, every street and square in Beuvron-en-Auge seems to be in bloom, and the houses are so decked out with geraniums that their ancient half-timbering itself seems to be blossoming. The Boule d'Or is a small, modest inn well known for its traditional cuisine. There is no reception area as such, so you should go straight into the dining room, which is rustic in style, with pink table cloths striking a note of simplicity. A small staircase leads up to the hotel's three bedrooms, which are small but comfortable, bright and neat, and have pleasant bathrooms. This is a friendly, unpretentious address in one of the most beautiful villages in Normandy. Special mention should be made of the excellent traditional cuisine.

How to get there *(Map 8): 25km west of Lisieux via A13, exit Dozulé in 7km.*

Hostellerie du Château de Goville ★★★

14330 Le-Breuil-en-Bessin (Calvados)
Tel. 31.22.19.28 - Fax 31.22.68.74
M. Vallée

Rooms 12 with telephone, bath or shower, WC and minibar. **Price** Double 425-695F, suite 795F. **Meals** Breakfast 55F, served 8:30-11:30; half board 445-625F (per pers., 2 days min.). **Restaurant** "Le Baromètre". Closed Tuesday in low season except by reservation. Service 12:30-14:00, 19:30-21:30; menus 140-245F, also à la carte. Specialties: Traditional cuisine. **Credit cards** All major. **Pets** Dogs allowed (+75F). **Facilities** Parking. **Nearby** Bayeux tapestry and cathedral, châteaux of Vaulaville and of Fontenay-Henry, beach of debarquement, church of Saint-Loup-Hors, abbey of Mondaye – 27-hole Omaha Beach golf course. **Open** All year.

This château, owned by the Vallée family since 1813, has retained the charm of a private house. The interior decor is elegant: there is hardly a piece of furniture, objèt d'art or picture which is not an original. There is something of the atmosphere of an English country house here. The spacious dining room is lit, by a huge crystal chandelier, and you will be enchanted by the lounge while you enjoy your aperitif or perhaps a glass of Calvados. Your hospitable hosts will ensure your enjoyment of a stay at one of the most charming hotels in Normandy.

How to get there *(Map 7): 38km northwest of Caen via N13 to Bayeux, then D5 towards Molay-Littry.*

Ferme Hôtel La Rançonnière **

Route d'Arromanches
14480 Crépon (Calvados)
Tel. 31.22.21.73 – Fax 31.22.98.39 – Mmes Vereecke and Sileghem

Rooms 35 with telephone, bath or shower, WC and TV. **Price** Single and double 180-380F. **Meals** Breakfast 42F, served 7:45-10:00; half board 205-315F (per pers.). **Restaurant** Service 12:00-14:00, 19:00-21:30; menus 60-235F, also à la carte. Specialties: Homard frais flambé, salade champêtre. **Credit cards** All major. **Pets** Dogs allowed. **Facilities** Parking. **Nearby** Bayeux tapestry and cathedral, châteaux of Creullet and of Creully, church of Saint-Loup-Hors, abbey of Mondaye – 27-hole Omaha Beach golf course. **Open** All year.

The Bessin region is full of old manor houses and Crépon has more than its share in terms of both numbers and quality. You enter this old farm through a crenellated carriage gate into a vast courtyard around which are the reception, restaurant and the bedrooms of the hotel. The interior is decidedly rustic with wooden furniture and exposed timbers everywhere. Comfortable bedrooms have small windows and old furniture whose dark tones are at times a little heavy. We particularly like rooms 2, 3, 5, 6, 7, 9, 18, 24, 28, 29 and for families we like rooms 8, 23, 25, 31 and 32. The rooms above the restaurant are a little small but very pleasant. The food is good and abundant and served in a vast hall, often brightened by a cheerful wood fire. In summer you can dine in the courtyard. The cordial staff will make you feel at home.

How to get there *(Map 7): 21km northwest of Caen via D22 towards Arromanches, then D112 towards Couseulles.*

La Chenevière ★★★★

Escures-Commes
14520 Port-en-Bessin (Calvados)
Tel. 31.21 47 96 - Fax 31 21 47 98 - M. Neutelings

Rooms 18 with telephone, bath, WC, TV and minibar - Wheelchair access, elevator. **Price** Double 700-1100F. **Meals** Breakfast 80F. **Restaurant** Closed Monday in low season. Menu 150-350F, also à la carte. Specialties: Fricassée de langoustines aux girolles, agneau de prés-salés au jus de truffes, feuillantine de pommes au caramel de cidre. **Credit cards** Amex, Visa, Eurocard and MasterCard. **Pets** Dogs allowed (+100F). **Facilities** Parking, garage (150 F). **Nearby** Epaves museum in Commes, Port-en-Bessin, cathedral of Bayeux – 27-hole Omaha Beach golf course. **Open** Feb 11 – Jan 2.

Very near Port-en-Bessin, Arromanches and Omaha Beaches, this is an elegant mansion surrounded by a beautifully kept park. The interior resembles a private home which has been furnished to please the eye as well as to provide the comfort you crave after a tiring drive. You will find a succession of very pretty, bright rooms which are generously decorated with light fabrics, collections of paintings (old seals, architectural drawings) and handsome objects. The bedrooms, with efficient soundproofing, are furnished in the same tasteful style; bathrooms are luxurious. All the windows look out on the lawn and flowers.

How to get there (Map 7): 8km south of Bayeux via D6, in the direction of Port-en-Bessin.

Hôtel l'Ecrin ★★★

19, rue Eugène-Boudin
14602 Honfleur (Calvados)
Tel. 31.14.43.45 - Fax 31.89.24.41 - Mme Blais

Rooms 21 with telephone, bath or shower, WC, TV and 10 with minibar. **Price** Double 350-900F, suite 900F. **Meals** Breakfast 45-50F, served 8:00-11:00. No restaurant. **Credit cards** All major. **Pets** Dogs allowed. **Facilities** Sauna (65F), parking. **Nearby** Old dock, church of Sainte-Catherine, Eugène Boudin museum in Honfleur, Deauville, Trouville – 27-hole New-Golf, 18- and 9-hole Saint-Gatien golf courses in Deauville. **Open** All year.

You can truly relax in the courtyard and lovely gardens of this elegant Napoleon III mansion. Although in the center of the town, the hotel is out of the way of the hordes of tourists who head for Honfleur when summer begins. The ground floor rooms still retain their original layout and much of the style of their period. In the Proustian lounge the gilt of the plasterwork echoes the gilt on the armchairs, and the delicate tints of the numerous paintings are repeated in the silks, the curtains and the carpets; there's even an adjoining conservatory. The bedrooms are a little overdone (number 2 is extraordinary) but very comfortable. Avoid the ones on the *deuxième étage* but do not reject the ones in the front pavilions where the cheaper rooms are not necessarily the least pleasant. Breakfast is served in a room full of paintings, many in the style of the school of Honfleur, or in the glassed-in veranda which opens onto the pretty garden. For restaurant we recommend: *La Lieutenance, La Taverne de la mer* for fish and shellfish and *L'Assiette Gourmande*.

How to get there *(Map 8): 97km west of Rouen via A13, Beuzeville exit, then D22(in the town center).*

Auberge Saint-Christophe **
14690 Pont-d'Ouilly (Calvados)
Tel. 31.69.81.23
M. Lecoeur

Rooms 7 with telephone, bath or shower, WC and TV. **Price** Double 260F. **Meals** Breakfast 40F, served 8:00-9:30; half board 275F, full board 370F (per pers., 2 days min.). **Restaurant** Service 12:00-13:30, 19:30-21:00; menus 92-240F, also à la carte. Specialties: Nonnettes de saumon au beurre de cidre, salade tiède de queues de langoustines, crème brûlée. **Credit cards** Amex, Visa, Eurocard and MasterCard. **Pets** Dogs allowed (+25F). **Facilities** Parking. **Nearby** Castle of Falaise, 'La Suisse Normande', Thury-Harcourt, Clécy (châteaux of La Pommeraye and Placy), Oëtre rock, gorges of Saint-Aubert, château de Pontécoulant – 18-hole Clécy-Cantelou golf course. **Open** All year, except Nov 1 holidays and Feb 15 – March 13 (closed Sunday evening and Monday).

This hotel is in an elegant house in the Suisse Normande. Its interior has been carefully designed to provide every comfort. Plants and flowers adorn every corner. There is a small lounge, a breakfast room which becomes a bar in the evening, and many places to sit, talk and read. The bedrooms are small but charming and have recently been renovated in a modern style. They look out over peaceful gardens, but the soundproofing in the hotel could be better. During the summer, lunch can be enjoyed on the terrace. The cuisine is excellent and the young owners will make you feel at home.

How to get there *(Map 7): 26km south of Caen via D562 towards Flers, or N158 towards Falaise, then D1; 1.5km from Pont-d'Ouilly via D23 towards Thury-Harcourt.*

La Chaîne d'Or ★★★

27, rue Grande
27700 Petit Andelys (Eure)
Tel. 32.54.00.31 - Fax 32.54.05.68 - M. and Mme Foucault

Rooms 10 with telephone, bath or shower, WC and TV. **Price** Single and double 395-740F. **Meals** Breakfast 60F, served 8:00-9:30. **Restaurant** Closed Sunday evening and Monday and one week in Sept. Service 12:00-14:00, 19:30-21:30; menus 135-295F, also à la carte. Specialties: Raviolis de coquillages, charlotte de rognon de veau au vin de Madiran, croquant à la vanille et aux pommes, sorbet au cidre. **Credit cards** Amex, Visa, Eurocard and MasterCard. **Pets** Dogs not allowed. **Facilities** Parking. **Nearby** Church of Notre-Dame and Château Gaillard in Les Andelys, Giverny – 18-hole Vaudreuil golf course. **Open** Feb 1 – Dec 31.

This friendly hostelry was founded in 1751. From the wing in the inner courtyard there is a stunning view of the Seine. Most of the bedrooms are large and light. The ones overlooking the river have just been entirely refurbished; very elegant and refined, they have gained in comfort what they have lost in traditional style. The rooms looking out over the church or the courtyard have period furniture, rugs and engravings; foreign guests prefer them for their "old France" atmosphere. The breakfast room has a high ceiling with polished beams, and is sometimes used in the evening as a lounge. In the dining room, half timbering, paintings and flowers combine to create a warm and cozy ambience, while the pink tablecloths compliment the silvery green of the Seine. The traditional cuisine is delicious.

How to get there *(Map 8): 72km northwest of Paris via A13, Gaillon exit, then D316.*

Relais Moulin de Balisne ★★

Baline
27130 Verneuil-sur-Avre (Eure)
Tel. 32.32.03.48 – Fax 32.60.11.22 – M. Gastaldi

Rooms 10 and 2 suites with telephone, bath, WC, 8 with TV and minibar. **Price** Double 350-400F. **Meals** Breakfast 50F, served 8:00-11:00; half board 350-380F, full board 450-480F (per pers., 2 days min.). **Restaurant** Closed Monday noon in winter. Service 12:00-15:00, 19:30-22:00; menus 135-280F, also à la carte. Specialties: Duo de sole et langouste, cassolette d'escargots et gambas aux petits lardons, 'œuf d'autruche farci'. **Credit cards** All major. **Pets** Dogs allowed. **Facilities** Lake and river fishing, supervised parking. **Nearby** Senonches forest, châteaux de Beauménil and d'Anet – 9-hole golf course in Coulonges. **Open** All year.

When you first see this hotel you may worry about its proximity to the road, but as soon as you enter, you will be reassured by the beautifully quiet surroundings. The only sound is that of the waters converging here from the Rivers Avre and Iton. The Moulin is surrounded by 25-acres of land with a small lake; boats are available for fishing enthusiasts. The bar dining room is furnished with antiques, Persian tablecloths and a splendid fireplace. The bedrooms are just as appealing. Some of them in the attic seem to be "perched in the trees". You will be warmly welcomed at the Relais and its proximity to Paris makes it an appealing place to stay.

How to get there *(Map 8): 75km west of Paris via Autoroute-Ouest (in the direction of Dreux), Bois d'Arcy exit, then N12 to Dreux, Alençon. 45km southwest of Evreux via N154 to Nonancourt, then N12 dir. Verneuil-sur-Avre.*

Château de la Rapée ★★★

27140 Bazincourt-sur-Epte (Eure)
Tel. 32.55.11.61 - Fax 32.55.93.65
M. Bergeron

Rooms 14 with telephone, bath or shower, WC and 8 with TV. **Price** Single and double 410-510F, suite 680F. **Meals** Breakfast 48F, served 8:00-10:00; half board 650-750F, full board 750-840F (per pers., 3 days min.). **Restaurant** Service 12:30-14:00, 19:30-21:00; menus 160-215F, also à la carte. Specialties: Tarte légère au livarot, douillons, anguille en matelote au cidre brut. **Credit cards** All major. **Pets** Dogs not allowed. **Facilities** Parking. **Nearby** Château of Harcourt and Gisors, A.G. Poulain museum in Vernon and Nicolas-Poussin in Andelys, Monet museum in Giverny – 18-hole Bertuchère Golf Course. **Open** All year except Feb 1 – 24 and Aug 16 – 31.

This 19th-century Norman mansion is less than an hour from Paris and a few kilometers from Gisors. Lost in the midst of woods and fields, with a stud farm its only neighbor, it is ideal for those who love tranquillity in a beautiful setting. The bedrooms are comfortable (the largest are on the *premier étage* and number 15 has a terrace) and there are two dining rooms: one for summer and another with a large fireplace for the winter months. Monsieur Bergeron is a good cook and Madame will make you feel like one of the family. Tables in the garden allow you to have breakfast and drinks there, weather permitting.

How to get there *(Map 9): 70km northwest of Paris via A15, Pontoise exit, then D915 to Gisors. 4km north of Gisors by D915.*

Auberge de l'Abbaye ★★★

27800 Le Bec-Hellouin (Eure)
Tel. 32.44.86.02 – Fax 32.46.32.23
Mme Sergent

Rooms 10 with telephone, bath and WC. **Price** Double 360-390F, suite 480F. **Meals** Breakfast 40F, served from 8:30; half board 380-400F. **Restaurant** Service 12:15-14:30, 19:15-21:30; menus 125-250F, also à la carte. Specialties: Cassolette de homard, lapin au cidre, ris de veau aux morilles, tarte aux pommes. **Credit cards** Visa, Eurocard and MasterCard. **Pets** Dogs allowed. **Facilities** Parking. **Nearby** In Bec-Hellouin: abbey, Piano and Car museum; château of Harcourt and of Champ-de-Bataille; insect collection at the Canel museum in Pont-Audemer – 18-hole Champ-de-Bataille golf course in Neubourg. **Open** All year (closed Monday evening and Tuesday in low season).

This hotel is in an 18th-century building close to the abbey and in the center of a very pretty village. There are ten bedrooms furnished in a rustic style, all small but comfortable and quiet and with full bathroom facilities. The dining room is attractive, with whitewashed walls and a fireplace, and the cuisine is excellent. There is an interior courtyard blooming with flowers, a small terrace on the front where you can enjoy the fresh air and watch the life of the village square, and hospitable proprietors who have built up a loyal clientele and are full of enthusiasm for their auberge. This is a good, simple inn, which is charming and authentic.

How to get there (Map 8): *40km southwest of Rouen via A13, number 24 Maison Brulée exit, in the direction of Alençon/Le Mans then D138 toward Bec-Hellouin.*

La Ferme de Cocherel

Route de la vallée d'Eure
Cocherel 27120 Paçy-sur-Eure (Eure)
Tel. 32.36.68.27 – Fax 32.26.28.18 – M. and Mme Delton

Rooms 3, 1 with bath, 2 with shower and WC. **Price** Double 350-400F **Meals** Breakfast incl. **Restaurant** Closed Tuesday and Wednesday. Service 12:00-14:00, 19:30-21:15; menu 195F, also à la carte. Specialties: Flan de foie gras à la crème de calvados, chausson de homard crème safranée, rognons de veau au cassis et au cidre. **Credit cards** All major. **Pets** Dogs allowed **Facilities** Parking. **Nearby** Historique village of Cocherel, château of Bizy, Monet museum in Giverny, château of Anet – 18-hole Vaudreuil golf course. **Open** All year except in Jan, 1 week in sept (closed Tuesday and Wednesday).

There is only a small country road between the Ferme de Cocherel and the peaceful Eure River. The Ferme consists of several picturesque Norman houses with old tile roofs. The largest is reserved for the acclaimed gastronomic restaurant, where the tables are set in a room decorated like an elegant winter garden. You will enjoy succulent meals made with fresh products bought in the local market or from nearby farms. The three bedrooms, opening onto a carefully tended flower garden, are located on the ground floor at independent houses; they are decorated with several pieces of rustic or lacquered cane furniture, floral fabrics and a few engravings. The breakfasts are excellent. This is truly a beautiful country inn, located in the peaceful hamlet where Bertrand Du Guesclin won a historic victory over Anglo-Navarre troops in 1364.

How to get there *(Map 8): 7km northwest of Pacy-sur-Eure via D836, towards Louviers. On A 13, number 16 exit towards Vernon, then Cocherel.*

Le Moulin de Connelles ★★★★

40, route d'Amfreville-sur-les-Monts
27430 Connelles (Eure)
Tel. 32.59.53.33 - Fax 32. 59 21 83 - M. and Mme Petiteau

Rooms 7 and 6 suites with telephone, bath, WC, TV and minibar. **Price** Single and double 500-600F, suite 800F. **Meals** Breakfast 60F, served 7:30-10:30. **Restaurant** Closed Sunday evening and Monday. Service 12:00-14:30, 19:30-21:00; menus 135-280F (child 70F), also à la carte. Specialties: Foie de canard au vieux calvados, saumon soufflé en portefeuille, rognons de veau sauce Meaux, délice noix de coco et chocolat chaud. **Credit cards** All major. **Pets** Dogs allowed. **Facilities** Heated swimming pool, tennis, parking. **Nearby** Centre de loisirs Lery Poses (water skiing, golf, sailing...), church Notre-Dame in Louviers; cathedral of Rouen; Monet museum in Giverny – 18-hole Vaudreuil golf course. **Open** All year except Jan 2 – 31 (closed Sunday evening and Monday Oct – May).

A beautiful lawn and flower gardens on the banks of the Seine surround the Moulin de Connelles, an old mill which was converted into a lovely home and, then, into a luxurious hotel. The Moulin is extremely comfortable, with thick carpets, a handsome decor of soft green and gold-yellow tones, coordinated fabrics, and superb bathrooms. Many bedrooms, and the restaurant, look out on an enchanting river scene, where the Seine winds in and out of its course and finally forms several lush green islands. It's a lovely place for strolling or having a drink before dinner, and the hotel will happily lend you a boat to explore it all up close, including the resident moorhens.

How to get there *(Map 1 and 8): 30km south of Rouen via A13, exit Louviers. 100km from Paris.*

Château de Brécourt ★★★★

Douains
27120 Pacy-sur-Eure (Eure)
Tel. 32.52.40.50 - Fax 32.52.69.65 - M. Savry and Mme Langlais

Rooms 29 with telephone, bath, shower and WC. **Price** Single 390-470F, double 640-990F, suite 1100-1600F. **Meals** Breakfast 65F, served 6:30-12:00; half board 650-1500F, full board 1590-1830F. **Restaurant** Service 12:00-14:00, 19:30-21:30; menus 225-350F, also à la carte. Specialties: Salade tiède de langoustines à l'huile d'olive et au romarin, minute de bar dans une marinière de coquillage, pigeonneau de la ferme farçi à ma façon, pommes croquettes au chitake. **Credit cards** All major. **Pets** Dogs allowed (+50F). **Facilities** Swimming pool, whirlpool, tennis, parking. **Nearby** A.G. Poulain museum and church of Notre-Dame in Vernon, château de Gaillon, Monet museum in Giverny – 9-hole golf course in Gaillon. **Open** All year.

The Château de Brécourt is an ideal place for a weekend; it is a Louis XIII building only 60km from Paris on the borders of Normandy. The lovely 17th-century moated château has a 55-acre park where it is a pleasure to stroll at any time of the year. More active guests will enjoy the swimming pool and tennis courts. There are two dining rooms, both with a beautiful view of the woods and the countryside and both with a menu featuring good Normandy specialties. The decor is in keeping with the elegant and comfortable atmosphere of the chateau.

How to get there *(Map 8): 21km east of Evreux via N13, Pacy-sur-Eure exit, then D181 and D533. 70km west of Paris via A13, number 16 Vernon exit.*

Auberge du Vieux Puits **

6, rue Notre-Dame-du-Pré
27500 Pont-Audemer (Eure)
Tel. 32.41.01.48 – M. and Mme Foltz

Rooms 12 with telephone, bath or shower, 10 with WC and 6 with TV - 2 wheelchair accessible. **Price** Single 160-360F, double 260-410F. **Meals** Breakfast 42F, served 8:00-9:30. **Restaurant** Service 12:00-14:00, 19:30-21:00; menus 180F (weekday lunch only)-290F, also à la carte. Specialties: Canard aux griottes, truite 'Bovary'. **Credit cards** Visa, Eurocard and MasterCard. **Pets** Dogs not allowed. **Facilities** Parking. **Nearby** Insect collection in the Canel museum in Pont-Audemer, Risle valley, bidge of Normandie, abbey of Le Bec-Hollouin – 18-hole Champ-de-Bataille golf course in Neubourg. **Open** Jan 28 – Dec 20 (closed Monday evening and Tuesday in low season).

This inn, located in Pont-Audemer, easily accessible by the highway, is perfect for travelers who want to get aquainted with Normandy. The buildings, in typical 17th-century Norman timbered style, surround a flower garden, with an old well and two impressive willows, where you can have cocktails, coffee, and excellent afternoon snacks in summer. Inside, there are several cozy little lounges where you can have tea or read by the fireplace. The dining room is slightly larger and is decorated with antique china and gleaming copper. The savory cuisine is innovative yet based on traditional Norman recipes. You can choose between the simple, rustic, charming bedrooms in the old houses, or the modern comfort of those in another building, which is built in the same style.

How to get there *(Map 1 and 8): 52km west of Rouen via A13, Pont-Audemer exit, then D139 and N182 (300m from the town center).*

Hostellerie du Moulin Fourest

27300 Saint-Aubin-le-Vertueux (Eure)
Tel. 32.43.19.95 – Fax 32.45.55.50
M. and Mme Deduit

Rooms 8 with shower and WC. **Price** Single 200F, double 230F. **Meals** Breakfast 35F, served 7:30-9:30. **Restaurant** Service 12:00-14:00, 19:30-21:30; menus 98-270F, also à la carte. Specialties: Lapereau à la crème camembert, flan de foie gras au confit de poireaux, feuillantine de mousse au chocolat. **Credit cards** Amex, Visa, Eurocard and MasterCard. **Pets** Dogs allowed (+35F). **Facilities** Parking. **Nearby** Lisieux, Bernay – 18-hole Champ-de-Bataille golf course. **Open** All year (closed Sunday evening and Monday).

The small river flowing past the foot of the mill winds in and out, creating small spurs of land perfect for fishing or simply relaxing. Inside the hotel the rustic decor of the bar and the dining room combines beautiful pieces of furniture, ancient beams and paintings to create a warm and cozy atmosphere. François Deduit, who is both the chef and the owner of the hotel, is a promising young cook, and his traditional cuisine has gained him a solid reputation throughout the region. The comfortable bedrooms command beautiful views of the surrounding countryside. Their modern furnishings, however, are a disappointment after the charm and authenticity of the period furniture in the reception rooms and on the landings. In the spring, parasols are set up on a neat and flowery terrace which becomes the ideal setting for breakfast and dinner, enhanced by the distant babble of water gushing through the floodgates.

How to get there (Map 8): 3km south of Bernay via D833.

Le Manoir des Saules

2, place Saint-Martin
27370 La Saussaye (Eure)
Tel. 35.87 25 65 - Fax 35 87 49 39 - M. Monnaie-Metot

Rooms 4 with telephone, 1 with bath, 3 with shower, WC and TV. **Price** Double 300-
600F **Meals** Breakfast 65F. **Restaurant** Closed Sunday evening and Monday. Service
12:00-14:00, 20:00-21:30; menu 175-350F, also à la carte. Specialties: Foie gras,
ragoût de homard frais, fish. **Credit cards** Amex, Visa, Eurocard and MasterCard
Pets Dogs allowed. **Meals** Parking. **Nearby** Château of Champ-de-Bataille, château
and arboretum of Harcourt, collégiale de La Saussaye, Abbey of Bec-Hellouin – 18-
hole Champ-de-Bataille golf course. **Open** All year (closed public holidays in Feb and
beg Oct).

With its half-timbering, turrets and recessed walls, the Manoir
could not be more Norman. The associates who run it have
named the bedrooms after their grandmothers: Marie, Germaine,
Albertine and Joséphine. (We especially like the first three). These
are very delightful rooms decorated with a mixture of antiques and
Louis XV copies, amusing old objects and heavy drapes which are
coordinated with silky bedspreads. All the rooms are beautifully
kept, including the bathrooms. A lovely lounge in blue and cream
colors is an intimte, cozy place for a drink. Adjacent to it, the dining
room with its smartly set tables serves excellent cuisine which is
based on fresh, seasonal products. In charming weather, you can
of course have meals outside on the terrace amidst the flowers.
You will always receive very friendly and attentive service.

How to get there *(Map 8): South of Rouen, 4km from Elbeuf via D840,
towards Le Neubourg. On A13, Pont-de-l'Arche exit.*

Hôtel du Golf **

Golf du Vaudreuil
27100 Le Vaudreuil (Eure)
Tel. 32.59.02.94 - Fax 32.59.67.39 - Mme Launay

Rooms 20 with telephone, bath or shower, 17 with WC and TV, 10 with minibar.
Price Single 160-220F, double 220-350F. **Meals** Breakfast 30-45F, served 7:00-
11:00. No restaurant. **Credit cards** Amex, Visa, Eurocard and MasterCard. **Pets** Dogs
allowed (+20F). **Facilities** Parking, 18-hole golf course. **Nearby** Rouen, Château
Gaillard. **Open** All year.

The Château de Vaudreuil was destroyed during the Revolution
and all that remains of it are two buildings beside an avenue
that leads nowhere. The château's large park is now a golf course
and one of the buildings a hotel. It is quiet here, and you can enjoy
views over the greens from the breakfast room and the living room.
The bedrooms, with big windows and almond-green wallpaper,
are simply furnished but pleasant. They are small on the *premier
étage* but considerably larger on the second. The decor is modern
but elegant. There is no restaurant at the hotel but golfers can eat
at the golf club.

How to get there *(Map 8): 15km southeast of Rouen via A13, number 18
or 19 exit; then D77 to the entrance of Le Vaudreuil.*

Hôtel du Château d'Agneaux ★★★

Avenue Sainte-Marie
50180 Saint-Lô - Agneaux (Manche)
Tel. 33.57.65.88 - Fax 33.56.59.21 - M. and Mme Groult

Rooms 12 with shower, WC, TV and 10 with minibar. **Price** Double 360-680F, suite 850F. **Meals** Breakfast 55-65F. **Restaurant** Service 19:30-21:00; menus 185-268F, also à la carte. Specialties: Fish and the chef's desserts. **Pets** Dogs allowed (+50F). **Facilities** Tennis (30F), sauna (80F), parking. **Nearby** Church and museum in Saint-Lô, château de Torigni-sur-Vire – 9-hole golf course in Courtainville. **Open** All year.

Leaving the ugly suburbs of Saint-Lô, you'll find that the Château d'Agneaux has escaped the town planners. A narrow gravel lane leads away from the main road to the old chapel, the château and the watchtower which look out over the unspoiled and peaceful valley, with nothing in view but trees and the River Vire flowing gently through the green countryside. M. and Mme Groult owned a farmhouse inn for many years, and now Agneaux is their dream come true; they have refurbished it with love. The bedrooms are very comfortable and prettily though not overwhelmingly decorated, with some four-poster beds and lovely parquet floors. Room 4, with it's five windows, is well-lit all day.

How to get there *(Map 7): 1.5km west of Saint-Lô via D900.*

Hôtel Le Conquérant ★★
16/18 rue Saint-Thomas-Becket
50760 Barfleur (Manche)
Tel. 33.54.00.82 - Fax 33. 54 65 25 - Mme Delomenède

Rooms 16 with telephone, 11 with bath or shower, 5 with cabinet de toilette, 10 with WC and TV. **Price** Double 150-350F. **Meals** Breakfast 25-45F, served 8:00-10:00. **Crèperie** Service 19:00-21:00; menus 75-100F, also à la carte. Specialties: Galette camembert sur beurre d'escargot, galette manchotte, crêpe Le Conquérant. **Credit cards** Visa, Eurocard and MasterCard. **Pets** Dogs not allowed. **Facilities** Parking (20F). **Nearby** Ile Tatihon, Valognes, Thomas-Henry museum in Cherbourg – 9-hole golf course in Fontenay-en-Cotentin. **Open** All year except Nov 15 – Dec 15 and Jan 5 – 31.

If you are one of the surprisingly few tourists who appreciate the beauty of this splendid region, the Conquérant will be an ideal place for you to stay. Located at the road's edge, this very simple hotel reveals a charming garden behind its walls, where there is direct access to the port. As the modern conveniences of its rooms are variable, we recommend numbers 9, 10, 11, 16 and 17. (The latter has a vast terrace overlooking the garden). The overall decoration is unremarkable but the prices are reasonable, the people are very friendly, and the breakfasts are delicious. (This is also a very good *crêperie*). Finally, should you want to set out to sea, Madame Delomenède's father will take you for a cruise or a fishing expedition on his boat. From the sea, you can admire the lovely Norman farms dotted with manor houses along the coast between Querqueville and "Jobourg's Nose." The charming Conquérant is, of course, named after William the Conqueror.

How to get there *(Map 7): 30km east of Cherbourg via D901.*

Manoir de Roche Torin ★★★
50220 Courtils (Manche)
Tel. 33.70.96.55 – Fax 33.48.35.20
Mme Barraux

,**Rooms** 12 with telephone, bath or shower, WC, TV and 3 with minibar. **Price** Single and double 400-650F, suite 800F. **Meals** Breakfast 50F, served 8:00-10:30. No restaurant but snacks available. **Credit cards** All major. **Pets** Dogs allowed (+40F). **Facilities** Parking. **Nearby** Jardin des Plantes in Avranches, Mont Saint-Michel. **Open** March 15 – Nov 15.

This turn of the century gentleman's residence combines old and contemporary styles. Flowered fabrics brighten the lounge, and in the dining room there is a splendid fireplace where the chef grills lobsters, beef and salt-meadow lamb. The bedrooms reflect the style of the rest of the house, mixing modern furniture with cane chairs and period pieces. They are all very comfortable. The terrace and garden are very pleasant and in good weather a bar and meal service is provided there. Between the hotel, its lovely 5-acre park and Mont Saint-Michel, which can be seen in the distance, there is nothing but fields crossed by small inlets and dotted with sheep.

How to get there *(Map 7): 12km southwest of Avranches via N175, then towards Mont Saint-Michel via D43.*

Auberge de la Sélune ★★

2, rue Saint-Germain
50220 Ducey (Manche)
Tel. 33.48.53.62 – Fax 33.48.90.30 – M. Girres

Rooms 19 with telephone, bath and WC. **Price** Double 255-275F. **Meals** Breakfast 38F, served 7:30-9:30; half board 280-290F, full board 400-405F (per pers., 3 days min.). **Restaurant** Service 12:00-14:00, 19:00-21:00; menus 75-190F, also à la carte. Specialties: Pie au crabe, paupiettes de saumon au poiré, rable de lapereau farci au vinaigre de cidre. **Credit cards** Visa, Eurocard and MasterCard. **Pets** Dogs not allowed. **Facilities** Parking. **Nearby** Jardin des Plantes in Avranches, Mont Saint-Michel. **Open** All year.

The Auberge de la Sélune is a former almshouse of spacious proportions. It is set in the country on the edge of the village in a large garden by the River Sélune (where you might be lucky enough to catch a salmon). The auberge has large, high-ceilinged rooms and the pleasant bedrooms are furnished with cane furniture and pretty fabrics. A good number of them look out on the delightful flowering garden and tranquil river. The rooms located in the small annex are also very attractive and open onto the lawn. The auberge is well kept, elegant and comfortable.

How to get there *(Map 7): 10km southeast of Avranches via N175, then N176 towards Saint-Hilaire-du-Harcouët (follow signs as you enter Ducey).*

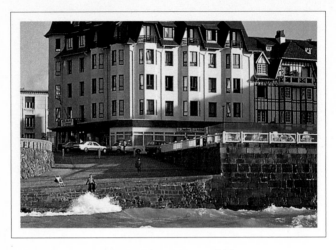

Hôtel des Bains ★★★

50400 Granville (Manche)
Tel. 33.50.17.31. – Fax 33 50 89 22
Mme Collette

Rooms 50 with telephone, 35 with bath witch 6 balnéo, 15 with shower, WC and TV.
Price Single and double 350-800F, suite 800-1000F. **Meals** Breakfast 45F, served
7:00-12:00; half board 480F (per pers., 3 days min.). **Restaurant** Service 19:00-
22:00; menu 80-160F, also à la carte. Specialties: Filets de sole au camembert,
homard de Chausey. **Credit cards** Amex, Visa, Eurocard and MasterCard. **Pets** Dogs
not allowed. **Facilities** Parking. **Nearby** Mont Saint-Michel, îles anglo-normandes,
Avranches, La Lucerne abbey, cathedral of Coutances – 9-hole and 18-hole Bréhal
golf course. **Open** All year.

This town hotel is dramatically located overlooking the English
Channel, very near a long quay where you can take a lovely
walk and watch the waves crash onto the shore. The interior has
just been very elegantly and imaginatively renovated. The bedrooms
are bright and cheerful and decorated with contemporary furniture
and fabrics. On the ground floor, there is a small tea room next to
the dining room, which also has a corner lounge. The traditionally
Norman cuisine, featuring lots of fresh fish and local cheeses, is
succulent and the service is efficient and courteous. The tables are
well spaced, and here too, the decoration is attractive. Ask for a
room facing the sea, for a view of spectacular sunsets. Service with
a smile adds a final positive note to this excellent hotel.

How to get there *(Map 6): 25km north of Avranches via D973.*

Château de la Roque

50180 Hébécrevon (Manche)
Tel. 33.57.33.20 – Fax 33.57.51.20
M. and Mme Delisle

Rooms 15 with telephone, bath or shower, WC and TV - Wheelchair accessible.
Price Single 230F, double 310F, suite 420-490F. **Meals** Breakfast incl.; half board
250F (per pers., 3 days min.). **Restaurant** Evening meals. Service 20:00; menus 95F
(wine incl.). Specialties: Regional cuisine. **Credit cards** All major. **Pets** Dogs allowed.
Facilities Bicycle rentals, fishing, hunting, tennis, parking. **Nearby** Church and
museum (Tenture des Amours de Gombault and Macé) in Saint-Lô, château of Torigni-
sur-Vire – 9-hole golf course in Couttainville. **Open** All year.

In the midst of the gentle Norman countryside, this very pretty
chateau has been opened to guests by Raymond Delisle of cycle
racing fame. It's a great success: All the rooms are comfortable and
beautiful, with special attention paid to the choice of fabrics, which
are complemented by antique furniture. Bread is made every day
in an old oven here; it is served at the breakfasts which guests enjoy
at a large communal table in the charming dining room. Meals are
served by reservation.

How to get there *(Map 7): 6km northwest of Saint-Lô. Before Saint-Lô,
take D972, towards Coutances, to Saint-Gilles, then towards Pont Hébert
(D77) for 3km.*

Hôtel de France et des Fuchsias **
18, rue du Maréchal-Foch
50550 Saint-Vaast-la-Hougue (Manche)
Tel. 33.54.42.26 - Fax 33.43.46.79 - M. and Mme Brix

Rooms 33 and 1 suite with telephone, 29 with bath or shower, WC and TV. **Price** 290-395F. **Meals** Breakfast 40F, served 8:00-10:30; half board 275-335F, full board 355-410F (per pers., 3 days min.). **Restaurant** Closed Monday except in June – mid. Sept; Tuesday lunchtime Nov – end March. Service 12:00-14:00, 19:00-21:15; menus 75-230F, also à la carte. Specialties: Choucroute de la mer au beurre blanc, ravioles de homard et son coulis, salade tiède de queues de langoustines. **Credit cards** All major. **Pets** Dogs allowed (+40F). **Facilities** Bicycle rent. **Nearby** Ile Tatihon, Valognes, Barfleur, Thomas Henry museum in Cherbourg – 9-hole golf course in Fontenay-en-Cotentin. **Open** April – Jan 5 (closed Monday in low season).

At Saint Vaast-la-Hougue on the eastern side of the Cotentin Peninsula the climate is so mild that mimosas flourish. The bedrooms in this old coachmen's inn are simple but elegant, with muted colors and handsome furniture (though Room 14 is a bit small). The food is excellent and combines products of the sea with those of the nearby farm at Quettehou. There is a small fishing port quite close by, a sandy beach, and pretty countryside with hedgerows and woods. In the last two weeks of August there are open-air chamber concerts in the garden (free for hotel guests).

How to get there *(Map 7): 37km southeast of Cherbourg via N13 to Valognes, then D902 and D1 to Saint-Vaast-la-Hougue (it's in the town center).*

La Verte Campagne **
50660 Trelly (Manche)
Tel. 33.47.65.33 – Fax 33.47.38.03
M. and Mme Bernou

Rooms 8 (4 with bath, 1 with shower and 3 with WC). **Price** Single 100F, double 200-350F. **Meals** Breakfast 30F, served 8:30-10:00; half board +170F, full board +270F (per pers., 3 days min.). **Restaurant** Closed Monday lunchtime in low season. Service 12:30-14:30, 19:30-21:30; menus 140-350F, also à la carte. Specialties: Filet de canette aux épices et aux figues, vinaigrette tiède de rougets aux artichauds, moelleux au chocolat et mousse chicorée. **Credit cards** Visa, Eurocard and MasterCard. **Pets** Dogs not allowed. **Facilities** Parking. **Nearby** Mont Saint-Michel, valley of the Vire (G.R. 221) – 18-hole Granville golf course in Bréhal. **Open** Feb 1 – Nov 15 and Dec 14 – Jan 10 (closed Sunday evening and Monday in low season).

This hotel is in an authentic Normandy farmhouse of the 18th-century and, located as it is in the heart of wooded countryside, it deserves its name: "Green Countryside." This is not a large place but its size gives it an intimate, atmosphere. The stone walls, beams and furniture, antique ceramics and copperware create an ambience which is rustic yet civilized, comfortable and welcoming. All the bedrooms are different, but whether large or small they are furnished with an eye to harmony and comfort. There is an air of English elegance in the delightful fabrics used and the charming furniture. When they took over the hotel, Monsieur and Madame Bernou conserved the charming features which we found so attractive. And they have added a big plus: gastronomy. The *Verte Campagne* has become a leading restaurant in the area.

How to get there (Map 7): 42km southwest of Saint-Lô via D972 to Coutances, then D971 towards Bréhal to Quettreville-sur-Sienne, then D35 and D49.

Moulin de Villeray ★★★★

61110 Condeau (Orne)
Tel. 33.73.30.22 – Fax 33.73.38.28
M. Eelsen

Rooms 16 and 2 apartments with telephone, bath or shower, WC, TV and minibar.
Price Single 390-740F, double 450-850F, suite 750-1150F. **Meals** Breakfast 60F;
half board 960-1150F. **Restaurant** Service 12:00-14:00, 19:00-22:00; menus 130-
320F, also à la carte. Specialties: Regional cuisine. **Credit cards** All major. **Pets** Dogs
allowed (+45F). **Facilities** Swimming pool, parking. **Nearby** Hills of the Perche (about
150km), museum of the philosopher Alain in Mortagne-au-Perche – 18-hole Perche
golf course. **Open** All year.

The Moulin de Villeray is an old mill on the banks of the peaceful
River Huisne in a charming hamlet of the Perche region. It
is surrounded by a large and carefully tended park with lovely
flower gardens. The bedrooms located in two charming houses
(which have just been added) are individually decorated with terra
cotta floors, thick carpets, stunning cotton fabrics, and glossy pine
furniture. In the mill itself, the rooms are more classic but have
equally modern amenities; it's now their turn to be redecorated.
There is a pleasant lounge off the terrace, and a delightfully rustic
dining room built around the large paddle wheel of the mill. The
regional cuisine is delicious and the young owners are especially
pleasant and attentive.

How to get there *(Map 8): 9km north of Nogent-le-Rotrou; on A11, Chartres-
Est exit, Luigny or La Ferté-Bernard.*

Manoir du Lys ★★★

La Croix Gauthier
61140 Bagnoles-de-l'Orne (Orne)
Tel. 33.37.80.69 - Fax 33.30.05.80 - M. and Mme Quinton

Rooms 23 with telephone, bath or shower, WC, TV and minibar - Wheelchair accessible, elevator. **Price** Single and double 300-650F, suite 650-1000F. **Meals** Breakfast 50F; half board 350-550F, full board 500-680F (per pers., 3 days min.). **Restaurant** Service 12:30-14:30, 19:30-21:30; menus 130-350F, also à la carte. Specialties: Raviolis de grenouilles, duo de boudin, carré d'agneau de pré-salé. **Credit cards** All major. **Pets** Dogs allowed (+35F). **Facilities** Tennis, golf (3 greens), parking. **Nearby** Andaine forest, Bonvouloir lighthouse, château de Carrouges, Sées cathedral – 9-hole golf course in Bagnoles-de-l'Orne. **Open** March 1 – Jan 8 (closed Sunday and Monday March 1 – Easter and Oct 1 – Jan 8).

Lying in the midst of the Andaine Forest very near the Bagnoles-de-l'Orne spa, the Manoir du Lys is beautifully quiet. The bedrooms are light and very well equipped. Special mention should be made of the most recent, which are large and feature antiqued or lacquered furniture, prettily colored fabrics and magnificent bathrooms. They are perfectly soundproofed. Some have terraces and those under the mansard eaves have a lovely view of the orchard. Throughout the hotel, you will find contemporary paintings, which add to the charm. Meals are occasionally served in the lovely garden, or you might prefer to dine in the very pretty dining room with a panoramic view. Monsieur Quinton and his son Franck preside over the excellent Norman cuisine.

How to get there *(Map 7): 53km west of Alençon via N12 to Pré-au-Pail, then N176 and D916.*

Château de Landel ★★★

76220 Bézancourt (Seine-Maritime)
Tel. 35.90.16.01 - Fax 35.90 62 47
M. Cardon

Rooms 17 with telephone, bath or shower, WC and 4 with TV. **Price** Double 450-720F. **Meals** Breakfast 55F. **Restaurant** Service 12:30-13:30, 20:00- 21:30, also à la carte 180F. Specialties: Regional cuisine and game. **Credit cards** All major. **Pets** Dogs allowed (+70F). **Facilities** Heated swimming pool, tennis (70F/hr), Parking. **Nearby** Le Pays de Bray: church of Gournay-en-Bray, church of Aumale, abbaye of Beaubec in Forges-les-Eaux, château of Mesnières-en-Bray, Forêt de Lyons; abbey of Moretmer – Golfs at Chaumont-en-Vexin, Saint-Saens, Vivier Danger. **Open** March 15– Nov 15.

This is a former 18th-century glass factory on the edge of the glorious Forest of Lyons. The Château du Landel is a superb family mansion which has been converted into a hotel and where the members of the Cardon family work in various capacities. Madame Cardon is at the reception desk while one of her sons is in the kitchen preparing refined dishes which will be served to you in a very elegant salon (with a fireplace in winter). The bedrooms are all furnished with antiques. The chateau has recently been soundproofed. With the first sunny days of spring, drinks are served on the terrace overlooking the peaceful park.

How to get there *(Map 1 and 9): 90km northwest of Paris, towards N14 Rouen; 5km after Pontoise, towards D53 Dieppe, then D915; in Neufmarché, towards Bézancourt.*

Auberge du Val au Cesne

Le Val au Cesne
76190 Croix-Mare (Seine-Maritime)
Tel. 35.56.63.06 - Fax 35.56.92.78 - M. Carel

Rooms 5 with telephone, bath, WC and TV. **Price** Double 350F. **Meals** Breakfast 50F, served 8:00-11:00; half board 550F, full board 620F (per pers., 3 days min.). **Restaurant** Service 12:00-14:00, 19:00-21:00; menu 150F, also à la carte. Specialties: Terrine de raie, tête et fraise de veau, sole farcie à la mousse de langoustines, escalope de dinde 'Vieille Henriette', feuilleté aux pommes. **Credit cards** Visa, Eurocard and MasterCrad. **Pets** Dogs allowed. **Facilities** Parking. **Nearby** Rouen cathedral, church and museum in Yvetot, abbey of Saint-Wandrille – 18-hole golf course in Etretat. **Open** All year.

Primarily this auberge is known for its restaurant. M. Carel set up five comfortable bedrooms in a nearby house at the request of his clientele. The Auberge is in a pretty valley and is tastefully furnished in the style of the region; you'll feel quite at home here. You will find some of the garden occupied by animals; there are a couple of peacocks, an aviary and a cat breeding farm. The nearby road will not disturb you, for there is hardly any traffic when night falls.

How to get there (Map 1 and 8): 30km northwest of Rouen via A15 towards Yvetot, then D5 for 3km in the direction of Duclair direction.

Le Donjon
Chemin de Saint-Clair
76790 Etretat (Seine–Maritime)
Tel. 35.27.08.23 – Fax 35.29.92.24 – Mme Abo Dib

Rooms 8 with telephone, bath or shower, WC and TV. **Price** With half board 500-700F (per pers.). **Meals** Breakfast 50F, served 8:00-10:00. **Restaurant** Service 12:00-14:00, 19:00-22:00; menus 160-260F, also à la carte. Specialties: Seafood, fish, duck. **Credit cards** Amex, Visa, Eurocard and MasterCard. **Pets** Dogs allowed (+50F). **Facilities** Swimming pool, parking. **Nearby** Etretat cliffs, châteaux of Valmont and Bailleul, Trinity church and Bénédictine museum in Fécamp – 18-hole golf course in Etretat. **Open** All year.

Overlooking the charming town of Etretat, with its cliffs and pebble beach, this small ivy-covered château is a seductive place. The lounge, the beautiful blue and yellow dining room and the circular bar overlooking the Channel are all decorated with shimmering fabrics, paintings and antique furniture. The bedrooms are decorated in good taste. We particularly recommend the Suite Orientale and the Chambre Horizon, both of which enjoy a magnificent view over the Aiguille Creuse cliff, and the Marjorie Room, with a view of the sea. You must take *demi-pension*, but you will not regret it – the cuisine is excellent. Madame Abo Dib's hospitality is charming.

How to get there *(Map 8): 17km west of Fécamp via D940.*

Auberge du Clos Normand **

22, rue Henri IV
76370 Martin-Eglise (Seine-Maritime)
Tel. 35.04.40.34 - Fax 35.04.48.49 - M. and Mme Hauchecorne

Rooms 7 with telephone, bath or shower, WC and TV. **Price** Double 270-370F, suite 460F. **Meals** Breakfast 35F, served 8:00-10:00; half board 347-397F (per pers., 3 days min.). **Restaurant** Service 12:15-14:00, 19:30-21:00; à la carte. Specialties: Tarte aux moules, filets de sole dieppoise, turbotin sauce crème estragon, tarte aux pommes. **Credit cards** All major. **Pets** Dogs allowed (+50F). **Nearby** Castle and museum in Dieppe, church and graveyard in Varengeville, château de Mesnières-en-Bray, Saint-Säens, valley of the Varenne and Eawy forest – 18-hole golf course in Etretat. **Open** All year except April 3 – 12 and Nov 15 – Dec 15 (closed Monday evening and Tuesday).

This is a beautiful little hotel dating back to the 15th-Century; it is on the edge of the Forest of Arques a few kilometers from the sea. From the pretty, rustic dining room you can watch the chef at work. The garden borders the river; you can have lunch outdoors. There are seven bedrooms in the annex at the bottom of the garden, all of them individually decorated, with floral wallpaper, and views over the green landscape. Their decoration is somewhat old-fashioned, except in the suite. One room also has a small terrace. In this part of the auberge, there is also a lounge which is entirely at guests' disposal. As is often the case with overnight stops, you will be asked to dine in the hotel.

How to get there *(Map 1): 5km southeast of Dieppe via D1 towards Neufchâtel-en-Bray.*

Château de Sassetot-le-Mauconduit
Sassetot-le-Mauconduit
76540 Valmont (Seine-Maritime)
Tel. 35.28.00.11 - Fax 35.28.50.00 - M. Devaux

Rooms 30 with telephone, bath or shower, WC and TV. **Price** Double 415-730F.
Meals Breakfast 50F, served 7:30-9:30; half board 760F (2 pers.). **Restaurant** Service
19:30-21:30 (closed Sunday evening and Monday); menus 115-300F, also à la carte.
Specialties: Foie gras and home-smoked salmon. **Credit cards** Amex, Visa, Eurocard
and MasterCard. **Pets** Dogs allowed (+60F). **Facilities** Parking. **Nearby** Church of
the Trinité and Benedictine museum in Fécamp, Saint-Valéry-en-Caux, Châteaux of
Valmont and Bailleul, church and château of Cany-Barville – 18-hole golf course in
Etretat. **Open** All year.

This elegant classical château once welcomed Empress Sissi of
Austria. The interior is composed of charming, beautifully
proportioned rooms overlooking the vast English-style park. The
bedrooms, reached via a double wooden staircase, have green or
pink upholstery and have been thoroughly and comfortably
refurbished. The furniture – antique and reproduction – varies
from room to room. You will enjoy refined, creative cuisine, which
is served in a beautiful panelled dining room or, in summer, on
the terrace. In the evenings you can enjoy the bar with its billiard
table.

*How to get there (Map 8): 74km northwest of Rouen via N15 to Valliquerville,
then D926 and D17.*

Hôtel de la Terrasse **
Route de Vastérival
76119 Varengeville (Seine-Maritime)
Tel. 35.85.12.54 - Fax 35.85.11.70 - M. and Mme Delafontaine

Rooms 22 with telephone, bath or shower and WC. **Price** Double 240-290F.
Meals Breakfast 32F, served 7:45-9:30; half board 220-245F (per pers.).
Restaurant Service 12:00-13:30, 19:00-20:15; menu 80-160F, also à la carte.
Specialties: Shellfish and fish. **Credit cards** Visa, Eurocard and MasterCard. **Pets** Dogs
allowed. **Facilities** Tennis (35F), parking. **Nearby** Château and museum of Dieppe,
church and cemetery of Varengeville, château de Mesnières-en-Bray, Saint-Saëns,
vallée de la Varenne and forêt d'Eawy – 18-hole glof course. **Open** March 14 – Oct 14.

The views from this hotel's dining room and the flower-covered
terrace (which is opened or covered depending on the
temperamental Norman weather) stretch over the English Channel
to the horizon. Half of the bedrooms also offer this beautiful view;
the others look onto the back but they have the advantage of being
sunnier. All are pleasant and decorated with cheerful fabrics, and
the renovated rooms have elegant rattan furniture. The young
owners are friendly and the prices alone are enough to make you
want to stay.

*How to get there (Map 1): 15km west of Dieppe. In Varengeville, take D75
towards Vastérival.*

Hôtel Sud–Bretagne ★★★★

42, Bd de la République
44380 Pornichet (Loire-Atlantique)
Tel. 40.11.65.00 - Fax 40.61.73.70 - M. Bardouil

Rooms 30 with telephone, bath, WC and TV. **Price** Single 450F, double 600-800F, suite 1000-1500F. **Meals** Breakfast 60F; half board 500-850F, full board 750-1050F. **Restaurant** Menus 150-270F, also à la carte. **Credit cards** All major. **Pets** Dogs allowed. **Facilities** Swimming pool, tennis, parking. **Nearby** La Baule, La Brière and the Guérande marshes – 18-hole La Baule golf course in Saint-Denac. **Open** All year.

Ideally located not far from the beaches at La Baule, the Hôtel Sud-Bretagne has been in the same family since 1912, and to this day every member of the family joins in running and improving the hotel. Their contributions range from interior decoration to the organization of excursions aboard *La Orana*, a 17-meter teak-and-mahogany ketch. You will feel at home here. And a magnificent home it is, where each room has its own style. There is a lounge with a cozy fireplace, a billiard room, and several dining rooms over looking an indoor swimming pool. Outside, garden furniture invites you to relax in the sun. Each bedroom has a different theme reflected in the choice of fabrics, furniture and objects. There are some small apartments, with a lounge, a terrace, and typical Breton box beds for children. The Sud-Bretagne is one of a few luxury hotels which has retained all its charm and character.

How to get there *(Map 14): 5km east of La Baule.*

Auberge de Kerhinet **

Le Kerhinet
44410 Saint-Lyphard (Loire-Atlantique)
Tel. 40.61.91.46 – Fax 40.61.97.57 – M. and Mme Pebay-Arnauné

Rooms 7 with bath and WC. **Price** Single 250F, double 270F. **Meals** Breakfast 40F, served 8:00-11:00; half board 300F. **Restaurant** Closed Tuesday evening and Wednesday except July and August. Service 12:00-15:00, 19:00-23:00; menus 85-210F, also à la carte. Specialties: Emincés de pimpenneaux, anguilles au roquefort, persillade de cuisses de grenouilles fraîches, petits foies de canard aux pleurotes, matelote d'anguille à la Brièronne. **Credit cards** All major. **Pets** Dogs allowed. **Facilities** Parking. **Nearby** Medieval town of Guérande, marshes, La Brière regional park, Croisic aquarium – 18-hole La Bretesche golf course, 18-hole La Baule golf course in Saint-Denac. **Open** All year.

This lovely little auberge lies in a historically classified village which has been immaculately rebuilt and restored. Thatched roofs and stone walls add special beauty to the Auberge are all done in a rustic style. The bar, dining room and the bedrooms, which are in a separate and quiet pavilion.

How to get there (Map 14): 23km north of Saint-Nazaire via D47 to Saint-Lyphard via Saint-André-des-Eaux. In the village of Kerhinet (follown signs on D47).

Abbaye de Villeneuve ****

Route des Sables-d'Olonne
44840 Les Sorinières (Loire-Atlantique)
Tel. 40.04.40.25 – Fax 40.31.28.45 – M. Guillet

Rooms 24 with telephone, bath and WC (12 with TV). **Price** Single and double 390-935F, suite 1150-1310F. **Meals** Breakfast 65F, served 6:45-10:30; half board 430-970F, full board 645-1190F. **Restaurant** Service 12:00-13:30, 19:00-21:30; menus 160-340F, also à la carte. Specialties: Saumon fumé à l'abbaye crème de raifort, corne d'abondance de sandre aux beurres du Val-de-Loire, noisettes de canard de Challans aux pêches acidulées. **Credit cards** All major. **Pets** Dogs allowed. **Facilities** Swimming pool, parking. **Nearby** Art museum and Jules Verne museum in Nantes, valley of the Erdre, Clisson – 18-hole golf course in Nantes. **Open** All year.

The abbey was founded in 1201 by Constance of Brittany, partlially destroyed during the French Revolution and then restored in 1977. Today this old Cistercian abbey is a hotel. The great hall of the monastery is now the restaurant and the bedrooms retain the magnificent timbers of the building's frame. In the lounges, plaster ceilings and stone fireplaces give the room a grand air, but they are comfortable spots to relax – surely less forbidding then the austerity of the original abbey. The hotel, which is only ten minutes from the center of Nantes. The cuisine is classic and you will be looked after in grand style.

How to get there (Map 14): 10km south of Nantes via A83 towards Bordeaux, then Challans.

Château des Briottières ★★★★

49330 Champigné (Maine-et-Loire)
Tel. 41.42.00.02 – Fax 41.42.01.55
M. and Mme de Valbray

Rooms 10 with telephone, bath. **Price** Double 550-750F, suite 900F. **Meals** Breakfast 45F; Half board 1240-1590F (per 2 pers.). **Restaurant** Evening meals at 20:00 (on reservation); menu 300F (all incl.). **Credit cards** All major. **Pets** Dogs allowed (+50F). **Facilities** Heated swimming pool, bicycle, parking. **Nearby** Abbey of Solesmes, abbey of Fontevrault, château of Angers (tapisserie), Loire Valley (châteaux de la Loire) – 18-hole Anjou country club golf course. **Open** All year (by reservation in winter).

Off the beaten path and surrounded by an immense English-style garden, the Château des Briottières is a private chateau which hosts guests. It alone is worthy of a trip to the Loire. The young owners are warm and friendly. On the ground floor, a vast gallery leads to the reception areas. The lounges are furnished in 18th-century style, and the large dining room is brightened by pearl-grey woodwork and pink drapes. The owners join you for the excellent, friendly dinners, which are served on a magnificently set dining table. There is a library with a French billiard table. Upstairs, the comfortable bedrooms are all tastefully decorated with lovely fabrics and very beautiful antique furniture. Some rooms are intimate, while others are vast. The bathrooms are luxurious, and all have a view of the park. The swimming pool is located in a beautiful garden. And if you stay on, the sixth night is free!

How to get there *(Map 15): 32km north of Angers via A11, Durtal exit, then D859 and D770 in the direction of Le Lion-d'Angers.*

Hôtel Anne d'Ajou ★★★

32, quai Mayaud
49400 Saumur (Maine- et-Loire)
Tel. 41.67.30.30 - Fax 41.67.51.00 - M. and Mme Touzé

Rooms 50 with telephone, bath or shower, WC and TV - 1 wheelchair accessible.
Price Single 280F, double 450F, suite 650F. **Meals** Breakfast 48F, served 7:00-10:00;
half board 425-475F. **Restaurant** "Les Ménestrels". Closed Sunday and Monday in
low season. Service 12:15-13:30, 19:30-21:30, also à la carte. **Credit card** All major.
Pets Dogs not allowed. **Facilities** Parking. **Nearby** Notre-Dame church of Nantilly,
Horse Museum in Saumur, Château of Montsoreau, abbey of Fontevraud, Montreuil-
Bellay (château), Mushroom Museum in Saint-Hilaire-Saint-Florent, Château of
Boumois. **Open** All year except Dec 23 – Jan 3.

The Anne d'Anjou is a beautiful 18th-century mansion which
is ideally located between the Loire and the imposing medieval
Chateau of Saumur. A magnificent Louis XVI stairway surmounted
by a stunning *trompe l'oeil* ceiling leads to the bedrooms. Those on
the *premier étage* still have much of their original charm, particularly
the room with Empire *bas-reliefs* covered with gold leaf. The rooms
are beautifully decorated with elegant fabrics, many with antique
furniture or rugs. The price of the rooms varies according to their
size and the floor they are on. (We are less enthusiastic about those
on the *troisième étage*). Some rooms have a view on the garden and
the chateau rising in the immediate background; others look out
over the immense span of the Loire. Effective double-windows
muffle the noise of the traffic. With the first warm days of spring,
tables are set out in the beautiful garden for breakfast.

How to get there *(Map 15): 66km west of Tours.*

Hôtel L'Ermitage ★★★
53340 Saulges (Mayenne)
Tel. 43.90.52.28 – Fax 43.90.56.61
M. and Mme Janvier

Rooms 36 with telephone, bath or shower, WC, TV and minibar - Wheelchair accessible. **Price** Single 270-330F, double 310-450F, suite 520F. **Meals** Breakfast (buffet) 50F, served 7:30-10:00; half board 300-420F, full board 390-520F (per pers., 3 days min.). **Restaurant** Service 12:00-14:00, 19:15-21:00; menus 98-260F, also à la carte. Specialties: Salade de gambas sauce orange, foie gras maison, coquilles Saint-Jacques au vin de Jasnières, rognonnade de lapereau à la sarriette, fricassée de volaille "pomme d'abeille", comté du maine. **Credit cards** All major. **Pets** Dogs allowed (+40F). **Facilities** Heated swimming pool, sauna (40F), health center, parking, garage (+suppl.). **Nearby** Caves of Roquefort and Margot in Saulges, basilica of Evron, fortified town of Sainte-Suzanne, château of Rocher, abbey of Clermont, abbey of Solesmes – 27-hole golf courses in Laval and Sablé. **Open** All year except Feb (closed Sunday evening and Monday in low season).

L'Ermitage is located in the region of the Evre and Vegre, two charming fishing rivers in the heart of the Mayenne. It is a modern building in the center of the small and quiet market town of Saulges. Major refurbishment has done much to improve the comfort of this hotel. The bedrooms have been completely renovated and all look out onto the countryside. The garden has been enlarged by the addition of a meadow, and the restaurant with its views of the park has also been refurbished to celebrate the arrival of chef Thierry Janvier, the son of the family, who trained with the best chefs in Paris.

How to get there *(Map 15): 37km east of Laval via A81, number 2 Vaiges exit, then D24 in the direction of Sablé for 4km, then CD554.*

379

Relais Cicéro ★★★

18, boulevard d'Alger
72200 La Flèche (Sarthe)
Tel. 43.94.14.14 - Fax 43.45.98.96 - Mme Levasseur

Rooms 21 with telephone, bath or shower, WC and TV. **Price** Single 380-425F, double 495-675F. **Meals** Breakfast 45F, served from 7:00. No restaurant. **Credit cards** Amex, Visa, Eurocard and MasterCard. **Pets** Small dogs allowed. **Nearby** Chapel of Notre Dame-des-Vertus, Tertre Rouge zoological park, château de Lude, Solesmes abbey. **Open** Jan 4 – Dec 17.

This hotel isn't really a country hotel since it is in the small, pretty town of La Flèche, yet the Relais Cicéro has various advantages that make it a first-class place to stay. It is located on a peaceful tree-lined street away from the bustle and noise of the town. Its large garden is tranquil and the beautiful 16th- and 18th-century building is both comfortably and elegantly furnished. There is a bar, a reading room and a television room. In the dining room a very good breakfast is served – in winter to the accompaniment of a blazing fire in the fireplace. The bedrooms are comfortable and tastefully furnished. Our favorite rooms are those in the main building. Try the traditional *Fesse d'Ange* and *Le Vert Galant*, two restaurants in the village.

How to get there *(Map 15): 52km northwest of Angers via A11, Durtal exit, then N23 to La Flèche.*

Auberge du Port-des-Roches ★★

72800 Luché-Pringé (Sarthe)
Tel. 43.45.44.48 – Fax 43.45.39.61
M. Martin

Rooms 13 with telephone, bath or shower (11 with WC, 6 with TV). **Price** Double
220-310F. **Meals** Breakfast 32F, served 8:00-9:00; half board 250-300F, full board
320-370F (per pers., 5 days min.). **Restaurant** Service 12:00-13:30, 19:00-20:30;
menus 135-160F, also à la carte. Specialties: Filet de sandre au vinaigre de cidre,
terrine maison, charlotte aux fruits. **Credit cards** All major. **Pets** Dogs not allowed.
Facilities Parking. **Nearby** Châteaux of Montmirail, Courtanvaux and Saint-Calais,
château of Lude, château of Bazouges – 18-hole Le Mans golf course in Luisanne.
Open All year (closed Sunday evening and Monday).

By the side of a pretty road in the valley of the Loir, this
comfortable, unpretentious hotel has a lovely terrace (on the
other side from the road) which overlooks the Loir. Madame
Martin will make you feel at home. Her husband is the chef,
specializing in traditional regional dishes made with fresh produce
from the market. The bedrooms are cozy, comfortable and well
kept; six have a view of the river. The lounge and dining room
are decorated in rustic style. There is a pretty, shady terrace with
flowers on the riverbank. This is a marvelous, reasonably priced
hotel in a region full of touristic attractions.

How to get there *(Map 16): 40km southwest of Le Mans in the direction of
La Flèche, then D13 to Luché-Pringé and D214 to "Le Port-des-Roches".*

Haras de la Potardière

La Portardière
72200 Crosmières (Sarthe)
Tel. 43.45.83.47 – Fax 43.45.81.06 – M. and Mme Benoist

Rooms 17 with telephone, 16 with bath, 1 with shower, WC, TV, 16 with minibar – Wheelchair accessible. **Price** Single 450F, double 550F. **Meals** Breakfast 40F, served 7:00-11:00. No restaurant but snacks available in winter. **Credit cards** Visa, Eurocard and MasterCard. **Pets** Dogs allowed. **Facilities** Heated swimming pool, billiards, 3-hole compact golf, tennis, horseback trips by reservation. **Nearby** Notre-Dame-des-Vertus chapel, Malicorne pottery, Rairies terra cotta, Tertre Rouge zoological park, château de Lude, abbey of Solesmes – 27-hole Sablé-Solesmes golf course. **Open** All year (by reservation Nov – March).

A countryside of forests and large green valleys surrounds this horse farm, a large part of which has been transformed into a hotel. *Haras* means "stud farm", so it is not surprising that the architecture of the stables is as handsome as that of the chateau. The bedrooms are beautifully furnished, with beautiful fabrics, antiques, lovely lighting and outstanding bathrooms. The suites, ideal for families, offer unbeatable quality for the price. The young owners are friendly and informal, making the Potardière a place as lovely and gentle as the Loire Valley itself. For restaurants, try *Le Moulin de la Barbée* in Bazouges-sur-le-Loir, *La Petite Auberge* in Malicorne, or *Le Vert Galant* and *La Fesse d'Ange* in La Flèche.

How to get there *(Map 15): 10km northwest of La Flèche. On A11, exit La Flèche/Sablé, Crosmières, then towards Bazouges to La Potardière.*

Hôtel du Martinet **
Place de la Croix-Blanche
85230 Bouin (Vendée)
Tel. 51.49.08.94 – Mme Huchet

Rooms 21 with telephone, bath or shower, WC and TV. **Price** Single 195-230F, double 265-330F. **Meals** Breakfast 35F. No restaurant. **Credit cards** All major. **Pets** Dogs allowed (+20F). **Facilities** Bicycles, swimming pool, parking. **Nearby** Church of St-Philbert-de-Grand-Lieu, Machecoul, oyster beds, Ile d'Yeu – 18-hole golf courses in Saint-Jean-de-Monts and in Pornic. **Open** All year.

You will be enchanted by this late 18th–century residence where the smell of wax mingles with that of bowls of cut flowers. The furniture in the bedrooms on the ground floor and *premier étage* is plain but very comfortable. There are two other bedrooms under the eaves which are ideal for families of four. In a small wing of the hotel, five beautiful bedrooms have just been added. They are prettily decorated, and are on the ground floor, looking onto a large garden at the rear of the house; the swimming pool is also located here, which has good views of the countryside and the marshes of the Vendée. There isn't a restaurant in the hotel but the husband of the owner, an oyster breeder, is pleased to let you taste the oysters from his oyster beds. For fine dining, try *Le Courlis*.

How to get there *(Map 14): 51km southwest of Nantes via D751 and D758 in the direction of Noirmoutier.*

Château de la Vérie ★★★

Route de Saint-Gilles-Croix-de-Vie
85300 Challans (Vendée)
Tel. 51.35.33.44 - Fax 51.35.14.84 - M. Martin

Rooms 17 with telephone, bath, WC, TV and minibar. **Price** Single and double 350-850F. **Meals** Breakfast 50-80F, served 7:30-10:30. **Restaurant** Closed Sunday evening and Monday in low season. Service 12:00-14:00, 19:30-21:30; menus 100-320F, also à la carte. Specialties: Pommes de terre de Noirmoutier farcies aux langoustines, canard de Challans aux sang en deux services, brioche vendéenne dorée aux framboise. **Credit cards** Visa, Eurocard and Mastercard. **Pets** Dogs allowed (+50F). **Facilities** Swimming pool, tennis, parking. **Nearby** Château of Apremont, church of Sallertaine, château and market in Clisson, church of Saint-Philbert-de-Grand-Lieu, Machecoul, Saint-Gilles-Croix-de-Vie, la Fromentine (boats for Ile d'Yeu). **Open** All year.

Recently converted into a hotel, the château boasts exquisite bedrooms, both comfortable and well renovated. Japanese wickerwork, vivid colors, charming little engravings and antique furniture – nothing is lacking: even the mirrors in the bathrooms have china frames. The dining room and lounge have been decorated in the same spirit; they are welcoming rooms, feel very much like a private house, and look out onto a large terrace where breakfast is served and you can view the lush park. There is a swimming pool not far away, useful because this is the second sunniest part of France. The sea used to come this far but has retreated, leaving behind lush marshland.

How to get there (Map 14): 60km south of Nantes via D65 to Saint-Philibert, then D117 to Machecoul, then D32 to Challans; it's 2.5km from the town hall in the direction of Saint-Gilles-Croix-de-Vie.

Hôtel de l'Antiquité ★★

14, rue Galliéni
85300 Challans (Vendée)
Tel. 51.68.02.84 - Fax 51.35.55.74 - Mme Flaire

Rooms 16 with telephone, bath or shower, WC and TV. **Price** Singles 210-350F, double 250-390F. **Meals** Breakfast 30F, served 7:30-10:00. No restaurant. **Credit cards** All major. **Pets** Dogs not allowed. **Facilities** Swimming pool, parking. **Nearby** Château of Apremont, church of Sallertaine, le marais breton, château and market of Clisson, church of Saint-Philbert-de-Grand-Lieu, Machecoul, Saint-Gilles-Croix-de-Vie, Fromentine (boat for Ile d'Yeu). **Open** Jan 2 – Dec 23.

On the street side, the Hotel de l'Antiquité doesn't look like much. Thus our surprise when we went into the reception area and glimpsed the lovely dining room with a handsome old china cabinet and charming tables, a lounge/winter garden which opens onto a flower-filled patio, and an inviting swimming pool. Friendly Madame Flaire is also an antiques dealer, which explains the beautiful furniture and tasteful decoration. She is gradually renovating each bedroom, carefully coordinating fabrics, wallpapers and antique furniture. The most beautiful rooms are the four large bedrooms on the other side of the patio, which are very well furnished and have luxurious bathrooms. (Reserve well ahead of time). This is a very welcoming small hotel in the farm town of Challans, which is famous for its ducks, and it is only a few minutes from the coast of Noirmoutier. In Challans, two good restaurants are *Le Dauphin* and *Le Pavillon Gourmand*.

How to get there *(Map 14): 60km south of Nantes via D65, Saint-Philbert, then D117, Machecoul, D32 to Challans.*

Flux Hôtel ★★

27, rue Pierre-Henry, Port Joinville
85350 Ile-d'Yeu (Vendée)
Tel. 51.58.36.25 - Mme Cadou

Rooms 16 with telephone, bath or shower and TV. **Price** Double 280F. **Meals** Breakfast 35F, served 8:30-9:00; half board 310F; full board 340F (per pers., recommended in July, Aug.). **Restaurant** Closed Sunday evening in low season. Service 12:00-14:00, 19:30-21:00; menus 80-160F. Specialties: Fish, shellfish, tarte aux pruneaux. **Credit cards** Visa, Eurocard and MasterCard. **Pets** Dogs allowed (+30F). **Facilities** Parking. **Nearby** Ker-Chalon beach, lighthouse, Saint-Sauveur church, ruins of the old château. **Open** Jan 15 – Nov 22.

Somewhat on the outskirts of Port-Joinville, the Flux Hôtel has an exceptional location, its garden giving onto a small coastal path overlooking the immense blue ocean. To take advantage of this beautiful view, the owners constructed a building twenty years ago whose *premier étage* bedrooms look out on this magnificent seascape. Those on the ground floor do not enjoy the same panorama but they all have a small garden just in front of the door. There are also two other guestrooms in the main hotel. Room 15 is immense and perfect for families, and number 16 has a vast terrace looking out over the superb landscape. The interior decoration is unremarkable but comfortable. The shellfish you in the afternoon are cooked and served to you in the evening. If your luck had run out, the magnificent platters of shellfish will console you. (The dishes in a sauce are disappointing). In summer, the island is irresistible and you should thus reserve well in advance and take half-board in July and August.

How to get there *(Map 14): Steamer connections with Port-Joinville (tel. 51.58.36.66) and Fromentine (tel. 51.68.52. 32).*

Hôtel du Général d'Elbée ★★★

Place d'Armes
85330 Noirmoutier-en-l'Ile (Vendée)
Tel. 51.39.10.29 – Fax 51.39.08.23 – M. Savry

Rooms 28 with telephone, bath and WC. **Price** Single and double 390-690F, suite 880-1500F. **Meals** Breakfast 55-60F, served 7:30-11:30. No restaurant. **Credit cards** All major. **Pets** Dogs allowed (+60F). **Facilities** Swimming pool. **Nearby** Art and folk museum in La Guérinière, L'Herbaudière, salt marshes. **Open** April 1 –Oct 1.

The Hôtel du Général d'Elbée is in a large old building on the edge of a small canal. It is named after the leader of the Vendée uprising who died on the Place d'Armes, where you will see *l'arbre de la liberté* (the tree of liberty). The hotel has 30 pretty, comfortable bedrooms, decorated with charming antique furniture. A walled garden contains a large, inviting swimming pool. The people are welcoming and helpful. For good seafood, try the *Coté Jardin*.

How to get there *(Map 14): 82km southwest of Nantes via D751 and D758. Access by the bridge from Fromentine. The hotel is in the center of the town.*

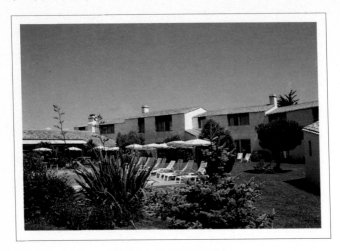

Fleur de Sel ★★★
85330 Noirmoutier-en-L'Ile (Vendée)
Tel. 51.39.21.59 – Fax 51.39.75.66
M. and Mme Wattecamps

Rooms 35 with telephone, bath, WC, TV, 22 with minibar - Wheelchair accessible. **Price** Single 325-510F, double 385-595F. **Meals** Breakfast 48F, served 8:00-9:30 in lounge, 10:30 in room; half board 370-510F, full board 470-610F (per pers., 2 days min.). **Restaurant** Service 12:00-14:00, 19:00-21:00/22:00; menus 120-230F, also à la carte. Specialties: Seafood, shellfish and fish, homards du vivier. **Credit cards** Visa, Eurocard and MasterCard. **Pets** Dogs allowed (+40F). **Facilities** Swimming pool, tennis (30-50F in hight season), sauna (60F), uva (50F). **Nearby** Château and museum of Noirmoutier, passage du Gois and the woods of la Chaize, Saint-Phibert church, salt marshes, oyster beds; 18-hole Golf Course in Saint-Jean-de-Monts, 18-hole golf course in Pornic. **Open** Mid. Feb – Nov 1.

Fleur de Sel is a large white house built around a turquoise swimming pool and a pretty garden. It is located somewhat outside the lovely island village of Noirmoutier. The bedrooms are bright and very pleasant. (Those on the ground floor have small private terraces). The furniture is of English pine, mahogany, and colored rattan, which is complemented by matching fabrics and attractive watercolors on the walls. The large dining room is bright and opens onto the sea in summer. Two small lounges decorated in blue and white lend a warm touch to the hotel. This is a beautiful, friendly hotel and the cuisine is excellent.

How to get there *(Map 14): 82km southwest of Nantes via D751 and D758. Road bridge as you leave Fromentine, 1/2 km behind the church.*

Hôtel Les Prateaux ★★★

Bois de la Chaize
85330 Noirmoutier-en-l'Ile (Vendée)
Tel. 51.39.12.52 - Fax 51.39.46.28 - M. Blouard

Rooms 22 with telephone, bath or shower, WC and TV. **Price** Single and double 340-680F. **Meals** Breakfast 50F; half board 270-362F, half board 330-590F,full board 390-660F (per pers.). **Restaurant** Service 12:30-13:30, 19:30-20:30; à la carte. Specialties: Fish and shellfish. **Credit cards** All major. **Pets** Dogs not allowed. **Facilities** Parking. **Nearby** Church of Saint-Philbert-de-Grand-Lieu, Machecoul, oyster beds, Ile d'Yeu — 18-hole golf courses in Saint-Jean-de-Monts and Pornic. **Open** Feb 15 – Nov 11.

L es Prateaux has been entirely renovated and nothing has been spared to make the new and old bedrooms beautifully comfortable. The newest rooms are larger, and one even has a private 144-square-foot terrace looking over the park. The other rooms have balconies. The principal building is composed of the dining rooms which open onto a vast terrace the lounge and some of the bedrooms. The other rooms are located nearby in the garden. The hotel is very attractively located; built in 1939 on the end of the Ile du Noirmoutier in the middle of the forest of La Chaize, it is totally quiet. The sea is only about 300 meters away and a walk through the woods will bring you to a pretty beach. The atmosphere is very summery and there is a scent reminiscent of the Côte d'Azur from the pines and mimosas.

How to get there *(Map 14): 82km southwest of Nantes by D751 and D758. Access by road bridge from Fromentine, 1.5km from Noirmoutier to Bois de la Chaize, then follow signs.*

Logis de la Couperie **
85000 La Roche-sur-Yon (Vendée)
Tel. 51.37.21.19
Mme Oliveau

Rooms 7 with telephone, bath or shower, WC and TV. **Price** Single 260-420F, double
285-470F, suite 420-470F. **Meals** Breakfast 38F, served 7:30-10:00. No restaurant.
Credit cards Amex, Visa, Eurocard and MasterCard. **Pets** Dogs not allowed.
Facilities Lake, parking. **Nearby** History museum and château of Chabotterie, Saint-
Sulpice-le-Verdon, Tiffauges, military Vendée. **Open** All year.

The Logis de la Couperie is a former manor house which was
rebuilt at the end of the 18th-century. It is located in open
countryside, five minutes from the center of town, and surrounded
by a 5-acre park with a small lake. Nature lovers will find peace
here. In the large entrance hall there is a magnificent staircase which
leads to the upper floors. The bedrooms are all comfortable and
tastefully furnished with antiques and regional furniture. There is
a well-stocked lounge/library, where a cheerful log fire burns in
winter. The excellent breakfast, which can include homemade
apple juice and the local brioche, is served in the dining room or
your room. *L'Halbran, l'Auberge de Noiron* and *Le Rivol* are among
the very good restaurants in La Roche-sur-Yon.

How to get there *(Map 14): On D80, five minutes from the town center,
via the Route Nationale from Cholet.*

PAYS DE LA LOIRE

Hôtel La Barbacane **
2, place de l'Eglise
85130 Tiffauges (Vendée)
Tel. 51.65.75.59 - Fax 51.65.71.91 - Mme Bidan

Rooms 16 with telephone, bath or shower, WC and TV. **Price** Single 230-295F, double 259-345F. **Meals** Breakfast 29-42F. No restaurant. **Credit cards** All major. **Pets** Dogs allowed. **Facilities** Swimming pool, billiards, garage. **Nearby** Ruins of château of Gilles de Retz ('Blue Beard'), spectacle of Puy-du-Fou, military Vendée – 18-hole golf course in Cholet. **Open** All year.

This charming little hotel is in a village the mention of whose name made the entire surrounding region tremble in the 15th-century. The fortress of Gilles de Retz, alias Blue Beard, is located here. You will go past its imposing ruins to get to La Barbacane, where you'll find the friendly welcome of Madame Bidan. The hotel is also her home, which is why each room has travel souvenirs and family furniture. On the ground floor there is a billiards room and a dining room where you can have generous breakfasts. The bedrooms are on several floors and in a ground-floor wing which opens onto the main garden; they are charming, often with exotic wicker furniture and pretty bathrooms (terracotta and blond wood), and are reasonably priced. Behind the hotel, there is another garden, with a beautiful terrace around a swimming pool. For dinner, the village restaurant, *L'Auberge du Donjon*, is right next door. If you don't mind going a little further, visit the castle at Clisson and the market before having dinner at *La Bonne Auberge*.

How to get there *(Map 15): 20km west of Cholet via D753 towards Montaigu.*

Auberge de la Rivière **
85770 Velluire (Vendée)
Tel. 51.52.32.15 - Fax 51.52.37.42
M. and Mme Pajot

Rooms 11 with telephone, bath and WC (6 with TV). **Price** Single 340F, double 400F.
Meals Breakfast 60F, served 8:00-10:30; half board 355-385F, full board 435-465F
(per pers., 3 days min.). **Restaurant** Closed Sunday evening and Monday in low
season. Service 12:15-14:00, 20:00-21:30; menus 95-215F, also à la carte.
Specialties: Feuilleté de langoustines, foie gras chaud, fish. **Credit cards** Visa,
Eurocard and MasterCard. **Pets** Dogs allowed (+30F). **Nearby** Church of Notre-Dame
and museum of the Vendée in Fontenay-le-Comte, Poitou marshes – 9-hole golf
course in Niort. **Open** Feb 21 – Jan 9 (closed Monday in low season).

This hotel is in the little village of Velluire on the banks of the
Vendée and is only a few kilometers from Fontenay-le-
Comte. The place is very peaceful and there are various types of
bedrooms. All are very pleasant; those in the main building are
decored with several beautiful pieces of antique furniture, while
those in the house next door are more functional, elegant, bright
and very comfortable. All except one look out on the river. In the
large, beautiful dining room, Madame Pajot serves excellent
seafood and regional specialities. This is a pleasant and
unpretentious place to stay, far from the tourist hordes. It is near
the Ile de Ré, famous for is salt marshes and network of canals
called "Venise Verte," Green Venice.

How to get there *(Map 15): 45km northwest of Niort via N148 towards
Fontenay-le-Comte, then D938 to Nizeau and D68 to Velluire*

Auberge de Maître Pannetier ★★

Place du Corps-de-Garde
85120 Vouvant (Vendée)
Tel. 51.00.80.12 - M. and Mme Guignard

Rooms 8 with telephone, bath or shower, WC and TV. **Price** Single 180-250F, double 200-270F. **Meals** Breakfast 26F, served from 7:30; half board 250-270F, full board 300F (per pers., 3 days min.). **Restaurant** Service 12:00-13:45, 19:30-21:00; menus 62-300F (children 38F), also à la carte. Specialties: Croustillant de langoustines à l'estragon, bar aux morilles, poêlée de ris de veau aux huîtres, nougat glacé sur coulis, fraises flambées sur glace vanille. **Credit cards** Diners, Visa, Eurocard and MasterCard. **Pets** Dogs allowed. **Nearby** Circuit of La Brière and the Guérande marshes – 18-hole La Baule golf course in Saint-Denac. **Open** All year (closed Sunday evening and Monday).

The hotel is on a small square not far from the church. The bedrooms are delightful, with English-style furniture in light, polished wood; the ones on the *premier étage* are the largest and lightest. Don't miss meals in the large dining room; the auberge has one of the best restaurants in the region. It is decorated in country style and has a splendid fireplace. While waiting for your meal you can watch the lobsters in their tank near the kitchen. Vouvant, which is huddled in a meander of the River Mère, is one of the loveliest villages in France, and you will be quite unable to resist strolling through its streets.

How to get there *(Map 15): 45km northwest of Niort via N148 to Fontenay-le-Comte, then D938; at Alouette take D30.*

Les Pigeons Blancs

110, rue Jules Brisson
16100 Cognac (Charente)
Tel. 45.82.16.36 – Fax 45.82.29.29 – Tachet Family

Rooms 7 with telephone, bath or shower, WC and TV. **Price** Singles 260-360F, double 300-450F. **Meals** Breakfast 40F, served 8:00-10:00. **Restaurant** Service 12:00-14:00, 19:30-21:00; menus 130-275F, also à la carte. Specialties: Poêlée de petits gris aux pleurotes, fricassée de morue charentaise, ris de veau au foie gras frais, voiture gourmandises. **Credit cards** All major. **Pets** Dogs not allowed. **Nearby** In Cognac: museum of Cognac, Chais of Cognac, festival du film policier; Romanesque churches of Cherves and Saint-Hérie in Matha, Le Marestay, Châtres, châteaux of Saint-Sauvan, Richemont and Garde-Epée; Randonnées en roulotte à partir de Matha; Road along the banks of the Charente de Jarnac in Angoulême, cruises on the Charente from June to Sept. **Open** All year.

In the same family since the 18th century, the Pigeons Blancs is a former postal relay station which is set in a quiet private park. The hotel is renowned for its restaurant, which is considered one of the finest in the region and is where merchants from the famous cognac houses often come for business lunches. But the Pigeons Blancs can also be proud of its lovely, comfortable bedrooms. They are decorated with elegant antique furniture, pretty coordinated fabrics and wallpaper. And they are kept immaculate, as are the bathrooms. There is a small, comfortable lounge with deep sofas, books and games which provide pleasant relaxation as you enjoy one of the region's famous brandies. Next to the lounge are two warmly decorated dining rooms with handsome family furniture.

How to get there *(Map 22): 40km west of Angoulême via N141; road to Saint-Jean-d'Angély, Matha.*

Les Trois Saules ★★

Saint-Groux
16230 Mansle (Charente)
Tel. 45.20.31.40 – M. Faure

Rooms 10 with telephone, shower (1 with bath), WC and TV. **Price** Single 180F, double 198F. **Meals** Breakfast 26F, served 8:00-10:00; half board 180F, full board 240F (per pers., 3 days min.). **Restaurant** Closed Sunday evening and Monday lunchtime. Service 12:15-13:45, 19:15-20:45; menus 58-160F, also à la carte. Specialties: Sole aux cèpes, feuilleté de Saint-Jacques au pineau, bar au beurre blanc, magret de canard aux choux. **Credit cards** Visa, Eurocard and MasterCard. **Pets** Dogs allowed. **Facilities** Parking. **Nearby** Cathedral of Saint-Pierre in Angoulême, romanesque churches in Saint-Armand-de-Boixe, Ruffec, Braconne forest, La Rochefoucault – 9-hole l'Hirondelle golf course in Angoulême. **Open** All year.

This is a real country auberge, simple but comfortable. The bedrooms are not large and their decor is fairly plain, but all of them have showers and one has a full bath. Regular guests meet here in summer to cycle, fish, relax or swim in the River Charente which flows at the bottom of the garden. The Faure family has owned the hotel for several generations and is the largest family in the village. They all devote themselves to hotel guests with great enthusiasm and kindness, and their restaurant is famous throughout the region.

How to get there *(Map 23): 26km north of Angoulême via N10 to Mansle, then D361 (3km northwest).*

Hôtel l'Ecailler ★★★

65, rue du Port
Ile d'Oléron - 17310 La Cotinière (Charente-Maritime)
Tel. 46.47.10.31 - Fax 46.47.10.23 - M. Rochard

Rooms 8 with telephone, bath, WC, TV and minibar. **Price** Single and double 330-400F. **Meals** Breakfast 38F, served 8:00-9:30, until 11:30 in room; half board 355-410F, full board 440-500F (per pers.). **Restaurant** Service 12:00-14:00, 19:00-22:00. Specialties: Boudin de Saint-Jacques, escargots charentais. **Credit cards** All major. **Pets** Dogs allowed (+35F). **Facilities** Parking (18F). **Nearby** Beachs of Le Coureau and La Giraudière, Aliénor d'Aquitaine Museum in Saint-Pierre-d'Oléron; from Boyardville, boat for Islands of Aix and Fouras; beach of Les Saumonards facing Fort Boyard – 9-hole Oléron golf course. **Open** Feb 7 – Nov 14.

L'Ecaillier is an ideal place from which to enjoy this delightful island fishing village. There is only a small street between the hotel and the picturesque fishing boats, and half the bedrooms have a view over this scene. The other rooms look out on a small garden and have the advantage of being quieter. All are well equipped. On the ground floor, you can enjoy a winter garden where there are a few tables covered with pretty floral cloths. In the adjacent large restaurant, there is a permanent exhibit of bright paintings and watercolors by local artists. The delicious fish on your plate (the *boudin* of scallops is special) is caught each morning. The atmosphere is relaxed and friendly at the Ecaillier, which means "oyster merchant".

How to get there *(Map 22): 10km west of Marennes via the viaduct bridge. 3km west of Saint-Pierre-d'Oléron.*

Hôtel Le Chat Botté **

Ile de Ré
17590 Saint-Clément-des-Baleines (Charente-Maritime)
Tel. 46.29.21.93 - Fax 46.29.29.97- Melles Massé

Rooms 19 with telephone, 7 with bath, 12 with shower and WC - Wheelchair accessible. **Price** Single 280F, double 340-480F. **Meals** Breakfast 40-55F, served 8:15-10:30. No restaurant. **Credit cards** Visa, Eurocard and MasterCard. **Pets** Dogs allowed (+35F). **Facilities** Small health center, parking. **Nearby** Museum and citadel of Saint-Martin-de-Ré, Baleines Lighthouse – 9-hole Trousse golf course. **Open** All year except Dec 1 – 15 and Jan 6 – Fev 10.

The Chat Botté ("puss in boots") is an adorable village house with a patio and a large flower garden on the delightful Ile de Ré. Bright wood paneling harmonizes with elegant terra cotta floors and fabrics. Everything is impeccably kept and decorated, including the bedrooms. Breakfast is served in a pretty room which opens onto the garden. There is also a small, well–equipped exercise room. The young owners and staff are very friendly and informal. There is no restaurant in the hotel but the excellent seafood restaurant *Le Chat Botté* is just next door; and in Portes-en-Ré, there is *L'Auberge de la Rivière* (try the langoustine ravioli). Both are run by other members of the Massé family. And there are many other good restaurants on this delightful island.

How to get there *(Map 22): 28km west of La Rochelle via the Pallice Bridge.*

Hôtel France et Angleterre et Champlain ***

20, rue Rambaud
17000 La Rochelle (Charente-Maritime)
Tel. 46.41.34.66 - Fax 46.41.15.19 - Mme Jouineau

Rooms 36 with telephone, bath or shower, WC, TV, 5 with air-conditioning and 28 with minibar. **Price** Single and double 310-535F, suite 655F. **Meals** Breakfast 42F, served 7:15-11:30. No restaurant. **Credit cards** All major. **Pets** Dogs allowed (+30F). **Facilities** Garage (35-48F). **Nearby** New World museum, Lafaille museum, Protestant and arts museum in La Rochelle, Ile de Ré, Esnandes, church portal and dungeon in Vouvant, Poitou marshes – 18-hole La Prée golf course in La Rochelle. **Open** All year.

This 17th-century former convent hides a beautiful garden behind its walls, which is a good place for breakfast. To get to the garden you cross a large hall and some lovely reception rooms. Period woodwork, antique statues and lovely old furniture create a warm and elegant ambience. The bedrooms, reached by elevator or by the splendid stone staircase, offer you the choice of a comfortable modern style or the charm and elegance of an earlier era. They are different in decor but all are comfortable, though you will probably prefer those which overlook the garden. There is no restaurant but the hotel has a *demi-pension* arrangement with a nearby restaurant. For the best seafood in La Rochelle, try *La Marmite,* or the bustling bistrot *La Marée*, for its giant platters of shellfish.

***How to get there** (Map 22): In the center of La Rochelle.*

Résidence de Rohan ★★★

Parc des Fées
17640 Vaux-sur-Mer (Charente-Maritime)
Tel. 46.39.00.75 – Fax 46.38.29.99 – M. and Mme Seguin

Rooms 41 with telephone, bath or shower, WC and TV. **Price** Single and double 300-670F. **Meals** Breakfast 49F, served 7:30-13:00. No restaurant. **Credit cards** Amex, Visa, Eurocard and MasterCard. **Pets** Dogs allowed. **Facilities** Tennis (+50F), parking. **Nearby** Lighthouse of Cordouan, La Rochelle, Sablonceaux abbey, Talmont-sur-Gironde, zoo of La Palmyre – 18-hole Côte de la Beauté golf course in Royan. **Open** Easter – Nov 13.

This pretty little family house is in a little wood which runs behind the beach at Nauzan. The pink and white 19th-century building has lawns sloping gently down to the beach, with chaises longues scattered among the pines. Inside, the decor is quite different from what you might expect to find in a seaside house; the velvet-covered armchairs in the lounge, the mahogany Charles X-style furniture in the bar, the carpets and rugs create a rather opulent ambience. All the bedrooms have their own style and beautiful fabrics; many are furnished with antique furniture. Some rooms, notably those in the annex, are very spacious, while others open onto the garden where you can have breakfast. The hosts are friendly and hospitable. *Le Chalet, Les Trois Marmites, Les Filets Bleus* and *La Sabotière* are good restaurants which will compensate for the hotel's lack of one.

How to get there *(Map 22): 3km northwest of Royan via D25, which follows the coast in the direction of Saint-Palais-sur-Mer.*

Au Marais ★★★

46-48, quai Louis-Tardy
79510 Coulon (Deux-Sèvres)
Tel. 49.35.90.43 - Fax 49.35.81.98 - M. and Mme Nerrière

Rooms 18 with telephone, bath, WC and TV. **Price** Double 250-600F. **Meals** Breakfast (buffet) 38F, served 7:30-10:00 No restaurant. **Credit cards** Visa, Eurocard and MasterCard. **Pets** Dogs allowed (+35F). **Nearby** Poitou marshes, museums and church of Notre-Dame in Niort – 18-hole golf course in Maziéres-en-Gatine. **Open** All year.

All the magic of the Poitou marshland is here in front of the hotel: the Sèvre River is directly in front of the hotel and the cruise boats are nearby. The hotel is built in classic Poitou style and has been totally restored without being spoiled. The interior decoration is very tasteful. In the bedrooms, there is a beautiful assortment of fresh colors and handsome furniture and fabrics. They are all remarkably well kept and the bathrooms are immaculate. The hotel is quiet despite the numbers of tourists in July and August. This is an excellent small hotel which is ideal for visiting "Green Venice" and where you will find a young, very friendly staff. Note that there is no longer a restaurant in the hotel but you can enjoy a range of local specialties at the pleasant *Les Mangeux de Lumas* three kilometers away.

How to get there *(Map 15): 10km west of Niort via D9 and D1 (beside the Sèvre niortaise).*

Le Logis Saint-Martin ★★★
Chemin de Pissot
79400 Saint-Maixent-l'École (Deux-Sèvres)
Tel. 49.05.58.68 - Fax 49.76.19.93 - Mme Verdier

Rooms 10 with telephone, bath or shower, WC and TV. **Price** Single 300F, double 400F, suite 450F. **Meals** Breakfast 50F, served 7:30-9:30; half board 360-610F (per pers., 3 days min.). **Restaurant** Service 12:30-14:00, 19:30-21:30; menus 120-160F, also à la carte. Specialties: Foie gras au torchon, andouille en papillotte. **Credit cards** Amex, Visa, Eurocard and MasterCard. **Pets** Dogs allowed (+40F). **Facilities** Parking. **Nearby** Local history museum, arts museum, Notre-Dame church in Niort, church in Melle, Tumulus of Bougon museum, Futuroscope in Poitiers – 9-hole golf courses in Mazières-en-Gatine, Sainte-Maxire and Les Forges. **Open** All year except Jan 2 – 23.

This large 17th-century stone house, so cool when it is hot outside, and so warm in the winter, is a great place to spend a weekend. From here you can walk along the Sèvre River which runs in front of the hotel, and through the countryside described by René Bazin in *L'Église Verte*. You can also enjoy the local architecture in this region rich in Romanesque art and buildings. The comfortable rooms look out on the river. They are all light, quiet, and very pleasant. The cuisine is very good and the hosts are warm and welcoming.

How to get there (Map 15): 24km northeast of Niort via N11.

Le Roumanin

Chemin des Plèches
04550 Esparron-de-Verdon (Alpes-de-Haute-Provence)
Tel. 92.77.15.91 - Mme Tellier

Rooms 10 with telephone, bath, shower, WC and 1 with TV. **Price** Double 300F.
Meals Breakfast 38F, served 8:30-10:30. No restaurant but snacks available.
Credit cards Not accepted. **Pets** Dogs not allowed. **Facilities** Swimming pool, parking.
Nearby Gorges du Verdon, lakes route – 18-hole golf course in Pierrevert. **Open** March –
Oct (closed Nov 1).

Here is a charming simple hotel for lovers of nature and beautiful landscapes. It was built recently and has a marvelous view of the turquoise waters of Lake Esparon. Because of the many nooks and crannies of its architecture, you'll feel as though you are in a private house. The interior of the building is uncluttered, almost austere; the white walls, old furniture and blue Provençal fabrics are delightful. The bedrooms are in the same simple style but are very comfortable and well cared for. Each has a private terrace. Six overlook the delightful garden of aromatic plants which slopes down to the swimming pool, and in the distance are the lake and the mountains. The other four do not have a view but are cooler. In any of them you will enjoy perfect quiet. You will also appreciate Mme Tellier's courtesy and kindness. This pleasant hotel has reasonable prices.

How to get there *(Map 34): 60km north of Aix-en-Provence via A51, exit Gréoux-les-Bains, then D952 to Gréoux-les-Bains and D82 (1km from the village).*

Auberge Charembeau ★★

Route de Niozelles
04300 Forcalquier (Alpes-de-Haute-Provence)
Tel. 92.75.05.69 - Fax 92.75.24.37 - M. Berger

Rooms 12 with telephone, bath or shower and WC. **Price** Single 260F, double 336F. Rooms with kitchenette 1540-2300F per week. **Meals** Breakfast 41F, served 8:00-9:30. No restaurant. **Credit cards** All major. **Pets** Dogs allowed (+20F). **Facilities** Swimming pool, tennis (+60F), mountain bikes, parking. **Nearby** Lure mountain, Salagon priory, Ganagobie priory, château de Sauvan, Saint-Michel-l'Observatoire. **Open** Feb 1 – Nov 30.

This little hotel in the middle of the lovely countryside of the Forcalquier region is run by a friendly couple who have given the old restored house a charming family atmosphere. The bedrooms, are simple and in good taste. Some of them have cooking facilities, which may be useful for families. In front of the house is a terrace which is perfect for those who want nothing more than to enjoy the Provençal landscape. For good Provençal country cooking, we recommend *L'Hostellerie des Deux Lions* in Forcalquier or *Bois d'Amon* in Sainte-Marie.

How to get there *(Map 34): 39km south of Sisteron via N85 (or A51, exit La Brillanne), then D12 towards Forcalquier. It's 4km from Forcalquier via N100 towards Niozelles.*

La Ferme Rose

04360 Moustiers-Sainte-Marie (Alpes-de-Haute-Provence)
Tel. 92.74.69.47 – Fax 92.74.60.76
M. Kako Vagh

Rooms 7 with telephone, shower and WC. **Price** Double 320-350F. **Meals** Breakfast 40F or brunch à la carte. **Restaurant** Service 20:00-22:00, menu 110F, also à la carte. Specialties: Provençal cooking with market produce. **Credit cards** Visa, Eurocard and MasterCard. **Pets** Dogs allowed. **Nearby** Church and Pottery Museum in Moustiers, the Grand Canyon of the Gorges of the Verdon via the road or GR4; Lake of Sainte-Croix. **Open** All year.

From the terrace of "The Pink Farm," you will have a beautiful view over the lovely village of Moustiers, which seems suspended between two cliffs. The hotel is charming. The owner has decorated it in a very personal style, combining his collection of l950s objects, paintings done by his grandfather – a well-known Provençal painter – and amusing pieces of furniture. Note the tables, chairs and bar banquettes which came from the old Brasserie Noailles in Marseilles. The bedrooms are very pleasant, bright and cheerful, with shower rooms decorated in pretty Salernes tiles from the region. The very helpful owner, Kako, will reserve a mattress for you on a private beach on Sainte Croix Lake, rent you an electric boat to ascend the Verdon Falls, or give you tips insider's for visiting this endearing village in the spectacular Alps of Haute Provence.

How to get there *(Map 34): 50km from Manosque, then D6 direction Valensole. In Moustiers, take the direction of Lac de Sainte-Croix for 1km.*

Auberge du Clos Sorel ★★★

Les Molanès
04400 Pra-Loup (Alpes-de-Haute-Provence)
Tel. 92.84.10.74 - Mme Mercier

Rooms 10 with telephone, bath, WC and TV. **Price** Single 400F, double 520-650F.
Meals Breakfast 48F, served 8:00-10:30; half board +200F (per pers., 3 days min.).
Restaurant Service 12:30-14:30; menu 165F, also à la carte. Specialties: Morilles,
ravioles, gigots. **Credit cards** Visa, Eurocard and MasterCard. **Pets** Dogs allowed
(+35F). **Facilities** Swimming pool. **Nearby** Skiing from hotel, Colmars, route de la
Bonette. **Open** Dec 15 – Sept 5 and June 30 – April 11.

Well located on a hillside, an old farmhouse has been converted
into the Auberge du Clos Sorel. The building has lovely
stone walls and an entranceway built of logs, and blends in perfectly
with the surrounding chalets. Inside, original features such as beams,
an impressive fireplace and sloping ceilings have been retained, and
these combine with the polished furniture to create the kind of
warm and cozy atmosphere one looks forward to after a long day
spent skiing or walking. In the evening, dinner is served by
candlelight in what used to be the main room of the farmhouse.
The tables are pretty and the cuisine is refined. In summer, a
swimming-pool and tennis courts add to the many attractions of
the inn. A relaxed and informal atmosphere prevails. Clos Sorel is
a hamlet which time truly seems to have passed by, although it is
on the ski slopes of Pra-Loup.

How to get there *(Map 34): 70km southwest of Gap via D900B and D900
to Barcelonnette, then D902 and D109 to Pra-Loup. (Les Molanès is just
before the resort.)*

405

Auberge de Reillanne

04110 Reillanne (Alpes-de-Haute-Provence)
Tel. 92.76.45.95
M. Bellaiche

Rooms 7 with telephone, bath, WC and minibar. **Price** Single 240F, double 340F. **Meals** Breakfast 40F; half board 340F (per pers.). **Restaurant** Closed Wednesday except for residents. Service 19:00-21:00; menus 115-140F. Specialties: Piccata de fois gras aux navets confits, soliman d'agneau à la menthe et au miel, home-smoked fish and duck breast. **Credit cards** Visa, Eurocard and MasterCard. **Pets** Dogs allowed. **Facilities** Parking. **Nearby** Manosque, priories of Salagon and Ganagobie, château de Sauvan. **Open** All year.

Located in a part of the Luberon which has remained unspoiled, this hotel is surrounded by greenery. The few bedrooms are large, plainly furnished, but warm and comfortable, with an emphasis on natural materials: light-colored wood or cane, unbleached wool and flowery fabrics. All the bedrooms have pleasant views and lovely bathrooms with terracotta floor tiles. There is no charge to use the minibars in the rooms, guests decide how much they want to pay for the drinks – obviously trust is the keyword here. Maurice Bellaiche chose the hotel business because he enjoys it, and has created a peaceful and above all friendly atmosphere. He does the cooking himself, and his good seasonal cuisine is based on fresh local produce, with a touch of exoticism. You will find it all the more delectable in the charming dining room where meals are served.

How to get there *(Map 33): 15km northwest of Manosque towards Apt, then N100 and D214 towards Reillanne.*

Le Pyjama ★★★

04400 Super-Sauze (Alpes-de-Haute-Provence)
Tel. 92.81.12.00 – Fax 92.81.03.16
Mme Merle

Rooms 10 with telephone, bath, WC, TV and minibar. **Price** Single 250-310F, double 300-420F, suite 450-550F. **Meals** Breakfast 39F. No restaurant. **Credit cards** All major. **Pets** Dogs allowed. **Nearby** Skiing from the hotel, village of Colmars, Beauvezer, gorges of Saint-Pierre, Guillaumes via the col des Champs, route de la Bonette. **Open** Dec 15 – Sept 10 and June 25 – April 25.

Having spent twenty years running another hotel in the resort, Geneviève Merle (ski champion Carole Merle's mother) has recently had this small hotel built, using materials and designs which blend perfectly with the surroundings. Eight of the ten bedrooms face south, their terraces overlooking a field of larch trees. They are tastefully decorated, with very pleasant bathrooms. M. Merle owns an antique shop nearby, and it has provided the hotel furniture. Four rooms have a mezzanine which can accommodate two extra people. In the annex there are four studios complete with kitchen areas which are very convenient for families. The hotel doesn't have its own restaurant, but there are many in the resort, or higher up. L'Optraken which is run by Madame Merle's children, is next door; otherwise, try Les Deux Mazots. This is an extremely comfortable establishment, at the foot of the slopes, offering a friendly and informal atmosphere.

How to get there *(Map 34): 79km southeast of Gap via D900B and D900 towards Barcelonnette, then D9 and D209 to Super-Sauze.*

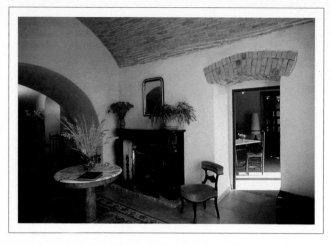

La Ferme Blanche ***
3, chemin de Villarobert
05000 Gap (Hautes-Alpes)
Tel. 92.51.03.41 - Fax 92.51.35.39 - M. Catier

Rooms 27 with telephone, bath or shower, 21 with WC and 20 with TV. **Price** Single and double 170-305F, suite 480F; half board 433F (per pers.). **Meals** Breakfast 38F. **Restaurant** Service 12:30-13:30, 20:00-21:30 (closed Sunday evening and Monday);menus 120-350F, also à la carte. **Credit cards** Amex, Visa, Eurocard, and MasterCard. **Pets** Dogs allowed (+30F). **Facilities** Parking. **Nearby** Sports nautiques sur le lac de Serre-Ponçon abbey et forêt de Boscodon près d'Embrun, château de Charance, Parc des Ecrins, Parc du Queyras - Stations de ski dans les environs – Gap Bayard golf course. **Open** All year.

You will find La Ferme Blanche hidden in the countryside just outside of Gap. The house was acquired in the 18th-century by Jean-René Catier's family, but its origins are much older, as you will observe from the vaulted rooms on the ground floor. They are very pleasantly decorated with antique chestnut furniture, handsome objects and framed inscriptions written by actors who have stayed here. There is a very friendly bar, a pretty room for breakfasts and next to it, the rustic restaurant. The bedrooms are simple and pleasant, but the nicest ones are those which look out over the terrace and the outskirts of this delightful Provençal village. This is a charming place to stay, greatly because of Jean-René Catier's hospitality. He is, by the way, an administrator of the Gap Theatre.

How to get there (Map 27): 100km south of Grenoble via N 85; north of the center of town, on D 92 to Romette.

Le Clos de Chantemerle **

33, rue du centre Chantemerle
05330 Serre-Chevalier - Saint-Chaffrey (Hautes-Alpes)
Tel. 92.24.00.13 - Fax 92.24.09.51 - Mme Loubier

Rooms 31 with telephone, WC ,16 with bath and 1 with shower. **Price** Double 200-450F. **Meals** Breakfast 35-60F; half board 340-450F (per pers., 7 days min.). **Restaurant** Service from 19:00 (in winter); menu 90-159F, also à la carte. **Credit cards** Visa, Eurocard and MasterCard. **Pets** Dogs allowed (+35F). **Facilities** Swimming pool in summer. **Nearby** Ski: 60m from the ski lift – 9-hole Montgenèvre Golf Course (18km), 9-hole Clavière Golf Course (21km). **Open** Dec – Sept (closed in May).

The origins of this old farm go back to 1732. In the 1940s, it was transformed into a hotel. Denise Loubier and her husband have now given a new start to this large, very charming house. Inside, antique furniture creates a lovely, traditional atmosphere; the bar is a popular place to gather. In the large dining room with skylights, there are beautiful bouquets of flowers and a view of the spectacular Provençal Alps as well as the hotel garden. The bedrooms vary greatly in size and the bathrooms have variable amenities. Rooms in the new wing are the best equipped and those on the ground floor looking onto the garden are recommended for families. Room 42 overlooks the village and the valley, while rooms 8, 9, 31 and 32 have a balcony and are very well kept. The hotel's well-known cuisine is a big plus.

How to get there *(Map 27): 4km northwest of Briançon via N91; in the village, next to the ski lift.*

Les Escondus ★★

Les Claux
05560 Vars (Hautes-Alpes)
Tel. 92.46.50.35 – Fax 92.46.50.47 – M. David

Rooms 22 with telephone, bath or shower, 1 with lavabo and 20 with WC. **Price** Double with half board 340-490F, with full board 380-530F (per pers., 3 days min.). **Restaurant** Service 12:30-14:00, 19:30-21:00; menu 70-150F, also à la carte. **Credit cards** Amex, Visa, Eurocard and MasterCard. **Pets** Dogs not allowed. **Facilities** Tennis, squash, billards, pianobar. **Nearby** Skiing from hotel, Queyras Valley (Montdauphin, Château-Queyras, Saint-Véran) – 9-hole Montgenèvre Golf Course (18km), 9-hole Clavière Golf Course (21km). **Open** Dec 20 – Aug 31 and July 1 – April 15.

Located in the heart of a ski resort and at the foot of the ski trails, the Escondus is one of the oldest hotels of Vars. In this tiny hamlet where their parents raised livestock, the owners are today hotel keepers and ski instructors. At the Escondus, you will enjoy not only comfortable, wood-paneled rooms, but also a simple and varied cuisine, served in a large, friendly dining room. There is a piano bar, billiard table and squash court. In the summer, you can relax on the edge of the stream amidst the larches, go horseback riding, take long walks in the forest. Because of Vars' microclimate, the snow is always powdery and abundant; and in the summer, the grass and flowers are as luxuriant as they are in Switzerland.

How to get there *(Map 27): 75km east of Gap via N94 to Guillestre, then D902.*

Mas de la Pagane

15, avenue du Mas-Ensoleillé
06600 Antibes (Alpes-Maritimes)
Tel. 93.33.33.78 – Fax 93.74.55.37 – Mme Ott

Rooms 5 with telephone, bath, shower, WC and TV. **Price** Single and double 550F.
Meals Breakfast 35F. **Restaurant** Closed Sunday evening. Service 12:00-14:30,
20:00-22:30; menu 130F, also à la carte. Specialties: Poisson à l'apicius, beignets
de cervelle sauce safran, poivron braisé et fondant d'aubergine. **Credit cards** Amex,
Visa, Eurocard and MasterCard. **Pets** Dogs allowed. **Facilities** Parking.
Nearby Picasso museum in Antibes, Cap d'Antibes, Villa Thuret, chapel of La
Garoupe, Fernand Léger museum in Biot – 18-hole Opio golf course in Valbonne.
Open All year.

This is the kind of address one likes to find in the Provence that
has charmed so many artists. Close to the yacht harbor, this
old house is tucked away from the rest of the town in beautiful
grounds. Inside, contemporary works of art, lovely fabrics and
antique furniture have been combined with consummate skill. In
the bedrooms, the decor is very elegant.   The cuisine is far from
second-rate: it is light, innovative... in short, delectable. In summer,
meals can be served on the flowery terrace. The bar opens out into
the garden, and provides the perfect setting for an evening drink.
The Mas is a friendly place.

How to get there *(Map 35): Take Avenue du Mas-Ensoleillé at crossroads
at entrance to Antibes, then signs for hotel.*

Hôtel de Paris ★★★

34, boulevard d'Alsace
06400 Cannes (Alpes-Maritimes)
Tel. 93.38.30.89 – Fax 93.39.04.61 – M. Lazzari

Rooms 45 and 5 suites, with telephone, bath or shower, WC and TV. **Price** Single 500-650F, double 550-750F, suite 900-1600F. **Meals** Breakfast 50F, served 7:00-11:00. No restaurant. **Credit cards** All major. **Pets** Dogs not allowed. **Facilities** Parking (80F). **Nearby** Massif du Tanneron, Auribeau-sur-Siagne, Mougins, Vallauris, îles de Lérins – 27-hole Cannes golf course in Mandelieu. **Open** Dec 17 – Nov 15.

This hotel is in a large white house near the highway. Its facade is decorated with columns and pediments in typical turn of the century Côte d'Azur style. Although the hotel is in the center of Cannes it has a garden (a bit noisy) with palms and cypresses around a very pleasant swimming pool. The interior is very smart. The bedrooms are decorated with prints. The suites are luxurious and have a private lounge. All the rooms are air conditioned and soundproofed and some have a balcony on which you can have breakfast. For restaurants, try *Gaston et Gastounette* for bourride or bouillabaisse; *Côté Jardin, Au Bec Fin* or *La Brouette de Grand-mère* for fresh cuisine and good chef's-special menu; and a interesting menu; *Chez Franco* for Italian cooking; *Le Café Carlton* on the beach of the Carlton Hotel, for an informal and chic buffet lunch; and *Le Rado-Plage* under the parasols on the Croisette.

How to get there *(Map 34): In the town center.*

Auberge du Soleil *
Quartier Porta-Savel
06390 Coaraze (Alpes-Maritimes)
Tel. 93.79.08.11 - Fax 93.79.37.79 - M. and Mme Jacquet

Rooms 8 and 2 suites in annex with telephone, bath or shower, WC and TV on request. **Price** Single 320-420F, double 340-495F, suite 495-940F. **Meals** Breakfast 44F, served 8:00-12:00; half board 350-425F, (per pers., 3 days min.). **Restaurant** Service 12:00-14:00, 19:30-21:00; menu 137F, also à la carte. Specialties: Tourte maison, gibelotte de lapin, caille aux raisins. **Credit cards** Amex, Visa, Eurocard and MasterCard. **Pets** Dogs allowed (+35F). **Facilities** Swimming pool, boules, table tennis. **Nearby** Mercantour reserve, valley of the Merveilles, Turini forest, villages of Lucéram, Peille and Peillon – 18-hole Agel golf course in La Turbie. **Open** March 15 – Nov 15.

This hotel is only half an hour from Nice and not far from the magnificent nature reserve of Mercantour. It is splendidly located in a medieval village 640 meters up on a rocky outcrop. The maze of narrow village streets ensures total peace and calm: you may need to call on the hotel to help with your luggage up the steep slopes. You will find an informal, almost bohemian atmosphere in the hotel but it is all in elegant good taste. There is a summer lounge located in a cool vaulted cellar and an attractive dining room which extends out over a covered terrace with panoramic views of the valley. The cuisine is simple and good. The garden slopes down in steps to the swimming pool and orchard, where you can pick the fruit without feeling guilty.

How to get there *(Map 35): 2km north of Nice via A8 exit Nice-Est, then "voie rapide" (highway) towards Drap-Sospel. At the Pointe des Contes, left towards Contes-Coaraze.*

La Tour de l'Esquillon ★★★

Miramar
06590 Théoule-sur-Mer (Alpes-Maritimes)
Tel. 93.75.41.51 - Fax 93.75.49.99 - M. and Mme Dérobert

Rooms 25 with telephone, bath, WC, TV and minibar. **Price** Single and double 400-800F. **Meals** Breakfast 60F, served 8:00-10:00; half board 520-720F. **Restaurant** Service 12:00-14:00, 19:00-21:00; menus 120-145F, also à la carte. Specialties: Fish, bouride, aïoli. **Credit cards** All major. **Pets** Dogs allowed. **Facilities** Swimming pool, private beach, parking. **Nearby** Château of Napoule, Estérel Mountains, point of l'Esquillon, bight of Napoule – 18-hole Cannes-Mandelieu golf course. **Open** Feb 1 – Oct 14.

At the edge of the winding road overlooking the deep-red Esterel Mountains, the Tour de L'Esquillon is perched like a bird's nest. Brilliant yellow broom, pink oleander, hydrangeas and fruit trees covering the terraced garden lie between the hotel and its private beach which you can reach by minibus, and where you can enjoy light meals. The Esquillon has a kind of old-fashioned charm, which is accented by its 1950s furniture and its discreet, friendly service. The 25 bedrooms are large and cool, and they face the Mediterranean. Some more expensive rooms have a balcony, which is a pleasant place to have breakfast. In the restaurant, you will enjoy the savory, spicy specialties of Provence. From the dining room, you will have a panoramic view over Cannes. It's a shame that the background music somewhat spoils this lovely place; at least it covers the sound of the traffic on the road, which certainly can be disturbing.

How to get there (Map 34): Between Saint-Raphael and Cannes, on A7, exit Mandelieu, then in the direction of Théole Miramar.

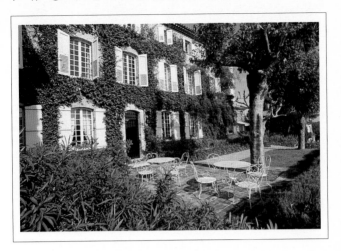

Le Manoir de l'Etang ★★★

66, allée du Manoir
06250 Mougins (Alpes-Maritimes)
Tel. 93.90.01.07 – Fax 92.92.20.70 – Gridaine-Labro Family

Rooms 15 with telephone, bath or shower, WC, TV and minibar. **Price** Double 600-850F, suite 1300F. **Meals** Breakfast 55F, served 8:00-11:00. **Restaurant** Closed Sunday evening and Tuesday in low season. Service 12:00-14:00, 20:00-22:00; menus 145-190F, also à la carte. Specialties: Canelloni de homard au jus de favouilles, lapereau mijoté à la niçoise, millefeuille de framboise et chocolat, nougat glacé au miel du manoir. **Credit cards** Amex, Visa ,Eurocard and MasterCard. **Pets** Small dogs allowed. **Facilities** Swimming pool, parking. **Nearby** The Riviera and her villages – 18-hole Cannes-Mougins golf course. **Open** All year except Nov and Feb.

This superb 19th-century house, surrounded by cypresses and oleander, overlooks a lake in a rolling 17-acre park. On the ground floor there is a warmly decorated lounge with terracotta-tiled floor, piano and cane furniture, and an airy dining room overlooking the pool framed by olive trees. Beyond the pool there are extensive views over the Provençal landscape. The comfortable bedrooms are brightened by cheerful materials with flower and fruit patterns. You will enjoy the tranquil atmosphere and the good humor of the owners, who will give you a real family welcome. This is a delightful and charming place to stay.

How to get there *(Map 34): 5km north of Cannes via "voie rapide" (highway).*

Hôtel La Pérouse ★★★★

11, quai Rauba-Capeu
06300 Nice (Alpes–Maritimes)
Tel. 93.62.34.63 - Fax 93.62.59.41 - M. Mercadal

Rooms 65 with air-conditioning, telephone, bath or shower, WC, TV and minibar. **Price** Single 360-1210F, double 595-121F, suite 1480-2000F. **Meals** Breakfast 75F, served 6:30-11:00. **Restaurant** Closed Sept 15 – May 15. Service 12:00-15:00, 19:30-22:00; à la carte. Specialties: Grills in the hotel gardens. **Credit cards** All major. **Pets** Dogs allowed. **Facilities** Swimming pool, sauna, whirlpool, solarium. **Nearby** Turini forest, valley of La Tinée (Roure, Roubron), valley of La Vésubie, villages of Utelle, Belvédère, le Boréon, Venanson – 18-hole Opio golf course in Valbonne, 18-hole Bastide-du-Roy golf course in Biot. **Open** All year.

La Pérouse is in a large Mediterranean–style mansion at the foot of the château that dominates old Nice and the Baie des Anges. It is surrounded by aloeplants and lemon trees and to reach it you have to take one of the two elevators from the quayside. The bedrooms are spacious and quiet, and prices vary according to whether you have a view of the garden or the sea; some have a terrace with deck chairs. In summer you might take advantage of the barbecue, swimming pool, and solarium, and enjoy a drink on the terrace.

How to get there *(Map 35): In the town center.*

Hôtel Windsor ★★★

11, rue Dalpozzo
06300 Nice (Alpes-Maritimes)
Tel 93.88.59.35 – Fax 93.88.9457 – M. Ridolfi-Strizzot

Rooms 60 with telephone, bath or shower, WC, TV and minibar - Elevator.
Price Single 350-525F, double 460-670F. **Meals** Breakfast 40F, served 7:00-10:30;
half board 390-495F (per pers.). **Restaurant** Closed Saturday noon and Sunday.
Service 12:00-14:00, 19:00-22:30, also à la carte. **Credit cards** All major. **Pets** Dogs
allowed. **Facilities** Swimming pool, sauna (70F), whirlpool, parking (60F).
Nearby Turini forest, valley of La Tinée (Roure, Roubron), valley of La Vésubie, villages
of Utelle, Belvédère, le Boréon, Venanson – 18-hole Opio golf course in Valbonne,
18-hole Bastide-du-Roy golf course in Biot. **Open** All year.

From the street, the Windsor seems like a classic mid-town hotel.
Once you step inside, however, this impression soon fades. In
the modern reception area, there is an ornate Oriental bed
encrusted with mother-of-pearl and an ancient gilt shrine with a
seated Buddha in the center. Just outside, you will also discover a
luxuriant exotic garden with an aviary in the hollow of an old tree;
here, a few tables are hidden away not far from a small swimming
pool. In the bedrooms, the furniture is deliberately 1950s-60s hotel
style. Many are large, all are comfortable and some have interesting
frescos on the walls. If you have avant-garde taste, ask for the
"Numéro" room. There is a very well equipped gym and a
hammam with a luminous skylight. Finally, while there is no
restaurant as such, you can enjoy the chef's special at the bar: It,
too, is often exotic!

How to get there *(Map 35): In the center of town.*

Auberge de la Madone ★★★
06440 Peillon (Alpes-Maritimes)
Tel. 93.79.91.17
Millo Family

Rooms 20 with telephone, bath, shower and WC. **Price** Double 400-780F, suite 850-1100F. **Meals** Breakfast 50F, served 8:00-10:00; half board 420-700F. **Restaurant** On reservation. Service 12:30-14:00, 19:30-20:30; menus 130-280F, also à la carte. Specialties: Bouillabaisse froide, carré d'agneau aux petits légumes fondants. **Credit cards** Visa, Eurocard and MasterCard. **Pets** Dogs not allowed. **Facilities** Tennis, parking. **Nearby** Nice, valleys of La Tinée and La Vésubie – 18-hole Mont-Agel golf course. **Open** All year except 20 Oct – 20 Dec and 7 Jan – 24 Jan (closed Wednesday).

The Auberge is a good place for those with a taste for adventure. All around it are deep ravines and rocky summits which you would hardly suspect existed only twenty minutes from Nice. From the hotel's sunny terraces you will have all the time in the world to look out on Peillon, one of the most spectacular villages in the Niçois hinterland, perched on a steep crag and with superb views all around. You can explore it on foot, up the steep stairways which lead up to the Chapel of the Pénitents Blancs. The hotel has an attractive decor with all the refinements for a comfortable stay. The excellent regional cooking is reasonably priced and encourages visitors who prefer the tranquillity of Peillon to the tourist frenzy of the Nice coast.

How to get there (Map 35): 19km north of Nice via D2204 towards L'Escarène, then on the Peille bridge D21 towards Peillon. On the left as you enter the village.

Hôtel Les Deux Frères **

Place des Deux-Frères
Roquebrune Village, 06100 Cap-Martin (Alpes-Maritimes)
Tel. 93.28.99.00 – Fax 93.28.99.10 – M. Inthout

Rooms 10 with telephone, bath or shower, WC and TV. **Price** Single 385F, double 495F. **Meals** Breakfast 45F. **Restaurant** Service 12:00-14:00, 19:30-22:00; à la carte. Specialties: Fish, duck, foie gras. **Credit cards** Amex, Visa, Eurocard and MasterCard. **Pets** Dogs allowed (+40F). **Nearby** Rue Moncolet in Roquebrune, La Turbie church, footpath to Cap Martin – 18-hole Monte-Carlo Golf Course in La Turbie. **Open** Dec 15 – Nov 15 (closed Thursday).

The two brothers of the hotel name are the two rocks that gave their name to the village of Roquebrune. The square named for them is on one of the best sites in the medieval village, protected by its Carolingian castle, and was chosen for the school built here in 1854. This was just in front of the *Café de la Grotte* and overlooked the bay of Monte Carlo. The school was eventually closed and for fifteen years it was abandoned until a Dutch architect decided to restore this house with its green shutters. He turned the classrooms into pretty white-walled bedrooms, and the courtyard into a restaurant. Around the great fireplace he installed comfortable leather covered sofas and created a place that most guests find it difficult to tear themselves away from in the evenings. The decor is delightful, there are always plenty of flowers, and you will receive a warm welcome.

How to get there *(Map 35): 5km south of Menton via A8 or N98.*

Auberge du Colombier ★★★

06330 Roquefort-les-Pins (Alpes-Maritimes)
Tel. 93.77.10.27 – Fax 93.77.07.03
M. Wolff

Rooms 18, 2 suites with telephone, bath, shower, WC and TV **Price** Single 200-350F, double 350-550F, suite 680F. **Meals** Breakfast 50F; half board +170F, full board +340F. **Restaurant** Closed Tuesday in low season. Service 12:00-14:30, 19:00-22:00; menus 155-190F, also à la carte. Specialties: Salade gourmande de caille tiède au foie gras, chariot de patisseries maison. **Credit cards** All major. **Pets** Dogs allowed (+40F). **Facilities** Swimming pool, tennis (+50F), parking. **Nearby** Nice, Grasse, gorges of Le Loup and Gourdon – 18-hole Opio golf course in Valbonne. **Open** All year except Jan 10 – Feb 10.

This old stagecoach stop on the route from Nice to Grasse (once a two-day journey) still makes a good overnight halt or a pleasant base from which to explore the many attractions of the French Riviera. The auberge was modernized in 1980 but preserves its old charm. Today it has a beautiful swimming pool, a tennis court and some more recently built bedrooms in which, however, some of the atmosphere has been lost. You will find a pleasant welcome here and a restaurant which is renowned for its cuisine and its *spécialités de la maison*.

How to get there (Map 34): 25km west of Nice via A8, exit Villeneuve-Loubet, then D2085 towards Grasse.

Bastide de Moustiers ★★★

04360 Moustiers-Sainte-Marie (Alpes-de-Haute-Provence)
Tel. 92.74.62.40 - Fax 92.74.62.41
M. Ducasse

Rooms 7 with air-conditioning, Tel., Fax, bath, shower, WC, TV, safe and minibar.
Price Double 450-850F. **Meals** Breakfast 65F. **Restaurant** Service 12:00-14:30,
19:30-22:00, menus 225-335F. **Credit cards** Amex, Eurocard and MasterCard.
Pets Dogs allowed. **Facilities** Heated swimming pool, parking. **Nearby** Church and
Pottery Museum in Moustiers, the Grand Canyon of the Gorges of the Verdon via the
road or GR4; Lake of Sainte-Croix. **Open** From April 15

Great names in French gastonomy are regularly mentioned in this
guide. Far from changing our criteria for selection, we have
included the great chefs who have opened a charming hotel or inn
along with their prestigious restaurant. This year, three-star chef A.
Ducasse has opened a Provençal auberge in Moustiers which reflects
the loveliest tradition of this region. It is a tradition of hospitality, and
you will be received as friends. The kitchen is open to you; you can
have dinner at the same table or enjoy a romantic *tête à tête* in one of
the dining rooms; and you can browse quietly through the books in
the library. You will also find tradition in the decor, with its elegant
and comfortable furnishings, antique Provençal furniture. There is
tradition, too, in the environment in this part of Provence, where
cypresses intermingle with poplars, oaks with olive trees, chestnut with
almond trees, and of course, there is the traditional country vegetable
garden. Simplicity, charm and the outstanding Ducasse quality are so
many reasons you will be enchanted with the Bastide de Moustiers.

How to get there *(Map 34): 50km from Manosque (A51), towards Gréoux-
les-Bains, Riez, Moustiers. From Nice (A8) Le Luc exit.*

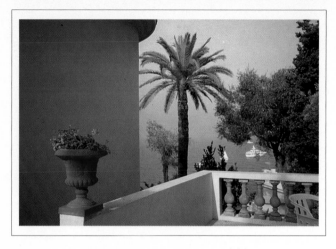

Hôtel Brise Marine ★★★

58, avenue Jean-Mermoz
06230 Saint-Jean-Cap-Ferrat (Alpes-Maritimes)
Tel. 93.76.04.36 - Fax 93.76.11.49 - M. Maîtrehenry

Rooms 16 with telephone, bath or shower, WC and TV. **Price** Double 625-680F.
Meals Breakfast 55F, served 8:00-10:00. No restaurant. **Credit cards** Visa, Eurocard
and MasterCard. **Pets** Dogs allowed. **Nearby** Saint-Pierre chapel (Cocteau) in
Villefranche, Villa Ephrussi-de-Rothschild in Saint-Jean-Cap-Ferrat, Villa Kerylos in
Beaulieu – 18-hole La Bastide-du-Roy golf course in Biot. **Open** Feb 1 – Oct 30.

Among the luxurious villas, grand hotels and noble residences
in Saint-Jean-Cap-Ferrat, this is a little Italian house built in
the 19th century. The Hôtel Brise Marine has a delightful garden
with flowers, palm trees, espaliers, stone balustrades, fountains and
terraces. The owner has personally looked after the hotel and its
sixteen elegant and comfortable little bedrooms for forty-five years.
All of them look out on the gardens of an inaccessible château and
the surrounding sea. You will enjoy a very friendly welcome here
as well as excellent breakfasts. *La Voile d'Or* and *Le Provençal* are
among the chic, expensive restaurants of Saint Jean. *Le Sloop* is a
simpler, reasonably priced fish restaurant.

How to get there *(Map 35): 15km east of Nice via N98.*

Hôtel Le Hameau★★★

528, route de La Colle
06570 Saint-Paul-de-Vence (Alpes-Maritimes)
Tel. 93.32.80.24 - Fax 93.32.55.75 - M. Huvelin

Rooms 12 and 3 apartments with air-conditioning (except one), telephone, bath or shower, WC and minibar (some with safe). **Price** Single 380F, double 420-580F, suite 670F. **Meals** Breakfast 48F, served 8:00-10:00. No restaurant. **Credit cards** Amex, Visa, Eurocard and MasterCard. **Pets** Dogs allowed. **Facilities** Swimming pool, garage (35F), parking. **Nearby** Chapel of Le Rosaire (Matisse), perfume museum, Maeght Foundation, church of Saint-Charles-Borromée in Saint-Paul-de-Vence, les Clues de Haute-Provence – 18-hole Opio golf course in Valbonne. **Open** All year except Jan 8 – Feb 15 and Nov 15 – Dec 22.

This white 1920s house looks over the valley and the village of Saint-Paul-de-Vence, and is up a path bordered by lemon trees in a flowering garden. The hotel is terraced and arcaded and almost hidden by honeysuckle, fig trees and climbing vines. The bedrooms are large and prettily decorated, and the furniture is traditional Provençal. Numbers 1, 2 and 3 have a loggia and an impressive view of Saint-Paul. The old iridescent green tiles of some of the bathrooms are superb. In the adjoining 18th-century farmhouse there are other smaller attic rooms but they all have a lovely view. The friendly welcome you will find here will explain why so many guests return. There is no restaurant but apart from a gastronomic pilgrimage to the famous *Colombe d'Or*, you can enjoy delicious Provençal cuisine at *La Brouette*.

How to get there *(Map 34): 20km west of Nice via A8, exit Cagnes-sur-Mer, then D7 towards Vence via La Colle-sur-Loup; it's 1km before Saint-Paul-de-Vence.*

Auberge des Seigneurs et du Lion d'Or **
Place du Frêne
06140 Vence (Alpes–Maritimes)
Tel. 93.58.04.24 - Fax 93.24.08.01 – M. and Mme Rodi

Rooms 10 with telephone, shower, WC and TV. **Price** Single 280F, double 314-344F.
Meals Breakfast 50F, served 7:30-10:30. **Restaurant** Service from 12:30 and 19:30;
menus 210-230F, also à la carte. Specialties: Carré d'agneau à la broche, tian vençois.
Credit cards All major. **Pets** Dogs allowed. **Nearby** Chapel of Le Rosaire (Matisse),
perfume museum, Carzou museum in Vence, Maeght Foundation, church of St-
Charles-Borromée in Saint-Paul-de-Vence, les Clues de Haute Provence – 18-hole
Opio golf course in Valbonne. **Open** All year except July 1 – 10 and Nov 15 – Dec 12.

This is a very lovely, almost timeless auberge. Some parts of it
date from the 14th-century and some from the 17th. In its
day it has welcomed many famous guests such as King Francis I
and, more recently, Renoir, Modigliani, Dufy and Soutine. M.
Rodi knows the exact dates of their visits and will enjoy telling
you about them. The hotel is situated in a wing of the Château
des Villeneuve de Vence, which is mostly occupied by the Carzou
Museum. It is on the square where the ash tree planted by Francis
I flourishes still. The reception rooms contain an eclectic collection
of objects (a 16th-century washstand, an olive oil press, modern
lithographs, etc.) all of which have a history. The bedrooms are
large, furnished plainly but appropriately for the building, and there
is always a basket of fruit and flowers awaiting every guest. The
most attractive rooms look out on the square, the quietest over the
rooftops. The whole Auberge is full of character and very
welcoming.

How to get there *(Map 34): 10km north of Cagnes-sur-Mer via D36.*

La Roseraie ★★

Avenue Henri-Giraud
06140 Vence (Alpes-Maritimes)
Tel. 93.58.02.20 – Fax 93.58.99.31 – M. and Mme Ganier

Rooms 12 with telephone, bath or shower, WC, TV and minibar. **Price** Double 380-480F. **Meals** Breakfast 45F, served 8:30-12:00. No restaurant. **Credit cards** Amex, Visa, Eurocard and MasterCard. **Pets** Dogs allowed. **Facilities** Swimming pool, parking. **Nearby** Chapelle du Rosaire (Matisse), fondation Maeght, Saint-Charles church, Borromée in Saint-Paul-de-Vence, les Clues de Haute-Provence – 18 hole Opio golf course in Valbonne. **Open** All year.

Dating from the turn of the century, the "Rose Garden" is a beautiful old Mediterranean-style residence in the heart of picturesque Vence. Graceful palm trees, magnolias, yucca, eucalyptus, banana trees, and lovely roses, combined with a spectacular view over Vence and Baou Hill, create a veritable oasis of beauty and charm here. There are only twelve bedrooms, all decorated in the loveliest Provençal style; although all have a beautiful view, the best is to be enjoyed from rooms 4, 5, 8, which have balconies, and from number 12, which has a terrace. The bathrooms are comfortable and prettily decorated with the famous Provençal tiles from nearby Salernes. The breakfasts are very special, with homemade croissants and traditional preserves. Monsieur and Madame Ganier make every effort to please you. *La Farigoule*, a small restaurant near the hotel, offers good Provençal cuisine, and the *Auberge de Seigneurs* serves an outstanding rack of lamb grilled in the fireplace.

How to get there *(Map 34): 10km north of Cagnes-sur-Mer via D36.*

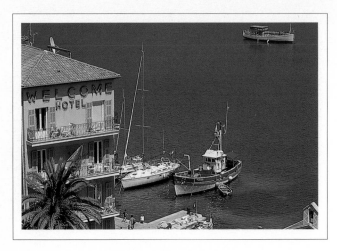

Hôtel Welcome ★★★
1, quai Courbet
06230 Villefranche-sur-Mer (Alpes-Maritimes)
Tel. 93.76.76.93 - Fax 93.01.88.81 - M. and Mme Galbois

Rooms 32 with air-conditioning, telephone, bath or shower, WC and TV; 30 with minibar. **Price** Single and double 350-820F. **Meals** Breakfast 45F, served 7:00-10:30; half board 390-820F (per pers.). **Restaurant** Open June 15 – Sept 30, service 19:30-24:00. Open Oct 1 – June 14, service 12:30-14:00, 19:30-22:30; menus 150-230F, also à la carte. Specialties: Raviolis de homard cuisiné dans son jus, tatin de rouget vinaigrette d'olives, blanc de saint-Pierre rôti à l'aïl, pêche caramélisée aux 4 épices. **Credit cards** All major. **Pets** Dogs allowed (+25F). **Nearby** The Lower Corniche, St-Jean-Cap-Ferrat (Villa Ephrussi de Rothschild), Beaulieu (Villa Kerylos) – 18-hole Opio golf course in Valbonne. **Open** Dec 19 – Nov 20.

On the quayside of the old port of Villefranche you will find colorful fishing boats, a chapel decorated by Jean Cocteau and a hotel in the pedestrian area which is built on the site of a 17th-century monastery. The hotel is modern with many balconies and large, comfortable, sunny rooms, all of them air-conditioned. The balconies have *chaise longues* and small tables on which you can enjoy your breakfast. On the top story the rooms are in a nautical style with copper fittings and exotic woodwork. They are smaller than the other rooms but very lovely and warm.

How to get there *(Map 35): 6km from Nice via N559.*

Villa Gallici ★★★★

Avenue de la Violette
13100 Aix-en-Provence (Bouches-du-Rhône)
Tel. 42.23.29.23 - Fax 42.96.30.45 - M. Gil Dez

Rooms 17 with air-conditioning, telephone, bath, WC, cable TV, safe and minibar. **Price** Single and double 850-1750F, suite 1750-1950F. **Meals** Breakfast 110F. **Restaurant** "Le Clos de la Violette", menus 300F. Specialties: Filets de rouget aux croutons, râble de lapereau en pébrade, mille-feuille de chocolat blanc aux framboises. **Credit cards** All major. **Pets** Dogs allowed. **Facilities** Swimming pool, parking. **Nearby** Place d'Albertas, Hôtel de Ville, Saint-Sauveur Cathedral (burning bush triptych by N. Froment) in Aix-en-Provence, Roquefavour aqueduct – 18-hole Club des Milles golf course, 18-hole Fuveau Golf Course. **Open** All year.

In the Villa Gallici, Gil Dez found a bastide in which to exercise his talents as an interior decorator and create an elegant *hôtel de charme*. The villa has been decorated with exquisite style, and designed like a home rather than a hotel. The bedrooms are spacious, comfortable and individually decorated. *Toile de Jouy* and gingham have been used in one, while another boasts a flowery cotton canopied bed along with boldly striped fabrics. In each room styles, colors and materials have been subtly and successfully combined. In the immaculate bathrooms earthenware tiles, Carrara marble and glossy white wood panelling create an elegant decor. Breakfast beneath the planetrees is a delight. The cuisine at *Le Clos de la Violette*, the restaurant next door, is probably the best in Aix. This is a truly charming place.

How to get there (Map 33): *near the Archbishop's Palace.*

Hôtel des Quatre-Dauphins **
54, rue Roux-Alphéran
13100 Aix-en-Provence (Bouches-du-Rhône)
Tel. 42.38.16.39 - Fax 42.38.60.19- MM. Darricau and Juster

Rooms 12 with telephone, bath or shower, WC, TV and minibar. **Price** Single 280-320F, double 320-380F, suite 480F (3 pers.). **Meals** Breakfast 38F, served 7:00-10:00. No restaurant. **Credit cards** Visa, Eurocard and MasterCard. **Pets** Dogs allowed. **Nearby** Place d'Albertas, Hôtel de Ville, Saint-Sauveur Cathedral (burning bush triptych by N. Froment) in Aix-en-Provence, Roquefavour aqueduct – 18-hole Club des Milles golf course, 18-hole Fuveau golf course. **Open** All year.

This three-story family house in a quiet side street near the famous Place des Quatre Dauphins in Aix has recently been converted into a hotel. On the ground floor there is a small reception area and a lounge which also serves as a breakfast room. The bedrooms are on the upper floors. The decor is in the Provençal style, with pretty fabrics which go well with the painted wooden furniture. The rooms are not very large and the furnishings are simple but they are functional. The bathrooms are well equipped. Everything is in good taste in this charming small hotel. For restaurants, try *Maxime, Côté Cour* on the cours Mirabeau, *Le Bistro Latin*, or *Chez Gu*, and don't forget to take a drink *Aux Deux Garçons*.

How to get there *(Map 33): In the center of the town.*

Hôtel d'Arlatan ★★★

26, rue du Sauvage
13200 Arles (Bouches-du-Rhône)
Tel. 90.93.56.66 - Fax 90.49.68.45 - M. Desjardin

Rooms 41 with air-conditioning, telephone, bath, WC, TV and minibar. **Price** Double 455-695F, suite 795-1350F. **Meals** Breakfast 58F, served 7:00-11:00. No restaurant. **Credit cards** All major. **Pets** Dogs allowed. **Facilities** Parking (+55F). **Nearby** Saint Trophime church, les Aliscamps, Réattu museum in Arles, abbey of Montmajour, the Camargue – 18-hole Servanes golf course in Mouriès. **Open** All year.

This hotel, like Arles itself, is almost a museum of the past and contains traces of many different eras. It was built on the site of the basilica and baths of Constantine and is a patchwork of architectural styles. This is a very unusual hotel, owned for three generations by the same family, who refurbish and restore the bedrooms constantly. It would take a whole book to describe the bedrooms. In suite 43 there are fragments of a 4th-century wall and 17th-century wooden beams. In suite 41 there is a monumental 17th-century fireplace. We recommend that you ask for the recently refurbished bedrooms, among them rooms 23 and 27 which have a view of the Rhône; or number 34, one of the least expensive which has beautiful stone walls. Whichever you choose you will love this charming hotel hidden away in a little street facing the gardens. The most popular restaurants in Arles are *L'Olivier* and *Le Vaccarès*. For a very fashionable spot, try the restaurant or bar of the famous Hôtel Nord-Pinus or *Le Café de la Nuit*.

How to get there *(Map 33): In the center of the town, signposted.*

429

Grand Hôtel Nord-Pinus ★★★★

Place du Forum
13200 Arles (Bouches-du-Rhône)
Tel. 90.93.44.44 - Fax 90.93.34.00 - Mme Igou

Rooms 23 with telephone, bath, WC, TV and minibar. **Price** Single 650F, double 750-890F, suite 1500F. **Meals** Breakfast 60F, served 7:00-11:00. **Restaurant** Service 12:00-14:00, 19:30-22:00; menus 120-180F, also à la carte. Specialties: Provençal cooking. **Credit cards** All major. **Pets** Dogs allowed. **Nearby** Saint-Trophime church, les Aliscamps, Réattu Museum in Arles, abbey of Montmajour, the Camargue – 18-hole Servanes golf course in Mouriès. **Open** March 1 – Dec 31.

Like Giono, you might wonder; "Why Pinus? Nord, I understand, but Pinus? It was simply the name of the founder. Nothing is more logical. I now realize that I have entered the land of the imagination and fantasy." Picasso, Cocteau, Dominguez are just some of the famous names in the visitors' book. The hotel was run for some time by Germaine, a chanteuse, and Nello, a famous clown, both of whom were well known characters in Arles. When they died the hotel lost its soul. It has returned under the care of Anne Igou, whose love for the place has brought back the magic and atmosphere with a skillful restoration which combines sensitivity and good taste. The bedrooms are large, with pretty furniture and Provençal fabrics, and the bathrooms have every facility. It is worth remembering to ask for suite 10 or the bedrooms looking onto the courtyard. These are recommended for people who are concerned about the noise on the Place du Forum in summer. This is truly a charming hotel.

How to get there *(Map 33): In the town center.*

Hôtel Castel–Mouisson ★★

Quartier Castel Mouisson
13570 Barbentane (Bouches-du-Rhône)
Tel. 90.95.51.17 – Fax 90.95.67.63 – Mme Mourgue

Rooms 17 with telephone, bath and WC. **Price** Double 270-310F, suite 390F.
Meals Breakfast 32F, served 8:00-10:30. No restaurant. **Credit cards** Not
accepted. **Pets** Dogs not allowed. **Facilities** Swimming pool, tennis, parking.
Nearby Barbentane, Avignon, Villeneuve-lès-Avignon, abbey of Saint-Michel-de-
Frigolet – 18-hole Châteaublanc golf course, 18-hole Vedène golf course in Grand
Avignon, 4-hole Lou Compact golf course in Barbentane. **Open** March 15 – Oct 15.

This peaceful and reasonably priced hotel is at the foot of the
Montagnette Mountain not far from Avignon. It was built
twenty years ago in the style of a Provençal farmhouse and is
surrounded by tranquil countryside. There are cypresses and fruit
trees growing beneath the grey cliffs of the Montagnette, which
overlooks the valley. The bedrooms are simple but reasonably
comfortable. In hot weather you will enjoy cooling off in the pretty
swimming pool. In Avignon, there are numerous good small
restaurants such as *La Fourchette, Le Bain Marie* and *Simple Simon*,
as well as the *Les Félibres* tea room and bookshop. For a charming
dinner try the restaurant in the Mirande or the Europe Hotels.

How to get there *(Map 33): 8km southwest of Avignon via N570, then
D35 towards Tarascon along the Rhône.*

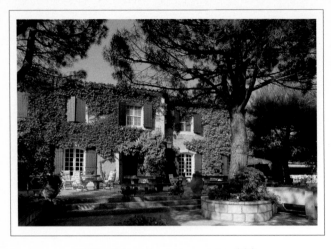

Hôtel Le Benvengudo ★★★

13520 Les Baux-de-Provence (Bouches-du-Rhône)
Tel. 90.54.32.54 – Fax 90.54.42.58
Beaupied Family

Rooms 20 with telephone, bath, WC and TV. **Price** Double 520-680F, suite 780-900F. **Meals** Breakfast 58F, served 8:15-10:15; half board 1060-1230F (per 2 pers., 3 days min.). **Restaurant** Closed Sunday. Service 19:30-21:00; menu 225F. Specialties: Soupe de poissons de roche, loup grillé sauce béarnaise, carré d'agneau à la crème de romarin. **Credit cards** Amex, Visa, Eurocard and MasterCard. **Pets** Dogs allowed (+50F). **Facilities** Swimming pool, tennis, parking. **Nearby** Contemporary art museum at the Hôtel des Porcelets in Les Baux, Queen Jeanne's pavilion, Alphonse Daudet's windmill in Fontvieille, the Val d'enfer – 9-hole golf course in Les Baux, 18-hole Servanes golf course in Mouriès. **Open** Feb 5 – Nov 15.

The Benvengudo hides at the foot of a small range of mountains. The hotel was built twenty-one years ago but has the air of always having been there. The bedrooms, some of which are air-conditioned, are very comfortable; each one has individual style and some have small private terraces. There is a rustic touch to the lounge and dining room. In summer you can dine outdoors by the swimming pool under the olive trees. The jagged outline of the Alpilles recalls some of the highest mountain ranges in the world, and their white rocks and dry vegetation give this part of Provence a look of Greece.

How to get there *(Map 33): 30km south of Avignon via A7, Cavaillon exit, then D99 to Saint-Rémy and D5.*

Le Mas d'Aigret ★★★

13520 Les Baux-de-Provence (Bouches-du-Rhône)
Tel. 90.54.33.54 – Fax 90.54.41.37
M. and Mme Phillips

Rooms 16 with telephone, bath, WC, cable TV and minibar. **Price** Double 450-850F.
Meals Breakfast 70F, served 8:00-11:00; half board 495-785F (per pers.).
Restaurant Closed Wednesday lunchtime. Service 12:15-13:30, 19:15-21:00; menus
90F (wine and coffee incl. for lunchtime only)-190-280F, menu-carte 350F.
Specialties: Foie gras de canard aux mendiants, filets de rouget grondin au pistou,
tarte au chocolat. **Credit cards** All major. **Pets** Dogs allowed (+40F).
Facilities Swimming pool, parking. **Nearby** Contemporary art museum at the Hôtel
des Porcelets in Les Baux, Queen Jeanne's pavilion, the Val d'enfer, Alphonse
Daudet's windmill in Fontvieille – 9-hole golf course in Les Baux, 18-hole Servanes
golf course in Mouriès. **Open** Feb 25 – Jan 5.

This old farm, built in 1730 and recently restored, stands in an
old cave dwelling. All the bedrooms have their own terrace
and TV with three satellite channels. Room 16 and Apartment 15,
are the most attractive. There is a vaulted lounge and library with
large tables. The dining room with its stone walls is built into the
rock and so are the lounge bar and music room. The furniture is
a pleasant blend of old and new with Provençal fabrics. The
restaurant serves excellent cuisine at very affordable prices. The
hotel also offers golfers a special package rate. The Mas d'Aigret is
truly a charming place to stay.

How to get there *(Map 33): 30km south of Avignon via A7, Cavaillon
exit, then D99 to Saint-Rémy and D5.*

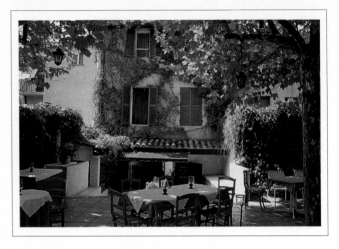

Le Clos des Arômes **

10, rue Paul-Mouton – Rue Agostini
13260 Cassis (Bouches-du-Rhône)
Tel. 42.01.71.84 – Fax 42.01.31.76 – Mme Grinda

Rooms 8 with telephone, bath or shower and WC. **Price** Double 295-570F.
Meals Breakfast 45F, served 8:00-12:00. **Restaurant** Service 12:00-14:00, 19:30-
22:30; menus 95-140F, also à la carte. Specialties: Provençal cooking.
Credit cards Amex, Visa, Euracard and MasterCard. **Pets** Dogs allowed (+35F).
Facilities Garage (+50F). **Nearby** The Calanques: Port-Miou, Port-Pin and Envau –
18-hole La Salette Golf Course in Marseille-La Valentine. **Open** May 1 – Oct 3.

Though located in a little street in the village, this doll house
of a hotel is surrounded by a garden that is a riot of blue and
white with lavender, peonies, arum lilies and marguerites. In
beautiful weather this makes a fragrant setting for breakfast and for
dinners of light and delicious Provençal dishes. Indoors the
ambience is just as delightful, with lavender painted furniture,
flowered tablecloths and a large fireplace. The bedrooms, with blue
and yellow Provençal fabrics, all look out on the garden. The hotel
is very quiet though in the middle of the village and only a few
meters from the old port. You will enjoy the warm and friendly
hospitality of Mme Grinda, the owner.

How to get there *(Map 33): 23km east of Marseille via A50 towards Toulon,
Cassis exit.*

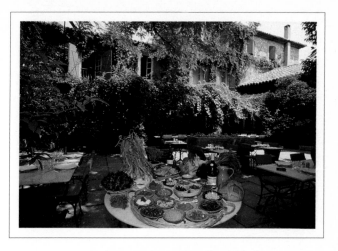

Auberge Provençale ★★★

Place de la Mairie
13810 Eygalières (Bouches–du–Rhône)
Tel. 90.95.91.00 – M. Pézevil

Rooms 7 with telephone, bath or shower, WC and TV. **Price** Double 250-485F. **Meals** Breakfast 40F, served 8:30-10:30; half board 330-450F (per pers., 2 days min.). **Restaurant** Service 12:00-13:30, 19:30-21:30; menus 125-185F, also à la carte. Specialties: Plateau de hors d'œuvre, marmite du pêcheur au safran, pavé de morue fraîche à la purée truffée. **Credit cards** Visa, Eurocard and MasterCard. **Pets** Dogs allowed (+30F). **Facilities** Parking. **Nearby** Les Baux, Saint-Rémy-de-Provence, Fontvieille – 18-hole Servanes golf course in Mouriès. **Open** All year (closed Wednesday).

The auberge is in the center of a beautifully preserved village of the Alpilles. Formerly a restaurant in an 18th-century postal relay station, it has recently become a small five-room hotel. The most comfortable bedrooms (our favorites are numbers 1, 3, 4 and 5) look out over a tree shaded courtyard. The other two are smaller and overlook the Place de la Mairie. A bistro area also serves as a lounge for hotel guests. The young owner is the chef. Meals are served on the terrace in beautiful weather or in the restaurant, which has a handsome fireplace. The excellent cuisine is copious and mouthwatering, with specialties from various regions. There is grilled fish, magret of duck and *turbot à la crème*, and of course the famous platter of *hors d'oeuvres*. You will receive a very cordial welcome.

How to get there *(Map 33): 13km southeast of Cavaillon via A7, Cavaillon exit, then D99 and D74a.*

435

Mas dou Pastré

Quartier Saint-Sixte
13810 Eygalières (Bouches-du-Rhône)
Tel. 90.95.92.61 - Fax 90.90.61.75 - M. and Mme Roumanille

Rooms 8 with telephone, bath or shower, WC, TV and 3 with minibar. **Price** Double 300-500F. **Meals** Breakfast 45F, served 8:00-10:30. No restaurant. **Credit cards** All major. **Pets** Dogs not allowed. **Facilities** Swimming pool, parking. **Nearby** Les Baux, Saint-Rémy-de-Provence, Fontvieille – 18-hole Servanes golf course in Mouriès. **Open** All year.

Madame Roumanille, who has just renovated this old farmhouse as she would have her own home, is a friendly and hospitable hostess. Throughout the house, the ceilings and walls are decked out in the colors of Provence, and there is a wealth of antique furniture, paintings, engravings, prints, bunches of dried flowers and local curios... enough to make you feel at home, and even better. The evocatively named bedrooms are all different: their decor owes much to carefully chosen features, and to the owners' boundless imagination in adding a touch of exuberance and humor. You can also sleep in an authentic, elaborately carved wooden trailer, which is very old but equipped with air-conditioning and every modern comfort. Breakfast is delicious (there are always fresh fruit juices) whether you have it outside or in the charming dining room. This is an excellent and very Provençal hotel. *L'Auberge Provençale* is the famous restaurant in Eygalières, and the fashionable spot is *Sous les Micocouliers*.

How to get there *(Map 33): 13km southeast of Cavaillon via A7, Cavaillon exit, then D99 and D74a.*

Le Relais de la Magdelaine ★★★★

Route d'Aix-en-Provence
13420 Gémenos (Bouches-du-Rhône)
Tel. 42.32.20.16 – Fax 42.32.02.26 – M. and Mme Marignane

Rooms 24 with telephone, bath or shower, WC and TV. **Price** Single 395-520F, double 545-750F, suite 1100F. **Meals** Breakfast 69F, served from 7:15; half board 565-850F, full board 785-1050F (per pers., 3 days min.). **Restaurant** Service 12:00-14:00, 20:00-21:30; menu 240F, also à la carte. Specialties: Galettes de grenouilles à la provençale, pavé de canard au miel de lavande, griottes au chocolat sauce pistache. **Credit cards** Visa, Eurocard andMasterCard. **Pets** Dogs allowed (+30F) but not in the swimming pool. **Facilities** Swimming pool, parking. **Nearby** Marseille, Aix-en-Provence, Cassis and the Calanques – 18-hole La Salette golf course in Marseille-La Valentine. **Open** March 15 – Nov 30.

To find this beautiful 18th-century country house covered in ivy and roses, you leave the highway, drive along an avenue of century-old plane trees and cross a formal garden designed by Le Nôtre. Here you will find M. and Mme Marignane, who have been welcoming an international clientele for thirty years. Their dedication and good taste in creating a very special holiday hotel is evident in the bedrooms. These have lovely old furniture and are superb; those that look out on the terrace are the largest. Their son is the chef and turns out refined Provençal food. The garden and swimming pool are very pleasant and you will be delighted by the cordial welcome.

How to get there *(Map 33): 23km from Marseille via A50 towards Toulon, Aubagne-Est or Aubagne-Sud exit, then D2 to Gémenos.*

New Hôtel Bompard ★★★

2, rue des Flots-Bleus
13007 Marseille (Bouches-du-Rhône)
Tel. 91.52.10.93 - Fax 91.31.02.14 - M. Antoun

Rooms 46 with air-conditioning, telephone, bath, WC, TV and minibar. **Price** Single and double 350F. **Meals** Breakfast 42F, served 7:00-11:00. No restaurant. **Credit cards** All major. **Pets** Dogs allowed. **Facilities** Swimming pool, solarium, parking. **Nearby** Vieille Charité, Art museum, Cantini museum, M.A.C. in Marseille, Cassis and the Calanques: Port-Miou, Port Pin and Envau, Aix-en-Provence – 18-hole La Salette golf course in Marseille-La Valentine. **Open** All year.

The Hotel Bompard, which is located on the Corniche which runs around the Bay of Marseille, has the unusual advantage of having a large garden though it is in the city. The bedrooms, most of which have a large balcony which looks out over the acacias and palm trees in the grounds, are charming. The best rooms are those in the main building which are tastefully furnished, combining elegance, practicality and comfort. For longer stays, or if you are a family, there are bungalows, some with kitchenettes. The tranquillity and the cordial welcome at the Hotel Bompard make it a good place to stay, but as it is ten minutes from the center of the city you will need a car or taxi to get to and fro. You can rent a car at the hotel. For the best *bouillabaisse* in town, try *Chez Michel, Le Chaudron Provençal, Chez Foulon* or, more reasonably priced, *Chez Etienne*. For a beautiful view, there are also *La Nautique* and *Chez Péron*.

How to get there *(Map 33): On the J F Kennedy Corniche, follow signs from Le Ruhl restaurant.*

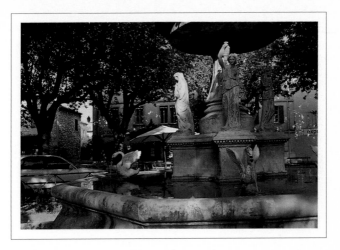

L'Oustaloun **

Place de l'église
13520 Maussane-les-Alpilles (Bouches-du-Rhône)
Tel. 90.54.32.19 - Fax 90.54.45.57 - M. Fabrégoul

Rooms 10 with telephone, bath or shower, WC and 8 with TV. **Price** Double 260-390F. **Meals** Breakfast 34F, served 7:30-9:30. **Restaurant** Service 12:15-13:45, 19:15-21:30; menu, also à la carte. Specialties: Provençales and italian cooking. **Credit cards** Amex, Visa, Eurocard and MasterCard. **Pets** Dogs allowed. **Facilities** Garage (20F). **Nearby** Avignon, Arles, St-Rémy-de-Provence, Les Baux and le Val d'enfer, Alphonse Daudet's windmill in Fontvieille – 9-hole golf course in les Baux, 18-hole Servanes golf course in Mouriès. **Open** All year except Jan 8 – Feb 6.

In 1792, this was the first town hall of the village, then the gendarmerie (and the prison). Today, L'Oustaloun is a typical small Provençal auberge looking out on - what else? - a square shaded with towering plane trees and a tinkling fountain. The bedrooms are lovely and comfortable; all are decorated with Provençal fabrics and antique furniture. Although the carpets and some bathrooms are somewhat old-fashioned, that will soon change because the hotel has just been bought by new owners and much renovation has been planned. With the first beautiful weather, the Oustaloun spills out to the center of the square, where a bar-terrace is set up, shaded by large parasols. This is a charming spot just several minutes out of spectacular (and gastronomic) Les Baux. The prices are reasonable and you will be welcomed with a very warm Provençal smile.

How to get there *(See Map 33): 40km south of Avignon via A7, exit Cavaillon, then D99 to Saint-Rémy and D5.*

Le Berger des Abeilles ★★
13670 Saint-Andiol (Bouches-du-Rhône)
Tel. 90.95.01.91 – Fax 90.95.48.26
Mme Grenier

Rooms 6 with telephone, bath or shower, WC and TV. **Price** 300-350F.
Meals Breakfast 50F, served 8:00-10:00; half board 450F (per 1 pers.), 680F (per 2
pers., 3 days min.). **Restaurant** Closed Sunday evening and Monday except for
residents. Service 12:30-14:00, 20:00-21:30; menus 120-270F, also à la carte.
Specialties: Provençale cooking, mousse au miel de lavande, vieux marc de Provence.
Credit cards Amex, Visa, Eurocard and MasterCard. **Pets** Dogs allowed (35F).
Facilities Parking. **Nearby** Les Baux, Saint-Rémy-de-Provence, Avignon. **Open** March
4 – Dec 31.

L e Berger des Abeilles is as welcoming as a hotel could possibly
be. There are only six bedrooms and the owners thus provide
a personal style of service. All the rooms are perfectly comfortable,
but you should choose our favorites if they're available, *Alexia* or
Caroline. (The rooms are named after the women in the family.)
A few items of period furniture set the trend for the cheerful,
intimate decor. Mme Grenier does the cooking herself and her
cuisine has an excellent reputation. Dinner is served in a beautiful,
rustic dining-room or outside in the shade of a gigantic planetree.
The noise of traffic on the main road, muffled by luxuriant
vegetation, can hardly be heard in the hotel garden, and not at all
indoors (thanks to the thick walls). This is a lovely place to stay.

How to get there *(Map 33): 13km south of Avignon via N7 (2km from
north of Saint-Andiol). On A7, Avignon-Sud exit, 5km south.*

Hostellerie de Cacharel ★★★

Route de Cacharel
13460 Les Saintes-Maries-de-la-Mer (Bouches-du-Rhône)
Tel. 90.97.95.44 – Faxs 90.97.87.97 – M. Colomb de Daunant

Rooms 11 with telephone, bath or shower and WC. **Price** Single and double 500F. **Meals** Breakfast 45F, served 8:00-10:30. **Restaurant** Snacks available: 75F "assiette campagnarde". **Credit cards** Amex, Visa, Eurocard and MasterCard. **Pets** Dogs allowed. **Facilities** Swimming pool, horse trekking, parking. **Nearby** Church of Saintes-Maries-de-la-Mer, gypsy pilgrimage (May 24 and 25), sea wall (30km), Arles – 18-hole Servanes golf course in Mouriès. **Open** All year.

The Hostellerie is an old farmhouse on the borders of the Camargue, a land of nature reserves, placid lakes and white horses. The ground-floor bedrooms are furnished charmingly and look out either on a flower-filled inner courtyard or on the lakes and salt marshes. As the hotel is part of the farm, guests can walk or ride on the property. There is no restaurant but snacks can be served. You will receive a good welcome at this tranquil and genuine Camargue house in what is a popular tourist region.

How to get there *(Map 33): 38km southwest of Arles. 4km north of Saintes-Maries-de-la-Mer by D85a, called the Route de Cacharel.*

Mas du Clarousset ★★★

Route de Cacharel
13460 Les Saintes-Maries-de-la-Mer (Bouches-du-Rhône)
Tel. 90.97.81.66 - Fax 90.97.88.59 - Mme Eyssette

Rooms 10 with telephone, bath, WC, TV and minibar. **Price** Single 730F, double 750F. **Meals** Breakfast 50F, served 7:00-11:00; half board 675-1050F, full board 925-1300F (per pers., -10% from 3 days). **Restaurant** Closed Sunday evening and Monday. Service 12:00-14:00, 20:00-22:00; menus 250-350F, also à la carte. Specialties: Sufrigi aux croûtons, terrine de canard sauvage, loup en croûte, terrines à la provençale, Aïgue Saoü. **Credit cards** All major. **Pets** Dogs allowed (+50F). **Facilities** Swimming pool, gypsy evenings (on request), parking. **Nearby** Church of Saintes-Maries-de-la-Mer, gypsy pilgrimage (May 24 and 25), sea wall (30km), Arles – 18-hole La Grande Motte golf course. **Open** All year.

The very pleasant Mas du Clarousset is an ideal place to absorb the spirit of Provence. Here, Henriette gives a special welcome to lovers of the Camargue and likes to introduce them to the local way of life with gypsy evenings, walks on little-known beaches and a midnight Christmas mass to which everyone rides on horseback. She can also reserve a horse or a boat for you. The pretty and comfortable bedrooms all have private terraces and views over the Carmargue. Each room has a separate private entrance and there is room for your car in front of the door. After a day's excursion in the area you can relax and cool off in the swimming pool in the garden. Afterwards, you can enjoy the very good restaurant at the Mas, where Henriette offers traditional cuisine, rich in regional specialties.

How to get there *(Map 33): 38km southwest of Arles, then D85a (7km from Saintes-Maries).*

Lou Mas doù Juge ***
Quartier Pin Tourcat
13460 Saintes-Maries-de-la-Mer (Bouches-du-Rhône)
Tel. 66.73.51.45 – Fax 66.73.51.42 – M. and Mme Granier

Rooms 7 with bath or shower, WC and 4 with TV. **Price** Single with half board 750F
(1 pers.), 1100F (2 pers.). **Restaurant** Table d'hôtes on reservation. Service 12:00-
13:00, 20:00-21:00; menus 350F. Specialties: Anchoïades, terrine maison, salade
frisée à l'aïl avec fromage frais de brebis, sandre et turbot grillés, gardianne pâtes
fraîches. **Credit cards** Not accepted. **Pets** Dogs not allowed. **Facilities** Parking.
Nearby Church of Saintes-Maries-de-la-Mer, gypsy pilgrimage May 24 and 25, sea
wall (30km), Arles – 18-hole Servanes golf course in Mouriès. **Open** All year.

As you drive through the Camargue you will see a giant bottle
at the side of the road; this tells you that you are on the right
road and that the farm hotel Lou Mas doù Juge is not far off. It is
known for its true Camargue spirit, its cuisine and the parties put
on by your convivial host. The large farm has several bedrooms,
all of them pleasant, spacious and prettily furnished with old
furniture. Each one has a large bathroom and a good view of the
Camargue countryside. There is what some might consider a slight
snag, namely that the Mas is very much sought after for receptions.
However, the proprietors are very good at creating a friendly
atmosphere among all the guests.

How to get there *(Map 33): 38km southwest of Arles, then D85, the route
du Bac du Sauvage.*

Château des Alpilles ★★★★

Ancienne route des Baux
13210 Saint-Rémy-de-Provence (Bouches-du-Rhône)
Tel. 90.92.03.33 – Fax 90.92.45.17 – Mmes Bon

Rooms 19 with telephone, bath, WC, TV and minibar (some air-conditioned). **Price** Single 810-860F, double 860-1030F, suite 1290-2000F. **Restaurant** Snacks available on reservation, also à la carte 180-220F. **Meals** Breakfast 70F, served 7:30-12:00; . **Credit cards** All major. **Pets** Dogs allowed (+40F). **Facilities** Swimming pool, tennis, sauna, parking. **Nearby** Frédéric Mistral museum in Maillane, Eygalières, Les Baux, Avignon, Arles – 9-hole golf course in Les Baux, 18-hole Servanes golf course in Mouriès. **Open** All year except Nov 13 – Dec 19 and Jan 9 – March 24.

The château was built at the beginning of the 19th-century by one of the oldest families of Arles and became the meeting place of politicians and writers staying in the region. It still has the feeling of a holiday château. The lounge, the bar and the dining room, richly decorated with plasterwork and mirrors, are all very pleasant rooms and open out onto the garden. The comfortable bedrooms have period furniture, and large bathrooms. The large park, in which there is a swimming pool and tennis court, is planted with hundred-year-old trees and rare plant species. The Château des Alpilles is very well adapted to the chic clientele who are coming more frequently to the villge.

How to get there (Map 33): 14km west of Cavaillon via A7, exit Cavaillon, then D99; 1km from Saint-Rémy-de-Provence.

Château de Roussan

13210 Saint-Rémy-de-Provence (Bouches-du-Rhône)
Tel. 90.92.11.63 - Fax 90.92.37.32

Rooms 21 with telephone, bath or shower and 18 with WC - Handicap access. **Price** Double 360-750F. **Meals** Breakfast 50-60F in room, served 7:30-10:00; half board 365-610F (per pers., 3 days min.). **Restaurant** Closed Wednesday, Thursday noon. Service 12:00-13:30, 19:30-21:00; menu 135F, also à la carte. Specialties: Magret de canard aux olives, cuisses de grenouilles à la provençale. **Credit cards** Amex, Visa, Eurocard and MasterCard. **Pets** Dogs allowed. **Facilities** Parking. **Nearby** Museum Frédéric-Mistral in Maillane, Eygalières, les Baux, Avignon, Arles – 9-hole golf course in Baux, 18-hole Servanes golf course in Mouriès. **Open** All year.

An avenue of superb, century-old plane trees leads up to this fanciful and splendid house which was built at the beginning of the 18th-century by the Marquis of Ganges. A hotel since 1951, the château has nevertheless retained all its original character. The salons, the dining room, the library and many bedrooms are still furnished with beautiful antiques; and the floors still have their beautiful old parquet and terra-cotta floors. If you like modern accommodations, ask for the bedrooms located behind the library, or the rooms named *Laurier-Rose, Lilas* or *Lavande*. History buffs should ask for the rooms named *Alix, Mistral* or *Marquise*. The château is surrounded by a 15-acre park, an orange grove, a basin and a lake on which there is a small island. It is said that the elegant Marquis used to give sumptuous suppers here.

How to get there *(Map 33): 14km west of Cavaillon via A7, exit Cavaillon, then D99; 2km from Saint-Rémy, take road to Tarascon.*

Le Mas des Carassins ★★★

1, chemin Gaulois
13210 Saint-Rémy-de-Provence (Bouches-du-Rhône)
Tel. 90.92.15.48 - M. and Mme Ripert

Rooms 10 with telephone, bath and WC - Handicap access. **Price** Single 350-450F, double 380-520F. **Meals** Breakfast 48F, served 8:00-9:30. No restaurant. **Credit cards** Visa, Eurocard and MasterCard. **Pets** Dogs not allowed. **Facilities** Parking. **Nearby** Frédéric Mistral museum in Maillane, Eygalières, Les Baux, Avignon, Arles – 9-hole golf course in Les Baux, 18-hole Servanes golf course in Mouriès. **Open** March 15 – Nov 15.

This 19th-century farm is now a small family hotel. It is located a little outside the center of Saint Rémy-de-Provence in what has become the residential quarter. In its pretty garden, however, you can imagine yourself in the middle of the country. The bedrooms are all different. In *Magnaneraie,* for example, there is a rustic ambience with stone walls, while the *Jassé* room is the only one with a terrace. There is a pretty dining room and a small, pleasant lounge with cane furniture. There is no restaurant, but if you are staying in the hotel the helpful Mme Ripert will prepare a snack for you. The restaurants we recommend are: *Bistrot des Alpilles, Café des Arts, Jardin de Frédéric* in the village or *L'Oustalet* in Maillane.

How to get there *(Map 33): 14km west of Cavaillon via A7, Cavaillon exit, then D99.*

Le Mas de Peint

Le Sambuc
13200 Arles (Bouches-du-Rhône)
Tel. 90.97.20.62 – Fax 90.97.22.20 – M. Bon

Rooms 8 and 2 suites with telephone, bath, WC and minibar. **Price** Double 950-1500F, suite 1700-2300F. **Meals** Breakfast 75F, served 8:00-10:00; half board 695-995F,full board 825-1125F (per pers., 3 days min., on request per suites). **Restaurant** Service 12:00-14:30, 20:00-22:00; menus 165F (lunch), 210F (dinner). Specialties: Produits de la ferme, taureau de notre élevage, riz du marais. **Credit cards** All major. **Pets** Dogs allowed (+75F). **Facilities** Swimming pool, parking. **Nearby** Saintes-Maries-de-la-Mer (gypsy pilgrimage, May 24 and 25), sea wall (30km), Arles (féria for easter) – 18-hole La Grande Motte golf course. **Open** March 20 – early Jan.

The Mas de Peint is a formidable compromise between the friendliness of a Camargue guest house and the modern accommodations of a luxurious hotel of character and charm. The owner of a famous herd of horses and bulls, Jacques Bon is always proud to discuss (and show) his 1235 acres devoted to growing rice and breeding horses and bulls. Madame Bon has contributed her art as a talented architect and interior decorator to the Mas de Peint, which feels like a house for entertaining friends. There is a large table with a bouquet of fresh flowers in the entrance, and a comfortable sofa surrounded by bookshelves. You will find a small reading room and a larger room with a fireplace. In the kitchen, guests gather for an informal meal offering regional specialties. The bedrooms are extraordinarily large, some have bathrooms located on a mezzanine and every room has its personal charm.

How to get there *(Map 33): 20km south of Arles via D36, direction Salin de Giraud; at the exit from Sambuc, 3km to the left.*

Hôtel Le Chrystalin ★★★
83600 Les Adrets-de-l'Estérel (Var)
Tel. 94.40.97.56 – Fax : 94.40.94.66
Mme Butor Blamont and M. Pandelle

Rooms 15 with telephone, bath, WC and TV - Wheelchair accessible. **Price** Single and double 380-430F, triple 480-530F, quadruple 580-630. **Meals** Breakfast 40F in room, 50F in bedroom, served 8:00-10:00; half board 350-385F (per pers.). **Restaurant** Service 11:30-15:00, 18:30-23:00; menus 95-170F, also à la carte. Specialties: Fish, aioli, bouillabaise, bourride. **Credit cards** Amex, Visa, Eurocard and MasterCard. **Pets** Dogs allowed. **Facilities** Swimming pool, tennis, parking. **Nearby** Lake of Saint-Cassien, Estérel Mountains between Saint-Raphaël and La Napoule, Saint-Tropez – 18-hole golf course in Valescure. **Open** Feb – Oct.

This lovely hotel is made up of three buildings located in the heart of the spectacular unspoiled Esterel Mountains. In the first, facing the church, you will find the friendly village bar and the Chrystallin's panoramic restaurant. Ask for a table near the large bay window and you will enjoy a stunning view out over one of the most beautiful regions of Provence. The bedrooms are located in two other buildings away from the street, surrounded by flowers and looking out over a superb swimming pool and, in the distance, the craggy red escarpments of the Esterel. All the rooms are comfortable and bright, and decorated with cheerful Provençal fabrics; all have large terraces with a magnificent view. There are also duplex suites which are beautifully decorated and perfect for a group.

How to get there *(Map 34): 14km west of Fréjus via A8, exit Les Adrets. On the Place de l'Eglise.*

Logis du Guetteur ★★★

Place du Château
83460 Les Arcs–sur–Argens (Var)
Tel. 94.73.30.82 - Fax 94.73.39.95 - M. Callegari

Rooms 10 with telephone, bath or shower, WC, TV and minibar. **Price** Double 450F.
Meals Breakfast 45F, served 8:00-10:30; half board 430F, full board 550F (per pers.,
2 days min.). **Restaurant** Service 12:00 and 19:15; menus 130-330F, also à la carte.
Specialties; Saumon fourré à l'écrevisse, Saint-Jacques au beurre de muscat, pigeon
de ferme aux truffes, ris de veau aux oranges, bourride. **Credit cards** All major.
Pets Dogs allowed (+30F). **Facilities** Swimming pool, parking. **Nearby** Sainte-
Rosaline chapel (4km from Arcs), château d'Entrecasteaux, abbey of Le Thoronet,
Seillans, Simon Segal museum in Aups – Saint-Andiol golf course. **Open** All year
(closed Jan 15 – Feb 15).

The old 11th-century Château du Villeneuve in which the Logis
is situated was restored in 1970, but its rough stone medieval
walls have been preserved. In your comfortable, pleasantly
furnished bedroom, you can be assured that no enemies will scale
the castle walls. On the contrary, you can relax and take in the
magnificent, panoramic views. The dining room, which is in the
old cellars, has a covered terrace that looks out over the charming
belltower and rooftops below. There is a lovely swimming pool,
delicious cuisine and a very kind welcome.

How to get there *(Map 34): 12km south of Draguignan via N555 and
D555; in the medieval village.*

Hostellerie Bérard ★★★

Rue Gabriel-Péri
83740 La Cadière-d'Azur (Var)
Tel. 94.90.11.43 - Fax 94.90.01.94 - Mme Bérard

Rooms 40 with telephone, bath or shower, WC, TV and minibar. **Price** Single 320-390F, double 517-595F, suite 750-900F. **Meals** Breakfast 65F, served 7:30-9:30.
Restaurant Closed Sunday evening and Monday in low season. Service 12:30-13:30, 19:30-21:30; menus 115-390F, menu lunchtime in the garden 90F, also à la carte.
Specialties: Mille-feuille de coquilles Saint-Jacques aux pousses d'épinards à l'aceto balsamico, Saint-Pierre rôti à la peau au jus court de lapereau à la badiane.
Credit cards Amex, Visa, Eurocard and MasterCard. **Pets** Dogs allowed (+40F).
Facilities Swimming pool, tennis, cooking school, parking. **Nearby** Sanary exotic garden, Bandol, village of Le Castellet, beach (3km) – 18-hole La Frégate golf course in Saint-Cyr-sur-Mer. **Open** All year except Jan 10 – Feb 20.

You will enjoy the festive atmosphere of the Thursday market but don't worry about being disturbed by it: the hotel has a quiet garden behind medieval walls. The bedrooms in the former convent are large, cool in summer, and decorated in varied tones of brown, with beautiful bathrooms. The rooms in the *bastide* are more traditional, but also more colorful with their pretty Provençal curtains and bedcovers. All are comfortable and well furnished. You can have a view of the rooftops, the garden, the ramparts, the village itself or the countryside with the medieval village of Le Castellet in the distance. You will be charmed by Danièle Bérard's friendly welcome, and the highly reputed cuisine is excellent.

How to get there *(Map 34): 24km north of Bandol via D559 and D266.*

Hostellerie Les Gorges de Pennafort ★★★

83830 Callas (Var)
Tel. 94.76.66.51 - Fax 94.76.67.23
M. Bador

Rooms 16 with telephone, bath, WC, TV and minibar. **Price** Single 475-525F, double 575-650F, suite 800-1000F. **Meals** Breakfast 50F, served 8:00-11:00; half board 500F (per pers., 2 days min.). **Restaurant** Closed Sunday evening and Monday in low season. Service 12:00-14:00, 19:30-21:00; menus 190-310F, also à la carte. Specialties: Pistes sautées aux courgettes et tomates à la fleur de Thymet et son risotto à l'encre, pommes de ris de veau sautées en cocotte grand-mère, tarte légère au chocolat et sa purée de poire. **Credit cards** Amex, Visa, Eurocard and MasterCard. **Pets** Dogs allowed (+50F). **Facilities** Parking. **Nearby** Le Malmont, villages of Bargemon, Seillans, Salernes, Tourtour, Aups (Simon-Segal museum), Les Arcs (Sainte-Roseline chapel), château of Entrecasteaux, Thoronet abbey. **Open** March 15 – Jan 15 (closed Sunday evening and Monday in low season).

This pretty, ochre-colored Provençal hotel lies in the heart of dramatic mountain gorges. At night, the trees, the craggy cliffs and the nearby lake are beautifully illuminated by invisible projectors. Decorated with colorful fabric wall coverings, the bedrooms are prim and modern, impeccably kept, and very comfortable; all have gleaming bathrooms. The lounges, the bar and the dining room, where you will enjoy excellent Provençal specialties, are decorated in the same charming style. There is a ravishing shady terrace, and the service is attentive.

How to get there *(Map 34): 20km northeast of Draguignan via D56 and D25. On A8, exit Le Muy and then D25.*

Auberge du Puits Jaubert ★

Route du Lac de Fondurane
83440 Callian (Var)
Tel. 94.76.44.48 - M. Fillatreau

Rooms 8 with bath or shower and WC. **Price** Double 250-300F. **Meals** Breakfast 35F, served 8:00-11:00; half board 300F, full board 420F (per pers., 3 days min.). **Restaurant** Service 12:00-13:30, 20:00-21:30; menus 145-260F, also à la carte. Specialties: Feuilleté d'escalopes de saumon, tournedos au thym. **Credit cards** Visa, Eurocard and MasterCard. **Pets** Dogs allowed. **Facilities** Parking. **Nearby** Saint-Cassien lake, massif du Tanneron, chapel of Notre-Dame-de-Peygros, Auribeau-sur-Siagne – 18-hole golf course in Valescure. **Open** Dec 15 – Oct 31 (closed Tuesday).

To the west of Cannes lies the massif of Tanneron, the land of mimosa, and it is in this beautiful area, in the middle of the countryside, that you will find the Auberge du Puits Jaubert. Converted from a 15th-century farm, it lies at the end of a track winding along the banks of Lake Saint-Cassien. It is a lovely dry stone building roofed in round Genoese tiles. The same lovely stonework is found in the large dining room where a collection of old farming implements adds to the country atmosphere. In summer it is a real pleasure to dine under the foliage of the verandah or in the shade of the plane trees. The cooking is good, and the bedrooms simple but not lacking in comfort. They have just been completely renovated and prettily decorated in pastel colors. The service it variable.

How to get there *(Map 34): 33km from Fréjus via A8, exit Les Adrets-de-l'Estérel, then D37 towards Montauroux and D560; follow signs.*

Hostellerie Lou Calen ★★★

1, cours Gambetta
83850 Cotignac (Var)
Tel. 94.04.60.40 – Fax 94.04.76.64 – M. and Mme Mendes

Rooms 16 with telephone, bath or shower, WC and TV. **Price** Double 290-620F.
Meals Breakfast 45F, served 7:30-10:30; half board 650-985F, full board 920-1256F
(2 pers.). **Restaurant** Closed Wednesday in low season. Service 12:00-14:30,
19:30-21:30; menus 105-250F, also à la carte. Specialties: Foie gras maison.
Credit cards All major. **Pets** Dogs allowed (+40F). **Facilities** Swimming pool,
parking. **Nearby** Abbey of Le Thoronet, château d'Entrecasteaux, Verdon gorges,
Sainte-Croix lake – 18-hole Barbaroux golf course in Brignoles. **Open** March 15 –
Jan 2.

The hotel is at the entrance to the village, near the old wash
house; it is in the center of things but surrounded by
countryside and has a garden hidden behind its façade. The dining
room extends into a garden terrace with the swimming pool below.
The bedrooms are in various styles, sizes and prices but they are
all charming and comfortable. Some have a loggia, while others
have fireplaces where fires are lit in the autumn. However, the
soundproofing in some of the rooms is not good. All around
Cotignac there are cliffs topped by Saracen towers. The village
itself, with its squares shaded by plane trees, its pavement cafés and
moss-covered fountain, is an ideal place for enjoying the life of a
Provençal village.

*How to get there (Map 34): 24km north of Brignoles via A8, Brignoles exit,
then D562 towards Carcès and D13 towards Cotignac.*

453

Château de Valmer ***
Route de Gigaro
83420 La Croix Valmer
Tel. 94.79.60.10 – Fax 94.54.22.68

Rooms 42 with telephone, bath, WC, TV and minibar - Wheelchair accessible, elevator. **Price** Double 700-1200F. **Meals** Breakfast 75F, served 8:00-10:30. **Restaurant** Grill on the beach, service 12:30-15:00 – "La Pinède", service 19:30-21:00. **Credit cards** All major. **Pets** Dogs allowed (+50F). **Facilities** Swimming pool, tennis, parking. **Nearby** Saint-Tropez gulf, Les Maures, islands of Porquerolles and Port-Cros. **Open** April – Sept.

A comfortable, elegant and luxurious hotel, the Château de Valmer is surrounded by a 12-acre park with a century-old palm grove and a private beach. The interior of the Valmer has just been magnificently renovated. In the lounges, there are antiques and deep sofas which are elegantly covered with printed fabrics coordinated with those of the drapes. The décor matches the handsome paintings. The bedrooms are beautiful and impeccably kept, and they have very luxurious bathrooms. Prices vary according to the size of the room and the view. Lovely terraces with stone colonnades lend charm to the façade of the château, and there are tables there where you can have breakfast.

How to get there *(Map 34): A8, Le Muy exit, direction La Garde-Freinet, G assin and La Croix-Valmer.*

Moulin de la Camandoule ★★★

Chemin Notre-Dame-des-Cyprès
83440 Fayence (Var)
Tel. 94.76.00.84 – Fax 94.76.10.40 – M. and Mme Rilla

Rooms 11 with telephone, bath, shower, WC and TV. **Price** Single 260-450F, double 445-685F, suite 685F. **Meals** Breakfast 50F, served 8:00-10:00; half board 500-575F (obligatory March 15 – Oct 31). **Restaurant** Closed Tuesday. Service 12:30-15:00, 20:00-22:00; menus 180F, also à la carte. **Credit cards** Visa, Eurocard and MasterCard. **Pets** Dogs allowed (+40F). **Facilities** Swimming pool, parking. **Nearby** Seillans, Bargème, Sainte-Roseline chapel (4km from Arcs), château d'Entrecasteaux, abbey of Le Thoronet – 18-hole golf course in Roquebrune-sur-Argens. **Open** All year.

This old olive oil mill has been well preserved and today belongs to an English couple who run it like an old-fashioned English guest house. You will enjoy a warm, friendly welcome and all the services and comforts of a good hotel. The interior decoration is in excellent taste. The bedrooms are furnished in an attractive Provençal style, although the attention to detail is uneven. In the unusual lounge the old machinery of the oil press has been cleverly incorporated into the decor. Around the hotel are large grounds through which the River Camandre flows. A look at the menus on the walls of the swimming pool bar will tell you much about the care given to the cooking. Mme Rilla, who has worked on many radio and TV food programs, has made La Camandoule a favorite destination for travelers with a passion for good food.

How to get there (Map 34): 31km north of Fréjus via D4, then D19.

La Grillade au feu de bois ★★

Flassans–sur–Issole
83340 Le Luc (Var)
Tel. 94.69.71.20 – Fax 94.59.66.11 – Mme Babb

Rooms 16 with telephone, bath or shower, WC and TV. **Price** Single and double 400-550F, suite 900F. **Meals** Breakfast 50F, served 8:00-10:30. **Restaurant** Service 12:00-13:45, 19:30-21:00; menu 180F, also à la carte. Specialties: Traditional Provençal cooking. **Credit cards** Amex, Visa, Eurocard and MasterCard. **Pets** Dogs allowed. **Facilities** Heated swimming pool, parking. **Nearby** Abbey of Thoronet, tour of Luc, abbey of La Celle, La Loube mountain – 18-hole Barbaroux golf course in Brignoles. **Open** All year.

This very well restored 18th-century Provençal *mas* is surrounded by lush vegetation and a terrace shaded by beautiful trees, the oldest of which is a 100-year-old mulberry. Inside, the various living areas and the long vaulted dining room, with a fireplace at one end, are remarkably furnished. (Madame Babb, who is also an antiques dealer, has personalized the decor with numerous lovely objects, paintings and pieces of furniture.) The bedrooms are superb, large and comfortable, in fact immense; they are very quiet despite the proximity of the N7 highway (500m away). We can heartily recommend them. The bathrooms are also lovely. You will enjoy good Provençal cuisine and, as you would expect, there are delicious grills.

How to get there *(Map 34): 13km east of Brignoles via N7. On A8, Le Luc exit.*

La Vieille Bastide
83780 Flayosc (Var)
Tel. 94.70.40.57 – Fax 94.84.61.23
M. and Mme Isaia

Rooms 7 with telephone, bath, WC, TV and minibar. **Price** Double 300-500F.
Meals Breakfast 30F, served 7:30-12:00; half board 270-350F (per pers.).
Restaurant Service from 12:30 and 19:30; menu 145F, also à la carte. Specialties:
Provençal cooking. **Credit cards** All major. **Pets** Dogs allowed. **Facilities** Swimming
pool, parking. **Nearby** Seillans, Bargème, Sainte-Roseline chapel (4km from Arcs),
château d'Entrecasteaux, abbey of Le Thoronet, Simon-Segal museum in Aups.
Open All year (closed Monday).

This hotel is in an old *bastide* which has been rebuilt, extended
and generally improved. The bedrooms are comfortable, many
of them with cheerful pink wallpaper and pastel fabrics. The view
from them varies: some look out on the garden and others on the
swimming pool, and their prices (all very reasonable) vary
accordingly. In the lounge a large sofa and two armchairs are by
the fireplace, where a wood fire burns in winter. Adjoining it is a
spacious dining room. You can also dine or have your breakfast
on the shaded terrace looking out on the countryside with its olive
and cypress trees.

How to get there *(Map 34): 7km west of Draguignan via D557 through*
Salernes.

Auberge du Vieux Fox **
Place de l'Eglise
83670 Fox–Amphoux (Var)
Tel. 94.80.71.69 – Fax 94.80.78.38 – M. Martha

Rooms 8 with telephone, bath or shower, WC and 4 with TV. **Price** Double 280-380F.
Meals Breakfast 35F, served 8:30-10:00; half board 600-750F, full board 750-850F
(per 2 pers.). **Restaurant** Service from 12:30 and 19:15; menus 115-245F, also à la
carte. Specialties: Agneau de Haute-Provence, galette du berger. **Credit cards** Amex,
Visa, Eurocard and MasterCard. **Pets** Dogs allowed (+35F). **Facilities** Parking.
Nearby Abbeys of Le Thoronet and La Celle, Verdon lake and gorges – 18-hole
Barbaroux golf course in Brignoles. **Open** All year (closed Tuesday and Wednesday
noon in low season).

The old village of Fox–Amphoux, perched on its wooded crag,
was first a Roman camp and then became a headquarters of
Knights Templars. The hotel is in the old presbytery adjoining the
church in the center of the village. The interior will instantly charm
you: there is a delightful dining room with prettily laid tables
alongside lovely old furniture. In summer you can also have dinner
on the enchanting little terrace in the shade of a large fig tree. The
bedrooms and bathrooms have been recently renovated. They are
comfortable and look out on the massifs of Sainte-Victoire and
Sainte-Baume. In addition to the comfort and charm of this small
hotel (where *demi-pension* is recommended), you will enjoy very
good cuisine and reasonable prices.

*How to get there (Map 34): 32km north of Brignoles via A8, Saint-
Maximin-la-Sainte-Baume exit, then D560 to Tavernes, D71 and D32.*

La Boulangerie ★★★

Route de Collobrières
83310 Grimaud (Var)
Tel. 94 43.23.16 – Fax 94.43.38.27 – Mme Piget

Rooms 11 with telephone, bath, WC, 2 with TV and 1 with minibar. **Price** Single 560F, double 660-690F, suite 780-1320F. **Meals** Breakfast 50F, served 7:45-11:00. **Restaurant** For residents only. Service 12:00-13:30; à la carte. Specialties: Aïoli de poissons, poulet fermier aux truffes. **Credit cards** Amex, Visa, Eurocard and MasterCard. **Pets** Dogs allowed (+60F). **Facilities** Swimming pool, tennis, table tennis, parking. **Nearby** La Garde-Freinet, ridgeway to the Notre-Dame-des-Anges hermitage, Collobrières, Carthusian monastery of La Verne, Saint-Tropez – 9-hole Beauvallon golf course in Sainte-Maxime. **Open** April 1 – Oct 10.

This place has nothing to do with bakeries as its name would suggest – it is named after a small village – but it has a very different atmosphere from a traditional hotel. Far from the crowds in a tranquil spot in the Massif des Maures, it is more like a holiday house in the interior of Provence. Everything conspires to produce this impression: both the terrace where you can have meals, and the dining room, which is part of the lounge. There is a happy informality that makes you feel instantly at ease. The bedrooms have the same homey atmosphere and are more like guest rooms in a friend's house. This is a beautiful hotel where you will warmly received.

How to get there *(Map 34): 10km west of Saint-Tropez via D14; 1km from the village.*

Le Verger

Route de Collobrières
83310 Grimaud (Var)
Tel. 94.43.25.93 – Fax 94.43.33.92 – Mme Zachary

Rooms 9 (first floor with air-conditioning) with telephone, bath or shower, WC, TV and 3 with air-conditioning. **Price** Double 550-850F. **Meals** Breakfast 60F, served 8:30-11:30. **Restaurant** Service 12:00-14:30, 19:30-23:30; à la carte. Specialties: Fleurs de courgettes sauce mousseline, médaillon de lotte au curry, carré d'agneau au miel, feuilleté de saumon au basilic, bourride. **Credit cards** Visa, Eurocard and MasterCard. **Pets** Dogs allowed. **Facilities** Swimming pool, parking. **Nearby** La Garde-Freinet, ridgeway to the Notre-Dame-des-Anges hermitage, Collobrières, Carthusian monastery of La Verne, Saint-Tropez – 9-hole Beauvallon golf course in Sainte-Maxime. **Open** March – Nov.

This pretty house looks like a private dwelling. The bedrooms have French windows which open onto a terrace or a lawn with fruit trees. The tasteful Provençal decor is enhanced with lovely fabrics and beautiful bathrooms. You will find your bed turned down every evening, and bouquets of flowers add a pleasant touch. Every day the restaurant is filled with loyal followers of M. Zachary who remember him when he was the excellent chef at the Bigorneaux in Saint-Tropez. His delicious cuisine is made with aromatic herbs and vegetables from the kitchen garden. Shielded by a bamboo grove on the small river in back, the Verger is very quiet. And the hospitality is charming.

How to get there *(Map 34): 9km west of Saint-Tropez. From A8, exit Le Luc, then D558 towards Saint-Tropez; before Grimaud take D14 for 1km towards Collobrières and follow signs.*

Le Manoir ***

Ile de Port-Cros
83400 Hyères (Var)
Tel. 94.05.90.52 - Fax 94.05.90.89 - M. Buffet

Rooms 23 with telephone, bath or shower and WC. **Price** Double with half board 760-960F (per pers., 3 days min.). **Meals** Breakfast 60F, served 7:45-10:00. **Restaurant** Service from 13:00 and 20:00; menus 250-300F, also à la carte. Specialties: Bourride provençale, baron d'agneau à la broche, fricassée de gambas au whisky. **Credit cards** Visa, Eurocard and MasterCard. **Pets** Dogs not allowed. **Nearby** Nature trails in the Port-Cros national park, Porquerolles. **Open** Mid April – beg. Oct.

The eucalyptus, palm trees, white walls and graceful columns of the Manoir evoke an exotic dream, a lost island. And yet Toulon is so close. The island of Pont-Cros is a nature reserve and no vehicles are allowed. The hotel was opened just after the war in this private house and it still preserves a family atmosphere, blending conviviality with elegance. There is a large lounge and several small ones, which card players frequent towards the end of the summer season. The bedrooms are cool and charming and some have little loggias; from Room 4 you can see the sea through the trees. A beautiful, quiet 30-acre park adds to the considerable charm of this lovely hotel.

How to get there *(Map 34): Ferry connection from Le Lavandou and Cavalaire (tel. 94.71.01.02), from Hyères (tel. 94.58.21.81). Cars not allowed on the island. Airport Toulon-Hyères.*

Les Glycines ★★★

Place d'Armes - Ile de Porquerolles
83400 Hyères (Var)
Tel. 94.58.30.36 - Fax 94.58.35.22 - M. Fanara

Rooms 12 with air-conditioning, telephone, bath or shower, WC and TV. **Price** Double 500-650F. **Meals** Breakfast (buffet) 50F, served from 8:30; half board 450-900F (per pers.). **Restaurant** Service 19:30-22:30: menu 140F, also à la carte. Specialties: Loups au gros sel grillés, thon grillé, sardines rôties, souris d'agneau. **Credit cards** Amex, Visa, Eurocard and MasterCard. **Pets** Dogs not allowed. **Nearby** Bike rides along island paths, beaches, boat rental. **Open** All year.

The hotel has been completely refurbished and is located on the main square of the village, but as there are no cars on the island it is very peaceful. Set back in its garden, which has a century-old fig tree, the hotel with its whitewashed walls and blue shutters still has the peaceful atmosphere of Provençal houses of yesteryear. The bedrooms, all comfortable and air-conditioned, open onto the garden or the square, and have a pleasant atmosphere with pastel tinted walls, Provençal fabrics and ceramic floor-tiles. The bathrooms are also elegant and have every facility. The meals include Mediterranean specialties and are served in the cool shady garden on tables with brightly patterned tablecloths.

How to get there *(Map 34): Ferry connection from Hyères or La Tour Fondue (tel. 94.58.21.81) or boat-taxi (tel. 94.58.31.19) at any time. Cars not allowed on the island. Airport Toulon-Hyères (7km).*

Hôtel Le Calalou ★★★

Moissac-Bellevue
83630 Aups (Var)
Tel. 94.70.17.91 - Fax 94.70.50.11 - Mme Vernet

Rooms 36 with telephone, bath, WC, 5 with shower, 31 with TV and minibar.
Price Single 320-380F, double 510-600F, 800F with salon. **Meals** Breakfast 60F,
served 8:00-10:00; half board 515-560F, full board 715-760F (per pers.).
Restaurant Closed Sunday evening and Monday in March, April, Oct and Nov. Service
12:00-14:00, 19:30-22:00/23:00; menus 150-250F, also à la carte. Specialties: Petit
clin d'œil piémontais, carré d'agneau à la broche avec sa mijotée de légumes, abricot
rôti et son sorbet aux pêches. **Credit cards** All major. **Pets** Dogs allowed (+40F).
Facilities Swimming pool, tennis, parking. **Nearby** Aups: Simon-Segal museum,
villages of Salernes (pottery), Tourtour, Cotignac Château d'Entrecasteaux, abbey
of Thoronet, gorges du Verdon, lake of Sainte-Croix – 18-hole Barbaroux golf course.
Open March 18 – Nov 12.

L e Calalou looks way out over splendid countryside and a flower
garden. Inside, antique furniture, pretty regional fabrics, old
tiles and immense bouquets of flowers all create a warm and cheerful
atmosphere in the vast reception rooms. Out of season, meals are
served in a fine, sunny colored dining room; in summer, it opens
onto the garden, The cuisine turned out by young Olivier is refined
and savory. The bedrooms detract somewhat from the charm of
the place. They are certainly comfortable but some are small for
the price and they would be improved with prettier bathrooms.
But improvements are in the works and you should ask for those
which have already been redone: they are very charming.

How to get there *(Map 34): 35km northwest of Draguignan; via A8, Le
Muy or Saint-Maximin exit.*

Mas des Brugassières ★★
Plan–de–la–Tour
83120 Sainte–Maxime (Var)
Tel. 94.43.72.42 – Fax 94.43.00.20 – M. and Mme Geffine

Rooms 14 with telephone, bath or shower and WC. **Price** Double 420-550F.
Meals Breakfast 38F, served 8:30-10:00. No restaurant, but snacks by the pool at
lunchtime. **Credit cards** Visa, Eurocard and Mastercard. **Pets** Dogs allowed (+60F).
Facilities Swimming pool, tennis, parking. **Nearby** Massif des Maures – 9-hole
Beauvallon golf course in Sainte-Maxime. **Open** March 15 – Oct 31 and Christmas
holidays.

The Mas des Brugassières lies in the heart of the Massif des
Maures by a quiet road; and if you dream of spending a few
days by a swimming pool in the peace of these wooded mountains
behind Saint-Tropez, this is the place. The white-walled bedrooms
are light and airy and open out onto the swimming pool or small
private terraces. Breakfasts are copious but the hotel does not have
a restaurant. On certain days, however, there are buffet meals and
barbecues available by the pool. The atmosphere is simple and
relaxed, which is greatly due to the hospitality of the young owners.

How to get there *(Map 34): 15km northwest of Sainte-Maxime via D25*
and D74; 1km from the village.

La Maurette

83520 Roquebrune-sur-Argens (Var)
Tel. 94.45.46.81
M. and Mme Rapin

Rooms 9 with telephone, bath or shower and WC (5 with kitchenette). **Price** Double 350-450F. **Meals** Breakfast 45F, served 8:00-10:00. **Restaurant** Occasional meals for residents only. **Credit cards** Visa, Eurocard and MasterCard. **Pets** Dogs not allowed. **Facilities** Swimming pool, parking. **Nearby** Roquebrune, Fréjus cathedral, massif de l'Estérel – 18-hole golf course in Roquebrune. **Open** Easter – mid-Oct.

Monsieur Rapin may well owe his vocation as a hotelier to a grandfather who owned a hotel in Cannes. But is "hotelier" the right word in his case? For La Maurette is really more like a guest house. It is the kind of place where you will almost feel you have been invited. And anyway, would a hotel really choose such a secluded location, so removed from the crowds? This could be the setting for a monastery, facing the rock of Roquebrune and the foothills of the Massif des Maures. And in the back, there are the Estérel, the Mediterranean and the valley. The bedrooms are bright, cheerful and very comfortable, with charming, carefully chosen furniture, curios and paintings. The *table d'hôte* meals are delicious, with good family-style Provençal gratins, meats roasted in a woodburning oven and desserts. Then there is the large swimming pool and your hosts' warm, friendly hospitality. Who could ask for more?

How to get there *(Map 34): 10km west of Fréjus via N7 and D7; then after the Pont de l'Argens follow signs; from A8, Le Muy or Puget-sur-Argens exit.*

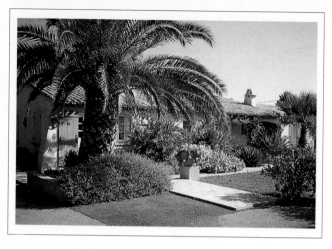

Hôtel Le Pré de la Mer ★★★

Route des Salins
83990 Saint-Tropez (Var)
Tel. 94.97.12.23 - Fax 94.97.43.91 - Mme Blum

Rooms 3 and 9 studios (with kitchenette) with telephone, bath, shower, WC, TV and minibar. **Price** Single and double 490-660F, studio 640-875F. **Meals** Breakfast 55F, served 8:30-12:00. No restaurant. **Credit cards** Visa, Eurocard and MasterCard. **Pets** Dogs allowed (+50F). **Facilities** Parking. **Nearby** L'Annonciade museum in Saint-Tropez, Ramatuelle festival in July, La Nioulargue in October, la Garde-Freinet, ridgeway to Notre-Dame-des-Anges hermitage, Collobrières, Carthusian monastery of La Verne – 9-hole Beauvallon golf course in Sainte-Maxime. **Open** Easter – Sept 30.

This is a low-roofed white house built in Saint-Tropez-Mexican style. The bedrooms are large and comfortable, cooled by large fans. Some have a kitchen (which helps you forget the prices of the restaurants in Saint-Tropez) and all have a private terrace with white wooden table and chairs, perfect for breakfast and meals. The terraces lead out into a pleasant garden where lemon and pomegranate trees and oleanders bloom. But to get into this peaceful haven just minutes from Saint-Tropez you will have to charm Joséphine Blum, the owner, who likes to choose her clientele. Restaurant fashions come and go here, but there are always *Le Gorille* and *Le Sénequier* on the port; *Le Bistrot des Lices* and *Le Café des Arts* on the Place des Lices; *Chez Fuchs* and *La Table du Marché*; and on the beaches, *Le Club 55*, *Le Nioulargo* for his Thai cuisine. Or try *Les Jumeaux*.

How to get there *(Map 34): 3km east of Saint-Tropez on the Salins road.*

La Ferme d'Augustin ★★★

83350 Ramatuelle – Saint-Tropez (Var)
Tel. 94.97.23.83 – Fax 94.97.40.30
Mme Vallet

Rooms 46 of which 30 with air-conditioning, with telephone, bath (5 with shower), WC, TV, safe and minibar - Elevator. **Price** Double 580-1600F, suite 1800F. **Meals** Breakfast 75F, served 6:00-14:00. No restaurant but snacks available. **Credit cards** Amex, Visa, Eurocard and MasterCard. **Pets** Dogs allowed (+70F). **Facilities** Heated swimming pool, parking. **Nearby** L'Annonciade museum in Saint-Tropez, Ramatuelle festival in July, La Nioulargue in October, la Garde-Freinet, ridgeway to the Notre-Dame-des-Anges hermitage, Collobrières, Carthusian monastery of La Verne – 9-hole Beauvallon golf course in Sainte-Maxime. **Open** March 25 – Oct 15.

This former family farmhouse and has now been completely renovated. As soon as you arrive, you will be captivated by the pine grove and the garden full of wisteria, bougainvillea, rambling roses and the great parasol-shaped mulberry trees. In the lounges, antique country-style furniture is tastefully combined with modern sofas. The bedrooms have pretty bathrooms with wall tiles from Salernes. They all overlook the garden and have a balcony or terrace commanding sea views. The hotel occupies a truly enviable position, just off Tahiti Beach, 200 meters from hiking paths and overland biking trails. If you want to stay on the beach all day, ask for a box lunches; the bar serves light meals and provides 24-hour room service. Ask your hotel for restaurant recommendations; or see ours on page 465.

How to get there *(Map 34): 5km from Saint-Tropez on the Tahiti Beach road.*

Hôtel Les Bouis ★★★
Route des Plages-Pampelonne
83350 Ramatuelle - Saint-Tropez (Var)
Tel. 94.79.87.61 - Fax 94.79.85.20

Rooms 14 plus 4 duplexes with air-conditioning, telephone, bath, WC, TV, safe and minibar. **Price** Double 750-1150F, duplex +350F. **Meals** Breakfast 68F, served 8:00-12:00. No restaurant, but grill by the swimming pool at lunchtime. **Credit cards** Visa, Eurocard and MasterCard. **Pets** Dogs allowed (+50F). **Facilities** Swimming pool, parking. **Nearby** L'Annonciade museum in Saint-Tropez, Ramatuelle festival in July, La Nioulargue in October, la Garde-Freinet, ridgeway to the Notre-Dame-des-Anges hermitage, Collobrières, Carthusian monastery of La Verne – 9-hole Beauvallon golf course in Sainte-Maxime. **Open** March 22 – Oct 25.

Les Bouis' special attraction in this town of many charming hotels is its exceptional location, high in the hills yet only a kilometer from the sea, commanding an impressive view out over Pampelonne and Camarat Beaches, and one of the most beautiful gulfs of the Côte d'Azur. Of recent construction, the hotel has only a few bedrooms; some open directly onto the garden and have a private terrace with a panorama of the swimming pool and the coast. All the rooms are very comfortable. Breakfast, which is special, can be served in your room or around the swimming pool until noon. Here also, a grill is set up in the summer. The atmosphere is relaxed and the service is charming. The owner will give you good restaurant recommendations; our own are given on page 465.

How to get there *(Map 34): 5km from Saint-Tropez, on the road to Pampelonne Beach.*

La Ferme d'Hermès **

Route de l'Escalet - Val de Pons
83350 Ramatuelle - Saint-Tropez (Var)
Tel. 94.79.27.80 – Fax 94.79.26.86 – Mme Verrier

Rooms 9 with telephone, bath or shower, WC, TV, minibar and 9 with kitchenette. **Price** Double 600-900F, suite 850-1100F. **Meals** Breakfast 70F, served 9:00-12:00. No restaurant. **Credit cards** Visa, Eurocard and MasterCard. **Pets** Dogs allowed (+50F). **Facilities** Swimming pool, parking. **Nearby** L'Annonciade museum in Saint-Tropez, Ramatuelle festival in July, La Nioulargue in October, Grimaud. **Open** April 1 – Oct 31.

A dirt path through the vineyards, a fragrant garden full of rosemary bushes and olive trees, a pink house: this the address in the Midi you have always dreamed of, a place where you want to welcome your friends. Madame Verrier, the owner, has thought of every detail. The fireplace, homemade preserves and pastries for breakfast, bouquets of flowers – all make this house thoroughly charming. The rooms are lovely, and some have a small terrace right on the vineyard. Most have a pleasant kitchenette. Madame Verrier can advise you on restaurants; otherwise, see our note on page 465.

How to get there *(Map 34): 2km south of Ramatuelle on L'Escalet Road.*

La Figuière ★★★

Route de Tahiti
83350 Ramatuelle – Saint-Tropez (Var)
Tel. 94.97.18.21 – Fax 94.97.68.48 – M. Béraud and Mme Chaix

Rooms 45 with air-conditioning, telephone, bath (3 with shower) and WC (31 with TV, 42 with safe and minibar). **Price** Double 500-900F, suite 1300-1400F. **Meals** Breakfast 60F, served 8:00-11:00. **Restaurant** Service 12:00-15:00, 20:00-23:00; also à la carte. Specialties: Grills. **Credit cards** Visa, Eurocard and MasterCard. **Pets** Dogs allowed (+50F). **Facilities** Swimming pool, tennis, parking. **Nearby** L'Annonciade museum in Saint-Tropez, Ramatuelle festival in July, La Nioulargue in October, La Garde-Freinet, ridgeway to the Notre-Dame-des-Anges hermitage, Collobrières, Carthusian monastery of La Verne, Saint-Tropez – 9-hole Beauvallon golf course in Sainte-Maxime. **Open** April 7 – Oct 10.

Opening the shutters in the morning to a vista of sunny vineyards is one of the many charms of this hotel in the countryside a few kilometers from Saint-Tropez. La Figuière is composed of five small typical Provençal buildings in a garden full of fig trees. The bedrooms are spacious, quiet and open onto a small private terrace. The regional decoration is sober and the bathrooms are comfortable-some have a double washbasin, shower and bath. Our favorites have numbers ending in 30 and 40 and enjoy pretty, private terraces surrounded by lavender and lantanas; they have a panoramic view over the vineyards and hills covered with parasol pines. Good breakfasts are served with the morning newspaper. Grills are served at lunchtime around the swimming pool bordered with pink oleander and japonica. A tennis court is hidden behind the hotel, and the staff is very friendly.

How to get there *(Map 34): 2.5km south of Saint-Tropez on the Tahiti Beach road.*

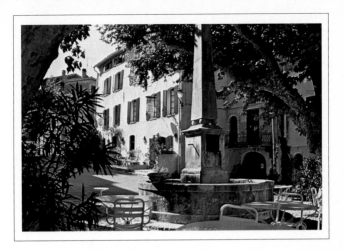

Hôtel des Deux Rocs ★★★

Place Font d'Amont
83440 Seillans (Var)
Tel. 94.76.87.32 - Fax 94.76.88.68 - Mme Hirsch

Rooms 15 with telephone, bath or shower, WC and minibar. **Price** Double 250-520F.
Meals Breakfast 43F, served 8:00-10:00; half board 300-440F, full board 390-520F
(per pers., 3 days min.). **Restaurant** Closed Tuesday and Thursday lunchtime. Service
12:00-14:00, 19:30-21:00; menus 90F (lunchtime in week)-140-220F, also à la carte.
Specialties: Crotin de chavignol en croûte, filet de loup à la crème de basilic, feuilleté
aux pommes. **Credit cards** Visa, Eurocard and MasterCard. **Pets** Dogs allowed.
Nearby Chapel of Saint-André in Comps-sur-Artuby, Fayence, les Arcs and the
Sainte-Roseline chapel (4km), château d'Entrecasteaux, abbey of Le Thoronet – 18-
hole golf course in Roquebrune-sur-Argens. **Open** April 1 – Oct 31.

Standing at the top of the splendid village of Seillans, close to
the city walls and the old castle, the large Provençal style Hôtel
des Deux Rocs, with its rows of windows, recalls to some Italian
houses. Variety is the keynote of the decor, which is exquisite.
You will feel at home and relaxed in the small lounge with a
fireplace. The bedrooms are all individually designed: period
furniture, wall fabrics, curtains, everything down to the bathroom
towels gives a personal touch to each one of them. Breakfast can
be served at tables set up in the pleasant little square, and homemade jams are just one among many thoughtful details which make
a stay here memorable. You will love this hotel, and prices are very
reasonable.

How to get there *(Map 34): 34km north of Fréjus via A8, Les Adrets exit,
then D562 towards Fayence and D19.*

Auberge Saint-Pierre ★★★
Quartier Saint-Pierre
83690 Tourtour (Var)
Tel. 94.70.57.17 - Fax 94.70.59.04 - M. and Mme Marcellin

Rooms 18 with telephone, bath or shower and WC. **Price** Double 360-510F.
Meals Breakfast 50F, served 8:00-11:00; half board 760-910F (per 2 pers., 3 days
min.). **Restaurant** Closed Wednesday. Service 12:00-13:00, 20:00-20:30; menus
170-200F. Specialties: Brouillade aux truffes, pigeonneau truffé, jambonnette
d'agneau à la broche, lapereau farci sauce sariette. **Credit cards** Not accepted.
Pets Dogs allowed (+30F). **Facilities** Swimming pool, tennis, sauna (80F), riding,
bikes, archery, table tennis, parking. **Nearby** Caves of Villecroze, chapel of Saint-
André in Comps-sur-Artuby, Bargème, Simon-Segal museum in Aups. **Open** April 1 –
Oct 15.

The Auberge is a 16th-century *bastide* which once belonged to
the lords of Tourtour. Its secluded position in the middle of
the lush countryside make it just the place to relax. In the lounge,
country furniture is arranged around the fireplace and there is a
collection of prehistoric objects, which were found on the
property. The dining room, decorated in Provençal style, was once
the courtyard of the *bastide*. The bedrooms are comfortable. The
Marcellin family's warm welcome and the good Provençal cooking
made with natural products make the Auberge a delightful place
to stay.

How to get there *(Map 34): 19km west of Draguignan via A8, Le Muy
exit; 3km from Tourtour.*

Château de Trigance ★★★

83840 Trigance (Var)
Tel. 94.76.91.18 – Fax 94.85.68.99
M. Thomas

Rooms 10 with telephone, bath, WC and TV. **Price** Double 520-700F, suite 850-900F. **Meals** Breakfast 65F, served 7:30-10:00; half board 550-720F (per pers.). **Restaurant** Closed Wednesday lunchtime in low season. Service 12:00-14:00, 19:30-21:00; menus 190-360F, also à la carte. Specialties: Salade de rouget barbet aux légumes croquants et sa vinaigrette framboisée, panaché de la mer au fumet d'anis vert en cocote lutée, étuvée de pigeonneau du haut Var aux saveurs provençales. **Credit cards** All major. **Pets** Dogs allowed. **Facilities** Parking. **Nearby** Verdon canyon, ridgeway from La-Palud-sur-Verdon, Moustiers-Sainte-Marie – 9-hole château de Toulane golf course in La Martie. **Open** March 20 – Nov 7.

Originally a fortress built in the 9th-century by the monks of the Abbey of Saint-Victor, the château de Trigance became a castle of the Counts of Provence two hundred years later. It is a massive stone building occupying an impregnable position at the top of a hill. The lounge, dining-room and bar area, all with vaulted ceilings, occupy one of the wings. The bedrooms surround the huge and magnificent terrace, thus ensuring more peace and privacy. They are extremely comfortable: the decoration is simple (in keeping with the character of the building) and shows taste and flair, enhanced by personal touches. The restaurant serves excellent local specialties. Drinks can be served on the terrace facing the breathtaking scenery. In summer plays are performed on the esplanade by the ramparts. The owners extend a warm welcome.

How to get there *(Map 34): 44km north of Draguignan via D995 towards Verdon gorges, at Comps-sur-Artuby D995, then D90.*

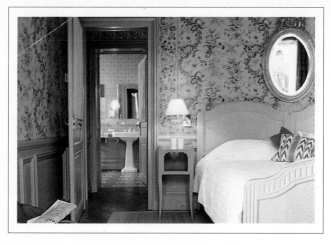

Hôtel de la Mirande ★★★★

Place de la Mirande
84000 Avignon (Vaucluse)
Tel. 90.85.93.93 – Fax 90.86.26.85 – M. Stein

Rooms 19 with air-conditioning, telephone, bath, shower, WC, TV and minibar.
Price Double 1400-2100F, suite 2800F. **Meals** Breakfast 95F, served until 11:30.
Restaurant Service 19:00-21:45; menus 190-350F, also à la carte. Specialties: Filet
rouget barbet dans son croustillant Provençal, raviolis de homard aux poireaux.
Credit cards All major. **Pets** Dogs allowed (+80F). **Facilities** Parking (+80F).
Nearby Palace of the Popes, Notre-Dame des Doms, Campana collection at the Petit-
Palais, Calvet museum, theater festival at Avignon in July, Villeneuve-Lès-Avignon,
la Provence romaine and les Alpilles, le Lubéron – 18-hole Châteaublanc golf course
in Avignon. **Open** All year.

This marvelous hotel in Avignon is charming, to say the least.
The inner courtyard has been turned into a delightful
conservatory, where the wicker armchairs in delicate caramel colors
set the tone. Off the courtyard there is a stunning sequence of
rooms richly decorated with beautiful antiques, Provençal style
fabrics, and chintzes. The bedrooms are spacious, elegant and
comfortable, and all have a lounge or anteroom. Those on the
premier étage are more spacious, while those on the mezzanine and
deuxième étage are more intimate. Some rooms on the last floor have
a lovely terrace which is very pleasant at lunchtime. The ancient
– and baroque – music evening concerts in the autumn will perhaps
give you the opportunity to discover this exquisite, sumptuous
hotel. Last but least, the people are very charming.

How to get there *(Map 33): In the town center, at the foot of the Palais des
Papes.*

Hôtel d'Europe ★★★★
12, place Crillon
84000 Avignon (Vaucluse)
Tel. 90.82.66.92- Fax 90.85.43.66 - M. Daire

Rooms 47 with air-conditioning, telephone, bath, WC, TV (24 with minibar).
Price Single and double 610-1600F, suite 1990-2300F. **Meals** Breakfast 90F,
served 6:30-11:00. **Restaurant** Closed Saturday noon and Sunday. Service 12:00-
14:00, 19:30-22:00; menu, also à la carte. **Credit cards** All major. **Pets** Dogs allowed
(+50F). **Facilities** Garage. **Nearby** Palace of the Popes, Notre-Dame des Doms,
Campana collection at the Petit-Palais, Calvet museum, theater festival at Avignon
in July, Villeneuve-Lès-Avignon, la Provence romaine and les Alpilles, le Lubéron −
18-hole Châteaublanc golf course in Avignon. **Open** All year.

The seigneurial 17th-century Hôtel d'Europe was once the
mansion of the Marquis de Graveson. The refinement of the
hotel has been carefully preserved: handsome antique furniture and
paintings along with brilliant Aubusson tapestries decorate the
salons and the very beautiful dining room. The bedrooms, which
are of varying size, are all furnished with antiques and have very
comfortable accommodations. Three suites have been opened and
from their private terrace in the evening, you will enjoy a unique
spectacle offered by the illuminated Palace of the Popes and the
medieval ramparts surrounding the town. In summer, you can have
meals in the pretty patio, shaded by plane and palm trees, which
are planted in huge traditional pots made in the nearby village of
Anduze. The cuisine is excellent, and there is a very good wine
cellar. Note the private garage, which solves the thorny problem
of parking in the old town.

How to get there (Map 33): Inside the ramparts.

475

L'Anastasy

Ile de la Barthelasse
84000 Avignon (Vaucluse)
Tel. 90.85.55.94 – Fax 90.82.94.49 – Mme Manguin

Rooms 4 with bath or shower. **Price** Single and double 300-350F. **Meals** Breakfast incl.
Restaurant For residents only. Service from 13:00 and 20:30; menu 100F. Specialties:
Provençal and Italian cooking. **Credit cards** Not accepted. **Pets** Dogs allowed.
Facilities Swimming pool, parking. **Nearby** Palace of the Popes, Notre-Dame des Doms,
Campana collection at the Petit-Palais, Calvet museum, Villeneuve-lès-Avignon – 18-
hole Châteaublanc golf course. **Open** All year.

L'Anastasy used to be a farm typical of the area surrounding
Avignon, where animals and harvests were the sole concern.
Now the barns and stables have been converted to make a large
family house where friends and guests can be welcomed. On the
ground floor there is now a spacious lounge and kitchen-dining
room which is the very heart of the house, for the warm and friendly
hostess, Olga Manguin, enjoys nothing more than cooking for her
guests; indeed, the Provençal and Italian specialties she excels at
are delicious. The bedrooms are pretty. The attractions of the house
are many, including the terrace leading into the garden planted
with lavender and rosemary, hollyhocks and acanthus. Although
the atmosphere is convivial, you nevertheless can be left on your
own; but it would be a shame not to join in the activities here.
Olga's friends, including journalists, directors, stage designers and
actors, wouldn't dream of staying anywhere else during the
Avignon Festival.

How to get there *(Map 33): 6km north of Avignon; from Avignon head for
Villeneuve-lès-Avignon over the Daladier bridge.*

476

Les Géraniums **

Place de la Croix
Le Barroux - 84330 Caromb (Vaucluse)
Tel. 90.62.41.08 - Fax 90.62.56.48 - M. and Mme Roux

Rooms 22 with telephone, bath or shower and WC. **Price** Single and double 210-250F. **Meals** Breakfast 35F, served 8:00-10:00; half board 230-250F, full board 310-330F (per pers., 3 days min.). **Restaurant** Service 12:15-13:30, 19:15-21:00; menus 80-250F, also à la carte. Specialties: Omelette aux truffes, lapin à la sarriette, chevreau au romarin, terrine maison aux pruneaux. **Credit cards** All major. **Pets** Dogs allowed (+30F). **Facilities** Parking. **Nearby** Château de Barroux, pharmacy museum at the Hôtel-Dieu in Carpentras, Mazan Gallo-Roman cemetery, dentelles de Montmirail – 18-hole Le Grand Avignon golf course. **Open** All year (closed Wednesday in low season).

Le Barroux is a village set high on a hill between the Ventoux and the jagged peaks of Montmirail, commanding stunning views of the whole Avignon area. The place has a charm of its own, and this small hotel provides pleasantly comfortable accommodation. It also serves as that typical French institution, the *café de la place*, thus offering first-hand insight into local village life. The bedrooms are simple but pleasant and have recently been improved. The nicest have a small terrace. The menu features good local dishes based on fresh products and is likely to include game in season. Meals can be served on the terrace or in the dining room.

How to get there *(Map 33): 9km from Carpentras via D938; between Carpentras and Malaucène.*

Château de Rocher–La Belle Ecluse ***

42, rue Emile Lachaux
84500 Bollène (Vaucluse)
Tel. 90.40.09.09 – Fax 90.40.09.30 – M. Carloni

Rooms 18 with telephone, bath or shower, WC and TV. **Price** Single and double 220-370F. **Meals** Breakfast 45F, served 7:30-10:30; half board 260-380F, full board 320-440F (per pers., 3 days min.). **Restaurant** Service from 12:00 and 19:00; menus 110F (lunchtime)-150-250F; also à la carte. Specialties: Huîtres au champagne, ris d'agneau à la provençale. **Credit cards** All major. **Pets** Dogs allowed (+30F). **Facilities** Parking. **Nearby** Arc de triomphe and old theatre in Orange, Henri Fabre museum in Sérignan – 18-hole Grand Avignon golf course. **Open** All year.

A beautiful aristocratic mansion built in 1828, the Château is set in the middle of a lovely 10-acre park containing both domestic and wild animals and a large garden. The bedrooms are big, comfortable and light and have been recently refurbished by the new owners. They now all have fully-equipped bathrooms. The most attractive is room 6, with a terrace overlooking the garden, and the most amusing is room 8, in the former chapel, which has stained glass windows. The elegant cuisine can be served outside on the terrace, in summer, or in the Richelieu dining room, which has a painted wooden ceiling, a beautiful carved stone chimney and a portrait of the famous Cardinal above the mantel.

How to get there *(Map 33): 25km from Orange via A9, Bollène exit, towards town center then towards Gap, Nyons road.*

Château de Saint-Ariès

Route de Saint Ariès
84500 Bollène (Vaucluse)
Tel. 90.40.09.17 - Fax 90.30.45.62 - M. de Loye

Rooms 5 with bath, shower and WC. **Price** Double 610-740F, suite 990-1090F.
Meals Breakfast 55F, served from 8:45; half board rates on request.
Restaurant Table d'hôtes menu 250F. Specialties: Caillettes à la provençale,
estouffade de bœuf, blancs de vollaille sauce au curry, charlotte au chocolat, crème
caramel. **Credit cards** Visa, Eurocard and MasterCard. **Pets** Dogs allowed on request.
Facilities Swimming pool, bicycles, parking. **Nearby** Arc de triomphe and old theatre
in Orange, Henri Fabre museum in Sérignan – 9-hole Grand Avignon golf course.
Open On request only.

The Château de Saint-Ariès looks like a Tuscan villa lost in the
Provençal countryside. Indeed, the present structure was built
about 1820 by an ancestor of Michel de Loÿe and was designed like
an Italian villa to replace the old chateau. Tucked away in 50-acres
of parkland, it is hidden from view, and as soon as you walk through
the door, you will be surprised and delighted with its beauty. The
lounge, dining-room, library, bedrooms and 1930s bathrooms have
all been recently refurbished and beautifully decorated with family
portraits and furniture, Souleïado fabrics, books and curios. The
conviviality of his *table d'hôte* dinners charmingly exemplifies
Michel de Loÿe's friendly hospitality. Breakfast is excellent, and in
summer it is served on the terrace facing the beautiful landscaped
grounds. This is a very lovely place.

How to get there (Map 33): 22km from Orange via A7, Bollène exit; in
city center, direction Mondragon D26; on leaving Bollène, on the left, take
direction Saint-Ariès. The lake.

Hostellerie du Prieuré ★★★

84480 Bonnieux (Vaucluse)
Tel. 90.75.80.78 – Fax 90.75.96.00
Mme Keller and M. Chapotin

Rooms 10 with telephone, bath, WC and TV. **Price** Single 350F, double 500-590F. **Meals** Breakfast 40F, served 8:00-11:00. **Restaurant** Closed Tuesday and Wednesday noon; Tuesday, Wednesday, Thursday noon in July, Aug and Sept. Service 12:00-13:30, 19:00-21:00; menu 145-200F. Specialties: Feuilleté d'escargot à la crème d'aïl, carré d'agneau rôti aux herbes de Provence, râble de lièvre en civet. **Credit cards** Visa, Eurocard and MasterCard. **Pets** Dogs allowed (+suppl.). **Facilities** Parking. **Nearby** Avignon, Aix-en-Provence, Lubéron villages – 18-hole Saumane golf course. **Open** Feb – late Oct.

L'Hostellerie du Prieuré is in the village, but the main reception rooms and bedrooms face the garden and the valley. The interior decoration is very comfortable and elegant – indeed opulent – creating an atmosphere that is both intimate and cozy. The bedrooms are delightful; all are different, but Number 9 has a terrace with a view of the valley. In summer there is a bar and restaurant service in the garden. There is no à la carte menu, but there are two set–price menus which, although unimaginative, do offer a good choice of specialties.

How to get there *(Map 33): 27km east of Cavaillon via D2 and N100 towards Apt, then D36.*

Hostellerie de Crillon-le-Brave ★★★★

Place de l'église
84410 Crillon-le-Brave (Vaucluse)
Tel. 90.65.61.61 - Fax 90.65.62.86 - M. Chittick

Rooms 22 with telephone, bath or shower, WC and TV on request. **Price** Single and double 750-1150F, suite 1250-1450F. **Meals** Breakfast 75F, served 7:30-11:00; half board +250F, full board +420F (per pers., 3 days min.). **Restaurant** Closed in week for lunchtime. Service 12:00-14:00 (grills on the swimming pool in summer), 19:30-21:30; menus 210-340F, also à la carte. **Credit cards** Amex, Visa, Eurocard and MasterCard. **Pets** Dogs allowed (+60F). **Facilities** Swimming pool, garage. **Nearby** Bédoin, dentelles de Montmirail, chapel of Le Grozeau, château du Barroux, pharmacy museum at Hôtel-Dieu in Carpentras – 18-hole Grand Avignon golf course. **Open** April – Dec.

Just next to the church stands this beautiful hotel: formerly a large family house, its bedrooms are still named after the former occupants. The building still has its worn flagstone floors and is tastefully decorated with terracotta objects and Provençal antiques found at nearby Isle-sur-la-Sorgue. The bedrooms are extremely comfortable and cozy, and their yellow-ochre walls evoke the Midi sun. The two lounges contain shelves loaded with old books, comfortable sofas and windows looking over the pink rooftops of the village. A terraced garden, with pretty wrought-iron furniture in its many shady corners, leads down from a waterlily pond to the swimming-pool, where a grill has been set up.

How to get there (Map 33): 15km north of Carpentras via D974 and D138.

Hostellerie La Manescale

Route de Faucon
Les Essareaux – 84340 Entrechaux (Vaucluse)
Tel. 90.46.03.80 – Fax 90.46.03.89 – Mme Warland

Rooms 6 with telephone, bath or shower, WC, TV and minibar. **Price** Double 350-560F, suite 800F. **Meals** Breakfast 55F, served 8:30-10:00; half board 400-625F (per pers., 2 days min). **Restaurant** For residents only, closed Monday evening. Service at 19:45; menu 170F. Specialties: Cooking with fresh local produce. **Credit cards** All major. **Pets** Dogs allowed (+60F). **Facilities** Swimming pool, parking. **Nearby** Cathedral of Notre-Dame-de-Nazareth in Vaison-la-Romaine, dentelles de Montmirail, Séguret – 18-hole Grand Avignon golf course. **Open** Easter – Oct.

Formerly a shepherd's house and now carefully rebuilt and restored, this pleasant inn stands among vineyards and olive trees between the Drôme and the Vaucluse, facing Mont Ventoux. The bedrooms are luxuriously equipped and tastefully decorated, providing every thoughtful detail. Some of them are small suites (the *Provence* room, for instance). The pleasure of a hearty breakfast on the terrace is enhanced by the magical scenery: a peaceful valley, crowned by the Ventoux, displaying a subtle and ever–changing palette of colors and light. Hotel facilities also include a superb swimming pool. This is a place one would like to keep to oneself, but enthusiastic readers' letters have made sharing the secret a pleasure.

How to get there *(Map 33): 8km east of Vaison-la-Romaine via D205. From A7, take Bollène exit.*

482

Les Florets ★★

Route des Dentelles
84190 Gigondas (Vaucluse)
Tel. 90.65.85.01 – Fax 90.65.83.80 – Mme Bernard

Rooms 13 with telephone, bath or shower, WC and TV. **Price** Double 345-410F.
Meals Breakfast 45F, served 8:00-10:00; half board 780F (2 pers., 3 days min.).
Restaurant Service 12:00-14:00, 19:30-21:00; menus 95-210F, also à la carte.
Specialties: Pieds et paquets maison, aïolade du comtat, lapin au miel et citron.
Credit cards All major. **Pets** Dogs allowed (+40F). **Facilities** Parking. **Nearby** Chapel
of Notre-Dame-d'Aubune, Séguret, dentelles de Montmirail, cathedral and Roman
bridge in Vaison-la-Romaine – 18-hole Grand Avignon golf course. **Open** March –
Dec. (closed Wednesday).

Les Florets occupies an enviable position in the middle of the
countryside at an altitude of 1200 feet facing the peaks of
Montmirail and overlooking the Gigondas vineyards. This is a
simple country hotel, traditional in style, with a pleasant family
atmosphere. The jagged peaks above can be viewed from the terrace,
where an arbor provides welcome shade. The bedrooms are simple
and unpretentious, but comfortable enough and have a view of the
trees. We recommend the new and very charming bedrooms in the
annex. Each opens directly onto the garden and the decoration is
very lovely, with coordinated fabrics throughout; the furniture is
tasteful and the rooms and baths have modern conveniences. The
restaurant serves regional specialties accompanied by local Gigondas
wines. The staff are very friendly and the owner will be happy to
show you his cellars and have you taste his wines.

How to get there *(Map 33): 25km east of Orange via D975 towards Vaison-
la-Romaine, then D8 and D80; on the Route des Dentelles de Montmirail.*

Ferme de la Huppe

Route D 156
Les Pourquiers - 84220 Gordes (Vaucluse)
Tel. 90.72.12.25 - Fax 90.72.01.83 - Mme Konings

Rooms 8 with telephone, bath, shower, WC, TV and minibar. **Price** Single 400F, double 500F. **Meals** Breakfast incl., served 8:00-10:00. **Restaurant** Open Saturday and Sunday. Service 12:00-13:30, 19:30-21:00; menus 140-190F, also à la carte. Specialties: Seasonal cooking. **Credit cards** Visa, Eurocard and MasterCard. **Pets** Dogs not allowed. **Facilities** Swimming pool, parking. **Nearby** Les Bories, Sénanque abbey, Roussillon, l'Isle-sur-la-Sorgue, Fontaine de Vaucluse – 18-hole Saumane golf course. **Open** April 1 – Nov 7.

The small road winding across the Luberon plain gradually turns into a track, leading to this beautifully restored, extremely secluded old farmhouse. The hoopoe bird which gives its name to the place still nests in an old tree-trunk nearby. Everything revolves around the fig tree, the olive trees and the well in the middle of a small inner courtyard. It gives access to the six delightful bedrooms named after the old parts of the building: *La cuisine, L'écurie, La cuve...* the kitchen, the stables, and the wine vat. Their terracotta floors, thick walls and typically small windows ensure both privacy and coolness. They are decorated with old objects and elegant fabrics, and all are very comfortable. A covered patio adjoining the dining room looks onto a beautiful swimming pool screened by flowers and lavender. Young chef Gérald Konings' inspired cuisine is fast gaining him a reputation. The Ferme offers excellent service and reasonable prices.

How to get there *(Map 33): 25km northeast of Cavaillon via D2 (2km from Gordes).*

Hôtel Les Romarins ★★★

Route de Sénanque
84220 Gordes (Vaucluse)
Tel. 90.72.12.13 - Fax 90.72.13.13 - Mme Charles

Rooms 10 with telephone, bath or shower, WC, TV (8 with minibar). **Price** Single and double 400-670F. **Meals** Breakfast 50F, served 8:00-10:00. No restaurant. **Credit cards** Amex, Visa, Eurocard and MasterCard. **Pets** Dogs not allowed. **Facilities** Swimming pool, parking. **Nearby** Les Bories, Sénanque abbey, Roussillon, l'Isle-sur-la-Sorgue, Fontaine de Vaucluse – 18-hole Saumane golf course. **Open** Feb 16 – Jan 14.

This 200-year-old house has just been fully refurbished and turned into a hotel; it is the only establishment in Gordes commanding a view of the old village more houses. That is a beautiful asset indeed if you delight, as we do, in that breathtaking assemblage of ancient walls, terraced gardens and cypresses. Most of the bedrooms have this view, but make sure when you reserve. They are neat and comfortable, and simply and elegantly decorated in either Directoire or contemporary style. The delicious breakfast – with the view of Gordes – can be served in a small, bright dining-room, or outside in the shade of an ancient mulberry tree. The atmosphere is friendly and informal (all the more so because of the a talking parrot on the staff!). The bird, however, is not in sole charge, and M. and Mme Charles extend an urbane and congenial welcome. There is no restaurant but those previously mentioned for Gordes will delight you. Don't forget *Le Mas Tourteron* on the Imberts road.

How to get there *(Map 33): 25km northeast of Cavaillon via D2.*

Domaine Le Moulin Blanc ★★★★
Chemin du Moulin
Les Beaumettes – 84220 Gordes (Vaucluse)
Tel. 90.72.34.50 – Fax 90.72.25.41 – Mme Diez

Rooms 18 with telephone, bath, WC, TV and minibar. **Price** Single and double 450-950F, suite 880-1200F. **Meals** Breakfast 65F, served 7:00-11:00; half board 450-660F, full board 610-820F (per pers., 2 days min.). **Restaurant** Service 12:00-14:00, 19:00-22:00; menus 160-350F, also à la carte. Specialties: Foie gras frais de canard, salade de langoustines aux artichauts, petite brandade de rouget et ses filets grillés, noisette d'agneau et purée d'olives. **Credit cards** All major. **Pets** Dogs allowed. **Facilities** Swimming pool, tennis, parking. **Nearby** Les Bories, Sénanque abbey, Roussillon, Isle-sur-la-Sorgue, Fontaine de Vaucluse – 18-hole Saumane golf course. **Open** All year.

Formerly a postal relay station and then a flour mill, the Moulin Blanc has been superbly restored. The bedrooms are magnificent. The ones opening onto the garden are quieter than those overlooking the road. A superb vaulted hall houses a dining room and lounge. The grounds, planted with pinetrees and cypresses, are also lovely. The restaurant serves good food using fresh local produce. Ideally located between Gordes, Roussillon and Bonnieux, the Moulin Blanc stands at the very heart of historic Provence.

How to get there *(Map 33): 20km northeast of Cavaillon via D2 and N100 towards Apt.*

Mas de Cure Bourse ★★★

Carrefour de Velorgues
84800 Isle-sur-la-Sorgue (Vaucluse)
Tel. 90.38.16.58 - Fax 90.38.52.31 - M. and Mme Donzé

Rooms 13 with telephone, bath, WC and TV. **Price** Single 290-500F, double 320-550F. **Meals** Breakfast 45F; half board 400-470F. **Restaurant** Closed Sunday evening and Monday except Easter – Oct. Service 12:00-13:30, 20:00-21:30, also à la carte. Specialties: Fleurs de courgettes farcies aux champignons, rascasse coulis de crabe, melon d'agneau aux haricots blancs, petits chèvres pané aux noisettes, nougat glacé. **Credit cards** Visa, Eurocard and MasterCard. **Pets** Dogs allowed (+30F). **Facilities** Swimming pool, parking. **Nearby** l'Isle-sur-Sorgue, flea market and Provençal market on Sunday, Fontaine de Vaucluse, Gordes, les Bories, abbey of Sénanque – 18-hole Saumane golf course. **Open** All year.

The Mas de Cure Bourse is a former postal relay station which was built in 1754 in the plain of Isle-sur-la-Sorgue. And it is in this very charming old Provençal *mas,* surrounded by orchards and a 5-acre park, that Monsieur and Madame Donzé receive their visitors. Françoise Donzé is a renowned chef and will make outstanding meals of succulent regional specialties. You will be served in the pretty dining room in front of a large fireplace or on the shady terrace. Through the large glassed-in opening between the reception area and the kitchen, you can even watch the chef and her helpers at work. The decoration and the modern amenities in the bedrooms are impeccable. We prefer *La Chambre du Bout,* the Room at the End, with its small balcony and view over the swimming pool.

How to get there *(Map 33): On A7, exit Avignon-sud or Cavaillon. 3km from Isle-sur-la-Sorgue, on D938, road from Carpentras to Cavaillon.*

Le Mas des Grès ★★
Route d'Apt
84800 Lagnes (Vaucluse)
Tel. 90.20.32.85 - Fax 90.20.21.45 - M. and Mme Hermitte

Rooms 12 with telephone, bath, WC and 6 with TV. **Price** Double 400-550F, suite 950F. **Meals** Breakfast 50F, served 8:00-11:00. **Restaurant** Residents only. Menu 130F. Specialties: Provençal cooking. **Credit cards** Visa, Eurocard and MasterCard. **Pets** Dogs not allowed. **Facilities** Swimming pool, parking. **Nearby** Isle-sur-la-Sorgue, Fontaine de Vaucluse, Gordes, les Bories, Sénanque abbey – 18-hole Saumane golf course. **Open** March 1 – Nov 31, Dec week-end, Christmas and New Year's day.

Set among orchards, this beautiful place is a truly marvelous hotel, a bit like your own home in the Luberon, full of joie de vivre and even a touch of eccentricity. The owner, an interior decorator from Savoy, jokes about the "rustico-Byzantine" style, but the decoration has in fact been very tastefully handled. The lounge and bedrooms are elegantly simple and as charming as the guest room you would expect to find in a friend's house. Room 8 can accommodate a whole family, and Room 6 is perfect for children. The restaurant, for guests only, serves good food, which can be enjoyed under an arbor. Monsieur Hermitte's warm and friendly hospitality makes dinner a special pleasure. Meals are available on a half-board basis.

How to get there *(Map 33): 5km southeast of Isle-sur-la-Sorgue via N100.*

Mas des Capelans

84580 Oppède (Vaucluse)
Tel. 90.76.99.04 – Fax 90.76.90.29
M. and Mme Poiri

Rooms 8 with telephone, bath, WC (4 with TV). **Price** Double 400-800F, suite 600-900F. **Meals** Breakfast 50F, served 8:30-10:30; half board 400-600F (per pers., 3 days min.). **Restaurant** Evening meals. Service at 20:00; menu 155F. Specialties: Lapereau au romarin, navarin aux petits légumes, pintade aux cerises. **Credit cards** All major. **Pets** Dogs allowed (+70F). **Facilities** Heated swimming pool, billiard, parking. **Nearby** The north of Luberon (Ménerbes, Lacoste, Bonnieux, Saint-Symphorien priory, Buoux, Saignon, Apt) – 18-hole Saumane golf course. **Open** Feb 15 – Nov 15 (closed Sunday).

The Mas des Capelans once belonged to the monks of the abbey of Sénanque, who used the building to breed silkworms. The guest bedrooms are large and very comfortable, and have been carefully decorated. Each one is named after the view it commands – *Roussillon, Gordes* – or simply after the vineyard it overlooks, like some of the ground-floor rooms (which have private entrances). The pine furniture and duvets on the beds are quite unusual in this area, and the decor tends towards that of a Swiss chalet lost in the land of lavender! The surroundings are pleasant, and dinner in the courtyard beneath the mulberry-trees and acacias is one of the highlights of a stay.

How to get there *(Map 33): 10km east of Cavaillon. Via A 7, exit Avignon-Sud, direction Apt, N100 between Coustellet and Beaumette, then follow signs.*

Hôtel Arène ***

Place de Langes
84100 Orange (Vaucluse)
Tel. 90.34.10.95 - Fax 90.34.91.62 - M. and Mme Coutel

Rooms 30 with air-conditioning, telephone, bath or shower, WC, minibar and TV.
Price Single and double 320-420F. **Meals** Breakfast 42F, served 7:00-12:00. No
restaurant. **Credit cards** All major. **Pets** Dogs allowed. **Facilities** Garage. **Nearby** Old
theatre and Arc de Triomphe in Orange, Mornas, Henri Fabre museum in Sérignan,
gorges of Ardèche, Vaison-la-Romaine – 18-hole Grand Avignon golf course.
Open Dec 15 – Oct 31.

Ideally located close to the Roman Theatre in a small pedestrian
square shaded by hundred-year old plane trees, the Arène is the
most sought-after hotel in town. M. and Mme Coutel devote lavish
amounts of care to their guests' well-being and are constantly
refurbishing and embellishing the hotel. The bedrooms, all
different, are comfortable and cheerful, though some are a little
dark. There is no restaurant, but there is a pleasant lounge with a
large fireplace and period furniture. This is a very popular place
and it is necessary to reserve well ahead, especially during the
Festival. *Au Goût du Jour* is a charming restaurant with very
reasonable prices.

How to get there *(Map 33): In the old town center.*

Mas des Aigras

Chemin des Aigras
84100 Orange (Vaucluse)
Tel. 90.34.81.01 – Fax 90.34.05.66 – M. and Mme Pernelle

Rooms 11 with telephone, bath or shower, WC and TV. **Price** Single 350F, double 350-410F. **Meals** Breakfast 50F. No restaurant but dinner. **Credit cards** All major. **Pets** Dogs allowed. **Facilities** Swimming pool, tennis, parking. **Nearby** Old theatre and Arc de Triomphe in Orange, Les Chorégies of Orange in August, Mornas, Henri Fabre museum in Sérignan – 18-hole Grand Avignon golf course. **Open** All year.

With a limited number of rooms and a beautiful garden with swimming pool, this hotel has all the appeal of a private house. Beyond the vineyards lies the road to Orange, which is only minutes away. The bedrooms are pleasant and extremely comfortable. Although it lacks diversity, the olive-wood furniture creates a warm atmosphere. Breakfast is served in an elegant dining room leading out into the garden. Hotel facilities also include a tennis court, so a stay in the Mas des Aigras provides the opportunity to relax or to exercise. For dinner, residents can enjoy the *table d'hôtes* meal at the Mas. Otherwise, the owners will give you expert recommendations on restaurants in the Orange area. We would recommend the charming, reasonably priced *Au Goût du Jou*r. The welcome is inconsistent.

How to get there *(Map 33): In the north of the town.*

Hôtel L'Hermitage ★★

Route de Carpentras
84210 Pernes-les-Fontaines (Vaucluse)
Tel. 90.66.51.41 - Fax 90.61.36.41 - Mme Oury

Rooms 20 with telephone, bath, WC and TV. **Price** Single and double 340-400F. **Meals** Breakfast 45F, served 7:30-11:00; half board 310-340F (per pers., 3 days min.). **Restaurant** (1km away) Service 12:00-14:00, 19:00-22:00; menus, also à la carte. **Credit cards** Diners, Visa, Eurocard and MasterCard. **Pets** Dogs allowed (+20F). **Facilities** Swimming pool, parking. **Nearby** Venasque church, Gallo-Roman cemetery in Mazan, Carpentras – 18-hole Grand Avignon golf course. **Open** All year.

Conveniently close to the many local places of interest, L'Hermitage is a beautiful country house set in a 5-acre park. The Provençal-style furniture and many personal objects found around the house add to its charm. The bedrooms are very well kept; those on the top floor command beautiful views of the Ventoux; Rooms 6, 7 and 14 have a large terrace; and Rooms 8 and 10 a small balcony. The wisteria shading the terrace, the tall plane trees and the terracotta urns full of flowers lend special beauty to the gardens. You can take meals on a half-board basis in a restaurant 1km away which belongs to the same family.

How to get there *(Map 33): 4km south of Carpentras via D938.*

L'Orangerie
4, rue Pasteur
84420 Piolenc (Vaucluse)
Tel. 90.29.59.88 – Fax 90.29.67.74 – Mme Delarocque

Rooms 5 with bath or shower, WC and TV. **Price** Single 180-240F, double 240-380F.
Meals Breakfast 40F, served 8:30-11:30; half board 280F, full board 350F.
Restaurant Service 12:00-14:00, 19:30-21:30; menus 85-200F. Specialties: Foie
gras, crabe farci, ossobuco de langouste, zarzuela, magret aux airelles.
Credit cards Visa, Eurocard and MasterCard. **Pets** Dogs allowed (+30F).
Facilities Parking. **Nearby** Henri Fabre museum in Sérignan, old theatre and Arc
de Triomphe of Orange, Chorégies of Orange in July and August, Mornas – 18-hole
Moulin golf course. **Open** All year.

The vegetation has overrun the interior courtyard of the
Orangerie where everything is in charming disorder. Set back
in a tiny street of Piolenc, a small village only 6km from Orange,
the hotel is very quiet. The dense tangle of flowers and climbing
plants makes the house delightfully cool in summer. Once the
principal attraction of the property, the restaurant is in a beautiful
vaulted room at the back. The simple bedrooms, decorated with
several regional antiques, have an endearing provincial charm; and
one room has a small, pretty terrace. The hospitality is very friendly,
as are the prices.

*How to get there (Map 33): 6km north of Orange. Via A7, exit Orange
(or Bollène if you are coming from Lyon), N7 direction Bollène.*

Auberge de Cassagne ★★★★

450, allée de Cassagne
84130 Le Pontet - Avignon (Vaucluse)
Tel. 90.31.04.18 - Fax 90.32.25.09 - MM. Gallon, Boucher, Trestour

Rooms 25 and 5 apartments with air-conditioning, telephone, bath, WC, cable TV, safe and minibar. **Price** Single 420-490F, double 490-1380F, suite 1380-1780F. **Meals** Breakfast 85F, served 7:30-10:30; half board 710-1155F, full board 900-1345F (per pers.). **Restaurant** Service 12:00-13:30, 19:30-21:30; menus 210-440F, also à la carte. Specialties: Terrine provençale au coeur de foie gras, filets de rouget au citron vert, émincé d'agneau et côtelettes de lapereau panées aux petits légumes farcis. **Credit cards** All major. **Pets** Dogs allowed (+60F). **Facilities** Tennis, parking (+20F). **Nearby** Palace of the Popes, Campana collection at the Petit Palais and Calvet museum in Avignon, Avignon festival in July, Villeneuve-les-Avignon – 18-hole Grand Avignon golf course, 18-hole Châteaublanc golf course in Avignon. **Open** All year.

Jean-Michel and Françoise Gallon will greet you in this beautiful old Provençal house only a few kilometers out of Avignon. In summer, in the magnificent flower-filled garden, you can enjoy the renowned cooking of the young chef Philippe Boucher, who trained under Georges Blanc and Paul Bocuse. The outstanding wine cellar has been entrusted to André Trestour. The bedrooms, pleasantly decorated and furnished in Provençal style, are comfortable, though rather small. Some are located in the main building and others around the lovely swimming pool.

How to get there (Map 33): 5km east of Avignon via A7, Avignon-Nord exit, then 5 mins. and left on small road before the lights.

Mas de Garrigon ★★★
Route de St-Saturnin
84220 Roussillon (Vaucluse)
Tel. 90.05.63.22 – Fax 90.05.70.01 – Mme Rech-Druart

Rooms 9 with telephone, bath, shower, WC, TV and minibar. **Price** Single 700F, double 750F, suite 950F. **Meals** Breakfast 75F, served 7:30-10:30; half board 700-900F, full board 850-1050F (per pers.). **Restaurant** Closed Sunday evening and Monday. Service 12:00-14:00, 20:00-21:30; menus 175-320F, also à la carte. Specialties: Asperges vertes en vinaigrette de truffes, filets de loup sauce vierge, langoustines rôties à l'estragon, agneau du Luberon, tartes aux fruits de saison. **Credit cards** All major. **Pets** Dogs allowed (+65F). **Facilities** Swimming pool, parking. **Nearby** Gordes, les Bories, Sénanque abbey, Isle-sur-la-Sorgue, Luberon – 18-hole Saumane golf course. **Open** All year.

This charming *mas* is typically Provençal in style. Lying at the foot of the Luberon, it is a pleasant place to stay in all seasons. The swimming pool and deckchairs are an invitation to relax in the sun, and lunch can be served there. The lounge has a magnificent fireplace and is perfect for listening to classical music or reading a book from the bookshelves. The bedrooms are tastefully furnished and all have their own terrace facing south over the Luberon. The cooking is refined and made with fresh products from the market. The Mas is ideally situated for touring Provence, as all the principal places of interest are within a 100km radius.

How to get there *(Map 33): 48km east of Avignon via N100 towards Apt, then D2 towards Gordes and D102.*

Auberge du Presbytère

Place de la Fontaine
Saignon – 84400 Apt (Vaucluse)
Tel. 90.74.11.50 – Fax 90.04.68.51 – Mme Bernardi

Rooms 10, 5 with bath and WC. **Price** Double 180-300F. **Meals** Breakfast 45F, served 8:30-10:00. **Restaurant** Service 12:30-14:00, 20:00-21:00; menu 150F. Specialties: Provençal cooking. **Credit cards** Amex, Visa, Eurocard and MasterCard. **Pets** Dogs allowed (+30F). **Nearby** Saignon church, Luberon, Buoux, Saint-Symphorien priory, Bonnieux, Lacoste, Ménerbes, Oppède, Maubec, Robion – 18-hole Saumane golf course. **Open** All year except Nov 15 – 30 and 15 days in Jan (closed Wednesday).

The Auberge du Presbytère is made up of three village houses joined together, making for an entertaining variety of floor levels. The decoration is that of a country house, with period furniture and Pierre Frey and Souleïado Provençal-style fabrics. The bedrooms (not all of which yet have bathrooms) are charming and have lovely curtains made by Mme Bernardi herself. The restaurant offers two daily menus featuring delicious traditional and local dishes. The Auberge is a charming and friendly place to stay in the heart of the Luberon where Monsieur and Madame Bernardi will greet you like friends.

How to get there (Map 33): 3.5km southeast of Apt; in the village.

Hostellerie du Vieux Château

Route de Sainte-Cécile
84830 Sérignan (Vaucluse)
Tel. 90.70.05.58 - Fax 90.70.05.62 - M. and Mme Truchot

Rooms 7 with telephone, bath, WC, TV and minibar - Wheelchair accessible.
Price Double 300-800F. **Meals** Breakfast 40F, served 8:00-10:00. **Restaurant** Closed
Sunday evening and Monday in low season. Service 12:30-13:30, 19:30-21:00;
menus 140-180F, also à la carte. Specialties: Jambon persillé, foie gras au Beaume
de Venise, canard aux cassis, agneau de la Drôme, truffes au chocolat et raisins au
marc. **Credit cards** Amex, Visa, Eurocard and MasterCard. **Pets** Dogs allowed (+50F).
Facilities Swimming pool, parking. **Nearby** Arc de triomphe and old theatre in Orange,
Chorégies of Orange in July and Augut, Mornas, Henri Fabre museum in Sérignan.
Open All year except late Dec, 1 week in Feb (closed Sunday evening and Monday in
low season).

This was originally a farmhouse with a mill in the back whose
only remaining trace is a canal which flows by the house.
Today, the hotel is a large village house flanked by a small vegetable
garden and a pleasant flower garden filled with fragrant lavender
around the swimming pool. The owners run a very traditional
hotel, with Monsieur Truchot in the kitchen and his wife at the
reception. The atmosphere is that of a quiet, family-style provincial
auberge. The bedrooms are all individually decorated, with the
decor occasionally overdone. Our favorite is Number 6, with the
poppies. In summer, meals are served in the shade of the beautiful
plane trees in the garden, making for a very Provençal setting.

How to get there *(Map 33): 7km northeast of Orange. Via A7, Orange*
exit, (or Bollène if you are coming from Lyon), in the direction of Bollène and
D976 in the direction of Sérignan.

497

Hostellerie Le Beffroi ★★★

Haute Ville - Rue de l'Evêché
84110 Vaison-la-Romaine (Vaucluse)
Tel. 90.36.04.71 - Fax 90.36.24.78 - M. Christiansen

Rooms 22 with telephone, bath or shower, WC, TV and minibar. **Price** Single 320-415F, double 435-630F, suite 630-725F. **Meals** Breakfast 45F, served 7:30-9:45; half board 430-525F, full board 525-685F (per pers., 3 days min.). **Restaurant** Closed Monday, Tuesday noon in winter. Service 12:00-13:45, 19:15-21:30; menus 98F, 185F, also à la carte. Specialties: Terrine d'agneau aux pommes, confit de pintade à la graine de moutarde, crème brûlée au miel de lavande. **Credit cards** All major. **Pets** Dogs allowed (+30F). **Facilities** Minigolf, games, table tennis, parking. **Nearby** Arc de Triomphe and old theatre in Orange, Mornas, Henri Fabre museum in Sérignan. **Open** March 15 – Nov 15 and Dec 15 – Feb 15.

This hotel high up in the medieval part of Vaison, consists of several mansions joined together. The buildings' character has been preserved, with tiled floors, polished paneling, spiral staircases and beautiful antiques, paintings and curios. The bedrooms are all different; antique lovers will be especially taken by the quality of the period furniture. The lounges are also pleasantly furnished and have open fireplaces. A superb terrace garden gives lovely views over the rooftops of the town. In summer, meals are served here, along with very reasonably priced salads.

How to get there *(Map 33): 30km northeast of Orange via D975; at the top of the town.*

Auberge de la Fontaine

Place de la Fontaine
84210 Venasque (Vaucluse)
Tel. 90.66.02.96 – Fax 90.66.13.14 – M. and Mme Soehlke

Rooms 5 suites with air-conditioning, telephone, bath, WC, TV and minibar. **Price** Suite 700F. **Meals** Breakfast 50F. **Restaurant** Closed Wednesday and from mid-Nov to mid-Dec. Service every evening 20:00-22:00 and Sunday 12:00-14:00; menu 200F, also à la carte. Specialties: Assiette du pêcheur, choucroute au foie gras, gibier frais en saison, pigeonneau aux airelles. **Credit cards** Visa, Eurocard and MasterCard. **Pets** Dogs allowed. **Facilities** Mountain bike rental, parking. **Nearby** Venasque church, Gallo-Roman cemetery in Mazan, Pernes-les-Fontaines, Carpentras – 18-hole Saumane golf course. **Open** All year.

The Auberge de la Fontaine is a beautiful old village house which Ingrid and Christian Soehlke have completely restructured inside, creating an amusing maze of mezzanines, terraces and stairways. While conserving the structure's noble appearance, they particularly sought to create the informal atmosphere of a house for friends. And it would be difficult not to feel at ease: each suite includes a bedroom and a lounge with a fireplace, tastefully decorated and furnished in very Provençal style and equipped with a direct-dial phone, television, and cassette, CD players, fax and minitel. Each has a secluded terrace and a kitchenette, but the charming dining room and the Soehlkes' succulent cuisine should not be missed. There is a dinner concert each month, and in the low season, the hotel proposes a 5-day package with cooking lessons.

How to get there (Map 33): 11km south of Carpentras via D9.

Auberge Les Bichonnières **

Route de Savigneux
01330 Ambérieux-en-Dombes (Ain)
Tel. 74.00.82.07 - Fax 74.00.89.61 - M. Sauvage

Rooms 9 with telephone, bath or shower and WC. **Price** Single 210F, double 230-300F. **Meals** Breakfast 35F, served 8:00-10:00; half board 240F (per pers., 3 days min.). **Restaurant** Service 12:15-14:00, 19:30-21:00; menus 98-240F, also à la carte. Specialties: Grenouilles fraîches, volaille de Bresse. **Credit cards** Amex, Visa, Eurocard and MasterCard. **Pets** Dogs allowed. **Facilities** Parking. **Nearby** Trévoux, bird reserve in Villard-les-Dombes, Montluel, Pérouges – 18-hole Le Clou golf course in Villard-les-Dombes. **Open** All year (closed Sunday evening and Monday in low season).

Not far north of Lyon, this roadside (yet quiet) inn is an old farmhouse that has been restored but still retains its rustic character – not a fake, kitsch version of rustic, as is too often the case, but the genuine article with all its charm. The flower-filled courtyard where meals can be enjoyed in the shade of large white parasols brings to mind Italian sidewalk cafés. The bedrooms are comfortable, with pleasant decor in keeping with the rural character of the building. This hotel provides a good stopping place just before Lyon and an ideal base for exploring the picturesque, lake-dotted Dombe area. Chef Marc Sauvage trained with Fernand Point and prepares regional specialities using fresh local produce.

How to get there *(Map 26): 30km north of Lyon via A6, Villefranche exit, then D904 towards Bourg-en-Bresse, then Villars-les-Dombes.*

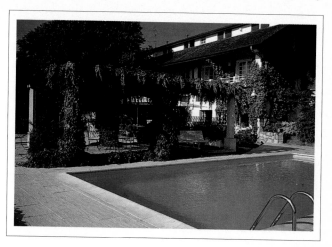

Auberge des Chasseurs ★★★

Naz–Dessus
01170 Echenevex (Ain)
Tel. 50.41.54.07 - Fax 50.41.90.61 - M. Lamy

Rooms 15 with telephone, bath or shower, WC and TV. **Price** Single 350-500F, double 400-600F. **Meals** Breakfast 50F, served 8:00-10:00; half board 480-600F (per pers.). **Restaurant** Service 12:00-13:30, 19:00-21:30; menus 175-300F, also à la carte. Specialties: Filet mignon de porc bigarade, escalope barbue au basilic et brocolis, filet de truite rose au gingembre. **Credit cards** All major. **Pets** Dogs allowed (+40F). **Facilities** Swimming pool, tennis, parking. **Nearby** Le Pailly and col de la Faucille, château of Fernet-Voltaire – 27-hole Maison Blanche golf course in Echenevex. **Open** March 10 – Nov 15.

Standing on the slopes of the Jura, amidst fields and woods, and yet just 15 minutes from Geneva, the Auberge des Chasseurs is an old farmhouse which has been very well restored. The homey atmosphere inside is very charming. The beamed ceilings, chairs and bedroom doors are decorated with floral frescos recently done by a Swedish artist. In the restaurant, there is a magnificent series of photographs by Cartier-Bresson. Upstairs, you will find a very inviting lounge and bar. The bedrooms are beautifully decorated with Laura Ashley fabrics and wallpapers, English-pine furniture and their charming bathrooms are as lovely. Outside, the oak garden furniture was designed by an artist, as was the mosaic of the terrace floor. The garden is full of flowers and shady spots, and the view is splendid. The cuisine is excellent, the service attentive and Dominique Lamy is a very hospitable owner.

How to get there *(Map 20): 17km northwest of Genève via D984 towards St-Genis-Pouilly, then D978c towards Echenevex; at Chevry head for Naz-Dessus.*

Hostellerie du Vieux Pérouges ★★★★

Place du Tilleul
01800 Pérouges (Ain)
Tel. 74.61.00.88 – Fax 74.34.77.90 – M. Thibaut

Rooms 28 with telephone, bath, shower, WC and 4 with TV. **Price** Single 390-700F, double 450-900F, suite 980F. **Meals** Breakfast 60F, served 8:00-12:00. **Restaurant** Service 12:00-14:00, 19:00-21:00; menus 170-390F, also à la carte. Specialties: Filet de carpe farci à l'ancienne, volaille de Bresse, panaché pérougien, galette de l'hostellerie. **Credit cards** Visa, Eurocard and MasterCard. **Pets** Dogs allowed. **Facilities** Parking. **Nearby** Trévoux, bird reserve in Villard-les-Dombes, Montluel – 18-hole Le Clou golf course in Villard-les-Dombes. **Open** All year.

The hotel lies among the narrow streets of the medieval part of the town. The bedrooms in the *Pavilion des trois saisons* are charming; not unexpectedly, the *Printemps* room is bright and fresh. The annex has great old-fashioned charm. The bedrooms in it overlook the garden and the countryside. Room 2 has warm colors and antique furniture and is very attractive although it faces the street. The bedrooms in the main building are more expensive, stone stairways, stained-glass windows and four-poster beds combine to create a medieval effect. Whether seigneurial, as in the *Noble* bedroom, or more modest, as in the *Remparts* bedroom, each one takes you back to the Pérouges of the Middle Ages. The same atmosphere is found in the restaurant, where local specialties are served by staff in traditional dress. The antique furniture is exceptional.

How to get there *(Map 26): 35km northeast of Lyon via A42, Pérouges exit.*

Hôtel de la Santoline ★★
07460 Beaulieu (Ardèche)
Tel. 75.39.01.91 – Fax 75.39.38.79
M. and Mme Espenel

Rooms 7 with telephone, bath, WC and minibar (some with air-conditioning).
Price Double 290-370F, suite 530F. **Meals** Breakfast 40F, served 8:00-10:00; half
board 310-425F, full board 375-495F, (per pers., 3 days min.). **Restaurant** Service
19:30-21:30; menus 155-240F, also à la carte. Specialties: Blinis au saumon et aux
épinards, assiette d'agneau, pieds et paquets. **Credit cards** Visa, Eurocard and
MasterCard. **Pets** Dogs allowed (+30F). **Facilities** Swimming pool, parking.
Nearby La Cocalière cave, bois de Païolive, corniche du Vivarais, Les Vans to la
Bastide-Puylaurent. **Open** March – Nov.

Standing right in the middle of Provençal Ardèche, la Santoline is a converted stone hunting lodge. It is a haven of peace and commands views as far as the Cévennes. A beautiful vaulted cellar has been turned into a dining-room, and the simple decor of the bedrooms, all of which have pretty bathrooms, is perfectly in tune with the unadorned style of the building. Our favorites are Room 5 and especially Room 4, under the eaves; both have marvelous view of the surrounding country side and are equipped with air conditioning. The swimming pool is much appreciated in summer, as is the pleasant flowery terrace where breakfast and dinner can be served. Pierre and Marie-Danièle Espenel are friendly hosts, and prices are very reasonable.

How to get there *(Map 32): 84km north of Nîmes via N106 to Alès, then D904 and D104 to La Croisée de Jalès, then D225.*

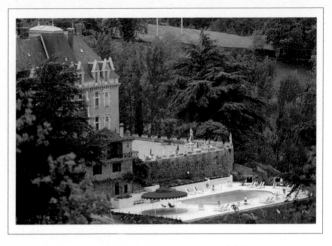

Château d'Urbilhac ★★★

07270 Lamastre (Ardèche)
Tel. 75.06.42.11 – Fax 75.06.52.75
Mme Xompero

Rooms 13 with telephone, bath or shower and WC. **Price** Single 450F, double 500-650F. **Meals** Breakfast 65F, served 8:00-11:00; half board 500-575F (per pers.). **Restaurant** Closed lunchtime except weekends. Service at 12:30 and 19:30; menu 200F. Specialties: Chartreuse de langoustines crème au cocombre, blanquette de lotte à l'orange et au gingembre riz sauvage, trilogie d'oranges à la mandarine impériale, croustade de frangipane glace à la vanille coulis café. **Credit cards** All major. **Pets** Dogs allowed in bedroom. **Facilities** Heated swimming pool, tennis, parking. **Nearby** Tournon, Vivarais steam train between Tournon and Lamastre – 18-hole golf course in Chambon-sur-Lignon. **Open** May 1 – Oct 5.

The Château d'Urbilhac, built in the last century in Renaissance style over the cellars of a 16th-century fortified house, is set in 148-acres of parkland. A weekend here is like a dream of 19th-century living, without a false note, for the Château could be a museum of the furniture of that age. The emphasis here is on character and authenticity, and a vivid period atmosphere prevails throughout. Whether in the bedrooms, the living rooms or dining room, the use of velvet and damask fabrics is in perfect harmony with the tapestries. Engravings, paintings, mirrors, chandeliers – even the elegant china – take you back a century in time, without sacrificing modern bathroom comforts. A peaceful setting and a warm welcome are other noteworthy features of the *vie de château* awaiting you in this hotel whose gastronomic reputation is growing.

How to get there *(Map 26): 36km west of Valence via D533.*

504

Grangeon

07800 Saint-Cierge-la-Serre (Ardèche)
Tel. 75.65.73.86
Mme Valette

Rooms 5 of which 4 with bath, 2 with shower and 2 with WC. **Price** Double 290-480F. **Meals** Breakfast 37F, served 8:00-9:00. **Restaurant** Evening meals for residents only. Service 19:30; menu 160F. Specialties: Agneau au miel, papillotes de lapin à l'aneth et au pastis. **Credit cards** Not accepted. **Pets** Dogs not allowed. **Facilities** Parking. **Nearby** Valence museum, villages romanesque church and châteaux of the Ardèche – 18-hole Valence golf course in Saint-Didier-de-Charpey. **Open** On reservation April 10 – Nov 1.

Grangeon is the ideal place for those seeking a peaceful retreat and for nature lovers. It is an estate of 155-acres of parkland and forests, 4km away from the nearest village, and is reached by a small road winding through hills and woods. The house itself was built at the beginning of the 18th century and has seven bedrooms. The decoration combines wood and stone to create a warm country atmosphere. (Guests can play the piano.) All kinds of vegetables grow in Mme Valette's lovely terraced garden, and as she bakes her own bread and raises sheep, she is almost self-sufficient. Set in the heart of the Ardèche region and yet only 15km from the motorway, Grangeon provides an opportunity to relax in the countryside.

How to get there *(Map 26): 35km south of Valence via A7, Loriol exit, then N104 towards Privas-Aubenas; at Les Fonts-du-Pouzin D265 towards Saint-Cierge (follow signs).*

Hôtel Bellier **

Avenue de Provence
26420 La Chapelle-en-Vercors (Drôme)
Tel. 75.48.20.03 – Fax 75.48.25.31 – Mme Bellier

Rooms 12 with telephone, bath or shower, WC and TV. **Price** Single 150-180F, double 300-440F. **Meals** Breakfast 40F, served 8:00-11:30; half board 280-370F, full board 400-490F (per pers., 3 days min.). **Restaurant** Service 12:30-13:45, 19:30-21:15; menus 90-210F, also à la carte. Specialties: Truite Bellier, poulet aux écrevisses, pintadeau au genièvre, poulet aux morilles. **Credit cards** All major. **Pets** Dogs allowed. **Facilities** Swimming pool, parking. **Nearby** Pont-en-Royans, road des Petits and Grands Goulets, La Luire cave, Col of Rousset, Lente forest, Draye Blanche cave – 9-hole golf course in La-Chapelle-en-Vercors. **Open** All year.

This hotel is built in chalet style and stands on a slope above the edge of the village. Its terrace and flower-filled garden have a lovely view of the fields and mountains. As this is a mountain hotel, the interior is Alpine in design. The bedrooms are quiet and comfortable. In the restaurant, the menu is both refined and varied, and meals can be served outside. There is a lovely swimming pool and you will enjoy a friendly welcome.

How to get there *(Map 26): 63km east of Valence. 62km southwest of Grenoble via D531 to Villard-de-Lans, then D103.*

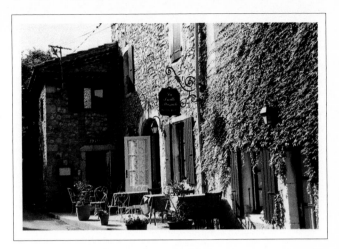

La Treille Muscate ★★★

26270 Cliousclat (Drôme)
Tel. 75.63.13.10 - Fax 75.63.10.79
Mme Delaitre

Rooms 10 with telephone, bath, WC and TV. **Price** Double 280-400F. **Meals** Breakfast 40F, served 8:00-10:00. **Restaurant** Closed Tuesday. Service 12:00-13:30, 20:00-21:30; menus 85-125F, also à la carte. Specialties: Beignets d'aubergines, dos de saumon poêlé aux herbes fraîches, crème de potiron aux moules et coriandre fraîche. **Credit cards** Visa, Eurocard and MasterCard. **Pets** Dogs allowed. **Facilities** Swimming pool. **Nearby** Mirmande, Poët-Laval; le quartier des Forts in Nyons – 18-hole Valdaine golf course. **Open** All year except Jan and Feb.

L a Treille Muscate is exactly the kind of small hotel you hope to find in a Provençal village. Beautiful sunny yellow walls brighten the on the ground floor rooms; here you will find the dining room with its bright Provençal table linens, the corner bar and the small TV room. There are several pieces of handsome regional furniture, large watercolors, varnished jugs and splendid dinnerware crafted by a skilled potter, a neighbor and friend; all create a decor that makes you feel truly at home. Upstairs, pretty bedrooms have recently been installed and beautifully decorated. They have a lovely view out over the quiet village or the countryside. The excellent cuisine is enhanced with aromatic herbs and local products. In good weather, a few tables are set out on the village side or in a small garden, bordered with terraced walls. "The Muscat Arbor" is a hospitable, charming small hotel with extremely reasonable prices.

How to get there *(Map 26): 16km north of Montélimar via A7, Loriol exit, then 5km. On N7 Montélimard direction*

Manoir de la Roseraie ★★★

26230 Grignan (Drôme)
Tel. 75.46.58.15 – Fax 75.46.91.55
M. and Mme Alberts

Rooms 15 with telephone, bath or shower, WC and TV - Wheelchair accessible.
Price Single and double 630-1050F, suite 1600F. **Meals** Breakfast 85F, served 8:00-
10:30; half board 595-805F (per pers., 3 days min.). **Restaurant** Service 12:00-
13:30, 20:00-21:15; menus 170-220F. Specialties: Croustillant de filet d'agneau au
miel de tapenade, filet de sole à la graine de moutarde, foie gras maison, belle cave
de côte du Rhône. **Credit cards** All major. **Pets** Dogs allowed (+60F).
Facilities Heated swimming pool, tennis, sauna, parking. **Nearby** Château and
museum of Mme de Sévigné in Grignan, Poët-Laval, Dieulefit – 9-hole Valaurie golf
course. **Open** All year except Jan 5 – Feb 14 and Nov 6 – 13 (closed Monday in low season).

In this beautiful private mansion built in 1850 by the mayor of
Grignan, Michèle Alberts and her husband have tastefully
refurbished and decorated the bedrooms and the suite. Those on
the ground and first floors are imposingly large with their high
ceilings, and are bright and comfortable, while the ones on the
deuxième étage are more intimate. They have colorful and sometimes
unusual bathrooms. (The *Baccara* room, for instance, has a circular
bath.) The elegant salmon-pink dining room looks out onto the
ravishingly beautiful park, which is planted with cedars,
bougainvillea and 350 rose bushes. The heated swimming pool is
prettily integrated into the design of the park. Meals and the
breakfast buffet are served on the large terrace in summer. The staff
is very friendly.

How to get there *(Map 33): 90km north of Avignon via A7, Montélimar-
Sud exit, then N7 and D133.*

Domaine du Colombier ★★★

Route de Donzère
Malataverne - 26780 Montélimar (Drôme)
Tel. 75.90.86.86 - Fax 75.90.79.40 - M. and Mme Barette

Rooms 20 and 5 suites with telephone, bath, WC and TV. **Price** Single 400-580F, double 450-860F, suite 860-1200F. **Meals** Breakfast 70F, served 7:30-11:00. **Restaurant** Service 12:15-14:15, 19:15-21:30; menus 190-230F, also à la carte. Specialties: Omelette aux truffes et foie gras, pot-au-feu de mer aux ravioles de Royans, noix de ris de veau au champagne. **Credit cards** All major. **Pets** Dogs allowed (+50F). **Facilities** Swimming pool, bowling alley, bicycles, parking. **Nearby** Poët-Laval, Nyons, château and museum of Mme de Sévigné in Grignan, villages of the Drôme between Montélimar and Orange. **Open** All year.

Formerly a 14th-Century abbey, the Domaine du Colombier maintains its tradition of hospitality to travelers to this day, as it is now a pleasant hotel conveniently located on the road south. Although only minutes off the highway, it seems to be in the middle of the countryside. When you walk through the door be prepared to find furniture and fabrics piled up in the entrance hall, for it is also a shop. The bedrooms are bright, colorful and comfortably decorated; three of them have a small mezzanine. In the garden, the swimming pool, surrounded by chaises longues, is a lovely place to relax. The lavender-blue furniture in the dining room is Provençal in style, and dinner or an evening drink can also be served on the patio.

How to get there *(Map 33): 9km south of Montélimar via N7 and D144a (2km after Malataverne).*

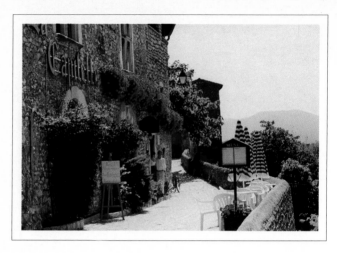

La Capitelle ★★
Rue du Rempart
26270 Mirmande (Drôme)
Tel. 75.63.02.72 - Fax 75.63.02.50 - M. and Mme Melki

Rooms 10 plus 2 apartments with telephone, bath or shower (10 with WC). **Price** Single and double 260-550F. **Meals** Breakfast 45-50F, served 8:00-10:30; half board 315-445F. **Restaurant** Service 12:00-13:30, 19:30-21:30; menu 85-175F, also à la carte. Specialties: Brouillade aux truffes du Tricastin, demi pigeon farci au foie gras de canard, tulipe de fruits rouges, nougat glacé. **Credit cards** Diners, Visa, Eurocard and MasterCard. **Pets** dogs allowed (+35F). **Facilities** Garage (+70F). **Nearby** Mirmande church, Pöet-Laval, Nyons – 18-hole Valdaine golf course. **Open** Feb 15 – Jan 10 (closed Tuesday and Wednesday lunchtime).

La Capitelle is a tall Renaissance building with mullioned windows. The lounge and dining-room have vaulted ceilings and handsome stone fireplaces. Items of period furniture combine well with more simple contemporary furnishings to create an elegant and yet warm atmosphere. A sober and sure taste is also in evidence in the bedrooms, which are all different. The hotel stands in the center of Mirmande, a historic landmark. Although it has no garden, its leafy setting provides peace and quiet. In the restaurant, a friendly and attentive chef prepares excellent gourmet cuisine and regional specialities.

How to get there *(Map 26): 17km south of Valence via N7, then D204; at the entrance to Mirmande.*

Auberge du Vieux Village ★★★

Route de Gap
Aubres - 26110 Nyons (Drôme)
Tel. 75.26.12.89 - Fax 75.26.38.10 - Mme Colombe

Rooms 23 with telephone, bath, shower, WC, TV (13 with minibar). **Price** Single and double 300-780F, suite 1100F. **Meals** Breakfast 52F, served 8:00-10:30; half board 360-657F, full board 440-737F. **Restaurant** Closed Wednesday lunchtime in low season. Service 12:00-14:00, 19:30-21:00; menus 80-240F, also à la carte. Specialties: Agneau au miel, poulet fermier à l'estragon, selle d'agneau aux champignons, gratins de légumes. **Credit cards** All major. **Pets** Dogs allowed. **Facilities** Heated swimming pool, health center, sauna and sunbed (60F), parking. **Nearby** Château and museum of Mme de Sévigné in Grignan, Drôme villages (La Garde-Adhémar, Clansayes, Saint-Paul-Trois-Châteaux, Saint-Restitut, Suze-la-Rousse, Montségur-sur-Lauzon, Saint-Turquoit, Visan). **Open** All year.

This hotel is built on a high lookout point where a castle once stood, which explains its exceptional views over the village and the whole valley. The Auberge has a terrace with lounge chairs where the panorama can be enjoyed to the full. The bedrooms are subdued in style, comfortable and quiet. They are all equipped with color television and have wonderful views. The lovely old dining room (with smoking and no-smoking areas) is furnished with period furniture, including a beautiful tall clock. It also offers spectacular views from its large picture windows.

How to get there *(Map 33): 55km southeast of Montélimar via A7, Montélimar-Sud exit, then D133, D141, D538 and D94 towards Gap. 7km from Nyons.*

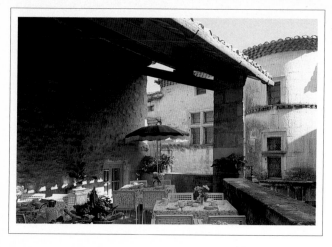

Auberge des 4 Saisons ★★★

Place de l'Eglise
26130 Saint-Restitut (Drôme)
Tel. 75.04.71.88 – Fax 75.04.70.88 – M. Fritsch

Rooms 10 with telephone, bath or shower, WC (5 with TV). **Price** Single 250-340F, double 300-450F. **Meals** Breakfast 40-45F, served 8:00-10:00; half board 300-360F (per pers., 7 days min.). **Restaurant** "36 Soupières". Service 12:30-13:30, 19:30-21:30. Closed Saturday lunchtime. à la carte. Specialties: Feuilleté d'escargots à la sauce roquefort, carré d'agneau aux herbes, menu-truffes. **Credit card** All major. **Pets** Dogs allowed. **Nearby** Château and museum of Mme de Sévigné in Grignan, Drôme villages (La Garde-Adhémar, Clansayes, Saint-Paul-Trois-Châteaux, Saint-Restitut, Suze-la-Rousse, Montségur-sur-Lauzon, Saint Turquoit, Visan). **Open** All year except Jan.

Several ancient Roman stone houses covered in Virginia creeper have been converted to accommodate the Auberge des 4 Saisons and, next to it, the very good Restaurant des 36 Soupières. Set in the medieval part of the village, they give onto the small square where the church stands. The bedrooms are all very comfortable, pleasant and quiet. They are furnished with antiques and everything is well coordinated and tasteful. Some are like small apartments, and in one room a closet has been made into a child's bedroom. Served in beautiful vaulted rooms, the cuisine is excellent, featuring traditional recipes made with the freshest produce. This is a very charming auberge, where you will be greeted with warm hospitality.

How to get there *(Map 33): 9km north of Bollène via D160 ; in the village.*

Ferme Saint-Michel **

26130 Solérieux (Drôme)
Tel. 75.98.10.66 – Fax 75.98.19.09
M. Laurent

Rooms 15 with telephone (13 with bath and WC, 10 with TV). **Price** Single 300-330F, double 310-350F. **Meals** Breakfast 38F, served 9:00-10:00, half board 310F (per pers., 3 days min.). **Restaurant** Service 12:30-14:00, 20:00-21:15; menus 130-180F, also à la carte. Specialties: Menu-truffe. **Credit cards** Visa, Eurocard and MasterCard. **Pets** Dogs not allowed. **Facilities** Swimming pool, tennis, parking. **Nearby** Château and museum of Mme de Sévigné in Grignan, Forts in Nyons, Poët-Laval, Dieulefit, villages of the Drôme – 9-hole Valaurie golf course. **Open** Jan 24 – Dec 23 (closed Sunday evening and Monday).

Partially renovated and under new ownership, the Ferme Saint-Michel is a traditional old Provençal *mas*, isolated from the road by thick vegetation, whose origins go back to the 16th century. The Ferme opens onto an inviting terrace where, in summer, a few tables are set for dinner. You will savor excellent local products such as the truffles harvested on the property, and game in season. Large trees afford lovely shade over the terrace, while a few steps away, there is the swimming pool. For the moment, we can recommend only the bedrooms which have been renovated. They are simple with modern conveniences, and they are decorated with local Souleïado fabrics, which harmonize beautifully with the Provençal furniture. On the ground floor, there is a cool dining room, a small bar and inviting lounges with fireplaces.

How to get there *(Map 33): North of Bollène. On A7, Bollène or Montélimar-Sud exit, direction Saint-Paul-Trois-Châteaux.*

Auberge de la Rochette

La Rochette
26400 Vauvaneys-la-Rochette (Drôme)
Tel. 75.25.79.30 - Fax 75.25.79.25

Rooms 5 with telephone, 13 with shower, WC, TV and minibar. **Price** Double 350-550F. **Meals** Breakfast-brunch 50F, served 7:30-10:00; half board 345F (per pers., 3 days min.). **Restaurant** Service 12:00-13:30, 19:30-21:00; menus 120-190F. Specialties: Foie gras de canard maison, agneau de la Drôme au jus d'aïl, pigeonneau au miel and vinaigre de framboise, crème brûlée à la lavande. **Credit cards** Visa, Eurocard and MasterCard. **Pets** Dogs allowed (+40F). **Facilities** Swimming pool, parking. **Nearby** Shoe Museum in Romans, Facteur Cheval's Palace in Hauterives, Massif du Vercors, villages of the Drôme. **Open** All year except 15 days in Feb and Wednesday.

Located in the stunningly beautiful setting of Provençal Drôme, the Auberge is an old barn which has been restored in the regional style. The small size allows the owners to receive guests informally, like friends. The beautiful rooms have been carefully designed down to the last detail. (A room with a mezzanine and high ceilings was designed with families or groups of friends in mind). The decor includes warm sand-colored walls, Provençal quilted bedspreads and matching drapes, terracotta-tile floor and antique furniture. An elegant small dining room opens onto a flower-filled terrace where regional specialties are served. This is a charming, very friendly inn.

How to get there *(Map 26): 20km south of Valence, on A7 exit Loriol or Valence-Sud, direction Crest; before Crest, take road for Vauvaneys, then La Rochette on D538 coming from Valence.*

Château de Passières ★★
38930 Chichilianne (Isère)
Tel. 76.34.45.48 – Fax 76.34.46.25
M. Perli

Rooms 23 with telephone, bath, shower and 20 with WC. **Price** Single 280F, double 280-420F. **Meals** Breakfast 35F, served 7:30-9:30; half board 310F on request (per pers., 3 days min.). **Restaurant** Closed Monday in low season and Nov – Jan. Service 12:15-13:30, 19:15-21:00; menus 95-200F, also à la carte. Specialties: Fricassée de cèpes et escargots, escalope de saumon du miel de pissenlit. **Credit cards** Visa, Eurocard and MasterCard. **Pets** Dogs allowed (+20F). **Facilities** Swimming pool, tennis, sauna, parking. **Nearby** Mont Aiguille, Vercors plateau, Grenoble. **Open** Feb 1 – Nov 1 (closed Sunday evening and Monday in low season).

This hotel occupies a truly exceptional position at the foot of the Mont Aiguille, an extraordinary mountain which dominates the entire area. This 15th-century castle, skillfully restored by Yvon Perli, has 23 bedrooms. Three of them are magnificent, with superb antique panelling and truly royal furnishings. The other ones offer modern amenities at reasonable prices. The dining room is spacious and sunny, and the menu features traditional but inventive cuisine, which can also be enjoyed on the terrace. The lounge is very romantic, with lovely sofas and a wealth of curios, as well as a collection of portraits. The swimming pool is surrounded by beautiful scenery. The Château de Passières is a must in this little-known region.

How to get there *(Map 26): 50km south of Grenoble via N75 towards Sisteron until Clelles, then D7 and D7b.*

Domaine de Clairefontaine **
38121 Chonas-L'Amballan (Isère)
Tel. 74.58.81.52 - Fax 74.58.80.93
M. Girardon

Rooms 14 and 2 apartments with telephone and 13 with bath and WC (TV on request).
Price Single and double 180-380F, suite 360-710F. **Meals** Breakfast 40F, served
7:30-9:00. **Restaurant** Closed Sunday evening and Monday. Service 12:00-13:45,
19:00-21:00; menus 130-350F, also à la carte. Specialties: Brochette de noix de
Saint-Jacques poëlées, papillonade de rouget beurre au basilic, rosace d'agneau
rôti au romarin. **Credit cards** All major. **Pets** Dogs allowed. **Facilities** Tennis, parking,
garage. **Nearby** Saint-Pierre church and lapidary museum in Vienne, wine tasting.
Open Feb 1 –Oct 31.

Clairefontaine is run by Mme Girardon and her two sons, who
are responsible for the excellent cuisine here. One makes of
the morning croissants, pastries and desserts, while the other does
the main dishes, from stocks to sauces. The delicious meals are
further enhanced by the beautiful view from the dining room across
the grounds, where peacocks parade on the lawns beneath age-old
trees. The bedrooms differ greatly in style and furnishings and will
appeal to all tastes and pocketbooks. In the main building the high-
ceilinged rooms with creaking floors and period furniture have a
distinctive country house atmosphere. (Room 3 is probably the
the most beautiful, but they all are charming.) Those in the annex
have more modern amenities.

*How to get there (Map 26): 12km south of Vienne via A7, Vienne exit,
then N7 or N86 and D7 towards Le Péage-en-Roussillon or Chanas exit
then N7 Vienne direction.*

Chalet Mounier ★★★

38860 Les Deux-Alpes (Isère)
Tel. 76.80.56.90 – Fax 76.79.56.51
M. and Mme Mounier

Rooms 48 with telephone, bath or shower, TV and 44 with WC. **Price** Single 290-510F, double 335-780F. **Meals** Breakfast incl., served 7:30-9:30; half board 295-565F, full board 375-645F (per pers., 3 days min.). **Restaurant** Service 12:30-14:00, 19:30-21:00; menus 120-280F, also à la carte. **Credit cards** Visa, Eurocard and MasterCard. **Pets** Dogs allowed. **Facilities** Heated swimming pool, covered swimming pool, sauna, hamman, health center, garage (+40F). **Nearby** Ski lifts (100m), village of Venosc, Bézardé valley, Ecrins park, massif of La Meije. **Open** June 24 – Sept 5 and Dec 17 – May 3.

This chalet was originally a mountain refuge and farm but since 1933 has grown into a large and modern hotel while retaining its charm. The welcoming entrance hall immediately establishes the atmosphere of the hotel. You will be charmed by the decor of the lounge and the restaurant, whose large windows open onto the garden and the swimming pool and onto the snow-clad slopes in winter. The bedrooms are all comfortable and have balconies with unrestricted views of the mountains. Chef Robert Mounier prides himself on his hearty, succulent cuisine, which is very professionally served. There is also a newly opened small restaurant for gourmet fare. The hotel is very quiet and the people are very friendly.

How to get there *(Map 27): 74km southeast of Grenoble (detour from Grenoble via Pont-de-Claix) via N85 to Vizille; then N91 to the barrage (dam) on the Chambon via Bourg-d'Oisans, then D213 to Les Deux-Alpes.*

Château de la Commanderie ★★★
17, avenue d'Echirolles
Eybens- 38320 Grenoble (Isère)
Tel. 76.25.34.58 – Fax 76.24.07.31 – M. de Beaumont

Rooms 25 with telephone, bath or shower, WC, TV and minibar. **Price** Single 375-590F, double 415-630F. **Meals** Breakfast 52F, served 7:00-10:00. **Restaurant** Closed Saturday and Sunday lunchtime. Service 12:00-14:00, 19:30-21:45; menu 139-165F, also à la carte. **Credit cards** All major. **Pets** Dogs allowed (+50F). **Facilities** Swimming pool, parking. **Nearby** Grenoble museum, massifs of Vercors, Chartreuse and Oisans – 18-hole Bresson-Eybens golf course. **Open** All year.

Formerly a hospice of the Knights of Malta, the Château de la Commanderie is ideally located just 5km from the center of Grenoble and half an hour from the Olympic ski slopes. A large, lovely walled garden planted with centuries-old trees gives it an air of space and tranquillity rare in a town hotel. The bedrooms combine modern comforts and facilities with period furniture, old engravings and carefully chosen fabrics. Breakfast is a substantial affair served on the terrace in summer, or in vast 18th-century rooms decorated with family portraits. Next to it is a large dining room decorated with pastoral Aubusson tapestries. The superb cuisine is intelligently innovative and respect ful of its ingredients. A friendly, family atmosphere prevails.

How to get there (Map 26): 4km east of Grenoble via the bypass (south), exit Eybens (Route Napoléon); 500m from Eybens.

Le Lièvre Amoureux ★★★

38840 Saint-Lattier (Isère)
Tel. 76.64.50.67 – Fax 76.64.31.21
M. Breda

Rooms 14 with telephone (12 with bath and 5 with TV). **Price** Double 320-450F, suite 380F. **Meals** Breakfast 55F, served 7:30-10:30. **Restaurant** Menus 175-195F, also à la carte. Specialties: Game, hare on the spit. **Credit cards** All major. **Pets** Dogs allowed (+40F). **Facilities** Swimming pool, parking. **Nearby** Saint-Bernard college in Romans, Facteur Cheval palace, Saint-Antoine abbey. **Open** Feb 15 – Dec 15 (closed Sunday evening and Monday in low season).

This comfortable and welcoming small hotel is nestled in the countryside facing the foothills of the Vercors, to the east of Valence. The bedrooms are in different buildings; those by the swimming pool are large and have a living area. Though modern, they are very charming; their large windows open onto a private terrace. (In the distance, a plantation of walnut trees reminds you of the local speciality.) The other bedrooms, in a small turn-of-the-century house, are also faultless and have a lovely old-fashioned atmosphere. One slight drawback is that they are within earshot of the railway line, so visitors who like total silence should ask for the modern accommodations by the pool.

How to get there *(Map 26): 15km north of Romans via N92.*

Hôtel des Artistes ★★★

8, rue Gaspard-André
69002 Lyon (Rhône)
.Tel. 78.42.04.88 – Fax 78.42.93.76 – Mme Durand

Rooms 45 with telephone, bath or shower, WC, TV and 36 with minibar. **Price** Single 330-390F, double 370-430F. **Meals** Breakfast 45F, served 7:00-11:30. No restaurant. **Credit cards** All major. **Pets** Dogs not allowed. **Nearby** Hôtel de Ville, art museum in Lyon, Yzeron, Mont d'Or Lyonnais, Trévoux, Pérouges – 18-hole Lyon Verger golf course, 9-hole Lyon Chassieux golf course. **Open** All year.

The Hôtel des Artistes (a favorite haunt of artists, as its name and many autographs indicate) is in that old quarter of Lyon, which lies between the embankments of the Rhône and Saône, close to the Place Bellecour and the Célestins Theatre. The bedrooms are decorated with very simple, modern furniture, and differ only in their soft colors. They are all comfortably equipped, with television and good soundproofing, and some have air conditioning. Breakfast is very good, and there is a friendly atmosphere. Special weekend rates are sometimes available. As Lyons has a number of world-famous restaurants, here are several simpler traditional bistros, which also are famous in Lyon: *Le Bistrot de Lyon, Le Bouchon aux Vins, Le Garet,* the *Brasserie Brotteaux,* the *Café Comptoir Abel,* the *Café des Fédérations,* and the *Café des Négociants, Assiette et Marée.*

How to get there (Map 26): *In the town center near Place des Célestins.*

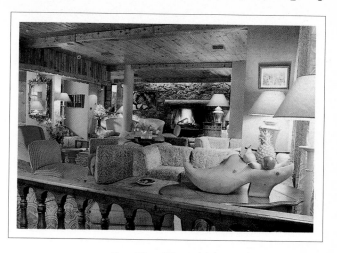

La Sivolière ★★★

Quartier des Chenus
73120 Courchevel (Savoie)
Tel. 79.08.08.33 – Fax 79.08.15.73 – Mme Cattelin

Rooms 30 with telephone, bath, WC and TV. **Price** Double 770-1830F.
Meals Breakfast 75F, served at any time; half board 710-1250F. **Restaurant** Service
12:00-14:30, 19:00-23:00; menus 120-250F. Specialties: Savoyard dishes, côte de
bœuf à la cheminée. **Credit cards** Visa, Eurocard and MasterCard. **Pets** Dogs not
allowed. **Facilities** Sauna, jacuzzi, hamman. **Nearby** Skiing, cable car to La Saulire –
9-hole Courchevel golf course, 18-hole Méribel golf course. **Open** Dec 1 – May 1.

Lying sheltered by trees at the foot of the ski runs is Courchevel's
hôtel de charme. Although quiet and tranquil, it is within walking
distance of the village center. The hotel's friendly atmosphere
reflects the personality of Mme Cattelin, who looks after her guests
personally and has spent twenty years creating what some would
call a little paradise. Everything in the chalet is in good taste: the
decor, the food, the hospitality. Its success is due to a thousand
small touches such as potpourris, fresh flowers and pretty
tablecloths, the delicious *plats du jour* and homemade tarts. The
same care and attention to detail is found in the ski room and living
rooms. This is the kind of place that visitors tend to keep secret.

How to get there *(Map 27): 50km southeast of Albertville via N90 to
Moûtiers, then D915 and D91.*

Lodge Nogentil Hôtel ★★★

73123 Courchevel 1850 (Savoie)
Tel. 79 08 32 32 - Fax 79 08 03 15
Mme Kollmann

Rooms 10 with telephone, bath, WC, TV and minibar. **Price** Double 1100-1550F, suite-duplex 1700-2100F. **Meals** Breakfast incl., served 8:00-14:00. No restaurant. **Credit cards** Amex, Visa, Eurocard and MasterCard. **Pets** Dogs not allowed. **Facilities** Swimming pool, sauna, fitness center, parking. **Nearby** Skiing from hotel – 9-hole Courchevel golf course, 18-hole Méribel golf course. **Open** Nov 27 – May 1.

The new architectural policy of Courchevel is designed to encourage the construction of hotels in the traditional Savoyard style, and the Lodge Nogentil is one of the latest of its new charming chalet-hôtels. Well located at the edge of the Bellecôte ski run, the Nogentil offers only a few rooms, all very pretty indeed. They are bright with luminous wood paneling. The pleasant décor includes rustic furniture, which complements the handsome armoires from Afghanistan. There is the same exotic touch in the lounge. And you're sure of after-ski relaxation, what with the sauna and gym at your disposal. There is no restaurant in the hotel, but a free shuttle will take you to the center of the resort, where there are many beautiful gastronomic restaurants as well as simpler Savoyard bistrots.

How to get there *(Map 27): 50km southeast of Albertville via N90 to Moûtiers, then D915 and D91 to Courchevel 1850.*

La Tour de Pacoret ★★

Montailleur
73460 Grésy-sur-Isère (Savoie)
Tel. 79.37.91.59 – Fax 79.37.93.84 – M. Chardonnet

Rooms 10 with telephone, bath or shower, WC and TV. **Price** Single and double 280-450F. **Meals** Breakfast 45F, served 8:00-10:00; half board 300-400F, full board 390-490F (per pers., 3 days min.). **Restaurant** Service 12:00-13:30, 19:30-21:00; menus 90-120F, also à la carte. Specialties: Délice de Savoie, home-smoked salmon. **Credit cards** Visa, Eurocard and MasterCard. **Pets** Small dogs allowed (+30F). **Facilities** parking. **Nearby** Conflans, fort du Mont, château of Miolans – 27-hole Giez-Faverges golf course. **Open** Mid-April – Nov 1.

This beautiful 14th-century watchtower, standing in the middle of the countryside on a hilltop at the foot of the Alps, has been transformed into an intimate and elegant hotel. A cheerful lounge devoted to reading and music, a dining-room with chalet-style panelling, and carefully chosen watercolors and drawings make a harmonious ensemble. The bedrooms are individually decorated, with well-chosen furnishings and fully-equipped bathrooms. The terrace gardens command splendid views of the snow-capped Alps and of the Isère Valley below, and meals and drinks can be served there in the shade of the wisteria and garden umbrellas. The kitchen garden supplies fresh produce for the table. You will be warmly welcomed by the extremely friendly hosts.

How to get there *(Map 27): 19km southwest of Albertville via N90 towards Montmélian until Pont-de-Grésy, then D222 and D201 towards Montailleur.*

Adray-Télébar ★★

73550 Méribel-les-Allues (Savoie)
Tel. 79.08.60.26 - Fax 79.08.53.85
M. Bonnet

Rooms 26 with telephone, bath or shower (24 with WC). **Price** Single and double 450-750F. **Meals** Breakfast 50F, served 8:00-11:00; half board 500-670F, full board 550-720F (per pers., 3 days min.). **Restaurant** Service 12:00-16:00, 20:00-22:00; menu 190F, also à la carte. Specialties: Escalope à la crème, steak au poivre, tarte aux myrtilles, fondue savoyarde, raclette. **Credit cards** Visa, Eurocard and MasterCard. **Pets** Dogs allowed. **Nearby** Ski ing from hotel, Les Trois Vallées, mountain excursions – 9-hole Courchevel golf course, 18-hole Méribel golf course. **Open** Dec 20 – April 24.

This pretty chalet is only a few steps from the chairlift and the ski runs but it is well located above the valley, with spectacular views of pinewoods and mountains. You reach it via Méribel 1600, where you must leave your car; the hotel staff meets you and to take you to the chalet. The Adray is unrivalled at Méribel, and at lunchtime the large sunny terrace is invaded by skiers. The atmosphere is cheerful and the home cooking excellent. The bedrooms are simple but welcoming, with comfortable rustic furniture. The service is friendly and attentive. This is the place for making the most of the mountains without paying the higher prices of hotels in the village center.

How to get there *(Map 27): 39km south of Albertville via N90 and D95, then D90.*

Le Yéti ★★★

73553 Méribel-les-Allues (Savoie)
Tel. 79.00.51.15 - Fax 79.00.51.73
M. and Mme Saint Ghilhem

Rooms 37 with telephone, bath, WC and cable TV. **Price** Room with half board in winter 780-970F, in summer 590-750F (per pers.). **Restaurant** Service 12:00-15:00, 19:30-22:00; menus 150-210F, also à la carte. **Credit cards** All major. **Pets** Dogs not allowed. **Facilities** Swimming pool, sauna, hammam. **Nearby** Skiing from hotel, Les Trois Vallées, mountain excursions – 9-hole Courchevelle Golf Course, 18-hole Méribel Golf Course. **Open** All year except April 21 – June 30 and Oct 1 – Dec 17.

This chalet-hôtel is located on the western slopes of Méribel, just next to the ski runs. Sophie and Frédéric Saint Guilhem, who are both mountain guides, have decorated the hotel lovingly, and it shows. The walls are panelled in rough, hand-polished wood; the handsome furnishings include pretty objects, kilims, and comfortable armchairs in the bar and in front of the fireplace. The view is magnificent from all vantage points. The bedrooms are extremely comfortable and furnished in the loveliest mountain-chalet style. The panoramic restaurant has a terrace facing due south over a small swimming pool. Finally, when you set out for the lofty summits, Frédéric is there to advise you and to share the adventure.

How to get there *(Map 27): 39m south of Albertville via N90 and D95, then D90.*

Les Châtaigniers

Rue Maurice-Franck
73110 La Rochette (Savoie)
Tel. 79.25.50.21 – Fax 79.25.79.97 – Mme Rey

Rooms 3; 1 suite and 1 apartment with telephone, bath, WC (2 with TV). **Price** Single and double 390F, suite 650-950F. **Meals** Breakfast 65F, served 7:45-10:00; half board from 3 night min. **Restaurant** Service 12:00-13:30, 19:45-21:30; menus 130-270F, also à la carte. Specialties: Foie gras mi-cuit au torchon maison, fish, crème brûlée de homard, andouillette de saucisson chaud maison. **Credit cards** All major. **Pets** Dogs not allowed. **Facilities** Swimming pool, parking. **Nearby** Saint-Pierre-de-Chartreuse, château of Miolans, Charmant Som, belvédère des Sangles, la Grande Chartreuse convent, Wine Route of Savoie – 18-hole Aix-les Bains golf course. **Open** All year except first two weeks in Jan (closed Saturday noon, Sunday evening and Monday in low season).

This family home, which is now a guest house, is as charming as the surrounding valleys and mountains. From the elegant lounge with its grand piano to the beautiful dining-room and the spacious, comfortably furnished bedrooms, throughout the house, you will feel relaxed and at home. The lovely decor and ambience have been created by your two remarkable hosts, Philippe Roman and Madame Rey. Philippe a chef and poet, has trained with several renowned chefs. Ask about his "poetic dinner". Madame Rey is a charming hostess with impeccable taste, and speaks several languages. The atmosphere is lively and light-hearted, and you will certainly want to stay for a while.

How to get there *(Map 27): 30km north of Grenoble via A41, Pontcharra exit, then D925; at La Rochette (opposite Hôtel de Ville) towards Arvillard.*

526

Hôtel Le Calgary ★★★

73620 Les Saisies (Savoie)
Tel. 79 38 98 38 - Fax 79 38 98 00
M. Berthod

Rooms 40 with telephone, bath, TV and minibar. **Price** Double and triple in half board 260-540F, full board 330-610F (per pers.). **Restaurant** Service 12:15-13:30, 19:15-21:00; menu 135-250F, also à la carte. Specialties: Croustade de ris d'agneau aux chanterelles, morille farçie matignon de légumes coulis pistache au génepi, escalope de foie gras frais de canard, loup de mer cuit au vert, gratin de poire dans son sabayon au calvados. **Credit cards** All major. **Pets** Dogs allowed (+40F). **Facilities** Swimming pool, hammam, sauna, garage (40F per day). **Nearby** Skiing from hotel, Olympic cross-country stadium in 200 m – 18-hole Mont d'Arbois golf course in Megève (15 km). **Open** All year except May, Oct and Nov.

Le Calgary was built in Tyrolean style by the French ski champion Frank Piccard, who returned from Austria in love with the hotels there. And thus the reason for the flower-covered balconies which run along the façades and the two traditional oriel windows. Inside, the lounge recalls an Austrian pub and the dining room, with its colorful tablecloths, is very cheerful. Although the bedroom decor is somewhat standard, the rooms are spacious, and some can accommodate three people. All have a balcony with a lovely view over Beaufort and the ski trails of Les Saisies. In summer, the hotel offers a large choice of study sessions, including some for children. Le Calgary, by the way, is named after the town where Frank Piccard won an Olympic medal.

How to get there *(Map 27): 31km northeast of Albertville via D925, direction Beaufort, and D218, direction Col des Saisies.*

Le Blizzard ★★★★

73150 Val-d'Isère (Savoie)
Tel. 79 06 02 07 - Fax 79 06 04 94
M. Cerboneschi

Rooms 74 including 14 suites with telephone, bath or shower, WC and TV, minibar in suite - Elevator. **Price** Single and double 470-1210F (450-550F in summer). **Meals** Breakfast incl.; half board 355-705F per pers. (325-375F in summer). **Restaurant** Service 12:30-14:30, 19:00-2:00; menu from 150F, also à la carte. Specialties: Regional cooking. **Credit cards** All major. **Pets** Dogs allowed (+40F). **Facilities** Swimming pool, sauna, hammam, jacuzzi, parking. **Nearby** Ski lift (100m), Parc de la Vanoise. **Open** All year except beg May – June and Sept – Nov.

This has long been "the" hotel of Val d'Isère. Frequented by a chic clientele of habitués and famous people, there is nevertheless a sporty atmosphere marked by everyone's passion for skiing; if guests stay late at the bar, they are ready to go the next morning when the cable cars start up. The Blizzard has just had a face lift. All the bedrooms have been redone in a style which is both modern and warm. Those on the south side are quieter and have a large balcony with a beautiful view. A large swimming pool has been built and is be open in both winter and summer. The restaurant serves excellent cuisine – on the terrace in summer and winter. Note also *Le Knack*, the hotel's nightclub; and *La Luge*, the restaurant which is open until 2 AM.

How to get there *(Map 27): 85km southeast of Albertville, voie express toward Moûtiers, then N90 to Bourg-Saint-Maurice, then D902 to Val-d'Isère. Airport: Genève, Lyon Satolas, Chambéry. SNCF: TGV every Fridays Paris-Bourg-Saint-Maurice.*

La Savoyarde ***
73150 Val–d'Isère (Savoie)
Tel. 79.06.01.55 – Fax 79.41.11.29
M. and Mme Marie

Rooms 44 and 2 suites with telephone, bath, WC, cable TV and 3 with minibar.
Price Single and double in half board 500-850F (per pers.). **Restaurant** Service
19:30-23:00; menu 195F (lunchtime 100F), also à la carte. **Credit cards** All major.
Pets Dogs allowed. **Facilities** Sauna, jacuzzi, solarium, fitness center, massage,
parking. **Nearby** Skiing from hotel, Col de l'Iseran. **Open** Dec 1 – May 5.

The Savoyarde is in the heart of the Espace Killy in the old
village: it is the "classic" hotel of Val d'Isère and has been
owned by the same family for four generations. Each has added its
personal touch, but with the constant aim of putting comfortable
furnishings first. The bedrooms have been recently refurbished, in
simple good taste. Some have exposed beams, which fit in well
with the pine furniture and patchwork bedcovers; others have
pleasant balconies with unrestricted views of the ski runs and the
Manchet Valley. All have pleasant bathrooms. The dining room
is also very pleasant and lively at dinner, and the cooking is refined.
This hotel is a favorite with the loyal clientele of Val-d'Isère.

*How to get there (Map 27): 85km southeast of Albertville via N90 to Bourg-
Saint-Maurice, then D902 to Val-d'Isère.*

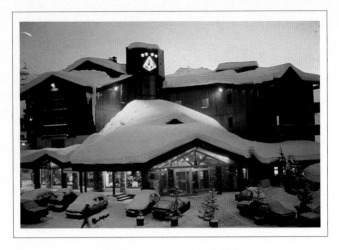

Hôtel Fitz Roy ★★★★
73440 Val Thorens (Savoie)
Tel. 79 00 04 78 – Fax 79 00 06 11
Mme Loubet

Rooms 36 with telephone, bath, TV and minibar. **Price** Double in half board 700-1500F, full board 880-1680F (per pers.). **Meals** Breakfast 90F, served 8:00-11:00. **Restaurant** Service 12:00-15:00, 19:00-22:00; menu 220-500F, also à la carte. Specialties: Regional cooking. **Credit cards** Amex, Visa, Eurocard and Mastercard. **Pets** Dogs allowed (+90F in rooms only). **Facilities** Swimming pool, sauna, health center, beauty salon, garage (350Fper week). **Nearby** Skiing from hotel. **Open** Nov 15 – May 6.

Located in the heart of Val Thorens, the Fitz Roy is a luxurious modern chalet. The interior is decorated very elegantly, with blond woodwork, predominantly white and pastel fabrics, and tasteful furniture. The large lounge, where vast sofas surround the fireplace, looks out due south over the ski runs. The bedrooms, which are all different, are spacious, with very refined décor and accommodations. Each has a balcony and a bathtub with whirlpool. In the evening, enjoy traditional Savoyard country cooking and professional service by candlelight. From the large terrace-solarium, you will also enjoy the superb sunsets over the resort. For *l'après-ski*, there is a swimming pool and excellent exercise equipment. In a resort which can be criticized for being artificial, the Fitz Roy has successfully combined luxury, modernity and the finest hotel tradition.

How to get there *(Map 27): 62km southeast of Albertville via N90 to Moûtiers, then D915 and D117.*

Chalet Rémy *

74170 Saint-Gervais (Haute-Savoie)
Tel. 50.93.11.85
Mme Didier

Rooms 19 with basin. **Price** Double 220F. **Meals** Breakfast 30F, served 8:00-10:00; half board and full board 280-340F (per pers., 3 days min.). **Restaurant** Service 12:00-14:00, 19:00-21:00; menu 90F, also à la carte. Specialties: Family cooking. **Credit cards** Visa, Eurocard and MasterCard. **Pets** Dogs allowed. **Nearby** Ski lift (300m), Chamonix, Megève – Mont-d'Arbois golf course in Megève (15km). **Open** All year.

This exceptional hotel is housed in an 18th-century farmhouse which through the centuries has preserved all its old woodwork. Panels, ceilings, moldings and the staircase leading to the superb gallery serving the bedrooms, all create a lovely harmony of dark red tones. The dining room is set with small tables lit by candles, and the family cuisine is excellent. Madame Didier loves classical music, which accompanies meals. It is the simplicity of the bedrooms that makes them charming; and though the bathroom facilities are merely basic, the bedrooms are absolute jewels with their lovely wood walls, floors and ceilings. The location of the Chalet Rémy is another major asset. It is on the outskirts of Saint-Gervais and is reached by a winding road surrounded by pine woods and meadows facing the impressive snowy peaks of Mont Blanc.

How to get there *(Map 27): 50km northeast of Albertville via N212 and D909 to Robinson and Le Bettex. By A40, Le Fayet exit.*

Hôtel La Savoyarde ★★★

28, route des Moussoux
74400 Chamonix (Haute-Savoie)
Tel. 50.53.00.77 – Fax 50.55.86.82 – Mme Janin

Rooms 14 with telephone, bath, WC and TV. **Price** Double 480-600F. **Meals** Breakfast 46F, served from 7:00. No restaurant. **Credit cards** Amex, Visa, Eurocard and MasterCard. **Pets** Dogs allowed. **Facilities** Garage (+40F), parking. **Nearby** Skiing, mountain excursions – 18-hole Praz golf course. **Open** Dec 15 – Nov 13.

This hotel at the foot of Mount Brévent is surely one of the best located hotels in Chamonix. It overlooks the village and has a superb view of the Aiguille du Midi. Refurbished in the last two years, its style evokes both an English country cottage and an Alpine chalet. There are two adjoining buildings, both well cared for and, in summer, surrounded by flowers. The attractive entrance hall sets the tone of the house: painted ceilings, white walls and a cozy atmosphere. The owners have resisted the temptation to go in for a pseudo-rustic decor. The bedrooms are light and airy and have specially designed furniture. All have balconies or terraces and only two are at the back of the hotel. Among our favorites are Room 5, which has a large balcony, and Room 14, with its exposed beams. One drawback: in the bedrooms near the stairs, early-morning skiers can sometimes wake guests who are less enthusiastic early risers. This is a marvelous place to stay in Chamonix. A few restaurants are *Le Chaudron, L'Impossible,* and *Le Peter Pan* in Les Houches.

How to get there *(Map 27): 67km northeast of Albertville via N212 to Saint-Gervais, then N205. By A40, Le Fayet exit.*

Hôtel du Jeu de Paume ★★★★

705, route du Château – Le Lavancher
74400 Chamonix (Haute-Savoie)
Tel. 50.54.03.76 – Fax 50.54.10.75 – Mmes Prache and Blanc

Rooms 24 with telephone, bath, shower, WC, TV, hairdryer and minibar. **Price** Single and double 770-980F, suite 1250F. **Meals** Breakfast 55F, served 7:30-10:30; half board 630-735F (per pers.). **Restaurant** Service 12:00-14:30, 19:30-21:30; menu 190F, also à la carte. **Credit cards** All major. **Pets** Dogs allowed (+50F). **Facilities** Swimming pool, tennis, sauna, car rental, parking. **Nearby** Skiing in Argentières (Les Grands Montets, 3km), and in Chamonix – 18-hole Praz golf course. **Open** Dec 15 – Nov 10.

Elyane and Guy Prache, who own the elegant Hôtel du Jeu de Paume in the heart of the Ile Saint-Louis in Paris, have just opened this delightful chalet-hôtel at Lavancher, 7km from Chamonix, on the edge of a pine wood overlooking the Argentière Valley. The hotel is luxurious, refined and very comfortable; it is the chalet "re-invented", with wood playing a major role in the decor. The bedrooms are all very functional and furnished with warmth and good taste; nearly all have balconies. There is the same comfortable coziness in the bar and lounges. Throughout the hotel there are lovely pieces of antique furniture, mirrors and paintings. The traditional cooking is excellent and is served in a convivial atmosphere. The staff is very welcoming and in winter the hotel car will take you to the departure points for the ski runs.

How to get there *(Map 27): 67km northeast of Albertville via N212. By A40, Le Fayet exit.*

Chalet-Hôtel Beausoleil **
74400 Chamonix - Le Lavancher (Haute-Savoie)
Tel. 50.54.00.78 - Fax 50.54.17.34
M. Bossonney

Rooms 15 with telephone, bath or shower, WC and TV. **Price** Single 280F, double 320-540F. **Meals** Breakfast, served 7:30-11:00; half board 280-390F, full board 340-450F (per pers., 3 days min.). **Restaurant** Service 12:30-13:30, 19:30-20:30; menu 90-150F, also à la carte. Specialties: Entrecôte sauce morilles, escalope de veau savoyarde, filet de truite à l'oseille, fondue, raclette.**Credit cards** Visa, Eurocard and MasterCard. **Pets** Dogs allowed in rooms. **Facilities** Tennis. **Nearby** Ski lift (3 km), overland skiing from hotel – 18-hole Praz golf course. **Open** Dec 20 – Sept 20.

This peaceful hotel has been run by the Bossonney family for fifty years. Lying at the foot of the Aiguille du Midi and Mont Blanc, it is surrounded by gentle fields and peaceful tranquility. The recently renovated bedrooms are small but all offer modern accommodations and pleasant bathrooms; the rooms upstairs have balconies. The dining room opens onto a terrace which in turn gives onto a lovely flower garden bordered with evergreens. You will enjoy good family cooking at the Beausoleil, along with a friendly welcome.

How to get there (Map 27): 67km northeast of Albertville viaN212. Via A40, exit Le Fayet. (4km north of Chamonix via N506, direction Argentière).

Hôtel Le Labrador ★★★

Route du Golf, 101
74400 Chamonix – Les Praz (Haute-Savoie)
Tel. 50.55.90.09 – Fax 50.53.15.85 – M. Bartoli

Rooms 32 with telephone, bath, WC, TV and minibar. **Price** Double 500-830F.
Meals Breakfast incl., served until 10:30; half board 430-565F, full board 530-695F
(per pers., 3 days min.). **Restaurant** Service 12:00-22:30; menu from 75F, also à la
carte. Specialties: Saumon fumé maison, côte de bœuf gros sel. **Credit cards** All
major. **Pets** Dogs allowed. **Facilities** Sauna, fitness center, whilpool, parking.
Nearby Skiing from hotel, Alpine skiing: La Flégère (250 m), Chamonix (3 km) – 18-
hole Praz golf course. **Open** Dec 15 – Oct 15.

Built on the Chamonix Golf Course facing Mont Blanc, the
Labrador enjoys an outstanding location. A combination of
Scandinavian and Savoyard architecture, the various buildings of
the hotel fit harmoniously into the natural setting. The bedrooms
are not very large but they are comfortable, and those on the front
have balconies. The restaurant, *La Cabane*, is more typically
Finnish, with a traditional *kelo* roof which is made of an actual turf.
(It is mowed every week!) The *Cabane* offers simple, hearty cuisine
with specialties which vary with the seasons. (Try the roast beef
ribs with coarse salt). The only drawback is its large size, which
makes it somewhat lacking in intimacy. The service is attentive.
And the hotel will also suggest ski, golf or mountain package trips
if you wish.

How to get there *(Map 27): 67km northeast of Albertville, via N212. Via
A40, exit Le Fayet. (3km north of Chamonix via N506, direction Argentière;
on the golf course).*

Au Cœur des Prés ★★★

74920 Combloux (Haute-Savoie)
Tel. 50.93.36.55 – Fax 50.58.69.14
M. Paget

Rooms 34 with telephone, bath, WC and TV. **Price** Single 310-380F, double 420-480F. **Meals** Breakfast 40F, served from 7:30; half board and full board 380-440F (per pers.). **Restaurant** Service 12:30-14:00, 19:30-20:30; menu 140-180F, also à la carte. **Credit cards** Visa, Eurocard and MasterCard. **Pets** Dogs allowed. **Facilities** Tennis, sauna, whirlpool, garage (28F), parking. **Nearby** Ski lifts (1km), Megève, Chamonix – 18-hole Mont d'Arbois golf course in Megève. **Open** Dec 20 – April 15 and June 1 – Sept 25.

This hotel has the advantage not only of a superb view of Mont Blanc and the Aravis Mountains, it is also surrounded by a large meadow which isolates it from neighboring traffic and noise. The majority of the bedrooms looking out towards Mont Blanc have balconies and are comfortable, though their decor is a little impersonal. The ones or the third floor have more character. The lounge offers comfortable armchairs and a big fireplace, and the dining room is charming with its tiled floor, exposed beams, pink tablecloths and panoramic view. The hotel has been awarded prizes by the community for its summer flower display and is ideal for those who like peace and tranquillity amid impressive scenery. During the winter-sports season, the hotel has a shuttle to take clients to the various ski areas.

How to get there *(Map 27): 36km northeast of Albertville via N212 to Combloux through Megève. By A40, Le Fayet exit.*

Les Roches Fleuries ★★★

74700 Cordon (Haute-Savoie)
Tel. 50.58.06.71 - Fax 50.47.82.30
J. and G. Picot

Rooms 28 with telephone, bath, WC and cable TV. **Price** Double 460-650F, suite 750-950F. **Meals** Breakfast 55F, served 7:30-10:00; half board 390-545F (per pers., 3 days min.). **Restaurant** Service 12:30-14:00, 19:30-21:30; menus 130-265F also à la carte. Specialties: Tartiffle de lapin au Beaufort, pigeon fermier mi-cuit aux pousses d'épinard, "la boite à fromages". Regional restaurant 160F. **Credit cards** All major. **Pets** Dogs allowed (+35F). **Facilities** Heated swimming pool, health center, whirlpool, hamman, Mountain bikes rental, mountain guides, parking, garage (30F). **Nearby** Ski lifts (700m), Megève, Chamonix – 18-hole Mont d'Arbois golf course in Megève. **Open** Dec 14 – April 31, April 17 – Oct 1.

Cordon lies between Combloux and Sallanches on the threshold of Mont Blanc and is a delightful village all year round. In summer the chalets nestle among cherry and walnut trees, and in winter there are sensational views of the Aiguilles de Chamonix and the Aravis Mountains. The bedrooms are prettily furnished and most have terraces on which you can enjoy the magnificent view, the peace and the sun. Like the bedrooms, the lounge and dining room are furnished in a comfortable rustic style. In winter the blaze in the fireplace creates a warm and cozy ambience. The cooking is good and the service attentive and friendly.

How to get there (Map 27): 43km northeast of Albertville via N212 to Sallanches, then D113. By A40, Le Fayet exit.

Marceau Hôtel ★★★

115, chemin de la Chappelière
74210 Doussard (Haute-Savoie)
Tel. 50.44.30.11 – Fax 50.44.39.44 – M. and Mme Sallaz

Rooms 16 with telephone, bath or shower, WC (14 with TV). **Price** Double 450F, suite 660F. **Meals** Breakfast 50F, served 7:30-10:00; half board 450-735F, full board 480-810F (per pers., 3 days min.). **Restaurant** Service 12:30-14:00, 19:30-21:00; menus 130-330F, also à la carte. Specialties: Longe de veau Marceau, féra du lac au chignin, blanquette de homard. **Credit cards** All major. **Pets** Dogs allowed (+50F). **Facilities** Tennis, parking. **Nearby** Lake of Annecy, le Semnoz by the ridgeway, gorges of Le Fier – 18-hole Annecy golf course in Talloires. **Open** Feb 1 – Oct 10.

In one of the most touristic areas of France, how lovely it is to find a peaceful haven well off the beaten track! Set in the middle of the countryside with a beautiful view of the lake and valley, this elegantly comfortable hotel is precisely that and much more. In the dining-room, subtle shades of pink blend perfectly with the colors of the wood, and large windows open onto beautiful surroundings. There is an attractive lounge for watching television or reading by the fireside. In summer, both view and sunshine can be enjoyed on a delightful terrace next to the kitchen garden. The bedrooms are tastefully decorated, with carefully chosen furniture. There are fresh flowers everywhere and the welcome is warm.

How to get there *(Map 27): 20km south of Annecy via N508 towards Albertville.*

Chalet-Hôtel Crychar ★★★

74260 Les Gets (Haute-Savoie)
Tel. 50.75.80.50 – Fax 50.79.83.12
Mme Bouchet

Rooms 12 with telephone, bath, WC and TV. **Price** Double 360-560F, suite 630-790F.
Meals Breakfast 45F. No restaurant. **Credit cards** All major. **Pets** Dogs not allowed.
Facilities Sauna (60F), solarium, garage (+40F), parking. **Nearby** Skiing from hotel,
Séous, Morzine, Avoriaz, Chamonix, Evian. **Open** Dec 15 – April 15, June 30 – Sept 15.

In the middle of the ski slopes in winter (yet only 100 metres from the center of the village) and surrounded by green Alpine meadows in summer, this modern hotel feels like a traditional mountain chalet because it has a limited number of rooms. The bedrooms are light, airy, well decorated and comfortable, with balconies and bathrooms. The hotel is well provided with leisure facilities including table tennis, a swimming pool, an authentic Finnish sauna and various kinds of exercise equipment. The lack of a restaurant makes for peace and quiet in the hotel and there are many restaurants close by.

How to get there *(Map 27): 86km northeast of Annecy via A41, then A40 Cluses exit, then D902 to Les Gets via Taninges.*

Chalet-Hôtel Peter Pan

74310 Les Houches (Haute-Savoie)
Tel. 50.54.40.63
M. and Mme Bochatay

Rooms 13 (2 with bath, 4 shower and 2 with WC). **Price** Double 190-255F.
Meals Breakfast 32F, served 8:00-10:00; half board 215-335F, full board 250-265F
(per pers., 3 days min.). **Restaurant** Service at 12:30 and 19:30; menus 85-135F,
also à la carte. Specialties: Saumon frais à l'oseille, braserades, tarte tatin, nougat
glacé. **Credit cards** Not accepted. **Pets** Dogs allowed. **Facilities** Parking. **Nearby** Ski
lifts (1km) – 18-hole Praz golf course in Chamonix (7km). **Open** All year except in
May and Nov 1 – Dec 14.

Michel Bochatay and his wife have been in this beautiful
converted 18th-century farm for seventeen years. It is on a
hilltop near Les Houches and has a superb view of the valley of
Chamonix. In this delightful place the owners have created an
original and welcoming ambience, with excellent food at
reasonable prices. The two chalets are constructed entirely of wood
and are veritable small museums. Meals are served by candlelight
on prettily set little wooden tables bright with bouquets of flowers.
The bedrooms vary in size and style. Rooms 1 and 2 are spacious
(2 has a bathroom) and Room 6 on the top floor is more intimate;
the three look out on the valley. The rooms in the annex are smaller
and four of them have only a washbasin. Nevertheless, thanks to
the tranquillity, the charming ambience and the warm welcome,
the Peter Pan is a great place to stay.

How to get there *(Map 27): 59km northeast of Albertville via N212, then
N205. By A40, Le Fayet exit. 7km west of Chamonix.*

540

Hôtel de La Croix Fry ★★★

Manigod - 74230 Thônes (Haute-Savoie)
Tel. 50.44.90.16 - Fax 50.44.94.87
Mme Guelpa-Veyrat

Rooms 12 with telephone, bath, WC and cable TV. **Price** Double 550-1500F(suite). **Meals** Breakfast 80F, served 8:00-10:00; half board 550-750F (per pers., 3 days min.). **Restaurant** Service 12:30-13:30, 19:30-20:30; menus 140-360F, also à la carte. Specialties: Tartifflette maison, viande et omelette avec bolets et chanterelles, foie gras cuit maison, desserts aux fruits sauvages. **Credit cards** Amex, Visa, Eurocard and MasterCard. **Pets** Dogs allowed (+25F). **Facilities** Heated swimming pool, tennis, parking. **Nearby** Skiing in La Croix-Fly/l'Etoile (1km), La Clusaz, Manigod valley, village of Chinaillon, gorges of Le Fier, Annecy lake – 18-hole Annecy golf course in Talloires. **Open** June 15 – Sept 15, Dec 15 – April 15.

This is the kind of hotel we would like to find more often in the French Alps without having to go to the five-star establishments. It is comfortable and cozy and its bedrooms – all named after mountain flowers – have had great care lavished on them over the years: beamed ceilings and old furniture create a snug chalet atmosphere. The ones facing the valley have breathtaking views and are very sunny. All have either a balcony, a terrace or a mezzanine to make up for the tiny bathrooms. (Some have balneotherapy bathtubs.) The former stables, converted into a bar with seats covered in sheepskin, lead into the dining-room, which faces the Tournette Mountains. This is a great spot in summer or winter, and you are strongly advised to reserve well in advance, for the hotel has a large and faithful following.

How to get there (Map 27): 27km east of Annecy via D909 to Thônes, then D12 and D16 to Manigod, then La Croix Fry.

Les Fermes Marie ★★★

Chemin de Riante Colline
74120 Megève (Haute-Savoie)
Tel. 50.93.03.10 – Fax 50.93.09.84 – M. Sibuet

Rooms 52 with telephone, bath, WC and TV. **Price** Single and double in half board 745-1000F (per pers.). **Restaurant** Service 12:00-14:00, 19:30-22:30; carte 250 F. Specialties: Regional cooking, fish. Cheeses restaurant: menu 220F. **Credit cards** Amex, Visa, Eurocard and MasterCard. **Pets** dogs allowed (+suppl.). **Facilities** Steam bath, fitness center, hammam, sauna, jacuzzi, health center, swimming pool, jacuzzi. **Nearby** ski lifts (500m), Chamonix valley – 18-hole Mont d'Arbois golf course. **Open** Dec 17 – April 15 and June 23 – Sept 15.

After opening their delightful hotel in Rochebrune, Le Coin du Feu, and the chaming restaurant Le Saint-Nicolas, Jocelyne and Jean-Louis Sibuet recently opened Les Fermes de Marie. This is in fact a small hamlet composed of several chalets which have been reconstructed from old mazots - tiny traditional Savoyard mountain chalets - and built entirely with old wood. The reception area, the two restaurants, the library, and the bar occupy the main building. All the bedrooms face due south and are delightfully decorated in the most attractive mountain style; they are very comfortable and have a balcony-terrace along with a corner lounge. Scouring the region for antiques, Jocelyne found more than 450 pieces of traditional furniture to decorate the hotel. Similar care has been paid even to the breakfasts, which include delicious homemade preserves, country bread and crusty baguettes. The evening meal is simple but nutritious and succulent. Here is yet another charming hotel in Megève.

How to get there *(Map 27): 34km northeast of Albertville via N212. Take A40, exit Le Fayet. (The hotel is on the road to Rochebrune).*

Le Coin du Feu ★★★

Route de Rochebrune
74120 Megève (Haute-Savoie)
Tel. 50.21.04.94 - Fax 50.21.20.15 - M. and Mme Sibuet

Rooms 23 with telephone, bath, WC and TV. **Price** Single and double 500-1000F.
Meals Breakfast 35F; half board 595-745F (per pers.). **Restaurant** Service 19:30-
22:30; menu 250F, also à la carte. Specialties: Regional cooking and fish from the
lake. **Credit cards** Amex, Visa, Eurocard and MasterCard. **Pets** Dogs allowed.
Nearby Ski lifts (200m), Chamonix valley – 18-hole Mont d'Arbois golf course.
Open Dec 20 – April 5 and July 20 – Aug 31.

This hotel has long been known as the most appealing place to
stay in Megève for those who like tradition. Its success lies in
its handsome pine furniture, oak panelling, the flowered fabrics
and above all its welcoming fireplace. The hotel's restaurant, the
Saint-Nicholas, attracts Megève regulars who come here for its
simple but delicious cuisine or the traditional *raclettes* and fondues.
The bedrooms are cheerful and pretty and you will receive a very
friendly welcome.

How to get there *(Map 27): 34km northeast of Albertville via N212. By
A40, Le Fayet exit. (The hotel is on the road to Rochebrune).*

Le Fer à Cheval ★★★
36, route du Crêt-d'Arbois
74120 Megève (Haute-Savoie)
Tel. 50.21.30.39 - Fax 50.93.07.60 - M. Sibuet

Rooms 41 with telephone, bath, WC, TV and 35 with minibar. **Price** Double with half board 675-890F (per pers.). **Meals** Breakfast 50F, served 7:45-11:30. **Restaurant** Service 19:30-21:30; menu savoyard, also à la carte. **Credit cards** Amex, Visa, Eurocar and MasterCard. **Pets** Dogs allowed (+45F). **Facilities** Swimming pool, sauna, whilpool, hammam, health center, parking, garage. **Nearby** Ski lifts (450m), Chamonix valley – 18-hole Mont d'Arbois golf course. **Open** Dec 14 – Easter and July 1 – Sept 11.

This is one of the most charming hotels in Megève, from every point of view. The chalet has been very well refurbished; exposed beams and lovely wood panelling create a warm and comfortable décor, as do the patinated and polished antique furniture and the variety of fabrics and *objets d'art*. We can't recommend any particular bedroom – they are all delightful and any variation in price is only due to size. In winter, meals are served by the fireplace in the dining room, and in summer by the swimming pool. If there isn't enough snow, a hotel shuttle will take you to the nearby resorts, Les Contamines or Chamonix. You can also make an excursion into the mountains (La Vallée Blanche, for example) with a guide. Guests receive a warm welcome.

How to get there *(Map 27): 34km northeast of Albertville via N212. By A40, Le Fayet exit.*

Ferme Hôtel Duvillard ★★★
Le Mont d'Arbois
74120 Megève (Haute-Savoie)
Tel. 50.21.14.62 – Fax 50.21.42.82 – Mme Mouroux

Rooms 19 with telephone, bath or shower, WC and cable TV. **Price** Single 642-763F, double 767-998F, triple 844F, duplex (4 pers.) 932F. **Meals** Breakfast 60F, served 7:30-9:30; half-board 560-689F (per pers. in double room). **Restaurant** Service 12:00-14:00, 19:30-21:00; menu 150F, also à la carte. Specialties: Pierrade, fondue, raclette, pela, farcement. **Credit cards** All major. **Pets** Dogs allowed (+60F). **Facilities** Heated swimming pool, sauna, parking. **Nearby** Skiing from hotel with Mont-D'Arbois chairlift – 18-hole Arbois golf course. **Open** Dec 20 – April 15 and July 1– Sept 15.

This is an old family farm which has been converted into a lovely mountain hotel. It is very conveniently located at the foot of the ski trails, the cable car, ski lift and the Mont d'Arbois Golf Course. The interior is warm and inviting. The bedrooms are not very large but they have full modern accommodations, which are welcome in the mountains: television, hair dryer, and there is a sauna upstairs. In the restaurant, the cuisine is simple, with the emphasis on hearty Savoyard specialties, which are served in a half-Savoyard, half-Tyrolean décor. And the owners know something about skiing and running a hotel: Adrien Duvillard is a native son of Megève and a member of the French Ski Team, and his wife, Eva, is a graduate of the Innsbrück Hotel School. The service is somewhat distant at first but quickly becomes friendly.

How to get there *(Map 27): 34km northeast of Albertville viaN212. Take A40, exit Le Fayet. (The hotel is at the foot of the Mont d'Arbois cable car).*

La Bergerie ★★★
Rue de Téléphérique
74110 Morzine (Haute-Savoie)
Tel. 50.79.13.69 – Fax 50.75.95.71 – Mme Marullaz

Rooms 27 rooms, studios or apartments with telephone, bath, WC, TV (21 with minibar).
Price Room 250-400F, studio 450-700F, apart. (2-4 pers.) 600-900F. **Meals** Breakfast
50F, served 7:00-11:00. **Restaurant** Table d'hôtes 1 day by week. **Credit cards** Visa,
Eurocard and MasterCard. **Pets** Dogs allowed. **Facilities** Swimming pool, sauna,
solarium, health center, games room, parking, garage. **Nearby** Ski lifts (50m), Avoriaz,
Evian – 9-hole Morzine golf course, 18-hole Royal Hôtel golf course, Evian. **Open** Dec
19 – April 20 and July 1 – mid. Sept.

This is the favorite hotel of Morzine residents, although it has
changed somewhat. There are now studios and apartments
as well as individual bedrooms, all sharing the hotel's services. The
Mourgues armchairs and the orange–and–yellow check fabrics on
the Knoll-style chairs in the lounge make for a delightful 1970s
style. The best bedrooms are those facing south which look out
over the garden and swimming pool. There is no restaurant but
light snacks are served. The most popular restaurants with the
resort's regulars are *Le Cherche Midi* on the road to Les Gets, or *La
Crémaillère* in Les Lindarets-Montrionds, which you can also get
to in winter via the ski trails. *La Taverne des Dromonts* in Avoriaz
is also very charming.

How to get there *(Map 27): 93km northeast of Annecy via A41 and A40,
Cluses exit, then D902. The hotel is near the E.S.F (ski school).*

Hôtel Beau Site ***

74290 Talloires (Haute-Savoie)
Tel. 50.60.71.04 – Fax 50.60.79.22
M. Conan

Rooms 29 with telephone, bath or shower, WC and TV (10 with minibar). **Price** Single and double 410-765F, suite 900-950F. **Meals** Breakfast 52F, served 7:30-10:30; half board 410-600F, full board 430-640F (per pers., 2 days min.). **Restaurant** Service 12:30-14:00, 19:30-21:15; menus 150-250F, also à la carte. Specialties: Fish from the lake. **Credit cards** All major. **Pets** Dogs allowed. **Facilities** Tennis (+60F), private beach, parking. **Nearby** Ermitage Saint-Germain, château de Menthon-Saint-Bernard, Thorens and Montrottier, château, lake, museum and olg city in Annecy – 18-hole Annecy golf course in Talloires. **Open** May 17 – Oct 13.

With grounds reaching right down to the banks of Lake Annecy, the Hôtel Beau Site is reminiscent of a hotel on the Italian lakes. A family estate converted into a hotel at the end of the 19th century, it has retained many gracious features: a vast, sunny dining-room-cum-verandah decorated with old plates; a delightful lounge with period furniture; and lawns well provided with deck chairs. The charming bedrooms have been completely refurbished; they have a terrace and many look out on the lake. Some are decorated with antiques, others are more modern, and some have a mezzanine. The food is excellent. The hotel is specially noted for its warm and friendly welcome.

How to get there *(Map 27): 13km from Annecy via A41, Annecy exit. At Annecy, take east bank of lake towards Thônes until Veyrier, then Talloires.*

INDEX

B

ILE DE FRANCE - CHAMPAGNE-PICARDIE

CENTRE

Notes

Notes

ALSO IN THE RIVAGES SERIES

Hotels and Country Inns of Character and Charm in Italy

Over 400 of the most charming places to stay all over Italy are included in this guide, from small hotels in country towns to inns in farmhouses and villas alike. There is an appealing color photograph and an unfussy description of each hostelry, along with a delightful section of brief restaurant reviews and detailed color road maps.

$18.00 ($25.00 Canada)
ISBN:0-679-02874-9

Bed & Breakfasts of Character and Charm in France

The over 300 B&Bs in this guide range from cottages deep in the unspoiled countryside to lavish châteaux, converted mills, and manors by the sea. For each property, readers will find a luscious color photograph and staightforward description, along with Rivages's signature road maps.

$17.00 ($23.50 Canada)
ISBN: 0-679-02873-0

Available in bookstores. Or call 800/533-6478.

Printed in CEE